MW00809407

The Bleeding Wound

Edited by James G. Hershberg

Published in collaboration with the Woodrow Wilson International Center for Scholars

THE BLEEDING WOUND

THE SOVIET WAR IN AFGHANISTAN AND THE COLLAPSE OF THE SOVIET SYSTEM

Yaacov Ro'i

STANFORD UNIVERSITY PRESS
STANFORD, CALIFORNIA

Stanford University Press
Stanford, California

Printed in the United States of America on acid-free, archival-quality paper

Library of Congress Cataloging-in-Publication Data

Names: Ro'i, Yaacov, author.
Title: The bleeding wound : the Soviet war in Afghanistan and the collapse of the Soviet system / Yaacov Ro'i.
Description: Stanford, California : Stanford University Press, 2022. | Includes bibliographical references and index.
Identifiers: LCCN 2021029240 (print) | LCCN 2021029241 (ebook) | ISBN 9781503628748 (cloth) | ISBN 9781503631069 (ebook)
Subjects: LCSH: Afghanistan—History—Soviet occupation, 1979–1989. | Soviet Union—Politics and government—1945–1991.
Classification: LCC DS371.2 .R65 2022 (print) | LCC DS371.2 (ebook) | DDC 958.104/5—dc23
LC record available at https://lccn.loc.gov/2021029240
LC ebook record available at https://lccn.loc.gov/2021029241

Cover design: Kevin Barrett Kane

Contents

Tables and Figures

Tables

Figures

Acknowledgments

It is my pleasant duty to express my gratitude to the many people who helped me in the research for this book and its eventual production. My first round of thanks goes to the Israel Science Foundation, which financed the interview project that I undertook in the early to mid-1990s, on the findings of which the research essentially rests. My second is to the numerous individuals who agreed to be interviewed in the FSU and Israel, some of whom I interrogated for long hours. A few of them, whom I interviewed separately from the mass survey, I have mentioned by name in the course of the book (chiefly in the endnotes); I promised the interviewees in the mass survey that I would not divulge their identity. Third come those who conducted the survey according to my questionnaire and in constant consultation with me, most importantly, Roman Zolotovitskii, then a PhD student in sociology, who went the rounds of eleven of the independent states that inherited the former Soviet Union and had frequent helpful insights; I was extremely lucky to have found him. Roman Fishman and Alik Yakubov implemented the Israeli part of the survey. My next debt is to Eyal Bar-Haim, a statistician at Tel-Aviv University, who prepared the tables and figures and had to put up with a great deal of badgering on my part.

I also received assistance from a number of fellow academics and students of either the Soviet-Afghan War or topics that touch on some aspect about which I requested their expert advice. I hope I have thanked them all specifically in the relevant endnotes: Rodric Braithwaite; Artemy Kalinovsky; Natalia Danilova; Marlène Laruelle; Ivan Radikov; my late friend and colleague Murray Feshbach, who diligently saved for me every source that he thought might be relevant and was always generous with his time; and, above all, Markus Göransson, who was invariably helpful and happy to share his data and extensive knowledge. I am also deeply indebted to my nephew Yoram Gorlizki of Manchester University, who was always there to offer me helpful practical advice whenever I ran into trouble, which was not infrequently, and to my niece Vera Tolz, also at Manchester, who read a draft of Chapter 6 and gave me some very valuable insights.

Finally, I thank the people who assisted with the final stages of the book. Here I must mention the people at Stanford University Press, especially Margo Irvin, the acquisitions editor for history, and Jim Hershberg, under whose auspices the series in which this book appears is published; the anonymous readers who called for some important corrections that definitely improved the manuscript; and my editor, Ruth Leah Kahan, who did the incredible and succeeded in record time to edit the manuscript, and cut it down by ten percent in so doing.

Glossary and Abbreviations

agitprop—agitation and propaganda

APC—armored personnel carrier

Basmachi—the Islamist peasant "Basmachi" (lit. bandits) had fought the new Soviet regime in Soviet Central Asia in the 1920s and into the 1930s

BMD—assault vehicle (*boevaia mashina desanta*)

BMP—tracked infantry fighting vehicle (*boevaia mashina pekhoty)*

BRDM—four-wheeled armored reconnaissance-patrol vehicle (*bronirovannaia razvedyvatel'no-dozornaia mashina*)

CC—Central Committee

CGS—Chief of General Staff or Chief of Staff

CPSU—Communist Party of the Soviet Union

CRA—Council for Religious Affairs

CWIHP—Cold War International History Project

dedovshchina—hazing (lit. "grandfather rule")

DM—Defense Minister

DOSAAF—Voluntary Society for Assistance to the Army, Aviation, and Fleet

DRA—Democratic Republic of Afghanistan (renamed Republic of Afghanistan in 1985)

DShB—air-assault brigade ((*desantno-shturmovaia brigada*)

dushman—enemy, Farsi (plural: *dushmany*)

Glavlit—Main Directorate for Literary and Publishing Affairs (*Glavnoe Upravlenie po Delam Literatury i Izdatel'stv*) that also acted as censorship for radio and television

GPW—Great Patriotic War (World War II)

GRU—Main Intelligence Directorate of the Soviet Armed Forces (*Glavnoe Razvedyvatel'noe Upravlenie*)

GS—General Staff of the Soviet Armed Forces

IMEMO—Institute of World Economy and International Relations

KGB—Committee of State Security

KIA—killed in action

kishlak—Afghan (and Central Asian) village

kolhoz—collective farm

Komsomol—Young Communist League

MD—military district

MIA—missing in action

MoD—Ministry of Defense

MPA—Main Political Administration; the CPSU CC military arm, which appointed political officers in every unit (down to regiment or battalion) and streamlined political activity in the armed forces

MRD—motorized rifle division (*motostrelkovaia diviziia*)

MRR—motorized rifle regiment (*motostrelkoviy polk*)

MRB—motorized rifle battalion (*motostrelkoviy batal'on*)

MRC—motorized rifle company (*motostrelkovaia rota*)

MRP—motorized rifle platoon (*motostrelkoviy vzvod*)

mujahidin—the Afghan resistance (lit. "holy warriors")

MVD—Ministry of Internal Affairs

MZhK—young people's housing complex

NTS—Narodno Trudovoi Soiuz rossiiskikh solidaristov (émigré association)

nomenklatura—top-level officials in the Soviet establishment: in the Communist Party of the Soviet Union, the state and government apparatus and academia

Oblast—region or state

OG—Operations Group

OMON—(*Otriad militsii osobogo naznacheniia*) Special-purpose militia detachment of the MVD, used as riot police; first formed in 1979 and formally established in October 1988

PDPA—People's Democratic Party of Afghanistan

POW—prisoner of war

PTSD—posttraumatic stress disorder

RFE—Radio Free Europe

RL—Radio Liberty

samizdat—uncensored, and therefore illegal, publications passed from hand to hand (lit. "self-publication")

shuravi—Afghan name for Soviets (derived from *shura*—council, in Russian, *Sovet*)

spetsnaz—GRU forces trained for long-range reconnaissance, commando, and special forces type combat (lit. "troops of special designation")

SVA—Union of Veterans of Afghanistan (*Soiuz veteranov Afganistana*)

tamizdat—Russian-language publications that came out "there" (*tam*), that is, abroad, and smuggled into the Soviet Union

unit (*chast*)—regiment or independent battalion with its own colors

UVA—participants of the Afghan War (*uchastniki voiny v Afganistane*)

VIZh—military history journal; organ of the MoD (*Voenno-istoricheskii zhurnal*)

voenkomat (*voennyi komissariat*)—military registration and enlistment office

VDV—elite airborne force (*vozdushno-desantnyi voisk*)

VPV—military-patriotic education (*voenno-patriotichsekoe vospitanie*)

YCL—Young Communist League, the Komosmol

The Bleeding Wound

Introduction

In the words of one of the most redoubtable Western analysts of the Cold War, the Soviet-Afghan War became a "death-knell" for the Soviet Union, "signaling its international isolation, its leadership's inconsistency and fragmentation, and its public's growing disbelief in the purpose and direction of Soviet rule."[1] It is therefore not surprising that the various aspects of the Soviet-Afghan War, which lasted almost a decade—from December 1979 to February 1989—have engendered a fair amount of analysis. The events of the war have received considerable attention; so too have the war's implications in the international arena—Soviet-U.S. relations, the Cold War, Soviet relations with other communist regimes and with the Third World—and for the history of Afghanistan itself, notably in light of subsequent developments in that conflict-ridden land.

This book surveys and analyzes the significance of the war for the evolution of Soviet politics, society, and the military in the last decade or so of the Soviet Union's existence and—albeit indirectly—in the evolution of its successor states. It studies the verdict of the first Soviet journalist to publish extensively and concurrently with the Soviet-Afghan War. "With a mere wave of Brezhnev's elderly hand," he writes, the Soviet people who worked and fought in Afghanistan "were thrown into a country where bribery, corruption, profiteering and drugs were no less common than the long lines in Soviet stores. These diseases can be far more infectious and dangerous than hepatitis, particularly when they reach epidemic proportions." Even more far-reaching than the loss of life and the war's economic cost were "our moral losses. It often seems to me that war and violence had crossed the border into our country. In

Afghanistan we bombed not only the detachments of rebels and their caravans, but our own ideals as well. With the war came the reevaluation of our moral and ethical values. In Afghanistan the policies of the government became utterly incompatible with the inherent morality of our nation. Things could not continue in the same vein. It is hardly coincidental that the ideas of perestroika took hold in 1985—the year the war reached its peak." Nor was the war itself "the only thing that chipped away at our morality. The official lies about the war, in newspapers and on television, also took a heavy toll. . . . Even when one of us tried to report the truth the military censors masterfully made it into a lie."[2]

In other words, the Soviet-Afghan War affected not just the large number of Soviet citizens who served in Afghanistan during its course, as either soldiers sent to uphold the People's Democratic Party of Afghanistan (PDPA) Marxist regime that had taken power in Kabul in April 1978 or advisers and civilian specialists dispatched to Afghanistan to modernize the country on the Soviet model and bring it closer to the Soviet Union. The war had a major impact on the evolution of Soviet politics and society in the crucial final years of the Soviet Union's existence, almost certainly precipitating processes that tore the country asunder in 1991, highlighting, undercutting, and reflecting the weaknesses of its regime.

This book addresses the crucial issue of the flaws of a political system that enabled a small group of men to embroil their country in a civil war beyond its borders. Two other spheres that our story necessarily reflects are trends within Soviet society in the 1970s and 1980s and ethnic relations within the Soviet empire.

By 1979, Soviet society had suffered a loss of direction for some years. As he administered and navigated destalinization, Nikita Khrushchev's large-scale reforms undercut the ideological base of the party-state that had engendered Stalin's misdeeds, all duly embedded in "Marxism-Leninism." The party continued to rule—with the ongoing support of the security forces, whose mandate, however, no longer included mass terror—but the harm done to the ideology on which its authority rested inevitably weakened that authority. The de-ideologization, for it was no less, that accompanied Khrushchev's promises to improve living standards led to a growing consumerism, disenchantment, widespread misbelief and cynicism, and a devaluation of the "values" that had characterized the earlier generations of Soviet rule, such as patriotism and collectivism. The partial breakdown of the Iron Curtain enabled a certain opening to the West. Western fashions and music became increasingly popular and the "Voices," as people called the Western broadcasts, gained ground. The maladies of society that pervaded in the 1970s and increasingly in the 1980s also included low production, a result not only of the economic centralism of the command system, but also of absenteeism, alcohol, and lack of incentive. A sophisticated discussion of the inherent paradoxes of late or "binary" socialism must analyze the Soviet Union's demise against the background of the anomalies intrinsic to its fundamental perceptions, which could not withstand the onslaught of glasnost.[3]

In addition, ethnic unrest was beginning to surface, particularly in the union republics that were traditionally troublesome: Ukraine, Georgia, and the three Baltic republics. (The raison d'être of all fifteen republics of the Union of Socialist Soviet Republics—the USSR—was the overlap of nationality and territory.) The Russians' role as Elder Brother in the Soviet family of nations and their "Great Russian" nationalism had not been conducive to *druzhba narodov* (the friendship of nations) that was to support that family. Indeed, Soviet nationalities policy had been one of the regime's anomalies and inherent contradictions from the start. As French scholar Hélène Carrère d'Encausse wrote in the late 1970s in her *Decline of an Empire*, "The obliteration of national differences and their fusion in a new and superior historical community—the Soviet People—has not succeeded."[4] "The fiction of a united *sovetskii narod* ('Soviet people')," Ron Suny tells us, "was belied by powerful identification with nationality. . . . As the Soviet economy ground down after the mid-1970s, one nationality after another began to express a profound anxiety about the threat to their culture, language, demographic, economic, and ecological future."[5] Our survey of both *afgantsy* (the Soviet soldiers who participated in the war) and regular citizens does not indicate that either group believed the war exacerbated national tensions in the Soviet Union. However, considerable anecdotal evidence attests to the prevalence of ethnic identity and mutual animosity on the basis of ethnic differences in the Fortieth Army—the "Limited Contingent" of Soviet troops that fought in Afghanistan. Moreover, in the context of the mounting ethnic unrest in the national republics during the 1980s, both samizdat and public protest addressed issues connected to the Afghan War as they contended against the Kremlin.

Any study of the Soviet role in the Soviet-Afghan War and the war's impact on the Soviet domestic scene must bear in mind the political, social, and economic backdrop against which the war was fought and which shaped the mentalité of all those who played their part in its unfolding—the political and military leadership, the officer corps, and the troops.

This book, then, looks at the decision to introduce Soviet troops into Afghanistan. Most specifically, it analyzes the background of that decision and its significance for later developments within the Soviet leadership. It looks at the Fortieth Army, formed for the purpose of upholding the Marxist regime in Kabul, deployed in late December 1979 and kept there until mid-February 1989. It bears out some of the statements of the participants in a 1995 symposium on the war (held under the auspices of the Oslo-based Nobel Institute) who played a role in the Soviet (and U.S.) policymaking process in the late 1970s. After discussing the decision to introduce troops, they provided insights into the interaction between the ailing Brezhnev and his entourage (described as "manipulative courtesans") and the importance of built-in political structures and stereotyped thinking that precluded creative thinking or initiative. They also spoke about the ignorance, prejudices, and misconceptions of the inner group of decision makers who did not read the relevant reports and so were unaware of their content and, in particular, their exaggeration of the capabilities of the rival superpower.[6]

The book examines the lessons of the war for the Soviet military, public morale, the Soviet population's image of the world's Communist superpower and, in particular, Soviet Central Asia. Above all, the book studies the meaning of the war and the way the Soviet media reported it as an indication of and stimulus to the evolution of Soviet public opinion, as Gorbachev's glasnost took root in the latter 1980s. I discuss one specific aspect of this special attention—the lot of the Soviet soldiers who participated in the war, the so-called afgantsy, both in Afghanistan and after their return home. Since this is the main thrust of the book, I touch only briefly on the war itself—merely to provide the context for the questions it discusses—and address neither the Afghan domestic scene nor the war's international implications and significance.

Two other books have addressed similar questions—Mark Galeotti's *Afghanistan: The Soviet Union's Last War* (written in 1992 and published in 1995) and Manfred Sapper's *Die Auswirkung des Afghanistan-Krieges auf die Sowjetgesellschaft* (1994). In his introduction, Galeotti writes, "Certainly the war was important in its effect on the people of the old USSR and, indeed, its successor states." Yet "it did not destroy the Soviet Union. For this was a relatively minor . . . military adventure. . . . Its real importance is two-fold: as a myth and as a window. In the context of the collapse of the Soviet system, the war became used [sic] as a symbol for a variety of issues, from the cost of supporting such a huge and seemingly useless army to the arrogant foolishness of the old regime. Scattered, politically marginalized, ostracized, disempowered, the veterans and the other victims of the war could not make their views heard, and thus the mythological picture of the war, conjured from the prejudices, perceptions and political needs of . . . journalists, politicians, academics and propagandists, came to dominate." The war influenced a wide range of issues, from the spread of informal political movements, through the shift away from conscription, to the rise of Russian vice president (and afganets), Aleksandr Rutskoi. It also led to widespread calls for leadership accountability.[7]

Sapper's work—published in a series of Studies in Conflict and Cooperation in the East—focused on the military's loss of legitimacy under perestroika, although it too covers much of the same ground as my study. The main difference is in the source material, for Sapper made no use of the press (as distinct from journal articles) and did not conduct interviews.

As a historian, my approach and emphases differ from those of Galeotti, and I use source material that neither Galeotti nor Sapper touched. I find myself in agreement with the verdict of a Russian political-scientist-cum-social psychologist who served in a civilian capacity in Afghanistan from 1985 to 1987: "The truth about Afghanistan emerges [only] in a polyphony of varying points of view [all] grounded in authentic knowledge and interpretations of what people saw and experienced."[8] It is for this reason that I have permitted myself to examine many of the same issues as did Galeotti and Sapper.

Other works in the Western literature on the war—Rodric Braithwaite's *Afgantsy: The Russians in Afghanistan 1979—1989* (2011); Artemy M. Kalinovsky's *A Long Goodbye* (2011); and Markus B. Göransson's PhD thesis, "At the Service of the State; Soviet-Afghan War Veterans in Tajikistan, 1979–1992" (2015)—focus on rather narrower fields. *Afgantsy* tells a compelling story based on a wealth of mostly Russian-language material that the author collected over the years. (Braithwaite served in the British embassy in Moscow in the 1960s and as the British ambassador from 1988 to 1992.) The book does not purport to be an academic study, and so of the Western works that I consulted frequently, it stands in a category of its own. *A Long Goodbye* spotlights Soviet decision making and policy and aims specifically to analyze and explain the seemingly inexplicable dragging out of the conflict; it deals with other aspects of the Soviet domestic arena only as they relate to this central theme. The work that most resembles mine in approach and methodology is that of Göransson, which, however, is a study on the afgantsy in a single Soviet union republic and one of the smallest ones at that, although probably the one that the war affected most directly.

Another book that I use extensively is Svetlana Alexievich's *Zinky Boys: Soviet Voices from the Afghanistan War*, which she wrote to highlight the horrors of the Soviet-Afghan War. True, she had an agenda, but the voices she recorded tell a broad gamut of authentic stories.

My most important source material is the extensive survey that I conducted in 1992 and 1993, with the assistance of a small team of interviewers, in eleven of the Soviet Union's successor states (all except the Baltic states and Georgia, which together contributed less than 5 percent of the soldiers who fought in Afghanistan). We based the survey on fixed questionnaires that enabled the preparation of tables and figures, which provide a picture of the broad spectrum of views and attitudes among both the war's veterans and civilians. We designed the veterans' questionnaire to recapture the experiences of the Soviet soldiers who served in Afghanistan and the atmosphere within the Limited Contingent. The intention in interviewing civilians was to gauge public opinion regarding the war and its implications and consequences. We aimed to do so before it became too distant and too hazy a memory in the whirl of changes that overcame the Soviet Union in the early 1990s, but after waiting sufficient time for public opinion to ripen—given that until approximately 1989, the year the Soviet troops finally withdrew from Afghanistan—the overwhelming majority of Soviet citizens were not only extremely wary of expressing opinions but also hesitant about forming them.

In all, we ran three surveys, each based on a separate questionnaire. The first consisted of 221 afgantsy; it was based on snowball sampling methods, starting with afgantsy clubs around the former Soviet Union. The second used a (nonrepresentative) quota sampling of 229 former Soviet citizens resident in the Former Soviet Union (FSU). The third survey relied on convenience sampling in Israel of 266 immigrants from all over the FSU who resided in the Soviet Union at the time of the war, a few of whom were also afgantsy. The respondents lived in a wide range of cities and towns, with a disproportionately small sample in the countryside (as Jews were the most urbanized ethnic group in the Soviet Union, the countryside was hardly represented in the third survey). The second and third surveys contained different questions, and I refer to these separately in the text.

The aim of the questionnaires was to embrace the spectrum of topics that the book covers: attitudes toward the decision to intervene, the conduct of the war, the behavior of the soldiers in Afghanistan, and the decision to withdraw; the war's influence on the Soviet Union's international prestige, the media, and the political developments within the Soviet Union, specifically in the context of glasnost and perestroika, ethnic relations in the Soviet empire, and ultimately its demise; and the soldiers' reception on returning home, the challenges they encountered, and their impact on the society around them.

I have supplemented the data from the surveys with a number of in-depth interviews from the same time period and a few more interviews from 2012 to 2017. These are the interviews in which I name the respondent.

I made extensive use of contemporary media, particularly the press, which, at least as of 1984, showed growing interest in the war; some newspapers sent correspondents to Afghanistan to cover it. I have also examined art forms—movies, songs, and literature—which frequently conveyed criticism that was otherwise impossible to express. And of course I have read a broad gamut of studies of the war and reminiscences in both Russian and English (many of them published since Galeotti and Sapper completed their works). In so doing, I have borne in mind the backdrop to the various testimonies and the unquestionable fact that not a few of their authors had an axe to grind and a need to justify their own actions—for example, the last commander of the Fortieth Army, Lieutenant General Boris Gromov.

The Woodrow Wilson Center's Cold War International History Project has preserved and declassified some official Soviet documentation. This material includes Politburo discussions that provide insight into the positions of the top Kremlin leaders. However, knowledgeable sources have stated that the Ministry of Defense, the KGB, and the Ministry of Internal Affairs (the MVD) transmitted many of their instructions only orally.[9] (For one crucial oral directive, that of Minister of Defense Dmitrii Ustinov, see Chapter 1.) I have not been able to ascertain whether this was because these instructions testified to Moscow's crossing permitted bounds of intervention in Third World confrontations (to use Academician Oleg Bogomolov's description of the activity). Be that as it may, historians of the way governments act have to be wary of relying unduly on documentation, because it cannot reflect such all-important aspects of decision making as personal characteristics, conduct, and interrelationships. Documents tend to show what Marshall Shulman described as "a pattern of coordination and rationality" that "misses the messiness and the disorder of decision-making and that overlooks the informal communications" that carry great weight. They tend, too, to focus on specific moments in time and to disregard processes, although every development has to be seen in the context of its time, such as what Bill Odom called the Soviet system's "bureaucratic degeneration."[10]

My primary goals were to get the broadest possible spectrum of views regarding the war, collect a broad sample of evidence, and analyze and quantify the testimonies that the surveys provided.

I do not believe that this book will unequivocally answer the leading question: How meaningful was the war's role in precipitating the Soviet Union's disintegration? I hope that it will, however, provide a comprehensive picture, convincing readers that the war served as a catalyst for the developments that led to the collapse of the Soviet state and both highlighted and exacerbated its fallibility and many of its intrinsic shortcomings.

Chapter 1

The Decision to Intervene Militarily in Afghanistan

In early December 1979, the Kremlin leaders decided to send Soviet forces into Afghanistan. The reasoning behind this step, what little there was, provoked years of debate, notably in the glasnost era, and led to significant acrimony between liberals and conservatives. Much of the relevant documentation has since been published, making the picture relatively clear.

To understand the background of this decision, however, it will be useful to review the process of decision making in the late Brezhnev years, as well as the composition of the Soviet leadership, the power that each of the main actors held, and the relationships among them. Brezhnev had been ailing since his first stroke in 1975.[1] Thanks, however, to the persistent buildup of his personal position and his ability to bring into the Politburo men who accepted his leadership status and had a vested interest in not rocking the boat, his immediate entourage made no attempt to replace him. Instead, a trio, or *troika*, of three Politburo members—KGB Chairman Yuri Andropov, Defense Minister Dmitrii Ustinov, and Foreign Minister Andrei Gromyko—took control; Andropov, at least, seems to have been laying the groundwork to become Brezhnev's successor.[2]

This chapter examines the decision to intervene militarily in Afghanistan and the reactions at the time. Later, when Gorbachev was preparing to withdraw Soviet troops from Afghanistan and glasnost began to take hold—1986 to early 1989—the "ideological" considerations that influenced the Kremlin gerontocrats who made the decision, their dismissal of the military's advice, and their failure to consult experts regarding Afghanistan, became a cause célèbre, demonstrating the inadequacy of policymaking in the Soviet system and the flaws of the regime.

How and Why the Decision Was Made

In April 1978, a military coup brought Afghanistan's Marxist party, the People's Democratic Party of Afghanistan (the PDPA), to power in Kabul. The new Afghan regime turned to Moscow for every form of assistance a superpower could be expected to render to a small, undeveloped neighbor with a seemingly similar ideology. (Even before the coup—as a result of trade agreements with and economic aid to the Daoud regime that had ousted the monarchy in 1973—the Soviet presence in Afghanistan was greater than that of any other foreign power.) In 1978 and 1979, Soviet aadvisers and representatives flocked to Kabul to aid the Afghan economy and education system and the regime's military and security forces.[3] The Soviets increased their military aid; the KGB sent personnel to "collect information and to cooperate" with their Afghan counterparts; and the Communist Party of the Soviet Union (CPSU) helped the PDPA with organizational matters and its propaganda network.[4] In short, "all sorts of Soviet structures were being actively implanted" in the country. In December 1978, the two countries signed a twenty-year Treaty of Friendship, Good Neighborliness, and Cooperation that American sources said contained "more specific language regarding military and security cooperation than is usually found in similar Soviet treaties."[5]

By spring 1979, the radical Marxist regime, which sought to impose orthodox Marxist land and social reforms, was evoking armed opposition from the country's many tribes, which composed its social backbone. As a result, over the following months, it sent Moscow eighteen appeals for military assistance, most of them specifically requesting the dispatch of troops.[6]

For over half a year, Moscow resisted the requests to send Soviet troops into a country where a civil war was raging. Instead it made do with supplying materiel and providing additional military advisers and training. Andropov adamantly opposed direct military intervention. He insisted that Afghanistan was not yet at a stage in which it could solve its problems "through socialism" and that it would be "entirely inadmissible" to suppress the insurgency "with the aid of our bayonets," for that would mean "waging war against the people." Yet the Kremlin's determination to maintain the "revolutionary" regime in Kabul was unequivocal; in the words of Prime Minster Aleksei Kosygin, "All of us agree—we must not surrender Afghanistan." Thus, the Politburo did not rule out the possibility of sending troops "as a last resort." Its initiation of a major propaganda effort to "unmask the interference of the U.S., Pakistan, Iran and China in the internal affairs of the Democratic Republic of Afghanistan [DRA]"[7] clearly indicated that the Soviet Union was preparing for every possible contingency.

The first appeal for Soviet military intervention came in a telephone conversation between DRA President Nur Muhammad Taraki and Kosygin on March 18, 1979, following the first major insurrection against the Marxist regime, in Herat, where an angry mob murdered—among others—some 100 Soviet personnel and their families. Although the Soviet leadership advised Taraki that introducing troops would be politically inexpedient, Moscow promptly sent eight Mi-8 troop transport helicopters, a transport squadron of AN-12s, a signal center, and, in July, a 600-man paratroop battalion (of the 105th Guards Airborne Division), deployed as "technical specialists," to the Bagram airbase near Kabul. Their dispatch required a further consignment of maintenance personnel and a force to protect training and maintenance areas. The Soviets disguised the aircraft with Afghan markings, and the crews, including the paratroopers, wore Afghan uniforms.[8]

The Soviet military presence in Afghanistan grew markedly even before the introduction of the Soviet army. By August 1979, the Soviet advisory contingent had increased from approximately 1,200 before April 1978, to at least 4,500, of whom 1,500 were military advisers to the DRA armed forces. The massive buildup of military hardware included MiG 21 fighters, SU-20 bombers, over 100 T-62 tanks, Mi-8 helicopters, and rocket-armed Mi-24 helicopter gunships. The Soviet role had evolved from supplying arms, training, and technical expertise to offering day-to-day operational guidance. By December 1979, Soviet military and KGB advisers had pervaded the structure of the Afghanistan armed forces.[9]

In addition, although Ustinov told the Politburo in March 1979 that he did not support "the idea of deploying troops in Afghanistan," the Soviet Union was already forming two divisions in the Turkestan Military District (MD) and one in the Central Asian MD.[10] Moreover, the Soviets conducted military exercises in the Turkestan MD, near the border with Afghanistan. First Deputy Minister of Defense (MoD) Valentin Varennikov later explained that as "military people," they had to prepare for any decision the political leadership might make.[11] In April, Nikolai Ogarkov, chief of the general staff (CGS), despite his opposition to sending in troops, instructed several senior officers from the Turkestan MD to fly to Kabul to see the situation for themselves.[12]

In April 1979, the men heading the four relevant organizations—Ustinov, together with Andropov, Gromyko, and Boris Ponomarev, CPSU Central Committee (CC) Secretary and head of its International Department—signed a report explaining the decision to offer only economic and military assistance—in the form of weaponry and advisers—and refrain from sending Soviet troops to repress the counterrevolution. Such a measure would "seriously damage the international authority of the USSR and would set back the process of disarmament. In addition, the use of Soviet troops would reveal the weakness of the Taraki government and widen the scope of the counter-revolution both domestically and abroad." The document also detailed the Kremlin's dissatisfaction with the PDPA regime's handling of the deteriorating situation in the country.[13]

Between March and December 1979, a number of Soviet officials visited Afghanistan. The first was the Main Political Administration (MPA) head, General Aleksei Epishev.[14] From August 17 through October 22, 1979, the deputy defense minister and C-in-C of the Soviet Ground Forces Army, General Ivan Pavlovskii, and a large, high-level military delegation helped the DRA army organize combat operations and improve its combat capabilities.[15] (Interestingly, Epishev had visited Czechoslovakia before the Soviet invasion in August 1968, and Pavlovskii had commanded the invasion force.)

A coup d'état in September 1979 led to the murder of Taraki and brought to power his assassin and former colleague, Hazifullah Amin. This put new pressure on the Kremlin to change its stand. Brezhnev took Taraki's assassination as a personal affront, occurring as it had within days of his personal promise to support Taraki. To his close circle, he described the murder as "a slap in the face." According to one knowledgeable expert, Igor' Beliaev, Brezhnev's emotional reaction was the critical factor in the subsequent dynamic. The decision to intervene was his response, even though it countered his original assertion to Taraki that "The Soviet Union will not introduce troops into Afghanistan. The appearance of our troops will undoubtedly set a large part of the Afghan people against the revolution." Beliaev went on, "Naturally, [Brezhnev's] closest circle should have held him back from the fatal decision. But '*vozhdizm*' [the cult of the leader] bred by all the flaws in our state administration . . . did its bit."[16] While some have suggested that "keeping Brezhnev on a higher pinnacle of prestige than any of his Politburo colleagues" was "a device of his supporters and of others who stood to gain from his continued presence" despite his frail health,[17] these same colleagues found themselves committed to the rules that they had laid down. Possibly, too, their personal and institutional interests played a role in determining their position.

Brezhnev's dissatisfaction at Taraki's murder implied a personal failure on Andropov's part, which the KGB chief undertook to rectify by pressuring "his" officials. Stories appeared about Amin's involvement with the CIA, the external threat to the DRA from Pakistan and Iran, the penetration of Islamic extremism into Soviet Central Asia, and the U.S. intention to place American SIGINT (Signals Intelligence) equipment and several types of missiles in Afghanistan if pro-Western forces came to power there."[18] In the words of a Soviet/Russian commentator, "The chimera that had found its way into the heads of the Kremlin gerontocrats had begun to take on a life of its own, and from their point of view was turning into a reality."[19]

By fall 1979, two members of the leadership troika, Ustinov and Andropov, together with Brezhnev's foreign policy adviser, Andrei Aleksandrov-Agentov, had come to present the situation in Afghanistan in the light of Soviet-American zero-sum-game competition. Based on the KGB reports flowing in from Kabul, they told Brezhnev of American involvement in the mounting fundamentalist Islamic opposition and President Amin's supposed pro-American orientation. Gromyko, the third member of the trio, probably acquiesced to this, given the breakdown of détente and the increasingly bleak chances of solving the problem through diplomacy. Toward the end of October, the special commission on Afghanistan, comprising the trio and CPSU CC Secretary Ponomarev, presented the Politburo with a report on the situation in Afghanistan, warning that Amin was showing signs of shifting toward the United States.[20] Brezhnev's cronies apparently emphasized this dynamic in order to legitimize Amin's removal, which they discerned was now the General Secretary's leading concern.

This theme became Andropov's main focus. In an undated personal memorandum to the General Secretary, attributed to the first days of December, Andropov emphasized the danger of losing the gains of the April 1978 revolution and the threat to Soviet positions in Afghanistan given the growing anti-Soviet sentiment there.[21] On December 4, he and CGS Marshal Nikolai Ogarkov wrote to Brezhnev recommending that the MoD send about 500 men to Kabul in uniforms that would not disclose their affiliation with the Soviet military, a proposal that the Politburo endorsed on December 6. On December 9 and 10, the "Muslim Battalion" left for the Afghan capital. The deputy chief of the KGB's First Main Directorate, Lieutenant General Vadim Kirpichenko, was already in Kabul to prepare the operation that would remove Amin from power.[22]

Before looking at the ultimate decision to intervene militarily, it is necessary to consider the international and regional background. In the course of the 1970s, the Soviet Union had lost three Third World allies—Egypt, Somalia, and Chile—and, seeking to rectify the balance vis-à-vis the United States, had endangered détente by resorting to aggressive measures in Ethiopia and Angola. By the end of the decade, Vietnam had scored a victory in Cambodia, as had Unità in Granada. Cuba and Vietnam encouraged Moscow to look for easy victories in the Third World. The future seemed to belong to socialism.

Closer to home, early in 1979, an Islamic regime had overthrown the shah of Iran. The Kremlin's fear of growing regional instability and its apprehension that the United States, which had close relations with the shah, would endeavor to regain its hold in "the area in neighboring Afghanistan almost certainly played a role in the Kremlin's change of mind. So too did information concerning the upcoming NATO decision to deploy a new class of medium-range nuclear—Pershing—missiles in Europe and Congress's postponement of ratification of the SALT II agreement that Brezhnev and President Jimmy Carter signed in June. These two developments apparently convinced the leaders in the Kremlin, who were concerned over the likely influence on détente of intervention in Afghanistan, that there was nothing to lose.[23] Moreover, the KGB suspected—or claimed to suspect—that Amin would allow the Americans to place their "control and intelligence centers close to our most sensitive borders."[24] According to Vasilii Safronchuk, an experienced diplomat sent to Kabul in mid-1979 as unofficial adviser to the Afghan foreign ministry, Moscow was also concerned about Amin's intention to redesign the Afghan state structure, making it more like that of the Soviet Union by creating nationality-based republics, which would place an Afghan Uzbek or Tajik republic on the Soviet border.[25]

By the end of November, the General Staff of the Armed Forces, the Foreign Ministry, and the KGB were all searching "feverishly" for solutions. The leadership, for its part, had resolved to remove Amin. Discussing decision making in Moscow, Aleksandr Liakhovskii, the leading Russian historian of the war in Afghanistan, says that Politburo procedure enabled it to make decisions without consulting other bodies. The prevalent "precise system of subordination" meant that there was no possibility of departure from the line that the Politburo laid down, even by those in "government posts." Moreover, "many leaders, including Politburo members," although they might have had their own views on any given situation, "always tried to 'see which way the wind was blowing' by trying to find out Brezhnev's opinion ahead of time, tailoring their opinions to him, and often ignoring the recommendations of analysts and experts. Such a flawed practice led to fatal mistakes." Liakhovskii writes that the decision "to deploy Soviet troops to Afghanistan to support an operation to remove Amin from power was made after long hesitation and an analysis of the unfolding situation. It was not impulsive, but many factors were not considered all the same."[26]

All commentators agree that those responsible for making the decision did not consult either civilian or military experts on the Middle East or on Afghanistan and ignored that country's particulars.[27] Karen Brutents, then deputy head of the CPSU CC's International Department, contends that the March 18 decision not to introduce troops was made after consultation with experts who were "unanimously and unquestionably" against doing so, whereas in December they were not asked.[28] The Soviet leadership likewise ignored its own experienced emissaries in Kabul, conducting a changeover of leading Soviet personnel in November. Tatar Obkom Secretary Fikrat Tabeev replaced Ambassador Aleksandr Puzanov, whom the DRA leadership had accused of colluding with Taraki against Amin;[29] First Deputy Commander of the Transbaikal MD, the Karachai colonel general, Soltan Magometov, took over from Chief Military Adviser General Lev Gorelov;[30] and Aleksandr Kosogovskii replaced the chief MVD adviser to the DRA, General Nikolai Veselkov. Their inexperience meant that they could offer little advice.[31] No one consulted Puzanov, who had spent seven years in Kabul and opposed any large-scale intervention.[32] The report that Pavlovskii gave Ustinov on his return recommended rejecting Afghan appeals for Soviet forces; he had told Amin in August that introducing Soviet troops would complicate the military and political situation in the region and encourage the United States to enhance its aid to the opposition.[33] But Ustinov concealed this report from the Central Committee.[34] Major General Vasilii Zaplatin, adviser to the chief of the DRA Armed Forces MPA, as well as most of the Soviet military advisers in Afghanistan,[35] disagreed with the report of the KGB's representative in Kabul, Boris Ivanov, who wrote that the situation in Afghanistan was near crisis. The Politburo disregarded his opinion as well.[36]

The issue at stake was therefore primarily political, not military. The decision rested on Moscow's assessment of whether the DRA leadership was capable of preventing the opposition from overrunning Afghanistan and implementing the April revolution.[37] By December 8, when he held his crucial meeting with the trio, Brezhnev had accepted their position that there was no alternative solution to the crisis that threatened the PDPA regime and consented to send troops into Afghanistan.

Mikhail Suslov, the party secretary responsible for propaganda and relations with socialist regimes, the leading ideologist in the Soviet leadership, and a known hardliner, apparently learned of the decision on the same day and provided it with the requisite legitimization; while clearly the Kremlin's verdict was based on strategic and practical considerations, the ideological framework and resultant mentality remained. According to Gromyko, Brezhnev told Suslov, "It seems necessary to make a decision immediately: either we ignore Afghanistan's request for aid or we save the people's power and act in accordance with the Soviet-Afghan agreement." Suslov considered "our obligations" under the treaty as binding. Were Moscow to withhold support from the DRA regime in Kabul, he said, it would forfeit any claim to promote other socialist states. Moreover, it was necessary to act on the decision immediately. "We will discuss it at the CC later on."[38]

Brezhnev stated categorically that the Soviet Union was in danger of losing Afghanistan. He feared that Amin's takeover and his relationship with the United States might lead to America's placing along the Soviet Union's southern border American monitoring technology capable of photographing "all the parameters" of Soviet weaponry on Central Asian testing grounds. In view of what they saw as the CIA's efforts to create a New Great Ottoman Empire that would include the Soviet Union's southern republics, and the lack of a reliable air defense system in the south, Andropov and Ustinov favored the deployment of troops. NATO's decision to station Pershing missiles in Western Europe was the last straw.

Andropov was also concerned about the formation of an Islamic autonomy in northern Afghanistan; if the counterrevolution succeeded, he noted, the Soviet Union would have a "Muslim problem." Those at the December 8 meeting resolved to remove Amin and replace him with Babrak Karmal, leader of Parcham, the rival faction within the PDPA. They discussed sending in 70,000 to 80,000 troops to stabilize the situation and then withdraw without fighting. This force would come primarily from Central Asia, as Ustinov opposed transferring troops from Europe or the Far East.[39]

The senior military command—CGS Marshal Nikolai Ogarkov; CGS First Deputy, Army General Sergei Akhromeev; Deputy CGS and Chief of the Main Operations Directorate, Valentin Varennikov; and Pavlovskii—opposed introducing Soviet armed forces into Afghanistan. They recognized that doing so was likely to involve the troops in military activity, even if the declared intention was only to buttress the PDPA's positions, and that the Soviet army was not prepared to fight guerrillas in a country like Afghanistan; its training had been for battle in Central Europe or East Asia. Further, by the Afghans' long tradition of resisting foreign intervention, the presence of Soviet troops would "pit all of eastern Islam against us" and alienate the whole world.

But the Kremlin leaders were not prepared to listen to the military or to dissenting voices within the party bureaucracy. The latter were silenced, while Brezhnev and Andropov overruled the chief of staff and his generals. Karen Brutents was preparing a negative report until Aleksandrov-Agentov stopped him, asking whether he wished Moscow to give Afghanistan to the Americans.[40] On December 10, Ogarkov told Ustinov that introducing Soviet troops was a reckless step. Ustinov nonetheless instructed him to prepare a force of 75,000 to 80,000 soldiers in accordance with the Politburo's "tentative decision to temporarily deploy troops to Afghanistan."[41] He wanted 75,000 troops for the initial operation to ensure that he could bring down the Amin regime and because he thought that using Soviet troops to protect Afghanistan's borders with Pakistan and Iran would foreclose external assistance to the Islamic guerrillas. The goal would be to "stabilize the situation"; there was no intention "to 'win,' to destroy, or to take over."[42]

It is possible that the GS's opposition to the intervention stemmed from its understanding that it would need thirty to thirty-five divisions to "conquer and control" Afghanistan, so that fielding the three comprising the initial force doomed the campaign to failure.[43] According to Varennikov, the calculation of the force's size rested on the need to establish garrisons in the twelve provinces along the Pakistani and Iranian borders where the mujahidin were "well established," in Kabul and at the Bagram airfield.

Yet there were people in "the top echelons" of the military establishment who supported the decision to intervene in order "to test our troops in combat, especially the officer corps," as well as assess "our battle equipment and new weaponry."[44] Indeed, senior KGB operative Leonid Shebarshin rejected Varennikov's testimony that the GS was unanimous in opposing the introduction of troops.[45]

Two days later, on December 12, a truncated Politburo made the formal decision to approve the introduction of Soviet troops into Afghanistan. At the meeting were Brezhnev; the trio, Suslov, Viktor Grishin, Andrei Kirilenko, Arvid Pel'she, Konstantin Chernenko, and Nikolai Tikhonov; all full Politburo members; and candidate member Boris Ponomarev.[46] Kosygin, the three full members not stationed permanently in Moscow (Volodymyr Shcherbytsky, Grigorii Romanov, and Dinmuhammed Kunaev), and the candidate members (except Ponomarev) did not participate. Romanov stated that the Politburo never voted on the intervention.[47] Kirilenko who, together with Kosygin, had vocally opposed the idea of sending in troops "signed after some hesitation."[48] More signatures were appended on December 25 and 26.[49] According to the testimony of his personal aide, although Ukrainian Party leader Shcherbytsky was asked to endorse the decision, he opposed the "adventure."[50]

Kosygin did not sign. According to Sergei Krakhmalov, the GRU official who became military attaché to the Soviet embassy in Kabul in spring 1980, the Soviet prime minister recognized that the Soviet forces would inevitably be drawn into combat. On December 11, Kosygin reportedly told Ogarkov to convince Ustinov that Moscow must not introduce troops into Afghanistan.[51]

Recalling those days a decade later, Gromyko, the sole remaining participant in the decisive meeting, insisted that "everyone knows that [Soviet] troops were introduced [into Afghanistan] solely as neighborly assistance between one country and another."[52] He told his son, however, that the decision had rested first on the U.S. aspiration to destabilize the Soviet Union's southern flank by placing in Pakistan, and if possible, in Afghanistan, armaments that it had removed from Iran; and, second, on Taraki's assassination, which the Politburo viewed as an attempted counterrevolution that the United States could use against the Soviet Union. The United States had plans to destabilize progressive countries friendly to Moscow and had enhanced measures for implementing them. Nobody in the leadership had any doubts as to the political grounds for the decision, and Brezhnev rejected Gromyko's proposal to bring it before the Supreme Soviet. The way the decision was made conformed to the prevalent decision-making mechanisms: who participated in the meeting and who did not depended solely on Brezhnev.[53]

Summing up his understanding at the 1995 Lysebu symposium on Afghanistan, Varennikov emphasized that the Kremlin did not make the decision hastily, and that a priori, the Soviet leadership had had no desire to introduce troops but that "the overall picture, and the views that our leadership held, forced them to make that decision. . . . Everything was filtered through the lens of the Cold War. Suspiciousness, mistrust, the expectation of grave consequences all dominated their thinking. That is why those ideological and strategic considerations that pressured them led them to take such a step."[54] Gorbachev aide Aleksandr Yakovlev used somewhat different language, but his point is similar. He attributed the intervention mainly to the Kremlin's living in a make-believe world, rejecting realistic assessments of the situation, and using ideological clichés to determine its positions. This, he stated, resulted from the leadership's dogmatism, unwillingness to consider objective facts, and reliance on force, violence, and arms.[55]

In the Turkestan Military District, the army formed a new combined-arms force—to be called the Fortieth Army—specifically for the purpose of entering Afghanistan It would include an airborne division, an independent airborne regiment, and five military transport aviation divisions, all of which now prepared for an airborne landing operation, while two divisions in the Turkestan MD increased their combat readiness. There was no official government resolution as the "USSR law on universal military service" stipulated; Ustinov issued instructions to the GS verbally.[56] On December 11, at a meeting of "the small Politburo," now including Chernenko and Kirilenko, Ogarkov recommended using only a small force that would protect certain objects and refrain from active participation in combat, on the assumption that the presence of Soviet troops would stabilize the situation and halt opposition attacks on the DRA army. This would free the DRA troops to fight. But Andropov silenced the CGS brutally,[57] and he was given his final orders.[58] In the words of Anatolii Cherniaev, then an official of the CC International Department, "I do not believe that ever before in Russian history, even under Stalin, was there a period when such important actions were taken without a hint of discussion, advice and deliberation. We have entered a very dangerous period when the ruling circle cannot fully appreciate what it is doing and why."[59]

Seventy-seven hundred men were flown into Kabul toward the end of that month, and beginning on December 25, 1979, the rest of the initial 50,000 went into Afghanistan by foot or in army transport from Termez.[60] The directive that Ustinov had signed the preceding day stated that "some contingents of Soviet troops" would be introduced into Afghanistan's southern regions in order "to give international aid to the friendly Afghan people and also to create favorable conditions to interdict possible anti-Afghan actions from neighboring states."[61]

A December 27 Politburo circular to the CPSU *nomenklatura* presented the Kremlin's steps as a response to the deteriorating situation in Afghanistan that resulted from Amin's repressive measures and foreign interference in Afghanistan's internal affairs on behalf of the forces of counterrevolution. Consequently, the Politburo was consenting to the Afghan government's approaches and introducing "a small military contingent" that would withdraw "as soon as the situation there stabilizes and the reasons that occasioned this action disappear." In adopting this measure, the Politburo was taking into consideration both its "international duty" and its own security in light of Afghanistan's strategic location, particularly its "direct proximity to our borders, neighboring on the Soviet republics of Central Asia."[62] Ustinov was said to have explained that the intervention also intended to test contemporary military technology in order to ensure Soviet capacity to counter the threat of NATO's midrange missiles.[63]

On the last day of the year, Andropov, Gromyko, Ustinov, and Ponomarev signed a letter to the CPSU Central Committee that attributed the need to overthrow Amin and "render additional military assistance to Afghanistan" to the situation there. Moscow introduced the requisite "contingent of the Soviet army,"[64] in accordance with the provisions of the Soviet-Afghan treaty of 1978, namely with the Brezhnev Doctrine, that justified the Soviet intervention in Czechoslovakia, where a socialist regime was apparently not toeing the Soviet line. The Kremlin had already applied the Brezhnev Doctrine to justify Soviet military intervention in Third World countries like Egypt, where a significant Soviet military presence existed from 1970 through 1972. The December 1978 treaty between the Soviet Union and the DRA spoke of Moscow's commitment to "guarantee [Afghanistan's] security, independence, and territorial integrity," thus providing a legal basis for the intervention.[65] As Varennikov testified, sending troops into a country with which one had a treaty and whose government had requested them was "completely normal"; aggression is when one wants to take over and pursue one's own goals.[66]

The operation that led to the killing of Amin was, according to a Western military analyst, "masterfully planned and well executed." But the Kremlin's intention to stabilize the country and then withdraw proved unrealistic. The leadership was thinking in terms of "a brief action"; Brezhnev reportedly contemplated withdrawing within a matter of weeks.[67] The commander of the first assault troops (VDV) testified that the Fortieth Army soldiers believed that they would be home by Army Day, February 23, 1980.[68] But the tribes across the country were in full revolt and the Afghan government's army proved incapable of fighting the ubiquitous guerrilla groups. "The specter of [its] defeat upon a Soviet withdrawal haunted the Politburo," and the failure to decide to withdraw meant a prolonged and hapless war.[69] In fact, it became clear after Andropov's visit to Kabul in January 1980 that Soviet troops would remain in Afghanistan for the indefinite future. On February 19, 1980, Moscow issued—but apparently did not publish—a document that seems to have contemplated a prolonged stay in Afghanistan; it included an instruction defining the "procedure of financing and granting privileges" to personnel serving there.[70]

Moscow started early on to contemplate a political settlement of the conflict (see Chapter 4). However the Politburo could not define the minimum requirements for a troop withdrawal. As Western positions hardened and it became increasingly clear that the Soviet force and the DRA army could not put down the resistance, Soviet demands grew more unrealistic. The "intervention" evolved into a war that lasted nearly a decade, leaving over a million Afghans dead or wounded and some 4 million more refugees, as well as a significant number of Soviet dead, wounded, and otherwise maimed.

Discussion and Evaluation of the Decision

In contrast to the international opprobrium that the intervention evoked, at home there was little or no public discussion of it. Public opinion carried little official weight with the leadership, although the Kremlin frequently sought tacit public acceptance of official policies. It strictly controlled media reportage. All that trickled out to the public about the war was that the Soviet Union was supporting the legal government of the DRA in its struggle to maintain the communist regime and to suppress the reactionary American-backed Islamic opposition (see Chapter 6). The public was aware that there were few sources of reliable information. The media routinely provided false reports, and the increased jamming of foreign broadcasts was an integral component of the hardening of domestic policy that accompanied the end of détente in 1979.

Officers and soldiers returning from the war, especially in the early weeks and months, tended not to discuss their experiences. They had committed themselves to total silence, first in their own military unit, again on crossing the border into the Soviet Union, and a third time at the KGB station or military commissariat (*voenkomat*) in their respective home towns. The army gave the families of those killed no information about how their sons or husbands had died.

Some information, however, leaked out. First, throughout the Soviet Union, there were the funerals of soldiers killed in Afghanistan (see Chapter 7). Second, soldiers who returned could not be isolated, and even those who did not talk afforded disquieting information; some had been wounded or contracted illnesses, and many had trouble sleeping and had nightmares. In addition to such scraps of actual information, rumor was rife. It was soon broadly known that Soviet losses were considerable.

Reservations regarding the introduction of troops persisted within the Soviet nomenklatura. On January 20, 1980, the USSR Academy of Sciences Institute of Economics of the World Socialist System, headed by Academician Oleg Bogomolov, addressed a thirty-two-page memorandum to the CPSU Central Committee and the KGB entitled, "Some Thoughts concerning the Foreign Policy Repercussions of the 70s." Regarding the intervention, it noted that "with the introduction of troops into Afghanistan our policy . . . crossed the permissible bounds of confrontation in the Third World. The advantages of this action" were "insignificant compared to the damage inflicted on our interests." Bogomolov later stated that his institute's memo "spoke of the futility and harmfulness of this action." It pointed out Afghanistan's "unfavorable geographic, social, and political conditions."[71] In 1988, Bogomolov also mentioned his institute's earlier reports "to the highest levels," which dwelled on the need for "restraint and caution in the turbulent zone of the developing countries."[72]

After the war's end, Varennikov noted that all reservations regarding the introduction of troops addressed solely the inexpediency of this measure for Soviet interests; only later might there have been doubts founded on moral or legal grounds.[73] This dictum ignored the few dissidents who protested the invasion, notably the most prominent one, Academician Andrei Sakharov. On January 17, 1980, he told an American correspondent that the main concern of the Soviet people and the rest of the world should be the war in Afghanistan and the danger that it would become yet more extensive. He called on the United Nations to persuade the Soviet Union to withdraw its troops from Afghanistan immediately, perhaps replacing them with a UN force. On January 22, Sakharov was arrested and exiled to the city of Gorkii, an industrial town 250 miles east of Moscow officially closed to foreigners. (His arrest was probably already in the cards, but his remonstrations regarding Afghanistan gave the security services a compelling pretext for convincing Brezhnev to order Sakharov's removal from the capital.)[74] In a July 1980 interview with American television, Sakharov reinforced his call for a Soviet withdrawal, backing it with an open letter to the Soviet leadership. Unlike Bogomolov, Sakharov also addressed the domestic implications of the intervention: "The war in Afghanistan has been going on for seven months. Thousands of Soviet people have been killed and maimed and tens of thousands of Afghans—not only partisans, but above all peaceful citizens. . . . More than a million Afghans have become refugees. There are sinister reports of the bombing of villages that helped the partisans, and of the mining of mountain roads, which threatens whole areas with starvation." At home, the war enhanced militarization and "the dangerous role of the repressive organs" and halted necessary reforms.[75]

In January 1980, Ukrainian activist Leonid Malyshev wrote an open letter to *Izvestiia* and to the CC CPSU entitled, "Get the Troops out of Afghanistan." Accusations that he had criticized the intervention figured in his trial that same year, as well as in those of two other Ukrainian activists, Anatolii Marchenko and Dmitrii Mazur.[76] Mazur, a teacher from Zhitomir Province and contributor to Ukrainian samizdat, had a relative who was killed in Afghanistan. He received a sentence of six years in camp and five in exile for dozens of statements against this "act of aggression," including letters to Soviet leaders, the CPSU, and major newspapers. A Kiev Jewish "refusenik" reportedly compared the intervention to the Nazi invasion of Poland in 1939 and feared that it might set off a third world war. One Yurii Popov, who was arrested for disseminating leaflets in Moscow demanding that the war be ended (and that the death punishment be commuted), was hospitalized in a psychiatric clinic. The same charge was brought in 1982 against Pavel Airepetov and one Nazarov of Dushanbe; Airepetov was also accused of contact with Afghan partisans.

Not surprisingly, there was protest in the camps. Valerii Abramkin of the editorial staff of the "thick" Moscow samizdat journal *Poiski*, who had been arrested in 1979, was charged with telling fellow prisoners that the Soviet Union was conducting an unjust war in Afghanistan.[77] A Leningrad women's group, Mariia, also expressed an "anti-Soviet" stance on Afghanistan early in the war; the authorities described this as "the last straw on top of their 'subversive' feminist agenda." The women called on Soviet conscripts to go to prison rather than serve in Afghanistan. At least two of them were punished with exile.[78] (For the occasional correspondent who criticized the intervention in the early years, see Chapter 6.)

Baltic activists were in the forefront of the opposition. The first collective protest condemning the intervention was an open letter that twenty-one Baltic activists sent to the USSR Supreme Soviet and the UN one month after the invasion, in the name of the Main Committee of the National Movement of Estonia, Latvia, and Lithuania (which had initiated its activity in Riga in 1977). In early 1982, leaflets protesting the war were disseminated in Latvia; one of them stated specifically that "our sons should not be killing Afghan sons and daughters. Freedom for Afghans and Latvians!"[79]

Criticism of the intervention in the three Baltic republics was not limited to dissidents. In the Baltics—perhaps alone of all regions of the Soviet Union—the general attitude to the war seems to have been negative; people compared the occupation of Afghanistan with that of Estonia, Latvia, and Lithuania in 1940. As the war continued, the Baltic peoples came to feel that they had contributed more than their share to the Soviet forces and had consequently suffered a disproportionate number of losses (see also Chapter 7).

It seems that people in other parts of the country felt similarly about the invasion. KGB operational reports from Ukraine noted the adverse attitude of both the local intelligentsia[80] and the man on the street. Already in 1980, people entertained doubts and questioned the expediency of military aid to Afghanistan, fearing an enhanced mobilization. After hearing Western broadcasts, they expressed dissatisfaction regarding the dearth of information in Soviet media. One woman said the intervention aggravated an already tense situation and anticipated workers' strikes. The spring of 1980 saw the zenith of anonymous protest—leaflets, letters, and inscriptions on walls calling for withdrawal. One leaflet read, "People! If the lives of your sons and husbands and altogether of our soldiers are dear to you, don't let them be sent to die in Afghanistan. Their lives depend on us, the peaceful population. Rise in struggle against the authorities."[81]

According to our interviews, taken admittedly in the early 1990s when later thinking might well have colored memories, the intervention upset Soviet citizens across the country from the start. Although they lacked information, they saw the war as an aggressive attempt by a major power to subdue a small nation that was trying to decide its own fate. Some discussed the issue with close friends, particularly in circles that managed to overcome the jamming and listen to foreign radio, a pastime that had become increasingly common in the 1960s and 1970s. One Soviet journalist recalled that as soon as he heard of the decision to intervene, a feeling of depression overcame him: "It seemed to me that I saw a dark tunnel into which my country was plunging. I felt as though I were choking. . . . The most amazing thing is that this reaction was shared by the vast majority of Soviet citizens. Of course, it changed nothing. Official approbation endowed the fateful step with a sort of triumphal rectitude. And so it was during all those long years of the war, the longest waged by Russia since 1813: the people lived in grief, and officialdom basked in the glory of doctrine."[82] *Pravda* dismissed its correspondent in Kabul, Leonid Mironov, for expressing doubts—orally, in a closed circle of the paper's staff—regarding Soviet policy in Afghanistan.[83] Announcer Vladimir Danchev at Radio Moscow in English was reportedly placed in a psychiatric hospital in May 1982 for repeatedly condemning the Soviet occupation of Afghanistan.[84]

In September 1981, people in the Russian city of Novocherkassk distributed leaflets calling on the Soviet government not to interfere in the domestic affairs of other countries. And as the November 7 celebrations of the October Revolution approached, inscriptions appeared on Moscow's Zhukovskii Street demanding freedom for Poland and Afghanistan.[85] The early years saw only a few group protests. In 1983, the government detained two hundred people after a pacifist demonstration in Moscow that disseminated leaflets calling for an end to the war in Afghanistan.[86] An economist from Latvia asserted that the occasional demonstration against the war ceased when people came to fear that their protest would increase the chances of their sons being sent to Afghanistan.[87]

Young intellectuals in Moscow also criticized the invasion though in the privacy of their apartments. Sergei Stankevich, later adviser to President Yeltsin but at the time a teacher at the Moscow Pedagogical Institute in his mid-twenties, told U.S. journalist Hedrick Smith a decade or so later that the invasion was a shock for him and his friends: "We were terrified, because we understood that when the war starts outside, the war also starts inside. The war against truth, openness, against liberals." His friends heard about Sakharov's protest on foreign radio, but nobody else dared protest openly. "Our reaction was blaming," but in the kitchen. "Afghanistan was a watershed for our generation . . . the funeral of hope." Yet even before Brezhnev died, Stankevich and his circle had come to believe that sooner or later "radical changes . . . would be inevitable. . . . When the government of a regime in crisis goes to war, it's also an attempt to postpone the crash. But in practice it accelerates the crash."[88]

In contrast, nearly half of our respondents from among the general population considered the intervention appropriate at the time; almost 40 percent thought that the Soviet Union needed to intervene, and 59 percent believed that there was a real danger to the Soviet Union's southern border (see Figure 7.1, and Table 7.4). It is likely that the majority of the Soviet population regarded the incursion of Soviet troops to Afghanistan positively or with indifference. Immigrants who arrived in Israel in 1980 and 1981 stated categorically that the dispatch of Soviet troops to Afghanistan had not evoked any manifest dissatisfaction within the Soviet Union—except in the Baltic republics. Many Russians approved of the step, and some expressed negative sentiments toward *inorodtsy* (a term used for some of the less respected ethnic minorities in the Russian Empire) and infidels. Others were completely disinterested or blamed the Afghans for the war, regarding them with exasperation and animosity, an apparent reflection of the widespread scorn with which Soviet Europeans looked on their own Central Asians.[89]

The more accepting or neutral perspectives changed as the war continued. Most Soviet citizens seemed resigned to the situation as long as it did not affect their stomachs. However, parents of newly enlisted sons and of boys approaching mobilization age did all they could to prevent their sons from being dispatched to Afghanistan, even appealing directly to the CPSU Central Committee and the Ministry of Defense.

Wide condemnation of the decision to intervene emerged only as time passed, and particularly after the end of the war. Now people considered it a mistake from almost every viewpoint—the arbitrary way in which it was made by a small number of old men unwilling to take advice from people who knew what it entailed; the almost automatic adherence to "old thinking" irrelevant to the situation in hand; the belief in supporting a neighboring socialist regime under any circumstances; and the failure to weigh the pros and especially the cons or to appreciate that the intervention would not only enhance the opposition to a regime that relied on a foreign power but also stimulate foreign aid to the "counterrevolution."[90] This was also the sense of the December 1989 report of the USSR Supreme Soviet Committee for the Affairs of the Soldier-Internationalists (see Chapter 4).

The verdict of former chief of the KGB First Main Directorate, Leonid Shebarshin, was no less harsh: "The entire undertaking was prepared in a situation of such secrecy that there was simply no critical data analysis of the situation in Afghanistan." Liakhovskii held that the decision resulted from "opportunistic approaches to the situation . . . mistakes, failures and the fatal miscalculations of our special services and missions in Kabul, and also superficial analysis . . . and insufficient forecasting of the development of the situation in and around Afghanistan by analysts in Moscow."[91]

The former Soviet military attaché in Kabul took a similar position. In his view, the intervention was

> inexpedient ... [it] complicated the USSR's political and economic situation and strained socio-political relations inside the country. This extremely serious measure was undertaken hastily without sufficient training of the troops, without creating the requisite

> foreign policy circumstances or considering its possible consequences. The [Soviet] political and military leadership had no clear goals and did not work out any strategic plan of action. Our force was not presented with any concrete military assignments when it entered Afghanistan. It was hoped that the very appearance of the Soviet army would be a stabilizing factor and sober up the mujahidin. [Yet] a civil war was raging in the DRA and, arriving to defend one side, the inevitability of confrontation with the other side ought to have been taken into account.[92]

Afganets Major General Kim Tsagolov was similarly critical. In an interview in the early 1990s, he censured the Soviet leadership for supporting the DRA regime's fundamental error in attempting to impose "a socialist paradise" on a feudal country. The Kremlin let itself be "dragged into an utterly hopeless, vicious, and cruel war." The responsibility of those who tutored the PDPA leaders was undeniable. Nor was it only the dead—Brezhnev, Andropov, Ustinov, Suslov, Gromyko—who were to blame, but all members of the Politburo, including Gorbachev and Shevarnadze, who lacked Sakharov's courage to protest.[93]

The decision to intervene in Afghanistan, then, was made by a very small number of the country's leaders, ignoring the advice of the military and without consulting civilian experts. In the words of one analyst, the fault was in "the internal balance of power, dominated . . . by old thinking and traditional conceptions of security" that "favored traditional notions of empire and commitments to client states," and the sense that not responding to PDPA requests for military support would jeopardize the Soviet Union's great power status. Certainly "ideology and systemic factors" were also significant, but they "were decisively mediated by domestic political constraints."[94] We can attribute the leading roles of Andropov and the KGB to the KGB chief's designs to succeed the ailing Brezhnev as General Secretary—as eventually happened. Interestingly, in Brezhnev's last three years Andropov increased his power and, with it, the tightening of controls. But the public that was subjected to the increasing limitations that accompanied this tended to attribute them instead to the Afghan War.

The Kremlin leaders decided to intervene militarily in what amounted to a civil war in a neighboring country because they interpreted, or felt they must interpret, it as an insurrection against a legitimate Marxist regime that they could not ignore. They did so without taking into account the fact that this regime was inflicting reforms for which the Afghan population was singularly unsuited and that therefore the intervention was likely to mean a protracted and unwinnable war.

Chapter 2

The Course of the War

The Soviet army was, in the words of a Western analyst, "probably the world's most operationally competent army in terms of theory, planning, and execution." The war in Afghanistan, however, was necessarily a tactical war and "Soviet tactics were initially inadequate for fighting guerrillas. ... The terrain, the climate and the enemy were entirely different from what they had prepared for . . . [so that] their equipment functioned less than optimally [and] their force structure was clearly inappropriate."[1] Or, as two former Soviet military personnel put it, "nothing" that Soviet troops in Afghanistan faced "could be found in field manuals and in the training programs of Soviet military academies and colleges. . . . In Afghanistan they had to learn again, to gain experience and knowledge. . . . Such experience was accumulated literally day by day in small doses, taking a long time."[2] One former military intelligence officer and *spetsnaz* (special forces) colonel attributes the lack of preparation for the war to ideological reasons and insists that the lack of written guidelines stymied their combat capabilities.[3]

The military, moreover, received no strategic overview of its assignment from the political leadership beyond the general outline of the intervention's goals (see Chapter 1), which it transmitted orally. Nor apparently did the MoD delineate any military assignments to the command of the Fortieth Army, the Soviet force in Afghanistan, and it never defined the tasks of the force's commanders. During December 1979, the MoD relayed over thirty oral directives relating to mobilization and the force's composition, but these never indicated what the Fortieth Army was supposed to accomplish.[4]

The cumbersome process of decision making further stymied the armed forces. The Fortieth Army was subordinated to the Turkestan MD, whose commander, at least in the early period, would come for a few days every month to be with "his Army."[5] The Turkestan MD command, together with the chief military adviser, under the general leadership of the MoD Operations Group (OG), drew up the army's monthly plans on the basis of their appraisal of the situation in Afghanistan. That they then had to send these to Moscow for confirmation "decidedly constrained the autonomy and initiative of the Fortieth Army command" while giving the DRA leadership a pretext for placing responsibility for the Afghan army's failures on the Kremlin.[6]

Like the Americans in Vietnam, the Soviets partly restructured and retrained their force during the war's course in order to meet Afghan conditions and the "requirements of the theater as [the Soviet command] came to understand them."[7] Military schools and training centers incorporated Afghanistan combat experience and trained personnel (see Chapter 5); indeed, the units that adapted were relatively more successful.[8]

Overall, however, these lessons were to little avail. "The Soviet Afghan military effort soon languished. Although appearing to have entered Afghanistan in seemingly surgical fashion and with overwhelming force, the Soviet military commitment was in reality quite limited, and the immense and stark terrain of Afghanistan swallowed the invaders up."[9]

This chapter discusses the evolution of this saga over the course of the war's three phases: invasion and consolidation (1979–1981), the search for victory (1982–1986), and withdrawal (1986–1989).

This discussion of the war outlines its general progress and dwells on the points essential for understanding its impact on the Soviet domestic scene. It does not examine details of the fighting, the Soviet propaganda effort to win the hearts and minds of Afghanistan's civilian population, or the multifaceted assistance to the DRA army that were inherent components of the war, as the war itself is extraneous to the focus of this book.

The Introduction of Soviet Troops

There is ample proof that Andropov and Ustinov contemplated the introduction of Soviet troops into Afghanistan well before December 1979. Ustinov spoke in March 1979 of forming three divisions in the Turkestan and Central Asian MDs, as well as of three regiments that could arrive in Afghanistan "in literally three hours." Within a month, the GRU (the Main Military Intelligence Directorate) was preparing a number of spetsnaz battalions for operations.[10] The three divisions were presumably the kernel of what even before the military intervention was designed the Fortieth Army, which would comprise the Soviet combat force in Afghanistan. In addition, a special limited call-up in June 1979 brought to Kushka, Turkmenistan, many of the Slavs and other Europeans who participated in the preliminary invasion force (recruiting was normally a strictly biannual event—in April and November).[11] That same summer, many officers were transferred from East Germany and Czechoslovakia to Central Asia, with an eye toward preparing for a campaign in Afghanistan. Boris Gromov, then deputy commander of an infantry division, learned in 1980 that preparations for the incursion had been underway throughout the previous year; the Turkestan MD had started drafting its reservists periodically and preparing them for such an event. It was the November draft that entered Afghanistan in December 1979.[12]

One month after the telephone conversation with Kosygin in which Taraki made the first direct appeal to Moscow for military assistance, the Soviet General Staff ordered the formation of the Muslim Battalion (signing the directive on April 26, 1979). By June 1, this battalion was fully staffed with soldiers of Central Asian ethnicity, as Taraki suggested. From June until August, led by their Uzbek commander, Major Habib Halbaev, they trained as paratroopers and carried out tactical exercises in which they would engage in Afghanistan: seizing mountain passes, capturing airfields, and practicing urban warfare, for example. The ethnic requirement aside, the battalion served as the prototype for the seven other GRU spetsnaz detachments that eventually deployed.[13] The Muslim Battalion went into Afghanistan in the second week of December.

Two months before the early December decision to introduce Soviet troops into Afghanistan, the Fortieth Army began organizing under the command of Colonel General Yurii Tukharinov, First Deputy Commander of the Turkestan MD. The commander of the first assault troops to enter Afghanistan in December 1979, General Ivan Riabchenko, was one of a group of officers sent to Afghanistan in September to prepare the ground, "not for an invasion or occupation but for providing assistance to friendly Afghanistan in its struggle against the counter-revolution" by preventing the flow of arms, ammunition, and equipment from Pakistan and Iran.[14]

Only in mid-December did Tukharinov receive operational plans for entering Afghanistan before the end of the month. His orders to bring the Fortieth Army up to strength arrived similarly late, so deployment was rushed. "Formations and units deployed in the Turkestan MD, which almost all had been cadre-strength and filled out, constituted its backbone." Using "local resources from the reserves," over 50,000 officers, sergeants, and soldiers were called up. Since the two relevant MDs had never experienced such "mobilization measures . . . local government, directors of enterprises and farms, draft boards, and military units turned out not to be prepared for them." Moreover, "everyone was convinced" that this was merely a "usual inspection," so "no one paid attention to the quality of the specialists filling out the subunits." There was indeed "a keen shortage of scarce specialists. . . . Due to poor knowledge of the

Russian language, soldiers from the Central Asian republics as a rule served out their draft obligations in construction or motorized rifle units where they could not acquire the requisite specialties."[15] Moreover, many reserve officers had never served in the army; they had trained in military departments of higher educational institutions." In the opinion of Aleksandr Liakhovskii, the war's semiofficial military historian, the disorder and haste of the mobilization process and the mishaps it encountered had dire consequences.[16]

Liakhovskii might have had in mind the ethnic composition of the original force. Yet given the short time frame—the decision to enter Afghanistan before the year's end—there was no way the Fortieth Army could have reached the requisite 75,000 to 80,000 soldiers other than by mobilizing reserves in the areas nearest to Afghanistan, most of whom were Central Asians. The consideration was purely logistical—the respective headquarters of the Turkestan and Central Asian MDs were in Kapchagay in the vicinity of Alma-Ata and Chirchik outside Tashkent; there was no intention of relying on Central Asians for the long term, as the Army could enlist reservists for only a limited period. However, this gave the GS time to mobilize a more ethnically balanced and professional force.

KGB defector Vasiliy Mitrokhin writes that in the period leading up to the intervention, the authorities imposed a state of emergency in the areas bordering Afghanistan and Iran. "Units and formations were brought up to full strength, put on military alert and holidays and leave were cancelled. It was forbidden to mention the planned invasion in any communications."[17] In Tajikistan, reservists were called up mostly at night, in an atmosphere of "panic-like excitement." The army was completely unprepared for war: provisions did not arrive, and armaments and other equipment were faulty (parts had been sold, bolts fell from tracks of moving tanks, engines had no gasoline).[18] The inability to locate many reservists—because of the draft boards' poor record keeping, violations of the residential passport system, confusion in street names, and the many who avoided the call-up notices by presenting false certificates of illness or fleeing their places of residence—further impeded the call-up.[19]

Two-thirds of the reservists enlisting from the Turkestan and Central Asian MDs—officers and men alike coming basically from Central Asian *kishlaks* (villages)—were in no way prepared for combat. Soldiers were also enlisted from the European parts of the Soviet Union. One Lithuanian officer was sent as a scout to "establish a path from the Soviet Union into Afghanistan before the war began." He returned to Vilnius, where he selected soldiers to lead into Afghanistan, arriving there with them in early 1980.[20]

The chaos surrounding the enlistment of older cohorts of reservists and the lack of elementary provisions, let alone arms and ammunition, made it inevitable that the troops would resort to "speculating in weapons, the use of narcotics," and a host of other "negative phenomena"[21] from the start. In other words, the mobilization not only proved the lack of any contemplated takeover of Afghanistan; it also went a long way toward establishing the atmosphere that prevailed within the Fortieth Army (publicly referred to as the Limited Contingent of Soviet Troops in Afghanistan) and the ethos of its soldiery.

A special group of generals and officers from all branches of the Soviet armed forces worked in the GS's Main Operations Directorate (GOU) to plan the deployment to Afghanistan. It prepared the draft directives of the defense minister and CGS for mobilization; planned and implemented the movement of troops across the border and the delivery of weapons and equipment to the DRA; carried out organizational measures; and kept track of the military-political situation in Afghanistan. In parallel with plans for removing Amin, to be carried out by a small group of elite troops who began moving into Kabul early in December, the army placed the 108th Motorized Rifle Division on alert on December 12 and moved its 180th Motorized Rifle Regiment to cover the border. December 13 brought the formation of a MoD Operations Group, headed by Army General Sergei Akhromeev. It included generals and officers of the GS, representatives of "all branches and troop arms of the armed forces," and the MoD's main and central directorates. By the following evening, it was in Termez, Uzbekistan, on the Afghan border, to begin coordinating operations to deploy troops into Afghanistan. After Akhromeev fell ill, First Deputy Defense Minister Sergei Sokolov took over command of the OG and the deployment of the Fortieth Army. (Sokolov was to command the largest military operations in the coming years.) The OG sent the troops that would carry out the plan to overthrow Amin from Bagram Airport near Kabul into the capital.[22] (Paratroopers had taken the airport in early December.[23])

The initial contingent arrived in Termez on December 17. Here, it received a quick, condensed training and, just over a week later, started moving into Afghanistan.

The original force was not alone in undergoing minimal training. The Sixty-Sixth Motorized-Rifle Brigade of the Central Asian MD was put on military alert on December 26, 1979, transferred to Termez on December 28, underwent combat training for seven days, and on January 4, 1980, crossed the border into Afghanistan, where it was subordinated to the command of the Fortieth Army.[24]

Invasion and Consolidation: The Early Stages of the War, 1979–1981

On the night of December 25–26, the force, under the command of Lieutenant General Boris Tkach, began crossing the Amu Darya River (the Oxus) that marked the frontier between the two countries, using pontoon bridges ("Friendship Bridge" was completed only in May 1982). Two motor-rifle divisions crossed over from Kushka in Turkmenistan. By December 27, airborne troops had secured the Salang Highway, while a further force of 15,000 had been airlifted into Kabul, paralyzed the capital, seized Amin's palace, and killed the president. On January 2, 1980, the Soviet force in Afghanistan numbered 50,000;[25] by mid-January, 81,800 (61,800 of them in infantry and air force combat units). In parallel to the takeover of Kabul, "general purpose forces poured down the Soviet-built road network to occupy the main cities and air bases that constitute the circular ring of urban Afghanistan."[26]

Sokolov and Akhromeev arrived in Kabul in the first week of January 1980 to head the Soviet military mission in Afghanistan; the mandate of the MoD OG was to coordinate the efforts of the various Soviet military formations in the country, specifically between the Fortieth Army and that of the DRA; cooperate with the KGB; and render practical assistance to the Fortieth Army Command, the general staff of the Turkestan MD, the DRA MoD, and the PDPA Central Committee. In periods when the head of the OG was away from Kabul, the chief military adviser planned operations, sent his plans to Moscow for approval, and then had to implement them.[27]

The first Soviet casualties occurred as the troops were entering Afghanistan. Four soldiers were killed in an ambush just 16 kilometers from Kabul.[28] A plane carrying troops in the original force crashed before landing, killing all thirty-three passengers. The chaotic nature of this preliminary stage, in which the Soviet force lacked state-of-the-art equipment to undertake a smooth transfer of a major force from Termez to locations in Afghanistan, led to further deaths. In January 1980, one unit (whose commanding officer, traveling at the head of the column, had no way of communicating with vehicles at the tail end) was held up for two days at Pul-i Khumri because of an accident in the Salang Tunnel that led to eighteen deaths.[29].

The Soviet losses that accompanied the takeover of Kabul seemed in retrospect to be a portent of things to come. For example, during a battle with Amin's guards, Soviet paratroopers shot a relief group of Soviet soldiers in an APC at point-blank range.[30]

As in Czechoslovakia in 1968, Moscow's first move included the rapid seizure of the major cities, radio stations, and power centers. But the Soviets discovered that Afghanistan would not be a repeat of Czechoslovakia, for Afghanistan was embroiled in a full-scale civil war that the Soviet intervention only exacerbated. Taking control of the capital could not address the main issue.[31]

Theoretically, once Amin had been eliminated and Babrak Karmal, a successor amenable to Moscow, installed in his place, the job of the Soviet force in Afghanistan would be to fortify Afghanistan's capital and main cities and ensure the stability of the country and the DRA regime. This would free the DRA army to suppress the opposition without involving Soviet troops in any fighting. As a senior GRU officer pointed out, the orders that the commanders of all stages of the intervention received were both "totally vague" and based on assumptions that did not fit the reality.[32] The outcome could hardly be auspicious.

Army General Valentin Varennikov testified that "when we introduced our troops, our orders were not to get involved in combat, and not to respond to provocations. But then the provocations became such that it was impossible not to respond. We had to defend ourselves."[33] Following an attack on the Soviet embassy in Kabul in February 1980, both the DRA leadership and local Soviet representatives sent messages to Moscow asking it to allow the Soviet troops to liquidate the enemy. Moscow accordingly ordered the Fortieth Army to conduct joint operations with the DRA armed forces to crush the insurgents.[34]

In this way, Soviet troops were drawn into combat, sometimes on their own, sometimes with DRA troops. As they proceeded along the highways (such as they were), they were attacked by "rebels" and became engaged, whether they sought a confrontation or not. One armored carrier driver who entered Afghanistan in December 1979 testified that hardly a day passed without an exchange of fire.[35]

The Kremlin seems not to have appreciated, either a priori or during the first months of the war, the extent of the DRA regime's alienation from the Afghan population and the dimensions of the insurgency. Nor did it envision the effect of the incursion of Soviet troops, which deployed the fragmented resistance against an enemy that was trampling on Afghan national pride. Although the ten major resistance groups failed to create a unified military command, this did not mean that the PDPA was capable of succeeding militarily or politically. It lacked a constituency outside the party, which itself was divided by internecine quarrels. The Soviet intervention denied the PDPA any chance of credibility and exacerbated the regime's unpopularity.[36]

The Soviet strategy centered around five major objectives, only three of them military. The first was to secure Kabul and the highways linking it to Kandahar in the south, Herat in the West, and, via the Salang Pass, Termez on the Soviet border. Next was to carry the war to the resistance, with the Fortieth Army conducting repeated operations into rebel-controlled areas. Aerial bombing, sometimes massive, typically accompanied these campaigns. Like the Americans in Vietnam, the Soviets targeted suspected resistance pockets, destroying entire villages, crops, and anything else that might sustain guerrilla activity. The third objective was to close the Pakistani frontier to rebel caravans bringing fighters and weapons to Afghanistan; the Soviets were no more successful at this than was the U.S. endeavor to close the Ho Chi Minh Trail. The two principal nonmilitary elements of Soviet strategy were no less vital, and it was the failure of these that frustrated Soviet endeavors to consolidate the infrastructure of the Afghan government and army. First, Moscow expended considerable effort on molding a competent officer corps in light of the severe hemorrhaging of the DRA army's ranks and on educating new cadres; it brought thousands of young Afghans to the Soviet Union for extended periods for courses of political indoctrination and military training. Finally, the Soviets sought to initiate a campaign of civic and political action to win adherents to the highly unpopular DRA regime; the very injection of Soviet troops stymied this effort.[37]

The presence of Soviet troops for a prolonged period in an alien country dictated a complex supply system. The MoD had not prepared for the complicated logistics of maintaining on foreign territory a relatively large force that it would have to equip over a lengthy period. All of the Fortieth Army's needs, from weapons and ammunition to food, clothing, and fuel, had to come from over the Soviet border. Roads were poor and dangerous, railways nonexistent, and the army spread throughout mountainous and difficult terrain. The Fortieth Army command, with its central HQ in Kabul, divided the country into seven military districts, each with its own HQ. It set up five field hospitals, which quickly proved incapable of treating the epidemic of contagious disease that hit the troops beginning June 1980 and necessitated further personnel and equipment to improve hygiene, sanitation (especially ensuring sufficient supplies of drinking water), and prophylactic antiepidemic measures.[38] Indeed, it seems that it was logistics that determined the size of the Fortieth Army, which could grow only as large as "could be supplied over the over-burdened Afghan road network."[39] The poorly developed logistical infrastructure plus the inhospitable climate and terrain created "major problems in command and control." Vehicles broke down frequently "owing to inferior maintenance, shortfalls in repair, driver inexperience, and general wear and tear."[40]

According to one Soviet military historian, 60 percent of the Soviet force was preoccupied with securing communication routes, preventing the opposition from using them to replenish manpower and supplies, ensuring the efficacy of the DRA administration, and providing the civilian population with basic necessities.[41] Western analysts described the occupation forces, namely most of the regular motorized infantry units, somewhat differently, as performing primarily "occupation- and security-related tasks . . . securing Soviet-controlled urban areas, as well as important lines of communications and logistics and individual military and civilian installations." The support force (20 to 25 percent of the Limited Contingent) included "construction troops (*stroibat*), transportation units, and various types of repair and maintenance units."[42] Gromov tells us that those who served in outposts and guarded restricted zones and the lines of communication—as distinct from those who actually accompanied convoys and served as drivers—accounted for 30 to 35 percent of the force.[43]

Throughout the war, the Soviet troops conducted combat operations on a comparatively limited scale in order to minimize Soviet casualties or avoid exacerbating international reaction, or both. Testimonies demonstrate that the commanders in the field, and perhaps some of their superiors, employed tactics intended to limit

Soviet casualties,[44] not a consideration that was in line with traditional Soviet military thinking.

From the very start, the Fortieth Army lost soldiers to mines, which proved a major source of casualties throughout the war. These took a heavy toll of sappers and drivers in the constant convoys—generally between 100 and 300 vehicles—transporting soldiers and goods along Afghanistan's poor roads. The mines were also a death trap for the infantry in their APCs unprotected by the armor that the Soviets had been trying for years to make impenetrable.[45] Mines were so ubiquitous in Afghanistan that every unit had unofficial (*neshtatnye*) sappers.[46] One sapper officer recounts, "Units [that] went out without sappers were known as 'suicide squads.' Mines were everywhere, on mountain paths, on the roads, and in houses."[47] Usually the mines were buried deep and disrupted an entire column, exploding when the fifth or sixth vehicle hit them. Some Soviet mine casualties stemmed from the uncharted minefields the Fortieth Army itself placed along the Pakistani border.[48] Mines killed 1,995 Soviet soldiers throughout the war and destroyed 1,191 vehicles.[49] (Gromov said that in 1988 alone, "the engineer corps detected, deactivated, and destroyed 4,882 anti-tank mines, 3,800 anti-personnel mines, and 1,162 land mines."[50])

In February and March 1980, the Soviets undertook their first major operation, employing some 5,000 troops with modern equipment and air support. The guerrillas disappeared into the mountains and ravines, while some 150,000 people abandoned their devastated villages. The Soviets demonstrated that they could go anywhere and wreak havoc, but that they were unable to rout the resistance or to prevent the *dushmany* (enemy) from returning once the forces withdrew. This scenario became a permanent feature of the war. The cities and daylight witnessed Soviet military successes; the countryside and nighttime belonged to the opposition. The Soviet military campaigns therefore had little lasting effect.

Often, too, the Soviet military campaigns were operationally unsuccessful—despite Gromov's and Liakhovskii's assertions. "Attempts of the command to organize an offensive and pursue dushmany by employing large military formations in accordance with the rules of classical war were without effect" for the mujahidin, finding that large groups were easy prey for a powerful conventional army, resorted to operating primarily in partisan detachments of 20 to 200 men.[51] Stories abound of the ludicrous conduct of operations in the early period. One soldier recorded "bungling" and stupidity as well as cowardice, including an incident where an officer abandoned his soldiers to die.[52] There were instances when Soviet planes and helicopters hit Soviet troops. One battalion was hit three times from the air in the course of one year; "we had no way of telling the pilots who we were."[53]

Memoranda regarding the war demonstrated the meaninglessness of Soviet reporting at the pinnacle of the hierarchy that both characterized and perpetuated the inefficacy of government. The Kremlin Afghanistan Commission, summing up the war's first months, reported in April 1980 that the Soviet troops were providing "decisive assistance in establishing control over the situation. . . . Together with the Afghan armed forces they have successfully carried out operations for elimination of armed rebel formations in several provinces . . . and thus the military threat to the existence of the new regime has been significantly reduced." Despite these declared accomplishments, the commission recommended and the Politburo concurred that "our troops will have to continue to carry out their tasks of defending the revolutionary regime in the DRA."[54]

Following this decision, which reinforced the resolve to remain in Afghanistan for an indefinite period, the army undertook to mend its early failings and incompetence. In summer 1980, it withdrew a number of combat units "whose presence is not required in Afghanistan at the moment."[55] These seem primarily to have been tank battalions, whose number far exceeded the exigencies of the Afghan War.[56] Clearly the Soviet force could not make much use of heavy weapons systems. The rocket battalions of motorized-rifle divisions and the artillery and antiaircraft rocket brigades also went home (the enemy had no aircraft).[57]

By this time, too, conscripts and experienced officers and noncommissioned officers (NCOs) from across the Soviet Union had replaced the 50,000 reservists.[58] The On Universal Military Service law envisaged large-scale recruitment, but it stipulated that reservists could be enlisted for training for periods not exceeding three months for regular troops and twelve months for officers, with an extension of up to two months. This meant that reservists recruited in November and December (except the officers) were all home by the end of May.[59]

In the early years especially, the GS's instructions often failed to take into account the circumstances that the Soviet force encountered, so that commanders on the spot had to risk either the ire of their superiors or the lives of their soldiers. Understandably, the mood among the Fortieth Army's senior officers was frequently morose, for they appreciated from the outset the hopelessness of the adventure in which they were engaged.[60]

Certainly the situation in the field gave little cause for sanguinity. However, reports from Afghanistan that did not restrict themselves to what Moscow wanted to hear seem rarely to have reached the Kremlin leaders; time and time again, official reporting presented a far rosier picture than was warranted. Varennikov, answering a question on the quality of reporting from Afghanistan, asserted that "in the time of stagnation"(at least until 1985), the system required reports that would please the Kremlin, which resulted in the leaders' inability to reach "the best decisions."[61]

The acknowledged role of the KGB in conducting the war explains a great deal of its complex nature and the military command's frustration that the Kremlin would not hear it. The chief military adviser in Kabul from June 1980 to November 1981, General Aleksandr Maiorov, noted that although formally he was subordinate to the MoD, the first signature on all his instructions was invariably Andropov's, with Ustinov's second.[62]

In summer 1980, the Soviets faced uprisings in Kandahar and Herat. Soviet troops surrounded both cities and combed their vicinities using planes and artillery. "The latest weapons and technology were used including chemical poisons in the form of gas bombs of short duration."[63]

The Soviet force's use of chemical weapons—it fielded chemical defense troops in the invasion team[64]—was a recurrent topic in Western reporting on the war. A U.S. State Department Bureau of Intelligence and Research analyst wrote that "reports of [Soviet] chemical and toxin agents" included "mycotoxins (poisons derived from natural biological sources), nerve gases, incapacitants, blister agents, carbon monoxide, and nonlethal gases delivered by a variety of means."[65] A vet who had served in the Chemical Engineering Corps said they used some kind of gas to paralyze villagers before switching to an incendiary mixture.[66] By late 1980, the Fortieth Army was also using flechette cluster bombs and thermobaric bombs on specific instructions from "the top authority" (*instantsiia*—Ustinov, Andropov, or Brezhnev).[67]

The chief role in the fight against the "counterrevolution" fell on the shoulders of the Fortieth Army. Three leading military personnel in Afghanistan sent a long memo to Defense Minister Ustinov in summer 1980, contending that the DRA leadership was detached from what was happening in the country, was dealing with ancillary issues, and was operating in a way injurious to the task of consolidating the April revolution. Although "events are developing on a positive level, and the authority of the new government is being strengthened," this was mainly through "the political authority of the USSR and our economic power," while in the principal task, the fight against the counterrevolution, the Fortieth Army remained "the decisive force." The officers demanded that Moscow "evaluate the real state of affairs [and] mark out a political and military strategy."[68] In other words, while it was clear to the senior military and civilian personnel that the war was pointless, everyone continued to do his part—the soldiers fought and defended communication routes, the advisers advised, the politicians composed and read out beautiful speeches—but all this served only to shore up a structure that was rotten and hollow within.[69]

Coordination between the Fortieth Army and the DRA's armed forces was critical, as the Fortieth Army generally fought side by side with its Afghan partner. It was also, however, consistently difficult. The Soviet high command sought to simplify matters by placing Soviet advisers in the Afghan units that were involved in joint operations, in addition to those already in place throughout the Afghan command system.[70] It was clear that the DRA army was incapable of engaging the opposition on its own;

its officers and soldiers lacked motivation, many of the former being preoccupied with infighting within the PDPA, and its manpower was always less than half of its official strength in light of disaffection and desertion to the rebels.[71] This flow of defectors from the DRA army—sometimes of entire units and senior officers—led to persistent betrayal. One soldier, who spoke of the low level of mutual trust and cooperation between the Soviet force and that of the DRA, noted both the latter's rejection of its allotted role as spearhead and the persistent leakage of information to the mujahidin that frequently affected an operation's outcome.[72]

Recalling the situation in fall 1980 when he arrived in Kabul as head of the Turkestan MD OG in Kabul, Lieutenant General Norat Ter-Grigor'iants commented on the irrelevance of the directive stipulating that the DRA army should conduct the fighting while the Soviet troops supported them. "Everything happened otherwise. Our troops went in front and behind—the Afghans." Ter-Grigor'iants described the Fortieth Army's activity during that period. First, it secured the unimpeded movement of columns bringing logistical equipment and provisions for the needs of the army and the local population: 35,000 vehicles traveled the roads of Afghanistan with their cargoes, although the trucks initially lacked both armor and the traction necessary in Afghanistan's heavy winter snow. Second, it ambushed the probable routes of the rebels in the country's interior. Third, it engaged in combat operations to help the Afghan army destroy the "rebel bands" in the provinces; in April 1983, they controlled 84 of the 286 districts and provinces, while DRA rule in many of the others was unstable.[73]

Reports by the military in Afghanistan at the end of the war's first year maintained that "power" was "being firmly held in all provincial centers," as well as in 70 percent of the country's rural districts; in other words, "significant results have been achieved in the matter of stabilizing the situation." CGS Ogarkov himself seemed to doubt the veracity of these reports, as his plan for the first quarter of 1981 included a number of comprehensive steps "to increase the effectiveness of combat operations," as well as "measures to upgrade combat equipment and weapons."[74] Clearly the GS believed that there was still a great deal to be done.

By now the war was in full swing, with no end in sight. Some improvement in the Fortieth Army's performance began to appear in the second year of fighting. It now included mountain rifle battalions trained in the mountain training center of the Turkestan MD.[75] Yet although guerrilla warfare is considered "a platoon leader's and company commander's war" because lower-level initiative is "essential for survival and success,"[76] junior commanders continued to demonstrate their lack of field sense, initiative, and ability to make decisions. Soviet efforts repeatedly came to grief because of inadequate reconnaissance, failure to ensure control of high ground, and failure to keep the enemy from escaping after combat. One study of the war devotes considerable attention to the general ineffectiveness of conventional military operations.[77]

Chief Military Adviser Aleksandr Maiorov accused Babrak Karmal of presenting a distorted picture at the Twenty-Sixth CPSU Congress in Moscow in February 1981. Karmal gave the impression that the war was effectively finished, DRA control ensured, and the country tranquil, when in fact the provinces were subordinate to the mujahidin.[78] In 1981, the Soviet army was instructed to suppress the resistance movement completely (an order that one former spetsnaz colonel described as irrelevant to the circumstances)[79] and to extend the DRA's control throughout the country. January saw an upsurge in Soviet military activity, and in March, the government sent in three more regiments and three border units. The Fortieth Army was "stretched to the limit in the fighting"; fifty-six of its seventy-three battalions were engaged in constant battle "with no breaks or change of men." The insurgents resisted desperately and dealt the Soviet and DRA government troops retaliatory blows. The population suffered great losses (with over 1 million killed, while 5.5 million—one-third of the population—fled the country and 2 million others left their homes for elsewhere within Afghanistan[80]), and the Soviets' actions aroused the people's hatred. A soldier recalled that when Soviet soldiers entered a kishlak, people threw bricks at them from the rooftops.[81] One officer "went to Afghanistan full of enthusiasm. I thought I could do something useful. . . . I expected to be needed." Instead, a wounded child he wanted to help ran away from him, screaming in terror. Village women with their hoes killed a lieutenant who found a baby while on patrol and brought it to them.[82] Altogether, the Soviets seemed to be making little headway. As Sokolov himself was forced to admit, all efforts to eliminate the adversary had failed. and the plan to crush him was postponed for yet another year.[83]

By 1981, Sergei Krakhmalov, military attaché to the embassy in Kabul, was reporting to "the Center" that it was impossible to solve the problem of Afghanistan solely by military means." After about two years of fighting, it "became clear that the presence of Soviet troops in Afghanistan and their conduct of combat operations, and our military, economic, and other comprehensive aid would not save the . . . regime and would not be conducive to ending the civil war. At this point, a decision should have been made: Is it expedient to continue maintaining our 100,000-strong army in Afghanistan? Should we discontinue completely or substantially reduce the inexhaustible economic and other assistance to the Karmal regime and limit the resolution of the Afghan problem to political means?"[84]

Ter-Grigor'iants, who flew to Moscow practically every month and reported to Ustinov and Ogarkov, held the same view.[85] So did Maiorov, who insisted that the war was futile and that the Soviet Union should withdraw its troops.[86] Colonel Leonid Shershnev of the Turkestan MD Political Administration prepared a report stating that even the ethnic groups in the north, which had hitherto refrained from siding with the opposition, had now joined it and that the rebel forces would be able to hold out for a long period. Neither his superiors in the Turkestan MD nor Akhromeev accepted this position. They told him that the army was in Afghanistan to fight, not to delve into politics.[87]

By the end of 1981, a *Pravda* correspondent wrote that the DRA government controlled all of Afghanistan's cities and the majority of its district centers, but less than 15 percent of its 35,000 hamlets. Operations aimed at destroying opposition bands and strongholds were having little effect; once the DRA and Soviet troops completed their operations and returned to their bases, the regions reverted to rebel hands. True, it was a war against counterrevolutionary forces backed by international reaction, but it was also a civil war. The rebels masked themselves as civilians and lived among the population, which was not sympathetic toward the government.[88]

In 1981 and 1982, the Soviets launched major offensives in the strategically situated Panjshir Valley. These were indecisive, with heavy losses of both personnel and military materiel, including large numbers of helicopters. The Fortieth Army had begun to use helicopters for assault, not merely for support missions, in late summer 1981. They became an essential component for protecting convoys, bringing supplies to isolated outposts, and transporting troops. Over the next five years—until summer 1986—the helicopter became the principal weapon in the Soviet arsenal. The Fortieth Army command relied increasingly on helicopter assault to support battalion-size maneuvers.[89]

In addition to offensive operations, the Soviet troops engaged in defensive warfare. To protect communication routes and guard convoys, soldiers were dispersed among small garrisons for months on end, leaving each division, regiment, battalion, and company too overextended to be effective. Their assignments entailed tasks for which no Soviet officers had training, so they relied on trial and error.[90]

This situation, combined with poor and often entirely nonexistent communication facilities, highlighted the inability of junior and middle-rank officers to make decisions and take initiative, a problem that Soviet commentators noted throughout the war. Although the army established a satellite communications link between its headquarters in Kabul and the GS in Moscow and between Kabul and most of the seven Afghanistan MD headquarters,[91] maintaining secure and efficient communications proved unfeasible, partly because Soviet equipment was antiquated and inadequate[92] and failed in difficult weather and terrain. One outpost commander complained that when he needed a helicopter, it was impossible to get the request through to anyone.[93]

A Western observer, summing up the war's first three years, noted that the Soviet army's "overcentralized bureaucracy and slow-moving command structure" deprived its officers of "the initiative or the authority to respond rapidly and creatively to mujahidin movements."[94] According to one Soviet military source, defeats in the early period made the Soviet command "arrive at some practical conclusions" regarding the need for changes. The wide gamut of Soviet failings included a lack of sufficient practical skills in dealing with personnel training; the unavailability of ammunition, training aids, and other supplies; the inability of officers to take initiative; difficulties in organizing and conducting reconnaissance missions against enemy ambushes; inexperience in conducting combat activity at night, especially in the mountains; poor knowledge of basic combat equipment; inadequate understanding of the logistics of evacuating combat vehicles under enemy fire and of the functioning of maintenance assets under field conditions; and lack of experience in coordination, command, and control of units in enemy-held territory. These lacunae forced the Soviet command to pay attention to "coordination among the different services. [It] started to emphasize mine-clearing and night operations." It also addressed "the problem of command" and of "providing the units with supplies consistent with their combat missions."[95]

The quantities of supplies needed to feed, clothe, and equip an army of over 100,000 men with a poor communications system and constant enemy attacks on convoys continued to challenge the GS and the MoD throughout the war. They had solved some of the problems by 1985, but never succeeded with others, such as transporting the requisite quantities of fuel.[96] Disruption of road communications was the main reason for the increased reliance on helicopters for transportation, although as early as spring 1981, the Afghan opposition had become adept at attacking even these.[97]

Another problem that the Soviet command was addressing by the end of the war's second year was the training of officers and troops. The motorized-rifle conscript units were ill suited to the mountainous terrain and the arduous task of engaging guerrillas with superior knowledge of both the topography and the population of which they were part. The MoD developed plans to improve training programs, reorient the assignments of the motorized-rifle regiments, and augment the elite troops.[98]

Once again, however, not everything put to paper was implemented due to institutional obstacles. The loss of prestige that the Soviet military incurred as a result of the war was manifestly justified. The reality was perhaps even grimmer than the Soviet public imagined.

The Search for Victory, 1982–1986

As of the mid-1980s, the Soviet command improved its planning, taking into consideration local conditions, seeking to outmaneuver the mujahidin by using helicopters to airlift troops into mountainous terrain and boosting secrecy.[99] It substituted mobile and offensive maneuvers involving aerial and artillery bombardment for European-style armored warfare. The goal of this massive use of firepower was—as for the Americans in Vietnam—to save Soviet lives and compensate for a lack of infantry, a policy that was "expensive, indiscriminate, and, probably, ineffective."[100] One analyst writes that the Soviet force began to adapt to Afghan requirements, relying more on "mobility, long-range ordnance from air power, vertical rather than tank-led encirclement, use of specially assigned forces (not just spetsnaz), greater emphasis on rugged physical and moral training, attempts to invest small unit commanders with more decision-making autonomy and boldness, and by moving to lighter forces."[101]

It was all too little or to no avail. The Soviets continued to overextend their columns when on the march, exposing themselves to ambushes with the dushmany firing on them from inaccessible points. Edward Girardet, an American war correspondent for the *Christian Science Monitor* and ABC News who made intermittent visits to Afghanistan during the war wrote, "Increasingly, armored columns have become sitting ducks for guerrilla mines, recoilless rifles, and grenade launchers." (By the mid-1980s, the mujahidin were placing mines in trees, where the carriers' radio antennas triggered them.[102]) The Soviet force resorted increasingly to aerial firepower, using Mi-24 helicopter gunships, MiG jet fighters, and SU-24 bombers to carry out an ever-growing number of operations from across the Soviet border. The Soviet force, having failed to crush the resistance, persisted in operating from "heavily-fortified bases by regularly launching major, and often highly destructive, military assaults against both guerrilla and civilian targets. The Kremlin [applied] a combination of psychological, economic, and subversive measures" to break the opposition."[103]

The Frunze Military Academy composed a small volume on the war in Afghanistan. It stated that the Soviet forces

> garnered valuable combat experience and significantly expanded the theory and practice of combat in mountainous-desert terrain. ... The war was fought under conditions where the enemy lacked any aviation capabilities, but, over time, had modern air defense systems and modern mines. A lack of front lines and advances along varied axes (which were not mutually supporting) characterized the decisive actions of the opposing sides as they attempted to seize the initiative and gain control over certain territories. . . .
>
> . . . The principal types of combat included company, battalion, and regimental raids; blocking off areas where the enemy was located prior to searching out and destroying guerrilla forces; and the simultaneous attack on several groups of the enemy located at various depths and locations. The specific combat conditions influenced the way in which the advance through mountains and inhabited areas was conducted; led to a change in air assault tactics; changed the methods of conducting marches and providing convoy security; and caused a change in the tactics of organizing and conducting ambushes.[104]

According to one Western expert, by 1984, "the war was primarily a logistics war, with each side trying to strangle the other's logistics while striving to stay supplied and viable."[105] The critical importance for the Soviets of keeping land transport routes open meant "a massive exercise in logistics and administration." They deployed no fewer than thirty new material support battalions simultaneously, as well as a transport brigade, in the effort to keep the supplies moving. Sometimes the Soviets had to resort to air bridges to supply urban centers within rebel territory. The Soviets proved their capacity to decentralize repair capabilities, and vehicle crews underwent trouble-shooting training.[106]

By now the Soviet military had developed considerable experience in conducting sweeps of separate regions and inhabited areas and coping with Afghanistan's terrain. Yet the mujahidin were still at an advantage in their knowledge of the country's topography. Throughout the war they remained more mobile; the Soviets dubbed them "spooks" (*dukhi*—spirits or ghosts), for they appeared and disappeared with incredible agility. One Soviet journalist noted that "attacks on Soviet armored groups were usually carried out without any prior warning. The spooks would emerge out of camouflaged manholes and open fire. Then they would disappear into the depths of . . . a network of underground tunnels dug for irrigation purposes. . . . [These tunnels] stretched under fields, alongside roads, and underneath villages" and "drove the Soviet soldiers mad. One minute you'd have concentrated fire from a village, but when you entered it, there wouldn't be a soul to be seen . . . the village would be deserted."[107]

The arbitrary use of heavy artillery and airpower to wipe out entire villages on the pretext that the civilian population sheltered the mujahidin continued to alienate the villagers (this made mujahidin efforts to enlist young men that much easier). The Soviets relied on a scorched earth policy, destroying entire villages, crops, livestock, and irrigation systems, leaving nothing alive; the tactic was "to eliminate everything and everyone."[108] Sometimes, however, the Soviets gave villagers the opportunity to evacuate a kishlak before moving in to eliminate armed fighters.[109]

By 1983, at least some in the Soviet command apparatus understood that moving large units of armored vehicles along valley floors in accordance with conventional Soviet operational thinking, was not only ineffective but actually a boon for the mujahidin. The terrain and the tactics dictated that the Soviets use small, dismounted units that could close in on the enemy in gorges and mountain passes and whose commanders had to act independently. Operational success in Afghanistan meant developing light infantry skills and tactics. Consequently, except in major operations, where the motorized rifle structures continued to participate, the brunt of the fighting fell on the elite airborne (VDV), air assault (DShB), and designated reconnaissance forces and the spetsnaz, all of which by 1983 were some 15 to 20 percent of the total force.[110] (Gromov asserts that the number of airborne assignments grew annually.[111]) These counterinsurgency formations, "preselected on the basis of athletic ability, psychological stability, and clean political records," were "subjected to rigorous and continuous training." They operated in the mujahidin's rear, setting up ambushes, conducting combat reconnaissance, initiating surprise air assaults, and performing "other high-risk operations."[112] A majority of the Soviet armed forces' airborne, air assault, and spetsnaz officers reportedly served in Afghanistan—versus barely 10 percent of all motorized rifle, armor, aviation, and artillery officers.[113]

The Soviet force "came closest to trying to win a military victory" under Konstantin Chernenko, who succeeded Andropov in February 1984. It stepped up its onslaught "from high-altitude carpet-bombing to massive major assaults such as attacks on refugee camps," and yet another (according to Jeanne Kirkpatrick, a sixth; according to the mujahidin, a seventh) Panjshir offensive, "which involved some 15,000 Soviet and 5,000 Afghan government troops, as well as heavy bombing by Tu-16 aircraft flying from bases inside the USSR and large heliborne landings, reportedly of up to 2,000 men at a time." Yet these "far more aggressive and brutal tactics" that the Fortieth Army, under Lieutenant General Leonid Generalov, now adopted led to no "convincing military success, just temporary victories," and "sparked a more assertive response from the USA and other backers of the rebels."[114] In fall 1984, an "analytical note" from the Main Directorate of Combat Training listed the marked improvement and increased flexibility and sophistication of rebel combat operations and the large quantities of high-quality weaponry that they were receiving from China, Iran, Saudi Arabia, and Pakistan, as well as Stinger and Blowpipe antiaircraft missiles.[115]

In mid-1984, the head of the MoD Operations Group in Afghanistan, Deputy Defense Minister Marshal Sergei Sokolov, reported home—in the traditional style—that "the military situation, as a result of conducting a whole series of operations against counter-revolutionary forces, has notably improved." He mentioned eighty-five operations in the course of the year's first five months, fifty-one of them joint operations of the Fortieth Army and Afghan units and the remainder of Afghan units alone, and pointed out that "the Fortieth Army continues to remain [the] decisive factor in stabilizing the situation in the DRA and takes on itself the main burden of the fight with the counter-revolutionaries. . . . The Army is combat ready. Combat operations . . . have shown the capability of the troops of the Army and aviation to carry out combat missions in difficult mountainous conditions. . . . The personnel have operated selflessly and bravely." At the same time, "The operations . . . permit several conclusions to be drawn about further improvement of [the] combat training and technical supplies not only of the Fortieth Army, but of the [Soviet] armed forces as a whole."[116]

Three months later, the chief of the Main Directorate of Combat Training of the Ground Forces reported the outcome of the twenty-two planned and nineteen unplanned operations, including ambushes and intelligence activity, undertaken in the previous five months. He noted "some improvement . . . in the organization and waging of combat operations and in the use of artillery and aircraft." According to this report,

> The main form of combat with rebel formations . . . remains conducting large planned and specific operations in order to eliminate rebels in vitally important regions, capture their bases and training centers, and also inflict defeat on groups in forested zones and villages. The primary method of troop operations consists of blockading bases and regions occupied by rebels with the wide use of tactical assault groups and subsequent combat sweeps with Afghan army subunits with constant artillery and air support.

The report bemoans the large number of operations conducted in "a stereotyped manner, according to a previously developed plan . . . straight-line operations" with poor results due to the "lack of concealment and deception and also a leak of information during joint operations with [Afghan] government troops that enabled the rebels to take preemptive measures." The report concluded with Soviet troop losses: 886 killed, 111 of them officers, and 1,958 wounded, 233 of them officers.[117] Altogether, late 1984 and early 1985 marked "the peak for combat operations."[118]

Ineffective "against a guerrilla that could not be targeted," the Soviet air force instead targeted the mujahidin "support structure" of irrigation systems, orchards, cropland, livestock, and villages, while the "helicopter gunships" attacked pack animals and trucks.[119] Thus, the air force gave the Soviets mobility, but, lacking the intelligence on the ground that would have allowed the soldiers to perform counterforce operations, it served mainly as countervalue—depriving the guerrillas of basic necessities and bombing that punished a supportive population.[120]

In 1985, General Mikhail Zaitsev, who that year took over command of the war, reportedly emphasized that encouraging more initiative from battalion and company commanders would let the army move more rapidly against the mujahidin.[121] Over time, indeed, some battalion commanders demonstrated considerable tactical flexibility.[122]

Another field that required attention was coordination between ground and air forces, for air resources had to be constantly allocated. Early in the war, officers assigned to ground units to provide forward air control and coordination were usually army officers ignorant of the basics of air force tactics and procedure and without the requisite signals training. Later, the Fortieth Army commanders began to integrate airpower into overall support plans; increasingly, they permitted ground officers direct contact with air units—contradicting the centralized command structure and the basic Soviet military principle that important decisions must be channeled through very senior commanders. Although Western observers noted built-in obstacles to effective coordination between air and ground forces,[123] a Soviet military source considered the extensive use of the former in providing all-around support to the latter to be among the chief achievements of the Soviet campaign in Afghanistan.[124]

At first, coordination was singularly lacking in the gathering and evaluation of intelligence, as each of the bodies involved kept its information to itself. Only in about 1985, Gromov recalls, did the Fortieth Army's GS start to hold daily meetings that included not only its own intelligence but also representatives of the KGB, the MVD, and the embassy to pool, verify, and analyze intelligence.[125]

The Soviets were less successful with their motorized rifle forces, apparently even the brigades designed for counterinsurgency and guerrilla warfare. "The conventional orientation, tactical rigidity, and generally poor quality of motorized rifle troops and their commanders precluded their effective use in a counter-insurgency role." The Frunze Military Academy manual of "lessons learned" gives examples of gross incompetence in tactical operations in the motorized rifle forces, contrasting them to the airborne and air assault troops. The lack of a professional NCO corps certainly affected block-and-sweep actions.[126]

By now, it was clear that there would be no decisive blow against the mujahidin. For a long time, Sokolov procrastinated in clarifying this to Ustinov. When he eventually did, the defense minister asked him whether he could at least close off Afghanistan's borders to prevent the continuous flow of arms to the mujahidin. Although Sokolov knew that this was impossible, as he admitted to Soviet advisers in Kabul in spring 1984—the mountainous terrain of the border with Pakistan precluded any such possibility—he answered that he could. This exchange highlights once again that it was impossible for the top command's to tell the entire truth to the political leadership[127] and therefore for the latter to reach pertinent conclusions.

In 1984, senior KGB operative Leonid Shebarshin visited Afghanistan to meet Sokolov and the Fortieth Army's senior staff. He criticized them for providing false statistics of casualties of both the Soviet troops and the opposition and for fabricating reports of successes because of personal interest.[128]

In addition to the enhanced capability of the mujahidin and the impossibility of sealing the borders, there were other troublesome issues. The commander of the Turkestan MD noted examples of carelessness, superficiality, and a lack of conscientiousness in organizing combat operations, as well as the low quality of operative missions and "the senseless death of people,"[129] referring undoubtedly to Soviet losses. Liakhovskii cites poor leadership at every level as a persistent problem, with only the commanders of the airborne and special-operations forces showing any ability to adapt to the opposition's changing tactics.[130]

The Soviet senior officers in Afghanistan felt generally stymied. They knew that all of the operations that the Soviet force initiated stemmed from DRA leadership requests to the Kremlin. The Kremlin then channeled these through the Politburo's

Afghanistan Commission, which thereupon issued orders to the Fortieth Army. Some of these orders were based on threats that the DRA leaders exaggerated in order to induce an operation; some called for the Fortieth Army to conduct such seemingly unnecessary operations that the command in Kabul ignored them without informing Moscow.[131]

The Soviet military attaché in Kabul claims that in 1983 he understood "finally" that "even with the help of Soviet troops, the Afghan armed forces were unable to cope with the opposition." In his reports to Moscow, he reiterated his assertion that the Soviets could not solve the Afghan problem by military means, but the Soviet and DRA leaders "still hoped to win the civil war."[132]

The increased frustration of the military command in Afghanistan is apparent in reports it dispatched to Moscow. Varennikov, who in late 1984 succeeded Sokolov as head of the MoD Operations Group in Kabul, later maintained that as of 1983, "and especially in 1984," the GS was categorically insisting that the "politicians and diplomats" unravel the knot by political means, and to make its point, it pulled out a small number of troops.[133] According to Gromov, who returned to Afghanistan in spring 1985 as commander of the Soviet GS group in Afghanistan, the senior officers in the country were by then calling for withdrawal.[134] One veteran officer testifies that Leonid Generalov, who commanded the Fortieth Army from November 1983 until April 1985, risked his military career several times by insisting that the situation in Afghanistan could only be solved politically, since it was militarily impossible to gain control of the country.[135]

In June 1985, Varennikov returned to the theme of the rebels' improved tactics and combat capability, as well as their increasing numbers. These meant that battles were prolonged and fierce and could succeed only with "powerful strikes of aircraft and artillery fire." In addition, all efforts of the Soviet force seemed in vain, as they did not result in the requisite political achievement by the PDPA and the DRA government. The Soviet attempt to stabilize the country could not be successful; the results of combat operations could only be temporary, and "with the passage of time the rebels are capable of regaining their lost positions." Varennikov said that getting results would mean an additional increase in the size of the Soviet contingent, although there had been such an increase just half a year before. "Everyone admits," he wrote to Defense Minister Sokolov (Sokolov had succeeded Ustinov, who died in December 1984) "that it is impossible to resolve all the issues of the April Revolution by military means alone." Due to the lack of "other effective measures, the scale of combat operations is expanding, which entails many negative consequences."

Viktor Dubynin stated later that he was convinced of the war's "hopelessness and senselessness" as soon as he arrived in Afghanistan in 1984 as the Fortieth Army's deputy commander for fighting. After becoming commander, his contacts with the

GS and with Defense Minister Dmitrii Yazov, who rebuked him for reporting the death in combat of soldiers who Yazov maintained had died from drinking bouts, only exacerbated his resentfulness. Moscow was far away and believed there was no fighting in Afghanistan. Like Generalov, Dubynin called repeatedly for withdrawal, only to encounter stony silence or "your job is to fight."[136]

Whether Gorbachev, the new General Secretary of the CPSU, at first believed that a military victory was possible (see Chapter 4), the pace of operations increased when General Igor Rodionov assumed command of the Fortieth Army in April 1985, the month after Gorbachev came to power. Indeed, 1985 was one of the harshest and bloodiest years of the war. Nonetheless, the senior military personnel in Afghanistan were convinced that the situation was deadlocked and there could be no military solution.[137] Toward the end of 1985, a detailed twenty-three-page U.S. State Department report described enhanced military activity on both sides, as well as great losses, with the Soviets adjusting "their numbers, weapons, and tactics to meet the improved capabilities of the mujahidin."[138]

A Western correspondent visiting Afghanistan in late 1985 noted that the Fortieth Army had modified its equipment to suit mountain and desert warfare—lighter, more mobile mortars, barrages of long-range artillery and rockets, increased use of clusters of seismic mines, and the expansion of security belts involving strings of new outposts.[139] Soviet soldiers who took part in operations, however, opined that even the improvements in training prior to Afghanistan and the experience of several years of fighting had prepared neither officers nor soldiers for the conditions of Afghanistan, where assignments could not be conducted according to MoD regulations.[140] Although there were officers who would not break the rules for fear of harming their chances of promotion, the reluctance of their superiors to violate rules and their insistence on playing by the book were causes of unhappiness within the officer corps. Air force officers, for example, complained that headquarters did not allow them to fly helicopters at low altitudes when circumstances clearly dictated this.[141]

By the end of this phase of the war, it had become apparent to the top echelons of the Fortieth Army that there would be no decisive defeat of the opposition, however much the Soviet force restructured its tactics and fighting capabilities. They continued the struggle since this was their assignment, but their covert goals became more restricted and realistic. They could only hope to minimize casualties, overcome some of the more antiquated perceptions of fighting, and lubricate their war machine.

Withdrawal, 1986–1989

At some point in 1985, Gorbachev became convinced of the need to move toward withdrawal. It took time, however, before this idea became a reality.

A first, minor, much-publicized withdrawal, however—of "more than 8,000 men" (six regiments)—occurred in October 1986.[142] The Soviet Defense Ministry report of this measure listed one tank regiment, two motor-rifle regiments, and three antiaircraft regiments, with their equipment and weapons.[143] *Pravda* said that the Kremlin hoped that "those who are organizing the armed intervention against Afghanistan will understand and evaluate the step correctly" and curtail external interference in Afghanistan's affairs.[144] The 1991 MoD appraisal of the war dubbed this measure "the first practical step" toward the withdrawal of the Fortieth Army.[145]

The Soviet political leadership's recognition that the Soviet armed forces' inability to achieve victory in Afghanistan reflected badly on the general capability of the Soviet military was an important reason behind Gorbachev's decision to opt out, together perhaps with the need to cut down on Soviet casualties in light of Soviet public opinion.

Meanwhile, the opposition's capabilities continued to grow, especially in the realm of antiaircraft missiles. In spring 1987, the Fortieth Army HQ noted that the number of attacks against fixed-wing aircraft and helicopters had increased from 62 in 1984—when the Stingers were first reported—to 141 in 1985, and 847 in 1986, in which year the mujahidin downed 26 fixed-wing aircraft and helicopters.[146] The relative value of fixed-wing aircraft in air combat changed as of 1987, when it became clear that the advance in mujahidin antiaircraft capability meant that helicopters could no longer fly securely at medium altitudes. The army henceforth excluded helicopters from participation in offensive missions.[147]

In March and again in April 1987, the mujahidin carried out attacks inside Soviet territory—in Tajikistan.[148] The Soviet media officially acknowledged these incidents, as distinct from earlier bombardments on Soviet territory—several attacks on the rail link between Samarkand and Termez and one on a power station in Tajikistan[149]—and later instances when the mujahidin "lobbed" rockets into Soviet territory. (As early as 1980, they had bombarded the Tajik township of Pyanj and Termez in Uzbekistan.[150]) Stories also circulated of groups of as many as sixty men crossing the frontier in order to conduct sabotage operations, such as cutting electric lines, aiming, in the words of one partisan, "to show the Soviets that we're not afraid of them; they fight with us on our territory and we on theirs." According to that source, the local Tajiks felt empathy for the Afghans: they helped them cross back into Afghanistan but were not prepared to join them in their operations.[151]

In 1987, the intensity of the Soviet military effort began to decrease as Gorbachev moved gradually but implacably toward withdrawal, in parallel with the announcement of Najibullah (Muhammad Najib), who succeeded Barak Karmal as president of Afghanistan, that he was opting for a policy of national reconciliation.[152]

By the time Gromov came to Afghanistan to command the Fortieth Army in May 1987, his third stint of service during the war, he knew he would be commanding the withdrawal. He notes that now the Fortieth Army's main objectives were to limit offensive initiatives and avoid losses.[153] The head of the CPSU CC General Department, Anatolii Luk'ianov, had instructed him to take care of the men, render all possible aid to the Afghans, and report truthfully.[154] Indeed, his command saw a reduction of loss of life by one and a half times (and of machinery by two times).[155] Varennikov attributed the instructions to spare lives and diminish losses to the CPSU CC plenum of April 1985, shortly after Gorbachev took over, which led the OG to review its tactics.[156]

The tension between the Fortieth Army command and Moscow persisted to the end. To achieve its strategic goals and tactical missions, the DRA leadership continued to rely "not on [its] own forces but on the international aid of the Soviet Union and the troops of the Fortieth Army."[157] The DRA government made this position clear throughout 1988 and even into 1989. Moreover, even in the war's last years, "the leaders of our various departments' missions in Kabul changed repeatedly," and "each new appointee began his work" with proposals to "prepare and implement," together with the DRA army, "large-scale operations against the gangs," failing as usual to appreciate that the opposition were not gangs but "the local male population taking up arms to defend their tribal interests."[158]

Consequently, the Fortieth Army continued to be involved in combat operations until almost the end. Gromov led a major operation (Operation Magistral; November 1987–January 1988) to considerable success as a result of careful and secretive planning, fastidious study of the terrain, and effective coordination among the various forces.[159] Following this, he undertook yet one more large-scale offensive in January 1989, one month before the final withdrawal (see below).

Nor was it solely the "representatives of the departments" who failed to learn. The military was similarly unable to internalize all of the requisite lessons. In the early stages of the war, Soviet soldiers went into combat carrying loads of 40, or, according to one source, almost 60 kilograms.[160] Discussing one operation in February 1988, a Western analyst noted that in the ninth year of the war, the Soviet troops still carried incredible weights—58-pound machine guns and 82mm mortars, for example—that hindered them from cutting off enemy escape routes, when the mujahidin already had an uphill advantage. He also noted that Soviet equipment frequently could not clear mines, particularly not nonmetallic ones, in mountainous areas.[161] There were constant problems with communication equipment and weaponry.

Ultimately the Geneva Accords (April 1988) stipulated the withdrawal of all Soviet troops from Afghan territory, beginning on May 15, 1988, and culminating on February 15, 1989.[162] The Soviet Union fulfilled its obligations to the letter. When the withdrawal began, "183 Soviet military townships and facilities were operating" in Afghanistan.[163] On May 14, Gromov announced that within the coming three months, over half of the Soviet contingent would leave nine of the fourteen provinces where "they have been stationed to date" and eleven of eighteen garrisons.[164] No new recruits arrived in the fall, as the GS ordered all those due for demobilization in the semiannual fall turnover to remain until the final withdrawal.[165]

Speaking to party activists at the Soviet missions in Afghanistan in April 1988, Viktor Polianichko, CPSU CC adviser to the PDPA Politburo from 1985 to 1988, and thus political adviser to both Karmal and Najibullah, said they must do everything to ensure that with the Soviet withdrawal, the Afghan and Soviet peoples "remain friends." The farewell for the Soviet force must be organized in such a way that "the Soviet soldier leaves not as a soldier with a sword [in hand] but as a soldier-internationalist." He wanted Fortieth Army personnel to be involved "more widely in the resolution of social problems (repairing roads, schools and mosques, and planting 'friendship gardens')."[166]

This dream was not reflected in practice. In August 1988, Varennikov prepared for Defense Minister Yazov a pessimistic appraisal of the situation in Afghanistan as Soviet troops withdrew. He pointed out the increasing demands and "even complaints" of the Afghan leadership who were trying to get from the Soviets "as much material and other resources as possible" and to force the Soviet military "to use maximally the men and equipment of the Fortieth Army." Instead of expressing gratitude, Najibullah emphasized the unreliability of his Afghan army and ministries of Interior Affairs and State Security and the constant failures to defend garrisons because of "insufficient assistance from the Fortieth Army." Although the Soviet troops did "not envision" combat operations—they were focusing their attention on withdrawal of troops—the Afghans frequently summoned Soviet artillery and aircraft to rescue them. Najibullah's attempt to involve the Fortieth Army in battles with the main opposition leader in northern Afghanistan, Ahmad Shah Massoud, would "place our troops in an extremely serious situation during the second stage of their withdrawal." There would be further losses and the entire "organized withdrawal . . . could be disrupted." Varennikov considered the whole idea a "mission impossible" and warned that it would harm Soviet prestige and evoke a "negative reaction" inside the Soviet Union.[167]

Although Varennikov had some support in the Kremlin, Gorbachev and his more hawkish advisers, led by Shevarnadze and KGB chief Vladimir Kriuchkov, overruled him. They ordered Gromov to initiate Operation Typhoon against Massoud's troops that involved massive bombing by fighter bombers and heavy bombers from bases inside the Soviet Union and led to numerous civilian deaths and negative political responses.[168]

Air strikes from the Soviet Union also accompanied the withdrawal. A senior Soviet officer who served in Afghanistan testified that Gorbachev "gave the order to use the whole might of the Soviet air force to carry out massive bombing and strafing strikes against Afghan villages that were believed to contain concentrations of rebels."[169] The Soviet Foreign Ministry spokesman, Gennadii Gerasimov, admitted in August 1988 that the Soviet Union sent planes "to give emergency support to a Soviet military unit engaged in combat with superior forces of the armed opposition."[170] Indeed, in summer 1988, the Soviets seem to have used a new and far more powerful type of bomb, the fuel-air explosive.[171]

In September 1988, after meeting with Najibullah, Varennikov wrote to Yazov that the Afghan leadership was doing everything in its power to halt the withdrawal of Soviet troops in response to violations of the Geneva Accords by the United States and Pakistan. Varennikov and his staff insisted that the Fortieth Army must not remain in Afghanistan "on any account," as it would cause the Soviet Union damage "difficult to predict . . . internationally and domestically."[172]

Withdrawal entailed the departure from Afghanistan not only of the Fortieth Army but also of Soviet advisers and specialists. As of January 1, 1988, there were over 1,000 Soviet military specialists, including 694 advisers, in the Afghan army. By November, approximately half had returned to the Soviet Union.[173]

The day before the last Soviet soldier left Afghanistan, the Soviet military command in Afghanistan issued a statement on the withdrawal. It noted that the main purpose of the decision to introduce troops had been to stabilize the situation in Afghanistan, help the DRA armed forces, and protect the country from "the rebel formations on Pakistani and Iranian territory and thereby create conditions for the defense of our southern borders." While "our soldiers came with a mission of peace . . . they were drawn into combat operations. This absolutely was not part of our plans and was not appropriate to our aspirations. . . . Therefore with time, the main accent increasingly changed to political settlement of the conflict." Najibullah's policy of national reconciliation envisioned the cessation of combat operations and settlement of differences "by negotiations and compromises." When, however, the counterrevolutionaries began disrupting and blocking this policy, Soviet soldiers became engaged in implementing it. Nonetheless, now the Soviet soldiers, "having completely fulfilled their internationalist duty," were returning home. They were doing so in "an organized manner, with honor and dignity . . . practically without losses, both in the initial and in the final stages." (In fact, mujahidin attacks leading to the killing and wounding of Soviet soldiers accompanied the withdrawal.[174])

The statement rejected the comparison between "the presence of Soviet troops in Afghanistan and the American actions in Vietnam. . . . We came not with the goal of occupying and splitting the country . . . but with the goal of providing internationalist assistance in the defense of [the] sovereignty and territorial integrity of Afghanistan." Now the withdrawal was occurring "according to the will of the Afghan and Soviet people."[175]

Officially, neither the political nor the military establishment acknowledged a Soviet defeat in Afghanistan—in contrast to the general sense among the Soviet public (see Chapter 7). Foreign Minister Eduard Shevarnadze told a press conference in Geneva on the day the accords were signed that while they created conditions for a Soviet withdrawal, "there is no defeat here."[176] The Soviet generals who participated in the war presented a similar picture. Gromov emphasized that it was irrelevant to speak of defeat, for the force had not gone to Afghanistan to win a war. This contradicts instructions given the Fortieth Army in both early 1981 and early 1982 to suppress completely or finish off the opposition in the course of the coming year. The Fortieth Army fulfilled its assignments, including supporting the PDPA regime, which, contrary to many expectations, did not collapse immediately upon the Soviet withdrawal.[177] Major General Kim Tsagolov was prepared to admit that the war had been lost, but not by the army: "Our soldiers and military leaders won the majority of battles. The war was lost by [the] politicians."[178]

CGS Akhromeev confessed, however, that the Soviet armed forces did not score a military success, explaining that the disparity between the assignments that they received from the political leadership and conditions in Afghanistan made this impossible.[179] An Uzbek officer who served in Afghanistan in the early 1980s wrote that Afghans of all ages fought against the *shuravi* (the Afghan name for the Soviets), just as they had fought all invaders throughout their history, and no army can conduct military operations against the people, whom history has shown are always victorious. Specifically, the Soviet troops frequently destroyed villages and killed innocent people because they answered fire with fire or because they were lured into doing so by the dushmany—or mujahidin—and opened fire without checking the misinformation they received, thus alienating the population. "That is why the war in Afghanistan ended with the withdrawal of the Soviet force."[180]

Indeed, in addition to its a priori unsuitability to conducting a war in the mountains of Afghanistan, especially against a guerrilla adversary, the Soviet force found itself dragged into what the Soviet military attaché in Kabul called the "quagmire of a civil war." It was committed to supporting a regime that was not popular with a meaningful percentage of the population, especially in the countryside, where most Afghans lived. During the first months, the Afghan people viewed the Soviet force sympathetically (*loial'no*), in the hope that it would quickly help the country to achieve tranquility. But this attitude changed radically when the Soviet force, at the persistent insistence of DRA President Babrak Karmal, began to fight the mujahidin. The losses in combat of "the Muslim mujahidin, combined with the active propaganda conducted by forces of the opposition, were conducive to many Afghans beginning to see us as invaders (*okkupanty*)."[181]

The commander of the first paratroop assault division to enter Afghanistan made an analogous assessment: had the regime focused on using the troops to close off the Pakistani border without involving them in the fighting, the outcome might have been more favorable. Once the Soviets undertook their first combat operation, the cause was lost. The DRA government conveyed the message: you've come, you act, you decide, and you fight, you're the stronger, whereas the civilian population saw the Soviet force as foreign infidels, killing and destroying.[182]

The MoD commission that later appraised the war came to a similar conclusion, admitting that rather than leading to the defeat of the opposition, as the Kremlin had hoped, the intervention catalyzed opposition to the atheist, imperialist-colonialist foreigner.[183]

Aleksandr Liakhovskii told the 1995 Lysebu symposium on the war that the Soviet side had analyzed the war's operations and found most of them successful: the Fortieth Army had achieved its goals. The withdrawal occurred because the situation changed, not because of Soviet losses of lives or equipment and not because it could not continue engaging the mujahidin. Both he and the former First Deputy CGS, General Makhmut Gareev, emphasized that had the Soviets intended to win, they would have entered Afghanistan in much greater force.[184] Later, however, Liakhovskii admitted that the war in effect was not "fought properly" and that this "low-intensity conflict" wore down the Soviet Union "economically and morally." Contradicting his previous statement, Liakhovskii added that the army did not achieve the declared goals of the intervention: it did not secure the DRA government's infrastructure, and its presence for the most part did not empower the Afghan army to conduct raids and operations independently. The PDPA government proved itself incapable of functioning or of repelling the armed attacks that threatened to endanger or—in the words of then Georgian First Party Secretary Eduard Shevarnadze in June 1980— "smother" the Afghan revolution "and create an imperialist base for military aggression at the southern borders of the USSR."[185]

Despite the fundamentally defensive nature of the Fortieth Army's mission, over the course of nine years of warfare, it found itself involved in no fewer than 416 combat operations, many of them extensive and most of them preplanned and undertaken with the DRA armed forces. In addition, it undertook 220 local operations, as well as an average of 20 to 25 raids per month.[186]

Given the virtual incapacitation of General Secretary Brezhnev by 1980 and the ailing of his two aged successors, Yuri Andropov (November 1982–February 1984) and Konstantin Chernenko (February 1984–March 1985), there was nobody at the helm to resolve the military impasse that evolved in Afghanistan, let alone to withdraw Soviet forces from that country, although the military leadership persistently pressed it to do so and the Kremlin discussed this possibility very early on. Mikhail Gorbachev began contemplating withdrawal soon after he became General Secretary in March

1985. Doing so, however, involved overcoming opposition within the Soviet leadership. It was only in 1987 that Moscow agreed to discuss withdrawal under the auspices of the United Nations secretary-general, which led ultimately to the Geneva Accords.

The Achievements of the Soviet Limited Contingent

Perhaps the Soviets did not lose the war, but they did not win it. Their massed artillery and battle drills could not rout the mujahidin. They rarely succeeded in working out tactics on site. Nor did the Soviets field adequate personnel strength in its line units; regiments were often at single battalion strength, battalions at single company strength, and companies at single platoon strength. Poor field sanitation and poor nutrition contributed considerably to the spread of disease (see Chapter 3). The first priority for replacing personnel went to drivers, gunners, and vehicle commanders, leaving few troops to do the fighting.

The Soviets failed to bring in sufficient helicopters and air assault forces to perform the necessary missions. Convoys did not always have helicopter support. Moreover, the Soviet force was stymied by its own built-in preferences for large, conventional operations, which were irrelevant to Afghan conditions, and by inappropriate equipment, from uniforms to cumbersome weapons.[187] True, this improved over time, giving the infantry a meaningful increase in firepower and reflecting the realities of counterinsurgency warfare, in which the infantry unit had to be independent rather than relying on battle plans delineated in Moscow.[188]

In addition, by 1984, the Fortieth Army had started to synchronize separate command structures, combining artillery units with systems such as mortars, howitzers, and rocket launchers that would "liaise far more closely with troops on the ground." In the use of airpower, which was "the key force multiplier" (as in Vietnam, Algeria, Nicaragua, and other counterinsurgency wars), the Soviets developed tactics and weaponry to meet changing operational requirements. This applied especially to helicopter pilots, whose craft had mobility, firepower, and flexibility. At least as significant was the way that the Soviets coped with hostile antiaircraft , especially light surface-to-air missiles, first Egyptian and Chinese versions of their own SAM-7 (notably the Chinese Hunin-5), then British Blowpipes and the American Stinger.[189] The Stinger brought down a large number of Soviet aircraft until the Soviets initiated a series of countermeasures. Besides the interception of caravans bringing in Stingers or their purchase from mujahidin, these included masking the infrared signatures of aircraft exhausts so that the missiles could not see them and blinding them with "ceramic 'hot bricks'" that put out a very strong infra-red signal or confused and misdirected them with flares."

In parallel, the Soviets "developed tactics to maximize their airborne edge." They replaced the indiscriminate carpet bombing of 1983–1984 with "increasingly precise attacks by new Su-25 attack jets with laser-guided bombs," while "helicopters acquired extra armored protection, flare dispensers, and often, extra guns or door-mounted weapons." The army elevated helicopter-borne assault landing brigades (DShB) to the status of a special service.[190]

Summing up the war and the achievements of the Fortieth Army, Sergei Krakhmalov, former military attaché at the embassy in Kabul, writes that the Soviet force conducted itself honorably and carried out its military duty in a dignified fashion, fulfilling all of its assigned tasks. The Soviet-Afghan War saw both "heroism, courage, and self-sacrifice, as well as baseness, cowardice, and faint-heartedness." "Riff-raff" could also be found among senior Soviet officials in Kabul, three of whom were tried in Soviet courts and sentenced to long prison terms. Yet Krakhmalov's overall picture plays down the negatives. He notes that the MoD made 86 people Heroes of the Soviet Union for bravery in the war and gave 200,000 awards and medals, 10,955 posthumously, including everyone wounded during its course (65,000 of those awarded were "officers and generals"; 20,000, warrant officers; 110,000, soldiers and sergeants; and 2,500, Fortieth Army's civilian employees, 1,350 of them women).[191] He too is adamant that "we did not lose this war."[192]

Boris Gromov emphasized in particular the success of the Fortieth Army's officers and political workers in "reshaping the men's awareness to a wartime footing," men who "yesterday were students, workers, *kolkhoz* members, even so-called 'heavy metalists' and rockers." Commanders and political workers received "many letters from parents of soldiers with words of profound gratitude for educating their sons." The brotherhood formed in the Fortieth Army, and the mutual ties of officers and men, the heroism, and the experience they gained "will be studied, generalized, and taken into account in training military specialists."[193]

In mid-1991, the MoD commission also considered it justified, for Najibullah's PDPA regime was still in power over two years after the Soviet withdrawal.[194] (Less than a year later, in April 1992, Najibullah was overthrown.)

Certainly the fact that no single ministry or organization coordinated it impeded the Soviet war effort. The representatives of the KGB, the foreign ministry, the defense ministry, and the MVD frequently sent conflicting reports to Moscow, where their bosses also often held incompatible positions. As Varennikov asserted, just prior to the final withdrawal, these representatives, specifically the ambassadors—of whom there were four in the four years he was in Kabul—had no understanding of Central Asia. Moreover, there was "the disease of the stagnation period; to inform the central offices only of what would be well received, rather than what was actually taking place." These "discrepancies caused Moscow to make decisions that weren't always sound.... Our dogmatism, inertia, and sluggishness also led to many problems." The real opposition to the Soviets and the PDPA was not the armed opposition, but the population at large. In Varennikov's words, there were many areas "whose inhabitants oppose the central government and at the same time refuse to allow rebel detachments on their territory. They're used to living independently and don't want to take orders from anyone. . . . During the first years of the war, in our effort to support the Afghan government, we thought that we had to implant the nucleus of a political organization in each district. But the kishlak dwellers resisted us at every turn. That's why military force was employed wherever there was opposition. Military units were used to support the 'people's' power."[195]

In 1990, Soviet military historian V. G. Safronov distinguished between the war's political and military lessons. Regarding the first, he wrote, the Soviet leadership should have analyzed more carefully the DRA leadership's ability to reform the country; because it could not, the decision to intervene militarily was clearly a mistake. Moreover, Safronov is adamant that military means are no way to solve acute domestic problems, making the war neither historically nor morally justifiable. Yet the errors of the Soviet leaders in no way belittled the military's heroic, honorable, and meritorious fulfillment of the tasks allotted it, in whose correctness it believed.[196]

Interestingly, none of the military personnel or military analysts at the time evaluated the war in terms of counterinsurgency warfare. Both the strategy and the tactics of the Limited Contingent frequently overlapped with elements of the theory and practice of counterinsurgency warfare, combining its classic enemy-centered and population-centered theories. Yet this appears to have occurred without conscious intention and without consulting any doctrine or model of counterinsurgency warfare, as this category did not appear in the lexicon of the Soviet military.[197] At the same time, the Soviet military command in Afghanistan instinctively appreciated that what David Galula calls the "intangible assets"—tactical initiative, the "ideological power of a cause," and political control of the population for which these were flesh and blood,[198] as well as a thorough knowledge of the terrain—were all in the hands of the mujahidin, the insurgents. The country's Marxist regime, representing a minute sector of the population and divided within, had no chance of success in face of these disadvantages. A force of the size of the Limited Contingent could not have tipped the balance, even if it had not been shackled with hefty obstacles, some of them built into the Soviet armed forces and some specific to the Fortieth Army.

Chapter 3

The Fortieth Army

The Kremlin created the Fortieth Army of the Soviet armed forces in 1979 specifically for Afghanistan (see Chapter 2). This chapter looks at the composition of the force, known during the war as the "Limited Contingent of Soviet Troops in Afghanistan"—its successes and failures, its morale, its conduct, and its casualties. [1]

There are various estimates regarding how many people served in the Fortieth Army. According to the MoD, 620,000 men served in Afghanistan: 525,000 in the armed forces, 90,000 in the KGB, and 5,000 in the MVD (the Interior Ministry), plus 21,000 civilians.[2] One well-informed source writes that of the "approximately one million" who passed through Afghanistan during the war's nine years, just 650,000 to 700,000 of them were military.[3] The civilians included interpreters, advisers, and construction engineers. Gorbachev himself spoke of "over one million,"[4] a figure that several observers accept.[5] One scholar found it probable that the official figures were distorted somewhere lower down in the reporting channel.[6]

At any given time, the force included anything between 85,000—the size it reached at some point in 1980—and 120,000. Possibly it grew as high as 150,000 in the peak period. For most of the time, the consensus figure is around 105,000.[7] According to MoD sources, the force never exceeded 108,800 soldiers—106,000 of them servicemen, 73,000 of them in combat units.[8] Varennikov himself noted that by 1985, the force numbered "over 100,000" without "construction, maintenance, and rear" personnel, medics, and other support services. In March 1988, the Afghanistan Commission spoke of withdrawing 109,000 troops—8,200 border troops, 513 planes and helicopters, and about 30,000 pieces of war materiel and vehicles.[9]

Galeotti, who opines that the maximum number of soldiers in the Fortieth Army at any one time was 120,000, points out that adding civilian specialists and "other 'honorary afgantsy'" brings the aggregate to the 730,000 that the Supreme Soviet Committee for Soldier-Internationalists claimed, although this might be "a slight underestimate."[10] My own assessment is close to that of Galeotti, around 750,000.

The average time of service in Afghanistan was eighteen months for soldiers. In May 1980, Ustinov required a statutory period of two years for officers.[11]

By December 24, 1979, according to Liakhovskii, "a total of about 100 formations, units, and installations, had been deployed, including the HQ of the 40th Army; a composite air corps," comprising apparently the squadron of fighter-bombers, transferred from the Transcaucasian MD to Mary in Turkmenistan, and placed under the command of the Turkestan MD; "four motorized rifle divisions (three in the Turkestan MD and one in the Central Asian MD), artillery, surface-to-air missile, and airborne assault brigades; independent motorized rifle and missile artillery regiments; and signals, intelligence, logistics, and repair units."[12] At its height, according to an MoD source, the force accounted for four divisions, five brigades, four separate regiments, six separate battalions, and four aircraft and three helicopter regiments, as well as rear, medical, maintenance, construction, supply, and "other units and departments."[13]

One officer, however, says that as of June and July 1980, the force held eight motor-rifle divisions, the 105th (Vitebsk) paratroop division, two or three VDV divisions, two spetsnaz brigades, and two border troop subdivisions. The army dispersed seven of the motor-rifle divisions along the ring of roads (Kushka–Herat–Kandahar–Gazni–Kabul–Mazar-i Sharif–Termez). The country's twelve airfields supported two airborne divisions with 270 fighter planes, as well as four regiments of fighter helicopters—approximately 250 Mi-8s and Mi-24s. Two air divisions at the Turkestan and Central Asian MD airfields reinforced them. In addition to fighter helicopters, the force in Afghanistan had about 350 transport helicopters.[14] The Fortieth Army rear held medical, maintenance, quartermaster, and construction units.

The spring and the fall draft call-ups regularly refilled the divisions, regiments, and battalions. The overall figures are, however, partially misleading, for formations failed to maintain "adequate personnel strength."[15] All of the units were chronically undermanned, as disease cut badly into present-for-duty strength; generally up to one-third of the soldiers were down with hepatitis, typhus, malaria, amoebic dysentery, or meningitis.[16] Boris Gromov tells of an epidemic of hepatitis toward the end of 1981 when every fourth soldier in his division, including Gromov, fell sick.[17] The temptation to drink unclean water was irresistible when no other water was available in heat that one Uzbek testified was unbearable even for Central Asians. "You wake up in the morning and your eyes and ears and nose and mouth are full of dust."[18] The official MoD data give an average of 4,269 personnel sick or wounded per month throughout the war.[19] Certainly early on, nobody replaced the wounded and sick,[20] although this might have changed later.[21]

Conditions of Service

All Soviet sources comment that the conditions in Afghanistan were arduous, even inhumane. The conditions of service in the Soviet armed forces were infamously substandard and rife with disease and hunger; this standard makes the picture for the Fortieth Army nothing less than appalling.[22] The Limited Contingent also brought from home two further blights, narcotics and hazing, both of which escalated in Afghanistan.

Unquestionably the inhospitable climate—extreme heat in the summer and cold in the winter in both the mountainous regions in the north and the desert in the south—were an objective disadvantage.[23] Added to this were poor sanitary conditions, inadequate nutrition, the lack of drinking water, and the unsuitability of Soviet army uniforms and other individual equipment. Many units lacked laundry and bathing facilities, and the general level of hygiene was low, adding to the risk of disease. One man reported brushing his teeth just twice during his service in Afghanistan.[24]

The stories of former soldiers abound with details that bring home the harsh realities of Afghanistan. One soldier in Kabul told a Soviet journalist in February 1980, "We live like animals. We haven't been able to wash even once. There's no firewood, so we freeze. And the food's hardly fit for pigs."[25] Some assert that everyone, even officers, had body lice.[26] "They were so short of things that we didn't even have a bowl or spoon each. There was one big bowl and eight of us would attack it."[27]

Uniforms were little better. The soldiers who went into Afghanistan in the early stages of the war looked like World War II fighters, with crudely made uniforms and overcoats.[28] One soldier, recruited to an intelligence unit in December 1980, recalled that "we were expected to do heavy building work—and sing as we worked—in 40 degrees Celsius while our feet were literally cooking" in multilayered waterproof boots of substitute leather.[29] In the winter, soldiers lost their feet for lack of sleeping bags and appropriate footwear. Some change for the better occurred later in the war; eventually the soldiers received camouflage battledress, armored vests, and, sometimes, newer helmets. Yet one soldier who arrived in Afghanistan in 1986 testified, "Our flak-jackets were so heavy we could hardly lift them," so "we looted enemy boots, clothes," food, trousers, even underwear.[30]

The paucity and poor quality of gear and the dearth of basic amenities led not only to stealing, smuggling, and other criminal activity but also to low morale. Soldiers stole cutlery and kitchen utensils from the mess and sold them at the local bazaars; some sold stolen weaponry to the local population. Stories of these misdemeanors abounded.[31] "We were hungry every minute of the day. . . . In my year and a half in Afghanistan I stopped being hungry only once, when I was wounded. You were looking for ways to get or steal food the whole time." All the soldiers climbed into gardens, orchards, and the army food store to steal at one time or another. Nor was the quality of the soldiers' food satisfactory: watery soup, "a gooey paste of dried potato mash or pearl barley, and tinned mackerel, the label saying, 'Year of manufacture: 1956. Consume within 18 months.'"[32] Soldiers who spent long months in solitary outposts that depended on regular supplies of provisions by helicopter would go without food if, for example, weather conditions prevented helicopters from flying. Medical equipment was similarly lacking. Two Soviet correspondents spoke with hundreds of soldiers; all confirmed that their daily conditions affected them as harshly as combat operations and dushman attacks.[33] At least one soldier was shot dead by the sentry when breaking into a food store.[34] The republican press wrote up the story of a soldier taken captive when he entered an apricot orchard.[35]

Not only was the Soviet army unsuited to the war, the individual soldier was similarly unready. Often he was neither adequately trained for combat nor psychologically prepared to fight. Soldiers enlisting early on spent their training period building officers' homes—and selling the building materials for vodka. They were given access to the firing range just twice, the first time with nine rounds; in the second, they threw one grenade each. In Afghanistan, they constructed a firing range. "Some of the boys never got to fire a weapon before their first taste of action."[36] Even after a statutory six-month training period became standard for those destined for the war, many of the soldiers and junior officers arrived in Afghanistan inadequately prepared for what awaited them. They had neither the basic know-how essential for combat nor even rudimentary information regarding the country, its population, and its customs.[37]

Correspondence with home was important for the soldiers, as in any other war. A letter from home brought with it the normalcy of another world. Letters from parents, wives, or girlfriends told of everyday life interspersed with anxiety and occasionally news of a fellow soldier brought home in a zinc coffin (see Chapter 7).[38] Some wrote home and to classmates frequently[39]—presumably in the hope of getting letters in return.[40] One journalist wrote from Afghanistan exhorting girlfriends to write to the soldiers.[41] A few of the men, mainly officers, sent money home. Although most knew that letters to family and friends would be censored, one soldier who served in 1985–1986 did not believe that private letters underwent inspection until an officer of the "special department" quoted to him by heart a passage from a letter he had written to his wife.[42]

Without mitigating the harshness of the conditions in Afghanistan, there was a difference between those of units that bore the brunt of the fighting and those that spent most of their time on garrison duty or accompanying convoys. The former included elite formations, which were better trained and had "a disproportionate share of professional soldiers and volunteers." These operational forces, which faced greater danger, were "cushioned by preferential treatment," and their esprit de corps was higher than among support and garrison forces. In contrast, garrison soldiers were confined to a unit outpost for months on end, with many of the posts simply "platoon bases watching stretches of roads or villages. . . . Groups as small as a dozen men could find themselves incarcerated in such posts for a full 18 months, without leave or remission." Convoy service involved a "constant and draining tension"; one just waited in one's lorry or personnel carrier for a mine or an ambush.[43]

Everyday conditions improved somewhat over time. Yet at no stage did uniforms, gear, and personal weapons meet the standards of Western armies. Nor could the troops' everyday existence be put right. One officer summed up the situation: "First of all, we had fallen into an uncivilized country. Indeed, we ourselves were not too civilized. This was the source of many misfortunes. Others resulted from our sluggishness, clumsiness, and negligence."[44]

The Command

The Fortieth Army was subordinated de facto to the "operations group" (OG) of the MoD and the Armed Forces GS. The OG was stationed in Kabul until November 1980 and thereafter went to Afghanistan periodically to coordinate the large combat operations of the Soviet and DRA troops. When Sokolov succeeded Ustinov as defense minister in December 1984, Army General Valentin Varennikov, First Deputy CGS, who had been in charge of operational planning under Sokolov, succeeded him as head of the OG. (Akhromeev had succeeded Ogarkov as CGS in September.) Varennikov remained in Kabul from January 1987 until the final withdrawal in February 1989.

The senior officer in Afghanistan, the head of the OG, communicated directly with Moscow. Yet the Fortieth Army commander was formally subordinated to the commander of the Turkestan MD in Tashkent, who was himself responsible to the CGS in Moscow. This duality of command was never formalized and was further complicated by the fact that the duties of the chief military adviser in Kabul included coordinating the operations of the DRA army with those of the Limited Contingent.[45] The Turkestan MD too had an OG in Kabul whose assignments included "planning and implementing combat operations and organizing cooperation with units of the Afghan People's Army."[46]

The officers of the OG gave "practical aid" to the commanders in "preparing and implementing combat operations, organizing combat training, considering accumulated experience, and also coordinating operations . . . with the Afghan army." Further, since the MoD OG only visited Afghanistan sporadically, a five-man group of GS representatives came to Kabul in March 1985, under Major General Boris Gromov, the CGS's general for Afghanistan-related special assignments. Major General V. S. Kudlai replaced him in April 1986.[47]

Second in rank to the Fortieth Army's commander were the head of its political department, a CoS, and a chief of intelligence, all of whom, at least at first, were major generals.[48] NATO sources claimed that the Fortieth Army command also included a deputy commander for the rear, who was "responsible for establishing rear area security, tasking units for specific support missions, assigning deployment areas to support units in Afghanistan, and coordinating rear area command and control in Afghanistan with the Chief of the Rear of the Soviet Armed Forces."[49]

However unrewarding and inhumane the war might have been for the conscripts, it was often a boon for the officers, who received two years' service credit for every year they served in Afghanistan.[50] "No one wanted to be posted to dreary Russian towns. . . . We begged to go to Afghanistan."[51] In addition, the war brought meaningful perks, including substantially higher salaries, as well as "the chance to hone military skills in battle and win a reputation that could propel the lucky few to higher, even the highest ranks." It was therefore not surprising that many officers, especially those with professional ambitions, volunteered for service in Afghanistan. Combat experience established "peer group credibility" and one's "understanding of military art."[52] As Aleksandr Prokhanov pointed out, in Afghanistan, "commanders who had greyed at the temples" were for the first time sending men into combat, seeing wounded soldiers, and becoming authentic warriors.[53]

The Fortieth Army had seven commanders during its nine years:[54] Iurii Tukharinov, who commanded it during its preparatory stage in the Turkestan MD, which he headed; Boris Tkach, who accompanied it into Afghanistan in December 1979 and took over in September 1980; Viktor Ermakov, as of September 1982; Leonid Generalov, from November 1983 until April 1985; Igor Rodionov, who commanded it during the crucial years of 1985–1986 and whom the Kremlin reportedly removed for refusing to undertake yet another Panjshir Valley campaign in 1986;[55] Viktor Dubynin, as of April 1986; and, finally, from May 1987, Boris Gromov, who orchestrated the withdrawal.

These men, like the eleven generals who served as senior advisers to the Afghan armed forces between 1975 and 1991, were "sophisticated professionals" who had managed military formations, run MDs inside the Soviet Union, and commanded armies abroad. They "shared with the political leadership the basic objective of maintaining strategic parity" with the United States. Some had seen service in the Far East, the Middle East, and Africa, where the Soviet Union had given military support to communist allies, "progressive" Third World regimes, and peoples seeking independence from colonialism. But they had "no recent experience in managing large numbers of troops in combat" and lacked "the equipment, the training, the doctrine, [and] the experience to fight a counter-insurgency war in the mountains of Afghanistan."[56]

In the words of three veterans, one private and two sergeants, the officers arrived in Afghanistan knowing nothing about conditions there and how to conduct the war. Junior officers knew far less than did sergeants who had been there for a year or more.[57]

Gromov, however, was an exception. He had filled posts in Afghanistan before being appointed commander of the Fortieth Army. He "cared genuinely about the men under his command . . . made no secret of his dissatisfaction with the all-pervasiveness of the military bureaucracy," and steered clear of perks with which the Soviet nomenklatura surrounded itself. "As a regular army man, [he] carried out his inhuman [sic] mission in Afghanistan with precision and efficiency. . . . [He] controlled the situation throughout." He too however, was unwilling to address the decision to send troops into Afghanistan: "'I'm commander of the army. This question should be addressed to others.'[58]

The senior officers in Afghanistan were generally frustrated by the no-win situation in which they found themselves. Their drinking toast put it in a nutshell: "To the success of our hopeless cause!" Seditious thoughts ran through their minds: "Are we fighting for a just cause?" One could hear comments about an anticipated Nuremberg trial for bombarding civilian settlements and shooting prisoners[59] despite Gromov's insistence that the Soviet side strictly observed the injunction not to bomb civilian settlements.[60]

The Fortieth Army command and other representatives of the Soviet MoD in Kabul were also frustrated by the conduct and ineffectiveness of the DRA leadership, the Soviet leadership's attempts to pander to its desires, and the KGB, which ran its own establishment in Afghanistan. According to Gromov, KGB personnel wrote their reports to suit the Kremlin.[61]

The political officers, who were placed in every unit, were a category unto themselves. They were generally titled "deputy commanders," but their assignment was completely different from that of the regular officers. Their job was to boost the troops' morale and imbue them with a sense of duty and commitment that would improve their combat abilities.[62] As one sergeant major put it, "The political education officers managed to convince us of things they didn't believe themselves."[63] However, when their falsehoods became transparent, they weakened the credibility of those who spread them and "undermin[ed] commanders' ability to maintain discipline and morale."[64] Some political officers worked with the population to attract Afghans to the PDPA.

Many testimonies addressed the corruption within the officer corps. One lieutenant colonel complained that only those who pandered to their seniors got promotions and spoke of officers selling weapons to the mujahidin, then writing them off as lost in combat. They could send anyone who countered these claims to a psychiatric ward.[65] Yet Major General Kim Tsagolov, who did not spare the top brass in his criticism of the war and was sacked for his pains, disagreed that the Fortieth Army officers were disproportionately corrupt. He said that while an army generally reflects society, the Fortieth Army was "on a much higher level" than Soviet society.[66]

The brunt of the fighting fell on middle and junior rank officers—colonels, majors, captains, and lieutenants—and on the ordinary soldiers. These officers believed in their professional duty, and most of them, certainly early in the war, trusted that they were in Afghanistan to protect it from outside interference and domestic rebellion and to defend their country's southern border.

Most officers had passed through the specialized military educational establishments that trained them for specific sections of the Soviet military. Others were reserve officers who had graduated from military training programs at institutions of higher learning. A third group were professional soldiers and warrant officers who had attained officer status after completing examinations and fulfilling other educational assignments.[67] In 1985–1986, no less than 64 percent of decorated Afghan veterans were captains or majors, coming predominantly from the airborne forces or the combat engineers.[68]

According to one Western appraisal, many of these officers were "reasonably well trained, or at least equipped to absorb the indispensable lessons they could only learn on the battlefield."[69] Liakhovskii, however, disagrees. Although admitting there were exceptions, he accuses company, battalion, and regiment commanders of poor performance and inability to learn the enemy's tricks and develop shrewd tactics in response (compare Chapter 2). He also recounts ignorance of local politics, political officers vying with one another for personal advantage, corruption at high levels, and higher commanders interfering with more competent lower ranking commanders.[70] He was surely in a position to know.

One captain asserted that many officers who served in Afghanistan had had problems in their previous units[71] so were not people of whom much could be expected. Objective conditions also operated to the disadvantage of junior officers. Since the Fortieth Army had to cover large sectors, "divisions were usually dispersed by regiments, battalions, and companies to cover an area of 250 kilometers. Each regiment, battalion, or company stationed in a separate garrison was assigned a sector of terrain, within the limits of which the commander was to conduct reconnaissance missions as well as operations against rebels in coordination with the Afghan army. But dispersing the troops in such large territories created difficulties in unit control. . . . Independent actions . . . became a necessity, frequently with bad results."[72] Complicating the situation was the impossibility of radio and other communication in mountainous terrain.

Relations between officers and soldiers appear to have varied, often as a result of the personality of the officer in question. On the whole, interactions were less formal in Afghanistan than was customary in the Soviet armed forces because officers were frequently drunk or doped, and because the "granddads" (senior conscripts; see below) held so much sway. Some officers cared for their men and managed to avoid creating bad feeling in their units. One soldier interviewed over twenty years after returning from the war remembered his commander for perceiving his primary task as teaching his troops how to survive.[73] A commander who was with the first troops to enter Afghanistan testified that once they started fighting, his primary concern was to preserve the lives of his men; his worst moments were returning from combat and ascertaining "how many?"[74] One officer refused an order by a general to send his men into combat when he considered it inexpedient and likely to cause unnecessary casualties.[75]

There was, however, another approach. Interactions between officers and soldiers could be tense, even brutal. There were cases where officers physically beat soldiers, and soldiers occasionally retaliated by killing officers.[76] In the words of one former soldier, "Many officers assumed it was the same here as back home, that they could hit and insult their men as much as they liked. Quite a few who thought that way have been found dead in battle, with a bullet in their back. The perfect murder!"[77] The officers' better living conditions, provisions, and financial opportunities bred bad feeling among their men.[78] A soldier who served in a paratroop unit in the latter half of the 1980s testifies to the tension, especially between officers and men. "The officers were for us, Enemy Number One." The Central Asians were frequently the most bitter about their commanders' attitude toward them; one Tajik afganets said that the officers, who were mostly Russians, "related to us as if we understood nothing and were completely unable to perform."[79]

A journalist testified that over the years, the soldiers' improved living conditions reduced the difference between officers and their men and that officers were the worst off in combat as the mujahidin aimed at them first, as proven by the relatively high proportion of officers killed in action.[80]

One junior officer insisted that they undertook assignments to save their soldiers and that an officer's responsibility for his soldiers' safety was more difficult than anything the troops had to undergo. They also had the frustration of being unable to explain why the war was necessary for the Soviet Union. Especially important was the role of the platoon commander who "teaches and educates, and organizes the life and daily existence of the troops whose fighting capacity depends on his competence, the level of his political awareness, and his moral and practical quality."[81]

In addition, the junior officers largely filled the role of NCOs. The Soviet armed forces traditionally had no professional NCOs capable of training troops for combat;[82] the conscript sergeants, basically just long-term servicemen, were incapable of doing the job. Yet in 1971, the army launched a warrant officer program that trained *praporshchiki*.[83] As Galeotti noted, "The long-service non-commissioned officers and warrant officers (praporshchiki) . . . showed their true worth in Afghanistan, where, amid the high turnover of semi-trained conscripts, they represented one of the few repositories of hard-won combat experience."[84]

Every platoon had three official NCOs. To the troops, they frequently seemed to have "unlimited power."[85] Indeed, asked about relations between command and troops, one interpreter testified that although there were many instances when drunken officers hit soldiers, notably Central Asians, sergeants and praporshchiki behaved especially inconsiderately.[86] (For humiliation of Central Asians by their superiors, see Chapter 9.)

The task of the KGB force, and of the much smaller MVD force, which were not formally part of the Fortieth Army, included forming networks of agents among the mujahidin, studying clan relationships, and discovering the whereabouts of opposition bases, supply routes, and army dumps. From the summer of 1980 through 1983, they operated in an approximately 1,000-strong organization called Kaskad stationed in eight places throughout Afghanistan. For most of the rest of the war, individual KGB officers were attached to various Fortieth Army spetsnaz units.[87]

The Troops

The Fortieth Army was composed of infantry and artillery regiments, airborne assault troops, reconnaissance or intelligence units, a tank force, helicopter squadrons, sappers, truck drivers, and rear echelon noncombat battalions.

Most of the soldiers were youngsters—eighteen- and nineteen-year-olds. As one former infantry platoon leader says, "It was a boys' war. It was kids not long out of school who did the fighting. It was like a game for us."[88] Some had completed a year or so of professional training in blue-collar occupations before conscription or had worked briefly. According to one source, "many of these young people were not motivated to serve the country."[89] One military correspondent wrote that approximately 40 percent of the soldiers in some units had criminal records.[90] Traditional recruiting practices underwent meaningful irregularities in the context of the Afghan War. New regulations waived the practice of giving automatic deferment to students enrolled in institutions of higher learning, so as at least of 1982, university students were conscripted, most of them after a year or two of studies.[91]

The troops suffered from their poor and unsuitable training, especially in the war's early stages, which left them unable to cope with the demands of military service under combat conditions. The Fortieth Army's last commander laid much of the blame on the prerecruitment training that the boys had received, both physical—"Not all, even strong young fellows are able to carry heavy loads"—and "moral-psychological."[92] Conscripts arrived with the poor physical condition of young Soviet citizens in the 1970s and 1980s—the outcome of defective nutrition, ignorance of ecological constraints, and a completely inadequate health system.[93]

By 1981, the army had extended the training course to six months "under the guidance of officers with combat experience."[94] The course had two parts. The first included strengthening the soldiers' motivation and their understanding of the importance of their mission. This involved emphasizing both the capabilities and the limitations of the adversary and ensuring that the soldiers were confident in the use of combat equipment. In the second stage, the soldiers were trained in "individual and collective combat skills," unit combat action, and psychological readiness for specific types of combat and for remaining at remote posts for long periods of time.

"The loneliness and boredom experienced in these remote outposts were extremely detrimental to . . . morale." For months at a time, soldiers were stationed on "dominant features, on heights far away from one another, surrounded by the enemy. We can only imagine the personal problems they had individually and with each other. Squads of seven to twelve lived in shelters constructed largely of the materials at hand." They had very little besides their combat equipment and weapons. Food, water, and ammunition came by truck or air every few weeks. Mail from home arrived only after long delays.[95]

The "moral and psychological indoctrination" was intended to teach them about the peculiarities of life in Afghanistan. But this was not always successful. There was no "theoretical doctrine" that might have been helpful, and the concealment of the truth about the war influenced the soldiers' "psychological condition" negatively; the knowledge that their families did not know what was going on there and could not understand the situation affected the soldiers' emotions.[96] Ultimately, whether because it was drummed into them so often or not, many seem genuinely to have believed that they were doing their internationalist duty. "Twice a week we attended a political 'seminar,' where we were continually told that we were doing our sacred duty to help make the [Soviet] border totally secure."[97] One NCO told a journalist that at the beginning, they were credulous, believed everything and everyone, as, for example, when told they had forestalled the Americans by a matter of hours.[98]

Some soldiers were more ambivalent. "The words revolution and internationalism did not, as concepts, arouse any special emotion in Nikolai's breast—either positive or negative."[99] Interviewed at a guard post, one twenty-year-old private admitted to a Soviet journalist that he felt nothing when shooting at people: "'You don't ask questions in the army.'" There was a war "'because of the revolution.'" It was the Americans who had started it, and he was there "'fulfilling my international duty.'" When pressed, he admitted he had no idea what that meant: "'I did try to find out. I asked the political officer. . . . He told me to stop bothering him. . . . He said that people should know things like that from childhood.'" As to whether sending troops to Afghanistan was the right decision, 'I don't know. . . . It's the generals who know.'"[100]

It was, then, not solely the military aspect of their initial training that worked

Table 3.1. Were relations within the Fortieth Army positive?

Between officers and soldiers	69%
Among the soldiers	75%
Between soldiers of different nationalities	58%

to the disadvantage of the average soldier in Afghanistan. His entire education was designed to deprive him of his ability to think for himself. Army discipline and the political officers' brainwashing further weakened the initiative he might need in order to survive. In addition, there was low morale, hazing, and often, the dictatorial rule of the sergeants.

Somewhat surprisingly, however, afgantsy tended to remember army relationships, both within the ranks and between the men and their commanders, positively (Table 3.1).

Had we been able to conduct a survey while they were in Afghanistan, our findings might have been somewhat less affirmative.

The Women

Women too saw service in Afghanistan; inevitably, some were killed.[101] They served mainly as nurses and civilian employees who worked on the larger bases and compounds as cooks, waitresses, storekeepers, typists, telephone and radio operators, and teachers.[102] A very few served in sniper regiments.[103] In the words of one woman who went as a civilian employee, "People like me . . . believed all the talk about the April revolution and accepted everything we'd been taught since our earliest schooldays. . . . We all had some practical reason for going, of course . . . but inside all of us there was still that . . . *faith*. We wanted to be needed and we wanted to help. . . . Those defenseless mutilated men needed [women], even if only for the comforting touch of a soft hand."[104]

One nurse recalled being summoned to the recruiting office in 1982, when she was a third-year nursing student: "'We need nurses in Afghanistan. How do you feel about volunteering? You'd get one and a half times your normal salary, plus foreign currency vouchers.'" She wanted to continue her studies and declined, but then she was told that if she didn't change her mind, the university would be informed what sort of *Komsomolka* (Young Communist League member) she was. She had no choice. A woman who apparently was employed in the security services left behind a daughter in her teens who spent the two years her mother was in Afghanistan in boarding school. "The CO called me in. 'You're needed over there,' he told me. 'It's your duty!' We were brought up on that word, it's second nature to us."[105]

In this way, although categorized as volunteers, many of the women were selected by the same military commissariats that sent the servicemen; others, however, volunteered. One woman from Moscow, for example, "wanted adventure and escape from everyday life."[106] In the view of the woman who, in 1991, set up the Moscow Committee of Women Disabled by the Afghanistan War, the rationale behind the enlistment of women for Afghanistan was that their presence would bring a sense of normalcy to relieve the stress of the war affecting so many young servicemen and officers.[107]

No one ever explained to them the reasoning behind their enlistment. "There was the eternal question," one nurse recalled, " . . . of why so many women were drafted into Afghanistan for the duration? To begin with, we were just a bit puzzled when dozens of 'cleaners,' `librarians,' and 'hotel workers' started arriving, often one cleaner for two or three prefabs, or one librarian for a few shelves of shabby old books." Well, why do you think? We professionals kept away from such women."[108] The women were inevitably "the source of constant youthful attention, ranging from jocular romanticism to rape. At least half the conscripts," according to one source, "had already had experience of sex by draft age." The same source notes that 11.8 percent of the prisoners serving sentences for crimes committed in Afghanistan had been convicted of rape.[109]

The women who served in the medical service did a job that evoked only praise for their devotion, hard work, and self-sacrifice. After taking the testimony of ten of them, one source remarked, "There is nothing to add. One can only bow low to those who endured all this and remained human, compassionate, and healers."[110]

The Medics

The doctors, nurses, medical attendants, and orderlies were critical to the Fortieth Army. The six military hospitals set up in Afghanistan were not fit to cope with the enormous dimensions of disease among the soldiery, let alone the large number of wounded. The army hospital in Shindand had 350 beds but regularly had to treat 1,200 to 1,300 people; beds would hold two people. Sanitary conditions were terrible, according to one nurse who contracted typhus.[111]

Although the treatment left much to be desired, the medical personnel gave everything they had. One of them testified before returning home, "I have a feeling that I'm going to the Soviet Union to live out the rest of my days. I have given all of myself here . . . who will I be when I return?"[112]

At the same time, the medical personnel's very qualifications stymied their performance. The Soviet armed forces' medical cadres were prepared for service in peacetime but lacked the knowledge to meet the needs that arose during a war, especially one with conditions like Afghanistan's. A former chief surgeon of the Fortieth Army, discussing the medical aid for the wounded early in the war, described young, inexperienced surgeons appointed heads of hospital departments, where they faced cases and dilemmas with which they were unable to cope.[113]

Medical equipment was generally poor and in short supply. A nurse who arrived in Kabul in early 1980 noted that "the hospital was the former English stables. There was no equipment—one syringe for all the patients, and the officers drank the surgical spirit so we had to use petrol to clean the wounds. They healed badly for lack of oxygen, but the hot sun helped to kill microbes. I saw my first patients in underwear and boots. For a long time there were no pyjamas, slippers, or even blankets. The first March, a pile grew up behind the hospital . . . amputated arms, legs and other bits of our men. . . . We didn't save everyone we could have. . . . We lost so many because we didn't have the right drugs, the wounded were often brought in too late because the field medics were badly trained soldiers who could just about put bandages on; the surgeon was often drunk. . . . The infectious department [sic] intended for 30 beds held 300 soldiers, mainly typhoid and malaria cases."[114]

Medical officers would return from leave with supplies bought on the black market and in Afghanistan itself. They would spend their precious hard currency vouchers on Japanese disposable syringes, Italian plastic plasma, and inflatable British splints. "Sometimes, they would don flak jackets and helmets and join commandos raiding rebel supply convoys simply to loot the caravans for Western-supplied medical goods." The nurses spent their free time preparing bandages.[115] Medical personnel washed bandages for reuse.[116]

"There was a general shortage of medication," a medical instructor in a reconnaissance unit recalled. "Even the iodine ran out. Either the supply system failed, or else we'd used up our allowance—another triumph of our planned economy. We used equipment captured from the enemy. In my bag I always had twenty Japanese disposable syringes. They were sealed in a high polyethylene packing which could be removed quickly, Our Soviet 'Rekord' brand, wrapped in paper which always got torn, was frequently not sterile. Half of them didn't work anyhow—the plungers got stuck. . . . Our ordinary Soviet-made sterile dressings were also bad. The packaging was as heavy as oak and weighed more than the dressing itself. . . . We had absolutely no elastic dressings, except what we captured. . . . And as for our splints! They were more like skis than medical equipment."[117]

A doctor of the medical battalion in Bagram near Kabul that treated about 13,000 patients a year and conducted a large number of amputations told war correspondent Artem Borovik that even toward the end of the war, it still did not have "a single piece of factory-made medical equipment or a conventional operating-room. I had to build everything with my bare hands." And speaking about the way medical supplies came in, he said, "We're doing things as they were done in World War II."[118]

Patients often saw things differently. One soldier wounded in the leg—which he refused to let the doctors amputate—spent two months in the hospital in Shindand. He reported that about half the patients had hepatitis, and there were many wounded, often as a result of accidents, including three attempted suicides. The doctors and nurses "were supposed to give shots every four hours but at night they were all having sex or getting drunk and would just give four shots at a time."[119]

A Soviet journalist treated in the Kabul hospital in 1987 for an infection gave a particularly vivid description of life—and death—on its precincts: "I do not believe that [people] suffered anywhere the way they did in that hospital. For here, they suffered for NOTHING. There was nothing purifying in the suffering of its inmates," although there was also "an acute sense of brotherhood. Here, people lost their minds, and gained insight."[120]

Over the years, the situation improved somewhat. In the words of one student of the war, toward its end, 93 percent of the wounded received initial medical aid within thirty minutes and full medical assistance within six hours, with the aid of airborne medical assistance and evacuation that linked main ground units to regional hospitals and airstrips and ultimately to Kabul and the main medical hospitals at Tashkent and Moscow, "using a variety of special 'casevac' aircraft."[121] Commanders began taking a surgeon and a medical assistant into combat, for even slight wounds at a high altitude could rapidly turn fatal and medical evacuation by helicopter was difficult in mountainous areas. Their comrades often carried wounded soldiers to lower altitudes to be picked up, but the wounded sometimes failed to survive the hours needed to reach treatment centers.[122]

A large number of soldiers were hospitalized because they contracted illnesses or because they had been wounded—52 and 50 percent, respectively, among my respondents. The highest percentage of those treated for infectious diseases was from 1984 to 1987, when it reached 31 to 34 percent of the Fortieth Army's entire force, while two-thirds of the force were treated by the various medical stations (*medpunkty*). Of the sick, 40.6 to 51.2 percent had hepatitis-C (the most prevalent of the diseases that plagued the Fortieth Army[123]); 14.6 to 20.2 percent had intestinal illnesses; and 9.6 to 26.9 percent suffered from typhoid fever and para-typhus A and B. Many developed complications—19.6 percent in Kandahar and Kunduz in 1983—and many died.

Because so many soldiers were flown for treatment to Tashkent (or Ashkhabad and Dushanbe), malaria, severe forms of hepatitis, and amoebic dysentery appeared in Central Asia, for the first time. But the frequency of illness in Afghanistan dropped as of 1985, when hospitalization and treatment within the Fortieth Army improved.[124]

Questioned about the quality of medical service in Afghanistan, to which most of my respondents had been exposed, 41 percent described it negatively: 13 percent labeled it terrible, another 13 percent said it was generally poor except in Kabul, and 15 percent replied that it was poor but added that it was satisfactory in military hospitals inside the Soviet Union, to which many of them had been consigned for further treatment (Table 3.2).

Table 3.2. How was medical treatment in Afghanistan?

Satisfactory	59%
Generally poor, except in Kabul	13%
Poor, but in military hospitals in the Soviet Union it was satisfactory	15%
Terrible	13%

A Moscow physician who knew people working in military hospitals in Afghanistan said officers received treatment far superior to that of ordinary soldiers.[125]

Social and Ethnic Composition

Who fought the war became an important aspect of the debates that arose in the 1980s regarding the morality and viability of the Soviet system. As public opinion became an increasingly significant factor in Soviet society and politics (see Chapter 7), the considerations behind the Kremlin's selection of soldiers for the Fortieth Army became a lightning rod regarding the equity of the entire political order. This applied to both the ethnic makeup of the Soviet force and its class nature.

We do not know whether the MoD had a discriminatory policy when conscripting soldiers for Afghanistan. Most agree, however, that the lower socioeconomic strata of Soviet society bore the brunt of service in Afghanistan.[126] According to the survey of a medical officer who arrived in Afghanistan in 1986 and interviewed 2,000 soldiers, Mikhail Reshetnikov, most soldiers came from villages, kolkhozy, and small towns, and were sons of blue-collar workers, farmers, and junior white-collar employees.[127] Official Soviet data, based on the Russian Federation MoD Book of Remembrance, tell us that 70 percent of the Soviet force in Afghanistan came from the countryside (although the country's rural inhabitants accounted for 38 percent of the total population), 61 percent were children of workers, and 31 percent of kolkhozniks, while 5 percent came from families of office workers. Over 20 percent grew up in single-parent homes.[128] While Moscow, Leningrad, and white-collar Novosibirsk, as well as the Baltic and Transcaucasian capitals (with Tbilisi at the top of the list), sent the fewest soldiers in proportion to their population, "the politically marginalized blue-collar centers of the Slavic proletariat," like Dnepropetrovsk, Arkhangel'sk, Liubertsy, and Tula, did far worse. In this way, the war was proletarianized, and the suffering and hardship it caused were primarily the lot of an underclass without money or connections.[129] One officer who served in the Fortieth Army and was awarded both the Red Star and the Red Banner noted that there were no sons of "highly-placed comrades" in Afghanistan.[130]

Those who did come from the large cities, moreover, were often not liked, apparently because of the socioeconomic distinction. One man from Moscow told Borovik that Muscovites were not popular because they often shirked combat. "When I arrived here, nobody expected anything good from me. So from day one I had to fight not only the dukhi, but also the attitude of others toward me."[131]

Despite the 1982 regulations abolishing automatic deferments for students at institutions of higher learning, the policy, especially at the periphery, was to send recruits from the less well-educated strata. Two soldiers with higher education who applied to go to Afghanistan were told specifically to let a peasant boy, a tractor driver, go instead because "the State's invested too much in your education."[132] Gromov points out that this proletarianization did not apply to junior officers, many of whom were sons of senior officers who specifically requested service in Afghanistan, probably with an eye to furthering their military careers.[133]

In the early stages of the war, according to one source, Central Asians accounted for no less than 90 percent of the force.[134] In addition to logistical considerations, there might have been further reasons for this. Gromov suggests that the MoD probably assumed that they would most easily adapt to the Afghan climate and terrain. Two other military men say that the Soviet government "considered [their ethnicity] a positive factor," since it facilitated "linguistic contact" with the Afghan population and the accomplishment of "combat objectives." Later, however, it "played a negative role, because in many cases these relations assumed the character of fraternization between Soviet soldiers and the mujahidin." There were, in fact, reports of Central Asian soldiers refusing to participate in combat and of the Afghan opposition's attempts to enlist them as informers and spies, perhaps, according to Gromov, because of religious affinity.[135] This was not the rule, however, and apparently reflected Gromov's ethnic prejudices.

Whatever the reasoning, during the course of 1980, the overrepresentation of Central Asians diminished. Perhaps this was the outcome of widespread disgruntlement in Central Asia at the large number of casualties, particularly in Uzbekistan, the most populous Central Asian republic and therefore the one with the most clout and the highest representation in the Fortieth Army. It has also been attributed to the Central Asians' inadequate fighting abilities. Their poor Russian must have interfered with their effectiveness as soldiers. This probably applied to Caucasian soldiers too. I met with Georgians, for example, who could not fill in my questionnaires because they had too little Russian; in 1986, Reshetnikov maintained that 30 percent of the troops had little knowledge of the language.[136]

By the end of 1980, the ethnic composition of most units within the Limited Contingent probably mirrored that of the general population. However the elite troops contained almost only Slavs, while ethnic groups with less Russian might have been overrepresented in ground force infantry regiments and construction battalions, which demanded less language fluency. (One student of the Soviet military has pointed out that while many claim that non-Slavs were frequently restricted to menial and nonsensitive posts, when asked to describe the ethnic mix of the units in which they themselves served, "informants typically reply with data that contradicts [sic] their own generalizations about minority troops."[137])

In any case, by 1982, again according to Gromov, 80 percent of the Soviet force was composed of soldiers from the European parts of the Soviet Union.[138] Yet while there was an intentional cutback in the number of Central Asians sent to Afghanistan after the first year, this policy changed around 1985 when more Central Asians reappeared in Afghanistan. This might have been because the Slavs were now reacting adversely to the large number of deaths among their soldiers or because the increasingly disproportionate birth rate between Central Asians and Europeans as of the 1960s (see note 91) led to the army recruiting more Central Asians.

If we extrapolate the number of those who served from each major ethnic grouping in the Soviet population by their proportion among those killed—and no particular ethnic grouping seems to have lost disproportionate numbers—we see that the Slavs (Russians, Ukrainians, and Belarussians) comprised just over 70 percent, Central Asians just under 15 percent, and other traditionally Muslim ethnic groups a further 7 percent. The aggregate of Russian casualties was almost identical to that of all the non-Russians put together, befitting their proportion of the population.[139]

Officially, the ethnicity of the soldiers was irrelevant to the way they served in Afghanistan. Three of the twenty-one Heroes of the Soviet Union honored in the Soviet press in early 1985 had Muslim names: the Tajik captain, Nabi Akramov; the Ingush major, Ruslan Aushev (see Chapter 10); and a presumably Tatar major, Viacheslav Gainutdinov. Two more Muslims—one Kazakh and one Uzbek—appeared among the war's seventy-one Heroes of the Soviet Union; fifty were Russians. As the chairman of the Soviet Peace Committee said in 1988, "The 'Soviet people' is not a fabrication."[140]

When there were significant numbers of soldiers from a particular ethnic background, they joined forces. One Uzbek testifies that when there were few Uzbeks in a unit, they tended to connect; if there were many, they split up by region.[141] An officer told of the terror that the Uzbek "mafia" had waged in one company, compelling him to counter with "reciprocal Russian terror."[142] Soldiers tended to settle problems unofficially, sometimes leading to racial and inter-unit violence.[143]

In our survey (see Table 3.1), almost 60 percent of Afghan War veterans reported that ethnic relations in the Fortieth Army were generally good.[144] Yet anecdotal evidence reflects many exceptions, certainly regarding relations between Slavs and others, especially soldiers from Muslim ethnic groups. (Sociologists claimed that every fourth conflict in the Soviet armed forces was nationality based;[145] there is no reason to suspect that the Fortieth Army was different.) Hostile relations between ethnic groups sometimes ended in murder. A military train carrying North Caucasian conscripts to

Afghanistan in summer 1985 was delayed when a fight over religion erupted between Muslims and Christians [sic].[146] One Leningrad paratrooper wrote to his mother, "Here, out of the whole unit (31 people), 7 are Ukrainians, Belorussians and Russians; all the others are Uzbeks—worms."[147] Such an attitude could hardly have been conducive to good relations.

Several veterans concede that relations between Slavs and Muslims were poor. An Estonian vet said the Central Asians in his unit had a "blind hatred" for soldiers from other ethnic groups.[148] A former soldier in a motor-rifle unit remembers frequent fighting between Bashkirs and Uzbeks (both "Muslim" peoples).[149] Ethnic animosity involved verbal abuse as well as physical. One Estonian veteran said he and other Balts had been the object of tongue lashings from Kazakhs who claimed that the Balts lived at their expense and that their food went to the Baltic republics.[150] Jewish soldiers claim that everyone hated them.[151]

Morale

Despite contrary official statements,[152] considerable evidence attests to the low morale among Soviet military personnel in Afghanistan.[153] There were any number of reasons for this: the composition of the force;[154] the officers' frustration at having to fight a counterinsurgency war against nonprofessional soldiers; the sense of deception that many soldiers felt at finding themselves fighting the Afghan population; the fact that even soldiers who identified with the war's official rationale considered it futile and not vital to their country's defense; the almost inhumane conditions that were aggravated by the evident bungling of the supply system and the inhospitable climate and terrible roads; the corruption of senior officers; the high rate of disease; the hazing, boredom, and unnecessary casualties; and, perhaps above all, the constant contact with death, almost every soldier fearing that his turn might be next.[155] Their outlook stands in sharp contrast to the motivation of Soviet soldiers during World War II, which Soviets euphemistically called "the Great Patriotic War," at least in their historiography and mythology.[156]

Some realized, even at the time, that the war hurt everyone who served in it: "Some are sick, in mind or body, others are wounded, but everyone's damaged in some way, no one escapes intact." One officer states that "only a madman" would tell the entire truth of what went on. "When the truth is too terrible, it doesn't get told." How low morale could drop was reflected in the casual attitude to death and killing, as evidenced by the smuggling of narcotics and fur coats in the "Black Tulips" (the code word for the planes that took the dead to the Soviet motherland), even in coffins, and by soldiers making trophy necklaces of dried ears.[157]

The fact that in 1983, the MoD believed that to reinforce military discipline in the Fortieth Army, it needed to appeal directly to the soldiers reflects the lack of control among the troops.[158] Certainly the overrepresentation of lower social strata in the Fortieth Army was not a recipe for high morale,[159] although village boys often made more conscientious soldiers than "the smart-asses" from Moscow, Kiev, and Odessa.[160] Nor was the knowledge that people bribed their way out of the war or that many were there in retribution for poor discipline and training records and, in the case of officers, following demotion in rank for drunkenness.

A senior officer in the original force said that initially there were no questions; soldiers believed that they were providing the DRA with "international assistance." The doubts arose after the first fights against irregular bands in late February and early March 1980. Soldiers began asking, "Why are we here? What sense is there in our actions? Why have we become involved in a war?" Then came the losses and, worse, the knowledge that the dead were being buried secretly. The soldiers were insulted that the country that had sent them was denying them the honor that "every civilized country" confers on its fallen.[161] One NCO who served from 1980 to 1981, said, "Nobody explained to us what was happening, what we were doing." Often they simply shot at and killed "regular people,"[162] "local Afghans," not the Chinese and Americans they had been told they would be fighting.[163]

The official propaganda simply did not conform to what the soldiers saw around them. One testimony stated that the brass considered the war a "political adventure," neither necessary militarily nor well thought out. They talked about it at every break. Nobody could answer the question, "Why are we here?"[164] A junior officer who served as an interpreter in a motor-rifle unit states that among themselves, the soldiers "discussed and argued the expediency" of their presence in Afghanistan. The majority, he contends, supported the "official version," that they were helping the Afghan people.[165] A soldier who entered Afghanistan at the war's beginning testified to the endless arguments among soldiers about the war's justification, but these stayed within the unit.[166] As the war wore on, the disillusionment and frustration increased. By 1985, letters from soldiers who "wonder, sincerely and simply, 'Why are we here?'" had reached the CPSU CC and *Pravda*. Similar letters "come from officers and even one general. They can't explain to their men what it's all for. They say that those in Afghanistan find it impossible to believe that they are really carrying out some 'internationalist duty.'"[167] The praporshchik of an NCO who was killed in action wrote to the boy's father from Afghanistan: "'I've been here two years and during this time have learnt the truth: There is no more stupid, unnecessary, absurd undertaking than this war. It's not just vandalism. It's madness.'"[168] One major, killed toward the end of the war and posthumously decorated Hero of the Soviet Union, wrote home that the war was purposeless.[169]

The deception and lies that surrounded their dispatch to Afghanistan were a constant source of humiliation and disillusionment. Most soldiers learned that they were going there only very shortly before they arrived (see Chapter 8). Some were never told outright that this would be their destination. The political officers frequently informed them that they would not be participating in fighting but would be doing garrison duty to free the DRA army for combat or building schools, hospitals, and roads. Those who learned part of the truth still did not know that they would be fighting a civilian population that they had been indoctrinated to believe the Soviet Union had come to liberate and that was defending its homeland, just as the Soviet population had done in 1941.[170] The violence and cruelty against the Afghan population contributed significantly to the low morale. The growing hatred of the population became another cause for disillusionment.

Another reason for the disenchantment was the sense that those back home in the Soviet Union were not giving the war proper attention. The administrative-command system insisted on keeping everything secret.[171] One veteran recalled coming back "from a battle . . . a hard battle, with much bloodshed. . . . That evening, I read the newspaper reporting how we and Afghans planted trees together as happy friends. There was not a single word about the war. I felt deeply offended."[172] *Frunzovets*, the paper of the Turkestan MD, was the troops' preferred paper, for it devoted the most space to the war. In early 1986, it too had no qualms about writing how "an orchestra" met the new arrivals in Afghanistan.[173]

Once the Soviet media began occasionally to address the war, the soldiers in Afghanistan—who read newspapers, listened to radio, and saw television[174]—felt an increasing distance between themselves and people at home (Figure 3.1). Life in the Soviet Union seemed to focus on trivialities; people there were having a good time while they were being killed in Afghanistan. Even when they mentioned the fighting in Afghanistan, the Soviet media downplayed or ignored the role of the Soviet troops and the casualties.[175] One soldier told journalist Artem Borovik that the Soviet papers wrote such "nonsense" about the war that "sometimes it's sickening."[176] Soviet troops were particularly enraged to read reports of operations in which they had fought as having been conducted by the DRA army. One political officer noted, "The contrast between what I saw and what I read" in the press that was "the complete opposite of the truth" made it extremely difficult "to tell our soldiers what we were doing there, whom we were fighting, what was right and what was wrong." It also "made me completely distrust our government."[177]

Over one-third of our sample remembered how the distortions in the Soviet media rankled. One option in my questionnaire (see Figure 3.1) turned out to be the disproportionately favored choice, although none of the respondents seems to have focused on it while in Afghanistan. This is probably the finding most influenced by thoughts they had after returning home.

Western sources noted the disheartenment: "The struggle against popular resistance

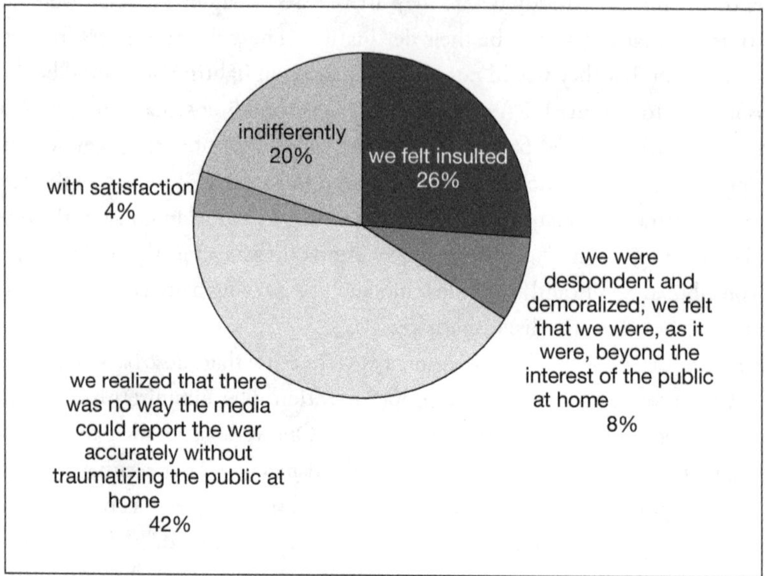

Figure 3.1. How did soldiers in Afghanistan react to Soviet media reporting on the war?

has produced the demoralizing effects . . . that other armies in other places have suffered—drugs and drunkenness, black marketing, desertions and dereliction, the fragging (to pick up a word from Vietnam) of over-zealous officers by their survival-minded subordinates. . . . There has been trouble between Afghan [DRA] soldiers and Russians, and inside the Russian army between European and Asian troops. No one who knew Vietnam can find any of this surprising."[178]

Desertion, self-inflicted wounds, and suicide often seemed to be the sole alternative to an impossible existence. Seeking to evade combat duty, soldiers would mutilate themselves to various extents, shooting themselves in the legs or hands. Some shot their fingers off. Alternatively, "for a few currency vouchers," one could get medics "to sell you a couple of glasses of urine from a hepatitis patient. You drank it, fell ill, and got yourself discharged from the army." One nurse recalls, "Such men were generally despised, even by us medics. 'There are lads getting killed out there, and you want to go home to Mummy.' . . . At the time they seemed the most contemptible cowards; now I'm beginning to realize that perhaps it was a protest as well, and an unwillingness to kill other people."[179]

The incidence of suicides among both soldiers and officers was the most dramatic manifestation of the low morale. They killed themselves as a result of the harsh conditions of service—the thirst and hunger, the hazing, and so on. (Official statistics regarding suicides naturally do not include instances where soldiers fought until the last bullet and then shot themselves or volunteered to cover their comrades' retreat, knowing that this meant certain death.)

Poetry and song were another—healthier—form of protest and escape. Artem Borovik who in 1987 and again toward the war's end spent long periods with the troops, constantly heard "pounding rock music" blasting out of cassette players. One young lieutenant explained to him, "You simply need to switch off from the fire and explosions, and rock can drown out everything."[180] Indeed, this was an inherent part of the daily routine. While "the generals felt that it was enough for soldiers to wear the uniform and bear arms . . . souls must be armed, too. Or, at least, supported. . . . So Afghan musical folklore was born."[181]

Many of the soldiers played an instrument—"a guitar is the only thing a soldier can hold in his embrace for two long years"[182]—sang, wrote, and composed songs. To the outside observer, these might have been "unofficial, often amateurish, ballads of bloodshed, bravado, and candid fear . . . of very young men caught up in a very hard war they understand very poorly."[183] They recoiled from songs of bravery and heroism designed to raise their morale. One officer remembers two fellow officers who played the guitar together or separately at every possible opportunity. "They sang primarily 'our' self-produced Afghan songs," but also those of the bards—Vladimir Vysotskii, Bulat Okudzhava, Sergei Nikitin—and songs from popular films. His company boasted about ten people who sang and played, "every unit [*vyvod*] having its own instrument."[184] The troops tended to be more appreciative of their own work than of professional creations.[185] Suppressed at first by the authorities, songwriters resorted to a variety of tricks they learned from Soviet revolutionary literature in order to circumvent censorship in their compositions.[186] An informal ensemble, Kaskad, formed in the summer of 1980, sang songs of Afghan vintage from the start.[187]

From time to time, Soviet artists of different genres came to perform before the troops, but such visits were rare, at least outside Kabul.[188] One artist who came several times was Aleksandr Rozenbaum, who also composed songs about the war. Another was Iosif Kobzon.[189] Sometimes, artists came from the national republics; one troupe from Kazakhstan that came in fall 1981 performed several times, apparently also before units stationed outside Kabul.[190]

Yet this entertainment could not cancel the boredom from which the troops suffered, especially in noncombat units and in the early years before the army provided TVs, enabling the troops to view the evening Vremia news or to see Rambo movies on videocassettes.[191] The ultimate panacea for inaction was hazing, euphemistically dubbed "nonstatutory relationships," the dimensions of which reflected the lack of discipline in Afghanistan and the dominance within the ranks of an unofficial hierarchy.

The hazing of first-year conscripts by their seniors, the notorious *dedovshchina* (grandfather rule), already infested the Soviet armed forces in the 1970s.[192] In

Afghanistan, it proved more traumatic for many soldiers than the conditions of their service.[193] Hazing involved beatings, brawls, physical injury, rape, and sometimes murder. This initiation rite had a rationale of its own in an army where NCOs and junior officers exercised little control.[194] In Afghanistan, where soldiers had no off-duty and no way of spending their idle time—few girls, no cinema, no sports facilities—this practice provided the sole pastime for hardened soldiers in their second year of service and awaiting demobilization. Recruits were at the mercy of their veteran fellows, while their officers turned a blind eye.[195] As one former soldier said, "Everything happened within the barracks" and what happened to them there, soldiers were ashamed—or afraid—of telling.[196]

"There are three classes of soldier in the Soviet army—new recruits, 'granddads' or veterans, and *dembels*, conscripts near the end of their two-year service," one afganets tells us. One evening in the barracks, soon after he arrived as a new recruit, "the dembels beat me up, eight of them, and gave me a good kicking with their army boots. My kidneys were crushed and I pissed blood for two days. They didn't touch me during the day. I tried not to antagonise them but they still beat me up. I changed tactics. When they came for me at night I was ready for them and hit out first. Then they beat me very carefully, so as not to leave a mark, with towel-covered fists in the stomach every night for a week."[197]

In "the big happy family" of soldiers, the new recruit "is an object," writes another former soldier. "He can be got out of bed at night and beaten up with chairs, sticks, fists, and feet. In the daytime, he's beaten up in the toilet, and his backpack, personal possessions . . . are stolen. There's no television or newspapers, so entertainment goes according to the law of the jungle. 'Wash my socks, sweetie-pie!' 'Now lick my socks, sweetie-pie, lick them good so that everyone can see you!' . . . It's more frightening than your first taste of action."[198] These experiences tarnished many soldiers for life. On arriving at the "clearing-center," one former soldier reminisces, "the dembels took everything of any value off us, including our boots, paratroop vests and berets. . . . They also stole our parade shirts which they traded with the Afghans for drugs," even opening up duffel bags and taking what they wanted. "All of us in our company had our uniforms taken and had to pay to buy old ones in return." This same soldier reflects:

> Within the year I was in hospital suffering from dystrophy. I was the only "new boy" in our unit, the other ten were "granddads." I was forced to do all their washing, chop all the wood, and clean the whole camp—I never got more than three hours' sleep in a night. . . . I eventually went back to my unit and got beaten up again, until my leg was broken and I had to have an operation. . . . The authorities were powerless against the unwritten rules of army life, which were literally life and death to us. If you tried to fight against them you always lost in the end.[199]

Almost certainly hazing was less rampant and vicious in elite units. Eighty percent of respondents in one survey of 320 afgantsy experienced hazing.[200]

In some units, hazing had an ethnic character. Hesitant about taking on Caucasians, especially when there was a group of them in the unit who would support each other, Slavs beat up Central Asians, whom they considered "easy meat." Occasionally Russians were a butt for minority nationals. A former soldier drafted and sent to Afghanistan in 1983 related, "Two Kazakhs served in my subdivision. They hated me just because I was from Moscow. They'd beat me until I was black and blue, until I'd lose consciousness and the ability to feel pain. . . . It seemed as if they were using me to avenge all the suffering that had befallen their people. . . . They used their boots, their fists; they hit me in the groin, in the stomach, on the head. . . . They hated me even before meeting me . . . if it hadn't been for them, I wouldn't have deserted my unit. . . . The thought of deserting sprouted in my subconscious during and after the beatings."[201] Another Russian soldier who deserted because of the hazing said, "Ukrainians beat Russians, Russians beat Tajiks, Turkmen, and Tatars, and Turkmen beat Tajiks."[202] Sixty percent of deserters reportedly took off because of hazing.[203]

The dembels and even the hazing also had a positive side, at least according to some. The dembels shared their experience and know-how with their juniors. In some units, one afganets who served in a VDV reconnaissance unit remembered, *dedovshchina* was "a system of mutual understanding" between greens and veterans—the former prepared the food for everyone and kept the barracks tidy; the dembels took the first bullets and stepped on the first mine.[204] Just one-third of the 320 afgantsy interviewed after the war's end in Krasnodar condemned the hazing as an evil that needed eradicating. Forty-eight percent considered it unpleasant but helpful in maintaining discipline.[205] Naturally, they took this position in hindsight as people who had themselves finished their service as granddads, so it does not refute the stories of soldiers in their first year.

Another outcome of both the boredom and the inhumane living conditions was the wide use of drugs (see the following section), which exacerbated yet another endemic problem in the Soviet armed forces: crime and corruption. Theft was commonplace, not just of food and clothing. Whether in order to purchase drugs or simply to "get rich," soldiers, whose pay was extremely poor, sold to Afghans whatever they could lay their hands on, especially military equipment—ammunition, weaponry, uniforms, field glasses, gasoline, vehicle parts, whatever came their way.[206] Too often, the robberies led to violent crimes, including murder.[207]

Both soldiers and officers smuggled drugs back into the Soviet Union.[208] Customs officials in Kushka found ammunition and narcotics in vehicles that brought troops home from Afghanistan.[209] "We once accumulated three broken-down armored carriers," one former soldier recalls. "We had to squirm around on the ground for three days so that we could unscrew the bottoms and hide all the contraband inside. . . . No one at the border ever bothered to take apart the frames to see what might be in there. . . . Two of our soldiers accompanied the carriers to Gorky" and "kept half the stuff for themselves. Do you think the officers could possibly remember exactly what they were bringing? It's scary to think how many weapons and drugs were smuggled into the Soviet Union."[210]

Not only drugs and weapons made their way into the Soviet Union. Soldiers' letters abound with stories of the shops they visited and the goods they found, of jeans and blouses, radios and videotape recorders.[211] Afghan sheepskins became "the rage. Women envied their friends whose husbands were in Afghanistan." A group of veterans who came to talk to school students wore Japanese watches they had purchased by selling a truckload of stolen fruit. The soldiers particularly envied their mates on oil-tanker duty.[212] Official records show 6,412 criminal charges against soldiers in Afghanistan, including 714 murders, 2,840 weapon sales to Afghans, and 524 drug trafficking cases.[213]

Fear was another factor that affected the morale of the Fortieth Army. Quite naturally, the fear of death haunted most new recruits. Thrown unexpectedly into combat with little moral preparation—often almost as soon as they landed in Afghanistan[214]—they saw fellow soldiers killed before their eyes; the MoD "Book of Memory" shows how many were killed within weeks of arriving.[215] The greatest fear seems to have been falling captive to the mujahidin. Some also feared sickness and disease-ridden areas. General Mikhail Zaitsev, commander of the Southern Direction of the Soviet Armed Forces, whose command included the Fortieth Army, was reportedly terrified of catching one of the diseases rampant in the force.[216] One veteran later recalled that fear "came at the beginning" when "emotions were very much on the surface. After the phase of acclimatization, there followed an almost complete atrophy of emotions. You just lived like a machine."[217]

Some soldiers turned to religion. In the copybook of one soldier were five pages, each with a prayer from the Russian Orthodox liturgy.[218] In April 1987, Soviet correspondent Artem Borovik "met a sniper who'd inscribed a passage from the Ninety-First Psalm in the underside of his dirty collar—'He who dwells in the shadow of the Most High, who abides in the shadow of the Almighty, will say to the Lord, 'My refuge, and my fortress, my God in whom I trust.'" Later in a Russian monastery Borovik met an Afghan War veteran who, when his unit unexpectedly came under heavy enemy fire, had "sworn that if his life were somehow spared he'd join a monastery," and that very minute all the other soldiers in his unit were killed.[219]

In letters written home, soldiers expressed similar sentiments. One major wrote to his wife, "Previously I didn't believe in God; now I've begun to believe." A colonel in his forties, the deputy commander of the Fortieth Army medical service, asked his wife to go to church and light a candle in memory of his mother and to give charity outside the building.[220]

Other soldiers began to reflect on their previous ways of life and on the Soviet value system and to elaborate their reservations regarding it. They developed more universal values and criteria than their Soviet education and surroundings had given them. Some, for instance, criticized the Soviet regime's culture of consumerism.[221]

Soldiers in the Limited Contingent viewed demoralization as one of the principal reasons for desertion. Indeed, reports of the soldiers' low morale leaked out through prisoners of war and defectors to the mujahidin.[222] One captured officer said that the Soviet soldiers were "demoralized, confused, and disappointed. Many . . . try to get a doctor's certificate proving that they are ill and must be sent to the Soviet Union for treatment."[223] Those able to go on leave in the Soviet Union would simply not return to the war.[224]

The low morale carried over to the officers as well, even among those who had volunteered to come to Afghanistan. They found that they had been given "an impossible task and would be the scapegoats for its failure."[225]

Nonetheless, there was, especially in units involved in combat operations, a clear sense of camaraderie. Many soldiers, perhaps especially fresh recruits, went on combat missions voluntarily and eagerly.[226] They all went into operations knowing that they depended on each other. "War trains you to think of others more than yourself," one soldier told a Soviet journalist. You have no right even to be killed. Four other guys would have to carry your corpse, and they have enough to carry without you. . . . You must be careful not to step on a mine. . . . If you [do], those ahead of you and behind you will also be wounded." As one lieutenant colonel put it, "We have a brotherhood here, maybe the only good thing to have come out of this war."[227] One observer noted that the war also brought out "marvelous human qualities in many, perhaps the majority of the soldiers—generosity, willpower, humility, a sense of duty, and amazing courage."[228]

Drugs

Alcohol and drugs are "classic forms of self-medication" in the face of the trauma, fear, and "some of [war's] baser, animal passions," in addition to the boredom. Since their use is often social, they also facilitate group bonding, enhancing "the survival prospects of members of the group by developing trust and their ability to work together." Since Afghanistan was a "dry" country, dope offered the "more accessible, portable, and effective escape"[229] and was undoubtedly the primary bane.

A large number of soldiers used drugs light and heavy—marijuana, hashish, opium—which were easy to obtain in Afghanistan. Often they acquired the drugs from the local population. All our afgantsy interviewees agreed that drugs were used (Table 3.3).

Table 3.3. It is widely known that the Soviet soldiers in Afghanistan used drugs.

Everybody used drugs, even officers	21%
Some used drugs, but not most	55%
Most used drugs	24%

A soldier who arrived in Afghanistan in December 1980 recalls that the soldiers "all smoked—it was the only way to keep going. . . . Somehow or other you had to unwind, to blot it all out. We'd put it in the rice or porridge. Your pupils got as big as saucers, you could see like a cat in the dark and you felt as light as a bat."[230] Taking drugs made the soldiers at least partially oblivious to their conditions and enabled them to bear the horror at what they were doing; not every young man found he could live with wiping out whole villages of Afghan peasants, men, women, and children or forget the mutilated bodies of fellow soldiers who had been wounded in combat or taken captive by the mujahidin.[231]

The soldiers learned that in Afghanistan, "life was impossible without drugs. They needed them there, because of the heat and because they had to carry 40 kilos up and down hills. Then there was the fear—drugs helped with that."[232] Veterans of the war "justified their use to relieve nervous tension before combat operations or night sentry duty near enemy positions."[233]

An artillery captain who arrived in Afghanistan in early 1980 said, "We smoked hash. One friend of mine got so high in battle he was sure every bullet had his name on it, wherever it was really headed." According to another officer, some got high on the hashish, "others got into the state we called *shubnyak*, where a bush turned into a tree, or a rock became a hill. . . . That made the world even more frightening for them."[234]

Hashish, one former soldier related, "gives you a great high, but you immediately develop a ferocious hunger. That's when you trudge over to the kishlak to get a lamb." "It's best to go into an operation stoned—you turn into an animal . . . taking a drug is like anesthetizing your soul; you stop feeling altogether. Later, when you come back, you just collapse. . . . As long as you're in combat, however, you just get high and run around like a maniac. Hashish stifles emotions, smoothes over nervous fits. . . . When you're stoned, you don't notice that you're tired. You run up and down the mountains and the *kishlaks* like a billy goat, without ever stopping."[235]

One officer testified that it was easy to discern which soldiers used drugs; they had to be kept under strict control for they were unreliable in combat.[236] Officers' attempts to cut down on drug use tended to be futile.[237]

Mujahidin commanders capitalized on the Soviet soldiers' demand for drugs. Western correspondents interviewing Soviet prisoners of war and defectors confirmed that mujahid commanders used narcotics to lure Soviet soldiers into captivity to get information.[238] One mujahid commander reportedly said he took no steps to obstruct drug sales to the Soviet troops, for the drugs enhanced their demoralization.[239] Perhaps this explains why "traders in the bazaar gave us [the stuff] for free. 'Go on, Russky, have a smoke!' they would say. The kids would run after us, pushing it into our hands."[240]

In addition to the drugs' direct damage, their use all too frequently meant crime. To purchase drugs, a soldier needed cash. And to procure cash, he had to sell something, which normally meant stolen goods. If an officer caught the thief, he might demand his share of the profit. One network that involved an officer and several soldiers led to the officer's execution and fifteen years in jail for the soldiers.[241] The manual for Soviet troops serving in Afghanistan absolutely prohibited all purchasing from Afghans using Soviet currency, the sale to them of any Soviet goods, and visits to bazaars and shops except on duty—to little avail.[242]

Social drinking was an integral part of Soviet officers' tradition, and officers found ways to drink in Afghanistan. An artillery officer remembered that "once a week we had bath and drinks night." They brought the vodka from home, in beer bottles, as customs regulations put no restrictions on beer (one study comments that vodka was the officers' "drug of choice"[243]). "Or else you might open a bottle of mineral water and find it was 40 percent proof. People drank used aeroplane kerosene and antifreeze. We'd warn new recruits not to touch antifreeze, whatever else they drank, but within a few days they'd be in hospital with their insides corroded."[244]

Excesses against the Civilian Population

One of the consequences of the lack of discipline and a reflection of the demoralization was the Soviet soldiers' attitude toward the Afghan population. In the early stages of the war, there seems to have been some mutual sympathy—at least in certain units—and soldiers distinguished between the "rebels"—the "Basmachi"—and the regular civilians they believed they had come to help.[245] In his first letter home, one soldier wrote, "Never in my life have I seen such dirty and tattered people. Many of them are like ghosts. But they are people, and some of them even drive around in cars. However, the majority push handcarts of wood around Kabul. I feel very sorry for them."[246] The hunger that the soldiers saw in Afghanistan, and especially the starving children, haunted them long after they returned home.[247]

Each unit in the original force boasted a group whose assignment was to explain to the Afghans the purpose of the Soviet military presence. The troops' instruction manual emphasized the need to preserve behavioral norms, as the soldiers were responsible for the way the Afghans would relate to the Soviet Union. Over time, these instructions included warnings that the army would prosecute any criminal deed.[248]

Soldiers were not supposed to touch civilians, let alone shoot them, and from time to time, a soldier was brought to justice for killing civilians.[249]

Testimonies of soldiers in the original force report satisfaction among Afghan civilians and hopes that the intervention would bring them peace and tranquility.[250] A soldier who served early in the war said that at first, they would go freely to the bazaar where relations with the locals were good.[251] "Our first people in Afghanistan were greeted with flowers and smiles . . . were welcomed as friends. Not always and not everywhere, but for the most part. Thus, the illusion was born that they were glad to see us." Soon, however, the dynamic of the war inexorably led to mutual hostility. On the one hand, the Soviet force had no qualms about pilfering. One vet recalled his regiment commander taking a sheep every night "because the food was so bad."[252] On the other hand, villagers whom "the soldiers had come to defend" and whom they considered friendly would shoot at them, and they had to return fire. Soon "the soldiers were no longer able to tell which Afghans were for them and which against."[253] The soldiers believed in their "internationalist duty," but as one military correspondent wrote, one had to know how to assist others, and this was impossible when the two sides inhabited different worlds.[254]

The Soviet propaganda campaign to win the hearts and minds of the Afghan population was generally a failure. Even when material assistance to the rural population—food, electricity, medical advice—preceded or accompanied the effort, the villagers tended to be unresponsive.[255] As CGS General Sergei Akhromeev told the Politburo in late 1986, they lost the battle for the Afghan people (see Chapter 4).

As cases of betrayal by villagers whom the Soviets had trusted multiplied and it became clear that they sheltered the mujahidin, the soldiers' anger against the mujahidin spread to the population at large. Testimonies tell of villagers being friendly during the day and hostile at night. Or, in the words of one Kazakh soldier, himself a rural inhabitant, they were amicable and peaceful at harvesttime; the harvest over, they began shooting.[256] The soldiers' anger and frustration led to frequent atrocities against the civilian population—looting, plunder, arson, and rape[257]—and, on many occasions, to the destruction of entire villages, either by Soviet troops or by the mujahidin themselves if they suspected the villagers of collaboration with the shuravi. Afghan civilians were often killed because of inaccurate bombing and shooting (for which the Fortieth Army rarely took responsibility).[258]

Killing in war was "'filial duty to the Motherland.' . . . We were told that we were reliving the achievements of the heroes of the Great Patriotic War against the Nazis, and who was I to doubt it? It was continually hammered into us that we were the best of the best, so why should I question whether what we were doing was right."[259]

The behavior of the Soviet troops, especially the indiscriminate killing, reflected not only the soldiers' general demoralization but also the ineffective command within combat units, which further undermined discipline. William Odom asked many former officers why they condoned such brutality. Uniformly they responded that a human life is not considered very valuable in Russia.[260] Chief Soviet military adviser General Maiorov recounts a particularly appalling incident in early 1981, when Soviet soldiers entered a village to take sheep for a barbecue and raped and shot villagers in the process. When he demanded that the perpetrators be punished, the MoD informed him that it accepted the KGB's contention that the crime was the doing of mujahidin dressed in Soviet uniforms to provoke the population's animosity toward the occupiers. Ustinov himself told Maiorov that "the investigation in Moscow" showed that it was a provocation by the mujahidin.[261]

The Soviet soldiers spoke a great deal about the way the mujahidin treated their prisoners of war, yet they too were not squeamish. "We captured some terrorists and interrogated them. 'Where are your arms dumps?' No answer. Then we took a couple of them up in helicopters. 'Where are they? Show us!' No answer. We threw one of them on to the rocks." Nor was there always the pretext of interrogation. "The prisoners we took somehow never got as far as regimental HQ[.] I saw them literally stamped and ground into the earth. In a year and a half I didn't see a single live dukh, only dead ones."[262] Again, early on, it was different: Soviet soldiers returned prisoners to their villages. Occasionally they kept some alive in order to exchange them for Soviet prisoners; in these cases, they received medical treatment no different from that of anyone else.[263]

Almost certainly, all semblance of friendship had dissipated after two or three years of warfare. In the words of one soldier who served from 1985 to 1987, there was little contact with the population. "They feared us and we—them. We didn't feel like missionaries and they felt no gratitude toward us."[264] Another soldier relates, "We couldn't afford to see each other as human beings. You blockade a village, wait 24 hours, then another 24, with the heat and tiredness driving you crazy. You end up being even more brutal than the 'greens,' as we called our allies, the Afghan National Army . . . we did what we did without thinking. . . . It was easier for us to fire our guns and throw our grenades." It was never a question of, "'Do I kill him or don't I?' . . . All you wanted was to eat and sleep and get it all over and done with, so you could stop shooting and go home." To kill or not is "a post-war question." At the time, "we were only doing our international duty. It was all quite cut and dried."[265]

Often the Soviet troops reacted out of revenge. Almost all veterans testified to this. As time passed and it became clear to the Soviet troops that Afghan men, women, and children were directing their arms not at the April revolution, as the political officers were constantly telling the soldiers, but against them, they wanted to retaliate, despite understanding that people did this because they received considerable sums for every killing.[266] The leading APC in one reconnaissance force caught a direct hit from a grenade-launcher. The remainder of the force, seeing their comrades being "carried away, their heads blown off like cardboard targets, hands hanging down lifelessly," fired all their mortars into the village from which the attack had come, "into every single house." Once, however, "I was struck by the horror of what we were doing . . . You fling open the door and throw in a grenade in case there's a machine-gun waiting for you. . . . I threw the grenade, went in and saw women, two little boys, and a baby in some kind of box making do for a cot."[267] Soldiers spoke later of memories that were "terribly painful" that would torment them "forever"—firing at peaceful inhabitants of the kishlaks."[268] Or, another testimony, "You watch your buddy knock a door down in a kishlak. Out comes a dark, bony hand with a sickle. It slashes his belly open and his guts fall to the ground. Your buddy is just standing there, looking—he can't believe it isn't a dream. Whenever you see something like that, you don't care who or what's in the house. You just throw a grenade at it, then another one."[269]

Some of the more gruesome incidents got out of hand or were the outcome of sheer boredom at checkpoints and on guard duty.[270] In reply to a question regarding the killing of peaceful population, one respondent observed, "We officers took an oath not to divulge concrete facts."[271]

Yet there were both commanders and troops who balked at killing civilians indiscriminately. Although one colonel, toward the end of the war, ordered the troops to kill all civilians, a battalion commander told his soldiers to kill only the dukhi. His division commanding officer reprimanded him. "'Why did you fail to comply with your orders. . . . Why were the kishlaki barely damaged, not entirely destroyed?'" The battalion commander replied,

> We did exactly what we were supposed to. Yes, . . . there was no butchery or unnecessary destruction in the zone that my battalion was responsible for. . . . We were firing only at the spots where the bandleaders were hiding and at the ammunition depots. The enemy didn't reciprocate because we'd eliminated all the leaders and destroyed all the ammunition dumps. So there was no resistance. As for destruction for the sake of destruction, just for pleasure, I wouldn't allow it.

Some of the soldiers were similarly "squeamish." One APC gunner said, "'We tried to shoot above people's heads so we wouldn't hit them . . . firing at people? No, I'm not ready for something like that.'" After they had shot at homes, the people came out, grateful that they hadn't been killed. "'I couldn't look them in the eyes. . . . It killed something in me. . . . Naturally, all of us—right down to the last man—received medals so we'd keep our mouths shut. But that didn't make it any easier. . . . Our soldiers and officers cursed the war, their orders, themselves, and Afghanistan."[272]

Some afgantsy, while not denying that numerous civilians were killed unnecessarily,

Table 3.4. What were the relations between the Soviet contingent and the Afghan population?

Generally friendly	22%
Friendly in the towns only	7%
Friendly in the villages only	5%
They looked upon us with hostility, but we viewed them with compassion	17%
We disliked them, but they had faith in us and relied on us	5%
Mutual animosity	23%
There were no real contacts	21%

tended to blame the Afghans for providing them with false information to get the Soviets to perform their own tribal reckonings.[273] A Tajik soldier who served from 1980 to 1982 in a unit that came into constant contact with locals called their attitude to the Soviet force ambiguous—hostile when their kishlaks were shot up yet ready to request Soviet assistance against their Afghan adversaries.[274]

The attitude of the Soviet troops toward the locals is probably the question on which we received the most varied answers (Table 3.4).

Throughout the war, some Soviet military personnel maintained contact with the Afghan population. These included officers, generally political officers, who were in regular touch with mujahidin commanders and local religious figures. Among other benefits, this enabled the force that withdrew from Shindand to Kushka at the war's end to receive a commitment that the mujahidin would not attack it on the way.[275]

Soviet Casualties: The Killed, Wounded, and Sick

Statistics for those who died in the war are disputed. The first official figure—which MPA head Aleksei Lizichev released before the war ended—gave 13,310 dead as of May 1, 1988.[276] But the number grew.[277] In 1989, after the war ended, the GS published the figure of 13,833 soldiers, including 1,979 officers, who were killed (presumably in combat) or died of wounds and sickness; 572 security service (KGB and border guard); 28 MVD personnel; and 190 military advisers, 145 of them officers. Of those who died, 62.5 percent were aged 18 to 20.[278] According to one source, anyone fit to be transported to the Soviet Union was sent there for treatment so as not to enlarge casualty statistics.[279] By the end of the 1990s, it was officially admitted that the total number exceeded 15,000 (15,051), plus 417 either missing in action or captured, of whom 130 had been liberated by January 1, 1999.[280]

Over 64 percent of those who died were killed in combat (9,661); 16.44 percent (2,475) died of wounds; 11.93 percent (1,795) as a result of "accidents and incidents";

and 5.53 percent (833) from disease.[281] In 1983 and 1984, 3,789 died either in battle or from wounds and sickness, 515 of them officers; and in 1985, 1,868 military personnel died—1,552 combat losses (1,194 killed in action, 202 of them officers, and 358 from wounds); 62 from disease; 45 from road accidents; 65 as a result of careless handling of weapons; 59 as a result of suicide; and 84 from "other causes." In addition, 36 were taken prisoner and 37 went missing.[282] One Russian source writing in the 2000s put the number of deaths at approximately 19,000.[283]

Unquestionably, deficiencies in experience and equipment cost the Soviet force unjustified losses of men, especially early in the war.[284] An unusually large number were killed because of mistakes, sometimes from inadequate information before going into battle, sometimes from sheer flippancy.[285] One battalion commander maintained that the dearth of knowledge about the war and its casualties gave rise to carelessness, while the soldiers' and junior and middle-rank officers' youth inclined them to prove bravery and register achievements, sometimes making them oblivious to risk.[286] Lack of appropriate training for combat in mountainous terrain, according to one air force colonel, caused the death of dozens of helicopter pilots early in the war.[287]

According to 1999 figures, 53,753 were wounded. Of these, 2,503 died, 7,194 were discharged from the army, and 44,056 returned to the ranks when they recovered. When the war ended, 869 were still being treated. Of the 415,932 soldiers who became sick, 4,100 were discharged, and 411,015 returned to serve. Of those who fell sick, 115,038 contracted hepatitis, 31,080 typhoid fever, and 140,665 other infectious diseases. Altogether, 469,685—over 70 percent of the entire force—were wounded or fell ill, and 10,751 were officially recognized as disabled.[288]

The official figures for wounded and sick, Western military analyst David Glantz comments, "are unheard of in modern armies" and say a great deal about Soviet military hygiene, the conditions surrounding troop life in Afghanistan, and the inadequate medical care.[289] Some suggest that the figures for invalids are "an underestimate, reflecting the generally low official figures for disability in the Soviet Union."[290]

Asked after the war ended whether, in their opinion, the number of soldiers killed and wounded could have been reduced, just 15 percent of the afgantsy in my survey answered in the negative.[291] The 85 percent who answered positively suggested various changes that might have resulted in fewer losses (Table 3.5).

Soldiers knew fellow soldiers who had been killed because of their own recklessness—for instance, men who went into villages to buy something—or because they had been improperly prepared for the war they were fighting.[292] The first two replies reflect the distrust between soldiers and officers. One soldier blames the junior officers for losing soldiers to field mines because there had been no reconnaissance of the area.[293] An officer lays the blame on "generals from Moscow," who came, "drew up a plan for an operation," received the award for which they had come, and returned

Table 3.5. Do you believe it would have been possible to decrease the number of killed and wounded?

If officers on the spot had taken more initiative and been better versed in the art of fighting	38%
If the Contingent's headquarters had been in closer touch with the soldiers and their problems	19%
If medical treatment had been more quickly available	11%
in other ways	17%
No	15%

home, noting that the "far-fetched, stupid plans of these rats from headquarters" were the cause of soldiers' deaths.[294]

A discussion of medical experience in Afghanistan in the MPA military-political bimonthly shortly after the final withdrawal reported similar findings. Many vets told the head of the Kiev military hospital that had they received effective first aid more quickly, there would have been fewer losses and complications during subsequent treatment. A medical officer who had served in an Afghanistan medical facility concurred. "The condition of the wounded indicated that they had not received skillful treatment. It frequently amounted to the administration of intra-muscular drugs from the first-aid kit. Wounded with fractured limbs were brought in without being immobilized. These cases were frequently fatal."[295]

My survey of afgantsy provides information about those who fell sick and were wounded in Afghanistan (Tables 3.6 and 3.7).

An army doctor with ten years' experience as a surgeon in a big city hospital recalls that "the first time a transport vehicle arrived with wounded men I almost went crazy. Arms and legs missing, just breathing torsos. It was far worse than anything you could see in the most brutal film. We did operations you can only dream about back home. The young nurses couldn't take it. . . . They often had to be sent home." Thousands lost legs and hands, and many their eyesight as well. A doctor saw how casualties "didn't arrive at hospital straightaway—they might have been lying for up to ten hours, or even a day or two, in the mountain sand before they were located, with the result that open wounds became breeding-grounds for every kind of infection. I'd examine a patient in reanimation, for example, and find he had typhoid on top of everything else."[296]

One soldier remembers how "we got hit by mortar-fire. . . . One hand was shattered." He "crawled out of the vehicle with the others. Someone applied a tourniquet." He lost a lot of blood and then heard someone say, "'They're surrounding us!'" and "another voice" 'We'll have to dump him or we'll all be killed.' 'Shoot me!' I begged.

Table 3.6. Were you sick in Afghanistan?

I had hepatitis	18%
I got typhus	4%
I had both	5%
I contracted other illnesses or combinations of illnesses	25%
No	48%

Table 3.7. Were you wounded in Afghanistan?

I was severely wounded and remain an invalid	20%
I was severely wounded but recovered completely	5%
I was slightly wounded	25%
No	50%

One lad just ran away, the other loaded his gun. . . . He threw the gun at me: 'I can't! Do it yourself!' I dragged it towards me, but you can't do anything with one hand." He managed to hide where he was, and the next morning, the two soldiers who had left him the previous day found him. "They made a stretcher out of my greatcoat and carried me on it to the dressing-station," and from there to the hospital where the surgeon ordered amputation. "Everyone in the ward was missing an arm or a leg, or both, or all."[297]

Many of the wounded were sent to hospitals in the Soviet Union. One doctor at the hospital in Termez reported that his division conducted 496 operations, nearly all of them emergency cases, in a single year. Most of the wounded were drivers in transport units who had hit mines.[298] In Tashkent, where most of the seriously injured were treated, it was a common sight to see young boys hopping around on crutches.[299]

Deserters, Prisoners of War, and MIA

One of the most troublesome issues for the Soviet military command was that of missing soldiers. Formally, it made every effort not to abandon soldiers in the field.[300] Already in 1981, the MoD was engaged in searching for the MIA.[301] Yet some were captured by the "spooks." The Russian émigré journal *Posev* contended that few people were interested in the captives, charging that the Soviets bombed precisely those villages and encampments where POWs were being kept so that they could not talk.[302] While there is no proof of this, it is clear that Gorbachev did not heed the request of the Fortieth Army Command and the MoD to include the freeing of POWs in the Geneva Accords.[303]

Table 3.8. Do you know of cases of desertion of Soviet soldiers?

Several	21%
One	52%
No	27%

Some of those captured were severely mutilated. One woman on her way to Afghanistan heard people saying, "'They do take prisoners. They cut off their limbs and apply tourniquets so they won't bleed to death. They leave them like that for our people to pick up the stumps. The stumps want to die but they're kept alive.'" A nurse could not forget the "dead bodies with gouged-out eyes, and stars carved into the skin of their backs and stomachs" by the mujahidin.[304]

Both sides killed captives. At first, the mujahidin kept some of their Muslim captives alive, reportedly relating better to Muslim prisoners and deserters than others. Eventually they realized that soldiers from other nationalities too looked askance on the war and that it was in their interest to take care of some of them as well. Two soldiers captured by the mujahidin early in the war told Western correspondents that they were being sustained just for show, to speak to journalists.

Despite the stories about what they could expect from the mujahidin, some soldiers deserted to them of their own accord. Many felt they simply had to quit, hoping to make it back to the Soviet Union or reach Pakistan and the West. Most soldiers knew at least one case of desertion (Table 3.8).

Few soldiers surrendered voluntarily to the mujahidin. Beside their belief that the enemy would torture them, they had grown up on the Soviet tradition that surrender equaled treason; Stalin had filled the camps with Soviet POWs brought back after the victory over Germany. It was clear to every Soviet soldier that the mother country could never accept the idea of active desertion.[305] Many preferred to kill themselves first. Most of those taken prisoner were wounded or otherwise incapacitated. Some were exchanged for captured mujahidin or ransomed. (One source speaks of ninety-eight Soviet soldiers whom the mujahidin captured, then sent back in trade for money and supplies.[306]) The army treated those who eventually returned to the Soviet Union with various degrees of severity. Some were court-martialed and received prison terms; none of them seems to have been executed.[307]

There are no authoritative figures for those who were taken captive, were simply missing, or deserted. Of the 311 whom the MoD listed as MIA in May 1988, TASS estimated that roughly one-third died in action and a further thirty-four in trying to escape from captivity; seventeen had received asylum in the West, and eight had returned to the Soviet Union.[308] According to Liakhovskii, thirty-eight of the MIA "were definitely identified as having been taken prisoner," while forty-four (seventeen of whom subsequently returned to the Soviet Union) had chosen to join the mujahidin.[309] Some vets believed that the majority of the MIA were soldiers who went over to the mujahidin who then killed them but that the Soviet authorities preferred to suggest they had fallen in action.[310] The card index of the People's Committee for Release of the Soviet Prisoners of War, "Hope,"[311] included 415 names, although when the war ended, the GS reported 330 soldiers, including 21 officers, as having been captured or missing in action.[312] (One of them was a soldier whose coffin had been delivered to his parents who, when they insisted on opening it, found another man inside.)

Of a February 1992 list of 304 MIA, nearly half (143) were Russians and another 68 Slavs (57 Ukrainians and 11 Belarussians); 25 were Uzbeks, 10 Tatars, 8 Kazakhs, 7 Azeris and Turkmen, and 5 Tajiks. The author of the note published with the list opined that approximately 200 were killed in combat or died of their wounds without anyone knowing their whereabouts. Some of them were advisers to the DRA army and interpreters; this explains the presence on the list of one colonel and two lieutenant colonels, and perhaps also the sole major. Apart from eight junior officers (and two civilians), all of the others were privates or NCOs. An article in the MoD daily paper estimated that 50 to 80 joined the Afghan opposition and that some of them participated in combat. The list did not include the 9 men whom the Soviets had succeeded in bringing home from Afghanistan after the war or the 19 known to be in other countries who refused to return to the Soviet Union.[313]

Stories abounded of Central Asians, especially Tajiks, deserting to the opposition,[314] but their percentage in this list was proportionate to their number in the Fortieth Army. Several of those captured—both Slavs and nominal Muslims—became practicing Muslims, some out of conviction, others under pressure.[315] After hearing that he was MIA in 1987, the family of one soldier from the Uzbek city, Chirchik, received a note from him through the Red Cross in Geneva; he had apparently become a practicing Muslim, dating his note with a (mistaken) hijrah year.[316]

Deserters' and POWs' refusal to return home, however much they yearned for their family, was understandable, perhaps inevitable. Not only did the Soviet military ethos demand a hero's death over captivity, soldiers and officers condemned those who deserted or were captured. A junior officer who fought in Afghanistan in 1983 and 1984, recalling how the soldiers had at the time perceived the dushmany as criminals, said their harshest judgment was for those who deserted.[317]

During the war about fifty men were freed, fifteen of them from Pakistan by a representative of Freedom House, a New York human rights organization. Thirty-one returned to the Soviet Union, and the rest reached, and remained in, the West. Two who returned to the Soviet Union as early as 1984 were the subject of a lengthy piece in the government daily, *Izvestiia*.[318]

The International Committee of the Red Cross had a program to intern Soviet prisoners in Switzerland "and eventually voluntarily repatriate them." A Russian émigré source pointed out that the situation was complicated by the Soviet Union's refusal to acknowledge them as POWs since it denied being at war in Afghanistan. Six Soviet soldiers asked for and received parole admission into the United States in 1983 and 1984; one returned to the USSR in 1985. At least twice—in 1980 and in 1985—a Soviet soldier entered the U.S. embassy in Kabul telling the American diplomats that he was fed up with the soldier's life and wanted to return to the Soviet Union. Eventually both agreed to leave with the Soviet ambassador if they could return home without retribution.[319]

In early 1984, Lord Nicholas Bethell interviewed fourteen Soviet prisoners, not a few of them from Muslim nationalities. Most had deserted; one was taken prisoner within days of arriving in Afghanistan, when he went to purchase cigarettes. Many of them were kept in terrible conditions and were in visibly poor health. Only one or two considered returning to the Soviet Union; most desired to live in the West, and some of the Muslims, in Turkey.[320]

The mujahidin held a number of Soviet soldiers captured between 1982 and 1984 in a prison near Peshawar in Pakistan, from which they tried to escape. They procured weapons, but were outnumbered and killed; the Soviets were unable to get their names from the Pakistani authorities.[321]

Those captured during the war included civilian advisers and experts. Sixteen engineers and technicians were at one point taken prisoner in Mazar-i Sharif. They were threatened with death if they did not adopt Islam. All seem to have been tortured and pressured to record anti-Soviet appeals, which were then broadcast. Their captors killed some of them; Soviet troops eventually freed the others.[322]

Western countries gave the POWs who reached them a platform to tell their tales. In July 1988, six former POWs held a press conference at Freedom House. They had all fought in Afghanistan and been taken prisoner, freed, and brought to the United States. At the event, Soviet journalist Artem Borovik noted that the Soviet public's attitude had changed during the course of the war from one of hatred for deserters who fought with the rebels against their own people to one of ambivalence. By this time, the United States had granted asylum to twelve other Soviet POWs, while Canada had taken in five; eight had returned to the Soviet Union.[323]

One POW who spoke at Freedom House was skeptical of the amnesty for POWs that the procurator-general had declared that month (see Chapter 4): What if there should be a change of policy? In that case, they would be helpless, like the former POW who had returned voluntarily to the Soviet Union after the Soviet consulate in New York had guaranteed his freedom but was then sentenced to twelve years' imprisonment.[324] One of the six men said, "I have been given amnesty now. What for? For honestly serving my two years and choosing the country in which I want to live? But what about the lie the system used to send us off to war?"[325]

At least three of the six had deserted. They related their story to Borovik. One came from a village in Ukraine. Enlisted in 1982, he was sent for training to Ashkhabad:

> They told us that we would be sent to Afghanistan, but I wasn't frightened. I believed the press, which carried picturesque accounts of how we were *not* fighting there. . . . At first, I didn't tell my parents anything, but I later wound up writing to them. I remember trying to comfort them by telling them that I was going to be eating watermelon and would send them some. "Son, my father had said to me, 'serve and obey.' . . . I ended up disobeying. . . .
>
> At first I had some doubts whether we were in the right; then I was overcome with a feeling of despair. Everyone around us was an enemy. I remember an intense feeling of anger toward the rebels because so many of our guys were getting killed. I wanted revenge. Then I began to doubt the goals and methods of international aid. I had a difficult time deciding what I really believed. I just knew what I had to say during the political instruction meeting: that we were fighting "'American aggression" and "Pakis." Why had we mined all the approaches to the regiment? I asked myself. Why were we aiming our machine guns at every Afghan? Why were we killing the people we came to help?

He stayed with the same dushman detachment for a year:

> I realized that all of our—er, I mean all of the Soviet—propaganda about the war . . . is a complete lie from beginning to end. . . . I was willing to do anything to atone for my sins before these people. . . . I couldn't see any difference between myself and a Nazi in my native Ukrainian land. It's the same thing: rolled-up sleeves, submachine guns, cries, villages." He ended up in America in 1984. "I tried writing to my family, but they . . . let me know that they were having problems. I stopped writing. I don't want them to suffer because of me. It's not their fault.[326]

The second man hailed from Kharkov. Enlisted in 1980, he too was sent to Turkmenistan for training. After two and a half months,

> we were lined up and told that we were lucky, that we had the great honor to be trusted by the Party to fulfill our international duty in Afghanistan. We had to help the Afghan people retain the conquests of the April revolution . . . and defend them from the bloodthirsty actions of imperialism, which, by invading the territory of our ally, threatened our southern border. . . .

> After six months of service, . . . my hands wouldn't shake anymore when I'd close the eyelids of a fallen friend. I smoked dope. . . . By January 1981 . . . I'd turned into a hardened wolf who was being eaten alive by lice and who was soon to disappear. . . . I didn't know what I wanted. I was the same person, yet somehow I was different. During the whole time of my military service, my submachine gun hadn't hit a single American. I'd wake up and think: Why won't the government tell us the whole truth? . . . They deceived us, their own soldiers. They played with us as if we were toys, while we were dropping like flies. . . . I decided to desert when there were only ten days remaining until my demobilization. . . . I wrote one last letter home, gathered all the weapons and ammunition I had, and left. The guerrillas in a nearby *kishlak* gave me shelter" [but then Soviet soldiers arrived and] grabbed me, returned me to the guardhouse in Kunduz, and began a four-month investigation.

In July 1982, he escaped again, spent four years in a rebel detachment and eventually reached the United States. Borovik asked for a short explanation of why he'd left: "I realized that I wouldn't be able to look the mothers of the soldiers who were killed in Afghanistan in the eye."[327]

One deserter related to Borovik how he—and another Russian—had deserted to escape the hazing. He "ran into a vineyard after one of the beatings." The spooks also beat him because he had come without his gun.[328] Another deserter had also been beaten by the granddads.

Finale

The last soldier of the Fortieth Army crossed back into the Soviet Union, as planned, on February 15, 1989. Its commander, General Gromov, who was that last soldier, remarks bitterly in his book, *The Limited Contingent*, that there was no official reception on the Soviet side; not a single representative of the central government or of the MoD was there to greet the returning soldiers. The locals showered flowers on them, but from the point of view of officialdom and the Kremlin, "this was not a war that need be remembered." The Fortieth Army, despite Gromov's hope to retain it, dispersed throughout the Soviet Union, each unit returning to its original posting.[329]

Their reception was an omen of a further saga of privation, humiliation, corruption, and frustration—this time at home, where they had waited so long to be.

Chapter 4

The Position of the Soviet Political Establishment

The failure of any senior Soviet official to welcome the returning soldiers in person, despite Gorbachev's making the withdrawal a feather in his cap, and the failure and apparent apathy to the lot of the Soviet POWs, were characteristic of the Kremlin's ambivalence about the war. It had sent over half a million soldiers to Afghanistan and seemed convinced it had done the right thing yet appeared to take little responsibility for their fate.

Official Statements and Politburo Resolutions, 1980–1985

After frequent discussions in the first months after the intervention, the Soviet leadership spent very little time debating the war, its conduct, and its implications. The semiannual CPSU Central Committee plenum in June 1980 raised it as part of its discussion of the international situation and Soviet foreign policy, but there was no debate. Every participant who addressed the issue expressed approval of the decision to introduce Soviet troops into Afghanistan. The plenum resolution noted that "the courageous step" that the Kremlin had taken with regard to Afghanistan "was received with satisfaction by every Soviet person."[1] As the Supreme Soviet Joint Committee on International Affairs reported in December 1989, "In accordance with [the] practice existing at the time," had "the decision in question . . . been submitted for discussion in any political or state forum," it "would most likely have been approved. Essentially, the party, the people, and our foreign friends were presented with a fait accompli."[2] (The "most likely" can surely be deleted.)

No official document spoke of the war in Afghanistan as one in which the Soviet

Union was participating, merely as the "undeclared war" of imperialism against the DRA.[3] In the first three years, the Kremlin usually referred to it euphemistically as "the events" and, after 1983, as "the military action," in Afghanistan. These misnomers had significant implications for the status of the war's veterans and for the attitude toward the war of both the Soviet establishment and Soviet society. Critics came to speak of "the war that never happened" or the "hidden war."

The Politburo concealed everything connected with the war behind a veil of secrecy. Almost immediately after the intervention, it adopted a resolution regarding its presentation in the media that *Pravda* itself quickly dubbed sheer fantasy (*vymysl' chisteishei vody*).[4]

In the first months, the Politburo regularly addressed the issue of maintaining troops in Afghanistan. Indeed, the Soviet leadership was under considerable international pressure to reconsider its decision, but it remained adamant that it had acted correctly.

In January 1980, the Politburo held two meetings to discuss the situation. The first, on January 17, confirmed the continued activity of the Commission on Afghanistan (Andropov seems to have been the dominant member and ex officio chairman[5]) of analyzing and preparing materials on Afghanistan. The second, on January 28, stipulated that "the necessity of providing for the broad foreign policy interests and the security of the USSR will demand the preservation of the offensive nature of the measures we are undertaking in relation to the Afghan events."[6] In other words, the Soviet force had to be retained in Afghanistan so long as the country was unquiet and the United States and the People's Republic of China supported the rebels. In fact, the United States had not given the Afghan opposition military equipment before the Soviet intervention. In its wake, however, Washington decided to take "punitive measures" against the Soviet Union and "provide lethal weapons to the rebels through the Pakistanis."[7] On January 25, the Soviet government sent the DRA government a detailed draft agreement stipulating "the conditions of the temporary stay" of up to 60,000 Soviet troops in Afghanistan, clearly indicating that no speedy withdrawal was in the cards.[8]

The following month, Andropov reported to the Politburo on his visit to Kabul (January 31–February 1). Although he asserted that the situation in Afghanistan was already stabilizing, Ustinov opined that "about a year will be needed, perhaps even a year and a half" until the situation is calm, "and before that we cannot even think about a withdrawal of troops." To this Brezhnev added that in his view, "we even need to increase the contingent of forces in Afghanistan somewhat."[9] According to Liakhovskii, the Kremlin discussed a possible withdrawal of the Soviet force in late February, but Ustinov and Andropov rejected this idea, as "perhaps [did] Gromyko," as it would be a concession to the aggressive policy of the Americans, damage Soviet international prestige, further destabilize the DRA, and boost Muslim extremism near the Soviet Union's southern border. Once again this view carried the day.[10]

In parallel, the Soviet leaders released several statements to the press. Brezhnev told a *Pravda* correspondent in January 1980 that "unending armed intervention and a well-developed conspiracy by external reactionary forces created a genuine threat that Afghanistan would lose its independence and be transformed into a military staging-ground for the imperialists on our . . . southern border. . . . We could no longer fail to respond" to Kabul's requests. The alternative would have been "to allow the forces of aggression to repeat there what they did in Chile . . . to look on passively while a hotbed of serious danger to the security of the Soviet state was created on our southern border. . . . It was not a simple decision for us," but Moscow had "acted in full awareness" of its responsibilities, and taking all circumstances into account. "The sole task facing the Soviet contingents is to assist the Afghans in repelling foreign aggression. They will be completely withdrawn as soon as the factors that made the Afghan leadership request their introduction no longer exist."[11] Addressing electors in a Moscow *raion* (district) in February 1980, Brezhnev insisted that there was no Russian intervention in Afghanistan, reiterated his statement that as soon as the reason that had led to the introduction of the Soviet contingent was removed, it would leave, and then he added that the United States was postponing that date by increasing its intervention in Afghan affairs.[12]

In election speeches earlier that month, both Andropov and Ponomarev had addressed the issue. Andropov explained that only Moscow's "timely" Soviet military assistance had prevented the United States from moving its regional military base into Afghanistan after losing its Iranian "bridgehead. . . . A dangerous hotbed of tension was developing on our southern border." The introduction of troops, a "step that was not simple for us," was "necessary in order to protect the interests of our homeland."[13] Ponomarev told his electors in Saratov, "There is no [Soviet] aggression against Afghanistan," despite the claims of American and Chinese propaganda. "The Soviet Union has not occupied that country. . . . Small military contingents have been introduced into Afghanistan at the request of its legitimate government" and would be "withdrawn as soon as the encroachment on Afghanistan's borders and state sovereignty cease." Ponomarev also stated that "no clashes are taking place between Afghans and our soldiers" and that Moscow was not interfering in the country's domestic affairs. Nor, he insisted, had the Soviet Union entered Afghanistan to "seize others' lands or raw materials, or to impose on anyone else a social or political system."[14] Brezhnev told the Indian foreign minister in June that the Soviet Union favored a political settlement of the situation in Afghanistan, one that would give trustworthy guarantees for a total cessation of all external interference in Afghan affairs.[15]

In March 1980, the Politburo endorsed a letter by the Commission on Afghanistan and First Deputy Head of the CC International Department, Oleg Rakhmanin, stating that "a successful resolution of the internal problems and the consolidation of the new structure in Afghanistan will demand not a small amount of effort and time, for the length of which the Soviet forces there will remain the basic stabilizing factor standing in opposition to the further expansion of the activity of domestic and foreign counter-revolutionary forces."[16] In April, the Politburo made a further resolution, confirming "the considerations" that the Afghanistan Commission presented (this time signed by the troika and another Ponomarev deputy, Vadim Zagliadin) and stating that "only when the situation in Afghanistan stabilizes, and the situation around the country improves, and only upon a request of the DRA leadership, may we consider the question of the eventual withdrawal of our troops from the DRA."[17]

The MoD instructions in late May stipulating that officers would serve in Afghanistan for two years (see Chapter 3) made explicit the expectation that the Limited Contingent would be there for a long time.[18] Nonetheless, the following month, the Politburo decided "to withdraw several military units whose presence in Afghanistan now is not necessary." It charged the Ministry of Defense with deciding "the number and composition of the troops to be withdrawn" as well as "the time frame and order of their withdrawal."[19] Yet, addressing the CPSU Central Committee plenum that same month, Gromyko clarified that while there was currently no need to maintain a military contingent "even of the size which it was when it was introduced . . . if the situation demands it, we at any time will be able to strengthen our contingent."[20] Following Sakharov's open letter of July 1980 (see Chapter 1), Brezhnev charged CGS Ogarkov with withdrawing the Soviet troops before the upcoming Twenty-Sixth Party Congress (February 1981) in light of "world public opinion and domestic opinion." This instruction implies that Brezhnev was still considering total withdrawal (Russian has no definite article, so one cannot be sure). However, the situation in Afghanistan degenerated, so the MoD brought home just "a first" 5,000 soldiers in 1980.[21]

In October, a joint statement at the conclusion of one of Babrak Karmal's frequent visits to Moscow referred once again to the terms for withdrawal: "As to the limited Soviet military contingent that is in the DRA at the request of the Afghan government and in accordance with the December 1978 treaty and the UN Charter, the question of timing [its] withdrawal can be examined in the context of a political settlement and not before the total cessation of the imperialist intervention in the DRA's internal affairs."[22] In the words of one scholar, the Politburo could not "make up [its] mind as to what constituted Soviet minimum demands for a troop withdrawal."[23]

Brezhnev told the Twenty-Sixth Party Congress that "imperialism launched a veritable undeclared war against the Afghan revolution. This created a direct threat to the security of our southern frontier. This situation compelled us to render the military aid requested by a friendly country." Moscow would withdraw the Soviet contingent "with the agreement of the DRA government" once incursions into the country of "counter-revolutionary bands" stopped and he received formal guarantees that there would be no new intervention.[24] Three months later, Brezhnev reiterated Moscow's support of a political settlement: he would withdraw troops only with the implementation of accords.[25]

In March 1981, the senior figures in the three branches represented in Kabul—Ambassador Fikrat Tabeev, KGB Major General Viktor Spol'nikov, and chief military adviser Army General Aleksandr Maiorov—came to Moscow to meet with the Afghanistan Commission, together with First Deputy DM Marshal Sergei Sokolov and First Deputy CGS Army General Sergei Akhromeev. Reporting on the war, Maiorov insisted that the problem of Afghanistan could be solved solely by political and diplomatic measures, that the Fortieth Army's presence played into the hands of the United States and NATO, and that Babrak Karmal had to be told that within six months, the Kremlin would withdraw half of the Fortieth Army and the second half in the following six months. Ustinov met Maiorov's report with hostility, stating that Moscow needed Afghanistan "as a military training-ground on a world scale"; Andropov and Gromyko were silent. It was clear to Maiorov that the commission had called the meeting to discuss ways of achieving a military victory and was rejecting his proposal. The following day, he was summoned to Chernenko, the person closest to Brezhnev, who informed him that the General Secretary remembered him from Czechoslovakia in 1968 and had great faith in him; that Moscow had to bolster the PDPA, whose fate depended on the outcome of the military action in Afghanistan; and that Maiorov's commission was to justify Brezhnev's confidence in his ability to achieve a military victory.[26]

Apparently, however, Ustinov's generals convinced him that there was no military solution to the Afghan situation. He submitted a memorandum to the Politburo in this vein, but it was transferred to the archives without comment, as if it had never existed.[27]

Over the months and years of the war, the Politburo touched occasionally on questions relating to it, but does not seem to have undertaken any major discussion of its conduct or its termination. At the end of December 1980, it resolved to decorate MVD (Ministry of Internal Affairs) agency workers and internal troops servicemen for the successful performance of a special assignment in giving international aid to the DRA (clearly the elimination of Amin and the capture of the palace exactly a year earlier).[28] In July 1981, the Politburo discussed the burial and epitaphs of soldiers killed in the war, debating how—and whether—to perpetuate their memory. While Andropov and Kirilenko opined that the time had not yet come to do so, Prime Minister Nikolai Tikhonov (Kosygin had resigned, and died, the previous year) suggested allocating one thousand rubles to each family for a headstone. Suslov, who chaired the meeting, asked, "What will we write on the epitaph?" In some cemeteries, he worried, there might be several headstones, drawing attention to the fact that Soviet soldiers were dying in Afghanistan. Ponomarev noted that "many letters are coming to the CC CPSU and other organizations; parents of the dead especially complain that their children and relatives died in Afghanistan." Suslov decided that replies to parents and relatives should be brief and standard: "We should not take liberties here." He appointed a committee to think about it.[29]

This unusual discussion touches on one of the cornerstones of Soviet policy regarding the war in Afghanistan: the utmost secrecy in which the Kremlin conducted it. While not a major issue at the time (the early 1980s), this became one over the next decade. In July 1981, the Politburo seems to have believed it could send a large contingent of conscripts to participate in combat operations without divulging the war's nature to the public. From the beginning, the official line was that Soviet soldiers were performing their "international duty" in Afghanistan and that this involved no fighting. Soviet television showed pictures of Soviet and Afghan soldiers embracing, Soviet doctors treating Afghan children, and Soviet soldiers giving Afghans food and medicine.

It is not clear to what extent the top Kremlin leaders in these early years were familiar with the situation in Afghanistan. The four institutions involved in the conduct of the war—the MoD, the KGB, the Foreign Ministry, and the party—each had its own representatives in Kabul who operated and reported separately.[30] The authors of all reports reflected the positions of their respective bosses in Moscow. Indeed, disagreements among the various Soviet "advisers and representatives" in Kabul and the pressing need for a single coordinating body "with appropriate authority" and for a long-term strategy were the kernel of the twelve-page report of *Pravda* correspondent, I. Shchedrov, which his paper's chief editor, Viktor Afanas'ev, forwarded to the Central Committee apparatus in November 1981.[31]

In February 1982, Andropov spent two days in Kabul, holding "intensive talks" with "several heads of Soviet institutions," Babrak Karmal, and his minister of state security, Mohamed Najibullah. The outcome was the formulation of a "strategic assignment," aiming to finish off the opposition by military means in the course of 1982.[32] Several military specialists and KGB operatives (*operativnye rabotniki*) in Afghanistan doubted that this was realistic (see Chapter 2), but few dared to assert that the concept behind Soviet policy—that the Soviets were fighting bandit groups rather than the Afghan Muslims (the kernel of the Afghan population)—was erroneous. Senior KGB operative Leonid Shebarshin stated that such insight was not pertinent in 1982 and attributed the failure to evaluate and analyze the situation to the "Soviet reality" that the Soviet leadership was stymied by its own propaganda labeling. The Kremlin began to rectify its "strategic mistake" only in 1986.[33] Two years later, Colonel Leonid

Shershnev wrote directly from Afghanistan to General Secretary Chernenko describing the punitive campaigns against the Afghan population—"We have been drawn into a war against the people, which is hopeless"—and revealing the "nonobjective" nature of the information Moscow was receiving from its representatives in Kabul.[34]

Critics later blamed the Soviet leadership for not changing tack and withdrawing the force in the early-mid 1980s. Former military attaché Krakhmalov writes, "Unfortunately, the Soviet leaders at the time did not manifest the political flexibility, the farsightedness, and the courage to state openly the need to review its policy with regard to Afghanistan. And so thousands of our boys had their lives rudely and ruthlessly cut short at their very start in a foreign land."[35] Writing shortly before his death, Gromyko contended that when Soviet losses in Afghanistan grew in the mid-1980s, no one gave the Politburo accurate information regarding casualties.[36] One Russian expert states that although many in the Soviet leadership "came to understand that a military defeat of the Afghan opposition was impracticable," withdrawal meant acknowledging their "miscalculations, impotence, and failure, which was why they chose to let events take their course."[37]

Nor does the Politburo seem to have addressed the decision to intervene. In one rare reference, in March 1983, to issues that later became the crux of a lively discussion, Andropov, who succeeded Brezhnev as General Secretary in November 1982, reminded the Politburo "how arduously and cautiously we decided the question of deploying troops in Afghanistan," with Brezhnev insisting "on a roll call vote" by Politburo members. Andropov told the Soviet leadership to remember that Afghanistan was "a feudal country where tribes have always been in charge of their territories and the central authority was far from always able to reach each kishlak." He recalled the years-long struggle against the Basmachi, who had resisted the imposition of Soviet rule in Soviet Central Asia in the 1920s and 1930s. Moreover, in Afghanistan, the Soviet Union was up against American imperialism. Therefore, "we cannot back off."[38] This was the sense of two Central Committee resolutions made in July and September that year. The former spoke of the ability of "rebel movements" with "small weapons" and "the comprehensive support of various governments" to achieve "global political goals" and bring down the ruling regime.[39] The latter pointed out that the withdrawal of Soviet troops would permit the establishment in Afghanistan of a government hostile to the Soviet Union, noting that it behooved the Kremlin to strive to consolidate the DRA regime and prevent this eventuality.[40]

True, in 1982, just after becoming General Secretary, Andropov had told UN Secretary- General Perez de Cuellar and his deputy, Diego Cordovez, that the Soviet Union was prepared to take "certain steps. . . . First, the conflict has affected Soviet relations not only with the West, but also with other socialist countries, Arab countries, and Third World countries. Second, it has affected our home life, our policy, and our economy." Soviet UN representative Gennadii Evstaf'ev contended that Andropov had an eight-month plan for a Soviet pullout.[41] But neither Andropov nor Chernenko mentioned Afghanistan specifically at the CPSU CC plenum in June 1983,[42] while Gromyko stuck to the mantra that the Soviet Union "holds to its position of full support for the program of a political settlement advanced by the DRA government," as the Afghans alone have to resolve the domestic affairs of the country.[43]

One student of the war notes the mounting evidence that Andropov appreciated the impossibility of a military solution in Afghanistan yet was "politically unable to initiate a withdrawal."[44] Given his various statements, the most that can be said is that he tried to satisfy whomever he was addressing.

Nikolai Egorychev, who became Moscow's ambassador to Kabul in 1988, testifies that by the second year of the war, he understood that the Kremlin had not determined what to do in Afghanistan.[45] However, he attributed this failure to actual shortcomings, not simply indecisiveness, because Moscow was endeavoring "to apply methods that don't work at home either. Based on our advice," the DRA leaders "undertook to destroy their petty capitalists and merchants," and later had to revise their policy. Soviet advisers to the PDPA "did not understand the situation."[46]

Economic Considerations

One of the most difficult questions is how much the war in Afghanistan cost the Soviet Union materially and the extent of the economic factor's role in the deliberations regarding a possible withdrawal. The available documentation offers none of the requisite information.[47] Whatever the cost and however small a percent of the total Soviet budget it might have been, we must examine this expenditure against the backdrop of the crisis of the Soviet economy, the growth of which was, in the 1970s and early 1980s, "the lowest ever recorded in Soviet peacetime history."[48] The question mark regarding the war's price tag applies even to its direct outlays, without considering any oblique and implied costs, like the Western technology of which the Soviet Union was deprived by virtue of its intervention in Afghanistan, which cannot be estimated.

The nine-year war cost the Soviet Union a good deal of money. One source tells us that the war "laid a heavy burden on the Soviet economy. . . . Just the cost of delivering military aid and civilian goods to Afghanistan during the years that the Soviet troops were in that country, according to official Soviet figures, came to 60 billion rubles, at least $2.4 billion."[49] (Converting rubles into dollars for the 1980s is no simple matter. The official rate was one for one, which was manifestly absurd.[50]) This was meaningfully different from probably the most professional estimate: that the intervention cost the Soviet Union some 30.4 billion rubles.[51] Egorychev, when asked whether the pullout was justified, maintained that there was no other choice given its economic cost.[52]

Whether or not this was a primary incentive, it must have been a consideration. In 1987, with an eye to cutting costs, Gorbachev charged Prime Minister Nikolai Ryzhkov with estimating the war's outlay.[53] At a Politburo session in April 1988, after affirming his primary concern for Soviet lives, he added, "not to mention the billions that this is costing us each year."[54] Ultimately the Soviet leadership extricated itself from Afghanistan by linking the withdrawal with domestic economic problems. In early 1987, Gorbachev stated, "Our international policy is, more than ever before, determined by domestic policy, by our interest in concentrating on constructive work to improve our country."[55]

In response to his assignment, the prime minister formed a group of economists and specialists from the various ministries connected with the war. To determine "precisely how much Afghanistan was costing us," the group took everything into account—the training of Afghan students in the Soviet Union, the work of Soviet specialists in Afghanistan, the quantities of military and civilian materiel supplied to the DRA government and army, even the Aeroflot flights to Afghanistan in the wake of the April revolution. The MoD provided precise figures, covering every item from food for the Fortieth Army to all types of ammunition. In 1988, Ryzhkov handed in a report for the years 1984 to 1987—his original mandate. He wrote that military aid had amounted to 1,578.5 million rubles in 1984, 2,623.8 in 1985, 3,197.4 in 1986, and 4,116 in 1987. By far the largest item was the "maintenance and provision" of the Soviet force.[56] By December 1990, when he was replaced, Ryzhkov had not completed the expanded assignment of estimating the total cost of the war.[57]

While not a significant percentage of either the Soviet Union's GDP or its national budget,[58] the war accounted for 18.8 percent of the budgetary deficit in 1985, 8 percent in 1986, and 10.2 percent in 1987. Clearly, the maintenance of a large force in a foreign country was costly. One Afghan vet calls the Fortieth Army a "golden duck." In addition to the weaponry and equipment, "we changed our uniforms every two or three months because they were unsuited to Afghanistan." Senior officers were highly paid. And there was "the oil and gas for the vehicles, the tanks, and planes."[59] In addition to the costs of its army, the Soviet Union had to pay the concomitant personnel it maintained in Afghanistan—advisers with the DRA forces, the KGB and MVD troops, and the many MoD representatives in Kabul. It also paid part of the expenses of the DRA armed forces, the KhAD (the DRA Intelligence), and the Tsarandoi (the DRA gendarmerie). And it covered the training of the thousands of Afghan officers at Soviet military establishments, in addition to the thousands of students who came to Soviet schools.

The Soviet press's frequent accounts of the extent of U.S. aid to the mujahidin served to legitimize Soviet spending on Afghanistan. In late 1984, the Soviet government daily reported that the Americans were stepping up their expenditure in Afghanistan, indicating that Moscow was doing the same for the DRA.[60]

By the time of the intervention in late 1979, Moscow had been giving Afghanistan economic and military aid for over two decades, ever since Khrushchev's visit there in 1955, when Moscow's involvement in the Third World became a major aspect of its constant striving for superpower status. This involvement required costly large-scale economic aid and investment and, frequently, military aid. Naturally someone had to pay for this, and the commodities with which Kabul paid Moscow for the economic aid and the arms it received (cotton, natural gas, uranium, precious stones, and fruit) did not come close to covering it.

In November 1980, DRA President Babrak Karmal stated that Moscow was supplying 80 percent of Afghanistan's foreign aid. The following year, *Pravda*'s correspondent in Afghanistan reported that trade turnover between the two countries had doubled in the past five years and would triple by 1985. Afghanistan's increasing dependence on the Soviet Union for economic assistance was making Afghanistan an expensive investment for Moscow.[61]

The civilian economic aid program to Afghanistan was considerable. It reportedly jumped from $13 million in 1977 to $264 million in 1982.[62] Ryzhkov testified in 1986 that the Soviet Union had constructed industrial enterprises, large irrigation complexes, and power stations; had drilled gas wells; and was building residential buildings, educational institutions, and hospitals.[63] Moscow expressed its readiness to continue providing assistance and to participate in constructing and operating "enterprises and facilities" and in extracting and refining natural gas and petroleum, among numerous other ventures.[64] Over the war's nine years, Soviet personnel "built or re-built" 84 schools, 25 hospitals, 26 nurseries, 326 residences, 35 mosques, and 53 bridges; dug 41 wells; dug or repaired 117 kilometers of canals and ditches; and electrified 6 villages.[65]

The Afghan students dispatched to the Soviet Union for higher education and technical training and the steady stream of Soviet technical and educational delegations to Afghanistan were also expensive. Whereas in 1978, 1,505 Afghan students and officials were reportedly training in the Soviet Union, their number in 1983 was estimated at 9,000.[66] By 1985, 70,000 Afghan "specialists" had trained in the Soviet Union.[67] Many of the teachers in any Afghan schools still functioning in 1986 were Soviet citizens, as was the majority of the staff at Kabul University. The Soviet Union was publishing tens of thousands of textbooks for the Afghan educational system.[68]

Some of the operations in which the Fortieth Army was involved related directly to the economic ties between the two countries. In late 1981, for instance, the Soviets engaged dushmans in the northern province of Kunduz who were trying to prevent the export of cotton to the Soviet Union. On another occasion, an air assault company provided escort for seventy trucks hauling cotton.[69]

Certainly the many, often huge, construction projects that the Soviet Union undertook during the war must have strained the Soviet economy. The Soviets supplied building and other materials and equipment and sent numerous experts and technicians to carry out the work.[70] According to the U. S. State Department, in 1985, for example, Soviet aid deliveries to Afghanistan reached $225 million (bringing deliveries since the invasion to $1.6 billion), with at least 5,000 Soviet economic technicians employed on sixty-three projects.[71]

Indeed, one of the underpinnings of "internationalism" was the use of aid, "from selling tanks at bargain prices to subsidizing 'fraternal' imports and outright charity, to bolster friendly regimes and buy uncommitted ones." Soviet foreign policy in the 1970s was "an object lesson in high-spending, cheque-book realpolitik." Even before public admission of the costs of this policy at the end of the 1980s, Afghanistan "had catalyzed public disquiet at spending money abroad when Soviet citizens lived so manifestly below their aspirations" (see Chapter 7).[72] At the end of the decade, discussions related to Soviet aid to developing countries took place in both the Congress of People's Deputies and the media.[73] The deputy chairman of the USSR Supreme Soviet, Anatolii Luk'ianov, said that even with the war over, the Soviet Union could not cut spending on Afghanistan: "We have to pay the peoples of that country for the fact that we did not listen to . . . Sakharov," who had opposed the introduction of Soviet troops into Afghanistan. Moreover, the war's veterans had to be "properly" paid so that "we won't be ashamed to look them in the eye."[74]

Twenty years after the final withdrawal of the Soviet Limited Contingent from Afghanistan, there was still no assessment of what the war had cost the Soviet Union. All that people in Russia knew was that the sum paid for "humanitarian assistance (the preparation of cadres for the economy, favorable credits, postponement of debts, gratuitous aid, etc.)" had, over the years between 1978 and 1990, reached over 8 billion foreign currency rubles. "The sum of expenses was undoubtedly several times higher."[75]

Moving toward Withdrawal, 1985–1989

On coming to power, Mikhail Gorbachev, who succeeded Chernenko as CPSU General Secretary in March 1985, resolved to find a solution to the impasse in Afghanistan. Clearly, as the first General Secretary not to have participated in the decision to introduce troops into Afghanistan, this was easier for him than for his predecessors.

Reportedly, Gorbachev first sanctioned an offensive to break the stalemate,[76] giving Army General Mikhail Zaitsev, Commander of the Southern Direction of the Soviet Armed Forces, a year or two to win the war.[77] Simultaneously, the new leader contemplated the option of withdrawal. Anatolii Cherniaev, one of Gorbachev's closest advisers, testifies that a flood of letters to the CC and *Pravda* protesting the war brought Afghanistan to his boss's attention as soon as he came to power. The new General Secretary realized that this was "his 'highest priority issue'."[78]

For Gorbachev, the decision to withdraw was in part a way to dissociate himself from the Brezhnev "stagnation." He "implied a readiness to make concessions and compromises and to reject many of the principles, methods, and ideologies" of his predecessors.[79] In the words of one scholar, the Soviet leaders "eventually succeeded" in extricating themselves from the war "by linking the need to get out of Afghanistan with domestic economic problems; reform at home became a sufficient condition for accommodation abroad. [Gorbachev's flag] programs of glasnost, perestroika, and new thinking . . . could not fully develop as long as the Soviets had troops in Afghanistan."[80]

The leadership, however, was divided over the issue of withdrawal. Viktor Kremeniuk, Georgii Arbatov's deputy at the Institute of the USA and Canada (ISKAN), claims that while some advocated stopping the war, others said withdrawal must be contingent on victory. Yakovlev attributes opposition to withdrawal to the military, including Akhromeev and Varennikov, who, he contends, passively resisted withdrawal right through early 1989.[81] This contention, however, is untenable in light of Varennikov's continued pressure for a political settlement (see Chapter 2) and Georgii Kornienko's claim regarding Akhromeev's flexibility. War correspondent Mikhail Leshchinskii said that the military was divided, with Defense Minister Yazov heading the opposition[82]—surely a more authentic opinion. Ultimately, Shevarnadze and Kriuchkov also joined those seeking to postpone withdrawal, aiming to retain a force to protect Najibullah, who in May 1986 succeeded Babrak Karmal as General Secretary of the PDPA, and in November, as DRA president. As long as people indulged in illusions of victory and hopes of America ceasing to support the mujahidin, there would be opposition to ending the intervention.[83]

Arbatov and Akhromeev concur that Gorbachev could not press for a political solution immediately,[84] yet in October 1985, Gorbachev indicated to the Politburo that intervening militarily in Afghanistan had been a mistake that must be corrected, and the sooner the better. Although Gorbachev refrained from making a direct proposal, the Politburo resolved to expedite the withdrawal of Soviet troops and simultaneously ensure a friendly Afghanistan. This would require a combination of military and political measures.

At a Politburo meeting that month, Gorbachev read aloud letters from mothers and soldiers. He summed them up, stating that they all had the same leitmotif: "International duty? In the name of what? Do the Afghans themselves want it? Is it worth the lives of our children, who do not understand why they were sent there, what they are fighting for, killing old people and children?"[85] The CPSU CC Administrative Department made a point of answering some letters addressed to the

Kremlin leadership.[86] Public opinion was becoming a significant consideration in decision making on major policy issues or at least a tool that Gorbachev frequently used to justify his chosen policies.[87]

"The principled decision" to withdraw the Soviet Limited Contingent, Shevarnadze tells us, had been made. The draft of the Political Report to the CPSU Central Committee that Gorbachev's foreign minister saw in February 1986, on the eve of the Twenty-Seventh Party Congress, however, contained no mention of it, although it had appeared in the previous drafts. This indicated the continuing influence of "opposition voices" within the Politburo itself.[88] Nonetheless, at the Congress, Gorbachev gave the first public hint that he intended to end the war. He declared that "counter-revolution and imperialism" had turned Afghanistan into a "bleeding wound," insinuating that Moscow's support of "that country's efforts at defending its sovereignty" was sapping Soviet society's health and strength. "We would like in the nearest future to bring back to the homeland the Soviet troops that are in Afghanistan at its government's request." Moscow had reached an agreement with Kabul "on a schedule for their staged withdrawal" as soon as "a political settlement is reached that will ensure a genuine cessation of external armed intervention in the DRA's domestic affairs."[89] In other words, the Soviet establishment was still making withdrawal dependent on Western guarantees to cease assisting the opposition, while appreciating that doing so was tantamount to rejecting the very notion of withdrawing.

In July 1986, at Vladivostok, Gorbachev promised to withdraw six regiments by the end of the year in order to provide a "stimulus" for a political settlement.[90] The CPSU CC's welcoming greeting to those regiments, which returned in October 1986 (see Chapter 2), emphasized that they had fulfilled their internationalist duty in Afghanistan honorably. "The Soviet people bow their heads before the memory of the courageous sons of our homeland who fell in battle. . . . To surround their families with attention and concern, to lessen the pain and bitterness of loss . . . is the duty of every Party, trade union, and YCL organization, and of the soviets."[91]

Gorbachev's reasoning was practical. He told the Politburo in November 1986, "We have been fighting in Afghanistan for . . . six years [sic]. If the approach is not changed we will continue to fight for another 20–30 years. This would cast a shadow on our abilities to affect the evolution of the situation." The war, he declared, must be ended within two years. CGS Sergei Akhromeev, however, contradicted Gorbachev's statement that the military "are learning badly from this war," pointing out to the Politburo that "there is no single piece of land in this country that has not been occupied by a Soviet soldier. Nevertheless, the majority of the territory remains in the hands of the rebels. . . . We have lost the battle for the Afghan people. The government is supported by a minority of the population." Akhromeev blamed the political situation in Afghanistan for the stalemate. According to Cherniaev, Akhromeev added that the Soviets had "lost touch with the peasants, who didn't gain anything from the revolution. 80 percent of the country is in the hands of the mujahidin, and the life of peasants is better there than in the areas controlled by the government." The Soviet armed forces were in a position to "maintain the situation on the level that it exists now," but this meant a long war. It was necessary to find a "way out." Even Gromyko now admitted that "there had been 'a lack of attention to social and other conditions when we agreed to provide military assistance,' . . . [but] time was against us and we could not wait any longer."[92]

In December, the Soviet and Afghan leaders made a timetable for withdrawal.[93] Gorbachev told Najibullah and his delegation that while Moscow would not abandon its "southern neighbor in distress . . . we don't intend to leave our troops in Afghanistan for any length of time." Despite the mantra that it was up to the other side, particularly the United States to curtail its interference in Afghanistan's domestic affairs,[94] his message was unequivocal: persisting in the search for victory carried unacceptable domestic and external repercussions.

Effecting withdrawal—like other measures that Gorbachev was intent on pursuing—required political reform. This called for far-reaching personnel changes to create a new political base and alternative sources of legitimacy. In October 1986, Gorbachev made Shevarnadze the head of a new Politburo commission that would "coordinate, make operative decisions, and make necessary proposals for solving the Afghan question."[95] He also empowered the expert community. Nodari Simoniia of the Institute for Oriental Studies emphasized in 1987 that unlike in December 1979, specialist opinion had to be involved in the decision to withdraw. Indeed, by 1987, "our specialists and our political figures [were] devoting great efforts to achieve a solution to this problem."[96] (The co-opting of experts under Gorbachev gave them access to people involved in the decision-making process; it also granted additional legitimacy to Gorbachev's leadership.[97]) But despite Simoniia's insistence that the whole country was unanimous that the war must be ended as soon as possible, the notion of withdrawal aroused "colossal opposition" among both politicians and senior commanders of the armed forces and "a significant stratum of Soviet society," as evidenced by "thousands of letters" to the CPSU CC and to newspapers, which were not published.[98]

Perhaps because of the Soviet conservatives' and Russian nationalists' opposition to any retreat or "betrayal" of the Afghan revolution, it was only in early 1987 that the Soviet leadership pushed publicly for reconciliation between the warring parties in Afghanistan, with an eye toward enabling a Soviet withdrawal. In April 1987, Gorbachev told the Politburo that

> we could get out of Afghanistan fast . . . and claim that we don't have to answer for the mistakes of the former leadership. But we have to think of our country's authority,

> about all the people who have fought in this war. How could we justify ourselves before our people if, after we leave, there followed a real slaughter and then the establishment of a base hostile to the Soviet Union? They'd say you forgot about those who suffered for this cause, about the state's authority! We'd only embitter everyone by abandoning our duty after losing so many people.[99]

In April 1987, Gorbachev told U.S. Secretary of State George Shultz that while the Soviet Union wanted to leave Afghanistan, the United States kept putting "sticks in the spokes," that is, not making counterconcessions.[100] Just as he needed political reform to implement withdrawal, Gorbachev needed withdrawal to implement domestic reform and convince the Americans that he was serious about "new thinking." Only this dual need can explain the Soviet fulfillment of the April 1988 Geneva Accords despite what Moscow perceived as both Washington's and Peshawar's continued violations.[101]

Undoubtedly Gorbachev had to maneuver between opponents to withdrawal and critics who accused him of dragging his feet. Regarding the former, his tactic was clear: he must focus public attention on the intervention itself, on the blunders of Brezhnev and others, most of -them conveniently deceased. At the other end of the spectrum, with Yakovlev as a CC Secretary and Afghanistan Commission member, he could now move ahead.[102]

At the Washington summit in December 1987, Gorbachev stated publicly that the Defense Council had made the formal decision to withdraw.[103] And in February 1988, he announced the timetable. It would begin May 1988 and be completed in February 1989.[104]

Shevarnadze stated that in the preparatory documents for the cease-fire agreement, the United States had agreed to discontinue aid to Afghan opposition forces.[105] But a Foreign Ministry statement, pointing to Pakistani violations of the Geneva Accords even after the withdrawal had commenced, said that these allowed Moscow "to draw the appropriate conclusions with respect to the schedule for troop withdrawal."[106] It is not clear whether the two men held divergent views or simply that Shevarnadze still sought to get the maximum return for withdrawing. But Gorbachev's position was resolute. He told the Politburo in April 1988, "We've decided to pull out anyway. . . . Our primary concern is that our boys are dying there. . . . No matter what . . . we'll start the pullout on May 15. . . . Whatever America or anyone else does, we are leaving. The decision is final and irreversible."[107] Yet in fall 1988, domestic political considerations and the demands of Shevarnadze and Kriuchkov, who in October became chairman of the KGB, impelled Gorbachev to support a last major operation in Afghanistan (see Chapter 2).[108]

Reassessing the Intervention

The withdrawal of Soviet troops that ended the nine-year Soviet-Afghan War was undoubtedly Gorbachev's most pressing issue. Reappraising the introduction of Soviet forces into a neighboring sovereign country was urgent in light of domestic politics and as a way to demonstrate the application of New Thinking. An American deputy assistant secretary of state said in late 1986, "Many Soviet spokesmen in private will frankly admit that the invasion of Afghanistan was a mistake."[109]

Indeed, once the decision to withdraw was set and implementation scheduled, a debate began–within both the establishment and the public sphere—regarding the intervention and the war. Shevarnadze, in his Geneva press conference after signing the accords, would not admit that the intervention had been a mistake. "Soviet troops," he said, "entered Afghanistan at the request of the legitimate government of Afghanistan at a difficult time for that country, and on a corresponding juridical and legal basis." At the same conference, however, he explained that the accords were "the result of new political thinking. All peoples must determine their fate themselves. The Afghans have this right as well."[110]

One month later, in May 1988, the CPSU Central Committee issued a "Letter on Afghanistan" to party organizations throughout the country that was designed to cancel the "negative mood" that had begun to surface within the party and among the population.[111] It said specifically that the April 1978 "revolutionary coup" had not had the economic or social basis from which to evolve into a "national democratic" revolution. This, coupled with the conflicts within the PDPA and its leaders' brutal repressions, had "created favorable conditions to intensify the counterrevolution." Moscow decided to intervene even though the Kremlin's "picture of the real social and economic situation" in Afghanistan was "insufficiently clear. We . . . did not even have a correct assessment" of its "unique geographical features. That found its reflection in the operations of our troops against small, highly mobile units, where very little could be accomplished with the help of modern military technology." Moreover, the Soviets "completely disregarded the most important national and historical factors, above all the fact that the appearance of armed foreigners was always met with arms . . . our military presence was associated with the forceful imposition of customs alien to the national characteristics and feelings of the Afghan people." Nor was this all: the Soviet "adviser apparatus . . . tried to transplant the approaches we are accustomed to onto Afghan soil." The war continued, "Our troops were getting engaged in extensive combat actions"; the situation "made any way out more and more difficult as time passed." The Soviet force suffered heavy losses, while the war "costs us 5 billion rubles a year."

Shortly after Gorbachev became General Secretary, Moscow undertook the requisite "deep analysis," the results of which Gorbachev transmitted to Babrak Karmal in October 1985, telling him "we cannot and will not wage war endlessly for the Afghans," although Moscow would continue to supply weaponry. Simultaneously, he ordered the Soviet command to take measures to reduce Soviet losses. In addition to the price the Soviet Union paid in the international arena, "the negative influence of the war . . . began to occur inside our country. And what other influence could the deaths of Soviet citizens in a foreign land have?" The Twenty-Seventh Party Congress in February and March 1986 "was unanimous that Soviet troops needed to be withdrawn . . . our people were expecting a word of truth and hope," and the new policy was put into practice.[112]

Gorbachev's statement to the Nineteenth CPSU Conference in June 1988 implied a definite dissociation from the intervention. "Our fighting men are leaving Afghanistan at the behest of the Homeland, which has displayed wisdom, having acquired in these years new political and moral experience, a deeper understanding of the present-day world, of its contradictions, and of the obstacles on the path into the future."[113]

Other members of the establishment who, however, did not hold official political positions decried the military intervention less equivocally at the conference. *Znamia* editor Grigorii Baklanov insisted that "it took both political wisdom and courage to pull our troops out of Afghanistan. It took neither of these qualities to send them in." Mothers of those who perished in Afghanistan "ask: how did this happen? Who was behind it? . . . We must create a mechanism that will prevent such things happening again." The head of the prestigious IMEMO, Academician Evgenii Primakov, told the conference, "Undoubtedly, the situation in neighboring Afghanistan, the interference in its affairs from without, and the international situation as a whole called for counteraction on our part in the interests of peace and stability in the region. But the nature of this counteraction was evidently determined without the requisite elaboration of alternatives for a political solution and, moreover, with a lack of realism in assessing the situation in Afghanistan as well as the inevitable consequences. . . . All this laid a heavy burden on our country and people. In light of this, such an achievement of the perestroika era as the withdrawal of our troops from Afghanistan cannot be overestimated."[114]

Some officials continued to justify the intervention, however. The deputy chief of the CPSU CC Propaganda Department, Vladimir Sevruk, said on the day of the first withdrawal that more than eight years of Soviet involvement had not been a mistake, as the Afghan economy and the situation of ethnic minorities had improved in its wake.[115] Similarly, Vladimir Kriuchkov, deputy KGB chairman responsible for Afghanistan, held that the intervention had been correct.[116]

Discussion of the pros and cons of the Soviet intervention became more pressing after the withdrawal was completed. At the Congress of People's Deputies, elected in spring 1989,[117] the chairman of the Ukrainian Council of Veterans, Serhii

Chervonopysky, charged Gorbachev with omitting "a political assessment of the war" in his report, although "all of us and perhaps the whole country and the whole world" were awaiting it.[118] Other delegates inquired why the issue of the intervention was being played down.[119] The congress suggested that the Supreme Soviet—the smaller and more permanent legislative body—form a commission and charged it with evaluating the decision to enter Afghanistan and reporting at the congress's fall convocation. Early that year, the Politburo authorized its Afghanistan Commission to prepare a summation based on documentation of "all stages of the events in Afghanistan," beginning with the decision to introduce Soviet troops.[120]

On a visit to Kabul in August 1989, Shevarnadze told the Afghan Bakhtar Agency that "no one in our country doubts that Soviet assistance was and remains vital to Afghanistan. But, like many others, I personally ask myself this question: Could the Afghan national-democratic revolution have defended its gains relying solely on the national armed forces and the support of the Afghan people—given, of course, our comprehensive political, moral and material support?"[121] Shevarnadze went on record as condemning the intervention, telling the Supreme Soviet in October 1989 that it had violated "our own legislation" and "Party and civil norms and ethics."[122] Later he called the war "a sin."[123]

In the framework of the mandated "political assessment" and after a thorough examination of documents and relevant individuals, on December 24, 1989, the USSR Supreme Soviet Joint Committee on International Affairs stated categorically that the decision to intervene in Afghanistan deserved "moral and political condemnation." The complicated international situation and the "excessive ideologization of Soviet foreign policy activity" did not justify sending Soviet troops into Afghanistan. The way the decision was made—by a small circle of four people: Brezhnev, Ustinov, Andropov, and Gromyko—contradicted the USSR's constitution. Yet it was insufficient to blame just these individuals. The crux of the problem lay in "serious flaws in the system of determining practical policy and in the decision-making mechanism."

The committee went on to note that New Thinking excluded any such action outside "the people's control" within the "highest bodies of power." The committee's condemnation of the 1979 decision "casts no aspersions" on the officers and soldiers dispatched to Afghanistan, who were "convinced that they were defending their mother country's interests and providing friendly assistance to a neighboring people; they were merely fulfilling their military duty."[124] The Congress of People's Deputies approved the committee's verdict and authorized the relevant bodies to take all necessary measures to prevent the recurrence of similar misdoings. It also empowered the Supreme Soviet "to consider" forming a commission to review the affairs of former servicemen in the Limited Contingent and instructed the Council of Ministers "to work out a state program aimed at resolving questions related to arranging [their] lives and living conditions . . . and those of the families of the fighting men who died."[125]

Another issue that the congress raised was the falsification of facts surrounding the war, specifically regarding official casualty figures. The people, one deputy insisted, must know the full truth. The Supreme Soviet also addressed the issue of remembering those who had fallen.[126]

The public discussion was not to the military's liking. A number of generals feared that it would drive a wedge between society and the army, whose prestige had suffered greatly from the war. In particular, it found the analogy between Afghanistan and Vietnam an anathema that implied the defeat of a superpower at the hands of a Third World guerrilla army.

But through New Thinking, Moscow concluded that military conflict was no longer an option—that even American involvement in Afghanistan did not warrant Soviet military intervention—and that victory for one side of a conflict inevitably led the other side to try to correct the situation. In other words, the debate about whether the Soviet force had been victorious had become irrelevant.

One scholar concludes that domestic pressure was what induced Gorbachev to pull out. But, she contends, the pressure came not from below but from "progressive elements in the Gorbachev coalition and from their understanding of economic and social realities." Andropov brought some of these people "in on the issue of the war in Afghanistan as early as 1983," but most of them came in late 1986. Their input carried weight, even though just three men—Gorbachev, Yakovlev (one of the men Gorbachev promoted), and Shevarnadze—made the decision to withdraw. By "empowering the experts who articulated the need for reform," Gorbachev enabled them to influence the "political environment, making old policies like the war in Afghanistan increasingly out of step with new policies of reform."[127]

The Authorities' Attitude toward the War's Veterans

The authorities' attitude toward the returning veterans fluctuated with the official position on the war, and was at best ambiguous. Both the media, which for most of the war were strictly controlled, and the material reality reflected this ambivalence.

In the early years, the afgantsy had participated in an unacknowledged war. Therefore, they could not be war veterans but were instead, "internationalists" or "internationalist fighters"; the halo of "veterans" was reserved for those who had fought in the Great Patriotic War. In this period, afgantsy's demobilization papers often failed to mention their participation in combat.[128]

On January 17, 1983, however, after three years of fighting, the party and General Secretary Andropov issued a special decree—"On entitlements (*l'goty)* to servicemen, workers, and employees within the structure of the Limited Contingent of Soviet Troops on the territory of the Democratic Republic of Afghanistan and their families,"[129] a de facto acknowledgment of the war. The decree was revised under

Chernenko on July 26, 1984, making the new text more specific about the sums and entitlements for each category of serviceman.[130] Yet while the regime now formally recognized that it owed them a debt, the decree lacked clear implementation procedures. It seems to have been distributed to local party organizations and *voenkomats* (military commissariats), allowing the civilian local authorities and factory managements responsible for distributing the material benefits to ignore it—if they were even aware of its existence and content.

In 1984, following the article "*Dolg*," the first article in a central newspaper to describe the hard lot of disabled *afgantsy* (see Chapter 6), and prior to the above revision, Chernenko, who had recently succeeded Andropov, instructed the party's political apparatus to review the returning veterans' situation with an eye toward helping them to receive their due material benefits and political legitimation. In the course of this "review," the party expelled thirty-two people in Ukraine alone for their "callous attitude to the afgantsy"[131] (the case of the invalid veteran behind *Dolg* had occurred in Ukraine). In summer 1987, CPU CC Secretary Aleksei Titarenko gave specific examples of officials in Ukraine who—following the *Pravda* article, "I Didn't Send You to Afghanistan" (see Chapter 6)—had been punished or reprimanded for "shortcomings" in this regard. The Ukraine CP CC, moreover, issued instructions to party committees to increase their monitoring of the fulfillment of decrees regarding benefits for the veterans and their families and advised party and Komsomol organizations "to involve internationalist soldiers more extensively in social and political life."[132] In this same period, the CC of Tajikistan's CP called on local officials to step up activity in order to give the vets their legal due.[133]

No longer able to sweep the war completely under the carpet, in 1984 and 1985, the authorities opted for a path that they hoped would appeal to the public and assuage the disaffected veterans—allowing the media to describe the heroic feats of soldiers of the Limited Contingent. While never equating them with the veterans of the Great Patriotic War, the party-state, and particularly the Komsomol, promoted this highlighting of the bravery of the current generation's "internationalist soldiers" who trod in the footsteps of their fathers and grandfathers four decades earlier. In the words of one scholar, the authorities encouraged Afghan War vets to succeed the GPW vets "as the guardians of military and patriotic tradition," even as it denied their legal status and therefore their entitlements.[134] In his February 1988 statement announcing the withdrawal timetable, Gorbachev praised the soldiers in Afghanistan who fulfilled their duty with "selflessness and heroism" and had the people's respect. The state, he maintained, "provides them with priority opportunities to obtain a good education and interesting, suitable work," while "Party and state agencies are obliged to ensure that the families of the dead, their relatives and loved ones, are surrounded with concern, attention, and kindness."[135]

Attributing valor to the Fortieth Army was tantamount to elevating the status of the veterans in the eyes of the public and the establishment. Gorbachev—while evading the issue of whom to blame for the intervention—told the Supreme Soviet that the soldiers in Afghanistan "fulfilled their duty; all that the state, the country, instructed them to do, they performed honorably. This is not an issue for discussion."[136] The state remained committed to providing them with material assistance. The May 1988 CPSU CC letter on Afghanistan emphasized that the CC CPSU, "considers its first duty . . . to display maximum concern for the people who underwent the most difficult trials in Afghanistan, to properly evaluate the combat exploits and the military service of Soviet soldiers and officers who fought and served there, and to display concern for their daily needs and to more actively involve them in public activity."[137] The CC CPSU address to the soldiers and civilian workers returning on May 15, 1988, praised their fulfillment of their "internationalist duty" in Afghanistan, and summoned them to participate in perestroika, "the renewal of socialism."[138]

The following month, at the Nineteenth Party Conference, Gorbachev expressed gratitude to the soldiers, officers, and civilian specialists—"all whose fate has been affected and who have been singed by this war."[139] In August 1988, the minister of health signed a decree improving medical services for Afghan vets,[140] and in October, the Politburo resolved to create centers where internationalist soldiers could regain their health and return to work and social activity.[141]

That July, for the first time, the procuracy addressed the issue of the 1983 decree guaranteeing afganets privileges. *Izvestiia*'s correspondent acquainted himself with an MoD Central Finance Administration sheet stating that all Afghan War veterans were enabled to take a vacation at a time convenient to them, as well as a two-week leave without pay, to receive housing on a priority basis, and "category one disabled veterans . . . to receive housing without reference to the waiting-list." They were to get one-time entitlements, interest-free loans, and priority in obtaining a telephone, medical treatment, pensions, and other benefits, as were the families of those killed in the war. A procuracy investigation found that few people knew about these rights; they were stamped "secret." The document had been sent to four or five provincial officials "and then shelved." Some of the few officials who knew the law deliberately refused to grant rights or did so in an inhumane fashion, even regarding the disabled. Procurator General Aleksandr Sukharev admitted that his office had "come to [its] senses late. . . . It's essential that we look into every case and initiate criminal proceedings" against those who violated the regulations.[142]

The following month, the Soviet government published a resolution obligating local governments to fulfill commitments—employment, housing, and pensions—particularly to the disabled and the families of those who died in Afghanistan.[143] Although in September 1988, the media detailed these benefits and privileges,[144] RSFSR

Minister of Social Security Viktor Kaznacheev confessed that the local government's responsibility was still expressed in very vague terms, making it necessary for veterans to rely on the goodwill of officials,[145] whose "inertia and inactivity" persisted.[146]

By this time, lack of funds, the increasingly chaotic Soviet administration, and the poor state of the Soviet health and welfare system often precluded adequate treatment even for invalid afgantsy.[147] Prime Minister Ryzhkov told the Supreme Soviet in 1989 that the government found it "very difficult" to implement instructions regarding measures for increasing pensions. The chairman of the USSR State Committee on Labor and Social Questions, V. I. Shcherbakov, pointed out—in reply to demands that the government pay Afghan veterans an amount equal to that of those of World War II veterans—that one can't compare a healthy young man able to work with older and weaker people who cannot.[148] Later that year, the Supreme Soviet allotted 2.4 billion rubles for the pensions of veterans of World War II and former soldier internationalists, that is, soldiers who had participated in later Soviet military interventions. Although "we don't have a great deal of money" and problems of implementation persisted, particularly regarding housing, the deputy head of the MoD Central Finance Administration, Major General Nikolai Bai, confessed, the state resolved to provide the pensions and benefits "to ensure that all veterans lead a normal life."[149]

Statements and resolutions clearly did not make privileges easier to come by. When one disabled veteran had finally assembled the necessary documentation to prove that he had the right to receive an apartment for himself and his wife and daughter, the chairman of the village soviet agreed to put him on the list, but said that he would have to wait at least ten years. When the man protested, the official told him bluntly, "Young man, your *l'goty* are a fiction. Everything depends solely on me. If you bristle and shake your rights at me, you will lose your turn completely."[150] In Cheliabinsk Region, 497 families of Afghan War veterans were still without apartments in 2015.[151]

L'goty included grants for professional training and retraining and lowering university admission standards in order to encourage afgantsy to study. One student believed this was in order to assuage their frustration at the difficulty of implementing their privileges. "They were frightened of us, because they knew that if we organized, we'd fight for our rights and they'd have to give us flats and so on."[152]

The afgantsy found even the medals they received to be a source of chagrin. In 1988, the USSR Supreme Soviet Presidium decreed that the veterans of the Afghan War would receive not a campaign medal but a diploma and badge for "fulfilling their internationalist duty." Generals Boris Gromov and Ruslan Aushev, both of whom had been decorated Hero of the Soviet Union, appealed this decision, which "in the stratified, prestige, and status-conscious world of the USSR . . . represented a clear devaluation of their experiences." Many of those awarded medals "had to campaign long and hard, often in the pages of newspapers or magazines," to receive them.[153]

Pravda published an article entitled "Afghan Pain" that included the announcement of Gorbachev's support of the request of a "regional gathering of parents and widows of Soviet soldiers who died while fulfilling their internationalist duty in the DRA." They asked for an official document confirming their right to veterans' benefits and publication of data on the Limited Contingent's losses so that those who died could be recognized posthumously and those who had decided to intervene be called to account. The article's author presented tenets that one can assume had official backing. The first was that no one held either those who died or those who returned responsible for "the actions of those who, behind the people's back, decided to send a force into a foreign country." The second, that under no condition might "a group of individuals, even those with supreme power, make such decisions without Supreme Soviet approval." And the third, "that attention and care . . . be lavished . . . on all international fighters and disabled veterans, along with their families, and on the families of those who died."[154] This had broad implications, as the campaign on behalf of the Afghan War veterans brought recognition to the vets of previous Soviet combat operations conducted under the guise of "international aid" (e.g., in North Korea, Algeria, Egypt, and Vietnam).[155]

In line with Gorbachev's expressed concern for the war's veterans and in contrast to Soviet tradition, in July 1988, Procurator General Aleksandr Sukharev announced an amnesty for POWs captured while serving in Afghanistan. The amnesty specified that afgantsy returning home from captivity "will enjoy in full all political, social, and other rights of Soviet citizens stipulated in the USSR constitution." This included those "who could not withstand hostile propaganda, who did not stand up to torture and the deprivations of captivity and committed unlawful actions to the detriment of our state."[156] The previous month, Major General Valentin Khrobostov of the MPA said that Stalin's time was over and no "repressions or punishments" would be inflicted "upon our officers and men who have seen action in Afghanistan, escaped, and returned home.. . . Back home they are guaranteed normal lives and jobs."[157]

This new, positive attitude toward those who fought was not strong enough to bring Gorbachev or any other member of the country's leadership to Termez to greet the returning soldiers during the withdrawal (see Chapter 3). They made do with official statements of welcome, lauding the honorable and courageous way the soldiers had defended their country's southern border and Afghanistan's people and sovereignty.[158]

In 1989, the USSR Supreme Soviet Presidium adopted a resolution reaffirming Sukharev's statement that servicemen captured in Afghanistan who returned to the Soviet Union would not forfeit their civil rights under the Soviet constitution and would be "relieved of criminal liability" for any crimes committed. The Politburo approved a draft Amnesty for Former Servicemen in the Limited Contingent of Soviet Troops in Afghanistan Who Committed Crimes and Were Captured by the

Afghan Opposition in August 1989; after lengthy debates, at which many delegates argued against unconditional amnesty for deserters, the Supreme Soviet passed it in late November.[159] The amnesty covered all soldiers who had committed crimes in Afghanistan, including the 2,540 already convicted.[160]

In 1989 too, a nationwide campaign attempted to help the soldiers who had returned from Afghanistan find work. The campaign, entitled "Trade Unions—For the Internationalist Soldiers," aimed, in the words of the secretary of the Turkmen Council of Trade Unions (TSPS), "to alleviate the situation of the internationalist soldiers who will now be able to join work collectives."[161] All union republic and oblast trade union councils and all trade union primary organizations were to participate in the campaign by initiating special concerts, trade exhibits, and sports events to raise money for rehabilitation centers.

While all republics were responsible for paying pensions, some seem to have taken the initiative to alleviate the lot of the returning soldiers.[162] But for the most part, as the Soviet Union fell apart and after its demise, the war's veterans received little assistance, apart from free public transportation, and some easing of entry examinations into institutions of higher learning. An analysis prepared for the Supreme Soviet Committee for the Affairs of Soldier-Internationalists stated that "the state, having created the 'afgantsy' . . . does not only not know how to rehabilitate them, to bring them back to a normal life, but for a long time did not seriously think that this needed to be done."[163]

The state, then, failed to provide adequate support for those who fought in the war and for their careers. By 1989, in the words of Galeotti, the afgantsy "had too low a priority" among the Soviet leadership, after "Chernobyl', food shortages, inter-ethnic violence, and the collapse of the Party's ability to govern."[164] In the words of Prokhanov, "that contingent, upon returning to the Motherland, was rejected by the state."[165]

Just as it was the Soviet political leadership that sent the Soviet troops into Afghanistan, so it alone could extricate the country from its intervention in the Afghan civil war. The decision to intervene simmered for months, but once made, implementation was immediate. It took longer to decide to withdraw, and that outcome was delayed repeatedly until domestic and international constraints unconnected to the war forced the Kremlin to act. The way the Kremlin reached and implemented both decisions reflected the Soviet domestic power constellation at the time, as did the leadership's conduct toward the officers and men it sent into Afghanistan.

Undoubtedly Gorbachev anticipated that the decision to withdraw would bring benefits in the international arena, especially in an era of a constant dialogue with the United States, specifically with President Ronald Reagan and Secretary of State George Shultz. Yet the evidence indicates that this was incidental to the domestic considerations. The decision to withdraw brought Gorbachev public support, although the statement that, "in this country, all were sincerely unanimous in giving their support to this decision"[166] was an exaggeration. The momentum of Gorbachev's reforms and the introduction of reform-minded new blood into the Soviet leadership meant drawing lessons from earlier leadership mechanisms inappropriate for the late 1980s.

Chapter 5

The Implications of the Soviet-Afghan War for the Soviet Military

Like the political leadership, the military establishment found that the war in Afghanistan created new challenges. This was the first war in which the Soviet armed forces participated since the Great Patriotic War,[1] and it affected every aspect of Soviet military thought and practice—from operational doctrine and concepts, to the use of new weapons and technologies in combat, to relations within the officer corps and between officers and men, as well as army morale and discipline, and the prestige of the military among the civilian population. By giving combat experience to "a younger generation of upwardly mobile officers," the Afghan War brought into the military elite new blood tried and tested in war.[2]

In Soviet doctrine, "local wars," which the West calls "low-intensity conflicts," occurred in the imperialist context as wars of national liberation. In the words of the first authoritative Soviet recapitulation of the Soviet-Afghan War, "Our own significant experience of dealing with banditry in Central Asia through the years of Stalin was totally forgotten . . . and the rich, modern experience of other countries in conducting guerrilla and counter-guerrilla operations in regional wars, 1945–1980" was not studied. "Besides, our army had never been intended to fight in such circumstances. . . . That is why our soldiers, officers, and generals, sent to Afghanistan, were forced to discover . . . the tactical ABCs of the science."[3] The failure to plan and fight a war in the conditions of Afghanistan emanated from the Soviet military's belief in fighting as a "'universally applicable' operational art."[4]

Iurii Grekov, former Fortieth Army CoS (February 1986–August 1988), said shortly after the war's end that although much of what they had learned was specific to Afghanistan, the lessons were relevant to the general training of officers and soldiers, provided they were applied "creatively" to match the circumstances. It was only because of Afghanistan that he understood, for example, what it meant to land an assault force and that he came to look "differently" at aspects of larger combat operations in the sphere of "organization of command and control, coordination and troop support."[5] When Sergei Sokolov became defense minister in 1985, he maintained that the Afghan War's testing soldiers under fire was a blessing; he wanted all army units to have combat experience there.[6]

Already during the war, it had become clear to the Soviet military that it could, and indeed should, draw important conclusions from the mistakes of the Fortieth Army and the MoD. Some of these, as Sokolov, then deputy defense minister and head of the MoD Operations Group in Afghanistan, wrote to his chiefs in mid-1984, were not relevant solely to the conduct of counterinsurgency fighting in mountainous areas but to the Soviet armed forces everywhere (see Chapter 2. Sokolov did not use the term *counterinsurgency*, which was absent from Soviet military terminology; he spoke of fighting "counterrevolutionaries," which has clear ideological connotations). Or, in the words of the Soviet Kabul embassy military attaché, the Soviet military must not ignore the experience gained in Afghanistan but instead must draw from it generalizations that it could apply to the training of future soldiers and officers.[7] The military's readiness to learn from its mistakes was not unlimited, however. In 1986, one medical officer surveyed some 2,000 soldiers. His report to the GS was harsh in its condemnation of the war, particularly the inadequacy of the supply operation and the lack of psychological assistance for the troops. In return, he was accused of disloyalty and of deliberately setting out to gather facts that brought shame on the Soviet Army. The report was shelved, appearing only in 2008.[8]

The endeavor to transfer the lessons of Afghanistan to the Soviet army as a whole applied "particularly for units training in or expected to operate in mountain theaters." The Soviet military press also showed "a concerted effort to pass the lessons learned" by special troops—for example, the engineering, communications, and reconnaissance troops that "appear to have benefited most thoroughly from the DRA experience."[9] Soon after the final withdrawal, the Frunze Military Academy in Moscow compiled a handbook for the command and general staff officers of the Soviet armed forces in order "to capture the lessons their tactical leaders learned in Afghanistan and to explain the change in tactics that followed."[10] The Introduction to the English version explains that the Soviet army was "hard pressed to devise military methodologies suited to deal with the Afghan challenge," especially against the backdrop of the "changing political-military and military technical realities" of the 1980s "in the form of a technological revolution in weaponry, which produced the looming specter of a proliferation of costly high-tech precision weaponry." Rising to the challenge, "the Soviets formulated new concepts for waging war in non-linear fashion" that "required the abandonment of traditional operational and tactical formations, a redefinition of traditional echelonment concepts, and a wholesale reorganization of formations and units to emphasize combat flexibility."[11]

From afar, it looked as if the Soviets were successfully using new high-tech and high-precision weapon systems, notably satellites, for real-time and long-range targeting via space tracking.[12] In the field, however, the situation looked gloomier. One soldier who fought early on noted bitterly that new arrivals ignored their predecessors' experience, which they had gained at great cost.[13] In the words of one Western military analyst, although Soviet military journals demonstrated an awareness of the failings of the Soviet effort in Afghanistan, a wide gap persisted between tactical doctrine and tactical proficiency, while the Fortieth Army, particularly the motorized rifle divisions that were its backbone, showed no readiness or ability to abandon ingrained deficiencies. Similarly, the analyst noted little improvement "in regard to initiative, decentralization of decision-making to lower levels, or imagination in training programs." [14]

A NATO assessment of the Soviet achievements in the first six years of the tactical and "logistics war" in Afghanistan opines that while the war "stretched the credibility of Soviet combat power," it highlighted its "ability to sustain combat forces in a protracted conflict. . . . Both the long-range area planning and the day-to-day logistics operations conducted by [the] Fortieth Army reflects [sic] a flexible logistics infrastructure tailored according to the guidelines of Soviet logistical doctrine." Consequently, Soviet logistics planners "developed a highly mechanized logistics support system" grounded in "centralized planning and tailoring for logistics units, prioritisation of supplies, and the forward positioning of support elements." Given the centrality of Afghanistan's "underdeveloped road network . . . repair work on roads, tunnels, bridges, and passes [has been] a continuous challenge for Soviet construction units," which included "engineer and specialized road and rail construction troops." It also dictated extensive use of helicopter transportation, especially to "units and outposts located on the fringes of the logistics supply network," while an "extensive series of tactical pipelines," bringing fuel for the Fortieth Army, reached from Termez to Kabul. The maintenance of vehicles and helicopters also improved as the war progressed, necessarily, perhaps, because of the constraints of long-distance support systems.

On the whole, "the rear services . . . performed extremely well." Thus, "sustaining the 120,000 men of [the] Fortieth Army has proven to be the consistently successful aspect" in what had seemed a military debacle. "The inherent flexibility of the system, as opposed to the soldier, coupled with a massive allocation of resources and almost total exclusion of media coverage . . . has enabled the

Soviet Army to sustain a long war with a conscript army against an ill-equipped but determined enemy."[15]

A year later, a group of U.S. experts on Soviet military affairs also noted improvement in the Soviet supply system. Logistics had been "dramatically" upgraded, often with the help of helicopters, which provided support for outlying garrisons. Support units had learned to play a more active role in defending rear areas, while "engineering and maintenance units" had been "beefed up to raise their combat capability."[16]

The medical services found themselves especially challenged in Afghanistan. Although the combat casualty rate was remarkably low, that of noncombat casualties was extremely high as a result of "improper sewage, refuse treatment, contaminated water, and poor hygiene" (see Chapter 3). This apparently stimulated the Soviet armed forces in late 1983 or early 1984 to establish "Extraordinary Anti-Epidemic Commissions" to control health and hygiene in Soviet army units.[17] Other aspects of military medicine under attention were first aid and the swift evacuation of the wounded.[18] Just months after the final withdrawal, the medical service was reviewing "the way medical support had been organized for combat operations in Afghanistan" in order to improve the "practical training" of soldiers in "medical self-assistance and mutual aid" for immediate treatment of the wounded.[19]

Although it learned lessons that would strengthen specific military capabilities, "the inability of the Soviet military to win the war decisively condemned it to suffer a slow bloodletting . . . that exposed the very weakness of the military as well as [of] the Soviet political structure and society itself."[20] The failure of the Soviet force against the Afghan opposition undermined the soldiers' morale. This engendered a breakdown of discipline, led to criticism of existing procedures, and accelerated calls for reform. The servicemen's loss of faith in Soviet military prowess and of pride in the armed forces' performance destroyed their main source of psychological satisfaction from military service. What remained were perceptions of military incompetence, a heightened sense of the injustice and inequality inherent in the Soviet system, and increasing disenchantment with their poor living conditions. The general dissatisfaction in the ranks of the armed forces by the end of the 1980s must not, however, be attributed primarily to the Afghan War but rather to the curtailment of the military's manpower and budget.[21]

Officers also agitated for improved circumstances—better military professionalism and less party interference in military affairs. These officers took advantage of available media platforms to criticize the shortcomings of the strategy and tactics of the Afghan expedition.

During the War's Course

It quickly became evident that fighting in Afghanistan put the Fortieth Army in a special quandary. Afghanistan's geography, topography, and climate, coupled with the nature, traditions, and history of its population, dictated fundamental changes in Soviet military theory and practice. As the Frunze Military Academy manual noted, the Fortieth Army gained valuable combat experience and significantly expanded the theory and practice of combat in mountainous and desert terrain.

Paying attention to local conditions included encouraging the initiative of the men on the spot. One battalion commander reported that nothing was worse than having to adhere to stereotyped regulations.[22] The rigid, inflexible preplanning and discipline of World War II were simply unsuited to Afghanistan. In that sense, Afghanistan provided a taste of what the army might expect of the individual soldier in the future.[23]

Between the start of the intervention and early 1988, military journals devoted over one hundred articles to mountain warfare as it affected tank, motorized infantry, signals, sapper, artillery, chemical warfare, transport, air force, and, above all, paratroop units. Rather than creating a special mountain warfare force, these emphasized training for all branches of the army and a coordinated effort with the air force. Numerous articles in the MoD military-tactical monthly *Voennyi vestnik* based new theories of mountain warfare on the Afghan experience. Military colleges taught tactical innovations, including the need to give small units permission to make decisions independently during combat. In fall 1987, the GS designed exercises in the Transcaucasian MD to enhance the coordination of the armed forces' different branches and combined-command fighting in unfamiliar territory, drawing on its Afghan experience with mountain warfare.[24]

At the Nineteenth Party Conference (June 1988) Gromov pointed out that the war "has undoubtedly forced us, the military, to draw certain conclusions. First, we had to bring the men's operational instruction up to scratch, especially for mountain combat, to pay far more attention to the training needed for long marches, to learn how to conduct anti-mine warfare, to improve the methods of interaction between different categories of troops and to operate at night." Moreover, preconscription groundwork required "radical improvement," and "we need a more systematic and complex resolution of the task of moral and psychological conditioning and basic military training."[25]

After the war, one commander confessed that "already in Afghanistan, we admitted that our mine detection equipment was inexcusably low-quality." A new mine detector had been developed, but it was "cumbersome." A sapper was supposed to cover 60 kilometers a day but after two hours was ready to drop. "Mine warfare forced us to change our tactics and the structure of the columns' battle formation" in order to attain "the current structure of a movement support detachment."[26]

Another area where the Afghan War led to far-reaching improvements was the use of aircraft, particularly helicopters. L. Batekhin, colonel general of aviation and head of the Soviet Air Force Political Administration, told an *Izvestiia* correspondent in 1988 that "the Afghan experience improved [our] aircraft and helicopter tactics."[27] The helicopter's weaponry and protection were enhanced. Changes in its design allowed it a more effective role in the "missions and operations" that the troops executed in Afghanistan. As a result of its achievements in Afghanistan, the helicopter became "one of the central elements around which Soviet operational art and strategy [were] redefined."[28]

Over the course of the war's nine years, Afghanistan became the testing ground for a new air echelon, the combined arms battalion, "new, more flexible, logistical support concepts . . . and . . . such innovative tactical techniques as the use of the *bronegruppa* [armored group]. . . . The brigade, the material support battalion, and the *bronegruppa* emerged on the Afghan field of battle, reconnaissance diversionary [spetsnaz] units sharpened their skills, and air assault techniques were widely employed."[29]

Extrapolating from the experience of the Afghan War, *Voennyi vestnik* wrote in early 1989 that, "a battalion reinforced with artillery and air defense weapons (in all, up to eight attached subunits) is the basic tactical entity on the battlefield."[30] The Combined Arms Reinforced Battalions that operated in Afghanistan, where conditions dictated the need for autonomous or semiautonomous motor-rifle battalions with extra artillery and air support, bolsters this conclusion:

> The Fortieth Army experimented with combined arms battalions and motorized rifle companies. All of this was done to come up with an optimum troop mix for counterinsurgency and independent actions. Materiel support brigades and battalions were [also] formed to provide more effective support to the combat units. Airborne, air assault and spetsnaz forces were refitted with roomier BTRs and BMPs instead of their BMDs. The post-Afghanistan force structure for the Russian Army [i.e., in the years after the disintegration of the USSR] . . . envisions a mix of corps and brigades for maneuver war and non-linear combat and divisions and regiments for conventional, ground-gaining combat."[31]

The Soviet army's experience with counterinsurgency warfare in Afghanistan made some of the armed forces' structure much less rigid.

The 1980s saw the deployment of new weapons systems able to meet the more mobile, flexible approach necessary for the Afghan War. One was the BTR-60 armored personnel carrier (APC), which, in the words of one war analyst, "went through several incarnations" in the form of the BTR-70 and BTR-80. The BMP-1 carrier-combat vehicle similarly underwent changes, as the original had proved extremely dangerous in combat. Reportedly, the Soviets also added two types of Hind helicopters and replaced the AKM-47 rifle, a refined version of a German weapon from 1943, with the new AK-74, equally reliable but much lighter. Underneath the rifle, a soldier might fit the new BG-15 grenade launcher, or he might carry one of the new RPG-18 or -22 rocket launchers, a squad rocket-propelled grenade launcher (the RPG-16), or the RPO-A flame-rocket launcher. The AGS-17 automatic grenade launcher replaced the RPG-7 (in use since 1962) whose qualities suited it particularly to mountain warfare. The war was thus "an opportunity for tactical and technical experimentation."[32]

One Soviet military analyst who wrote on the use of the air force in the Afghan War, focusing on coordination between the ground and air forces, noted the importance of studying the achievements and the failures of this most important aspect of modern warfare in the conditions of Afghanistan.[33]

Several articles in the paper of the Armed Forces' Main Political Administration noted the combat advantages that the advanced technologies brought those able to use them.[34] The commander of the political department of a helicopter regiment noted the extent to which the combat experience of pilots and navigators raised the quality and efficacy of training. He described how each operation was different and how on returning from operations to their base in Afghanistan, the pilots would share their experience with all of the crews. He elaborated on the need for the establishment to apply these lessons in contemporary conditions rather than hiding behind irrelevant pretexts to evade changes in perceptions and regulations.[35]

The army assigned officers who returned from Afghanistan to posts that enabled them to direct their experiences to the benefit of the Soviet armed forces—often with promotion in rank. This brought new, relatively young blood into the ranks of the senior officer corps, which had been filled with people of World War II vintage.[36] Thus, the war offered a core of young officers opportunities for promotion and visibility.

Iu. Kuznetsov, a lieutenant colonel in the paratroop forces in Afghanistan became a Hero of the Soviet Union, a full colonel, and commander of the Central Asian MD Panfilov Motor-Rifle Guards Division. Viktor Kot, who commanded a subdivision of fighter-bombers in Afghanistan, also returned a Hero of the Soviet Union and took over command of an air force regiment. Shortly afterward, he was promoted to the rank of major general and deputy commander of the Far Eastern MD air force.[37] Lieutenant General Igor Rodionov, who became the commander of the Transcaucasian MD, introduced military exercises closely simulating battle conditions in Afghanistan. In this way, despite opposition from older officers, officers who had served in Afghanistan passed on their experience to young graduates of officers' academies, NCOs, and regular soldiers.[38]

The commanders of the two MDs that played a crucial role in establishing the Fortieth Army and supervising the intervention were also promoted. Colonel General

Iurii Maksimov, who in December 1979 commanded the Turkestan MD, became a full general and, in 1985, commander of the strategic rocket forces. In 1980, Petr Lushev, commander of the Central Asian MD, became commander of the Moscow MD and a CC member; later he was nominated commander of the Group of Soviet Forces in Germany and thus of the Central European Theater of Military Operations. Within a year he became deputy defense minister, and in 1989, the last Warsaw Pact C-in-C.

The career of Major General A. P. Lebedev, commander of the Turkestan MD artillery forces in 1979 and responsible for coordinating operations in Afghanistan and deriving tactical lessons from them, reflects the importance of the artillery in Afghanistan. In 1983, he was promoted to the post of deputy chief of artillery troops with special responsibility for combat training: "Possessed of a reputation as an expert on mountain warfare, he brought to his new post a commitment to developing the artillery's responsiveness to technological and doctrinal change and its ability to operate in new and rapidly changing environments and situations."[39]

While the army learned significant lessons during the war, there were also areas in which it made little progress. Some of the basic challenges that had long troubled the Soviet armed forces persisted during the war, notably incompetent behavior in the deployment of forces. The conditions of the Soviet-Afghan War highlighted and intensified these issues. William Odom looks at the war's impact on the discipline, readiness, and morale of the Soviet armed forces as soldiers and officers who had served in Afghanistan were "recycled" into military units throughout the Soviet Union. Odom is convinced that although not a crucial component, it "must have been more than a trivial contributing factor" to the problems that surfaced in the Soviet military in its last years.[40]

Gorbachev himself criticized the Soviet armed forces' performance in Afghanistan. The fact that seven years after the intervention the army had not achieved a resolution to the war was not to its credit. "Our military should be told that they are learning badly from this war. Can it be that there is no room for our GS to maneuver? . . . Are we going to fight endlessly as a testimony that our troops are not able to deal with this situation?"[41]

A few officers on active service expressed their concerns about the war and the army's performance. One officer who could not contact headquarters when he needed a helicopter suggested that the talk about aviation support for ground troops was just "chatter and theorizing"; surveying Vietnam had taught military theorists nothing, simply producing "articles and doctoral dissertations."[42] Colonel Vladimir Kovalevskii lost his military rank and party membership in 1986 for comparing the Soviet involvement in Afghanistan with that of the United States in Vietnam,[43] while Major General Kim Tsagolov met the same fate following his harsh criticism in a much-publicized interview with *Ogonek* in 1988 (see Chapter 6).

The War's Impact and Long-Term Significance

Almost certainly the Afghan War played some part in the leadership's late 1988 decision to decrease military expenditures and the size of the armed forces. The official backdrop to this measure included the huge defense expenditure during an economic crisis and the Soviet military's falling prestige. The Afghan War contributed to both.

The war also contributed to the political crisis of the Soviet Union's last years, with the role of the military in politics and its relations with society as important factors (see Chapter 10). Military journals and senior officers addressed these issues. In a democratic state, the military-theoretical journal *Voennaia mysl'* wrote in 1991, the army must be used in the people's interests; the situation that arose within society in connection with the use of the Limited Contingent in Afghanistan highlighted the impermissibility of sending Soviet troops beyond the country's borders without the sanction of the statutory authority.[44] In summer 1989, a senior military historian called for universal military service, but only if the Soviet armed forces did not fight outside the country. The Soviet armed forces were an army of the people created to defend the mother country.[45]

While even before 1979, some had noted the trends that would trouble the military leadership in the Soviet Union's last years, the war brought them to the fore, especially against the backdrop of glasnost. These included the media's discussion of the military's problems, including hazing and the use of drugs; the lack of professionalism; draft evasion; and disinterest in military service to the point of antipathy and the growth of an antidraft movement. The term *refusenik* came to describe people who declined to serve in the armed forces.[46] (Georgia and Lithuania were the republics with the largest numbers of draft resisters, but these existed in all of the non-Slav union republics, as well as in Russia itself, particularly in Moscow and Leningrad.)

An apology by Defense Minister Dmitrii Yazov, following considerable political pressure, poignantly highlighted a new relationship between the military and society. In June 1990, Yazov addressed the mothers of those killed in Afghanistan: "We lost to some degree the prestige that the Soviet Union and its armed forces enjoyed after the victorious Great Patriotic War, and also to some degree inflicted terrible pain on families and friends, on our own Soviet people."[47] This was humble pie indeed.

The conclusion that it should not send the army beyond national borders carried over to the Russian Federation that claimed to be the Soviet Union's successor state. In his memoirs (2002), a former military attaché at the Soviet embassy in Kabul, wrote that "the Afghan experience" must not be in vain. In the event of any future question of using the military on foreign territory, "our government should study profoundly and comprehensively" the political and military situation in the world and in the region at issue, and not ignore the opinions of specialists and academics. Moreover, "the adoption of a decision to use our forces on foreign territory must comply with the Russian Federation's constitution and be legalized with necessary legal documentation." The Kremlin must remember that the success of military actions depends to a large measure on the clarity of their strategic goal and the provision of well-defined assignments.[48]

His experience in Afghanistan, where he had been the commander of the VDV, changed General Aleksandr Lebed's attitude toward war, hence his opposition to the Russian Federation's First Chechen War (1994–1996). "The way they sent the Soviet army into Afghanistan," he told a British journalist in 1994, "was simply a crime. They had no idea of what they were getting us into, they knew nothing of the country or its people. . . . We had no real idea why we were there, or what we were dying and killing for."[49]

The top brass, however, focused on the war's lessons in the military sphere. Just months after the final withdrawal, CGS and First Deputy Defense Minister Mikhail Moiseev said that the armed forces would use the experience acquired in Afghanistan. The war had highlighted problems requiring immediate solution and others that would take longer to fix. These included raising the low standards of predraft preparation and increasing the basic training of recruits from three weeks to six months. He wrote that units intended for operations in a given theater must be prepared for conditions there, and that certain provisions "in our regulations and manuals regarding combat operations should probably be amplified and broadened."[50] Indeed, Moiseev—with Varennikov, Rodionov, Gromov, and Akhromeev, men whose careers had brought them to Afghanistan—belonged to the circle of progressive technocrats who aspired to achieve and maintain technological parity and therefore supported Andropov's, and later Gorbachev's, plans for reform.[51]

Perhaps the most prestigious military journal, *Voenno-istoricheskii zhurnal*, announced weeks after the final withdrawal that it was initiating a rubric, "Afghanistan: Results and Conclusions." Gromov wrote its opening article: "They protected, they taught, they built." Predictably, one of his goals was to demonstrate how professionally he himself had performed. Another was to highlight the efficiency with which the army schooled conscripts in "patriotism and internationalism," sentiments that—according to Gromov—the troops' hardships in Afghanistan had reinforced. Gromov praised the officers and emphasized the soldiers' confidence in them and their decisions, downplaying the mounting criticism leveled against the Soviet military. "Clearly, for a long time to come, the Afghan events will be a matter of close study by politicians, military historians, and the like. . . . The combat experience gained in Afghanistan and paid for in the blood and sweat of our soldiers, sergeants, warrant officers, and officers should actively serve the cause of restructuring [perestroika] in the troops and the cause of enhancing the quality of the personnel's combat skills and without fail be considered in organizing the training process."[52]

Major General Grekov admitted that during the war, there had been no occasion to reach "meaningful general conclusions." Unquestionably, however, officers had no alternative but to "relearn skills and some principles of larger combat operations" that should be applied in Soviet military study, even if weapons and conditions changed from one theater of war to another. Moreover, "the war compelled me, a person with fixed ideas and values, to look at our youth and officers with different eyes" and to appreciate them. Grekov called for giving "meaning to the combat experience acquired in Afghanistan . . . and to link it up with [military] science." He understood that the outcome of a battle is "in many ways predetermined by the preparation for it," specifically in communication and coordination. Much, moreover, depended on the authority of a commander among his troops.[53]

A Western assessment of the war's lessons emphasized that a guerrilla war, that is, counterinsurgency warfare, "is a contest of endurance and will. The side with the highest moral commitment will hold the ground at the end of the conflict. Battlefield victory is almost irrelevant." Air domination too is irrelevant unless precisely targeted, whereas secure logistics and lines of communication are essential. Furthermore, conventional tactics, equipment, and weapons required major adjustment or replacement in Afghanistan, while the conventional "war force structure" was "inappropriate." In such a war, tanks were of "little value," while "light infantry and engineers [were] at a premium" and medical support "[was] paramount." Logistics determine "the scope of activity and the force size either side fields." Finally, the "information battle is essential to maintaining external and internal support."[54]

Not all of the war's after-effects in the military sphere involved lessons learned. Some were more general developments that the war expedited. Thus, the war accelerated the rise of new commanders, eager to make themselves felt in a time of change; it exposed problems and weaknesses within existing military thinking; it provided a reservoir of combat experience at a time when next-generation weapons, vehicles, and communications systems were affecting Soviet doctrine; and it compelled the MoD and GS to deal with low-intensity warfare at a time when perestroika was sparking severe unrest within the USSR.

Certainly there were different appraisals of the value of the Afghan experience for the Soviet armed forces as a whole. Many professional soldiers viewed the conditions there as so different from other potential theaters of war that long-term lessons were irrelevant. Facing irregular armed formations was considered so atypical that the new manual prepared for the spetsnaz in 1991 included no guidelines for fighting them.[55] The military press, however, advocated ensuring that the experiences of Afghanistan be reflected in the field, indicating that the MoD and GS attributed great importance to this. Indeed, several of the more senior officers became generals, either during the war—like former commander of a helicopter regiment, Vitalii Pavlov, and former commander of a paratroop division, Albert Sliusar'—or after it. Others were sent to various military districts,[56] most famously Igor Rodionov, who as commander of the Trans-Caucasus MD, had to cope with the Tbilisi demonstration in April 1989, and Boris Gromov, appointed commander of the Kiev MD three days after returning from Afghanistan.[57]

In addition, many afganets officers took teaching positions in military academies. Colonel General Rodionov became head of the Voroshilov GS Academy. Another afganets general who headed a military educational institution was Sliusar'—the Riazan' VDV Academy, where he emphasized the need for afgantsy students and teachers to promote the lessons of Afghanistan. Returning from Afghanistan, Colonel General Vladimir Ostrov was appointed chief of the Military Education Main Administration, with specific instructions to "revamp the system to take the new lessons into account."[58] Some officers of the tank corps proceeded from Afghanistan to the Moscow Malinovskii Academy of Armored Troops; several returned to the war after study.[59]

One officer brought from the war to teach at the Frunze Military Academy emphasized the human side—the qualities necessary for a commander who must win the confidence of his men and demonstrate initiative and daring. In his view, the more technology advanced, the greater were the demands on officer and soldier who had to undergo more professional and more arduous training.[60]

Thus, the opportunity to test theory against real combat and to develop new concepts for the high-mobility, air-land war of the late twentieth and early twenty-first centuries that Afghanistan provided prepared the ground for using the armed forces to keep the peace at home in the Soviet Union's last two years. It also laid down the doctrine, the intellectual framework, and military capabilities that would allow Moscow after 1991 to "adopt a forward policy in imposing its will on the successor states."[61]

When, however, the Russian Federation contemplated the First Chechen War in 1994, it appeared not to have internalized the lessons of Afghanistan. The Russian armed forces were again poorly trained, and their weaponry was still largely obsolete. The army again underestimated the fighting ability and determination of "backward" mountainous tribes, and the troops found themselves killing large numbers of civilians, including women and children. The main difference seems to have been that the Russian force in Chechnya had a lower percentage of eighteen- and nineteen-year old conscripts than had the Fortieth Army. Moreover, the extent of draft evasion was considerably higher in the 1990s than it had been a decade before as a result of sociological trends among Russian youth. A British observer noted that "Moscow's educated youth" had "a positively encyclopaedic knowledge of the various medical and legal ploys" by which to evade the draft. Widespread social protest against the use of conscripts in fighting garnered considerable publicity in the context of the mothers' movement, which had gathered momentum during the Afghan War and used its voice in January 1990 when women in southern Russian cities protested against sending local conscripts to suppress nationalist uprisings in Azerbaijan.[62]

The loss of faith in the military that was a direct and significant consequence of the Afghan War reflected the population's attitude to the entire Soviet system. The increasing skepticism regarding the regime reflected in turn on the military, which had always been a bulwark of the regime and subordinate to the party leadership. As the latter sought to reform the system, it was natural that the military should be one of its main victims. The army's "restructuring," notably, its reduction in size as Gorbachev cut military expenditures, also served to display the Kremlin's new face.[63]

The implications of the Afghan War for the Soviet military were multifaceted. They were technological—dictating the modernization of weaponry and equipment; administrative—with the war underscoring the imperative of greater efficiency, from mobilization procedures through the supply system and the need to heed nutrition and hygiene requirements; and social—affecting relations between senior and junior officers, between officers and men, and among the soldiers themselves. The lessons of Afghanistan pertained not solely to tactics, according to one analysis, but also to the higher levels of "operational and strategic thinking and practice," triggering changes in force structure, operational art, command and control, the role of intelligence and surprise in warfare and logistics, and the support services.[64] More broadly, the war underlined the deficiencies of a rigid hierarchy that prevented the military establishment from influencing the political leadership even when professional considerations were crucial, traditional "Marxism-Leninism" perceiving the military as a tool that the party could use to implement the policy *diktat* of the prevalent ideology. The war also undermined the military's prestige within Soviet society, ultimately contributing to the erosion of the party's authority and of the system with which the military was identified.

The media reflected some, but far from all, of these lessons, particularly in the war's last years and in its immediate aftermath. And even when it did not address them directly, acute observers could discern indications that the war was responsible for transformations in the role of the military and its relations with the political leadership and with society.

Chapter 6

Coverage of the War in the Soviet Media

Media coverage of the war became a major issue among the Soviet population, not solely within the country's leadership. This chapter looks at how and why this came about. Particularly it seeks to gauge the contribution of the media's coverage of the war to the evolution of glasnost, Gorbachev's policy of "openness" or transparency.

By the early 1980s, most of the intelligentsia recognized that the Soviet media were presenting a warped picture of events. As the saying went, "One could find no truth in *Pravda* (Russian for "truth") and no news in *Izvestiia* (Russian for "news")." (The former was the party's daily, the latter the government's.) Some people refrained from reading newspapers altogether (a Soviet physics professor at Moscow State University told me in summer 1979 that he never so much as looked at a paper for it contained only lies).

The Soviet-Afghan War brought the matter to the forefront. The Soviet media provided the main source of information regarding the war to the bulk of the Soviet citizenry. In 1984, a survey of the adult urban population demonstrated that over 50 percent got their news from the press, 42 percent from Soviet radio, 38 percent from agitprop meetings and word of mouth, and 33 percent from television. In that same year, however, 40 percent also tuned in to Western broadcasts.[1] By the end of 1985, the Soviet public was reportedly turning increasingly to non-Soviet publications and media, specifically, Western radio stations, samizdat publications, anti-Soviet literature smuggled in from abroad, and accounts of soldiers returning from the war.[2] Two years later, TV and the radio had changed places, reflecting Gorbachev's—and Yakovlev's—emphasis on television as the most powerful instrument of change;[3] the former now reached 50 percent of urbanites and the latter 26 percent, while word of mouth was up to 46 percent and agitprop meetings down to 15 percent.[4] Commenting (apparently in 1987) on these changes, Ellen Mickiewicz attributes "the very high place on the [TV] news agenda that Afghanistan holds" to the "ripples" created by "information about the fighting . . . seeping back through those who have suffered its effects," making "this issue a serious liability for Gorbachev's policy of persuasion and mobilization."[5]

Control of the media had always been critical to the Bolshevik regime, and all the more so during times of war. The party made mass media one of the fronts on which it waged the Afghan War, acknowledging propaganda as a major weapon. While it primarily directed this propaganda abroad, particularly to Afghanistan, a series of resolutions addressed the coverage in the domestic media of both the decision to introduce troops into Afghanistan and their retention there.[6]

This chapter shows how the war moved from being an "unknown war" (1979–1984) to becoming a "heroic war" (1985–1988), and ultimately (1989–1991) an "unnecessary and shameful war."[7] (The periodization—that of fifteen "expert" journalists, publicists, and writers—is inevitably an oversimplification.)

The Rules of the Game

Within days of the decision to intervene, conforming to standard Soviet practice regarding controversial issues, *Pravda* refuted reports from abroad regarding a Soviet military presence in Afghanistan as sheer fantasy.[8] During the week preceding Amin's assassination, party lecturers traveled the USSR reporting an anticipated American landing in Kabul. And almost immediately after the intervention, in January 1980, the Politburo adopted a secret resolution laying out precise guidelines regarding what the Soviet media could and could not mention. Above all, there was no war, just "internationalist assistance" to Afghanistan. Descriptions of military operations could not include more than one platoon, and in order to underline the small nature of operations, they could only mention privates and junior officers. They could report casualties only in exceptional cases.[9] Before this resolution, *Pravda* merely published verbatim a Radio Kabul announcement that in light of provocations by Afghanistan's enemies, the Soviet Union had "complied" with the DRA government's request to provide it "immediate political, moral, and economic assistance, including military assistance."[10] The Soviet troops there were fulfilling only peaceful assignments.

Until 1983, there was no official acknowledgment of Soviet participation in combat operations in Afghanistan. In the second stage, until 1987, the media publicized individual feats of Soviet "heroes." It was only in the last year and a half of the war that the hagiographic accounts ceded to investigative reporting and that the authorities sanctioned the publication of sentiments previously considered unpatriotic. Criticism of the war became widespread in the public discourse in the period immediately following the final withdrawal—from February 1989 until the disappearance of the Soviet Union in late 1991.

According to one Afghan veteran, who had meanwhile graduated from Tashkent State University's journalism department, the military press received instructions in January 1980 regarding what it could publish concerning Afghanistan; in particular, it was not to link the Turkestan MD to Afghanistan, military training, as it were, continuing there quite normatively. In mid-1980, a further directive sanctioned mention of individual courage in repelling dushman attacks but reiterated that DRA troops were conducting all military action. Early in 1983, the media were permitted to publish stories of Soviet soldiers accompanying convoys and repelling attacks while so doing, and to recount instances of bravery and of soldiers being wounded, but nothing about loss of life. Finally, in 1984, the censors let the media report on Soviet participation in fighting, but only at company level, raised at the end of the year to that of battalion—however, without any specifics.

Soviet journalists were allowed to fly to Kabul from the war's earliest stages. They were forbidden, however, to leave the capital. Censorship prohibited mention of Soviet units larger than the *pozdravlenie* (subunit); nor could correspondents refer to any commanders by name.[11] There were rare exceptions to these rules, however—one correspondent testified several years later that he had been in Kandahar in 1980.[12]

A journalist who visited Afghanistan "regularly" throughout the war described the quagmire in which correspondents found themselves as they sought to cover it. In both Kabul and Moscow, he writes, there were the journalists and "their bosses . . . those who wrote and those who controlled what was written." Articles were "edited mercilessly," with the "final touches . . . applied in Moscow by *Glavlit* and the central military censorship office of the General Headquarters of the Armed Forces of the USSR. Not a single news item, not a single article, could be broadcast or published without passing through these two obstacles." At one stage (apparently in the mid-1980s), he wrote a piece about a soldier who had lost both legs while saving the life of an officer. He took the article to the military censor, who told him to throw it away. "'Why?' 'Didn't you write a piece not so long ago about someone who got wounded? . . . That's quite enough. You've written about one, so there's no need to go on." 'But there are lots of wounded!' I exploded. 'Thousands of them!' 'And my limit for the number of pieces about them in the central Moscow press is four in the next six months. Four mentions of wounded. And nothing at all about anyone being killed.'"

In this way, two "propaganda rulings" of Mikhail Suslov, the CPSU CC Secretary responsible for ideology until his death in 1982, "proved to be especially resilient. The first was that 'Soviet forces were brought into Afghanistan at the request of the legal government of that country.' This axiom outlived its progenitor and the war.

The second, that 'Soviet soldiers take no part in military action, but merely stabilize the situation,' lasted for the first five or six years. After that, through force of circumstance and thousands of irrefutable deaths, it lost all credibility, and had disappeared from circulation by the war's end." Both the censors and the reporters did as the party ordered: "Collectively and individually, we did what was demanded of us . . . we drew an attractive picture of revolutionary Afghanistan, not forgetting to project the image of the Soviet soldier as a peacemaker." There were in fact instances of "soldiers' genuine kindness and generosity toward the Afghans, and sacrifices they made in their behalf. But removed from the main, tragic truth, even these instances seemed false."

When, in early 1983, the censors objected to a story about nurses saving the wounded, its author went straight to Akhromeev. The general told him that there was nothing to discuss: "We at the GS decide what and how the Afghan War is written about."[13]

One correspondent says that he and his colleagues became schizophrenics: "As a human being I want no part of the lies . . . that I accept as a journalist," but "it didn't work."[14] Other journalists also accepted the rules of the game; *Pravda* war correspondent Reserve Lieutenant Colonel Viktor Verstakov referred later to his resultant "silences" and "over-simplifications."[15] In 1987, another journalist wrote that his first working visit to Afghanistan had been in 1981: "I don't like to admit it, but it's true. The newspapers then wrote about the avenues of friendship that Soviet soldiers in Afghanistan were planting, about how Soviet physicians were delivering Afghan women's babies, and about how the Afghan army was successfully routing the dushman bands."[16] The armed forces of the DRA were doing all of the fighting, with Soviet troops providing support from the rear. Still, in 1990—in what were purportedly excerpts from the second edition of his diary—Verstakov insisted that not only did the Soviet troops not suffer in Afghanistan, they were happy to do battle on behalf of a just cause.[17] TV correspondent Mikhail Leshchinskii, who spent about four years in Afghanistan, stated after the war that he had not touched on fundamental issues—theoretical questions that belong to "Moscow salons"—but had tried to alleviate the feelings of citizens awaiting the return of "friends and relatives."[18]

As one analyst has said, glasnost–- might have happened without the war, but the war made it inevitable. Even before Gorbachev became General Secretary, growing public awareness of the war compelled the media to begin telling some of the truth—what came to be known as "glasnost from below." Official glasnost, moreover, descended on the world only gradually, with a dynamic of its own. Another stimulus to its evolution was the Chernobyl nuclear disaster in April 1986, regarding which information in the Soviet media was delayed and inadequate, making statements by Gorbachev and Yakovlev sound hollow.[19]

Gorbachev's growing emphasis on glasnost, however, enabled public figures to begin demanding the truth about the war. As Mark Galeotti has said, with information management a "key element in the maintenance of [elite] control," reporting on Afghanistan played its part in the "indirect struggle for power, role, and authority" that accompanied glasnost. "For professional soldiers, the war in Afghanistan underlined the folly of trusting military decisions to ill-informed civilians. For academics and analysts, it proved their point that they should be incorporated far more strongly into the decision-making process. For journalists, it presented the opportunity to invent [for] themselves credentials as independent-minded commentators by lambasting the very intervention that they had previously championed so obediently."[20] *Izvestiia* political observer Aleksandr Bovin, interviewed in mid-1989, dubbed glasnost as it was then as "semi-glasnost. One could now criticize what happened before 1985—for instance, the invasion of Afghanistan—but not developments or policy after Gorbachev came to power.[21] The military still controlled television reports from Afghanistan, censoring pictures sent by satellite and texts telephoned to Moscow, and war correspondents still depended on the Fortieth Army command to provide them with both information and transport. Yakovlev confessed that the political leadership resolved not to focus on the war's failure so there was little coverage of the aftermath of a failed war.[22]

Glasnost in its pure form implied telling the truth about the war, as it did about life in the Soviet Union. According to reformist sociologist Tat'iana Zaslavskaia, "We are, as it were, learning once again to look truth in the eye. . . . If one conceals from people information about the conditions under which they live . . . one cannot expect them to become more active in production or political life. People's trust and support can be acquired only if you show trust in them."[23] A long article in *Izvestiia* in late 1988 expounded on the dangers that result from concealing the truth from the public—erroneous decisions, the loss of accurate reference points, and people's disbelief when they finally learn the truth. It stated that politicians, scientists, officials—everyone—should know that times had changed and they could no longer get away with deceit; they would be accountable before the law.[24] Several months earlier, the article's author had censured "the super-secrecy with which the Afghan drama has been surrounded from the very beginning. . . . The war itself was, as it were, a military secret."[25]

USIA polls regarding the role that foreign broadcasts and rumor played in supplying information on the war emphasized the secrecy that enveloped it and the misinformation that encouraged rumormongering.

The Party Line

From time to time in the early period of the war, the Soviet media referred to the country's "limited military contingent" in Afghanistan, sent there in accordance with the Soviet-Afghan treaty of December 1978[26] and in response to Kabul's approaches.

Paradoxically, despite the stated danger to the Soviet Union's southern border, that contingent was not fighting but undertaking support assignments for the local population. This might explain why the theme soon disappeared from the press.[27]

The war was another example of the Cold War paradigm, with the Soviet Union supporting the "forces of progress," against local reaction backed by Pakistan, where the enemy was training, and which the United States armed and financed. In 1981, a justification for the as-yet-unacknowledged intervention appeared in *Pravda*, when it described the Afghan opposition as Basmachi.[28] The term evoked Soviet films about malevolent Basmachi engaging valiant Red Army soldiers in Soviet Central Asia in the 1920s and 1930s. Its use deliberately created the illusion that this was not an invasion of foreign territory and grew common when discussing the war in Afghanistan.[29]

By the time of Brezhnev's death, the media were "experiencing a growing crisis of legitimation as economic necessity, technological innovation, and international political developments combined to undermine the party's traditional approach to journalism and information policy."[30] Indeed, in 1983, media reporting on the war changed somewhat, with relevant items appearing more frequently. One scholar suggests that perhaps this was the result of the state's information management system succumbing to "the grapevine and foreign broadcasts." In these years—the early to mid-1980s—people gained access to a wide range of samizdat and even *tamizdat* materials. So while under Brezhnev there had been no fighting, under Andropov, Soviet soldiers were killed by mines[31] and there was "some fighting, invariably the result of perfidious attacks on Soviet soldiers on manoeuvres, and always concluded by a devastating Soviet riposte."[32] The Russian émigré paper, *Posev,* summed up the "new line" in reporting: "In principle, our soldiers are not participating in fighting but anything can happen—such is war. So, if you receive a coffin don't be surprised."[33]

During the short reign of Andropov's successor, Konstantin Chernenko, additional glimmers of truth began to appear in the Soviet media, although the new General Secretary was no reformer. A main breakthrough came in early 1984, when *Komsomol'skaia pravda*, the paper that seems to have devoted the most attention to the war, published the first article that addressed the problems of the war's veterans upon their return home. The article, entitled "*Dolg*," which means both duty and debt, detailed the tribulations of a seriously disabled veteran and the indifference of his hometown's officials. The concluding sentence pointed out that "scars form not only as a result of bullet wounds."[34] The piece was the harbinger of a number of articles decrying the lot of disabled and other alienated veterans. It had become impossible to sweep not only the war but also the lot of the returning soldiers under the carpet. CPSU CC Ideological Department official Vladimir Sevruk, who claims to have initiated this "slight lifting" of the "information veil," received a telephone call within ten minutes of the article's appearance: "Why is the

Party apparatus groundlessly finding fault, going against the army?" Sevruk went to Chernenko senior aide Arkadii Vol'skii, who asked him to draft a resolution in the General Secretary's name, instructing the Department of Party Organizational Work and the MPA (the Armed Forces' Main Political Administration—Glavpur) to spell out the facts in the article as a start to the necessary examination of the lot of internationalist soldiers throughout the country.[35]

This article proved to be a detonator. It drew attention not only to Afghanistan but also to the domestic scene. The returning soldiers became a weathervane for testing a system whose "faults" were becoming more blatant and "could be articulated in connection with the afgantsy."[36]

"*Dolg*" provoked a flood of letters to the newspaper's editorial office—969 within just two weeks. Apart from the sympathy of citizens all around the country, there were also "official replies," including one from the First Secretary of the relevant *obkom* (regional/oblast party committee), who stated that the officials guilty of callousness and indifference had been dismissed from their jobs and expelled from the party. He wrote that the insensitive treatment of the returning soldiers brought into the open "important moral problems." In a similar response, the First Secretary of the Ukrainian Komsomol Central Committee reported additional instances of officials whom the party had "sanctioned."[37] These admissions in turn brought the newspaper over 5,000 letters and telephone calls from afgantsy reporting that their problems with housing, employment, and holiday vouchers had suddenly been resolved.[38]

Within months of Gorbachev's coming to power, the party had loosened restrictions on information regarding the war, although it was still subject to the leadership's guidelines. On June 19, 1985, the KGB published a document signed by Valentin Varennikov, head of the MoD Operations Group in Afghanistan, and Vadim Kirpichenko, deputy head of the KGB First Department, entitled "A List of Information Permitted for Open Publication regarding the Activities of the Limited Contingent on DRA Territory." Reporters were now permitted to mention "the presence [there] of units and subunits, without describing their participation in military activity"; the "organization of and preparations for combat," but only up to company level; awards given to Soviet soldiers, but without specific mention of the activity for which they were being decorated; and the wounding and killing of soldiers in combat, but not more than once a month. They could mention soldiers' heroic deeds and instances of caring for disabled soldiers or the families of those KIA—but without any numbers.[39] The document was based on a list that Akhromeev at the MoD, Georgii Kornienko at the Foreign Ministry, and Vladimir Kriuchkov at the KGB had articulated following a CPSU CC decision of June 7. Deputy heads of the CPSU CC departments of foreign policy propaganda and administrative organs, Leonid Zamiatin and Nikolai Savinkin, endorsed it.[40]

Months later, without, however, mentioning glasnost, Gorbachev informed the Politburo that the party must change tack regarding information policy. The center would no longer tolerate reports that distorted reality with half-truths or sensationalism. It was time to present the stark facts.[41] Yakovlev followed up with a manifesto that called for "comprehensive glasnost."" "Exhaustive and operative information" was a prerequisite for society's further democratization.[42]

Gorbachev used glasnost as a weapon with which to pull Soviet troops out of the war. An article in *Izvestiia* in late 1987 said, "Of course our readers must be perturbed by . . . the presence of the Limited Contingent . . . on Afghan soil. This is evidenced by letters received in the editorial office."[43]

The greater laxity regarding media discussion of the war extended to other traditionally taboo topics as well. As the Gorbachev leadership allowed citizens greater freedom to express their opinions, the media began debating almost every controversial topic.[44] By the winter of 1986–1987, this included "the abortion epidemic," poverty, drug addiction, and Stalin's deportation of entire peoples.[45]

Yet editors still had to be careful about what they printed. In February 1988, Yakovlev conducted a meeting—apparently of the central press's chief editors and other key media figures—to issue guidelines regarding thorny issues. Yakovlev called Afghanistan "the most complex problem we are facing" both abroad and domestically. He quoted Gorbachev as saying that it affected many aspects of perestroika and transforming New Thinking into practical policy. Propaganda—the regime still regarded the media as an instrument of propaganda—had to be conducted with extreme tact, as the media presented the contours of the situation "to our people, to mothers, and to public opinion." It must portray Gorbachev's decision to withdraw as "a courageous step." There must be no talk of economic aid to Afghanistan, as if Afghanistan were yet another "hanger-on"; trade must be mutually economic trade. True, the war was not "particularly popular," but there must be no suggestion that it was "to no purpose," or "a mistake . . . God save us," or that Soviet boys had fallen or become maimed for nothing. Moreover, the media must defend the afgantsy, vindicate their "lawful interests," and give them a "tribune" so that through their stories, people would comprehend the complexity of Afghanistan.[46]

The First Five Years, 1980–1985

In this period, three main themes pervaded Soviet media reporting on "the undeclared war" that foreign aggressors had launched against the DRA.[47] First, the population had accepted the DRA regime; all opposition to it came from outside the country. Second, since the Soviet Union was assisting a popular regime, it could disclaim colonialist motives (which the United Nations attributed to it), as underlined by its commitment to leave as soon as the conditions that had led to the intervention disappeared.

And third, the Soviet Union's national security was at stake, and thus self-protection and self-interest coincided with its internationalist vocation.[48]

Within a week of the intervention, *Pravda* explained the Soviets' rationale, with the aid of a DRA government statement that spoke of U.S. hostility to the Afghan regime after it lost its bases in Iran. As a result of the threat to Afghanistan's sovereignty, Kabul had repeatedly requested Soviet moral, political, economic, and military assistance, to which Moscow had responded.[49] The newspaper also published excerpts of reports from various capitals (including Kabul) decrying opposition to the Soviet intervention.[50] Whether it intended this to assuage domestic opposition is unclear.

Less than a month after the intervention, *Izvestiia* correspondent Sergei Kondrashov spoke of "Moscow's forced and difficult decision to send troop contingents to Afghanistan" and disparaged the "widespread and false" canard that the decision was "a stage in some kind of long-term strategic plan" to reach warm waters and gain control of oil-rich regions.[51]

In summer 1980, Aleksandr Bovin wrote, "We would have ceased to be a great power if we refrained from carrying the burden of making unpopular but necessary decisions, extraordinary decisions dictated by extraordinary circumstances." The Soviet Union had had no option other than intervention in late 1979, when the achievements of the April coup were in danger. Moscow had to choose between sending in troops or letting the DRA collapse and the country become "a kind of Shah's Iran" with an American military presence that would challenge Soviet security. "There are situations when non-intervention is a disgrace and a betrayal. Such a situation developed in Afghanistan."[52] Eight years later, toward the end of the war, Bovin explained that he had perceived the introduction of troops as "an unavoidable evil that would produce maximum effect with minimum loss."[53]

The MoD and other publications followed the development of this "undeclared war unleashed by the forces of imperialist reaction." In 1981, the DOSAAF journal, *Voennye znaniia*, warned that Soviet soldiers might run into danger since "the counter-revolutionary forces paralyze the traffic on Afghanistan's roads, lay mines, put up road-blocks, stage ambushes." While helicopters had become the preferred means of transport, they too were "only relatively secure, for the insurgents are adept at making even this hazardous."[54] At the same time, throughout the first years of the war, the Soviet media persisted in emphasizing that only Afghan government troops were fighting and that the Soviet force was there just to help the Afghans repulse the external threat. A military correspondent's piece in *Pravda* in 1981 contained no indication of Soviet military activity. The only Soviet he mentioned was a military engineer assigned to oversee repair and restoration work on a war-ruined road.[55] Another piece, in 1984, described how a Soviet reconnaissance unit defended olive farmers from the insurgents, enabling them to harvest their crop. "All the dangers and tension the Soviet troops endured were more than compensated for by the peasants' friendship and gratitude. The Soviet soldiers were the first outsiders the Afghans saw as friends. . . . How can they regard as enemies Soviet soldiers who risk their lives to defend them and enable them to work and feed their families?"[56]

Thus the media mentioned dangers as if they were purely abstract. Reports focused on the soldiers' difficult living conditions, and even here they frequently softened the picture.[57] One 1981 piece in *Komsomol'skaia pravda* dwelled on the hard conditions of service in Afghanistan, playing down the element of danger and making no mention of casualties, although reporting a tank that had hit a mine.[58] Another tank had fallen into a pit—while delivering food to an Afghan village. Occasionally, however, the press indicated that the harsh conditions were adversely affecting morale and "political officers have to resolve quite a few difficult questions."[59] (Not surprisingly they did so successfully, as shown by the orders and medals they received.)

One unusual 1981 item by Vladimir Snegirev actually hinted that the Soviets were waging a real war in Afghanistan, with Soviet losses, and that there was meaningful resistance to the Soviet presence and the Babrak Karmal regime.[60] Yet it remained a cry in the wilderness. A lengthy article describing the 1982 offensive against the opposition in the Panjshir Valley focused on the DRA force and commanders; the sole mention of Soviet troops was a reference to military engineers and sappers clearing mines ahead of the Afghans' advance.[61] The Soviet reader had no way of knowing that many of those killed in the campaign were Soviet soldiers (Western sources told of the participation of 15,000 Soviet troops with between 300 and 400 killed).[62] Although this presentation completely distorted the reality, the Soviet press persisted in carrying pictures of happy Soviet soldiers building schools, hospitals, and orphanages, without mentioning that they were also engaged in combat that filled those orphanages. Soviet television spoke mostly of Afghan villagers offering Soviet soldiers kerosene and tea.[63]

When, for instance, opposition forces shot down Lieutenant General Petr Shkidchenko in early 1982, *Krasnaia zvezda* reported that he had died "in an airplane accident while fulfilling his official duty."[64] A short item in TASS that spoke of an "automobile accident" that happened "the other day" and led to a loss of life was in fact, the Salang Tunnel incident of October 30, 1982, in which there were 176 deaths, 64 of them Soviet servicemen. The article did not specify the number of casualties. or mention that any of them were Soviet soldiers, or that the cause was a Soviet officer's faulty command.[65]

Countless articles described the brutality of the dushmany toward their own countrymen,[66] told how the DRA forces enjoyed the upper hand in their war against the Basmachi,[67] and assured the Soviet public that the counterrevolutionaries were suffering defeat and that the situation was stabilizing.[68] Similarly, *Pravda* quoted Babrak Karmal's statement that "through the heroic advance of the Afghan army, the people's militia, and other security forces . . . there are no armed bands of any size left in Afghanistan today."[69] The public at home also learned that the dushmany laid mines that killed civilians, with the intent of stirring up the Afghan population against the Soviets. There was no suggestion that the Soviet troops were also laying large numbers of mines or that these were killing Soviet soldiers.[70]

Well into 1985, *Krasnaia zvezda* stated that there were no Soviet troops in "offensive units."[71] A sixty-minute documentary on Moscow TV in honor of the April revolution's seventh anniversary barely mentioned the Limited Contingent, which "is helping the Afghan soldiers guard the peaceful life of the population." It provided brief shots of Soviet soldiers clearing mines, doing medical checks on villagers, and talking informally with village youths, and showed Soviet soldiers at an awards ceremony in a field camp.[72]

Not everyone believed the media's distortions. A Soviet political officer serving in European Russia notes that in late 1980, a detachment was formed in his division to be sent to Afghanistan. "However much *Krasnaia zvezda* tried to reassure its readers that soldiers in Afghanistan were conducting regular training and maneuvers, the coffins that were coming in were testimony to something quite different—that a new war had flared up on the Soviet Union's southern border."[73]

After three years of fighting, partially truthful reports about the war began appearing in the Soviet media, albeit sporadically. People now learned officially that Soviet boys were being killed in combat in this bloody war against an unconventional enemy. In August 1982, the party daily mentioned feats of Soviet pilots in Afghanistan who risked their lives to save others, implying that such situations could arise.[74] *Trud* reported in February 1983 that Lieutenant Aleksandr Stovba, who had become a legendary figure after being killed in an operation against the dushmany in early 1981, had not died in a training exercise, as originally reported, but had sacrificed himself for his fellow soldiers, for which he was awarded the Order of Lenin.[75] In the same month, Snegirev reported in *Komsomol'skaia pravda* on three truck drivers losing their lives pulling a blazing truck loaded with TNT off the road, thus saving an entire column of trucks.[76]

At the end of 1983 and into 1984, the MoD daily admitted that Soviet helicopter pilots in Afghanistan underwent "combat training with daring strikes against the 'enemy'" and frequently carried "freights for Afghan friends . . . under dushman fire," and described in detail a dushman attack on a Soviet aircraft at a provincial airfield that left one person dead and several wounded.[77] In an article describing their routine, one Soviet helicopter pilot noted that while most of his assignments involved transportation of troops, equipment, provisions, and, of course, soldiers' letters home, they also included rescuing wounded servicemen, among them fellow pilots who had been shot down.[78] Indeed, in summer 1983, Soviet television ran a series called

Afghan Journal, which an American Moscow-based journalist described as "the closest Russia has come to telecasting a 'living-room war' . . . some of the violent scenes shocked the Soviets."[79] By 1984, there were stories in which Soviet troops were killed defending pipelines and highways.[80] Increasingly frequent reports spoke of sappers risking death to detonate dushman mines in Afghan villages.[81] While reportage of a 1984 campaign in the Panjshir Valley again attributed the actual fighting to the DRA army,[82] one article admitted that the Afghans turned for help "to their Soviet brothers, mine-clearing specialists" from the Limited Contingent, that one sapper had stepped on a mine, and that "everyone understood that he might be the next."[83]

Indeed, in the year 1984, several stories indicated hard fighting and casualties, describing the heroism of sappers, reconnaissance assault troops, and truck drivers,[84] and "difficult" situations in which soldiers took risks under fire.[85] Toward the end of 1984, *Izvestiia* recounted at length the story of two Soviet soldiers who had been taken captive, obviously as combatants, although the focus was on their captors' harsh treatment and the political and propaganda benefit that Western and émigré organizations sought to reap from them.[86]

Here and there, then, an item described Fortieth Army soldiers undertaking combat operations[87] or being awarded for "bravery and heroism." But these were the exception, not the rule.

Komsomol'skaia pravda was unusually forthcoming about the deleterious effect that the media's mendacity had on the soldiers in Afghanistan. Early in 1984, it published a letter from a soldier expressing his surprise how little the paper published about those "Soviet people who are honorably fulfilling their duty and not infrequently risking their lives for the sake of the bright future of the Afghan people," and who enable regular Soviet citizens to "live under peaceful skies" and go about their lives.

In short, in the months before Gorbachev became General Secretary, a change was gradually occurring. True, the media still transmitted the usual message that "the presence of the limited contingent of Soviet troops in Afghanistan combines the function of defending the Soviet borders from the approach of hostile imperialist and pro-imperialist forces with that of rendering internationalist assistance to the Afghan national-democratic regime, which repeatedly asked the Soviet Union for assistance in the struggle against the foreign intervention."[88] Soviet citizens read about the Afghan population's gratitude to their friends, the Soviet troops, and that this appreciation compensated the Soviet soldiers for what they were enduring. At the same time, the media continued to assert that "hostile propaganda" distorted the purpose of the Soviet presence and sowed hostility between the local inhabitants and the Soviet army.[89] Nor did it report the full horror of the war. One buried example was the fate of a motorized rifle division that was almost wiped out after a series of mistakes—it lost nearly 600 men in a single campaign in 1984. Many had frozen to death or been blown up by Soviet mines laid two years earlier; one battalion lost 70 men after misinformation led them into an ambush; Soviet pilots had bombed a division of paratroopers; and helicopter pilots had lacerated a motorized brigade, taking them for mujahidin. Such happenings simply could not appear in the press.[90]

Still, by New Year's Day 1985, there was more reporting about the war, even if pedantically censored, with the Komsomol press providing the greatest coverage.[91] One newspaper wrote that the word *Afghanistan* "worries and denies sleep to mothers whose sons in uniform, machine-gun in hand, are performing their sacred internationalist duty, helping the Afghan republicans in their encounters with the counter-revolution."[92] The Soviet press announced that the MoD had named twenty-one people serving in the Limited Contingent Hero of the Soviet Union, printing their pictures on the front pages of central newspapers. Twenty were officers and one a sergeant; seven served in motor-rifle units, seven as paratroopers, five were pilots—three of them helicopter pilots, one a motorist, and one unspecified.[93] Afghanistan was no longer simply a neighboring socialist country, where young Soviet men assisted friendly people in building a new life; it was a dangerous location where Soviet troops were being called on to demonstrate supreme courage, to the point of self-sacrifice.

The Last Four Years, 1985–1989: The Advent of Glasnost

Throughout the war, Soviet media remained the primary source of information for most Soviet citizens. Although disapproval of the war among those who had access to foreign radio remained meaningfully higher than among those who relied on Soviet reportage—with those using information passed by word of mouth somewhere in between— condemnation of the Soviet role in Afghanistan had grown markedly by 1987 among citizens who followed the Soviet media as well. Coverage of the war became increasingly realistic—perhaps as a result of complaints regarding the media's false narrative—"the graphic visual impact of television coverage" showing Soviet soldiers dying in combat clashed with previous idealized reporting. The media now revealed that the mujahidin were far from vanquished, reflected the domestic impact of the war, and probably fanned "the conviction that those troops should be withdrawn."[94] Yakovlev believed that presenting the war as an ongoing conflict would lead to "public distaste for fighting" and "disarm the political elites" who opposed withdrawal.[95]

The somewhat greater leeway accorded to war reporting that Gorbachev decreed just months after coming to power indicated that the new General Secretary and his advisers understood that the previous line had been counterproductive. Yet certain aspects of the war remained taboo. When a foreign correspondent enquired about Soviet losses at a press conference in October that year, the response was that Soviet troops were fulfilling assignments to protect the local population from the dushmany and defend important objects. They incurred losses when they were attacked and became involved in hostilities, but these were "insignificant."[96]

By now, even *Pravda* was reporting not only that Soviet soldiers were being wounded and killed but that some were taken prisoner, publishing an article on the killing of Soviet POWs in Pakistan after they revolted.[97] Another article reported losses to mines,[98] and yet another told the story of an exemplary officer, including the dangers and difficulties the Soviet troops were encountering.[99] MPA journal *Kommunist vooruzhennykh sil* published a self-congratulatory piece about Soviet soldiers conducting themselves valiantly in battle.[100] While still focusing on the bravery and courage of Soviet soldiers and officers, the media finally brought the war to the Soviet population with credible reportage showing that not all was going well.[101]

Toward the end of 1985, American correspondent in Moscow Nicholas Daniloff (accused a year later of spying) spoke of "shock waves from the long and costly conflict . . . beginning to rattle the homeland." Soviet forces were constantly being "stymied by the ill-trained, poorly armed mujeheddin." Gorbachev was allowing the media to "dramatically broaden coverage of the war, an about-face that has startled millions of Soviets." Gorbachev's "propaganda offensive" came "amid signs that Soviet citizens are growing tired of the steady casualties . . . in obvious response to increasing war weariness as the costs of the conflict are driven home." Public TV programs such as *I Serve the Soviet Union* highlighted "the courage, determination, and sacrifice of Soviet fighting men" with live scenes from the war. *Komsomol'skaia pravda* published a letter from a commanding officer to one boy's family: "You raised a real patriot . . . Excuse me that I wasn't able to save him"; and *Krasnaia zvezda* printed a letter from an Armenian mother who was proud to have raised such a son who "came through his greatest test with honor." Draft boards no longer required recruits to sign vows of silence when they returned home. "Now, quite the contrary," says a Soviet officer, "meetings are called to hear veterans tell how difficult conditions are in Afghanistan, how cruel are the attacks of the dushmany." Decorated Afghan veterans marched for the first time before the Soviet leaders in Moscow's Red Square on Revolution Day.[102]

Whether those who authorized the expanded coverage intended it or not, the army used the stories of heroism in battle to enhance the preconscript youth's identification with the "internationalist soldiers" and prepare them to serve. *Komsomol'skaia pravda*'s weekly supplement, *Sobesednik*, published pictures of those who died in Afghanistan and told of soldiers sacrificing themselves to save others. When a Moscow teenager asked, "Must everyone prepare himself for Afghanistan?" the paper replied that peace would come to Afghanistan and maybe not every young man would go to fight, but all had to prepare themselves for service to the mother country, for situations that demanded courage and selflessness.[103]

By summer 1985, the central press was reflecting official concern over draft evasion—not solely regarding Afghanistan—and insufficient "military-patriotic work" in preparing young men for army duty. Two generals wrote a *Pravda* article warning against "instances of lapsed vigilance and pacifist trends,"[104] while new regulations made it more difficult to evade the draft.[105] In 1983, *Turkmenskaia iskra* had reported that the legal adviser of the republic's Health Ministry was sentenced to five years of camp for getting her son released from military service and promising to do the same for another citizen in return for a bribe of 5,000 rubles.[106] In May 1987, *Pravda* admitted that sons of privileged party and government officials enrolled in academic institutions in order to avoid being drafted.[107] In November 1987, *Pravda* published a letter from a Moscow worker asking whether it was true that the war would have ended had children of the leadership gone to Afghanistan. The voenkomat commander explained that the army sent the most physically fit to Afghanistan and that the sons of the political elite tended to be weak. Yet, he confessed, "until recently, powerful pressure had been exerted to absolve the offspring [of party officials] from enlistment or at least to direct them to service nearer home."[108] In an "Open letter to those who attempt to protect their sons from the difficulties of military service," an officer of the Baltic MD condemned Lithuanians who forged medical records to gain deferment and parents who sought "'soft' assignments for their sons."[109]

The frequency of reporting on the war grew with the broadening of the topics that the media were allowed to cover. Until mid-1985, the MoD daily had run three to five articles and photographs per month. This doubled in the second half of 1986, and by early 1988 such items were appearing "almost daily."[110]

In 1987, the central press acknowledged two attacks that the Afghan opposition had conducted on Soviet territory, a report that would have been unthinkable earlier. The article's message highlighted the overlap between a soldier's "internationalist" duty to a "friendly people" or a new "people's democracy," and Soviet national security.[111]

Yet disinformation persisted even in the years from 1985 to 1987. The reports still emphasized the DRA army's triumphs against the dushmany[112] and attributed Soviet military successes to the DRA forces.[113] Two letters to *Pravda* from the crews of a tank and a helicopter said that *Pravda* published lies about "a battle in which, allegedly, our soldiers fought heroically. 'We were in that battle,' they wrote, 'and it was nothing like that.'"[114]

Some correspondents remained dissatisfied with the pace of change in reporting the war. Describing the increased attention to it in 1986, one journalist said that most items and articles were still dished up with the same old gravy.[115] Indeed, the censors in Kabul kept up the pressure until the war's end. In December 1987, reports of fighting around the besieged town of Khost did not hint that Soviet soldiers were involved.[116]

In summer 1987, a battalion commander in Afghanistan noted that Soviet TV was putting out false information about a successful cease-fire, the number of rebels surrendering, and so on, while Soviet soldiers and officers were being killed, and not a day passed without shooting. Of course, he added, it was easier to ignore the feats of men who died crawling under fire over a mine field to save wounded comrades.[117]

At the same time, most newspapers and correspondents, even while reporting the difficulties and price of the war, tended to defend the Soviet intervention and presence in Afghanistan. One ardent protagonist of the Soviet position contended that had the Soviet Union succeeded in saving the Spanish Republic in that country's civil war in the 1930s, Spain would have stood by it in the Great Patriotic War; ergo, the effort it was expending in Afghanistan was a strategic necessity.[118] The propaganda effort still entailed glowing pictures of the bright future that the April revolution was bringing the Afghan people.[119]

Yet the media seemed to be fighting a rearguard action. In late summer 1985, *Komsomol'skaia pravda* printed a letter from a citizen in Ukraine saying he failed to understand why his cousin was serving in Afghanistan. Colonel General F. Mazhaev read it out loud at a question-and-answer session in a plant in Kiev. He explained that Afghanistan was "our neighbor" with which the Soviet Union had "a vast border." The Limited Contingent was not merely enabling the Afghan people to protect the gains of their revolution, but was "also defending our country's interests. . . . Our soldiers, who are fulfilling their internationalist duty there, on Afghan soil, are defending their own Ukrainian, Siberian, and Kazakh homes as well."[120]

The dialogue between young Soviet civilians and the establishment was the backdrop to Gorbachev's dubbing the war "a bleeding wound" at the Twenty-Seventh Party Congress a month after *Izvestiia*'s Aleksandr Bovin called for changes in reporting that would reflect the transformations in the regime.

One or two newspapers took a special interest in the war and in those fighting it on behalf of the Soviet Union and lifted the curtain of silence, perhaps testing the new freedoms. In 1986, *Sobesednik*, of which Snegirev was the editor from 1985 to 1988, appealed to veterans to write to it about their war experiences.[121] During the course of that year, the paper published these personal stories, letters, and songs.[122] While the articles did not conceal the suffering and losses, they did not reflect the doubts that the soldiers might have entertained about their mission. But the year's end saw revelations that young people at home were disenchanted with the war in which "our boys are dying for nothing," and they had no wish to go and die. A young Muscovite doubted claims in the Soviet press that eighteen-year-olds were happy to fulfill their internationalist duty by fighting in Afghanistan. *Sobesednik* replied with an example of a boy whose "one dream" was to fight in Afghanistan, pointing out that, "duty is a measure of a person's freedom and happiness."[123]

In January 1987, the Ukrainian Komsomol *Molod' Ukrainy* published a letter from the mother of two draftees that criticized the Soviet role in Afghanistan and the way that the media depicted it. Having read an article about a soldier killed heroically in Afghanistan while fulfilling his internationalist duty, she stressed first that this was not the Great Patriotic War when soldiers died defending the mother country; second, only children of "simple workers" participated in the fighting, not children of officials; and third, journalists wrote of the war glibly, insensitively. The paper responded that journalists were not versed in dealing with this touchy subject; that it was important to remember the fallen; that many soldiers volunteered to go to Afghanistan; and that it was thanks to journalists that afgantsy, especially the disabled, were getting privileges comparable to those of World War II vets. In May, an article in the same paper indicated considerable opposition to the war and wide mistrust of the media.[124]

In summer 1987, *Pravda* published a letter from a father whose son had been killed in Afghanistan: "Our mass media . . . reflect the events taking place in Afghanistan very scantily, scrappily, even unrealistically in my view."[125]

Meanwhile, Gorbachev and his team were introducing personnel changes in the editorial staffs of a number of newspapers. In particular, Yakovlev brought Vitalii Korotich to edit *Ogonek,* which became the "most widely read source of investigative reporting."[126] These men, who departed from "old thinking," raised the circulation of their papers significantly.[127] In a 1990 TV interview, Yakovlev pointed out that glasnost was used to counter opposition to withdrawal from Afghanistan. "Suddenly, somebody had the idea of actually showing what was really happening. . . . Mikhail Sergeevich [Gorbachev] came down firmly on our side. 'Why not show it?' he said. 'Why keep it all secret? . . .' On the whole, this process of glasnost—applied to the war—helped us a very great deal in bringing closer the withdrawal."[128]

Writer Kim Selikhov published a generally conformist report in late 1987, although he included several critical comments; he bemoaned the Soviet public's indifference to the hardships of the Soviet soldiers and the lack of a memorial in Moscow to those who had fallen. He found the selling of Soviet uniforms and "all sorts of ammunition" at Kabul's bazaars "unpleasant" and was amazed that he "rarely encountered any grandchildren or children of writers, cultural figures, or high-ranking leadership officials in the subunits" he had visited.[129]

Ogonek pulled off something of a coup with Artem Borovik's stories from the war as he traveled from unit to unit in uniform. In July 1987, Hedrick Smith tells us, "Borovik caused a sensation by filing the first honest, graphic dispatches from the front. He described how the flower of Soviet youth was dying, their boots oozing with blood, their stomachs pierced by bullet holes, their armored vehicles crumpled by land mines. 'War tears the halo of secrecy away from death,' Borovik wrote in his 'Diary of a Reporter.'" For the first time, the readers of *Ogonek* could see the war from the inside. They could sit in the foxholes and feel the fear and loneliness of Soviet troops dying far from home. Borovik wrote about the cold terror of a night ambush. He quoted from the diary of a dead helicopter pilot, who described how his flight suit had smelled for two days of charred flesh from the corpses of three comrades he had recovered from the burned ruins of their downed helicopter."[130] Borovik said that he described the horrors in order to fight the Soviet public's apathy regarding the soldiers' suffering and to embarrass the regime into relating better to the veterans. He found it essential to open the eyes of the Soviet citizenry so that everyone understands "that we did send these people to Afghanistan" and thinks about "how to reintegrate them into society," lest they become "a lost generation."

To get his dispatches past the military censorship, Borovik enlisted Varennikov. He told Hedrick Smith that he "phoned the general and said, 'Listen, I've written a big, big documentary and these guys in censorship won't let it go because they think you guys are, you know, staging a ballet in Afghanistan, raising flowers, and nothing else. They don't want to show real life.'" Borovik recalled that the general got angry "because guys die there, they're risking their lives, and the press writes ridiculous things. So he helped me. He didn't read the articles. He just phoned [the censors] and said, 'Let Borovik publish what he saw. . . . ' This is how I got the visa . . . of approval from the military.'" Borovik's editor, Vitaly Korotich, "told me that the whole project had even higher-level political approval—from Gorbachev himself. 'I have a hot-line phone. . . . I called Akhromeyev, chief of the General Staff. . . . I pushed him, and for the first time, Akhromeyev gave me permission to send a reporter to the front. If he did not, he knew I would print that he refused. I understood that I must publish something about the end of this war to prepare the public.'" Gorbachev was using glasnost, and specifically Korotich, to prime public opinion for the withdrawal. "The pressure on public opinion continued for several years, turning the troop withdrawal from a political blow to Gorbachev into a public relations triumph." Nonetheless, TASS's revelation in May 1988, of official Soviet casualty figures "was almost unbelievable."[131]

The public, in fact, was not ready for too much exposure regarding the war. Mothers wrote that graphic articles made their lives more difficult; it had been easier before they knew what their sons were experiencing. At the same time, the materials politicized some of the mothers (see Chapter 7).[132]

The most popular television program was undoubtedly *Vzgliad,* which, after it first aired in October 1987, broke "more taboos and more exclusives" than any other show on television. During the war, *Vzgliad* "ran powerful shows on the carnage." (The program also described the violence of the hazing, including gang rapes.[133]) *Vzgliad* was at the vanguard of the far-reaching changes through which Gorbachev gradually transformed Soviet TV into "a genuine forum for a broad range of ideas."[134] This did not mean that all reporting was accurate. In late 1987, soldiers were still frustrated at the "safari-suited battle reports" where "a raiding party would have to shoot into the air to imitate a battle." *Sobesednik* printed scathing criticism of Moscow TV's presentation of a "false make-believe war." It described the war's true horrors and the lasting damage it inflicted on the soldiers whom its author followed on their return.[135]

Well before the end of the war, articles and news reports began to address the sensitive issues of draft dodging, drug abuse, and even the war's cost. The media left some topics virtually untouched, however, until the beginning of the final withdrawal in 1988. These included the return of POWs and the fate of the thousands of mothers, widows, and orphans. Only once the central press finally mentioned an official figure for casualties that included those MIA did the media take up the issue[136] or address the war's economic cost.[137]

While Gorbachev and his allies sought to guide public opinion toward favoring withdrawal, some of the old perspectives continued; one article addressing the withdrawal spoke only of the benefit the Soviets had brought to Afghanistan and the Afghans' gratitude.[138] Conservative platforms continued to focus on American involvement in Afghanistan, the need for "ideological rectitude," and Soviet heroism. However, when a television broadcast cut an Aleksandr Bovin commentary, it could appear in the radical *Argumenty i fakty*, as did an interview with Sakharov half a year after the war's end. And the veterans "ghettoized themselves" in their own press, like the All-Union *Pobratim* (1989–1991), Leningrad's *K sovesti* (which first appeared 1990), and Orenburg's *Kontingent*, which, while providing them with a forum for their experiences, remained "well out of the mainstream."[139]

Major General Kim Tsagolov, who had served in Afghanistan as a military adviser from 1981 to 1984 and again in 1987, gave an interview to Borovik for publication in *Ogonek* that Borovik compared to a bomb explosion;[140] in fact, it cost Tsagolov his job as chief of the Department of Marxism-Leninism at the Frunze Military Academy.[141] Tsagolov dubbed the April revolution "a military coup" and doubted that the Najibullah regime would survive the Soviet withdrawal. He agreed with Borovik that it had been "painful" for those serving in Afghanistan to read the reporting in the Soviet press in the early and mid-1980s of how well everything was going. "Our readers and television audiences got the impression that Soviet soldiers were doing everything under the sun but fighting a war . . . the Soviet people began to see in the luster of combat medals and decorations a certain fake window-dressing rather than an assessment of the hard, mortally dangerous labor of soldiers. This could not but be insulting to those who won their decorations in battle. . . . It is necessary to make up for the deficit in truth that has built up during the war."[142]

The combination of, on the one hand, Gorbachev's dissociation from the war at the Twenty-Seventh Party Congress and his announcement of the decision to withdraw and, on the other hand, of the greater freedom that glasnost created led inevitably to a debate in the media—and the public—about both the war's conduct and its initiation. This, in turn, sparked a discussion of the way that the Soviet system had enabled a small group of elderly men to make the fatal decision to intervene militarily in Afghanistan.

The discussion in the media began after the start of withdrawal. Calls for genuine analysis and more revelations concerning the war included a major piece in *New Times* noting that "only now is the veil being lifted to reveal [the war's] true face." Clearly, those who had initiated the intervention had not considered its effects and had not defined the "ends and means" of this confrontation, let alone its cost. They sent in a "limited contingent," so "there was nothing to worry about. It was as if there was no war at all." Society had paid the price in blood for censorship and the lack of openness. "The contingent of our news writers covering Afghanistan had no right to be limited. We too are to blame for Afghanistan. . . . Support of a lawful government and of popular movements is axiomatic, but . . . it must not take the form of the military involvement of a great power in the affairs of a small country," which "apart from everything else . . . has long proved unable to achieve the desired objective." Moreover, "it is wrong to impose one's own yardstick on others. Especially when it comes to military yardsticks."[143]

One of the first to take advantage of the new liberty was Russian nationalist Aleksandr Prokhanov, hitherto an ardent supporter of the regime's policy and generally viewed as its mouthpiece. In summer 1985, he had extolled the benefits for the Soviet Union of the war that had breathed new life into the armed forces, provided the younger generation with purpose, and promoted the Soviet Union's great power role.[144] But by 1988, he was addressing the decision to intervene—"and only God and our top politicians know how agonizing it was to make that decision"—as having been erroneous. Moscow had thought that the presence of Soviet troops would bring stability to the DRA, but Soviet military actions had exacerbated resistance to the PDPA. Moscow had erred due to "incorrect recipes for the implantation of socialism by directive 'in an 'un-Afghan,' and 'un-Islamic' form." Prokhanov blamed the experts for being "wrong in their assessments." Now that the PDPA had not only not achieved its original goals but had actually denounced them and had thwarted the Kremlin's hopes for a stable socialist Afghanistan, "the presence of Soviet troops . . . loses its point. Their departure is inevitable and logical." Yet it was "no defeat. The Army is in excellent fighting trim. The morale of officers and soldiers is high." The "Afghan topic," however, would remain "in culture, in domestic politics, and in social relations, for Afghanistan has tragically filtered through the greater part of our generation and has given rise to tragedy and pain in families and to a special 'Afghan spirit' in those who have returned from the villages where shooting is taking place." Prokhanov anticipated a prolonged polemic on the following questions: "Why we sent in the troops? What aims were we pursuing? Did we, or did we not, achieve these aims? What was the price of the presence in Afghanistan of our limited contingent?"[145]

Historian and political scientist Viacheslav Dashichev responded to Prokhanov's article by blaming the 1979 decision on the method of decision making: "It is our opinion that the crisis was caused mainly by errors and the incompetent approach of the Brezhnev leadership."[146]

Through 1988, the limitations on what one could publish meant that even Tsagolov could not say all he wanted. In 1992, when the Soviet Union was no more, he expanded his criticism, accusing Gorbachev's predecessors of entering a hopeless war, of deluding themselves into thinking that it was possible to transform the natural evolutionary process of Afghan history by force, and of allowing themselves historical amnesia. He placed responsibility on the Soviet Party advisers in Kabul for their reports to Moscow and for many of the PDPA leadership's mistakes. And he charged Gorbachev and other members of the Politburo for not having protested the intervention when they found out about it. Sakharov, he pointed out, had not been afraid to raise his voice in opposition. Gorbachev, moreover, would have to answer for those killed in the war while he played out his political game, that is, after he became General Secretary.[147]

Borovik, referring to the May 1988 CPSU CC letter on Afghanistan (see Chapter 4), sought to understand how there could be two "truths," the one designed for the party and the other for nonparty members.[148] Officials, however, maintained that caution was necessary in evaluating the war so as not to offend the veterans and bereaved families by declaring that their sacrifices were the outcome of a misguided policy.[149] Bovin said that he ceased writing that the war was unjust and contradicted Soviet interests after Soviet soldiers protested, exactly along those lines.[150]

The soldiers of the Fortieth Army also reacted sharply to press discussions of local officials' maltreatment of those who returned home; items about this appeared sporadically after "*Dolg*" was published. By early 1986, the press was running articles sympathetic to afgantsy who took the law into their own hands to combat antisocial elements. One correspondent commended these veterans as role models. Fighting in Afghanistan had imbued the vets with "high revolutionary purity," and they saw the world through "a powerful filter" that highlighted moral distinctions.[151] Local officials' failure to fulfill their obligations to the vets, especially invalids and families of the fallen, angered the republican media.[152] There were instances when the central party press itself criticized the cavalier fashion with which the bureaucracy related to the afgantsy.[153]

In 1987, one such article triggered a flood of letters expressing "pain and rage." They led to a follow-up article in the party daily—"I Didn't Send You to Afghanistan"—that castigated officials who sought to justify their indifference to the lot of the vets and blamed society too for not speaking out.[154] *Pravda* published a letter in which one soldier said that this second article had caused consternation in the ranks. A woman, he wrote, did not need a cripple, and if the vets were not going to get jobs, where could they get advancement? They would also not receive apartments. So what could a soldier expect from a mother country where he was unwanted? He was in fact needed solely by his mother who was killed from worry.[155] In summer 1988, the prestigious *Literaturnaia gazeta* published a lengthy piece sympathizing with the afgantsy and highlighting the failure of all sectors of society to understand their plight. The article concluded with a call to co-opt these badly needed "honest, socially keen" men who were capable of standing up to fire.[156] Altogether, the media undertook something of a campaign in summer 1988, calling on local officials to improve their treatment of the war's veterans.[157]

In this way, the media's depiction of the war focused not only on Soviet international prestige, the economy, and the standing of the military but also on social issues. Both the vigilantism and the cynicism of the returning soldiers reflected the attitudes of the younger generation, giving them legitimacy, while the vets' drug addiction, the glaringly inadequate care for the invalids, the bureaucracy's apathy, and the dearth of housing all related to problems that concerned the population at large. Discussion of the problems of the afgantsy brought to the fore themes that the media had hitherto glossed over.

The War's Aftermath, 1989–1991

Even after the war had ended, censorship persisted.[158] Borovik, who had witnessed the blood bath that accompanied the Soviet withdrawal (see Chapter 2), could not write about it at the time. Months later, he wrote that after a deputy division commander opened fire on civilians in order to avenge the death of one of his officers, a political officer in the Afghan capital had said to him, "If you know something of the incident . . . you have surely already forgotten, right?"[159] Even at the end of 1989, the press continued to publish misinformation, sometimes garnered directly from the MoD, as in the case of one POW whom *Izvestiia* reported had fallen captive in combat, while he recounted that he had been captured when treating himself to a watermelon.[160]

Following the final withdrawal, Borovik wanted to publish his "Hidden War" in *Ogonek*. A three-month battle ensued between the newspaper and the censor. "Both . . . sides employed powerful forces from their reserves. . . . On our side was the conviction that the country needed to know the truth about the war. On their side was something more material—power. But the circumstances surrounding the unpublished story became, thanks to glasnost, a cause célèbre. People began to speak and even to write about it. And the military retreated." Yet "a series of answering blows . . . in the form of articles and reviews . . . in the military and conservative civilian press" followed, accusing Borovik "of all sorts of mortal sins."[161] The paper eventually published the series in late 1989.[162]

On the day of the withdrawal, journalist Gennadii Bocharov outlined the evolution of the tragedy, from the initial welcome that the Soviet forces found to their eventual realization that the population included many who would fire at them. "Some people come out of battle stronger, while others went directly to the psycho wards." War breeds horrors and "circumstances that are not a justification for cruelty" but "an appropriate condition for it." When a small unit of Soviet soldiers killed innocent civilians, the court exonerated the officer who gave the command but not the soldier who carried it out. The soldier's friends, medical students in Leningrad, submitted a protest. Bocharov understood their complaint, but "they do not even try to think about what their comrade did. The letter crowns the immorality of the tragedy. . . . Society, when undertaking the Afghan action . . . was obligated to see what it would lead to, how it would end, including in the moral sense. But society did not undertake this."[163] In other words, concealing the war's true nature had morally deformed both the army and society. This was apparently the first time the Soviet media had spelled out Soviet excesses against the Afghan civilian population.

Journalists began to publish accounts that had until then remained in their notebooks. Days before the last soldier left Afghanistan, *Komsomol'skaia pravda* correspondent Vladimir Snegirev told of a Russian soldier who sold diesel fuel to the mujahidin before siding with them; when recaptured by Soviet troops, he recounted the hazing by "seniors" that had led to his actions.[164] The media, including Moscow television, relayed Sakharov's accusations that Soviet helicopters had opened fire on Soviet soldiers who were surrounded by the enemy in order to prevent their being taken captive (see Chapter 10). This time, the press reported his position, in sharp contrast to the situation a decade earlier, when few supported or had even known about Sakharov's protest at the intervention (see Chapter 1).

By 1990, even the MPA's journal questioned the intervention. A first study of the war explained that in order to decide whether it had been necessary to send troops into Afghanistan, one must bear in mind that the DRA leadership was incapable of preventing the opposition from overrunning the country. The crux of the question therefore was political: To what extent did the DRA administration rise to the assignment of implementing the revolutionary transformation of Afghanistan, which alone would justify the provision of international assistance. The author asserted that the way the troika made the decision was certainly faulty—the "secret thoughts" of a small group of politicians.[165] Interestingly, the journal did not mention any American threat or potential danger to Soviet security.

Table 6.1. How did you find out that facts about the war were being concealed from the public?

From the stories of soldiers who had fought in the war	35.0%
From the Soviet media	25.6%
From foreign sources of information	21.1%
Other	6.0%

Table 6.2. When did Soviet citizens begin to understand that the fact of the conduct of the war and its character were being concealed from them?

At the time of the intervention	9.4%
After about 4–5 years	33.5%
At the end of the war	40.6%
After the war was over	14.7%

Table 6.3. How did this discovery reflect on people's attitude to the authorities?

It made no difference	9.7%
It weakened people's confidence in the regime	75.0%
Don't know	15.3%

Three questions in our 1993 survey of Soviet immigrants to Israel who had lived in the Soviet Union during the Afghan War focused on Soviet media coverage of the war (Tables 6.1, 6.2, and 6.3). About 10 percent appreciated at the time of the intervention that Soviet citizens were not given the facts about the war. About 15 percent realized this only after the war was over. And the vast majority of the respondents claimed that disinformation concerning the war weakened people's trust in the Soviet regime.

In the final account, the policy of disinformation backfired. It contributed to discrediting the war effort and to undermining the legitimacy of the party-state. Gorbachev's glasnost unleashed a debate about the war's many sides and implications and provoked public indignation.

The question that begs resolution is, Was this transformation a sequitur to the greater freedoms of the media in the wake of glasnost, or was it an inevitable response to the dynamics of Soviet public opinion? Not that the two are mutually exclusive;

on the contrary, they are interrelated. The more the media reported, the more the war resonated among the population, and the more the public gave expression to its sentiments, the further some journalists and editors sensed they could push. The fact that by 1987 *Pravda* itself had admitted that the media's criticism of the war had elicited a torrent of letters from citizens throughout the country demonstrated that the party could no longer ignore public opinion. By then the party-controlled media were harnessing this disapproval for its own ends. Certainly the transformations in reporting the war—from the minimalism of the early years, through its advocacy for the soldiers and vets starting in the middle of the decade, to its critique and eventual disengagement in the Soviet Union's last years—reflected the power of public opinion.

This chapter highlights at least three important aspects of glasnost that are not always appreciated. First, in the year or so before Gorbachev's nomination as General Secretary, there were occasional articles that lifted the curtain of silence surrounding Soviet participation in the war; some even discussed of the lot its veterans, which inevitably reflected on that participation. Already then, a few journalists were breaking the bonds of censorship. Second, in 1987, the government's significant easing of restrictions evoked widespread public reaction, indicating that people had already been discussing—and forming opinions about—the war.[166] And third, whether or not Gorbachev was using glasnost to respond to the developments he sensed among the public, he made use of "glasnost from below"—public opinion—as well as the media to pursue his policies, specifically the goal of moving toward withdrawal.

Chapter 7

Public Opinion

Some have suggested that the Soviet-Afghan War created a situation in which glasnost was inevitable. This chapter addresses the following question: To what extent did the war create Soviet public opinion, affect its evolution throughout the 1980s, and contribute to the disintegration of the Soviet Union? It does so bearing in mind that the war occurred during a decade of transformations in Soviet society's acceptance of traditional perceptions, norms, and values. The attitude toward compulsory military service and the demand that young men be prepared to give their lives in defense of the mother country was a main focus of these changes.

The Black Tulip (the term for the planes bringing the coffins from Afghanistan[1]), the 1987 Soviet documentary, begins by stating that the Afghan War changed the Soviet Union. The returning veterans no longer simply accepted everything. Ordinary citizens too were speaking out, mothers asking questions just like their sons were.

We are told that after Gorbachev took over, the issue of media coverage of the war became "an acid test of the sincerity, feasibility, and reality" of glasnost.[2] Certainly it was not only those directly involved in or affected by the war who began to question the Soviet system with its in-built limitations and the constraints that prescribed withholding information concerning the war. As the media opened up and it became clear how much the government had concealed, long-suppressed grievances "magnified the reaction to each new offering."[3] In the words of a *New York Times* Moscow correspondent writing about the Afghan War, "Wars, especially prolonged foreign wars of questionable purpose, do not confine their damage to the battlefield. They leave physical and emotional scars; they tear at the social fabric; they cast doubt on official policies."[4]

We have seen how from the outset, the authorities did all they could to shroud the war in a heavy veil of secrecy. All the Soviet public knew about its inception came from the announcement that the Soviet government was responding to "urgent" requests for "immediate" aid in a variety of fields, including military, and from Brezhnev's explanations that this was necessary in view of the foreign intervention that aimed to reverse the achievements of the April revolution. The army instructed soldiers posted to Afghanistan to keep quiet when they returned. At the beginning, they were forbidden even to tell their parents of their whereabouts. As late as October 1986, soldiers returning home had to sign an oath: "I will never tell what I have seen, heard, and know about Afghanistan."[5]

According to one opinion, the social composition of the Soviet force in Afghanistan (see Chapter 3) was based on the establishment's not wanting coffins to return to the big cities,[6] apparently because it was only there that public opinion mattered or because it was only there that public opinion existed at all. The local *voenkomats* (military commissariats) ordered the families of those killed not to speak of the circumstances of their relative's death—which they themselves often did not know. Journalists too were subject to strict censorship regulations (see Chapter 6). The official news blackout and the in-built self-censorship that was an integral component of their mentalité inhibited many people from speaking out. "Many . . . who knew what was going on . . . were appalled by what they knew but kept their mouths shut."[7]

Nonetheless, people talked, and as often happens when censorship is imposed, hearsay ran rampant. Rumors, which played an important role in Soviet society, spread like wildfire and inevitably grew in the telling.[8] The Kremlin's attempts to impose secrecy began to fail almost at once. Soldiers returning from Afghanistan told of their experiences despite the prohibition. Only a month after the invasion, stories circulating in Moscow asserted that Tashkent's hospitals were full of wounded soldiers and that aircraft flying home held coffins.

As the war dragged on and ever more citizens saw their sons being sent to Afghanistan or likely to be sent there, protest, or at least discontent, mounted, directed against both the war and the endeavors to conceal it. While most Soviet citizens refrained from going so far as to transpose their complaints to the system in which they lived and those who controlled it, the realization that the Soviet force was not going to succeed in "liberating" Afghanistan bred complaint. The sense that the war was an "all-engulfing quagmire," a thorn in the Soviet side that had to be removed, grew. The flow of letters reaching the CC and the central press highlighted the "defects and lacunae" of the Soviet system. Moscow recognized that it had to neutralize this bomb before it exploded, so began the struggle to withdraw the Limited Contingent.[9] While this was not the sole cause for the withdrawal, many concur that it was the critical trigger.

Soviet society was not geared toward protesting the war as Americans were during the Vietnam era. Yet the KGB, tasked with monitoring public reaction to the intervention and reporting to the party leadership, reported early doubts and disgruntlement regarding the introduction and continued presence of Soviet troops in Afghanistan (see Chapter 1).[10] Instruments created under glasnost enable us to gauge Soviet public opinion about the war (as well as on a host of other topics), at least in its last years.[11] Certain groups were particularly likely to criticize the war. Beyond the families whom it directly affected, these included the intelligentsia in the major cities, some "national minorities" who did not identify with what they perceived as Russian expansionism, and the younger generation, whose commitment to "patriotic" causes had weakened by the early 1980s.

The Zinc Coffins

By and large, the funerals gave the first intimation of what was happening in Afghanistan. The zinc coffins carrying casualties from the war began arriving very quickly. One source, addressing the fact that there were nearly 1,500 soldiers killed in action while carrying out their "philanthropic mission" in the first year of the war, and in 1984, over 2,000, asks, "How could the government conceal numbers like these?"[12] True, the coffins were unloaded after dark, "so the public wouldn't find out," and the burials were carried out in secret, at night. Moreover, the gravestones, marked with a Red Star, the emblem of the Soviet armed forces, did not have "killed in action" engraved on them, just the date of death. Only after 1985 was it possible to inscribe killed "while fulfilling his internationalist duty" or even "while fulfilling a military assignment, true to his military oath, displaying determination and courage," and only in 1988, "killed in Afghanistan. The mother of the last soldier killed in the war, in January 1989, testified that when the family wrote on the tombstone, "died in Afghanistan," they feared the consequences.[13] Another safeguard against civilians knowing that many local boys were killed was burying them not only in different plots in the same cemetery but in separate cemeteries.[14] It seems that at first, some provincial areas did not realize or, perhaps did not implement, this. According to one testimony from Perm, at first, some graves bore small "tablets" with the inscription, "killed in Afghanistan," but by 1982 thes tablets had been removed.[15]

As early as 1980, KGB reports from Ukraine told of the harsh effect that these coffins were having on the villages. A worker at Rovno airport described the arrival, in March 1980, of seventeen coffins of soldiers killed in Afghanistan—in vain, on foreign territory.[16] The reports also relayed rumors of massive losses.[17] "And not just rumors. . . . One saw those coffins with increasing frequency although the Black

Tulips delivered them at the far end of the airfield." One couldn't bury the afgantsy with honors. It was done quietly, but everyone knew that the boy had been killed in Afghanistan.[18] In 1983, *Komsomol'skaia pravda* received a letter insisting that "there's no need to keep mum: a soldier sends a letter home—the whole village knows; they bring in a coffin—the entire region (oblast') knows."[19] In Tajikistan, where the first coffins arrived in January and February 1980, the burials were performed unobtrusively, but according to local custom, many people assembled for the funeral repasts.[20] In Silute (Lithuania), attempts in summer 1980 to conceal a soldier's burial resulted in a demonstration. The soldier's friends waited three days at the railway station, and when the coffin arrived, they took it from its military escort, fought off attempts by the police and militia to recover it, and staged a funeral procession through the streets with lighted torches.[21]

One woman who arrived in Israel in 1981, had taken part in one such funeral in Vitebsk; although there had been no discussion of what was happening in Afghanistan, everyone knew that the soldier being buried had been killed in the war. A taxi driver from Vilnius had driven from the airport a civilian pilot who, shortly before, had brought from Moscow the zinc coffins of several soldiers killed in Afghanistan. On arriving in Vilnius, he learned that one of them contained the body of his son. The boy's letters had not mentioned that he was in Afghanistan, and the father had not known he was there.[22]

Our survey of the general population indicates, however, that at least in many places, there was no knowledge about casualties at the time. Many people became aware that Soviet soldiers were being killed in Afghanistan only after the first news of this appeared in the Soviet media in 1984, and almost 40 percent found out only at the war's end (Table 7.1). (The respondents presumably understood "at the war's end" as referring to the time of the official announcement of the number of casualties just after the beginning of the first stage of the withdrawal.) At the same time, many knew of people killed or wounded in the war. The results of our survey of Soviet immigrants to Israel are in Table 7.2.

We can perhaps explain the apparent discrepancy between Tables 7.1 and 7.2 by the fact that Jews displayed greater interest and involvement in what was happening than did the general population, among whom apathy or nonchalance regarding public affairs was common (see Chapter 6). (Figure 7.2 seems to bear this out.)

By the mid-1980s, "whispered rumors" were circulating about letters reaching "jerry-built flats" and peasant cottages, "followed, a little later, by the zinc coffins themselves," too big to fit into the "rabbit-hutches" in which most people lived. Although the government was still trying to maintain the fiction that the Soviet troops were not engaged in action and was still delivering coffins to the families "at dead of night," the precaution was futile. Often the word got out in advance, and relatives,

Table 7.1. Did people in your town or vicinity know about Soviet soldiers being killed or wounded in the war?

They knew from the beginning	33.1%
Thy knew after 1984	25.9%
They knew only at the end of the war	38.7%

Table 7.2. Did you know soldiers who were wounded or killed in the war?

I knew none	18.8%
I knew none personally, but I heard of such cases	33.8%
I knew one	15.8%
I knew several	31.2%

neighbors, and friends were waiting when the truck drove up, the wooden box was broken open, and the zinc coffin delivered to the family. Frequently an officer escorted the coffin. When one young captain, a helicopter pilot, came with several soldiers to deliver the body of a comrade from his squadron, he found an angry crowd around the house. Someone punched one of the men in the jaw. "The women screamed, 'Murderers! Who've you brought with you! What have you done with our boy?' The men started to attack the soldiers as well, until the women shouted, 'Leave them alone. . . . It's not their fault!' The soldiers unpacked the wooden box and slowly took the coffin up to the apartment. It was crowded with relatives and neighbors, the mirrors were veiled in black, the women were wailing, and the men were drunk."[23]

There were cases in which crowds stoned to death the officers accompanying a soldier's corpse.[24] One father went to Moscow after shouting at the funeral that "if only the Afghans are fighting in Afghanistan, the way the papers say, let them explain . . . in Moscow why it's our boys who get sent back in coffins."[25]

"For more than eight years," one Soviet journalist wrote, "these planes landed on civilian and military airfields all over the USSR. No unauthorized persons saw them land." At first, "the traffic controllers who talked them down did not know what cargo they carried. . . . Before entering Soviet airspace, the charmed planes usually stuck to ordinary air corridors. However, once across the Soviet border, they would peel off to follow unexpected, frequently illogical routes. . . . Anyone rash enough to ask for explanations would have had cause to regret his curiosity."

The soldiers saw some of their comrades blown up, becoming "literally nothing. . . . When that happened they put empty full-dress uniforms in the coffin, and threw in a few spadesful of Afghan earth to make up the weight." One officer who lost five soldiers and a lieutenant in an operation went with the survivors to collect the remnants, "filled five crates and divided them so that there would be something of each man to be sent home." Many of the dead could not be identified before being put into coffins. "We [tried to] sort out which leg or fragment of skull belonged to whom. We weren't issued with identification tags because of the 'danger' of them falling into enemy hands. This was an undeclared war, you see—we were fighting a war that wasn't happening."[26] At some point. the army ordered the soldiers to carry a piece of paper with their name, parents' address, and blood type in a cartridge case around their necks.[27]

The bodies were prepared in the regimental or divisional morgue, where the corpse was cleaned, "repaired as far as possible, and dressed in its uniform." It was placed in a zinc coffin, and the lid soldered down and marked "Not to be opened." The coffin was then placed in a crude wooden box on which the name of the deceased was stenciled. One soldier taken to see the regimental morgue reported, "Inside, two soldiers, completely drunk, were picking through a pile of body parts. Another soldier wheeled in a trolley on which there was a long tin box. The two soldiers filled the box with a collection of human bits and pieces that seemed to bear some resemblance to one another." A doctor explained that the mujahidin had ambushed a twenty-five-man reconnaissance patrol: "'The mujahedin chopped them to pieces, put them in sacks, commandeered a lorry, and sent them back to us as a present." One soldier was sent to the airport in the Urals to accompany a "Cargo-200" to the city morgue: "No proper death certificates had been filled out. . . . [28] So, without any means of checking whether the contents of the boxes matched the names on the boxes, the morgue officials solemnly wrote out the documentation without which the coffins could not be delivered for burial to the relatives of the dead."[29]

At the Kabul airport in 1986, Soviet journalists encountered a film crew that had been filming "the loading of the 'black tulips,'" probably for the eponymous film. "They described how the dead 'sometimes have to be dressed in ancient uniforms, even jodhpurs and so on from the last century; sometimes, when there aren't even enough uniforms available, they're put in the coffins completely naked. The coffins are made of shabby old wood, held together with rusty nails. Casualties waiting to be shipped are put in cold storage, where they give off a stench of rotting wild boar.'"[30] The long time that passed before bodies were delivered to parents and the unprofessional way they were preserved explained both the stench and the instructions not to open the coffins.[31]

Many mothers and widows had serious doubts as to what and who lay there, doubts that were more than justified. A family in Leningrad that opened the coffin found someone else inside.[32]

One mother went to the local military commissariat to find out how her son had been killed; the officer in charge "got angry and even started shouting at me. 'This is classified information! You can't go around telling everyone your son has been killed! Don't you know that's not allowed?'" At the cemetery, the mother wanted her son to be buried near other Afghan graves, but the person accompanying them "shook his head. 'It's forbidden for them to be buried together. They have to be spread about the rest of the cemetery.'"[33] The mothers went regularly to the cemetery, finding some comfort in "the sisterhood of cemetery mothers."[34]

One father whose son was killed in late 1986 in fighting that the Soviet radio described as having been conducted by Afghan armed forces asked "the city authorities to have the district newspaper . . . carry an obituary; he was told: 'Writing in our newspaper about people who died like your son . . . just isn't done. . . . Your son isn't the first to be killed. What are we supposed to do—write in the newspaper about every one?'" The father was not placated: "What did my son die for?. . . [He] didn't just die—he was killed in battle." Moreover,

> on Soviet Army Day, no one came to his grave except relatives. . . . He attended two schools in the city, graduated from the DOSAAF school, where he was taught the people's military-patriotic traditions, worked at a plant, and was a member of the YCL. Wasn't this neglect because my son's gravestone is simply inscribed with the date of his birth and the date of his death . . . ? Why can't it be inscribed that he was killed performing his internationalist duty in Afghanistan?[35]

Although officially a secret, the large number of casualties evoked a widespread protest movement (see below). Even the policy of conscripting for Afghanistan largely from rural areas did not help; samizdat provided a breakdown of what it dubbed the large number of casualties from three raions in the Trans-Carpathian oblast. Radio Kiev broadcast the naming of a street after three boys from a village in Zhitomir oblast were killed in Afghanistan. [36]

Certainly the protest was one of the incentives that led Gorbachev both to move toward withdrawal and to instruct the army, in 1986 or 1987, to make every effort to decrease the casualties.

Public Awareness

Even the minimum estimate—that only just over half a million young Soviet men served in Afghanistan over the course of nine years—covers about 3.4 percent of that age cohort.[37] They and their million or so parents were clearly conscious of the war, even if the latter knew few of the particulars about it. Hardly less conscious were several million parents of adolescents nearing conscription age.

In the early years, it was not only the dead whom the authorities endeavored to

Table 7.3. How did people in your city react to the appearance of war invalids among them?

It caused great anxiety	55.3%
It caused some anxiety	31.2%
People were not very anxious	4.9%
People were indifferent	5.3%
People were not bothered by this at all	0.8%

conceal. They initially sent many of the wounded to hospitals in Poland, Czechoslovakia, and the German Democratic Republic, while the seriously wounded had "Invalid of the Great Patriotic War" written on their veterans' booklets.[38] Nor did the government inform parents if their sons were taken captive or went missing. One Swedish journalist who visited Afghanistan in 1983 called the parents of a Soviet POW to tell them their son had been captured; they had not even known that he was in Afghanistan.[39]

However, the gap between the awareness of those segments of the population whom the war affected directly and the broad population gradually dissipated. Over the years, the funerals, the invalids who appeared in the city streets, and the growing number of returning veterans brought the war home to an ever-growing number of civilians, making them realize that the government was not telling them the truth. When "the first young men began to return and we saw how psychologically damaged they were and heard about their experiences . . . we understood that a carnage was taking place and that things weren't at all as we presumed."[40] Our survey of Soviet immigrants to Israel disclosed that the wounded and maimed caused no little concern (Table 7.3).

Many people did not initially give the intervention much thought, preferring to believe what they were told. Early on, Soviet public opinion regarding the war tended toward indifference, as most citizens had more urgent concerns, especially the chronic Soviet problem of making ends meet. The population at large, especially outside Moscow and Leningrad, continued, as before, to be preoccupied with the dearth of food in the stores and the low standard of living; these were years when people traveled from Gor'kii or Kazan' to Moscow, a twelve-hour train journey, to buy sausage. Even in the mid-1980s, people in Moscow and other places were largely unconscious of the war. Any reporting about it was curt and uninteresting. One officer back from Afghanistan in 1983 found life in Moscow "going on as usual, as though we didn't exist. There was no war in Moscow." He asked people how long the war had been going on and got only vague answers, even, "Is there a war there? Really?"[41] For students in their last years of school and in institutions of higher learning, the war seemed irrelevant. Soviet young people in the 1980s were largely apolitical.

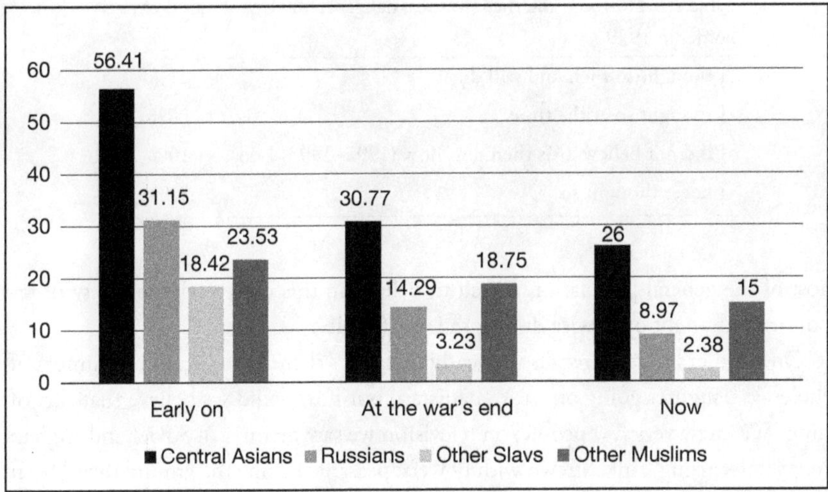

Figure 7.1. Did we need to intervene?

Nevertheless, some circles expressed dissatisfaction early on. A British Moscow correspondent, who might well have sought out such people, reported anxiety about casualties in late 1980 and wrote that while "the Russians do not know how many of their young men have been killed . . . there is widespread belief that the figure runs into thousands."[42] He noted further that "the Afghan campaign . . . is deeply unpopular . . . and [people] are skeptical of the need to send in the troops."[43]

In the first half of 1982, the Frankfurt-based Russian émigré journal *Posev*, which was obviously interested in reporting opposition of all kinds, printed a letter from Moscow describing the workers' negative attitude toward the war: "As the number of killed and wounded and the circle of those directly touched by the war gradually grows, so does dissatisfaction with our doings in Afghanistan."[44] People were especially upset about the country's fighting a war beyond the Soviet border.[45]

Although opposition existed, even if expressed chiefly in private conversation, many also supported the war, assuming that their leaders had good reason for it. Conversations in the 2000s between people in Moscow and Saratov, who had been about thirty years old in 1979, highlighted the "perplexingly contradictory nature" of late Soviet society.[46]

Our survey of the general population indicates that early in the war, many saw it as ineluctable (Figure 7.1). The acceptance that prevailed at first decreased as the war wore on.

Many accepted the claim that an American, Chinese, or Iranian threat existed on their southern border.[47] Our survey of the civilian population shows that eventually

Table 7.4. Do you think there was real danger to the USSR's southern border in 1979

I thought so then and still do	21%
I thought so at the time	38%
I did not believe this then, but now (1992–1993) I do	10%
I never thought so	31%

most of the general population ceased to believe in this danger, the majority of respondents thought otherwise during the war (Table 7.4).

One soldier's mother recalls that early in 1981, "there were all sorts of rumors of wholesale slaughter going on in Afghanistan, but how could we believe that sort of thing? We knew very few people; on television we saw pictures of Soviet and Afghan troops fraternizing, tanks strewn with flowers, peasants kissing the ground they'd been allotted by the Socialist government."[48]

Immigrants to Israel in 1981 and 1982 echoed this sentiment. People from sixteen cities throughout the country testified that the Soviet media offered only minimal information on the war; moreover, Western broadcasts were largely jammed, and soldiers divulged nothing. People who knew of soldiers killed in Afghanistan said that since their families had been told no details, they had nothing to relate. This began to change in late 1981. By then, rumors told of heavy Soviet losses, the opposition's cruelty to Soviet soldiers and officers, the Afghans' stubborn resistance, and Chinese interference in the fighting. Even so, most of the population remained indifferent. There was little evidence of displeasure at the war outside the Baltics (see Chapter 1).

Within the armed forces, however, awareness of the war seems to have been ubiquitous. An officer called for duty in Afghanistan in summer 1984 testified that by then, everyone "knew that our troops in the form of the Fortieth Army, the so-called Limited Contingent, were engaged in active fighting."[49]

Although people did not realize—or preferred not to realize—what the war entailed, by 1983, there were signs that public pressure on the press and the authorities was beginning to show results. That February, *Komsomol'skaia pravda* explained that after the paper published a reply to the letter of a mother of a recruit sent to render "fraternal assistance," readers' letters had provoked the paper's—relative—abundance of items on the war, including a special column on Afghanistan. The paper noted that the letters' authors had expressed admiration for the steadfastness of the Soviet troops in Afghanistan and asked for more information about their daily routine.[50] Colonel Leonid Shershnev, an officer of the Turkestan MD who had spent some time in Afghanistan and had criticized the war (see Chapter 2), saw the letters in the editorial offices of *Komsomol'skaia pravda* in spring 1983. Most of them were from relatives of soldiers killed in action, currently serving in Afghanistan, or likely to serve there, and preconscript youth. The letters rejected the idea of internationalism in the form of military assistance, considered the casualties suffered in defense of "foreign interests" unjustified, and deplored the indifferent attitude to those killed in action and their families and the partial nature of the information that the press reported.[51] Returning soldiers too were "bringing home feelings of bitterness, frustration, and horror."[52]

A year later, many newspapers were no longer concealing the floods of letters that they were receiving in response to items on the war and the soldiers; "*Dolg*," and "A Letter Home" (see Chapter 6) inspired 2,600 letters within less than six weeks.[53] The letters reflected the growing understanding that the Soviet Union was not going to "liberate" Afghanistan from the insurgency and that it was becoming engulfed in a quagmire. The year that saw the heaviest fighting and the most casualties also witnessed the growth—a "critical mass"—of public protest that, in highlighting its shortcomings, was dangerous for the entire system. The splinter had to be extricated before it decomposed. The process of liberating Afghanistan from the Soviet military presence began.[54]

William Odom writes that as word of what duty in Afghanistan was like got out, draft evasion increased (see Chapter 6). Bribing local voenkomat officials became a common way for the parents of a predraft youth to extricate him from service. Naturally, families with higher incomes and better connections were better able to do this, but even people from lower strata could pay their sons' way out of Afghanistan if they could scrape together the obligatory sum. Feigning illness or psychiatric issues could also work, and there was one reported case of self-immolation. "The MoD and its voenkomat bureaucracy" reacted by sending more conscripts from rural areas, where there were fewer means by which to evade the war.[55]

Throughout the war, draft-age boys "increasingly tried to avoid the draft and Afghanistan duty."[56] As the date of conscription approached, many parents faced the nightmare of their sons being sent to Afghanistan. One mother recalls how, when her son was called up, "my neighbor kept getting at me—and perhaps she was right: 'couldn't you scrape a couple of thousand rubles together and bribe someone?' We knew a woman who did precisely that, and kept her son out." In the end, the mother approached the battalion commander when she went to her son's oath-taking ceremony. He sent her to her local recruiting office: "If you can get them to send me an official request I'll have him transferred home." But the local military commissar refused to listen—perhaps because she did not offer money.[57]

In 1987, the Estonian SSR's leading military commander came under investigation, charged with receiving bribes for releasing men from service in Afghanistan.[58] (For draft dodging in Central Asia, where it appears to have been especially flagrant, see Chapter 9.)

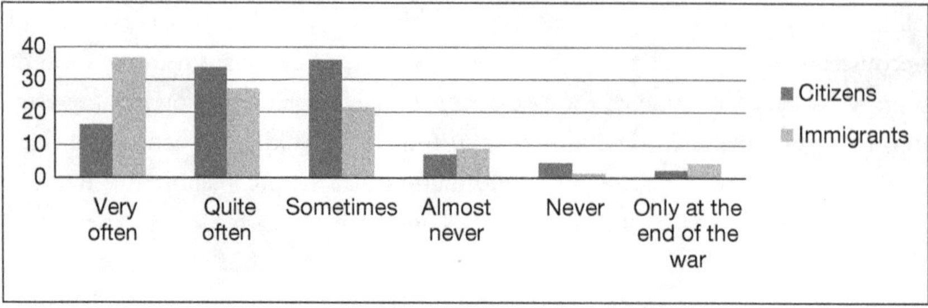

Figure 7.2. Did you and your friends discuss the war and its consequences?

In 1983, a Western reporter wrote that for fear of Afghanistan, teenagers and their parents increasingly sought to escape the draft.[59] In the latter half of 1985, reports told of private discussions of the war among citizens in the face of growing concern that their sons might be sent there. A foreign correspondent in Moscow was abruptly corrected by a Soviet acquaintance when he suggested that the war had not evoked public concern because "Soviet territory was not at stake. 'But lives are,' came the sharp reply. 'Everyone with a son or brother is concerned.'"[60]

Our own surveys—both of the general population and of Soviet immigrants to Israel—corroborate the findings concerning discussion of the war in the home and in intimate circles (Figure 7.2). (One must remember that the immigrants are distinguished by their nationality, that is, as opposed to most Soviet citizens; most of them were Jewish, and in the 1970s and 1980s, the Jews were the most urbanized and highly educated ethnic group in the Soviet Union.)

Our survey of the general population concerning the attitudes toward Moscow's moral justification for intervening militarily in Afghanistan, however, does not confirm the view of the correspondent just quoted—a further indication of the possible tendentiousness of some Western correspondents in Moscow, who might have drawn conclusions from unrepresentative segments of the population. (Interestingly, there seems to be no correlation between the perception of the need for the intervention—Figure 7.1—and of its moral justification.) The especially high acceptance among Ukrainians and Belarussians of the intervention's morality requires further analysis (Table 7.5).

Even before the announcement of glasnost and the holding of genuine public opinion polls, Radio Liberty attempted a quantitative opinion analysis—Radio Free Europe's Soviet Area Audience and Opinion Research (SAAOR). This 1984 survey of public attitudes to the war concluded that just over one-third (36 percent) of the adult urban population—and 55 percent of party members—favored it, while one-quarter (24 percent) disapproved; over 40 percent had no clear attitude. The poll surveyed Soviet visitors to the West, mostly educated urban men between the ages of thirty and forty-nine, and inhabitants of the European parts of the Soviet Union; 10 percent

Table 7.5. Your view of our moral right to intervene militarily in Afghanistan

	Russians	Other Slavs	Central Asians	Other Muslims
Early on	47.62%	62.5%	35.2%	46.67%
At the end of the war	52.54%	68.57%	38.71%	50.00%
Now (1992–1993)	64%	66.67%	43.48%	47.37%

of those asked refused to participate in the poll. An informal poll of Muscovites by Soviet sociologists reported 29 percent approval and 62 percent disapproval of the war.[61] The director of SAAOR or Radio Free Europe and Radio Liberty opined that in the war's "early years," respondents "tended either to minimize its importance and avoid expressing a viewpoint or to recite stereotyped responses based on domestic Soviet propaganda."[62]

Reports from different parts of the Soviet Union in the same period noted that opinions regarding the war varied. It was more unpopular among the general public than among the intelligentsia whose sons went from school to higher education and so, for the most part, did not draft into the army (although as of 1982 some students at institutions of higher learning were drafted into the Limited Contingent—see Chapter 3). A lecturer from Leningrad University said that people who did not have relatives or friends who went to the war spoke little about it and when they did, tended to support the "conventional position, namely that it's bad that our soldiers are dying but we cannot permit American bases to be established on our border." Others, notably military men and KGB personnel, said openly that the war was senseless and that the Soviet Union had entered into an unnecessary adventure that was "a preposterous farce." A second lecturer, also from Leningrad, said that people who had acquaintances and relatives killed in Afghanistan detested the war and those who had initiated it.

By early 1985, discussion of the war had spread to the provinces. A bookkeeper from the Russian town of Briansk reported a debate in a beer stall. Some said Soviet boys went into Afghanistan for nothing, that they were dying or returning home crippled. Others said, "We feed those beasts but they resist our help and kill our boys." And an Afghan vet spoke of how they had received orders to "destroy everything—cattle, grain, and crops, adults and children. . . . If we don't destroy everyone who resists us, there will be a big problem in our country. Where do you think our Chukchis, Uzbeks, and Turkmen are looking? We have more Muslims now than Russians." Many disagreed with him but stayed silent.[63]

In addition to instances of public protest (see below), samizdat publications, especially in the national republics, reflected public opposition. A pensioner from Lutsk said Ukrainians were comparing the intervention to the Russian conquest of Ukraine in 1918.[64] The *Chronicle of the Catholic Church in Ukraine* that had mentioned protests as early as 1984[65] protested in its sixth issue, in 1986, the "forceful and unlawful sending of our Ukrainian youth to the unjust war in Afghanistan." It published a letter complaining that Ukrainians were being used in colonial wars outside the Soviet Union. Baltic samizdat commented regularly on the war, speaking of the common fate of Afghanistan and all three Baltic republics and "of the way the flower of their youth was dying in distant mountains on Moscow's behalf."[66] The Lithuanian youth journal *Juventus Academica* wrote in 1985 that while information was being withheld from the public because "a dearth of information atrophies thought," the war "cuts across our hearts and destinies, and our children's future." The paper continued that this aggression would not be possible "if no one supported [it], if no one acquiesced in it, if the parents of the men drafted were to take to the streets, to stage peaceful demonstrations, if they were to shout to their country's citizens and to the entire world: No. Why must our sons and the innocent children of another country perish?" As long as this did not happen, "We are all guilty."[67]

Many recruits were reluctant to serve in Afghanistan; some resisted. "Among a recent group of recruits," a Western reporter wrote in late 1985 that "only one volunteered for Afghan duty. 'We all know how the Minsk Division was wiped out,' said one recruit. 'In our barracks, we figure the chances of being killed are 1 in 4.'"[68]

If by early 1985, things were already changing, disapproval of the war was even more marked by 1987 under the growing influence of glasnost. Radio Free Europe collected data revealing that the one-quarter of the population that had expressed disapproval of the war in 1984 had grown to nearly one-half (45 percent). Whereas official Moscow was advocating conditional withdrawal, a large number of citizens favored withdrawing unconditionally. The transformation was particularly notable in Soviet Central Asia, where disapproval of Soviet policy regarding Afghanistan now reached 49 percent. In the Baltic republics, where it had been strongest and most vocal throughout, it stood at 67 percent, with 58 percent in the Caucasian union republics. In the RSFSR, approval of the Soviet role in Afghanistan was still above 20 percent, yet here too, disapproval had grown, reaching 48 percent in Moscow and 54 percent in Leningrad.[69] Shortly after the war, a poll of Soviet youth showed 89 percent favoring withdrawal and just 5 percent against it.[70]

From "information sources on the war, it became apparent that those who received their information from Western radio or via word-of-mouth communications were considerably more critical of Soviet policy than those who relied on official sources." Users of all sources were more negative now than in 1984; "the critical rate for Western radio listeners" reached 71 percent, with 64 percent for word-of-mouth. Disapproval of the war among those who received their information from Soviet sources registered between 19 and 23 percent disapproval in 1984, while in 1987, the range was from 34 to 39 percent. Data gathered in 1988 and 1989 showed that 90 percent approved withdrawal and 69 percent felt that the USSR had failed to achieve its goals in the war.[71]

Before glasnost, the government had sentenced a number of Soviet citizens for their critical attitude to the war (see Chapter 1). Yet as Russian emigré writer, Vladimir Rybakov, pointed out in the second half of 1985, while only the Soviet population could force the government to end the war, the war's relatively minor proportions could hardly incite Soviet society to take up an open struggle against the regime. At the same time, coming on top of other (primarily social and economic) grievances, the war had provoked demonstrations and damage of voenkomats. The authorities conducted regular analyses of public opinion—although their findings remained secret—so they must have known of the increasing discontent regarding the war.[72]

Both the Soviet press and Western sources reported that public opinion was becoming vocal and that "ordinary citizens" were beginning to speak out. The turning point seems to have been 1985. Nodari Simoniia of the Institute of Oriental Studies wrote in mid-1987 that "during the past two years, the whole of my country has become unanimous that the Afghan war must be ended as soon as possible."[73]

By 1987, glasnost and Gorbachev's commitment to withdrawal further diminished the ranks of the war's adherents and enhanced the war's role in the public's political consciousness. There was a gradual rapprochement between the party members' attitudes to the war (only 8 percent of them opposed the official line in 1984) and those of other citizens. By now, almost as many party members disapproved the official line as supported it (39 and 37 percent, respectively).[74]

Letters to both the press and the country's leadership also reflected this public view. The Politburo had discussed letters from the citizenry, especially from parents of fallen soldiers, as early as 1981 (see Chapter 4) but seems not to have taken any measures in response to them. By the time Gorbachev came to power, it was no longer possible for him to ignore them, or perhaps the new General Secretary found it convenient not to do so, or perhaps both. One letter, from a World War II officer veteran addressed to Gorbachev in March 1986, protested sending very young workers and students to the war and suggested that units consist of volunteers aged twenty-five to forty with military experience.[75] Gorbachev adviser Anatolii Cherniaev tells us, "As soon as the new 'tsar' came to power the Central Committee and *Pravda* were flooded with letters. . . . Almost all were signed! The gist: 'What do we need this for, and when is it going to end? . . . If it's really necessary, send volunteers or professional soldiers, not freshly drafted boys whose souls are corrupted by what they do there'" (see Chapter 4).[76]

Although the Soviet media finally started to provide information on Soviet soldiers' participation in combat, it failed to mollify the people; even after the war, only 10 percent were fully satisfied with what they had learned about the problems connected with the war, with 55 percent partially satisfied and 16 percent not at all satisfied.[77] Nor did the information assuage public anxiety. In 1987, deputy chief editor of *Sotsiologicheskie issledovaniia*, Gennadii Batygin, called the war "our greatest problem" and the chief obstacle to implementing perestroika.[78] And once the war was over, one paper said that it had been "perhaps our people's greatest pain and anxiety."[79] As veterans moved into military-political education (see Chapter 8) and eventually into politics, they increased awareness of the war and its effects even further. A Moscow intellectual said about a year before the war's end, "The invincibility of Soviet power is the last great myth of our system. . . . We can accept sacrifice if we see a result, but we are psychologically unprepared to deal with the idea that we fought for nothing. That's why the real problem of Afghanistan will emerge after it's over."[80]

Images and Perceptions

In a closed, totalitarian, or authoritarian society, the rationale behind perceptions is often irrelevant and myth takes on a major role. Myths molded the foundations of the Soviet regime from the start—the building of socialism, the classless society, the friendship of peoples, and, somewhat later, the heroism of the Soviet soldier in the Great Patriotic War—legends with which three generations had been educated and indoctrinated. The party had not moderated these slogans despite the system's inherent internal contradictions, their increasing distance from the realities of Soviet life, and the prevalent atmosphere of apathy and disbelief.

It was, then, not surprising that myths regarding the war in Afghanistan pervaded a society in which the sons of every family could in theory be mobilized into the armed services, and so attain the pinnacle of all that the communist system represented. It was only in the war's last year or year and a half, as glasnost and informal organizations took root, that the freedom to articulate opinions and communicate information developed. But as one scholar points out, "It becomes an open question as to whether a few years of limited pluralism, accompanied as they were by their own distorting factors, from an immature political culture to the instrumental gambits of a new generation of public figures, could do much to counter early years of unopposed myth-building, and how far they merely revitalized and reflected them."[81]

Certainly the war debunked long-accepted perceptions, notably regarding the Soviet military. Under glasnost and as a direct outcome of the Afghan War, public criticism of the Soviet military establishment acquired dimensions that the party-state could no longer ignore.

"The military as an institution," writes an American political analyst who had served in the U.S. embassy in Moscow, "previously had very high prestige and a near sacrosanct status in the Soviet Union. Shifting attitudes under glasnost and Soviet failure in Afghanistan have resulted in a loss of influence and prestige for the Soviet military. . . . When the Soviets first invaded Afghanistan, most observers took for granted the ability of the military to achieve a quick victory."[82] Not only did this not occur, but the war led to a widespread discrediting of the Soviet military and adversely affected the morale of the soldiers and of young men on the eve of conscription. Inevitably this exacerbated draft evasion and evolved into a debunking of the entire military establishment—its basic concepts, its conduct, its relationship to conscripts, and discipline in the ranks.[83] By early 1988, one-quarter of the population felt that Soviet policy in Afghanistan had succeeded and approximately one-third that it had failed.[84] The revelation of Soviet fallibility led to an undermining of the army in public opinion. This in turn spurred pacifist feelings among the youth and carried over to criticism of a system that enabled some to prevent their sons from being sent to Afghanistan. The Afghan War aroused a sense of ignominy and humiliation in the Soviet public; it shattered the myths, cultivated and nurtured since World War II, of the Soviet armed forces' invincibility; the superiority of Soviet officers, soldiers, and arms; and the scientific nature of Soviet military planning.[85] In this way, the war played a significant role in Soviet society's debate in the second half of the 1980s over the military's place in the Soviet system, the relevance of a professional army at the close of the twentieth century, and the need to curtail military expenditure.

Military figures sought to mitigate the heavy shadow on the Soviet armed forces' public image of the Soviet armed forces and to argue for the army's continued centrality for the Soviet Union. In the summer of 1988, Gromov told the Nineteenth Party Conference that "concern for the defense of our homeland and for our readiness to come to its defense when necessary is as actual as ever." Gromov found "incomprehensible the position of some people who try to assert that the military threat to our country is an outdated concept." Nobody had "the right to destroy young people's faith" in the sanctity of military service, "to blacken our military traditions or disparage with words and deeds the sacred constitutional duty of protecting our homeland." It was, moreover, "irresponsible . . . to call the internationalist soldier's exploits into question."[86]

The people's loss of faith in the military, as an outcome of the war, both harmed its prestige and destroyed much of the satisfaction of military service. The press depicted a general demoralization within the military that was partly Afghanistan related, reflecting the impact of social and sociological trends within Soviet society.[87] What remained was a perception of incompetence, inequality, and brutality, as well as defiance in the ranks. As the final withdrawal date neared, the media depicted the retreating troops jettisoning their poor equipment as officers gritted their teeth in the face of jeering Afghans lining the roads.[88] The disillusionment of the Soviet civilian population affected the military tribunals that tried the soldiers for crimes and excesses committed during the war. In one case, in Tashkent, the court gave a soldier five years but exonerated the junior officer who had been on the spot and the commanding officer with whom he had communicated by phone. "Public opinion in Tashkent was outraged." Eventually, following complaints against the staff of the Turkestan MD "within the walls of the Central Military Procuracy of the USSR," the court reopened the case against the senior officer. The procurator general also received a letter from veterans demanding a retrial for the soldier on the grounds that his sole crime was to have carried out orders.[89]

The March 1989 elections to the Congress of People's Deputies demonstrated the diminished clout of the army; a number of high-ranking officers failed to win election, while some of their radical critics were chosen. Later that same year, the Congress's establishment of a commission to inquire into the causes and consequences of the Afghanistan War (see Chapter 4) allowed a civilian body to appraise the performance of the army for the first time. Generals, reeling under the criticism, joined the debate, feeling the need to justify army decisions. Indeed, they complained that people were using the war in order to embarrass them. Gromov, for instance, observed that a number of articles in the central media were trying "to drive a wedge between the army and society. *The sorest of sore points* [italics in original]—the war in Afghanistan—has been selected for this purpose."[90]

The war, then, became a symbol for the moral ills and political tensions gripping late Soviet society, a symbol "far more powerful than prosaic reality." What actually happened took "second place to what people *thought* had happened, *should* have happened, or *could* have happened."[91] In the early 1980s, dissidents considered the war the backdrop to the "tense" domestic situation that accompanied Andropov's ascendancy and that increased the pressure on their activities. Jews seeking to leave the Soviet Union believed it tightened the screws regarding Jewish emigration. Viktor Brailovsky, editor of probably the most important Jewish samizdat journal, *Jews in the USSR* (*Evrei v SSSR*), testified that its publication "became impossible after the Afghan invasion."[92]

During glasnost, public discourse regarding the war had "little direct connection with the real fighting." Afghanistan became a political symbol "defined principally" by the intelligentsia who had "minimal real contact with the war and political interest in distorting it." In 1989–1990, Afghanistan was an issue in the liberal press, which sought to use it to open up the policymaking process and "retreat from the global wargame of East versus West." In the public image, it was "what *Izvestiya*'s Stanislav Kondrashov called the 'imperial damn-foolishness of the septuagenarian leaders with their outdated mentality, stemming only from the lessons drawn from World War Two and in the Cold War environment.'" It was also a military defeat—the efforts to present it differently did not affect the war's public image—and the Soviet Union's Vietnam, which blighted a generation of Soviet youth. Since wars "as powerful foci for a wide range of emotions, are especially prone to mythology," the Soviet-Afghan War had "an obvious impact on the development of the policies and ideologies of the late Soviet (and post-Soviet) era, over a range of issues."[93]

Perhaps most significant, as the war underscored the blatant gap between what the authorities were telling citizens and real life, it impaired the former's credibility—in parallel with the irremediable damage Gorbachev earned by belittling the April 1986 Chernobyl disaster. Many were convinced, for example, that the regime doctored the casualty figures when it finally published them (see below).

In 1991, the Supreme Soviet Committee for the Affairs of the Soldier-Internationalists published a report based on its analysis of the Soviet press. It categorized society's appraisal of the war as either "orthodox" or "liberal." The former approved the introduction of Soviet troops into Afghanistan and claimed that the intervention was justified as the Soviet Union's "international duty" or for geopolitical reasons, or both—securing the Soviet Union from "the infiltration of Islamic extremism." Correspondingly, the latter condemned the intervention as a symbol of the period of stagnation that praised the soldiers' achievements in order to prepare adolescents to be gunpowder for future military crusades.[94] However, as the specter of Islam became an increasingly relevant factor in Soviet—and post-Soviet—politics (see Chapter 9), many on both sides of the political spectrum came to see the war as a response to the militant Islam that emerged with the rise of Ayatollah Khomeini in Iran.

Another convention that the war disrupted was the image of the adversary. From the Soviet regime's earliest days, it had been axiomatic that Soviet power's main enemy was big capitalism—the bourgeoisie, in all its aspects. This legitimized the Soviet citizens' low standard of living—they had to fulfill their internationalist duty to modernize and bring the light to backward nations. In Afghanistan, Soviet forces were fighting a rural population that lived in extreme poverty, the same primitive peasants whom communism was supposed to be liberating from the oppressive yoke of imperialism and capitalism. This contradiction became another fundamental question with which people had to grapple. Young Soviet citizens educated in the Soviet school system and simultaneously exposed to scenes of fighting in the heady days of glasnost simply could not reconcile the two.[95]

The perceived failure of the military in Afghanistan when pitted against the myth of its invincibility, on the one hand and, on the other, its role as representative of the might of the Soviet superpower and the validity of Marxism-Leninism severely undermined the entire system and the legends on which it rested.

For popular assessments of the impact of the Afghan War on various aspects of Soviet life and society, see the figures and tables in the appendix at the end of this chapter. Some of these assessments reflected the reality more than others, but even those that were less grounded in fact were politically important in a period of glasnost and of political, economic, and social instability.

Society's Attitude toward the Afgantsy

Both the establishment and the media presented the public with an image of the war's veterans that was intrinsically connected to the circumstances of Soviet society in the 1980s (see Chapters 4 and 6). It is noteworthy that respondents to a late 1989 survey attributed society's "unjust" reception of the afgantsy to the media's "deformation of information." Above all loomed the unacknowledged nature of the war—the authorities' insistence on burying those killed in action surreptitiously, abstention from erecting monuments in their memory, and the refrain, "I did not send you to Afghanistan." These elements kept society from recognizing the afgantsy as war veterans. Moreover, the more insistent the vets' demands were for acceptance, the more negatively people responded to them.

People frequently characterized the afgantsy as trigger-happy criminals, "a random but unredeemable collection of misfits, cripples, drug abusers, and vigilantes, heavy-handed riot policemen, or potential suicides." The activist minority of afgantsy who found jobs in the military (which, in the Soviet Union's last years, the regime increasingly used against civilians), the emergency services, and "the often violent and symbiotic juncture of private enterprise and private crime, as investigators, bodyguards, robbers, or racketeers" that surfaced in the social and economic chaos of Gorbachev's latter years necessarily influenced these stereotypes.[96]

Faced with "a colossal 'Afghan' problem" that it could not ignore, society could not simply blame the dead Brezhnev or rail against Sakharov (for Sakharov's 1989 condemnation of the war, see Chapter 10). The war influenced Soviet society as a whole, and the people's outlook on the war affected their attitude toward those who fought it. The status of the returning soldiers continued to worry society in the months (and years) after the war ended.[97] One psychologist who studied the lot of the afgantsy asserted that "people felt guilty" toward them.[98] Indeed, writer Ales' Adamovich wrote in 1989 that Soviet society had put immature souls in a complex situation, leaving them to choose between duty and conscience. One could see in their eyes, in their faces, that they were still living the war, so that coming to terms with its moral aspects was the problem of the whole society.[99]

Surveys conducted in the Soviet Union after the war indicated that according to the majority of the population, the personality of the afganets differed from that of the regular citizen. They perceived afgatntsy as more resolute, stronger, very moral, less sociable, and smarting from the widespread misunderstanding they encountered.[100]

The interviews I did in the first half of the 1990s in eleven of the Soviet Union's fifteen successor states confirm recognition of the vets as a composite unit. Yet most respondents refuted the idea that there was a typical afganets or characteristic afganets mentality. Many, however, were comfortable classifying them into groupings. While 26.9 percent denied that there was a typical afganets, 18.4 percent divided them into two subgroups—the so-called lost generation who resorted to drugs, crime, and violence and those determined to help transform society. More than half (54.8 percent) preferred three categories—those who returned with an active civic position, the so-called lost generation, and those indistinguishable from the population at large. One correspondent asserted that people should neither judge the veterans nor lump them together in a stereotype. They were simultaneously both "very different and very alike."[101] (The Latvian 1986 film *It Isn't Easy to Be Young*, described the afgantsy's predicament as "the return home of the lost generation."[102])

In a survey conducted in November 1989 that asked, "What are the veterans likely to become?" 52 percent of the respondents opined that the veterans would become active participants in the military-patriotic education of the youth; 31 percent, aides in law enforcement organizations; 27 percent, honest and efficient workers; 11 percent, leaders of informal political associations; 11 percent, outsiders and unwanted people; and 10 percent, criminals (racketeers, rapists, and hooligans).[103]

Public attitudes to the USSR's Afghan War veterans changed in response to the media's fluctuating assessments of the servicemen in the Fortieth Army. In the first stage, the public was indifferent because the media kept it ignorant of "what Soviet armed forces were doing in Afghanistan." In the second period, it welcomed them as heroes, when "the state sought to justify their role in Afghanistan and as glasnost shed light on their rehabilitation problems." In the 1989–1991 period, society was critical, "as the war was reassessed as a criminal or dirty one," and opinion changed again in 1991, reflecting pride in the veterans after they defended Russian democracy in the August coup (see Chapter 10).[104]

In Soviet jargon, at first the afgantsy were soldier-internationalists; later, the victims of a political mistake; and in 1990–1991, guilty of murder, "their hands bloodstained." Some attributed this "unstable" attitude to "propaganda extremities" reflecting the "manipulation of public opinion in conditions of a prolonged dearth of information regarding actual events: the war's image was modeled by a group of journalists enjoying special credibility regarding it. . . . The tragedy of the afgantsy's situation" lay in the desire of different political forces to use them "for goals that are not always honorable" and in society's fear of them as "a threatening and not always understood or predictable social force that it does not know what to do with."[105] One perspicacious World War II veteran attributed the difference in the attitude to the veterans of the two wars and the anomalous situation in which the afgantsy found themselves, to the fact that "the nation [now] lived a peaceful life" and so could not muster the requisite sensitivity toward the afgantsy.[106] Or, as Metropolitan Pitirim of Volokamsk and Iur'ev noted, the crux of the matter was that World War II had affected every individual and every family, while the Afghan War touched only its participants and their families.[107] One Moscow journalist said the afgantsy evoked no sympathy because they had fought for an unknown reason in an unknown cause in a foreign land.[108]

That attitudes toward the soldiers mirrored the wider issue of how the public understood the war, however, seems to be only part of the truth. There were also practical considerations. In a country where living standards were unbelievably low, local government officials sought to use their resources for ends other than caring for war veterans, while some saw afgantsy who were not disabled as availing themselves of their privileges in unwarranted fashion. The soldiers returning from Afghanistan inevitably seemed to be a further burden on a deprived population. Both the country's difficult economic situation and the already miserable standard of living deteriorated under Gorbachev, so the possibility that these new veterans would receive material benefits evoked envy and rancor.

Afgantsy were constantly running into instances of jealousy and misunderstanding. One veteran who lost an arm "met some old friends. 'Did you bring back a sheepskin? A Japanese cassette player? What, nothing? Are you sure you were in Afghanistan?' I only wish I'd brought my gun back with me!" After six years at home, the situation had not improved. "I have an invalid card—it's meant to give you a few privileges. So, at the cinema, for instance, I go to the window for war veterans. I hear someone say, 'Hey, you! Boy! You're in the wrong queue!' I clench my teeth and say nothing. Behind my back a voice says, `I defended the Motherland but . . . what's *he* done?' If a stranger asks me how I lost my arm, I tell him I was drunk and fell under a train and he's full of understanding and sympathy." When one woman who served in Afghanistan came home, "friends and neighbours—all women," came around to ask . . . what china, carpets, videos" she'd brought home. "More coffins came back than cassette-recorders, I can tell you, but that's all been forgotten."[109]

Every Soviet citizen, according to one writer, heard remarks addressed to the afgantsy such as: "You ass! It would have been better to sit in jail than become crippled."[110] The disrespect and failure to acknowledge them as veterans were manifest even in afgantsy songs.[111]

On the whole, then, the afgantsy were not being paranoid in sensing that the esteem that the public had shown World War II veterans contrasted sharply with its attitude toward these new war vets (see Chapter 8). True, there were notable exceptions. The first article that addressed the hardships of disabled veterans prompted a torrent of letters to the paper that had published it, expressing deep sympathy for and horror at the tribulations of the young man who was the focus of the article (see Chapter 6).

Unquestionably, however, society was neither friendly toward nor understanding of the returning afgantsy. As Galeotti put it, "There was certainly a considerable element of scapegoating: after all, to blame the hapless soldiers fighting a 'bad war' is [a] time-honoured . . . tradition . . . assuaging feelings of guilt and revulsion by externalizing them, projecting them onto another, clearly defined and politically powerless group and punishing them as proxies. For the street-smart, they were fools who had been unable to wangle their way out of the war, to patriots, simply losers, failures in battle." To the intelligentsia, "separated by a near-unbridgeable cultural divide from the veterans and their families," they were actively dangerous, "a new wave of Stalinists, fascists, vigilantes, and psychotics." Stories abounded of people accusing them "of having blood on their hands."[112]

It was primarily people's political perceptions that shaped their attitude toward the war and hence toward the afgantsy. At the turn of the decade, the conservative or "patriotic" view was that the heroic image of the afganets defending the mother country, prevalent in the early Gorbachev period, needed revision. And the "liberals" expanded their condemnation of the war to demand that those who had fought it repent publicly for having participated in it.[113] In the words of one veteran, when the second session of the Congress of People's Deputies issued its verdict on the war, the afgantsy became "the victims of a political adventure."[114]

While there were tensions between World War II veterans and those of Afghanistan,[115] some of the former were sympathetic toward the afgantsy. One insisted that the newer veterans had earned the gratitude of the Soviet people on whose behalf they had courageously spilled their blood.[116] Another remarked, "There's no denying that these kids had it rough. . . . [W]e have to help [them] move into civilian life. With patience and sympathy—but without permissiveness."[117] When it was time to go home, one soldier tells us, "We expected a warm welcome and open arms—then we discovered that people couldn't care less whether we'd survived or not." He encountered "kids I'd known before" and former teachers:

> This was the sum total of our conversation: I, solemnly: "We should perpetuate the memory of our school fellows who died doing their international duty.' They: "They were dunces and hooligans. How can we put up a plaque to them in school?' People back home had their own view of the war. "So you think you were heroes. . . . You lost a war, and, anyhow, who needed it, apart from Brezhnev and a few warmongering generals?" Apparently my friends died for nothing, and I might have died for nothing too. . . . I had a talk with an old lecturer at college. " You were a victim of a political mistake," he said. "You were forced to become accomplices to a crime." " I was eighteen then," I told him. "How old were you? You kept quiet when we were being roasted alive. You kept quiet when we were being brought back in body bags. . . . You kept quiet over here while we were doing the killing over there. Now all of a sudden you go on about victims and mistakes."[118]

People taunted afgantsy, suggesting they had stolen their medals.[119] Employers were reluctant to give them jobs because they were considered difficult.[120] One veteran from Minsk was not hired at a factory when it transpired that he had served in Afghanistan—"people were afraid of us. The press wrote that we were broken mentally." He ended up working in security at the airport.[121]

A lengthy article in summer 1988 spelled out the problems between a society that had retained its nonchalance and these young men who returned from the war scarred, united, and full of values that they wanted to impose on those who had remained behind. People were afraid of them and felt uncomfortable with their "pushiness,"[122] leading them to think of the afgantsy as people unduly prone to resort to force.

At the same time, many insisted that society owed the afgantsy a debt. They had been sent to the war, one correspondent wrote, but it could have happened to anyone.[123] Most had returned from the war physically or mentally damaged, and they needed society's material and moral support. By 1988, a few institutions and public figures had organized charitable activities for them. These included an All-Russia Society for the Disabled and a Health and Charity Fund that aimed to alleviate the problems of the disabled.[124] The editorial collective of the newspaper *Literaturnaia gazeta* appealed for funds to set up a rehabilitation center for invalids. In 1989, the Council of Trade Unions launched a Trade Unions for Soldier-Internationalists campaign (see Chapter 4). The Russian Orthodox Church also undertook initiatives on behalf of the afgantsy;[125] Metropolitan Pitirim became a member of their Supreme Soviet Committee and regularly appeared at events such as the founding congress of the Russian Union of Veterans of Afghanistan. Indeed, Pitirim envisioned a program to rehabilitate the afgantsy by finding them appropriate living housing and employment and doing everything possible to protect them from censure; in his view, they were not to blame for being "victims of a faulty appraisal of the situation and misguided policy."[126] In addition to the nationwide frameworks, similar organizations mushroomed in different cities.

As USSR Procurator General Aleksandr Sukharev noted in 1988, "The question is not just about charity. . . . It tests the preparedness of society to discharge its debt to those who showed courage, endurance, and heroism."[127] And in the months following the final withdrawal, the provincial press gave considerable space to items about the hard lot of disabled afgantsy and what society owed them.[128] The most common point made in the visitors' book at the exhibition about the war in Moscow's Manezh art gallery in 1991 was that there were no collection boxes for donations to the bereaved families, the disabled, and the veterans in general.[129]

Proposals at the Congress of People's Deputies to publish a book entitled "Memory" (*Pamiat'*) listing the names of all who died in Afghanistan,[130] indicated the debt society felt it owed those who had fought there. Throughout 1989, republican and local newspapers ran items describing the erection of monuments and various commemorations of soldiers who died in Afghanistan. Towns renamed streets, schools, and libraries after the local fallen; memorial books and albums mentioned the country's dead or those from a given region; districts established museums in schools where the soldiers had studied, in sov- or kolkhozes where they had lived, and through the agency of a variety of local initiatives.[131] Immediately after the last soldier left Afghanistan, the Komsomol adopted a resolution on the need for remembering those who died.[132]

In 1990, at the request of the Supreme Soviet Committee on the Affairs of Internationalist Soldiers, VTsIOM (Tat'iana Zaslavskaia's All-Union Center for the Study of Public Opinion) undertook a countrywide survey entitled, "Public Opinion on the Problems of the Participants of Military Activity in Afghanistan." Its purpose was to understand the opinion of the public in general, and that of certain social groups in particular, about "the moral cast of mind and mental character" of the afgantsy, their political profile, and the issue of their privileges. The survey found that public opinion was inconsistent but tended toward the positive: 44 percent believed that society related to the vets "with love and respect."[133] Almost half the respondents (48 percent) thought the vets' privileges needed to be augmented, while just under one-third responded that the afgantsy could apply their Afghan skills and experience whatever they took up. A full 78 percent approved of the fact that the vets had formed their own associations. Those with incomplete secondary education, workers, rural dwellers—and Russians—were particularly in favor of this.

Just 5 percent thought the war had made its participants indifferent and cynical, 11 percent (above all, older people) thought it had inclined the vets to use force, 16 percent—23 percent among party members and 37 percent among young preconscript males—that it had made them "stable and manly," 17 percent that it made them intolerant of evil (the percent was highest among older men, especially those with higher education, and lowest among women in their forties, the age when their sons served or would soon be drafted). Fifty-four percent believed the war had "crippled their souls." On the whole, people saw the vets as victims of the war and did not think that society was fulfilling its responsibility for their mental health.

Regarding the afgantsy's reintegration, nearly 20 percent suggested that they should turn to adolescent education; neither prearmy youth nor recently demobilized soldiers were enthusiastic about this (7 percent of the latter). Almost 20 percent thought the vets should play a role in "voluntary formations for preserving order," and a further 16 percent believed they should serve in "professional military formations."[134]

Our survey of Soviet immigrants to Israel in the early to mid-1990s demonstrated that a majority of Soviet citizens, certainly urban dwellers, read vets' speeches and stories, a fact that indicates a positive approach, even sensitivity, to the afgantsy and to questions

Table 7.6. Did you hear or read speeches of afgantsy in the media—in the papers, on the radio or TV, or at the movies?

Yes, frequently	22.2%
From time to time	35.3%
Just occasionally	35.0%
No	7.5%

Table 7.7. Did you read stories of afgantsy in books or journals?

Yes, frequently	13.5%
From time to time	28.2%
Just occasionally	44.0%
No	14.3%

arising from their difficult adaptation (Tables 7.6 and 7.7). These findings are also important because they testify to the availability of the relevant materials under glasnost.

Yet the disharmony between the afgantsy and society persisted. A psychologist who had served in Afghanistan made the penetrating analysis that this was the inevitable outcome of several factors. Above all, neither side was prepared for the encounter: the soldiers had undergone a profound psychological metamorphosis during their year and a half or two-year participation in a brutal war, while Soviet society, especially in the second half of the 1980s, was experiencing its own transformation, which involved new problems and tensions. The soldiers, who had a sense of pride for having done their "international duty" and believed that they deserved gratitude for their sufferings, returned to a society that rejoiced that an unpopular war had ended and was all too ready to blame the war on those who had fought it. The afgantsy, moreover, felt deceived at having been sent to a war nobody needed, while society was apprehensive that the returning veterans would be a destructive force that would further destabilize society. The result was that the afgantsy largely had to fend for themselves as they readapted. The crux of the problem, according to the psychologist, was the divergence between the veterans' perception of the war and that of society, and society's inability to distinguish between the war and those who fought it.[135]

The public's attitude toward the afgantsy inevitably affected their adaptation to civilian life. The tragedy of the veterans' situation, according to the report of the Supreme Soviet Committee, lay not only in the state's failure to fulfill its obligations toward them but also in the refusal of "a significant portion of society" to respect them. "This wounds their sense of self-esteem, deforms the meaning of life, and inculcates a feeling of guilt."[136]

The popular Moscow paper *Segodnia*'s defense correspondent wrote in 1994, "Russian society fenced itself off and rejected both the war itself and . . . the veterans who had taken part in [it]. . . . No one except the veterans ever much remembers the war. Society is trying to forget it, like a bad dream or a nightmare."[137]

Public Protest

Initially, the few public protests came from small groups—dissident intelligentsia in the larger cities, nationalists who drew parallels between the Soviet occupation of Afghanistan and of their own lands, and pacifist groups. (For early instances of protest, see Chapter 1.) Their primary demand was that the government bring the Fortieth Army home. KGB reports from Ukraine paid considerable attention to protests in the war's first year but gave them much less notice after that[138] (possibly because the KGB developed more pressing concerns).

By 1985, protest was becoming more vocal and more frequent. In Kalinin in 1985, some 500 people mounted an angry demonstration in front of party headquarters to protest the war and the deaths of Soviet soldiers.[139] Public rallies to protest the sending of young men to Afghanistan were reported in a number of cities throughout the Soviet Union. Clashes were said to have occurred in Astrakhan in the RSFSR in June 1985, when Chechen draftees refused to go to Afghanistan (see Chapter 9). It is perhaps not surprising that these incidents were especially widespread in the national republics. Agence France Presse reported that on May 20, about 200 people rallied in Erevan to protest the drafting of young Armenians to fight the mujahidin in Afghanistan. The agency maintained that the police had charged some forty protesters with hooliganism. It reported similar protests in Tbilisi.[140] The secret police reportedly broke up both demonstrations without difficulty.[141] People in Georgia were said to be grumbling about Georgians being sent to Afghanistan and complaining that the army considered Georgians "black."[142] (For protest in Central Asia and among other Muslim groups, see Chapter 9.)

As glasnost spread, protest mounted in both Russia and in the national republics, especially in Ukraine and the Baltics,[143] where people had condemned the war from the start. In December 1987, citizens demonstrated opposite the MoD in Moscow, and also in Leningrad, against the continued presence of Soviet troops in Afghanistan.[144]

Some protesters invested their disapproval with nationalist coloring, claiming that their particular ethnic group suffered disproportionately high casualties. Russian nationalist organizations, for instance, contended that Russians had higher-than-average casualties. Balts and West Ukrainians complained that the MoD sent their "politically unreliable" nationals to Afghanistan in proportionally higher numbers than draftees of other national groupings and that therefore their casualties were higher.[145]

Often the protest had an economic aspect. In May 1988, one paper published a letter from a concerned citizen, a schoolteacher from Krasnoiarsk, entitled "Is it necessary to help everyone?" She questioned the wisdom of international aid, given the difficulties of her own family in making ends meet. The same newspaper published a large number of responses, most of which concurred that the Soviet people "build and build for everyone, but [we] do not have enough for ourselves."[146]

This was also a central theme in Russian dissident protest. In September 1988, one democratic samizdat journal published an article entitled "Afghanistan Must Not Be Repeated! An Appeal to the Presidium of the USSR Supreme Soviet." It claimed that "the state, which does not have sufficient resources to build homes and hospitals, has wasted billions of rubles on a crime against its own and neighboring peoples."

The Democratic Union Party (founded in May 1988) demanded that the Supreme Soviet Presidium publicly acknowledge the war as an act of aggression; investigate and publish all the facts relating to the war's initiation and conduct; hand over to an open court those responsible for introducing Soviet troops into Afghanistan and those guilty of war crimes and crimes against humanity; rehabilitate all those sentenced for protesting the war; pay compensation to all veterans of the war; and condemn the offering of "so-called 'international aid' as a form of military intervention and arms supply." The same document called on all of the war's veterans to reject the awards and privileges they had received for participating in a criminal adventure.[147]

It is against this backdrop that we have to understand the claim made by Sergei Lukyanchikov, who directed *Bol* (Pain), a documentary on Afghanistan (see below), that "the War changed our psychology . . . helped perestroika."[148] Indeed, with the advent of glasnost, the protest expanded, although the fear of reprisals still restricted its extent. As late as April 1989, members of the Leningrad Independent Committee for the Liberation of "Afghan" Prisoners-of-War canceled a rally in central Moscow after the Supreme Court warned that demonstrators with banners outside public buildings would be prosecuted. They had planned to demand the prosecution of the top officials who had ordered the intervention.[149]

Toward the end of the war and in its aftermath, one topic that aroused considerable protest—and highlighted the evolution of a civil society—was that of the POWs; the government that had sent soldiers to Afghanistan must also bring them home. The opening shot was an April 1988 article in *Literaturnaia gazeta* entitled, "No One Is Forgotten—The Holy Commandment."[150] The first official announcement of casualties in May 1988 included a figure for those MIA, which people understood to mean POWs. In June, the USSR's Foreign Ministry announced that it would do everything possible "to learn about the fate of every one of them."[151] That same month saw the formation of the Soviet Public Coordinating Committee for the Release of Soviet Servicemen Taken Prisoner in Afghanistan to bring missing sons back to the motherland and their families. It included "as private persons, leaders of practically all major organizations of the USSR—pop stars, prominent writers, lawyers, journalists, religious figures, former soldier-internationalists, the mothers of soldiers killed in Afghanistan." From time to time "crowded public demonstrations" took place near the Pakistani embassy in Moscow.[152] However, one soldier who had defected, spent seven years in captivity, and returned home before the war's end evoked angry responses as people accused him of having been exchanged for "weapons and mines that crippled our men."[153]

In December 1988, staff members of the Soviet embassy in Pakistan and the ambassador to Kabul, Yurii Vorontsov, met with an Afghan opposition delegation to discuss the issue of the POWs as part of Moscow's official commitment to make every effort, "including all political and diplomatic means, to achieve the earliest possible release of our soldiers."[154] Almost 650 women from different Soviet cities and from the Soviet Women's Committee signed letters expressing concern over the fate of Soviet POWs. They gave these to the UN Information Center in Moscow, to be passed on to the UN secretary-general.[155] The media too devoted considerable attention to the issue (see Chapter 6).

In February 1989, the month of the final withdrawal from Afghanistan, Nadezhda (Hope), the People's Committee for the Release of Soviet Prisoners of War. came into being. It too sought to bring the surviving POWs back to the Soviet Union.[156] *Izvestiia* reported in June that its editorial office was receiving "hundreds of letters whose authors are worried about the fate of the Soviet soldiers taken captive by the Afghan opposition." MID Special Ambassador N. I. Kozyrev told the paper's correspondent about the efforts the ministry was making on their behalf. Altogether, eighty-six POWs were released—mostly in prisoner exchanges with the mujahidin—and repatriated to the Soviet Union.[157] Just a few had succeeded in escaping from captivity.[158] From time to time after the war's end, the media published stories of POWs who returned home.[159]

Another concern was the misinformation from official sources regarding casualty figures. Both the vets (see Chapter 8) and others questioned the statistics. One People's deputy based his doubts on "familiarity with the methodology" used to calculate combat losses, which excluded those who died not on the battlefield but "a week or two later in a hospital bed," and people other than MoD personnel. Extrapolating from the figure for a single republic, he concluded that the number of dead must have exceeded 20,000. Like many afgantsy, he was unwilling to accept the regime's lies: "We must know the truth."[160]

The Mothers

The war in Afghanistan was particularly hard on the mothers of the soldiers sent there. Some of them became physically sick from worry. A few died. One mother summed up what they all felt as their sons served in a war whose rationale they could not understand: "For us there was just no life whatever."[161]

It was hardest of all for mothers of those who never returned. The local bureaucracy offered them little or no support. One mother in Alma-Ata, whose son was killed in fighting in 1982, was hauled off to a psychiatric hospital for demonstrating her grief. Three years later, a committee of local officials asked her to cease wearing mourning and recommended that she be given an isolated apartment.[162]

The war in Afghanistan seems to have been the catalyst for many mothers' support groups, including, in spring 1989, the Committee of Soldiers' Mothers, also called Nadezhda. The proliferation of such groups is consistent with the broader context of the changes occurring in the Soviet Union and the breakdown of trust in state institutions, including the armed forces, where dedovshchina had reportedly resulted in thousands of casualties.[163]

One mother, who had been sick with worry about her afganets son, volunteered for Nadezhda as a way to help others in their distress.[164] Several mothers' organizations followed Nadezhda, among them the All-Union Organization of Parents of Sons Killed in Afghanistan. (This might be the same as the Council of mothers and widows of fallen afgantsy soldiers, set up in October 1989.[165]) It apparently operated under the auspices of, or in cooperation with, Nadezhda, whose secretary explained that their common goal was to give material and psychological assistance to parents of those who died in Afghanistan, had become invalids, or had committed suicide as a result of the Afghan War.[166]

The majority of the population attributed significance to the mothers' protests (Table 7.8). Only 16 percent of the sample viewed them as futile. This has wider implications, showing that Soviet citizens were coming to see or even believe that public opinion could influence official decision making.

One journalist asked several soldiers if she should give regards to their mothers, and on her return, she did so. She reported that the mother of a "soldier-internationalist" and a correspondent of Belarus television had gotten herself assigned to Afghanistan in order to find her severely wounded son. On her return home, other mothers of afgantsy joined her in demanding to know the whole truth about what was happening there.[167]

Feminist dissident groups such as Mariia became involved in protests against the Afghan War early on (see Chapter 1). The mothers' groups succeeded in uniting large numbers of women from different republics and social strata. In late 1983 or early 1984, one mother wrote to her son in Afghanistan about the "fraternity" of soldiers'

Table 7.8. How do you evaluate the protests of the mothers of those killed or taken captive?

They were very important in highlighting the hypocrisy of our leaders	24%
They were important in showing the significance of organized protest	14%
They were important in showing that people's efforts were not in vain and the regime had to meet them	25%
They were important in showing that protest was possible	21%
They were basically futile	16%

mothers" who helped each other "to live, wait, and have faith."[168] Broader-based movements that united the mothers or widows of Afghan veterans or even of conscripts soon overtook Nadezhda. The organizations acquired a mass base by extending their terms of reference beyond Afghan-related questions to larger issues, especially peacetime deaths in the Soviet armed forces. For example, the Council of Soldiers' Mothers and Widows undertook to monitor instances of bullying and maltreatment of soldiers and campaign for broad army reforms.

At the same time, organizations specifically catering to their Afghan constituency continued to exist. Their primary concerns were to give material assistance to the families of those killed in the war, provide medical rehabilitation, and erect monuments in memory of the fallen. Their message made headway even though in the long run, they were not particularly successful in aiding those whom they aspired to assist.[169]

The War in Popular Culture: Film, Song, and Literature

Fictional accounts of the war evolved, following the same linear development as media reportage. In the early years, such narratives as there were—"literary propaganda"—addressed solely the noncombatant activities of the Soviet contingent. In the mid-1980s, they portrayed the heroic feats of the Soviet troops in order, it seemed, to justify their losses. And as of 1987, writers began describing events and expressing views in both prose and poetry that were either critical of party policy or completely apolitical.

One early novel on the war was by Aleksandr Prokhanov—"the Soviet Kipling"—who accepted uncritically the imperialist message of "internationalism." In accordance with the official line, it addressed only Afghan infighting, with no mention of the presence of Soviet troops on Afghan soil.[170] A 1983 novel dedicated primarily to the April revolution similarly omitted any reference to the Limited Contingent, although it tells of two Soviet "internationalists"—an army doctor who dies saving an Afghan boy wounded by the dushmans and an army interpreter.[171]

Afghan War songs and poems circulated within the Limited Contingent from early in the war (see Chapter 3). The first three war poems to appear in print in the Soviet Union were by Ukrainian-born Lieutenant Aleksandr Stovba, who had been killed in action in early 1981 (*Molod Ukrainy*, 1982).[172] A 1983 Komsomol directive banned an album by the British rock band Pink Floyd because of a song whose opening line was, "Brezhnev took Afghanistan."[173] No other artistic expressions relating to the war appeared in print in the war's early years, apart from what critics of the war—and of the Soviet regime–called "pulp literature."[174] These were stories that appeared in military journals with specific audiences and were designed to suit the needs of the war machine and those who controlled it. (The stories described the cruelty of the mujahidin and the Afghan Communists' gratitude for the Fortieth Army's fraternal assistance as it fulfilled its international duty on foreign soil.)

The war began to appear in various art forms in the Soviet cultural space in the second half of the 1980s.[175] Some of the works were still literary propaganda—both pro- and anti-Soviet—sometimes as documentary tales, sometimes posing as pure fiction.[176] Aleksandr Prokhanov continued to be one of the USSR's most prolific writers. In 1986, he produced yet another novel, *Risunki batalista* (Sketches of a battlefield artist) and a short story, "*Svetlee lazuri*" (Brighter than the blue of the sky).[177]

The momentum, however, seems to have flowed from the afgantsy themselves as they sought to bring their experiences to a wider audience through art. By the end of 1988, the state record company, Melodiia, was preparing the publication of previously suppressed soldiers' songs.[178] There was an outpouring of both fiction and verse in 1989, including no fewer than nine short stories by Oleg Ermakov, who served from 1981 to 1983, and collections of poems by Aleksandr Karpenko (*Razgovory s smert'iu*—Conversations with death, published in *Molodaia gvardiia*), Aleksandr Vannikov ("*Iz afganskoi tetrad*"—From an Afghan notebook, which appeared in *Znamia*), and Valerii Rubin's *Reportazh* (published in *Novyi mir*). Perhaps the most significant instance of afganets art was an exhibition, The Incomprehensible War, at the Manezh, Moscow's Exhibition Hall Number One, which opened in July 1991 and was filled with Christian symbols—the Soviet troops bearing the cross in a variety of forms.[179] One picture portrayed an afganets "nailed to the cross to expiate the sins of a whole people."[180] This etching, or one similar, appeared on the cover of the booklet of poems of afganets paratroop officer, Dmitrii Semenov, *Bol'* (Pain), in which many of the poems had a manifestly Christian content. When wounded, he considered himself crucified: "We are brothers in Christ."[181]

The majority of those who devoted their artistic talents to the theme of the war appear to have fought in Afghanistan, yet there were others. These included—besides Prokhanov, who visited Afghanistan frequently as a war correspondent and dubbed himself an afganets—the singer Aleksandr Rozenbaum who performed before Soviet troops there on several occasions (see Chapter 3) and whose songs "The Black Tulip" and "We Will Return" remained popular long after the war. Among non-afgantsy songs on the war was the Siberian antiauthoritarian rock band Grazhdanskaia

Oborona's "Afghan Syndrome" (see Chapter 8). Evgenii Evtushenko's poem "Afghan Ant" drew official wrath with its refrain—"A Russian boy lies on Afghan ground, A Muslim ant crawls on his cheek," taunting and rebuking the corpse.[182]

Mostly though, the art toed the official line throughout the war and even after it. However, along with the Soviet public's growing sense of the war's futility, art forms began to dwell on its negative aspects. At first these were restricted to describing the adversary and the harsh conditions—such as climatic extremities and difficult terrain. But by 1988, even Prokhanov had changed direction, expressing in his fiction, as in his journalism, the realization that the Soviets were not going to win the war. His stories no longer reflected traditional party ideology but, dubbing the opposition "mujahidin" rather than the derogatory dushmany, contended that their position too was legitimate and conceded that many Afghans opposed the Kabul regime, while "positive" Soviet figures could engage in negative conduct such as torturing POWs.[183]

Others addressed the venality of the officers, the soldiers' low morale, and rampant disillusionment. One example was the "military-literary journal" *Podvig,* which, in 1989, devoted an entire issue to the war. It implicitly disparaged the Fortieth Army and the Kremlin but relegated the criticism to personal stories.[184] These themes are apparent even in the work of Lieutenant Colonel Nikolai Ivanov. His "'Al'kor' prinimaet vyzov" ('Al'kor' takes up the challenge, 1991) simultaneously offers official sanction and political protest, particularly of the corruption in both the armed forces and the party. Ivanov also published a "novel-chronicle" in the MPA's "social-political and literary artistic journal," *Sovetskii voin.* One scholar described it as a historical investigation, dramatized documentary, and fiction all in one, addressing young Soviet citizens' "social pathologies" such as nepotism, bribery, and disaffection with military duty.[185]

Despite Iurii Poliakov's 1987 book, *One Hundred Days until the Order,*[186] on Soviet soldiers' experiences, including hazing, the real change in the literary sphere came when, in 1989, Oleg Ermakov started to publish extensively in the "thick journal," *Znamia,* and, to a lesser extent, in *Oktiabr'* and *Novyi mir.* Ermakov's work, all of which addresses the Afghan War, "reanimates the legacy of Soviet dissident fiction about combat and its effect on the human spirit." Several of his stories focus on the Soviet domestic scene—the effect of a soldier's death on his family or the return of soldiers "spiritually transformed—and wounded—to re-enter society in yet another struggle for survival." In this way, the "selfless heroes and subhuman adversaries" of the early years gave way to a generally pessimistic, even satiric literature depicting the war's "psychological and moral effect" on its veterans.[187]

Other art forms (which the government found more difficult to control than the written word) were perhaps even more significant. The soldiers' own songs and poems were particularly popular and influential. Some have suggested that the two genres should be treated together, for some of the poems were put to music and some writers read their songs as poems.[188] At first, most units seem to have sung World War II songs or the bard songs of the 1960s, such as Vladimir Vysotsky's "On ne vernulsia iz boia" and "Synovia ukhodiat v boy" (He did not return from the battle and Sons leave for battle) . But Afghan songs appeared as early as 1980[189] (see Chapter 3). One of the most popular composers was Aleksandr Stovba, whose poems resounded throughout the ranks long after his death and were put to music posthumously.[190] Commenting on the poems of an officer of the Fortieth Army—many of the soldier bards (like Stovba) were officers[191]—Verstakov noted that Afghanistan convinced him that poetry was a far more forceful art form than he had realized.[192]

At first the songs, which focused on fallen comrades and the brutality of the fighting, were an underground phenomenon—"migrating from writing-pad to writing-pad and from notebook to notebook"—to avoid military censorship.[193] "They appeared and with lightning speed spread on hundreds of cassettes" and were sung in "garrisons, tents, headquarters." Soldiers quoted the songs in letters home and sang them before and during combat.[194] This underground folklore of soldier bards, some of whom later became well known (Iurii Kirsanov, Viktor Kutsenko, Igor Morozov, V. Pitriaev, A. Minaev) "ripped the soul apart."[195] By spring 1983, a Western correspondent was providing translated versions of some "often amateurish ballads of bloodshed, bravado and candid fear" that "stray a long way from the upbeat tenor of official Soviet propaganda. . . . The picture is one of very young men caught up in a very hard war they understand very poorly." One song is striking—a dying political officer imagines the approaching mujahid who'll say, "I've eaten many a pale-face before, Now for the first time I'll eat Russian"; the song's author thus compares the Soviet force with Afghanistan's previous unsuccessful imperialist invaders.[196]

Perceiving the songs as subversive, as they told of battles in a nonexistent war, the Fortieth Army authorities endeavored to suppress them in favor of songs from the Great Patriotic War and "sanitized variants." Political and other officers frequently confiscated the handwritten songbooks. Border guards too were instructed to impound the recordings that demobilizing soldiers brought home. Nonetheless, Afghan songs entered the Soviet Union very early; Verstakov heard them in youth groups and in military units, although the media pretended that they did not exist.[197]

Although from the start, the soldiers wrote Afghan music in order to voice, or at least imply, protest against the war, dwelling on its hardships and pain, by 1984 the authorities at home were trying to co-opt it—to harness some of the songs to their own ends, especially when the themes coincided with Russian and Slavic pride and Soviet patriotism. Through Afghan music, Moscow sought to revive patriotic and martial sentiments and maintain its legitimacy among disaffected youth. In the later 1980s, afgantsy songs became an important element in the education of Soviet children and adolescents.[198]

Afgantsy returning with the songs they had composed and sung in Afghanistan organized their own ensembles, such as Kaskad and the "muscular rock" of the paratrooper pop group Golubye berety (Blue berets),[199] creating a legitimate, or semilegitimate, "patriotic" rock style, as opposed to other rock troupes, which the government banned. In 1985, Aleksandr Prokhanov testified that the songs born in Afghanistan were aired in Soviet homes, and "young people, 10th graders, who only recently were tirelessly spinning Vysotsky, sternly and silently listen to these 'ballads.'"[200] In 1987, a first collection of these songs—Tkachenko's "When Soldiers Sing" (Kogda poiut soldaty)—appeared officially, after being censored (see above), and an Afghan song festival accompanied the Ashkhabad convention of Afghan veterans at the end of that year.[201] Over time, too, some songs appeared on Soviet TV; Mikhail Leshchinskii's reporting on the war included one song that a young officer sang in his unit's club, and another performed to the accompaniment of a guitar.[202]

By 1986, the "trickle of songs and poems . . . was threatening to become a flood," as the military-patriotic propaganda machine tapped this new resource. Yet while the military publishing house Voenizdat prepared its collection "Vremia vybralo nas" (Time chose us; see above), the authorities found themselves unable to control a musical phenomenon that sprang from experiences and emotions. A number of Afghan songs protested the war outright, especially when blended with non-Russian nationalism, as by the Latvian vocal group Zvaigznite.[203]

Thus afgantsy songs diverged from traditional military-patriotic music. Songs indicating disaffection—for instance, the refrain "Someone needs this merciless fighting"—were clearly intended to respond to the apathy and criticism that those at home leveled against the veterans and dwelled on the war nobody needed. Even the song that became, as it were, the soldiers' hymn in Afghanistan, Iurii Kirsanov's "A Battle Raged near Kabul," conveyed resentment at the Kremlin's ineptitude.[204] Kirsanov was the first to compose what became "famous and popular" Afghan songs and "is often regarded as the dean of the Afghan War bards.[205] Discontent and resentment were evident in other songs as well, such as Verstakov's satirical attack on the media, "Song about the Soviet Press," M. Smurov's "Soldier-Internationalist," Igor Koshel's "I'm Weary of Wandering," and Igor Morozov's "I Once Knew Two Brothers." Nikolai Shirayev in "A Night in the Hospital," spoke about invalids "discarded by calculating fiancées" and warned that they should not also be "discarded by you, the Mother country." In response to the disrespect that the veterans encountered at home, Vladimir Parygin's "Their Deathless Exploit" implied a threat of violent reaction: "We, with our soldiers' honor, will never yield." Some went as far as to express antiwar sentiment, for example, Iurii Pakhomov in "On the Road Tested by Death," and even Major General Viktor Kutsenko, who wrote that when going into battle, "there's no cry 'for the Mother Country,'" just a curse on parched lips.[206] While most songs were relatively one-sided, at least one poet, Aleksandr Karpenko, had the artistic talent to depict the multifaceted nature of the Afghan War and soldiers' experiences. Although he had been in Afghanistan less than three months when his BTR hit a mine, during the three years he spent in hospital (1981–1984), he gathered ample material from the experiences of other wounded afgantsy.[207]

These songs, whose main themes were the mountains and skies of Afghanistan and the Black Tulips, boasted "a purity and a vigour that could cut through the often over-stylised and -mannered cultural mainstream." Testimonies to their success were the 1990 All-Russian and All-Union Songs of the Afghan War Festivals in Yaroslavl' and Alma-Ata, and the Aist studio's mail-order cassette business, which within six months of opening had assembled thirteen collections of afgantsy music and had sold more than 8,000 cassettes. "For the veterans, [the songs] represented a form of self-medication, a safe way of expressing, externalizing, and purging their experiences. . . . For others, they could be a way into [the veterans'] closed and uncommunicative heads, offering some hope of understanding their lives. For yet others, they were the source of vicarious excitement or an infusion of primitive vitality into Russian culture."[208] Afgantsy continued to compose after their return home, some reflecting on the bitterness of their experience in songs like "Awards Are Not for Sale."[209] In Kirsanov's words, the songs were so popular because they reflected what the soldiers believed and so gave them faith.[210]

Like the popular soldiers' songs of World War II and the dissident underground songs of the guitar bards of the 1960s that inspired them, Afghan War songs went the rounds in the early stages in *magnitizdat* (cassette recordings of underground literature and song).[211] In the words of one critic of the war, these songs were the key not just to what happened in the war but also to Soviet society's response to it.[212] A Western study of Russian war songs, and specifically Afghan War songs—those composed during the war and those dating from the post-Soviet period—called them a "legitimate outlet to convey emotions in public," presenting "loss and trauma" in "publicly acceptable and socially familiar narratives and scenarios." As a pattern of actions in which "shared values, concepts of relations, are affirmed, explored, or celebrated," the songs, as "ready-made, repeatable, ritualistic structures," amalgamated the soldiers' individual and collective experience and "its meaningful expression."[213]

Soviet filmmakers also took up the challenge. What seems to have been the first documentary on the war to be shown in Soviet cinemas, *The Black Tulip* (1987) was a strange mixture of incriminating allusions and accepted propaganda: Here in Afghanistan we simply help the Afghan people. Unlike in Vietnam, where the Americans set up a puppet regime, we conquered nothing and don't interfere in domestic affairs. We're in Afghanistan so that the people here can return to normal lives. The guerrillas are all drug addicts who fight for the money they get from their foreign sponsors.

Another 1987 documentary, *How Difficult It Is to Be Young*, devoted considerable space to the Afghan War, discussing the Afghan problem and how it affected the Soviet Union; to quote Nodari Simoniia, playing on Gorbachev's aphorism, "how bleeding it is for us."[214] Two vets—one who served in 1983–1984, the other, 1986–1988—remember the documentaries of TV correspondent Mikhail Leshchinskii. The former vet spoke of *Zasada* (Ambush), in which half of the Soviet soldiers at whom the mujahidin shot at close range "surrendered into captivity." The latter recalled that Leshchinskii "came to our unit. We ourselves wrote the script for him. He trimmed it—nobody will show all the pain and blood."[215]

Three more documentaries—*Rana* (The wound), *Vozvrashchenie* (The return), and *Bol'* (Pain)—appeared in 1988; another was a joint Franco-Russian production, *Dorogie moi* (My dear ones, 1989), based on letters home of fallen soldiers. In January 1989, the film *Za vse zaplacheno* (Everything paid for) aired on television nationwide. In it, a group of afgantsy returns home to find corruption and crime. They organize, without the aid of the Communist Party or any other officials, and successfully fight social ills.[216]

"*Bol'* evoked considerable debate in the media and apparently also in society; it was discussed at movie theaters in Moscow, where the audience was "sharply divided in its emotions, assessments, and opinions," and Minsk, where the afgantsy passionately defended it.[217] In the words of one critic, "The picture is searing. Some scenes do not just scream, they really howl. . . . It is life in the raw . . . [w]ithout retouching or reticence," befitting the era of glasnost. It included scenes of crippled veterans and grieving mothers, and instances of the callousness of society and officialdom toward the afgantsy. The afgantsy, the critic claimed, thirsted for social justice and relied on support from society and the state.

Another film that appeared in 1989, *Crimson Land*, for which war correspondent Vladimir Snegirev wrote the script, sought to discuss the war "as correctly and objectively as possible" through "a new, more profound and comprehensive approach that rejected motifs "in which that which was desired was often passed off as actual" and showed the Soviet troops as both heroes and victims. Snegirev explained the film's purpose as "reflecting aloud and asking questions—of ourselves, of the audience, of our past and our future." The idea was to provide the viewer with "an opportunity to think for himself."[218] A 1991 film, *Afganets*, offered the agonies of the afgantsy and harsh criticism of the regime.

Some films were war movies in the accepted sense of the word, beginning in 1986 with *Solitary Voyage*. Calls for films on the war were heard at the 1987 Komsomol Congress. Many considered the joint Italian-Soviet venture, *Afganskii izlom* (Afghan fracture, 1991), which sought to underscore the war's purposelessness and brutality, the best film on the war. In one particularly poignant—and sophisticated—film, *Noga* (The Leg, 1991), a wounded soldier's amputated leg becomes his murderously angry and cynical alter ego, haunting him mercilessly. *Noga* underscores the suffering of the soldier's hospitalization and attempted rehabilitation; psychologically unable to return to his native Moscow, he opts for a provincial town, until finally, unable to cope, he lies prostrate on the ground (it's unclear whether alive or dead) while the Leg laughs wildly in the background.[219]

Petr Tkachenko, who compiled at least two volumes of afganets materials—one of letters, the other of songs—wrote in the MoD daily about the "stories, novellas, and even novels" about afgantsy that appear "all the time," and the films and poems, "to say nothing" of the afgantsy's own "already extensive and disturbing body of verse" and songs. He objected to depictions of the veterans as potential or actual criminals, as in Lev Khundus's "He Was My Best Friend" (*On byl moi samyi luchshii drug*) and Evtushenko's poem, "The Little Sorcerer" (*Koldunchik*; *Avrora*, no. 9, 1988); as seeking undeserved recognition of their tribulations for the mother country (as in an article in *Moskovskii komsomolets*); or as suffering from psychological trauma (as in the documentary *Vozvrashchenie*). Tkachenko insisted that the afgantsy perceived themselves less stereotypically, as their ordeals demanded a complex and frequently teleological treatment, like the balanced one in the documentary *Ozhidanie* (Expectation), which included both pain and faith or optimism. In order for the veterans not to "find themselves between the devil and the deep blue sea," it was essential to remain true to the "lofty concepts of military duty and internationalist exploit."[220]

It is not clear whether the afgantsy and civilians who used art forms and popular culture as a way to express their sentiments intended a priori to influence public opinion. Songs, in particular those written and composed in Afghanistan, aimed primarily to create a certain atmosphere. Yet there is ample testimony to the effect songs and films had, especially among young people in the 1980s who were seeking alternatives to the official culture drummed into them from early childhood; they now knew it was not the sole medium for entertainment.[221] The art forms relating to the Afghan War reflected the trends and sentiments prevalent among the younger generation, of resisting the centralization of authority and affirming the legitimacy of personal emotion and the need for individual expression—including the portrayal of negative phenomena: corruption, drug abuse, tactical defeat in combat, even the constraints of literary control, and at least implied criticism of a regime that betrayed the people's trust.

It is clear that the Afghan War had a significant impact on the evolution of public opinion as a social and political force within the Soviet Union. Just as it played a meaningful role in opening up the media by applying the theory behind glasnost, so it promoted the creation of a partly autonomous public opinion independent of the party and its teachings. The war highlighted ills of the Soviet system that people were coming to find increasingly intolerable, as glasnost and New Thinking encouraged citizens to think for themselves and to test the new freedoms of expression

A question mark remains regarding the relevance of public opinion to the withdrawal. Letters from mothers, veterans, and others to major newspapers and party organizations at various levels seem to have carried some weight, although Gorbachev and his reform-minded colleagues almost certainly sought to inflate their import in order to demonstrate the far-reaching nature of the democratization that they had initiated and to legitimize withdrawal. Manifestly, there is no comparison between the pressure to pull out of Vietnam in the late 1960s and early 1970s that civil society in the United States applied to the American administration, and that which the embryo of a civil society could bring to bear on the Kremlin in the latter half of the 1980s.

At the same time, Gorbachev seems to have based the decision to withdraw primarily on domestic constraints and considerations (see Chapter 4).

Appendix: The Impact of the War on the Soviet Union in Soviet Society's Perception

Tables 7.9 and 7.10 and Figures 7.3 and 7.4 are based on our survey of the general population and Figure 7.5 and Tables 7.11 through 7.13 on our survey of Soviet immigrants to Israel.

Table 7.9. Did the method and form of the introduction of our troops into Afghanistan strengthen the USSR's international prestige?

	Russians	Other Slavs	Central Asians	Other Muslims
Early on	19.64%	9.09%	50%	6.67%
At the end of the war	17.86%	10.53%	15.63%	6.67%
Now (1992–1993)	11.11%	6.98%	12.5%	15.79%

Table 7.10. Assess the influence of the Afghan War on national prestige, the economy, and living standards

	The USSR's prestige	The Soviet economy	The Soviet citizen's living standard
Negative	65%	59%	48%
2	20%	30%	31%
3 (no influence)	7%	7%	21%
4	6%	3%	0%
Positive	2%	1%	0%

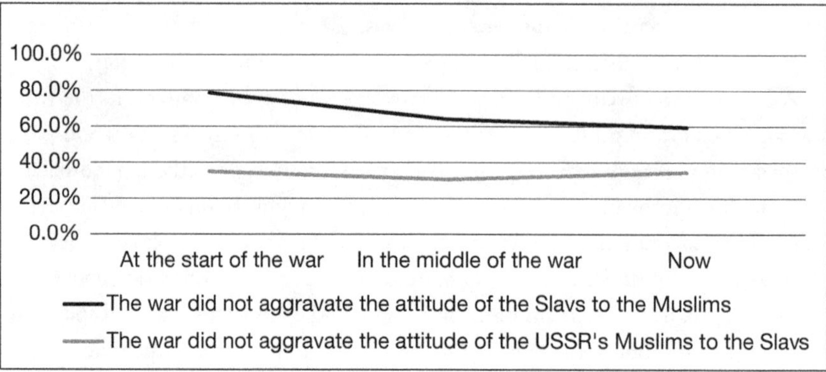

Figure 7.3. The effect of the war on ethnic animosity

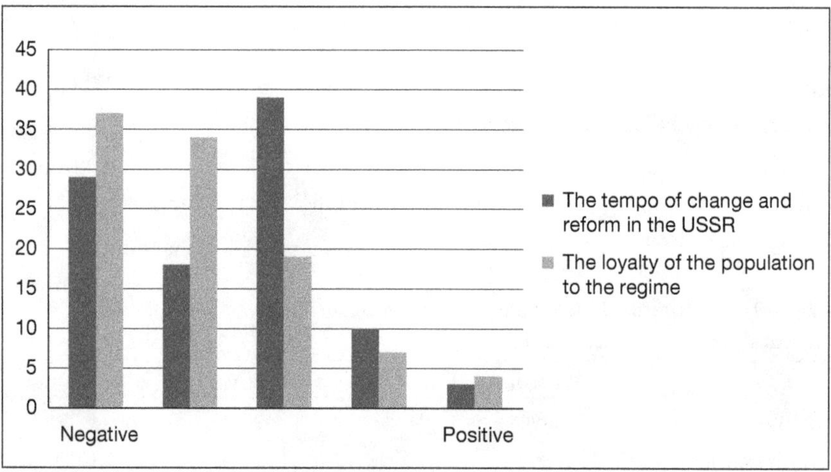

Figure 7.4. The influence of the Afghan War on

Most of the sample saw the war as having had a negative influence on the USSR in terms of prestige, the national economy, and the individual citizen's standard of living. Fewer people considered the war harmful in terms of the standard of living than in terms of prestige and the national economy.

While most Soviet citizens believed that the war did not adversely affect the Soviet Muslim population's attitude toward Slavs, they believed that the attitude of Slavs toward their Muslim fellow citizens deteriorated over its course. Soviet immigrants who arrived in Israel in late 1981 and early 1982 testified even/already then that the war was having a negative effect on the attitude of Slavs toward Soviet Central Asians (Figures 7.3 and 7.4).

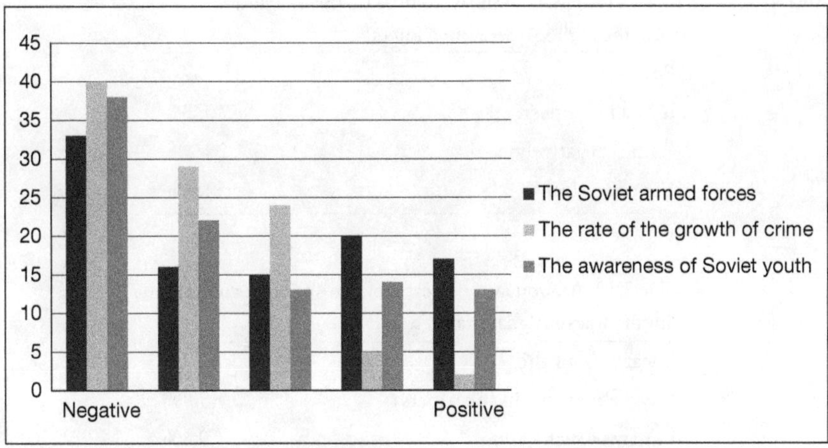

Figure 7.5. The influence of the Afghan War on

Respondents tended to believe that the war did not affect the pace of Gorbachev's domestic changes. At the same time, they claimed that the war decreased Soviet citizens' loyalty to the regime (Figure 7.4). This is similar to their perspective on the media's reportage on the war (see Table 6.3).

Over half of the respondents said that the war had a negative influence on the Soviet armed forces, and approximately one-quarter thought it had a positive or very positive influence on youth awareness. Less than 10 percent thought it affected the rate of crime growth (negative here means that it did not affect the rate at which crime grew).

Most of the sample thought that the war had at least some influence on the standard of living in the USSR (Table 7.11). This is similar to the results that we obtained from the general population (in spite of the different phrasing; see Table 7.10).

Table 7.11. What influence did the war's economic cost have on the standard of living of Soviet citizens?

A major influence	43.2%
Some influence	31.6%
No influence	9.4%
Don't Know	15.8%

Table 7.12. How did the war influence the morale and discipline of the Soviet armed forces?

Positively	6%
It had no impact	10.2%
Rather negatively	28.2%
Very negatively	52.3%

Table 7.13. Are you aware of cases of corruption in connection with the war in Afghanistan?

I heard about this	32.7%
I read about this in the papers	15.8%
I knew of such cases	9.4%
I heard nothing about this	37.6%

The majority of the sample believed that the war had a very negative influence on the armed forces (Table 7.12). Only 6 percent believed that the effect of the war was positive in this regard (note that among the general population, where the question did not limit itself to the issue of morale, the results were considerably more positive; see Figure 7.5).

It seems that the sample is split regarding cases of corruption in Afghanistan (Table 7.13). The most frequent answer is that the respondents had not heard of any cases of corruption. However, while less than 10 percent knew of such instances, over 50 percent had heard that they existed or had read about them in the press.

Chapter 8

The Afgantsy

The war's victims included every person who fought in it, physically wounded or not, according to leading afganets public figure Aleksandr Kotenov.[1] The afgantsy found themselves in

> a very complex psychological situation. They left home almost children and returned . . . far more mature than their peers. . . . Their character, views, values, and orientation formed in acute conditions. They therefore became an embarrassment for society, frequently withdraw into themselves or close ranks. . . . And all around are—bureaucratic "hurdles," obstacles, pits, walls of obsolete legislation that obstruct [their] adaptation. . . . In fulfilling our "international obligations," we, sadly, forgot our own national obligations. The time has come to settle accounts.[2]

Certainly the afgantsy had grievances. They had spent a meaningful period of their formative years fighting a hard war in harsh conditions. They returned feeling that the government and the society that sent them to that war owed them a debt, only to encounter a generally apathetic citizenry preoccupied with making ends meet and, in the war's last years, engulfed in the turbulence that accompanied perestroika and glasnost. Nor were their expectations regarding compensation unreasonable; since the Russian Civil War that followed the Bolshevik takeover in October 1917, the state had revered veterans as model citizens, honored for their contributions to the mother country. The Soviet regime had emphasized the strong connection between military service and the receipt of material privileges and status.[3]

"The bitter psychology of this conflict," writes one student of the Soviet-Afghan War, was

> very different from the positive mood of the nation as a whole during World War II (the "Great Patriotic War"). Afghanistan wrenched boys from their daily life of school and college, music and discos, and hurled them into a hell of filth . . . eighteen-year-olds, mere school-leavers who could be induced to believe anything. It was only much later that we began to hear such thoughts expressed as, "We went to fight a Great Patriotic War . . . but found something totally different." Or, "I wanted to be a hero but now I don't know what kind of person they've turned me into."[4]

The young people sent to Afghanistan, another observer commented, were caught in the midst of a "post-adolescent identity crisis." On the one hand, they had grown up in a communal society, had often never traveled beyond the nearest town or met people of different backgrounds; on the other hand, they had become increasingly educated and acquired a "combination of leisure time and freedom from all-embracing political control to develop [their] own cultures and attitudes." They were thrown unprepared into a framework of "brutality and hierarchy, fear and disaffection that maximized the initial trauma of the Afghan experience." Moreover, the military was singularly unprepared to train this new generation that had largely "drifted outside the ken of the Party and its Young Communist League, the Komsomol." The army's training program "presupposed a draft intake thoroughly prepared for military discipline and . . . possessing basic military skills," yet the edifice on which this assumption was based had crumbled and young people were immersed in their own distinctive subcultures, from hippies to heavy metal rock fans.[5] A study of "the last Soviet generation" that grew to adulthood in the 1970s dwells at length on the young "urbanites" who never attended Komsomol meetings and were uninterested in politics; with neither "overt support of, [n]or resistance to, the Soviet system," they perceived themselves as outside it.[6]

In Afghanistan, one former soldier commented, all the afgantsy had in common was "fear. We were all lied to in the same way, we all wanted to survive and . . . to get home." Another soldier said they were "all in the same boat there, but that didn't mean we all thought the same way. What we had in common was that we were trained to kill, and kill we did. We are all individuals but we've been made into sheep, first here at home and then over there."[7]

An internal army publication stated that what set the Afghan War veteran apart was the consequence of having had to fight in the midst of a foreign civilian population where it was difficult to distinguish between friend and foe, of having being cut off from his home surroundings where life was continuing as usual, and of the negative reception he encountered when he went home.[8] His chief characteristic, in the words of one vet, was reticence but "sometimes all of a sudden an as it were inexplicable aggressiveness would spill out from a sense of inferiority and their undefined position in society."[9]

This chapter suggests that the Afghan War vets retained common features and experiences when they returned home. As one afganets said, "I've left Afghanistan, but I am an afganets, and always will be. I can't walk away from what I have seen and done."[10] Self-appointed afganets Aleksandr Prokhanov contended that everyone who passed through Afghanistan shared something "in their soul, in their character."[11] Some have claimed that their shared painful memories actually shaped their collective identity; these memories were always "in the air" when vets came together, although they refrained from touching the hurt even among themselves.[12]

All Afghan War veterans, moreover, faced a shared dilemma. They needed to know who they were in the eyes of officialdom and of society—"internationalist soldiers" or the victims of a political blunder. This was the crux of their predicament as they commenced what one political officer called their struggle, one "no less complex than service in Afghanistan," to rebuild their lives in Soviet society.[13]

Yet the stereotypes that society conjured up (see Chapter 7) did not—indeed, could not—fit most afgantsy, a large and very diverse group.[14] One scholar who studied the vets in a single, small republic—Tajikistan—points out, "Socially fragmented and geographically dispersed, they were differentiated also by rank, function, and wartime experiences."[15] Indeed, most surveys of afgantsy highlighted their wide range of opinions, attitudes, and characteristics.[16]

Vets who responded to my questionnaire rejected outright the idea of there being a typical Afghan veteran. Yet up to 35 percent attributed certain specific inclinations to members of their group. We designed these categories—which the questionnaire specified—to throw light on the ways in which the afgantsy adapted to civilian life and the extent of their acceptance when they came home.

In short, whether the afganets answered to a clearly defined typology, most vets agree that one could speak of an afganets identity that was shaped by his experiences and sensations as he prepared for Afghanistan, while he served there, and upon his return home. This identity enables the researcher to study the afgantsy and to reach certain conclusions regarding their collective being and Weltanschauung.

Prior to Afghanistan

Although for logistical reasons, the soldiers in the initial intervention were predominantly from the regions bordering on Afghanistan, this disproportion soon evened out. However, even from the beginning, the selection of soldiers for service in Afghanistan seemed arbitrary.

Many soldiers—except those sent in in the very early stages of the war—learned about the war while still at school, as the local Komsomol or voenkomat frequently enlisted veterans to speak to pupils about their experiences, the prohibition against disclosing information on Afghanistan notwithstanding. Many afgantsy testified that they knew a great deal about the war from returning veterans. In addition to pep talks in schools, some vets gave interviews about the war during its course because "it mustn't be hushed up."[17] This was one of the instances where the afgantsy took the law into their own hands in an attempt—not necessarily conscious—to rectify situations in which they found themselves. A Ukrainian nurse, sent to Afghanistan in 1986, had heard about the war from relatives, neighbors, and friends; by then, even the television reported that Soviet soldiers were fighting there and being killed.[18]

Nonetheless, those without relatives, neighbors, or direct contact with vets often knew very little. One soldier sent to Afghanistan in 1986 said he had heard almost nothing about the war and had not given it any thought;[19] another who went in 1987 remembered that he was totally ignorant, for the media reported "almost nothing."[20]

Soldiers found out in different ways that they were being dispatched to Afghanistan. Some—close to 50 percent in our survey—were told at various stages of their training. Others found out at the last minute. The soldiers in a course in Omsk that prepared NCOs in 1982–1983 knew that 20 to 25 percent of those who finished it would be sent to Afghanistan and attempted to calculate the rate of losses. They learned from returning soldiers that discipline in the ranks of the Limited Contingent was deteriorating, that relations between officers and soldiers were often strained, and that the soldiers' main concern was to return home. At the end of the six-month course, the sergeants would spend five to ten days in Tashkent for political training before leaving for Afghanistan.[21] One afganets had attended a school for sergeants in Ashkhabad, where the soldiers were told they were being prepared for Afghanistan. He and some others were trained to shoot at tanks, although the mujahidin had no tanks (he ended up doing guard duty in Afghanistan in a motor-rifle regiment).[22]

A twenty-seven-year-old paratroop sergeant major who was among the first soldiers to go to Afghanistan in 1979 was called up for "reserve duty" and told his destination a few days in advance.[23] Another soldier testified that exactly one day before being sent to Afghanistan, the company commander simply informed the men with no additional comment.[24] Over 20 percent of our respondents learned their destination when they were on the way to Kabul.[25] Nor did they know to what purpose they were going to Afghanistan. A thirty-five-year old lieutenant was told in 1980 that they were being sent there for an inspection parade.[26] A soldier told a journalist interviewing Moscow afgantsy who had participated in the force that crossed the border in December 1979–January 1980 that they received no explanation whatever regarding the purpose of their mission but were told if they were shot at, they should respond by emptying the entire barrel.[27]

A boy enlisted in Zagorsk in the mid-1980s remembers that "by the time he was called to the local recruiting office, thirteen of his local contemporaries had already gone to Afghanistan. Two had returned almost immediately—in zinc coffins. A third came back later—without hands. . . . The other lads of the same age were scared. . . . Their parents were frankly alarmed."

Some soldiers tried to avoid going to Afghanistan. One mother who went to a swearing-in ceremony noted that the soldiers were required to stay in groups because when they "realised they were going to Afghanistan, some . . . hanged themselves in the toilets or slashed their wrists." After training in a camp in Samarkand in late 1980, a new troop of soldiers were lined up on the parade ground and read the "Order of the Day: We were being sent to the DRA 'in the execution of our international duty.' 'Anyone who doesn't wish to go—two paces forward—march!' Three boys stepped forward, but the CO kicked them back again. 'I was just testing your battle-readiness,' he said." Some afgantsy remembered the cowards. "'I won't go!' they'd say. 'Even prison's better than war.' . . . We'd make their lives a misery and beat them up. Some of them deserted."[28] My survey, however, demonstrated that post-factum, afgantsy tended to show more understanding, for "who wants to die?"

Theoretically, soldiers and officers alike were supposed to agree to go to Afghanistan. Several soldiers recalled that they had been asked whether they wanted to go there or not, but this was purely pro forma, to show that nobody was being compelled to go.[29] Clearly, *consent* was a flexible term. One soldier remembers,

> We were lined up and marched to a barbed-wire compound. . . . At lunchtime crates of vodka suddenly arrived. We were lined up in rows and informed that in a few hours' time we would be flying to Afghanistan to do our duty as soldiers in accordance with our military oath. It was incredible! Fear and panic turned [sic] men into animals—some of us went very quiet, others got into an absolute frenzy, or wept with anger or fell into a kind of trance, numb from this unbelievably filthy trick that had been played on us. That was what the vodka was for . . . to calm us down. After we'd drunk it and it had gone to our heads some of us tried to escape and others started to fight with the officers, but the compound was surrounded by troops from other units and they shoved us into the plane. We were just thrown into that great metal belly like so many crates being loaded.

When his wife inquired why he was in Afghanistan, she was told he had volunteered, just as they told "all our mothers and wives."[30] Some soldiers were ordered to write home they were volunteering for Afghanistan.[31]

Even some officers tried to refuse to serve in Afghanistan[32] despite the career opportunities that the war opened up for them. One battalion commander, for instance, "had to face a 'court of honor' which convicted him of cowardice," demoted him from major to captain, and posted him to a construction battalion. The party expelled him, and eventually the army discharged him with dishonor.[33] A professional soldier, a senior warrant officer in his forties, recollects that one day in 1985, his company was told they were being sent to Afghanistan to do construction work and give concerts. He personally was told that if he refused to go, he would get an early discharge or be declared a traitor; he added that the army discharged many professional soldiers who refused to go and deprived them of their pensions.[34]

Conversely, many soldiers, especially early in the war, volunteered for Afghanistan. The Komsomol daily wrote that soldiers in Afghanistan had told its correspondent that "back in our training unit, there was talk that we might have to serve in Afghanistan" and "basically all the fellows wanted to come here." They wanted to serve "where it would be harder" and "to be of use."[35] "I wanted to find out what I was capable of . . . and looked for a chance to be [a hero]. . . . It was like a game for us. Self-esteem and pride were terribly important—can I do it?"[36] One recruit told his mother he was volunteering for Afghanistan. "'That's the way you brought me up . . . there are higher things in life than a fridge full of meat.' He wasn't the only one, she recalls. Many other boys applied to go . . . all from the best families—their fathers were heads of collective farms, teachers, and so on."

Some "young men . . . were very keen to go to Afghanistan. . . . One of them was the son of a military man. . . . Another was the son of an alcoholic. A third was the son of the secretary of the regional party organization." That boy said that he would go on from Afghanistan to the West; his father, however, would not hear of his son going to the war, and ultimately the boy did not enlist at all but went to study.[37] A former group leader at a model Pioneer camp "naturally volunteered for Afghanistan" when he was called up. The political officer "told us that Soviet forces had forestalled the American Green Berets' airborne invasion of Afghanistan by just one hour. It was so incessantly drummed into us that this was a sacred 'international duty' that eventually we believed it." This was in 1986, and they were still lying.[38] One vet remembered that the stories he heard from a soldier demobilized after being wounded in Afghanistan only whetted his appetite.[39] Not a few afgantsy testified that prior to enlistment, boys were generally enthusiastic about the idea of going to Afghanistan. This was a recurrent theme in the narrative of twelve vets whose testimonies comprise the story of "Muscovites of the *'Dolg'* Club."[40]

One Afghan veteran who had been mobilized well into the war reflected, "When we were growing up we were never taught 'thou shalt not kill.' On the contrary—all those [World War II] veterans, with rows of medals pinned to their splendid uniforms, came to our schools and colleges to describe their exploits in detail. . . . [Afghan] veterans from the Special Forces described to us how they'd stormed villages and slaughtered all the inhabitants. It sounded romantic. We wanted to be as strong and fearless as they were. I love music and books but I also wanted to storm villages, cut throats, and boast about it afterwards."[41]

Their Experience in Afghanistan

Just as for many the humiliation of being deceived before their arrival in Afghanistan—and of having received inadequate training—continued to rankle and affect the vets' attitude toward Soviet society, so did many other aspects of their service in the war.

Very few letters from Afghanistan seem to have been kept. According to Colonel Petr Tkachenko, who edited a small volume of soldiers' letters, the soldiers were inclined to destroy their letters once they returned, as were the families of those killed.[42] Even letters that were preserved generally did not reflect what the writer experienced but what he sensed he could or should write home.[43] This section therefore rests primarily on the reports of Soviet journalists sent by their newspapers to cover the war and on the stories that soldiers recounted after returning home.

We have seen (in Chapter 3) that on arriving in Afghanistan, many soldiers believed that they were there to defend their country's southern border and to help the Afghans build socialism and a better life. This was the "internationalist duty" that the army had taught them. On the ground, however, the reality was more complex, even completely different, and the soldiers often found themselves wondering why and whom they were fighting. It was not always possible to distinguish between "the enemy" and the civilians who just wanted to go about their lives.[44] The soldiers found themselves fighting and killing Afghan peasants rather than American, Chinese, or Pakistani mercenaries. They were unable to rely on the DRA army with which they were supposed to cooperate and discovered that the population detested them.

Although he admits that then, "as now," there were many agonizing questions, one political officer reminisces, "At the time it entered the head of no one of us to call the war 'criminal.' Everyone did what he had to do and performed his military duty. . . . The soldiers, the NCOs, the officers, all understood that if one doesn't halt the war on the threshold," that is. on the border of the Soviet Union, "it will sooner or later enter the home."[45]

One battalion commander who made a point of explaining to his troops the importance of defending the Soviet Union's southern borders and of adding his own "ideological grounding" to the biweekly political education lectures admitted back home that he had been "terribly torn inside"; even while he was in Afghanistan, he did not believe that they were defending the April revolution. Coming back after seeing all the dead soldiers and always sensing that "someone was trying to kill you," he was unable to "adjust to this world. . . . I couldn't stand up in front of my lads nowadays and lecture them about how we're the finest and fairest in the world."[46]

Altogether, as one scholar has noted, in what he calls the *Gewaltraum*, the dangerous space that was all of Afghanistan outside Kabul, "Physical violence was the most important resource. It was used to communicate, to establish social hierarchies, and simply to survive." Back home, the afgantsy confessed that "there," they had been driven by emotions—fear, anger, revenge—had lived "another life, and we lived it as best we could. That life was lived by other values, other criteria."[47] The Ukrainian KGB registered statements by afgantsy in Lutsk who allowed themselves "politically immature judgments, misconstruing the essence of the international assistance to Afghanistan, stating that Soviet soldiers allegedly committed 'atrocities' against the peaceful population."[48]

Above all, they brought back the experience of living with death. Countless veterans spoke of the trauma of losing close friends. Their comrades were being killed, and they were well aware that their turn might come any time (see Chapter 3). Of the veterans I interviewed, just 5 percent had not known anyone who was killed in the fighting, over half knew between one and ten soldiers who had lost their lives in Afghanistan, and nearly 40 percent knew more than ten (Table 8.1).

Altogether, the soldiers and sergeants—but not the officers—frequently developed a sense of having been victimized. This was less because of the war and the traumatic impact of the constant proximity of death over a protracted period, and more from the formal and informal rules of army life that reflected the inequality, injustices, and corruption of life in the Soviet Union.[49]

Soldiers, for example, were ordered to write home that they were abroad, suggesting or even stating specifically that they were in Germany or Czechoslovakia or somewhere else where Soviet soldiers were serving. A few who had known where they were going ahead of time had told their parents or had agreed on a code word to inform their families that they were in Afghanistan.[50] Others wanted apparently to avoid worrying those at home, so censored themselves. One Soviet correspondent found a soldier reading a book on Mongolia so that he could write his mother about the country where he had told her he was serving.[51] Some families found out or divined that their sons were in Afghanistan during the course of their service; others learned that their sons had been in Afghanistan only after their demobilization—or when they received the zinc coffin.[52] Similarly, soldiers seem often to have refrained on their own accord from telling their families that they had been wounded.[53]

Moreover, soldiers were ordered not to talk about the war if they went home on leave (most of the rank-and-file soldiers never got leave[54]) and when they were demobilized (see Chapter 7). One soldier, who served from 1980 to 1981, was told not to tell anyone that fighting was taking place.[55] As late as 1986/1987 "the farewell

Table 8.1. Did you know people who were killed?

I personally knew many (more than 10)	39%
I personally knew a few	56%
No	5%

address from the political education officer . . . was a list of what we could and could not talk about back home. No mention to be made of fatalities, nor of any 'unofficial activities,' because we are a 'great' powerful and '*morally healthy*' army. We were to destroy all photographs and films. We did not shoot, bombard, use poisons, or lay mines here." The same happened when they arrived home. The authorities "tried to persuade us" not to "'talk too much about what you did and saw over there.'"[56]

Officers too reacted to the double-talk to which they were subjected. One Fortieth Army officer who served from 1979 to 1981 said, "I first began to doubt our press during the Afghan War. Most of our officers had the same experience. Our people were being killed and wounded, yet the newspapers said we were not taking part in combat. . . . It was impossible to explain to the soldiers why we were there."[57] One air force major participated in an operation in 1984, only to hear on Soviet radio that it had been conducted by Afghan troops: "Our press distorts reality and weakens people's trust in anything that is said or written."[58] (For the Soviet media's demoralizing impact on the troops in Afghanistan, see Chapter 3.)

When we asked what they had taken home from Afghanistan, officers and men alike answered, "a more serious attitude to life." They could not forget what they had seen and done, and especially their fallen comrades in arms.[59] Four years after leaving Afghanistan—after being wounded and losing a leg—one officer remembered his time there as "the most difficult and simultaneously the finest period of our lives."[60]

The Return Home

While in Afghanistan, most soldiers just wanted to survive and return home.[61] Nonetheless, some "guessed, even then, that when we got home, we'd be a lost and unwanted generation." A few, particularly in the war's later years, were scared that they'd find everything changed. "And a different view of the war. We'll stick out like a sore thumb." The seriously wounded, who'd lost arms and legs, were often reluctant to go home at all. "There were a lot of lads" in the hospital in Kabul who'd "smoke and crack jokes . . . but . . . didn't want to go home. They'd beg to stay till the last possible moment. Going home was the hardest thing of all, starting a new life." Some preferred suicide, like the man who tried to hang himself in the toilet of the Tashkent hospital after receiving a letter from his girlfriend saying, "You know, Afgantsi are out of fashion now."[62]

Most of the soldiers, however, expected a better, purer, and more equitable life. Instead, they—especially those returning in the second half of the decade—found themselves confronting a collapsing system, a shortage of everything, long lines everywhere, and people—the younger generation, their peers, and their parents—preoccupied with profit seeking and private entrepreneurship.

Their Reception

The veterans had anticipated a warm welcome (see Chapter 7). One soldier who returned in 1985 said he and his companions had felt like heroes, victors, and expected "gratitude, recognition, understanding." But they received nothing of the sort. The customs people at the border poured cold water on their expectations, looked on them as if they were "saboteurs." And that was just a portent of things to come.[63] The returning soldiers were not greeted as heroes. True, Soviet government policy dictated that local communities conduct welcome home ceremonies—"no doubt to the bafflement of officials since the troops were in Afghanistan engaged in 'public works.' The Afgantsi . . . called these largely meaningless, empty rituals the 'false face of welcome.'"[64] For even when they were welcomed with fanfare, they quickly had to face the problems of adaptation. One officer noted, "They are invited to a school and seated on the stage. Be grateful, soldier. But that soldier has neither house nor home."[65]

The withdrawal in May 1988 apparently occurred with considerable disorder, for in January 1989, Tashkent was trying to prepare for the final withdrawal in a way that would avoid "the muddle" of the previous spring;[66] the Turkestan MD formed a special Operations Group to orchestrate the withdrawal on the Soviet side of the border.[67] There were all the outward appearances of a warm welcome—including an official message of greeting from the regime[68] (although no member of the country's leadership came to either Termez or Kushka)—and the central press devoted considerable attention to the occasion.[69] *Pravda*'s special correspondents in Termez said the tension and excitement of the women awaiting their sons, husbands, and lovers were indescribable;[70] some of the relatives, who had come from all over the country, had been there for weeks.[71] (The withdrawal had been underway since late January although took on "intensive" proportions only on February 8.[72])

The returning soldiers ran immediately into the stark reality of Soviet existence. No one had made arrangements to transport them to their homes or even to feed and accommodate them until a train or plane could take them toward their destination. Officials at the entry points fleeced many of them of everything they had brought back. Several sources describe the chaos and hardships the soldiers encountered as soon as they reached Soviet territory.[73] A group of 300 paratroopers described how an officer of the divisional command greeted them as "swine and other unprintable names." After a month in the field in midwinter as they guarded the final withdrawal

Table 8.2. Official figures tell of 15,000 killed. What do you think of these data?

The real figures are higher	54%
They relate only to those who died in action, not to those who died of wounds or sickness	16%
They are probably correct	14%
I don't know	16%

at the Salang Pass, they were not able to wash or change their clothing before meeting their families.[74]

Not surprisingly, then, disillusionment at what they had encountered quickly superseded the positive feelings that the soldiers had entertained regarding the life that awaited them. The overriding sentiments of the returning afgantsy were anger and alienation, a sense that society was rejecting them. Still upset about the way they had been prepared for and sent to Afghanistan, the lies that continued to be told about the war incensed them.[75] "Many of my friends are dead," one soldier tells us, "and sometimes I envy them because they'll never know they were lied to about this disgusting war—and no one can ever lie to them again."[76]

If the government was determined to sweep under the carpet the shocking side of the war, including the fact that Soviet planes and helicopters sometimes attacked Soviet troops, and record only "exalted memories," one afganets said, regarding the reaction to Andrei Sakharov's call for the entire truth about the war (see Chapter 10), "Our children would perhaps want to go to fight somewhere else."[77]

The media's lies about the war opened their eyes to the realities of the Soviet Union. "Afghan," an afganets who came home in 1981, said, "cured me of the illusion that everything's OK here, and that the press and television tell the truth. . . . I wanted to do something specific . . . speak out, tell the truth, but my mother stopped me. 'We've lived like this all our lives,' she said."[78]

The afgantsy's disbelief in the figures the authorities gave for casualties reflects their lack of confidence in official publications (Table 8.2).

One woman who had worked as a nurse in Bagram said the figures did not include the many soldiers killed as a result of fights or quarrels with fellow soldiers, about which she knew from personal experience. Officers did not report even those wounded in such fights, fearing a demotion if they passed on such information.[79]

In addition to the falsehoods that surrounded the war, the revelation that those sent to Afghanistan came mostly from ordinary families and were not the children of state and party officials increased the resentment.[80] So too did the afgantsy's sense that as glasnost and the concomitant indictment of the war gathered momentum, neither the authorities nor society differentiated between the war and those who had fought in it. (For the insensitivity of the bureaucracy and its consequences for their well-being, see Chapter 6 and below.)

The afgantsy were infuriated by the way that society perceived them. Stories abound of the sense of cruel injustice that the veterans developed on their return home and in the following years. They resented the general refusal to acknowledge the hardships and sacrifices to which they had been consigned in a backward and unfriendly foreign country and felt humiliated by the accusations hurled at them by a society that looked on the war as a national disgrace and that blamed the soldiers who had fought it. This was in sharp contrast to the soldiers of the Great Patriotic War, who had been received as heroes. Young boys had been "taken from their homes, had a gun stuck in their hands and were taught to kill. They were told they were on a holy mission and that their country would remember them. Now people turn away and try to forget the war, especially those who sent us there in the first place."[81] In some places they encountered gibes, such as "Only fools go to Afghanistan"[82] (see Chapter 7). One vet, replying to a poll in late 1989, said that society's attitude to the afgantsy had driven many of them to take refuge in drugs and alcohol.[83] Another said, "How could we not be hooligans and brawlers after seeing our friends killed before our eyes? And if the Establishment didn't send us to Afghanistan, who did—the shopkeeper?"[84]

The afgantsy were particularly stung by charges that they had lost the war. "Who says we lost the war? Here's where we lost it, back home, in our own country. We could have won a great victory here too. We came back as strong as steel forged in the fire, but we weren't given the chance—or the power."[85] In the words of the song "Afghan Syndrome" of the punk-rock troupe Grazhdanskaia oborona, losing the war means to be embarrassed by one's awards, to be shunned like a thief, to live like a spring with a hand on the trigger.[86] The public's reaction made them ashamed to don the medals they had received for combat operations and to show their veterans' booklets to get their entitlements;[87] they preferred to pay for public transportation and stand in line.[88] At a Moscow demonstration in August 1988, thousands of veterans reportedly trampled their medals underfoot;[89] in Tajikistan, afgantsy set fire to their army papers, saying entering Afghanistan had been a mistake;[90] and in Vilnius, in December 1989, Afghan War vets participating in a 3,000-strong demonstration on the tenth anniversary of the intervention turned in their medals to the Lithuanian Supreme Soviet honors commission.[91]

One veteran

> got on a bus and heard two women talking. "Fine heroes they were! Murdering women and children. . . . They're sick. And just think, they get invited to speak at schools. They even get special privileges." I jumped off at the next stop and stood there crying. We were soldiers obeying orders. In wartime you can be shot for disobedience, and we *were*

> at war. Obviously it wasn't the generals themselves who killed women and children, but they gave the orders—and now they're blaming us. Now we're told that to obey a criminal order is itself a crime. But I trusted the people giving the orders. As far back as I remember I've been taught to have faith in authority. No one ever told me to judge for myself whether or not to trust the authorities, whether or not to shoot. . . . Yes, I was a killer and I'm covered in blood . . . but I saw him lying there, my friend who was like a brother to me, with his head cut off, and his arms and his legs, and his flayed skin. . . . I volunteered for the next raid. I watched a funeral procession in a village, there were a lot of people there . . . and I gave the order: "At the funeral—FIRE!"[92]

Some afgantsy admitted that the Fortieth Army had committed moral or ethical misdemeanors. But they tended to excuse them—especially the consumption of narcotics—by highlighting the hardships that the soldiers experienced in Afghanistan. They also insisted that misdeeds occurred only rarely and were inflated by rumor.[93]

Reality, then, slapped the afgantsy in the face. The worst came in December 1989 when the Congress of People's Deputies condemned the war as politically and morally wrong,[94] although it specifically excluded from the censure those who had fought in it (see Chapter 4).

Our survey showed that the afgantsy found themselves judged, unwanted and misunderstood, by their families, their friends, and, above all, by local officials (Table 8.3). (We did not ask them about the attitude of society as a whole.) Their resultant frustration was hardly a recommendation for a smooth acclimatization.

Questioned in the late 1989 *Komsomol'skaia pravda* survey about who displayed adequate concern for them, just 12 percent of afgantsy replied "society as a whole"; 18 percent, the government; 5 percent, both the party and soviet organs (the latter meaning local government); 14 percent, the Komsomol; 25 percent, those in their immediate surroundings; 33 percent, the older generation; 26 percent, young people; 48 percent, the press, which indeed was demonstrating considerable empathy by this time; and 26 percent, "they themselves."[95]

Acclimatization

There were three requirements for settling into civilian life: getting work or further education, finding accommodations, and learning to live with one's experiences.

For many afgantsy, the war did not end with their return to the Soviet Union. It followed them home, plaguing them as they tried to adapt to a new life.[96] Many were frightened to go out of the house for months or more. One boy from Leninabad who returned home in the middle of the 1980s in "a heavy depression" did not leave his room or speak to anyone.[97] A soldier who returned home in 1983 called his experience there "terribly obtrusive . . . like a crazy dream. I live and breathe as if I were

Table 8.3. Which people were least understanding of your difficult psychological situation?

The local authorities	49%
Family	30%
Friends	16%
Veterans of World War II	5%

two people"—one back home, the other there. "I don't know when I'll be able to shake it off."[98] Another soldier testified two years after returning home that he was still dreaming he was "at [his] own funeral . . . or else waking up in a panic because I had no ammo to shoot myself with." For years, they couldn't sleep or had nightmares: "All of us who were there have a graveyard of memories." "You try and live a normal life, the way you lived before. But you can't." One nurse testified that the men "came home, fell in love, had kids—but none of it really helped. Afghanistan was more important than anything else."[99] A vet who was able to raise a family testified ten years after returning home that Afghanistan just would not leave him.[100]

A nurse who went there in 1980 and presumably stayed about two years said a decade later, "Don't tell me the war's over. . . . I'll be haunted by Afghanistan for the rest of my life." In the words of a woman who had served as an NCO, "This war will never be finished—our children will go on fighting it."[101] After his second tour of the troops in Afghanistan, Artem Borovik thought "of all the subconscious associations you bring back with you from Afghanistan." Indeed, at times, "Afghanistan is reality, while everything around it is only an illusion, a dream. . . . If you're lucky, you learn to take it easy five or six months later."[102] In late 1989, 60 percent of afgantsy testified that they thought frequently of events connected with their Afghan experience, as against 12 percent who thought of them only rarely, and 3 percent who forced themselves to forget.[103] One vet explained that it was better if one forgot—it was easier to live.[104]

The war had transformed the afgantsy irremediably, become part of their identity. They felt they were not like everyone else. In one survey, half of the respondents felt that they had been changed for the better; one-quarter, for both the better and the worse; just 14 percent felt unchanged.[105] Many couldn't mingle with former friends. Many couldn't discuss their experiences in the barracks or in combat with anyone else.[106] They were more mature, more serious: "We had killed people and our friends had been killed before our eyes."[107] Unlike their contemporaries, they could not see new fashions or dances as issues that concerned them.[108] Many could not reconcile themselves to the materialism they saw around them of a generation that had grown up in an age of peace and relative prosperity and admired Western pop culture. Coming from a war and an "atmosphere of high revolutionary purity," he could not "believe his eyes," a correspondent from the Russian town of Togliatti wrote of an afganets. His friends wanted new records and cars, his parents argued over the site of their new dacha, and his girlfriend sported American jeans. He found himself wondering what his fellow soldiers had died for. Had his comrades given their lives "for these speculators, these complacent . . . scroungers?" asks another afganets.[109] One veteran wrote to *Sobesednik* in early 1986, "I cannot live as I used to, as many now live in the larger cities with their bourgeois ideology," refusing to take an interest in what goes on outside the home. "Was I really once like that? But now I'd [like to] show those vermin, those goody-goodies."[110] One veteran turned to drink "because I couldn't stand the sight of the speculators and wide-boys [wheeler-dealers]. They swagger about town like tin-pot gods. We've created them by our cult of materialism. The moment I see them I think of what our lads over there are suffering, the shells and mines, that terrible climate and homesickness. I feel more than intense hatred."[111]

Initially, the afgantsy tended to mix solely with their kind. "I could bear to be only with people who'd been there themselves. I spent my days—and nights—with them. Talking to anyone else seemed a futile waste of time. That phase lasted six months."[112] A woman who had worked in a Fortieth Army laboratory had taken sick with malaria and typhoid fever and had a ten-year-old son to raise found herself struggling to recover her dignity and sense of worth in a society that quickly forgot "we were there." She looked desperately for someone who had been in Afghanistan and had also not settled back into life with whom she could find understanding.[113] In the film *Afganskii izlom* (Afghan fracture), one vet felt alive, a human being with no shame, only when among fellow afgantsy, so spent all his time helping families of the fallen.

Many who returned before the war was over wanted to go back. According to one source, hundreds, perhaps thousands, of them "stormed" the military commissariats demanding to be sent back to the war because they longed for the action or the camaraderie of Afghanistan, felt unwanted at home,[114] or were unwilling to lead the bland and staid life that awaited them.[115]

Others could not look back with yearning. They were "ashamed to remember." Already in Afghanistan, they had been "struck by their own cruelty. We executed innocent peasants. If one of ours was killed or wounded, we would kill women, children, and old people as revenge. We killed everything, even the animals."[116] One man could not shake off the memory of a woman he had killed unintentionally.[117] "We were supposedly equated with the participants in the Great Patriotic War, but they defended their homeland, while what did we do? We played the role of the Germans."[118]

"The 'Afghan generation' missed the time when they should have been in colleges and universities improving their capabilities. . . . And when they came home, they were made to feel like outsiders. They were confused in trying to decide what to do in order to start a normal civilian life."[119] Nor were the stumbling blocks in their adaptation to civilian life a necessary consequence of the war. The bureaucracy with which they had to deal often dismissed their wants and problems out of hand. To a woman NCO's remark that she had returned "damaged inside," an official simply retorted, "Aren't we all? It wasn't us that sent you there."[120] No wonder the veterans called officialdom "the dushmans at home."[121]

One significant element of acclimatization was the timing; those coming home once perestroika was underway encountered increased difficulties. They found a breakdown of the existing order and an economic shortage that entailed "money-grubbing" while their public image was not that of heroes but of aggressors, marauders, loafers, and junkies, which complicated any possible social rehabilitation.

As a result of the moral disorientation they developed during the war, the soldiers returned home with a code of values different from that of their peers. Their suffering, one said, had made them comprehend the need for perestroika well before most other people.[122] The Krasnoiarsk survey found that 86 percent of afgantsy—as opposed to 44 percent of their peers—believed that Soviet society needed "radical improvement and change."[123] Some took up the cause of perestroika with enthusiasm, hoping to change the system. Major General Kim Tsagolov wrote in 1989 that the afgantsy's heightened sense of responsibility, honor, and duty made most of them "fighters in the struggle for perestroika."[124]

Others became compulsively violent, which led to criminal behavior, including murder. A social psychologist (cum-political scientist) who had worked with the Fortieth Army procuracy between 1985 and 1987 undertook an analysis of afganets' tendencies toward violence, attributing them to an "existentialist 'chaos' to which the personality was unable to adjust."[125] Another analysis explained the violence that frequently accompanied the afgantsy's reaction to what they encountered at home as a carry-over from their experience in Afghanistan. There, the chronic shortage and poor quality of the nutrition led them to theft and disregard of the law that undermined the idealism of their mission. At home, the frustration at the economic breakdown that excluded any adequate compensation for what they had endured "there" meant that "ominously," the vets again "envisioned violence as a currency with which they could redefine this broken exchange." Some "directed this violence against themselves in drug abuse, alcoholism, and suicide." For others, "the violence of war" that impregnated their "psyche" disrupted life on "the Russian home front."[126] Another psychologist attributed their "existentialist crisis," to the instability of the Soviet domestic situation and the constant transformation of values under glasnost, which particularly affected the afgantsy, with their special sensitivities.[127]

In other words, the traits that had helped them survive the war did not facilitate their adaptation to civilian life. They had little patience for its slow pace or for the vacillations of the Soviet leadership. Many felt that it was legitimate to use force to get results. One veteran wrote in a Ukrainian youth newspaper, "Among my comrades in arms you will not encounter money-grubbers or parasites, shirkers, or conformists. The ideas of honesty, duty, patriotism, and humaneness are not abstract for them." These values had become a part of those "whom it befell to fight for high human ideals not with words but with deeds."[128]

Loneliness, physical and societal, was a feeling that many—perhaps most—vets experienced. For some it was the predominant reaction. One vet asserted, "I had a feeling of being lonely and defenseless when I walked around in my hometown without a gun."[129] Some of them felt it necessary to leave their hometowns and villages. One soldier, who returned in 1985, wrote to an army newspaper, "I did not know what to do or where to go. I did not find understanding among my friends and all my family." (His mother had died while he was in Afghanistan.) "My nerves started to fail. I decided to leave my native village for some place as far away as possible." He found work in a cotton-spinning factory, where there were other afgantsy among whom he was more comfortable.[130] Another vet felt he had to leave his small hometown and go to a large city to create a new identity for himself. In this way, the war led to social mobility among its vets.[131]

Other veterans felt no need to be among their own. Sixty percent of the respondents in one survey of 320 vets rarely maintained contact with fellow afgantsy.[132] Some opted for solitude, closing themselves off entirely: "This feeling that I don't want to go on living gets stronger with every passing day. I have no desire to meet anyone or see anything."[133] Over two decades after the war's end, an article on the afgantsy noted that many were reluctant to have contact with other vets, and refused to be interviewed.[134]

We asked the vets about their relations with their peers after their return home; the results are in Table 8.4.

Medical personnel seem to have had an especially difficult time settling back into civilian life. Many of them had had harrowing experiences (see Chapter 3), yet when they returned home, they were taunted for seeking the entitlements granted afgantsy because most of them had not participated in fighting. Many encountered gibes that they had gone to Afghanistan to get "big money." In 1988, an All-Union Meeting of Internationalist Medics was held in Tashkent. Participants both sought adequate recognition for their services and discussed the social and medical rehabilitation of wounded and crippled soldiers.[135]

The veterans' psychological condition inevitably affected their personal, especially intimate, relationships. "Tales of estrangement and broken relationships were legion," writes Galeotti, whether in burgeoning relationships or with newly married wives.[136] One soldier married on his return. His wife said she'd save him "from Hell, from Purgatory." But she couldn't deal with his condition. She would tell him, "What a

Table 8.4. How did the war influence your relations with your peers at home?

It created a psychological barrier	30%
We discussed Afghanistan openly and reached understanding	35%
It made no difference	35%

Note: Our findings accord with those of a Soviet psychologist who studied the specifics of the afganets personality, Znakov, "Psikhologicheskoe issledovanie stereotipov ponimaniia lichnosti uchastnikov voiny v Afganistane." Znakov served in Afghanistan from 1985 to 1987.

night! You were shouting again, killing someone all night long." He would sit and watch the kettle smoldering on the gas, getting blacker and blacker until it burned completely because he liked the smell of burning. She left him and he continued hating himself, sometimes forgetting his name and address, scared to go out of the house or touch a woman, wishing he were dead.[137]

The self-hate, disgust, guilt, and social isolation, expressed through the difficulty in forming close relationships and reinforced by society's hostility, frequently led to suicide (the rate of which was already relatively high in the Soviet Union).[138] These same feelings brought other veterans into the fold of the church; some had already shown religious inclinations while on active service (see Chapters 3 and 7).

Not only were their l'goty (entitlements) often not forthcoming (see Chapter 4), many veterans lived in extreme poverty. The issue of housing was a particularly sore point. In view of the overall lack of housing in the Soviet Union, it was perhaps not surprising that many afgantsy, even the sick and the wounded, found themselves homeless. A group of afgantsy from the Russian town of Ivanovo wrote to a military newspaper that one of their number was without a home, although his wife was due to give birth. "Is it possible," they asked, that such a man, "marked with traces of the Afghan's bullets, who had to lie in a hospital for almost a year, does not deserve at least one room for him and his family?"[139] The painful odyssey of another disabled vet to get housing for himself and his family ended in suicide.[140]

Asked in a 1989 *Komsomol'skaia pravda* survey what was their most pressing issue, housing topped the list with 40 percent; restoring mental equilibrium, 35 percent; the search for a place in life, 32 percent; the restoration of health, 31 percent; material problems, 28 percent; consumer services, 10 percent; and beginning a family, 9 percent.[141]

The Afgantsy's Careers

Most afgantsy seem to have found work despite growing unemployment,[142] and, if we can judge from anecdotal evidence, they did so in all sectors of the job market. One study on afgantsy examined job advertisements in the veterans' organ *Pobratim* from 1989 to 1991 and determined that approximately one-third of them were for military-related work, one-third for sales and entrepreneurial opportunities, and one-third for conventional blue-collar jobs.[143]

Returning soldiers who had not completed their service when the withdrawal took place were not reassigned to units serving in the Soviet Union but were thrown into civilian life. (This presumably reflects Gorbachev's intention to reduce the size of the armed forces.) According to GS data, just 61,374 "people with combat experience in Afghanistan" were in the military months after the war's end.[144] Shortly before the Soviet Union broke up, Defense Minister Dmitrii Yazov stated that 70,000 veterans had found careers in the armed forces.[145] Probably the majority of these were officers who had chosen a military career before going to Afghanistan, had served there as officers or praporshchiki, and now, in the words of one senior commander, comprised "that force on which it is necessary to rely in the company and in the regiment . . . who show by deed."[146] Officers who continued to serve avoided the psychological shock of instant readaptation to civilian life, although some struggled with the rigorous discipline of routine army life.

A further 14,000 were recruited into the MVD and its Special Purpose Militia Detachment (OMON), where, according to Gromov, by now First Deputy Minister of the Interior, they applied the "professionalism acquired in Afghanistan."[147] Another 20,000 to 22,000 went into the emergency services of the Ministry for Extraordinary Situations,[148] criminal investigation units, the prosecutor's office, and special squads, or worked as security guards. "Alternative" law enforcement agencies where afgantsy served included the *druzhina*, the voluntary people's militia organized to assist the police in maintaining public order; workers' detachments formed to break up strikes and radical protests; and municipal and regional militias. Others were drawn to firefighting service and trauma medicine.[149]

A marked growth in the crime rate and a general feeling of insecurity accompanied the deterioration of the Soviet state. This might explain the explosion of interest in the late 1980s in martial arts, such as unarmed combat. Afganets groups frequently taught this, as it was a need to which afgantsy were well prepared to cater.[150]

Against the backdrop of the new economic freedoms, this sense of insecurity was also conducive to the mushrooming of "a private security business, providing bodyguards, private investigators, security experts, and even computer data crime specialists, culminating in the founding of the Independent Society of Private Detectives" (in 1991), whose chair was an afganets. They did not always enter security-related employment out of choice, however; one example was the afganets who returned home to Minsk in 1986, could not get a job in a factory because he was a vet, so he took up guard duty at the airport (see Chapter 7).

Because the more professional agencies refused to hire veterans, preferring people with experience in the MVD or KGB, many afgantsy found their way into "the shadowy world of bodyguarding, which so often shaded directly into criminality." Criminal subcultures in the early 1990s included many afgantsy, as their "heightened solidarity, geographically extended networks, and proficiency in the use of violence" made them well suited to the role. In Ekaterinburg, for example, a criminal group of afgantsy "specialized in protection services, insurance business, wholesale trade and swindling."[151] A psychologist who surveyed afgantsy found that 20 percent went into protection (*rekety*).[152] The Union of Veterans of Afghanistan (SVA) set up a firm to provide security for people and property. "Groups and individuals of every political complexion took to finding afganets minders, from the liberal Aprel' group . . . to . . . Russian nationalist icon," Aleksandr Nevzorov. "In the Baltic, the local Party supported the formation of the Viking cooperative, whereby local afgantsy would moonlight and protect party buildings from nationalists, at the taxpayer's expense."[153] Similarly, they were recruited to groups like Pamiat', whose leader surrounded himself with afganets bodyguards.[154]

One professor of psychology who studied stress and had served in Afghanistan explained the afgantsy's drive to go into private security organizations and criminal "setups" as their way to compensate for the loss of their youth and make the most of their lives. He believed they suffered from posttraumatic stress disorder, had to liberate suppressed impulses, and divided people into companions and aliens. They applied high moral standards toward the former and the converse toward the latter.[155]

Some Afghan veterans went to study in institutions of higher learning, which eased entrance requirements for them. (World War II vets had been entitled to get into college without exams.) They received grants for professional training and admission to college, while the disabled received extra funding and needed lower entrance marks. The presumable hope this would turn them into regular citizens was not always successful. A student who had lost an arm in the war remembers that the dean "called me in to see him. 'Look,' he said, 'we gave you a place even though your grades weren't really good enough. We gave you a grant. Now, don't go spending your time with that lot. Why do you keep going to the cemetery? It doesn't go down well here.'" In other words, he noted, they were discouraged from getting together and seem to have been under special supervision.[156]

Many went into blue-collar jobs. Some of those who came from kolkhozy found work in the kolkhoz. One veteran, who returned with one arm, had no choice other than to work on his kolkhoz in Belarus until his—and his family's—money ran out, at which point he resolved to go to study.[157]

The Invalids

The ones who had most feared going home, indeed who had the hardest time reacclimatizing, were those who returned crippled, especially those whose wives and girlfriends left them after they were wounded. For many of them, the war never ended. Medical care at home was not much better than it had been in Afghanistan. Medical facilities in the Soviet Union were, in the words of an American who visited Moscow in late 1989, "appallingly inadequate and woebegone—there is not enough of anything. There are no special facilities for wheelchairs or the blind and the engineering for artificial limbs—prosthetics—is abysmal, not to say medieval. . . . Several weeks before I arrived in Moscow eighty wheelchair Afgantsi gathered in Red Square . . . to protest the lack of decent health care and handicapped access. They were beaten up by the cops."[158] Fully 60 percent of those fitted out with Soviet-made prostheses could not walk with them; in mid-1990, 3,000 had not yet received artificial limbs at all.[159] A deputy to the Congress of People's Deputies, Serhii Chervonopysky, who had lost both legs in the war, complained that "our prosthetics industry remains on a stone-age level."[160] Indeed, a number of afgantsy were fitted with medical limbs made by foreign manufacturers, which also provided Soviet specialists with improved technologies.[161]

Those who returned maimed were often the angriest. One soldier who had lost his eyesight sometimes had "a desire to cut the odd throat." The blindness "doesn't stop me recognizing the people whose throats I'd like to cut: the ones who won't pay for gravestones for our lads, the ones who won't give us flats . . . the ones who try to wash their hands of us. What happened to me is still boiling inside."[162]

Many of the disabled saw their pensions reduced as the economic situation worsened. All pensions lagged far behind the rapidly rising prices of the Soviet Union's last years, and many afgantsy had to turn to their parents for material assistance. One man in a hospital told a visitor (who brought apples purchased with money schoolchildren had collected for afgantsy invalids) that the relevant organizations were moving with unbelievable slowness and he had to spend three to four months a year in the hospital because his pension was so small and his family had exhausted all of their means on him. The visitor called on the media to highlight the difficulties and privations of these men.[163] Denied the promised privileges and even humanitarian assistance and scorned by officials and citizens, they were reduced to leading a life more miserable and humiliating than that of the average Soviet citizen. The only people who regularly came to their aid were fellow afgantsy, who fought their battles with the local bureaucracy.[164]

A former soldier in the Soviet Far East described as "the last straw, that in our country, after this war, cripples are appearing in markets with outstretched hands:

'Please give alms for bread to a soldier-internationalist!' It's a scandal known all over the world! Let's not allow it!"[165]

Occasionally, however, the local media told optimistic stories, like that of a young woman from Khiva who, hearing that one of her fellow townspeople had returned without either arms or legs, resolved to marry him. Such incidents were a light at the end of a dark tunnel for families of the disabled.[166]

The Families

The families of the afgantsy, the parents who lived for two years in fear of the arrival of a zinc coffin, were also casualties of the war. Many parents became ill from the stress, and not a few died of heart failure. Motherhood is a strong symbol in Russia, and in light of the low birthrate, soldiers in Afghanistan tended to be only sons, often only children, so their ties to their mothers were particularly close. Their mothers' welcome appears as an absolute constant in afgantsy tales of their return. One vet recalls the support of his mother, who was herself a World War II vet; he believed that this facilitated his smooth transition to civilian life.[167] Families of those who had difficulties readjusting suffered with their vets.

For the mothers of those killed, and of those physically and psychologically disabled, the war never ended. Their wound continued bleeding and would until the end of their days.[168] Many afgantsy, when talking about the war, addressed the mothers of the invalids and the fallen. "You look at a dead soldier," said one officer of an artillery regiment, "and think of his mother. . . . This was the mothers' war, they were the ones who did the fighting."[169] The veterans continued to show concern for their disabled and the families of those who had fallen. They visited bereaved parents to tell them about their sons and how they had died.[170] While it was impossible to "explain to a mother the death of her son," they could show her that his memory lived on.[171] Indeed, the vets made every effort to have monuments erected in honor of their dead. As one afganets wrote to a republican Komsomol paper, "On the other side of the mountains, we would say that a soldier dies not when he is laid in a zinc coffin but when he is forgotten."[172]

Officialdom, however, made "no serious attempt to provide post-trauma care and support for the relatives of the fallen." On the contrary, since the war was hushed up for most of its duration—even after Gorbachev came to power—the bereaved were deprived of "the psychological support and catharsis of public approbation for the departed."[173] Months after the war's end, parents were still trying to find out the circumstances of their sons' death,[174] generally to no avail. Many bereaved mothers, moreover, became emotionally disturbed;[175] some refused to accept that their sons had died.[176]

Bereaved families were awarded pensions and benefits—except in cases of those who went missing; if a soldier disappeared and no body was found, his relatives could claim nothing.[177] But the families' benefits were inadequate and families frequently had to enter protracted negotiations with the local authorities in order to receive them at all. When one officer spoke with officials in a small Russian town to ask them to alleviate the lot of bereaved mothers, they responded that it would be "easier to resolve issues" if they received written instructions ("directive documents") regarding such entitlements.[178] Without them, families had to rely on the goodwill of local government, especially the financial services of the MDs and the voenkomats. *Pravda* singled out the initiative of the voenkomats of Moldova, Tatarstan, Primorskii Krai (in the Soviet Far East), and the oblasts of Dnepropetrovsk and Vinnitsa, which undertook to supplement the state's assistance.[179]

The parents, widows, and friends of those killed united to support each other against the meager amount of help that they received from state and society alike. There is ample anecdotal evidence of their solidarity at a grassroots level (see Chapter 7). In addition, against the backdrop of Soviet citizens' extensive return to religion in the 1980s, it was inevitable that widows and bereaved parents would look to the church for solace. One father, a communist, told his son when he visited him in the hospital that he had gone to church and lit a candle. "I need someone to put my faith in. Who else can I pray to for your safe return?"[180]

Despite their difficulties and their criticism of the war, many mothers of soldiers supported and even participated actively in the military-patriotic education of young people. They visited schools and colleges to speak about their sons' role in Afghanistan, emphasizing the duty of every young man to serve his country. Over time, however, many mothers became disenchanted with both the political and the military authorities (see Chapter 7).

In light of the failure of the post-Soviet states to provide meaningful assistance to the families of the fallen, the mothers' organizations continued to lobby for their rights and needs. Although they were not part of the main Afghan War veteran structures, the MoD and the CIS Committee for Internationalist-Servicemen gave them some support. Thus, those who had lost their family breadwinner were exempt from the privatization fee for their apartments and from income tax.[181]

Afgantsy Perceptions of the War

The veterans were neither homogeneous in their opinions of the war nor were their attitudes static. Our survey of over 220 veterans found that those who served in the first years were generally more positive than those who went to Afghanistan later. After the withdrawal, however, their overall view of the war frequently changed, sometimes completely. Many of those interviewed in the 2000s explained that then they were young, they had mostly not thought of anything except girls and discos

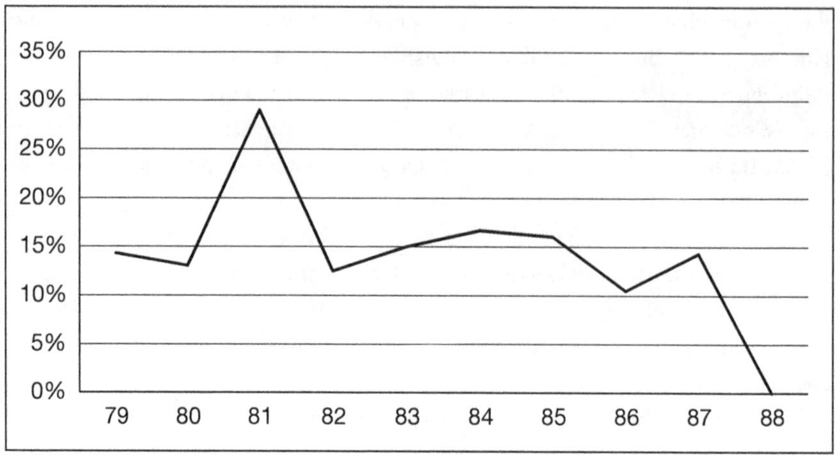

Figure 8.1. Related positively to the war in Afghanistan before going there

and had certainly never given any thought to politics or international affairs and relations.[182]

The great majority of those who served in the war said they had not related to it positively before being sent to Afghanistan. The highest approval rate—around 30 percent—was in 1981, before information concerning the war had leaked out—indeed when few people realized that Soviet soldiers were involved in a war (Figure 8.1).

In Afghanistan itself, the troops, especially regular soldiers, seem to have had neither the time nor the tranquility to think about the war and why they were there. They had to survive. In the words of one soldier, "It was as if thought was paralyzed. In front and behind, the guns rattle, rattle, and you yourself run, shoot. In front and behind you . . . is death. If you want to stay alive, you run, shoot."[183] Or, in the words of one nurse, "We kept our eyes shut . . . all we saw were our wounded, mutilated, and horribly burnt patients, and we learned to hate, but not to think."[184] An officer who had served in Afghanistan in 1983–1984 said that the soldiers there did not discuss why they were fighting this war. "We were fulfilling the command of our mother country and honestly considered ourselves internationalists"; the dushmans were enemies out to kill Soviet soldiers.[185] In 1986, one Soviet weekly asked veterans to write how the war had been for them. The recurrent theme of the responses was that the soldiers had been convinced that they were doing what they had been brought up to do: giving fraternal aid to a neighboring nation.[186] According to one deserter, the men did not have the strength to admit that it was an unjust war.[187]

There were, however, exceptions. In some units, discussion of the war and its purpose took place throughout its course (see Chapter 3). Unfortunately, however, we do not know the circumstances surrounding these exceptions—whether they depended on the unit, on the level of education or political awareness, or perhaps on ethnic affiliation or the amount of free time.

Most afgantsy seem to have shared the view of one junior officer who served as an interpreter in a motor-rifle unit: that the afgantsy had nothing to be ashamed of. He had thought so in real time and maintained that position two decades later.[188] Yet there were other positions. A soldier who served in 1985 and 1986, whose close friend was killed, who himself was severely wounded, and who was adamant that many people were killed for no purpose, changed his opinion about the justification for the Soviet military presence in Afghanistan over the course of his service.[189] A more widespread reaction was that they began to think about what they had seen and done only after returning home. On the whole, many found it difficult even then to disapprove of the war, basically, it seems, so as to avoid concluding that they had gone through it, and many of their comrades had paid the ultimate price, to no avail. Post-factum, however, one officer who fought early in the war summed up the Soviet effort: "We got drawn into a protracted, senseless war" that not only cost lives but also aggravated the situation in the DRA.[190] One of three vets interviewed in a book designed to analyze what the war did to Soviet society and to the individual said that "one could say, Afghanistan was a trap we fell into and our losses there were in vain."[191] The occasional soldier admitted that while it is difficult to avoid killing innocent people in wartime, "it is impossible to remove responsibility from soldiers" for killing civilians.[192]

Responding to our survey about three years after the war ended, veterans who went to Afghanistan before 1985 generally thought that the war answered Soviet interests, while those who arrived after 1985 were more likely to think otherwise: 40 percent of the veterans sent there in 1988 thought that the war had not met Soviet interests (Figure 8.2).

Even so, it was reported from Moscow in 1988 that the prevalent sense among the veterans was that had the Soviet Union not intervened militarily, the United States would have done so, or at least stationed missiles in the country.[193] A survey of veterans of the war in Cheliabinsk oblast and interviews in Central Asia in the second decade of the twenty-first century found that respondents had thought and persisted in thinking that the war corresponded to Soviet interests; that had the Soviet troops not entered Afghanistan, the Americans would have done so; and that it was necessary to both defend the Soviet Union's southern border and help the Afghan people build a new life. Only two in the Cheliabinsk survey said that they had thought so at the time but had since changed their minds and currently thought that the war could have been avoided.[194] One nurse said in the 2000s that the war was senseless, unnecessary, and took many lives, although she agreed it was not the mistake of those who participated in it.[195]

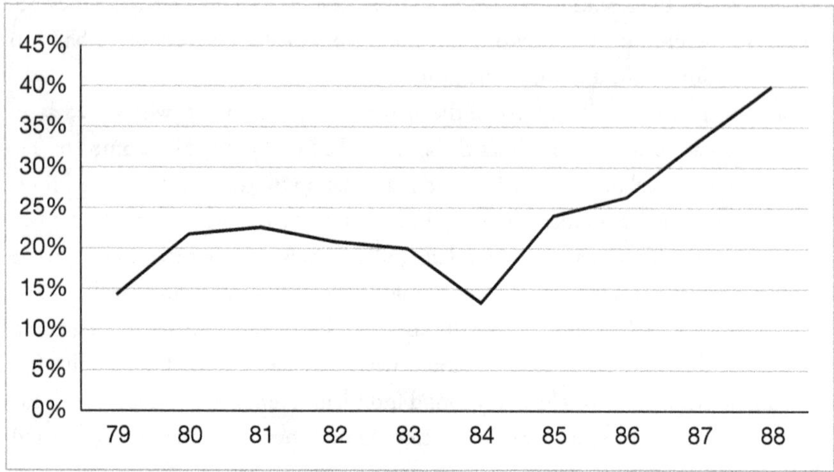

Figure 8.2. The war did not answer Soviet interests

One senior officer differentiated between discussion of the intervention and the role of the soldiers who fought the war. "We were needed both to help and to fight," but nobody considered the characteristics of the Afghans or the opposition's powerful foreign aid. Yet the army "fulfilled its duty."[196] Many soldiers genuinely believed that the Soviet Union was helping Afghanistan move out of the Middle Ages into modernity, which from a Marxist-Leninist perception was a positive assessment. One military adviser testifies, "I, personally, truly believed that their nomadic tents, their yurts, were inferior to our five-story blocks of flats, and that there was no true culture without a flush toilet."[197]By 1992–1993, many veterans considered the war a colonial and imperialist adventure and the intervention an occupation. (The later in the war they served, the more likely they were to think so.) Reflecting on what they had seen and done meant, in some cases, perceiving the mujahidin as freedom fighters and the Soviet force as occupiers (Figure 8.3).[198] This probably held especially for non-Russians.

When they were in Afghanistan, even those who did not ponder the war's political significance or implications might have perceived it as brutal and gory. Just 15 percent of the soldiers who came to Afghanistan in 1979 and only 5 percent of those who arrived in 1983 believed while there that it was a cruel war; almost 50 percent of the soldiers who began their service after 1986 thought so (Figure 8.4).

It was probably not merely a question of commitment to their military duty that prevented them from perceiving the war as such while engaged in it. It was also a function of the confusion that reigned in their minds. On the one hand, they were defending their country's southern border; on the other hand, they

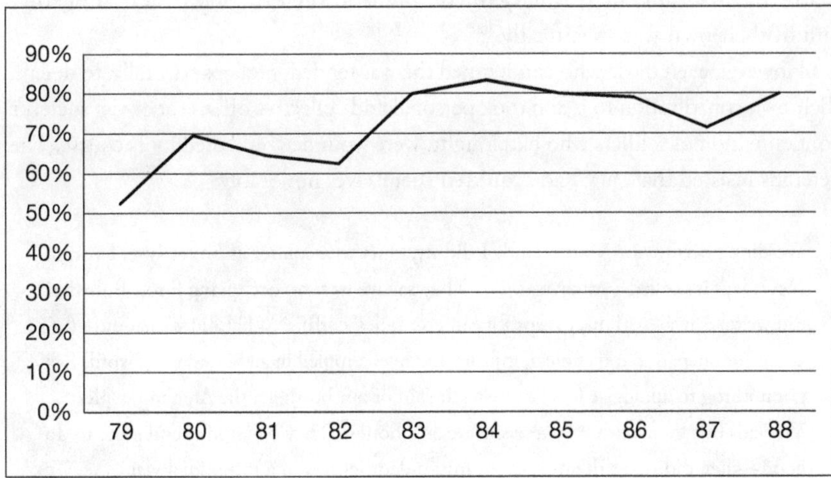

Figure 8.3. It was a colonial, imperialist war

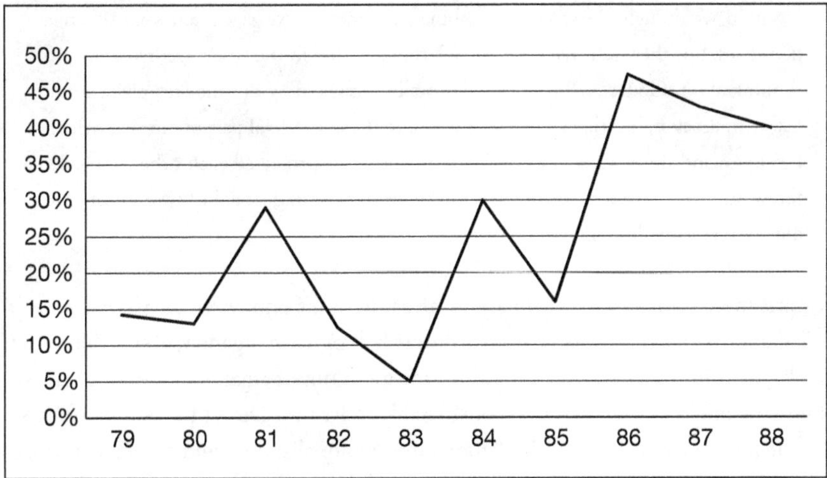

Figure 8.4. It was a cruel and bloody war

often found themselves fighting regular citizens, and some of those they killed were women and children—yet if you did not kill them, they might kill you. The confusion is perhaps best expressed in Igor' Morozov's song about the final withdrawal, "We're Leaving," which one scholar described as "a symbolic epitaph, an admission of surrender and failure . . . a poignant combination of bitterness [and] despair." It contemplated withdrawal as "an existential disaster."[199] Here clearly their age played a role: most soldiers were between eighteen and twenty. As they matured, they came increasingly to comprehend the brutality of war altogether and of their own war specifically.[200]

However, even those who condemned the war tended, perhaps naturally, to defend their own contribution to it and took personal and collective offense at Soviet society's condemnation of soldiers who had fought, were wounded, and died in its course. The veterans insisted that they had acquitted themselves honorably:

> We didn't betray our Motherland. I did my duty as a soldier as honestly as I could. Nowadays it's called a "dirty war." . . . They say we were an occupying force. But what did we take away with us, except for our comrades' coffins? What did we get out of it, apart from hepatitis and cholera, injuries and lives crippled in all senses of the word? I've got nothing to apologise for. I came to the aid of our brothers, the Afghan people. . . . The lads out there with me were sincere and honest. They believed they'd gone to do good—they didn't see themselves as "misguided fighters in a misguided war." . . . We thought the new government would give the land they had taken from the old feudal barons to the peasants, and the peasants would accept it with joy—but they never did accept it! We thought the tractors, combines, and mowers we gave them would change their lives, but they destroyed the lot! We thought that in the space age it was absurd to think about God. . . . But Islam was totally unshaken by our modern civilization. It was an illusion, but that's the way it was, and it was a special part of our lives which I treasure and don't want destroyed or tarnished. We protected each other in battle, threw ourselves between our friend and the mortar coming straight toward him. You don't forget something like that.[201]

Toward the end of 1989, nearly a year after the war's end, *Komsomol'skaia pravda* polled approximately 15,000 citizens, almost half of them afgantsy, about the Soviet involvement in Afghanistan, asking the same questions of afgantsy and non-afgantsy. Not surprisingly, the former were considerably more positive: 35 percent of afgantsy saw the involvement as the Soviet Union's internationalist duty and 19 percent called it "a difficult, but necessary action" (versus 10 and 19 percent, respectively, of regular citizens). Seventeen percent of soldiers and 46 percent of citizens considered the involvement "our national shame." Seventeen percent of vets said that they were "proud of the afgantsy" (compared with 6 percent of citizens). Nineteen percent of veterans and 30 percent of citizens believed that internationalist duty had lost its meaning.[202] (Aleksei Yurchak shows how questioning Soviet norms was part of the conceptual revolution of glasnost.[203])

"Nobody knows what internationalist aid means," one paratrooper explained shortly after the war's end. "Over the river" we understood only concrete notions—the next operation, a landing, or an ambush.[204] But when in 1986, one Muscovite wrote to a newspaper that "not everyone believes the old cliché that an 18-year-old youngster is happy to fulfill his internationalist duty in Afghanistan" (see Chapter 6) his doubts evoked "a torrent of 'ferocious and virulent letters'" from afgantsy who insisted that, "internationalism is not only a political concept, but first and foremost, a moral virtue, like honesty, decency, and intelligence."[205]

On the whole, the Soviet soldiers who returned from Afghanistan said it had "never occurred to them that they had been fighting against the Afghan people, who rose to defend their motherland."[206] The highest-ranking officer who fought in Afghanistan and was critical of its conduct in real time stated that although it had become "fashionable to throw stones at the army," the soldiers and officers had accredited themselves well. Maintaining that soldiers had died "by mistake" blasphemed "the memory of those who laid down their lives in honorably fulfilling their soldiers' duty." Most vets were proud to have helped the Afghan people move into modernity.[207]

A soldier who had been in the hospital with other wounded soldiers in 1982 had not heard a single soldier complain about being in Afghanistan or say that they were there by mistake. In the words of the chairman of a district Council of Internationalists in Turkmenistan, "Truth about Afghanistan is all very well. But many of us lose heart at the current opinion that Soviet troops were in Afghanistan by mistake, that we should have not been there. But we were there! And given that, what happened has to be appreciated." The chairman believed that all of the war's vets would endorse Varennikov's statement that one must not judge the intervention from the standpoint of 1989, for it had been undertaken when the international constellation had been quite different.[208]

"Don't try and tell me we were *victims* of a *mistake*. I can't stand those . . . words and I won't hear them spoken," one veteran is reported to have said:

> We fought well and bravely. Why are we being treated like this? I knelt to kiss the flag and took the military oath. We were brought up to believe these things were sacred, to love and trust the Motherland. And I *do* trust her, in spite of everything. I'm still at war, although it's thousands of miles away. If a car exhaust goes off outside my window or I hear the sound of breaking glass I go through a moment of animal terror. My head is a complete void, a great ringing emptiness. . . . I can't and I won't just stamp out all that part of my life, or my sleepless nights, or my horrors.[209]

Indeed, they could not bear the denial of any heroism in the war, the talk of the soldiers' cruelty to the Afghans, and the suggestion that the war had been a mistake.[210] Nevertheless, one-third of the respondents to a 1990 survey, especially those with higher education, considered the war to have been a political error.[211]

The afgantsy's attitude to the war inevitably affected their attitude to the

Table 8.5. The most repulsive features of the war

Its economic cost at a time when the standard of living at home was falling	56.98%
The fiasco—the failure we suffered in this war	48.02%
The fact of the invasion of a sovereign country	36.57%
The way the decision to invade Afghanistan was made	39.25%

government that had sent them to it and that shirked responsibility toward them after their return. One doctor in a Lvov clinic who had himself been wounded in Afghanistan was bitter about the "brainless idiots responsible for the deaths of tens of thousands of Soviet soldiers and Afghan civilians." He was duly called before the party committee and told to hold his tongue.[212]

Even though most afgantsy were unwilling to consider the war a political error, they admitted that it had negative aspects. The worst were its effect on citizens' standard of living, its having been a military fiasco, the way the decision to invade had been made, and the invasion of a sovereign country (Table 8.5).

Looking back about three years after the war ended, afgantsy assessments of the war denied it any long-term constructive effect; even if it prepared people mentally for glasnost and perestroika, in their view, it had little effect on political developments under Gorbachev Figures 8.5 to 8.7).

Their Attitude to Society

The afgantsy returned from the war but did not find the home for which they had been yearning. "You never really return home," one of them is recorded as saying. Humiliated and angered by society's accusations, they found that they could no longer tolerate the falsehoods on which Soviet society seemed to rest.

Their main ambition, Congress of People's Deputies afganets members Pavel Shet'ko and Vladimir Finogenov told a *Pravda* correspondent, was to earn the appreciation reserved for the veterans of the Great Patriotic War, to be treated on a par with them and receive the same material benefits.[213] They wanted recognition of the sacrifices they and their dead comrades had made. One vet said their main objective in all of their activity was to ensure that no afganets and no mother of a soldier who had not returned might think that she or her son had been forgotten.[214] They recognized that the state's economic situation was deteriorating daily and many World War II veterans were also being deprived of their material benefits. They understood the logic behind the contention that because of the state's financial constraints, the afgantsy should work. Nonetheless, the Afghanistan veterans' sense of discrimination rankled for years.[215]

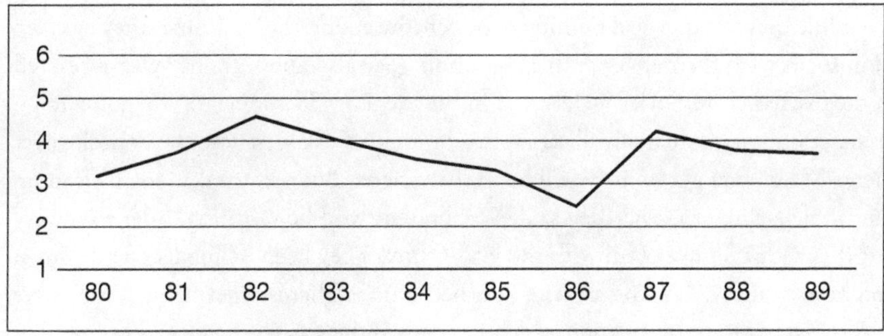

Figure 8.5. The war made people see the emptiness of many slogans (such as "internationalist duty") and in this way prepared the population and especially the intelligentsia for glasnost and perestroika

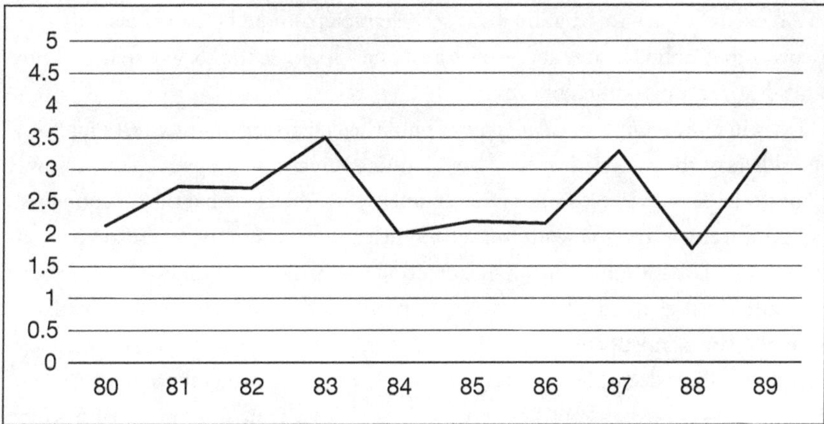

Figure 8.6. The war had virtually no influence on Soviet political life

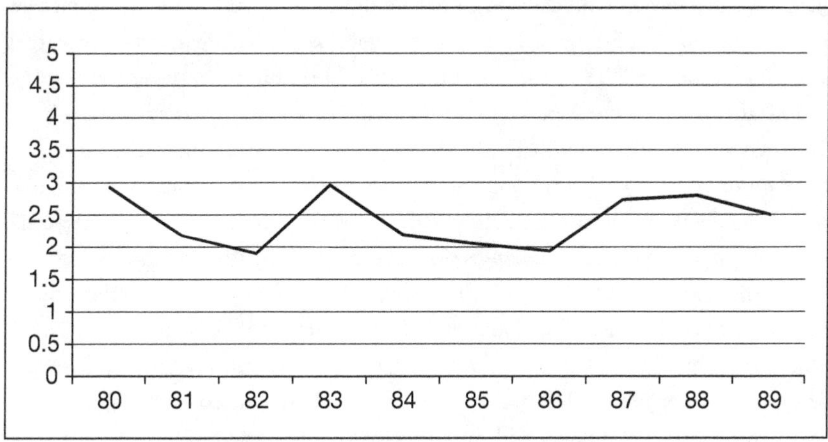

Figure 8.7. Do you believe that the war influenced domestic developments under Gorbachev?

While they felt they had nothing to be contrite about, the "welcome" they received from society fed their anger at their situation. (See also above.) One veteran reacted to the discussion in Soviet society and in the media: "How long are you going to go on describing us as mentally ill, or rapists, or junkies? We were told the opposite over there. 'When you get home you'll be in the vanguard of perestroika. You'll clean up the whole stagnant mess!' they said. We thought we'd be restoring order to society but they won't let us get on with the job. 'Study! They keep telling us. 'Settle down and have a family!'" A woman who returned from Afghanistan explained, "We were sent to Afghanistan by a nation which sanctioned the war, and returned to find that same nation had rejected it. What offends me is the way we've simply been erased from the public mind. What was only recently described as one's 'international duty' is now considered stupidity."[216] The Secretary of the Supreme Soviet Committee for the Affairs of Soldier-Internationalists (see Chapter 10) noted that when an afganets discovers that nobody cares about his future, he "'looks at the society that sent him to his death through different eyes."[217]

Early in 1986, *Komsomol'skaia pravda* published an article on the effect on returning soldiers of the materialism they saw around them and so despised. The press was full of stories about veterans who were genuinely perturbed by what they encountered, could not feel comfortable with former friends, and, wanting to cleanse Soviet society, took the law into their own hands, meting out justice to "money-grubbers" and other antisocial elements.[218] They ended up on the defendant's bench for carrying out lynch law against people whom they felt the authorities had not punished sufficiently for their deeds. Some attacked and even murdered members of a variety of subcultures—punks, rockers, heavy metal fans[219]—the same fraternities with which some of their fellow veterans had teamed up. One afganets from the elite spetsnaz killed a former soldier who claimed to have fought in Afghanistan when in fact he had been stationed in Ethiopia. The man's mother asked other afgantsy whether they too would be able to kill someone, and they all answered in the affirmative.[220]

The afgantsy, one correspondent wrote in spring 1987, "returned home with a sharpened sense of responsibility for the affairs and concerns of the mother country."[221] In the words of one young correspondent who visited Afghanistan, these soldiers came back imbued with revolutionary zeal, which tempted them to deal with "antisocial" elements. They joined other vigilantes similarly troubled by the corruption they saw around them and the official inactivity in face of lawlessness. The members of an "informal association of Young Communists" that called itself "Law and Order" seem to have been mainly Afghan War veterans, for one of its primary goals was to care for the families of men killed in Afghanistan.[222] "These lads come home and find themselves rubbing shoulders with unpunished bribe-takers, embezzlers, pilferers, and other riff-raff. The 'afgantsy'[s] . . . hatred of them is so intense that it has to be

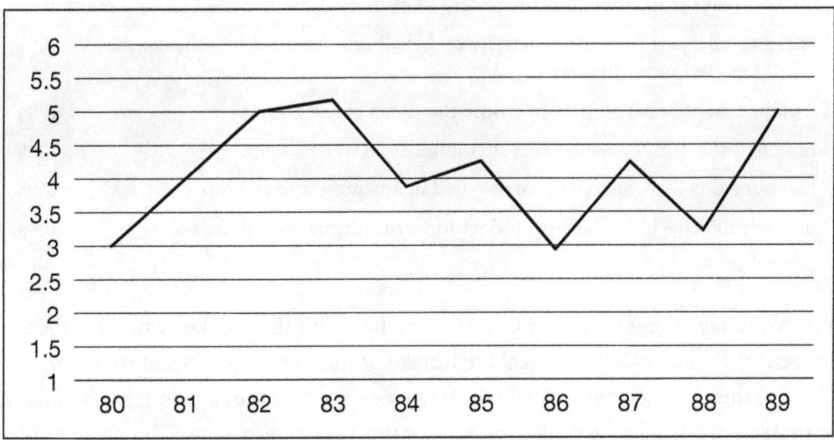

Figure 8.8. The afgantsy became the vigilantes of a society torn by corruption and immorality

restrained. It's fine when these lads are helped to organize in councils and clubs. But if they're left on their own, it's not long before there's trouble."[223] A Ukrainian youth journal reported that a student who had won a medal in Afghanistan was sentenced to eight years in prison for killing a teenager who led a Western way of life.[224] Certainly the veterans, or at least many of them, perceived themselves as committed to putting society to rights (Figure 8.8).

For years the afgantsy oscillated between the personal and collective hurt and the urge to make their mark in the domestic arena. Gromov told the Nineteenth Party Conference in July 1988 that with the advent of glasnost—as the traditional monologue became a dialogue—the soldiers of Afghanistan were developing an interest in Soviet political processes.[225] Many afgantsy undertook to improve the world. The chair of the student *profkom* at an institute in Ashkhabad, where 80 afgantsy were enrolled, spoke of them as the most socially active group in a student body full of initiative.[226]

In particular, they were prepared to fight to receive the l'goty that the government had promised them. According to the *Komsomol'skaia pravda* survey, 16 percent of afgantsy believed the entitlements were "the little that society was able and obliged" to give them, 17 percent opined that these l'goty were manifestly inadequate, and 71 percent that they were meaningless—existing on paper alone. (Just 7 percent of respondents thought them unwarranted.[227]) "No one gives a damn about us," said one afganets. "If we didn't stand up for our rights ourselves nobody would know a thing about the war. If there weren't so many of us, [1 million] in fact, they'd have shut us up, like they did after Vietnam and Egypt."[228] Some afgantsy eagerly took up challenges that came their way: "They want to transform us from a lost generation into reliable defenders of the status quo (we've already proved our faith in it after

Table 8.6. Events or manifestations in Soviet society that led you to protest on your return home

I began to take part in political activity on behalf of reform because the regime had involved us in this war	6%
I took part in political activity to ensure the rights of the afgantsy	19%
I protested the disinformation that surrounded the war	10%
I had some problems but never participated in any protest of any sort	45%
I had no problems in readjusting and within a short time everything was as usual	10%

all). Nowadays they're sending us to Chernobyl, Tbilisi, or Baku, wherever there's danger."[229] Some, "craving for real life instead of mere existence," went to hazardous places of their own accord—to Siberia to work on the pipeline or to join fire brigades, or to Armenia to help clear the damage after the November 1988 earthquake.[230] (For the role of the afgantsy in the period immediately prior to the demise of the Soviet Union, see Chapter 10.)

The vets, then, had an agenda. Asked in late 1989 where they preferred to apply their energies, they had clear answers: 34 percent said mutual help within their own group; 30 percent, educating the rising generation; 29 percent, creating order in general; 12 percent, participating in political activity; and 10 percent, the struggle against violations of the law.[231] In other words, they wanted to contribute to the general morass under perestroika and glasnost, yet primarily in areas where they could make a meaningful difference, not in the ongoing political conflict between conservatives and liberals.

Slightly over one-third participated in protests or other political activity outside their own group (Table 8.6).

The majority of those who replied to the *Komsomol'skaia pravda* poll agreed with the definition that they were among the few on whom their country could rely in hard times (72 percent) and that Afghanistan was indeed the best school of life (66 percent). Just 8 percent believed they were people on whom the opponents of perestroika would lean, and a mere 4 percent agreed that they were a lost generation,[232] although in our survey, a full 18 percent knew afgantsy who were unable to adapt to civilian life (see Table 8.8). The veterans felt contempt for the "dim-witted film-makers"—by late 1989, several films on the war had appeared on the screen (see Chapter 7)—who depicted them as cannon fodder. As for *Komsomol'skaia pravda*, the afgantsy respected it, but insisted that it must always stick to the truth; that was the primary assignment of the media.[233]

Notwithstanding their frustration in the face of the obstructionism they encountered, many soldiers were determined to help restructure society and eradicate some of its weaknesses. In the words of one vet, had there been no glasnost and

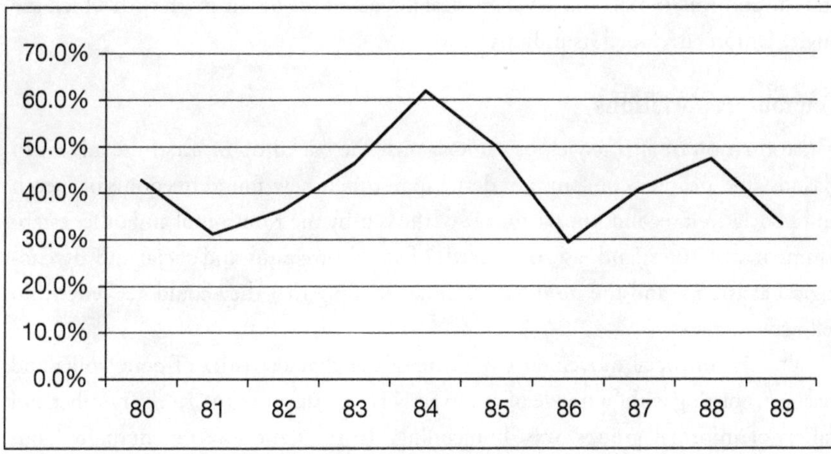

Figure 8.9. The afgantsy tended to take part in public activity

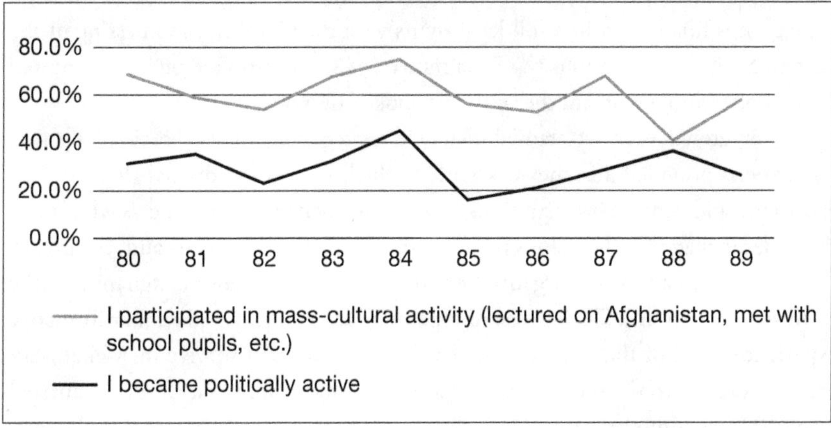

Figure 8.10. Did you take part in public activity after returning home?

democratization, the regime would have come up against a strong opposition in the afgantsy who could not go back to their old lives and "submissively approve the absurdities, nonsense, and crimes." [234] They therefore tended to take up various kinds of public activity (Figure 8.9).

This activity, however, was mostly not political and was largely restricted to their own group interests (Figure 8.10).

The veterans' different perceptions of society and the different paths they took, then, were likely to reflect their individual traits and the opportunities that came their way. Frequently, however, their views were the outcome of objective circumstances, notably society's mood in the mid- and late 1980s, to which the afgantsy reacted, and the political, moral, and psychological impact of the heroic myth with which the Soviet Union enveloped its military past.

Veterans' Associations

The formation of afgantsy clubs came against the backdrop of, first, the advent of glasnost and people's concomitant desire to test their new-found freedoms of speech and association; second, the patronage of the vets by the Komsomol and other establishment structures; and last, the dearth of social programs and social and psychological assistance and the need for an understanding that they could get only from fellow vets.[235]

The rise of social movements was one of the characteristics of perestroika and glasnost. Starting with "a trickle of group activity," by summer 1987, "the number and variety of 'informal' groups" was "burgeoning." In 1987, the government drafted, but did not enact, a new law on public organizations, and the first officially sanctioned national conference of "nonformal" associations (*neformal'nye*) took place in Moscow. (The groups finally acquired full legal rights with the October 1990 passing of the Law on Social Organizations.[236]) By summer 1988, one estimate put their number at 30,000; within a year, another estimate spoke of 60,000.[237]

An "outgrowth of the veterans' difficulty in reintegrating into civil society," afganets associations provided a framework within which they could discuss their Afghan experience and vent their frustrations among equally disenchanted peers who spoke the same language.[238] Their clubs provided the veterans with support and, eventually, the structure for a national organization, the Union of Veterans of Afghanistan (the SVA; see Chapter 10). Their sense of togetherness, of having had similar formative experiences, and of the camaraderie that had helped them survive in Afghanistan grew in reaction to the social ostracism and the stonewalling that they encountered from the local administrations.[239]

At first, most afganets' activity united veterans by hometown or by army unit; many who returned from the war in the early years have testified that they maintained contact with people with whom they served, often for years.[240] In 1985–1986, while the war was still raging, sporadic grassroots afgantsy clubs came into being, appearing "like mushrooms after the rain."[241] By 1986, there were already indications in the media that the veterans were maintaining a tight informal network and sought the establishment of an official organization.[242] As is inevitable in an authoritarian society, this required the assistance of a "state agency, with its huge mobilization and discursive powers. The Komsomol and military commissariats played an instrumental role . . . assisting the veterans in their transition into civilian life and representing them vis-à-vis the authorities."[243] Backing afganets' attempts to convene and cooperate[244] enabled the Komsomol—which was looking for new ways to attract young Soviet citizens[245]—to channel afganets activity according to party policy. True, there were limitations to the Komsomol's grip on the afganets associations; not infrequently, afgantsy organized themselves out of frustration at the inadequacies of the Komsomol and disillusionment with its reluctance to give them their place: "They don't welcome people dedicated in deeds, not words, to the Soviet system." Consequently, some of their associations engaged autonomously in "military-patriotic education of young people."[246] Yet the Komsomol ultimately prevailed over the majority by promising its policymaking influence regarding benefits and pre-army education. The ensuing council of military reservists came under a party steering committee.[247]

Even before Gorbachev's rise, the Voluntary Society for Assistance to the Army, Aviation and Fleet (DOSAAF), the Komsomol, and local voenkomats enlisted veterans to speak at schools about courage, the "lofty duty of a defender of the homeland, the sense of military comradeship, and [their] military service."[248] In 1986, the Komsomol set up the Administration for Afghan Questions. MPA head Colonel General Aleksei Lizichev cited the experience of the soldier-internationalists as a potent weapon in military-patriotic education (VPV) "to defeat 'pacifist tendencies' in Soviet youth" and to collaborate in the construction of what Galeotti dubs "the mythical Afghanistan."[249]

The All-Union Gathering of Young Reservists, held in Ashkhabad, the capital of Turkmenistan, in November 1987, under Komsomol auspices, assembled some 2,000 Afghan War veterans from associations throughout the country. The gathering discussed common issues, such as the erection of a national monument to those who fell in the war.[250] Twenty to 25 percent of the attendees were then engaged in VPV, but that percentage dropped over the following years. By the decade's end, 60,000 "internationalist soldiers," or approximately 10 percent, participated in VPV, and by 1991, the number was down to 5 to 8 percent.[251]

There was "money and hence power and *blat* (influence)" in VPV and its concomitant activities. It meant jobs and "extracurricular opportunities to collaborate with the system, which were an essential aid to lubricating the rest of one's life within the Party-State." Moreover, veterans enjoyed "the camaraderie of the groups, the macho heroism of stories and films shown at meetings, and the opportunity to test one's physical abilities."

Before the formal legalization of clubs, the *kollektiv* could enjoy rights in light of the "still essentially communal nature of Soviet law." By sanctioning the organizations, the state empowered them to conduct economic activity, exonerating them from possible charges of speculation. Associations "promised to provide not just moral and material support, but political and economic benefits."[252]

From the authorities' point of view, legalizing the clubs mitigated pressures for scarce or nonexistent state funds. The Soviet state, "economically unable to support the veterans . . . individually . . . set up a series of tax benefits for their associations.

The three major associations of veterans received a tax exemption for the import of goods and food products, facilities for banking, financial operations, and for various forms of entrepreneurial activities." (As a sequitur, some of "these organizations soon became involved in criminal activity."[253])

Thus, the veteran associations moved from answering social needs to becoming a caucus promoting the struggle to meet their material requirements. In Dushanbe, the afgantsy's need for a pressure group to ensure legislation of their rights gave birth to the city's afganets association.[254]

One in ten veterans in Donetsk oblast was a member of a Komsomol committee or bureau in 1987. They trained the young in military or paramilitary sports, the other face as it were of frontal education and VPV, and a common pastime for afgantsy. The vets also served in volunteer militia detachments; members of one such detachment took it upon themselves to maintain public order on suburban and passenger trains, leading to the detention of nine people for "conveying and selling narcotic substances."[255] This framework gave reservists brush-up training and provided preconscription teenagers with a "grounding" in military arts and instruction in such useful skills as driving, electronics, and first aid, along with the ideological and propaganda network around the party's monopoly of authority. Many of those who returned home threw themselves into Komsomol work with enthusiasm.[256]

The Perm association, inaugurated in 1986, had 100 ex-soldiers and afgantsy working for it. It set up three teenager clubs for the "working-class kids who would be the next generation of draftees and, had the war continued, afgantsy." Another, in Krasnodar, established in 1985, had about 200 members in 1988. The club in Vologda, established under Komsomol auspices, grew to 1,600 members by 1991. One of the Komsomol delegates to the first Congress of People's Deputies was Aleksandr Kolodeznikov, an invalid soldier who worked with the Council of Reserve Soldiers in his native Yakutsk. Although concerned that VPV was being used to "ghettoise and pacify the afgantsy," he "campaigned to develop their role in military-patriotic education, held fundraising concerts with afganets groups, and raised 100,000 rubles for his work." However, many members of these associations were not active, but were there simply to "ensure a place in the queue for a special flat or access to charitable food parcels without any real feeling of belonging to a community." Once out of uniform, many clearly preferred to perceive themselves primarily as "Soviets, Estonians, workers, students, Muscovites, Christians, or whatever."[257]

The best-known afganets club was Moscow-based Dolg (founded in 1987), which published its own booklet describing its significance for the vets.[258] Its chairman, Aleksandr Kotenev, delineated the many assignments Dolg undertook in order to provide whatever aid—financial, moral, physical—the afgantsy and the families of those killed and disabled required.[259] Indeed, the association's primary concern was

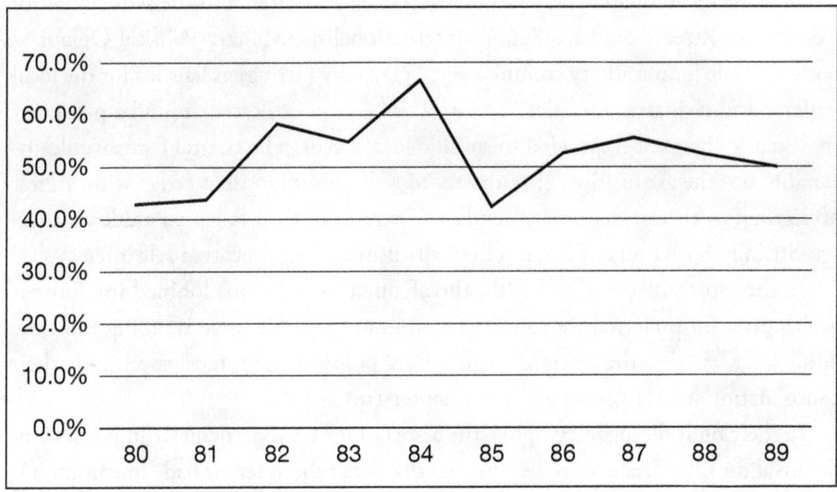

Figure 8.11. I personally joined a veterans' association

mutual assistance within the community and support for the invalids and the families of the fallen. As one veterans' association made clear, the soldiers would remain faithful to the oath they swore in Afghanistan: "One for all and all for one."[260] In Arkhangel'sk, for instance, they lobbied the local authorities to have their fallen comrades reinterred in a single area rather than dispersed among several cemeteries,and to erect a monument for them.[261]

Over half of the veterans we interviewed joined veterans' associations (Figure 8.11).

Well before the final disintegration of the Soviet Union, associations formed at the national level and at the republican, regional, municipal, and even raion (district or neighborhood) level. Not only did most cities boast an association of Afghan War veterans; in many cities, each *raion* had one.

Instances of afganets activity persisted outside the clubs' framework as well. In some places, afgantsy continued meeting and even operating informally.[262] In 1988, one newspaper published an appeal to Soviet institutions to exert every effort to attain the liberation of Soviet POWs in the name of "Soviet reservists who had fulfilled their international duty in the Republic of Afghanistan."[263]

In 1991–1992, Galeotti surveyed nine afganets groups, "ranging in size from 45 to 1,800 members, and geographically scattered from Kaliningrad to Karaganda," with over 4,400 members among them. Galeotti found the groups "strikingly homogeneous, combining the imperatives of self-help and military-patriotic education with a generous portion of shrewd economic and political entrepreneurship," designed to help the victims of the war and "other charitable causes." They were affiliated with both the Komsomol and the Union of Veterans, and often also the Association of Councils of Reserve Soldiers, Soldier-Internationalists, Military-Political Organizations, and the local military commissariat, "generally [acting] as liaisons for the local military and civilian authorities." Many of the groups coalesced around a particular charismatic figure or responded to specific local needs. The central focus would invariably be "the acquisition of resources to redistribute to the needy" within their peer group—"themselves, their friends, the parents of their fallen comrades, a characteristically Soviet mix of Robin Hood altruism and hard-hearted self-interest."[264]

In the words of Hedrick Smith, the afgantsy associations lobbied for "proper health care, for preferred treatment as consumers, and for understanding from the home folks."[265] (For the veterans' associations' political clout, most specifically their consolidation into larger unions, see Chapter 10.)

In their fight for afgantsy rights, the associations were particularly important for the invalids. One disabled soldier insisted that what the veterans had "in common is that we haven't got a thing to call our own. We all have the same problems—lousy pensions, the difficulty of getting a flat and a bit of furniture together, no decent medicines or prostheses. . . . If ever all that gets sorted out our veterans' clubs will fall apart. Once I get what I need, and perhaps a fridge and washing-machine and a Japanese video—however much I have to push and scratch and claw to get it—that'll be it! I won't need the club anymore."[266] Local Afghan veteran associations provided housing for vets and sought to work with the many who suffered from PTSD; one raion association in the Russian city of Cheliabinsk, for instance, undertook to talk with and listen to former soldiers who were sick and for whom no professional assistance was forthcoming.[267] The Uzbek SSR republican association was active in providing for health and other needs of the republic's afgantsy and of the families of those killed in action.[268] The "last hope" for housing of a pilot's widow after being turned down by the local authorities in Rostov-on-the-Don was the council of former internationalist soldiers.[269] (Table 8.7 sets out our afgantsy respondents' views of the associations.)

From time to time, the press reported on the obstacles to veterans' collaboration to secure their rights. They were ashamed to meet with their comrades when they were out of work, they had different personalities and different needs, and they had no tradition of voluntary cooperation. Many needed someone to push them, to give them moral support. Some of the local Komsomol organs filled the bill, but not all of them. When, in one Tashkent district, someone suggested giving the veterans privileges in purchasing food, the Komsomol leadership pointed out that the Chechen-Ingush ASSR, for example, had thirty-six stores for afgantsy.[270]

An article about the founding conference of the Uzbek SSR association in April 1989 detailed the grievances that the new organization intended to address. In addition

Table 8.7. The role of afgantsy associations

Were useful in defending our rights	34.6%
Provided a social framework	81.8%

to material problems, the veterans had encountered hurdles at every turn. They were sent from office to office and felt constantly insulted. The institute at which one man, who returned without his two legs, came to enroll, asked him, "How do you think you're going to study without legs?" Their kolkhozes did not give them accommodations. The parents of a fallen soldier were refused a telephone because they weren't receiving a breadwinner's pension.[271] (For veteran associations in Central Asia, see Chapter 9.)

The afgantsy associations' considerable economic activity focused on three main areas: enterprises to support their goals, paramilitary commercial undertakings, and housing. In 1987, the CPSU CC adopted a resolution designed to improve housing conditions and "social justice" in housing distribution. It addressed "callous, pro forma attitudes" on housing for World War II veterans, internationalist soldiers, and the families of soldiers and officers killed in combat.[272] But like so many other resolutions, it had little impact. In place of official support, some afganets clubs organized house-building cooperatives.[273] They "offered groups of young people the opportunity to build their houses themselves, at their own expense, but with the inducements of being able to sidestep waiting lists, live with friends, build to personal rather than shoddy and unimaginative State plans, and do so with generous government subsidy [sic]."[274]

In light of the state's mounting bankruptcy, veteran groups recognized the need to supplement membership dues and subsidies from the Komsomol and the local authorities. Thus, by 1989, the Moscow club was financially independent, largely thanks to "a lucrative enterprise manufacturing footwear, with 40 percent of the profits set aside straight away to support the invalids, families of dead soldiers, and similar causes." The Yaroslavl afganets commercial cooperative generated thirteen collections of songs on the war and published recordings of Afghan War songs for the First Russian Festival of Afghan War Songs, which was held in their town. Other groups produced books on the war, established their own newspapers, and held concerts of afganets music.[275]

Cooperation also existed among afganets associations in different parts of the country and in townships within a single oblast. Sometimes there was a specific purpose, like organizing summer camps for veterans or disseminating information regarding attempts to provide better artificial limbs.[276] One oblast association, for instance, supported invalids "through the collectives of industrial enterprises" and organized activities for the oblast's fifty-seven children of people killed in Afghanistan.[277] The associations also promoted the erection of monuments for their fallen comrades and initiated memorial ceremonies on February 15 of each year, which became the accepted Remembrance Day.[278]

A Living Memory of a Superpower's Failure: The Afgantsy's Rehabilitation as a Civic Concern

The war ended formally in February 1989. However, as long as there were former soldiers dying from their wounds and suffering materially, physically, and psychologically from the results of the war, it remained on the agenda of Soviet society, and particularly of those able to dissociate the war from the urgent problems of a crumbling economy and a flailing society. Afganets Supreme Soviet Deputy V. V. Yakushin reiterated that "many [vets] cannot find a place in civilian life" and must not be forgotten.[279] In the words of Svetlana Alexievich, "Our lives are forever tied to those red gravestones, with their inscriptions in memory, not only of the dead, but also of our naïve and trusting faith."[280]

Psychological damage is more complex in both diagnosis and treatment than physical disability. Its incidence is particularly high in wars where soldiers are fighting without faith in their cause and in modern counterinsurgency wars with their "blurring of the borders between civilian and non-civilian, 'hard' and 'soft' targets, legitimate and illegitimate." In these wars, "reprisal and atrocity become increasingly not just natural responses, but viable strategies," and "exposure to or participation in atrocities is far more stressful than simple combat."[281] In Afghanistan, the form and intensity of these disorders varied, depending on the type of unit (combat or support) in which the soldiers served, their experiences, and their individual character and social environment.

The afgantsy, like the veterans of Vietnam, "experienced prolonged emotional problems in the years following military service—Post-Traumatic Stress Disorder. . . . Simply put." An American who had experienced and studied the Vietnam War wrote:

> Because of the destructive nature of armed combat, the effects of delayed stress are irresistible and irremediable. The list of important symptoms includes recurring dreams and nightmares; a survivor's guilt that is most often expressed as an unshakable, debilitating depression; hyper-vigilance and an exaggerated startled response; and a purposeful self-destruction that might take the form of out-and-out suicide or the more punishing form of drug and alcohol abuse. . . . Until 1988, Soviet psychologists had never heard of PTSD, until American psychologists, experts with post-war trauma, visited and told them. Up till then their answer was behavior modification with [medication]—the way Soviet psychiatry had always dealt with mental illness.[282]

In the words of a Soviet psychologist a year after the war ended, not only was

Soviet psychology extremely unhelpful to the afgantsy, not a single Soviet psychologist was able to demonstrate scientifically what characterized them and how they differed from their peer group. Yet they had common traits resulting from their shared past and memories, the prolonged service in extreme conditions, and the fact that Soviet society regarded them as a special group in both positive and negative ways. It was incumbent on Soviet psychologists to analyze PTSD "scientifically" in order to be able to help the veterans and emancipate society from distortions and stereotypes that prevented it from understanding the afgantsy.[283]

The last chapter in an anthology of letters from soldiers in Afghanistan contained the writing of a soldier who served in 1983–1984 and committed suicide in 1988. His act of desperation, and similar suicides in various parts of the country in that and the following year, looked like "future retribution for [society's] inattention to progressive psychological sickness among the afgantsy," because nobody had ever put together the facts that would allow a diagnosis.[284] The proportions of the contributions of PTSD and the Soviet bureaucracy to these tragedies are surely irrelevant. Perhaps indeed "the Afghan syndrome"—the physical and psychological impact of the Soviet-Afghan War on those who returned from it—was often a combination of the two.[285] Certainly, the afgantsy's frustration was not paranoia. Many Soviet citizens accused the afgantsy of being killers, while society as a whole made them feel superfluous and betrayed and officialdom ignored their needs. One of the central goals of the rehabilitation effort, when it eventually began, was to help the veterans of this war with no fronts, and no defined enemy, assignment or goal, to "make sense of a senseless situation."

Soviet psychology, then, did not address the issue of war's influence on its participants until, the war over, Moscow State University (MGU) set up a team under Madridin Magomed-Eminov, the director of the SVA Psychological Service. It designed its survey of 15,000 afgantsy in different parts of the Soviet Union a year or so after the final withdrawal to create a database that would enable individual treatment of afgantsy. Working with American specialists who had studied the problems of Vietnam War vets, it focused on war's psychological influence on those who fought it, specifically the impact of stress and the meaning of life and death.[286] This effort reflected society's feelings of guilt toward the afgantsy and the widespread sense that it was not fulfilling its responsibilities toward them (see Chapter 7). In early 1990, Magomed-Eminov wrote an article, "The Syndrome of the Front-Line Soldier," suggesting that this syndrome hindered vets' adaptation and meant that on returning home, they had yet another war to fight.[287]

Addressing the Congress of People's Deputies' condemnation of the war as criminal, social psychologist Dmitrii Ol'shanskii, who had served in Afghanistan, noted that one could interpret this censure in two ways. It could mean that everyone who had participated in the war was a criminal or, alternatively, that society as a whole was duty-bound to share accountability for the crime with its direct participants, who represented the country's citizenry. "Then they will be able to feel what they need most of all, that they are understood."[288] The crux of the disparity between the psychology of those returning from Afghanistan and the social psychology of the environment to which they had returned, according to Ol'shanskii, was the parties' differing attitudes to the war and society's inability to distinguish between the war and those who fought it (see Chapter 7). In his view, the adaptation had to be mutual. It was incumbent on the government to reeducate the population so that it respect the veterans and their special status.[289]

In fact, Soviet society lacked the infrastructures to contend with the physical and emotional problems of young soldiers returning from Afghanistan, let alone to undertake their rehabilitation. This was particularly the case for soldiers returning in the war's early years. One vet who came back to his native Kazakhstan in 1984 recalled that there was no rehab program whatsoever: "The afgantsy undertook to console each other and would come together to sing songs and tell jokes. That was all there was."[290]

The failure of the establishment to support them exacerbated both the incidence and the consequences of PTSD. The attitude of one's surroundings and the state's "official policy" are "determining factors" in "the possibility of preserving or quickly restoring an order of values and a mental balance" among participants in military operations. The opportunity for Afghan War veterans to feel for a period "like haloed heroes . . . worked in favor of the improvement of their mental health at the beginning of the rehabilitation process if, thanks to social and economic benefits, they could feel more assured."[291] This temporary amelioration suffered a setback in 1988–1989 when censure of the war increased and the health care system became overtaxed and undersupplied. Rehab centers and specialists were few. This left soldiers with drug habits and severe psychological disorders, invalids, and alienated dropouts almost completely without treatment.[292] Those unable or unwilling to "collaborate in the construction of the mythical Afghanistan," who separated themselves from the collective, found themselves "pushed into various semi-pariah professions or activities . . . the state's victims and the poor saps at the bottom of the heap; scattered, shattered, silenced, cowed, bought, or marginalized."[293]

By the turn of the decade, many acknowledged that society's attitude toward the veterans and the war, and the afgantsy's recognition of this attitude, exacerbated the symptoms of PTSD. The return from the war, according to a report prepared for the Supreme Soviet Committee for the Affairs of Soldier-Internationalists, was inextricably linked to "the way the war is understood. The sequel of this understanding can lead to suicide, self-isolation, solitude, and time serving. The most desirable and radical way out is achieving a full life, incorporating the [vets] in the life of their generation, namely their socio-psychological rehabilitation." Life during the war was part of their present life; its memories influenced their decisions and conduct. PTSD was characterized by depression, anger, guilt feelings, insomnia, and numbness of the soul. Many vets pondered whether one may kill civilians, kill at all? How does one shake off the feelings of guilt? (The report did not address the even more profound guilt that every vet felt because he had returned and others had not.[294]) Their fellow citizens' attitude toward the veterans was crucial, the report continued. Many found intolerable the loss of their worth in the eyes of their compatriots, who judged them despite their impossible choice, either betray their oath—which for most was unthinkable—or collaborate in the crimes of a totalitarian regime they were not ready to oppose. Now they suffered because of the contrasts between there, where they had fought, and here, where they were misunderstood; and between we who suffered, and they who sent us and now want nothing to do with us. The more society judged the afgantsy, the greater was their desire to isolate themselves, to set up their associations.

Rehabilitation required comprehending the afganets personality, which involved combining theoretical typologization and empirical material based on their letters, reminiscences, diaries, and stories.[295]

In this vein, the journal of the Institute of Sociology published an article that stated, "An important factor in the re-adaptation of the participants of the war in Afghanistan to a peaceful life in a period of acute social change is their rehabilitation in social opinion. The problem arose when the 'heroic' image of the international warrior gave way to that of the image of the afgantsy as occupiers, members of a punitive expedition, marauders, and drug addicts." In late 1990, the institute undertook a research project on The social rehabilitation of a lost generation: A social defense of the vets of the War in Afghanistan. It surveyed fifteen "leaders" of public opinion, finding that their responses fell primarily into two opposing groups—the patriots, who said the afgantsy's heroic image had to be restored and that the mass media must cease disparaging them, and the liberals, who insisted that the vets must repent for having participated in a criminal war, but so too must society for having kept silent for nearly ten years, as this would enable the vets' moral rehabilitation. A few took a middle position. All, however, concurred in the importance of distinguishing between the war and those who fought it; responsibility for the war and its evolution lay solely with the politicians. The respondents also all agreed that the vets' moral-psychological problems, some of which arose in Afghanistan and others back home, were more acute than either their material or their medical ones. But they disagreed regarding the nature and treatment of these problems. Maximum information about all aspects of the war needed to be published, including official documents and vets' reminiscences. Until this happened, the media could manipulate public opinion.[296]

We asked our afgantsy respondents to address the following postulate, "The

Table 8.8. The afgantsy were portrayed as a "lost generation" (like the Vietnam vets in the United States)

Some were unable to make it back to civilian life even with help from psychologists	18%
Some of my acquaintances had to receive psychological treatment and that helped them	10%
I personally know afgantsy for whom it took several months to adapt to civilian life	35%
All of my personal acquaintances readjusted quickly without outside assistance	37%

afgantsy were portrayed as a lost generation (like the Vietnam vets in the United States)." Their responses are in Table 8.8.

When, in 1990, journalist Svetlana Alexievich published *Zinky Boys*, which included transcripts of interviews with veterans and their families, she received a barrage of letters and phone calls. The afgantsy were upset; so too were their families. One veteran wrote, "OK, we aren't heroes, but now we're murderers according to you. We murdered women, children, and their animals. Maybe in thirty years, I'll be ready to tell my son that not everything was as heroic as the books say it was. But I'll tell him myself, in my own words, and in thirty years' time. Now it's still an open wound that is only just beginning to heal and form a scab. Don't pick it! Leave it alone! It's still very painful." A mother wrote, "How could you? How dare you cover our boys' graves with such dirt? They did their duty by the Motherland to the bitter end and now you want them to be forgotten. . . . Who needs your dreadful truth?" Or another mother, "I call ours the 'obedient generation' and the Afghan war the acme of our tragedy. You've hit a nerve by daring to ask us and our children this question—'Who are we? And why can they do what they want with us?"[297] A group of veterans and mothers of veterans and fallen soldiers brought Alexievich to court in Minsk on charges that she was making money out of their misfortune, humiliating them, and taking their stories out of context. Some writers, journalists, and a few afgantsy came to her aid, saying that the authorities were hunting her down for publishing uncomfortable truths. The court acquitted her of most charges but recognized one: that of a veteran who said she had not given his story truthfully and demeaned him into the bargain.[298]

There is no consensus as to the extent of the Afghan syndrome. Those who returned with all their limbs, but discovered that the war had affected their health although no one at home recognized it, were a significant minority—maybe even a majority—of the vets. Just months after the war's end, Moscow State University's researchers found that 60 percent of veterans felt the war had had a psychological impact. For one-third of them, it was acute; they appeared "abnormally aggressive" and found it hard to readjust to civilian life.[299] Testing in the early 1990s reportedly showed that 35 to 40 percent of the war's vets were in urgent need of professional assistance.[300] According to the Ukrainian center for psychotherapy and medical ethics and the psychological service of the Union of Afghan Veterans (SVA), Soviet academics believed that 80 percent of afgantsy suffered some form of posttraumatic stress. (The same source described the impact of PTSD on the personality, values, and conduct of the veterans, emphasizing that it might well intensify with time.[301]) The chairman of the Leningrad Afghan Veterans' Association insisted that "everyone needs psychotherapy."[302] Kim Tsagolov agreed, contending that "there is practically not one person who returned from Afghanistan unharmed. All the troops without exception sustained psychological trauma. . . . We must heal everyone who was there."[303] A senior psychoanalyst who had served in Afghanistan as a medical adviser and specialized in the study of mass stress asserted that all afgantsy suffered from some measure of PTSD and bemoaned the fact that most Afghan veterans could not get private treatment. He too emphasized that the effects of PTSD increase over time.[304] Magomed-Eminov noted that the incidence of psychological problems was greater among soldiers than among officers, who did not lose their "social identification" and whose "life and service" continued. Their problem was a tendency toward aggression; many sought out risk and danger.[305]

A survey of the fate of the afgantsy in a single Russian region more than two and a half decades after the end of the war agreed that every veteran of the war suffered from mental trauma.[306] A generation after its end, veterans were still suffering from the war's psychological effects.[307]

PTSD led not only to suicide but also to physical problems and early death from a wide range of illnesses.[308] Some have claimed that five years after the war's end, 41.5 percent of the veterans had been diagnosed as suffering from various heart diseases, 53.7 percent from stomach illnesses, and many from nervous diseases, including hysteria, aggressiveness, and suicidalism. As their difficult adjustment to life at home drove many to drugs and alcohol, over 1,000 reportedly attempted suicide in 2005 alone.[309] A nurse in Afghanistan said that in the thirty years since returning to her native Kazakhstan, she had attended twenty funerals of afgantsy who had died from wounds or illnesses contracted in Afghanistan or as a result of their service there. There had been no rehabilitation. She personally was an invalid "of the second class"—presumably for PTSD—and still suffered sleepless nights, unable to obliterate the memories from her service in the medical unit.[310]

One former KGB officer who served as deputy commander of a special KGB unit in Kabul, from 1984 to 1987 claimed that the very term *Afghan syndrome*, which was widespread both within the establishment and among citizens, became an obstacle to the veterans' successful integration into society. It suggested, for instance, that would-be employers should think twice before hiring them (see Chapter 7). Thus, the term's use by nonprofessionals exacerbated the symptoms from which the afgantsy suffered, notably isolation, and social and official discrimination.[311]

Apparently the psychological disorders were particularly ubiquitous in Russia and other parts of the European USSR. Although there were cases in Central Asia and the Caucasus, they seem to have been less widespread and would not have been professionally treated,[312] although one Tashkenti told me Uzbek soldiers too returned *nervoznye* with their nerves on edge (see Chapter 9).

The afgantsy got the short end of the stick. Returning home after fighting a harsh war in extremely arduous conditions, they found themselves having to cope with a society that looked askance on their war as both immoral and a national disgrace and that transferred these sentiments to those who fought it. To add insult to injury, the country was undergoing far-reaching transformations that precluded providing the vets with an appropriate reception and the therapy that they needed. Even when the afgantsy created their own frameworks that might promote their acclimatization, the country's economic, political, and social turmoil undercut the chances of a meaningful solution to their problems. The result was that in every city and region, a large group of young men had to find ways to keep their heads above water with their own resources. In the words of one commentator, the system of exchange between the veterans on the one hand and the state and society on the other had faltered on every level—economic, social, moral, and personal.[313]

Chapter 9

Central Asia and the Soviet "Muslim" Peoples

Central Asia: The Soviet Union's Southern Border

One of the official reasons for the intervention in Afghanistan was the Soviet Union's need to protect its southern border. Specifically, the establishment contended that if the Soviet Union did not intercede to save the Marxist regime in Kabul, the United States would intervene militarily, which would allow it to threaten the Soviet Union with missiles from Afghan territory (see Chapter 1). Long after the war's end, Central Asians remained convinced that in light of the Cold War superpower rivalry, their region was in danger in 1979.[1]

The Soviet intervention did more than just transform the three Soviet Union republics that shared a border with Afghanistan—Turkmenistan, Uzbekistan, and Tajikistan–into a foremost strategic area. Under glasnost, it also led to Moscow's reassessment of its suppression of the Basmachi in the 1920s and 1930s. Because significant populations of each of the three republics' titular ethnic groups inhabited northern Afghanistan,[2] Moscow was reportedly apprehensive that if the Islamic opposition ousted the PDPA, it would endanger Moscow's rule in Soviet Central Asia by infecting its traditionally Muslim population with the spirit of Islam from across the border. Later, under glasnost, the government's general reassessment of its previous uses of the military led it to question both its campaign against the earlier Central Asian movement protesting Bolshevik rule and specifically, the methods that Moscow used to impose control on rural, Islamic Central Asia.[3]

Chapter 1 discussed the weakness of the first argument. This chapter addresses the validity of Moscow's concern that Islam might become a significant political and social force in Soviet Central Asia. It also examines the Soviet Central Asians' contribution to the war effort and the impact of the war on the Central Asian republics and other traditionally Muslim Soviet peoples.

The Islamic Threat to Soviet Central Asia

There is no written evidence that the Kremlin's policy regarding Afghanistan stemmed from concern that Islam might become a political and social force in the Soviet Union's Central Asian republics in the wake of the Iranian revolution in early 1979 and the consolidation of an Islamic opposition to the DRA regime. None of the Politburo resolutions or transcripts suggests that this factor played any role in either the decision to intervene militarily in Afghanistan or the failure to withdraw quickly. Karen Brutents, of the CPSU CC International Department, testified that nobody in the Soviet leadership at the time took any interest in Islam or even knew what an ayatollah was: "In our country the study of Islam at the level of political and scholarly institutions had practically stopped. . . . We probably thought that we had solved that problem once and for all. And, indeed, we were very successful in that. . . . [Or] perhaps we did not want to draw attention to that problem."[4]

However, a year after the Iranian revolution, the Moscow Institute of Oriental Studies established a department for the study of Islam. As of the early 1980s, the resultant Soviet analysis of Islam in the USSR focused on "Islamic extremism" and its endeavor to destabilize the country's Muslim peoples and areas, especially Central Asia. The accompanying political discourse became instrumental in legitimizing a security-driven approach to Islam.

Then deputy CGS and chief of the GS's Main Operations Directorate, Valentin Varennikov, moreover, maintained that Andropov, when trying to convince Brezhnev to intervene, claimed that if the counterrevolution succeeded in Afghanistan, the Soviet Union would have a "Muslim problem" at home (see Chapter 1).[5] A number of senior figures in the Soviet establishment who would necessarily have participated in discussions of strategy have also indicated that some circles paid attention to the issue of foreign Islam.[6] Writing in the 1990s, after the war was over, the last commander of the Soviet force in Afghanistan commented—in the context of the fall of the shah in Iran, which threatened to propagate Islamic fundamentalism—that a pan-Islamic perspective "could find considerable support in the Soviet Union's Central Asian republics." In such a situation, "a revolutionary Afghanistan constituted a serious obstacle for the penetration [into these republics] of such an ideology."[7] We have seen (in Chapter 7) that this was a feature of the support that conservative members of Soviet society showed for the war. Aleksandr Prokhanov, in his 1988 about-face on the war, claimed that its one success was that "the threat of the emergence on the USSR's borders of an extremist Muslim regime prepared to take its propaganda and practice onto the territory of our Central Asian republics . . . will not be fulfilled."[8] Possibly too, the war prevented any signs of tolerance toward Islam in the late 1980s when the Russian Orthodox Church was being feted.

Against the backdrop of the Afghan War, the possibility of enemies using Islam to destabilize the areas of the Soviet Union populated by traditionally Muslim peoples engendered a 1981 CPSU CC resolution, Measures to Counteract the Adversary's Attempts to Use the 'Islamic Factor' for Ends Hostile to the Soviet Union (September 24, 1981),[9] and, eighteen months later, a further resolution, Measures for the Ideological Isolation of the Reactionary Sector of the Muslim Clergy (March 25, 1983).[10] In 1984, officials in Uzbekistan feared that imperialist agents were trying to use the "Islamic factor" to stir up religious feeling in the republic and give it an "anti-Soviet nationalist direction."[11]

Khomeini's Iran and the war in Afghanistan suggested the potential of a politicized Islam to radical Islamic elements inside the Soviet Union. Hitherto a dialectical concomitant of the Marxist-Leninist tenet that every social phenomenon had political implications, and of its sequitur, by which every aspect of society that was not a component of "socialist construction" was by definition hostile to the Soviet system, this phantom took on concrete form in the 1980s. According to a history of the Islamic Renaissance Party of Tajikistan (the IRPT), the intervention in Afghanistan accelerated the politicization of the movement (*harakat)* that was the party's embryo and had existed since 1973 and that now decided it could not remain neutral regarding this "merciless aggression."[12]

"Political Islam" became an issue in Soviet discourse in 1986. In that year, the Central Asian media devoted unusual attention to Islam, and on November 24, Gorbachev himself lambasted Islam at a meeting with the Uzbekistan party elite in Tashkent. Anti-Islamic measures formally targeting "Islamic fundamentalism" followed. A "stormy protest by believers" in summer 1986 accompanied the arrest of itinerant mullah Said Abdullo Nuri, a cofounder of the harakat (which grew to become the Islamic Renaissance Party of Tajikistan). Because Nuri had reportedly called for the creation of an Islamic state in Tajikistan, the court sentenced him to eighteen months' imprisonment for slanderous provocations against the Soviet authority.[13] Some have suggested that during the war in Afghanistan, the suppression of any form of political Islam became a feature of the partnership between Moscow's Russian lieutenants in Tajikistan and the Khujandis who ran the republic.[14] The Afghan factor inevitably surfaced in the context of discussion of domestic Islam. In early 1987, an article blasted the activities of a self-styled radical "Wahhabi" mullah who went around kishlaks in Tajikistan's Qurghonteppa oblast preaching Islam. It censured him for negatively appraising Soviet international assistance to the Afghan people and, "in the spirit of Western radio voices, accusing the Limited Contingent . . . of intending to turn the Afghans into non-believers."[15]

Igor Beliaev's keynote article, "Islam and Politics" (May 1987), quoted mujahidin in Afghanistan as saying that "connections had been made with relatives and friends on the Soviet side. . . . 'We have taken the battle to the land of the shuravi.'" Beliaev contended that the interest in political Islam in the domestic context must be seen against the backdrop of the Alma-Ata demonstrations the previous December, which were "manipulated by Muslim fanatics and Sufis . . . senior students, and even professors." He would not be surprised, he wrote, to hear that some of the "cassettes with recordings of the holy Islamic texts and of Islamic authorities" being distributed in "Islamizdat . . . reach Tajikistan and Uzbekistan from over the border, and . . . can reach the rest of the Soviet Union."[16] (Beliaev's description of the Alma-Ata events was blatantly distorted and tendentious—it was the removal of the Kazakh CP's Kazakh First Secretary and his replacement by a Russian who did not even reside in Kazakhstan that sparked the demonstrations; reports from the scene made no mention of any Muslim factor.) Similarly, allegations that Afghan mujahidin gave meaningful backing to Tajikistan's Islamists emanated from KGB sources hoping to legitimize repression by highlighting the threat to the Soviet order from radical Islam as allegedly disloyal and the product of externally inspired subversion (and, later, from partisan sources interested in maintaining a Russian military presence in Tajikistan after that country's independence).[17]

Perhaps, however, the Soviet security forces—less sanguine by definition than other components of the establishment—genuinely feared that the country's Central Asian citizens, especially those with relatives in Afghanistan, might show signs of disaffection in solidarity with their Afghan brethren. Tashkent was said in summer 1980 to be packed with KGB agents, both visible and secret, which indicates doubts about the Central Asians' trustworthiness.[18] One Uzbek who had served in Kabul as an interpreter from 1979 to 1981 refrained from discussing Afghanistan for fear of the KGB.[19] In early 1987, the Afghan War was behind the KGB's stepping up of security in Tajikistan. The incursion of Afghan opposition forces into Tajikistan in spring 1987 prompted a visit by KGB chairman Vladimir Chebrikov, who instructed the Tajik security organs and border troops not to permit armed actions or "other hostile manifestations" at the border. In parallel, he prohibited "open and organized hostile manifestations on the part of religious extremists."[20]

In late 1987, the chairman of the Tajik SSR KGB, Vladimr Pektel', told a Tajik Party plenum that in 1986–1987, dozens of trials had taken place against "ringleaders" of anti-Soviet activity—"unofficial Muslim clerics who not only fanned religious sentiments but also called for a 'jihad' against the existing system."[21] Pektel' singled out the phenomenon of draft dodging and the disinclination of eighteen-year-olds to do army service, especially in Afghanistan. The draft dodgers would go to another region of Tajikistan, "where they began to study the dogmas of Islam" and, not registered there with the voenkomat, evaded military service.[22] Toward the end of the Soviet Union's existence, Pektel' returned to his theme of discrediting the Islamic opposition in Tajikistan as extremist and disloyal. He spoke about the penetration of Afghan fundamentalists into Tajikistan and maintained that the Soviet withdrawal from Afghanistan had led to "an outburst of subversive activity" in the republic's "local areas."[23] Military and KGB figures—Gareev, Kriuchkov, and Shebarshin—were concerned about the spillover effect in Soviet Central Asia of events in Afghanistan. In August 1989, Shevarnadze and Kriuchkov noted that "party leaders in Uzbekistan confirmed that 'Islamist fundamentalist" groups there "and elsewhere in Central Asia" were waiting to take advantage of a mujahidin victory in Afghanistan."[24]

For most Central Asians and other Soviet "Muslims," however, the Islamic component of their identity was an indicator of ethnic demarcation (primarily as opposed to Russians) and a safeguard for preserving local traditions and ways of life rather than a potential breeding ground for opposing the powers that be. People saw no contradiction in being simultaneously Uzbek or Tajik, Muslim, and Soviet. My own survey, which included forty-four Central Asian veterans and fifty regular citizens, uncovered no differentiation between them and other citizens or former soldiers in any way that regarded self-identity and sociopolitical attitudes. As a result of this, they felt little affinity with Afghans.

Soviet Central Asia and the DRA

The border with Afghanistan, while as vigilantly guarded as any other Soviet border, was traditionally one of the Soviet Union's more traversable frontiers. The mountainous terrain on both sides of the Amu Darya and its tributary, the Pyanj, which formed the border between the two countries, enabled smugglers to bring merchandise—especially narcotics—into Tajikistan and Uzbekistan. Drug contraband continued throughout the war, as did the smuggling of political and religious literature, making the proximity a constant headache for the militia who guarded the area.[25]

The Turkestan and the Central Asian Military District headquarters in Tashkent and Alma-Ata respectively, filled coordinating roles in the intervention (see Chapter 2). Not only were units from these two MDs deployed to Afghanistan, but over time, their bases—in Ashkhabad, Termez, Kushka, Charjou—became training centers for soldiers destined for the war.[26] And the Fortieth Army was formally subordinated to the commander of the Turkestan MD (see Chapter 3). The KGB, always active in the Soviet Union's border regions, increased its supervision in Central Asia in the context of the war.[27]

The five Soviet Central Asian republics had been role models for the Soviet Union's allies in the developing countries—including Afghanistan—since the mid-1950s, when Khrushchev orchestrated the Soviet penetration of the Third World, much of which was Muslim. There, Moscow had "a developmental model that has managed to achieve one of the highest levels of literacy, the best health care system, and the highest standard of living anywhere in the Muslim world."[28] By making Soviet citizens from traditionally Muslim ethnic groups integral to the intensive Soviet aid program, Moscow highlighted its successes in modernizing Central Asia. The widespread use of Soviet Muslims as representatives of the Soviet system deliberately showcased the success of socialist development among Muslims in order to disprove the idea that Islam and communism were incompatible. Long before the Soviet invasion, indeed well before the Marxist coup, many Soviet Muslim civilians, among them a high proportion of Central Asians, served in Afghanistan as experts and technical advisers.[29]

The Kremlin promoted this Central Asian presence with renewed verve after the 1978 communist takeover in Kabul, at which point Central Asia became a staging ground for civilian efforts in Afghanistan. The government extended its regional infrastructure into northern Afghanistan, strengthening the links between the two areas, and many Central Asians joined other Soviet specialists in the civilian Soviet state-building effort.[30] The ranks of the civilian experts in the country swelled even more after the intervention.[31] The Central Asian leadership and establishment maintained official ties with the DRA throughout the war. Uzbek Party First Secretary Sharaf Rashidov, for example, headed the Soviet delegation to the April Revolution's fifth anniversary celebrations.[32]

According to a former professor at Kabul University, the Soviet Union sought to transform relations in Afghanistan by severing the younger generation from their traditions and their affinities with Iranian and subcontinent civilizations and convincing them that Afghanistan was an integral component of Central Asian culture and society. To this end, the Kremlin dispatched to Afghanistan from the Central Asian republics educators, specialists in various fields, writers, and propagandists to implement the Soviet nationalities policy there. In Kabul, the Soviets orchestrated large gatherings with Uzbeks from Tashkent who brought abundant written materials that emphasized this connection between the Soviet Central Asian nationalities and the Afghans. In these, the Soviets exaggerated the size of "their" ethnic groups in the Afghan population.[33] It was perhaps in this context that Soviet propaganda presented fifteenth-century poet, Ali Shir Nava'i—born in Herat—as the founding poet of modern Uzbek literature, to symbolize the cultural links between Afghanistan and Soviet Central Asia.[34]

In August 1988 and again in January 1989, the Turkmen Komsomol organized a special train to Torgundi, across the border, to bring it a clinic and to facilitate meetings between members of the Turkmen "creative intelligentsia" and Afghan Turkmen; the town's inhabitants were basically Turkmen who had crossed over in the 1920s. During their two and a half week stay, Soviet doctors treated Afghans from near and far, while the artists found co-ethnics who had retained their native language and were acquainted with the works of Soviet Turkmen writers.[35] In February 1989, the chairman of the Soviet Committee for the Defense of Peace and vice president of the World Peace Council, G. A. Borovik, met with activists from Turkmenistan's Committee for Defense of Peace to discuss Turkmenistan's role in contributing to the regulation of the postwar Afghan situation by developing cultural, especially linguistic, ties with their Afghan compatriots.[36]

Nor was it solely cultural similarities between the inhabitants living on both sides of the border that the Soviet authorities used to bolster the DRA regime. They set up cooperative projects in a range of subjects "from seismology to the shared cultural heritage." The Tajik SSR government was particularly involved in cultivating patron-client relations with Afghanistan, specifically between neighboring provinces such as Tajikistan's Gorno-Badakhshan Autonomous oblast (GBAO) and the Afghan province of Badakhshan. Tajikistan sent the DRA books, newspapers, magazines, films, exhibits, cultural delegations, and entertainers.[37] The Soviet propaganda effort mobilized Central Asian materials in Afghanistan. These included films on Soviet Uzbekistan and Tajikistan, radio broadcasts, journals such as *Soviet Uzbekistan* or *Muslims in the Soviet East*, and Soviet publications in Dari and Pashtu, Afghanistan's two official languages.[38]

Tajik academics went to Afghanistan to teach and help build Afghanistan's Academy of Sciences. And the Tajik government sent a high-level delegation to Kabul in early summer 1988 to discuss aid in agriculture and trade relations, specifically with Afghanistan's northern provinces.[39] Kirghiziia's Talas oblast too established direct ties with an Afghan province, which entailed sending gifts from the former to the latter and led to economic aid.[40]

As an intrinsic component of Moscow's enhanced engagement in Afghanistan in the 1980s, Soviet Central Asia hosted a large cohort of Afghan citizens who, throughout the war, came to study and acquire civilian, as well as military, skills and professions. Many Afghan students came to study at Tajikistan's State University and polytechnic institutes. In 1987, 10,000 Afghans, including 3,000 children with their teachers, were studying in the Soviet Union—most of them almost certainly in Central Asia—while 15,000 or so youngsters toured the Soviet Union annually.[41] One Uzbek school of 700 children had, as of 1984, 100 Afghan pupils (75 of them boys) who studied there from the third grade and had a special curriculum, including the history and geography of Afghanistan, Pashtu and Dari, "and even the history of Islam."[42] Programs for Afghan students training in Central Asia, however, were not an unadulterated success. In January 1989, "Afghan nationals training in Tashkent, while under the influence of drugs and alcohol, ran wild at a kolkhoz market," throwing stones and killing and injuring citizens, after trying their hand at hustling foreign goods. The police "loaded them onto a bus and sent them to their dormitories," where "fighting broke out in earnest" with further physical injury to citizens.[43]

Within the framework of Soviet policy in the Muslim world, which sought to underscore the compatibility of socialism, and even communism, with Islam, Moscow traditionally harnessed the Spiritual Administration of the Muslims of Central Asia (SADUM) as a spokesman for the Soviet propaganda outreach. As of 1981, SADUM officials paid a series of visits to Afghanistan to emphasize its role as a model for institutionalizing Islam-state relations in a communist society and "to mould a cadre of pro-Socialist Afghan *ulama* in its own image."[44] A SADUM delegation, headed by Mufti Ziyautdin Babakhanov, arrived in Kabul in June 1981 to meet with the head of the DRA government.[45] SADUM also hosted senior Afghan officials, religious and secular, "to showcase the prosperity of Islam and Muslims in the Soviet Union."[46] A delegation of Afghan religious leaders visited Uzbekistan and Azerbaijan in 1980 and noted that their "Muslim brothers" there led "prosperous and free lives."[47] The heads of all four Soviet Muslim Administrations issued a joint statement in 1985, condemning the enemies of the April revolution who had burned down mosques and killed Muslim clergy.[48] A SADUM delegation, headed by Mufti Muhammad-Sadyk Muhammad-Yusuf, scheduled a July 1990 visit to Pakistan to meet Afghan opposition leaders and seek the release of Soviet POWs still held in Afghanistan.[49]

Afghan citizens also visited Soviet Central Asia in delegations of representatives from different Afghan tribes, which came to Turkmenistan in 1983, and to Tashkent in 1984,[50] while a festival of Soviet-Afghan friendship took place in Tajikistan with the participation of a representative delegation from the Democratic Youth Organization of Afghanistan and a delegation from the Afghan-Soviet Friendship Society.[51] Apparently these visits did not go entirely according to plan. In 1984, a group of children of Afghan communists who had perished during the war complained to their Uzbek bus driver in Samarkand that their Soviet instructors had forced them to eat pork, beaten them up during self-defense lessons, and required them to run 10 kilometers every night for their "physical development."[52]

Many Afghans who came to the Soviet Union to study—or on the pretext of doing so—remained in the Soviet Union or the FSU. There seems, however, to be little evidence of Soviet success in attracting them to Marxism-Leninism and imbuing them with Soviet values, just as hopes of Afghans to influence Central Asian or other "Muslim" ethnic groups to adopt Islamic tenets went largely unfulfilled. In this context, it must be borne in mind that in the 1960s and 1970s, Soviet Central Asia underwent a period of social stability, marked educational progress, and economic development. This was the backdrop against which the generation of those who fought in the Fortieth Army grew up. It was not solely the incessant brainwashing that promoted their gratitude to the Soviet power for these benefits. They sensed and lived them and accordingly identified with their Soviet mother country.

The 1980s, however, were a different story. Signs of flux were in the air, and not solely in connection with the Islamic revival. Uzbekistan was among the first republics to fall victim to Andropov's anticorruption campaign. The "cotton affair," accusing Uzbekistan's entire political elite of involvement in fabricating reports on cotton production to satisfy Moscow's ever-growing demands, shook the Uzbek establishment.[53] The December 1986 disturbances in Alma-Ata (see above) tore the political fabric in Kazakhstan. Thus, while the Central Asian leaders wanted the Afghan War to end, as Gorbachev's interpreter, Pavel Palazhchenko, testified, these were not days when they were banging on the table and making demands of the central powers.[54]

Central Asian Soldiers

The DRA leadership had specifically asked the Kremlin to dispatch Central Asian soldiers to Afghanistan. In his first request for military aid, in a telephone conversation with Soviet Prime Minister Aleksei Kosygin in March 1979 (see Chapter 1), DRA President Nur Muhammad Taraki inquired, "Why can't the Soviet Union send Uzbeks, Tajiks, and Turkmen in civilian clothing? No one will recognize them . . . because we have all these nationalities in Afghanistan. Let them don Afghan costume and wear Afghan badges." In this way, their presence would not lead to questions regarding the Marxist regime's collaboration with the hated foreigner (see below) or constitute a risk to the Soviet Union's international position.[55] (The first was probably the genuine concern, the second added in order to humor anticipated Soviet sensitivities.)

A disproportionately high percentage of the soldiers who entered Afghanistan in December 1979 and early 1980 were in fact Central Asians (see Chapters 2 and 3). The first reason for this was purely technical: the proximity of Soviet Central Asia enabled the Defense Ministry to mobilize a force within the extremely short period between the decision to intervene and the date fixed for doing so. A second reason was that Moscow thought that the Soviet Central Asians would be the most suitable for service in Afghanistan.[56] Some officials testified that Central Asians adapt to the Afghan climate more easily than Europeans do.[57] Furthermore, their potential common language with the Afghan population, notably with their co-ethnics, could help to create a favorable Afghan response to the Soviet intervention.

If the Soviet military authorities had hoped that introducing Soviet troops that resembled the local population would keep it from perceiving them as foreign invaders, that hope was in vain. The Pashtun tribes, which constituted almost half of Afghanistan's citizenry and were the backbone of the opposition to the PDPA, had a history of enmity toward the ethnic minorities inhabiting the country's northern regions. The very appearance in Afghanistan of foreign representatives of these minorities exacerbated the Pashtun revolt against the Kabul regime.[58]

There are no precise numbers regarding how many Central Asians served in Afghanistan during the war. We have figures for the number of soldiers from the Uzbek and Tajik SSRs, but these include Russians and Ukrainians and other nonindigenous populations. At the end of the war, Uzbekistan, for example, had 42,000 Afghan veterans.[59] The circumstantial evidence, however, suggests that a high proportion of the troops were Central Asians. Thirty graduates of a single school in Ashkhabad, for instance, served there, four of whom died.[60] Again, this might have been partly because the Fortieth Army was formally subordinate to the Turkestan MD command and because the Central Asian MD also played a significant role in the war—providing bases and training centers—so that whenever it was necessary to complement the force, these two MDs provided the relevant cadres.

The first soldiers sent into Afghanistan in December 1979 returned home early in the new year (the Muslim Battalion, see below); next came the reservists, who mobilized in November and December for their ninety-day term of active duty (see Chapter 3 and below). By summer 1980, men from all over the Soviet Union had replaced much of the original force. Some Central Asians allegedly told young Afghans whom they befriended in Kabul that they were being replaced because they were fraternizing with Afghans. The Afghans who reported this in Pakistan in early February 1980 told of contacts with Soviet soldiers who spoke Dari or Farsi, were apologetic of their presence in Afghanistan, and sold their Afghan friends small ammunition.[61] One mujahid told an American reporter that Central Asian soldiers, upon realizing that they were fighting Afghans rather than Chinese, Americans, and Pakistanis, as they had been told, would leave the rebels packages containing weapons and ammunition.[62]

A number of Central Asians indeed recalled amicable relations with local Afghans. One truck driver who served from 1980 to 1982, recalling that 70 percent of his company of thirty were Central Asians or Caucasians, opined that the Soviets believed Afghans would not shoot at other Muslims.[63] Tajik interpreters said Afghanistan was "very close" to them and that the local population welcomed them; Tajik soldiers met with people who knew their parents.[64] A Kazakh soldier encountered an Afghan Kazakh who wanted to hear about life in Kazakhstan and invited him to his home.[65] One Afghan Uzbek who reached Pakistan said that a Soviet Uzbek had told him that he and other Central Asians would deliberately misfire in encounters with mujahidin.[66] The West German *Der Spiegel* reported an incident in which Uzbek soldiers shot into the air when ordered to fire at Afghan villagers who hanged seventeen Russians in the center of Kabul in January 1980. Two Soviet deserters, who had been deployed to Afghanistan in 1980, claimed that all the Tajiks in their unit refused to fight and were sent home.[67] A Central Asian said his commander had punished him for refusing to kill civilians of similar ethnicity.[68]

There might well have been such instances, but careful scrutiny of the evidence demands that we refrain from drawing conclusions about widespread Central Asian disloyalty to the Soviet Union.[69] One popular story, which has not been corroborated, told of an incident in October 1985 when a Russian officer executed a Tajik soldier for fraternizing with Afghan civilians—or, according to one version, for trafficking in hashish—and as a result, Central Asian soldiers started firing at the Russians, initiating a full day of fighting and killing and wounding a large number of soldiers.[70]

The supposed unreliability of the Central Asian soldiers was not just Western Cold War rhetoric. The Soviet population took it seriously as well. Russians told Hedrick Smith, for instance, "that the Uzbeks were too friendly with their fellow Muslims the Afghans, and had to be replaced by more reliable Russian boys."[71] Even inhabitants of Tashkent believed this.[72] Certainly, Western analysts eagerly adopted the theme, as some of them had long been predicting discontent among the Soviet Central Asian population. The RAND Corporation, for example, immediately produced a paper contending that the Central Asians had to be sent home because of suspected disloyalty.[73] Much of the information on which these conclusions rested, however, emanated from the few deserters and POWs who reached the United States during the war (see Chapter 3) and whose testimony was presumably partial (in both senses of the word).

Whether these stories of active opposition to, or at least reservations regarding, the war are authentic, the great majority of former Soviet Central Asian soldiers assert convincingly that they remained loyal to the Soviet flag despite their contact with Afghans of their own ethnic group.[74] One of my interviewees, a Tajik from Bukhara who served in Afghanistan in 1982 and 1983, testified, "I am Tajik and we had friendly relations with the population. We talked with them and had no problems with them, they were like in parts of Uzbekistan," although, he pointed out, "we were more Europeanized."[75] An Uzbek who served as an intelligence officer in the 108th division felt that entering Afghanistan "was like going back to the 17th century," referencing his surprise at the burqas and the rampant poverty he saw there. He had joined the army because he "wanted to help the Afghans." However, when asked whether he felt kinship with Afghan Uzbeks there, he said no. "How could I feel kinship with them?" he asked. "Our lifestyle was like a fairy tale to them. They were all dumb and poor." He said he was not driven by any national or ethnic identity, but by a Soviet, international, humanitarian-motivated mission to help them.[76] The more "modernized" Soviet Central Asians' sense of superiority occasionally bred in them an intense dislike, not simply disrespect. One Tajik said the Afghans were a "dirty people" who could not be trusted.[77] A Tajik from Uzbekistan said all empathy with the Afghans dissipated when he saw how they tortured prisoners.[78]

Several accounts of Tajik afgantsy tell of them as go-betweens between the two sides, with some success.[79] Tajik officers were sometimes responsible for relations with the local population, and the Afghans liked them.[80] One man described winning the confidence of Afghans by insisting that he too was Muslim and that the Soviets were not there to fight Islam. He told them, "I am a Muslim myself. You saw me last night, I was reading the *namaz* (the basic Muslim prayer) together with you. It's like that in my homeland, too. People read the namaz, they keep their rituals. No one persecutes them." He asserts that they found this compelling.[81] Apart from serving as ad hoc interpreters, Central Asian soldiers who knew how to pray would dress in Afghan costume and mingle with the inhabitants of the local kishlaks in order to gather information.[82] Many soldiers from traditionally Muslim nationalities, however, dubbed themselves Muslims but had never opened a Qur'an.[83] Presumably these were the majority. Some Central Asian soldiers testified that service in Afghanistan, where they heard the call to prayer (the *muezzin*) five times a day, "awakened" religious sentiments in them.[84]

Central Asian Afghan veterans offered various testimonies regarding their Muslim affiliation. One Kyrgyz vet said that although educated in the spirit of atheism, he was always a Muslim at heart ("in my soul"), believed in Allah, and presented himself as a Muslim in conversation with locals.[85] Yet another former soldier, asked what he felt about being called *kafir*—infidel—by Afghans, said he didn't feel anything. "I've always believed in Allah," he said, "but I didn't think about it. I was just following Soviet orders."[86]

On the whole, my interviewees concurred that their Islamic affiliation was basically formal—they were circumcised and they celebrated the major Muslim festivals—but Islam was not a primary component of their identity. In the words of a veteran from Bukhara, "We were first of all Soviet citizens. We had nothing of Islam. Our grandparents went to the mosque, we never went. We wanted to go and study at an Institute. Our parents prayed at home, but we did not. To be a Muslim, you have to pray five times a day."[87] Another Bukharan veteran, however, gave a more complex response: "The war was part of our lives; we were Soviet patriots—that was our education. We were equally Muslims and Soviet citizens. Bukhara is holy territory, so there was no reason to look on the Afghans as better Muslims than us."[88] Ultimately, as a communications specialist who served in the last years of the war put it, "the mentality of Soviet Muslims and Afghans was totally different."[89]

While Central Asian soldiers entertained few illusions about the popularity of the Fortieth Army among the Afghan population, some testified that Afghans related more positively to them.[90] Others, especially those who served toward the end of the war, remembered only outright animosity. At most, Afghans would ask Central Asian soldiers why they as Muslims came to fight and were not sympathetic toward the reply that they had to fulfill their duty as soldiers.[91]

Their easier access to the locals made Central Asian soldiers inevitable intermediaries in trade with them. Some commentators blame the Central Asians for taking advantage of this trade,[92] although others suggest that European soldiers used Central Asians as go-betweens for procuring drugs.[93] Probably both are accurate: Central Asian officers and soldiers conducted these transactions on their own initiative and at the request of soldiers or officers from other nationalities (see Chapter 3).

Again, despite their contact and occasional sympathies, there seems to be no hard evidence that the bulk of Central Asians serving in Afghanistan were in any way disloyal to the Soviet Union. Indeed, Central Asian afgantsy testify that they did not question their identification with the Soviet mother country.[94] If we bear in mind that the majority of Soviet soldiers accepted that they were defending their country's southern border, we can expect the motivation of Central Asians who lived near that border to be especially high. The Soviet high command itself seems to have been convinced of their loyalty, for it assigned a considerable proportion of the Tajiks, for instance, to the northern, Persian-speaking provinces of Afghanistan, apparently so that the Soviet force could benefit from their linguistic and ethnic affinity with the local population.[95] One Uzbek junior officer who had studied Orientalistica before serving in Afghanistan and was able to converse in Dari would go to kishlaks, talk with the inhabitants, and answer their questions about life in the Soviet Union. Sometimes, not always, he was able to earn their sympathy and understanding.[96]

Undoubtedly, there were also many reasons not to hobnob with Afghans. First, there were the realities of war. It was often not clear who was a friend and who a foe. Stories abounded of soldiers—Central Asian and other—who paid with their lives for going into Afghan-populated areas, especially in the countryside. When Central Asian soldiers went alone to the bazaar, they risked assault and kidnapping. Second, army regulations strictly prohibited socializing. Soldiers were reluctant to risk punishment by violating them and to jeopardize their chances of earning letters of recommendation from political officers, which might prove helpful back home.[97]

If any skepticism existed regarding the Central Asian soldiers, it focused on their qualifications as soldiers. The unsuitability of many Central Asians for active participation in military activity was due in part to their poor Russian-language proficiency, which was a common problem for Central Asian draftees and potential draftees (see also Chapters 2 and 3). One Slav POW who reached the United States said that one-third of the Central Asians in his regiment did not understand even basic Russian, or pretended not to, and the others spoke haltingly.[98]

It is not surprising therefore that after those first few months, disproportionate numbers of Central Asians reportedly served in the support units. While they were approximately 20 percent of the Soviet force in Afghanistan, possibly as many as 50 percent served in these nonprestigious units, according to interviews with former construction unit servicemen, including some Central Asians. Alexiev and Wimbush (of the RAND Corporation) tell us that "close to 40 percent of the men in an automotive repair company in which a respondent served were from Central Asia."[99] At the same time, a scrupulous study of Tajik roles shows that Tajik soldiers filled a wide range of positions in the Fortieth Army, including large numbers in combat units, and that many of them were officers and NCOs.[100] One Tajik, who volunteered for Afghanistan and—together with eleven other Tajiks—as early as 1980 underwent a six-month special preparatory course, testified that Tajiks were selected for their language capabilities. Most of his unit's assignments involved contact with the civilian population, distributing material assistance, and liberating kishlaks from the dushmans. He was the only one of the twelve who survived the war.[101] One Russian vet singled out Tajiks as having proved themselves in the war as excellent and true soldiers.[102] One Tajik officer, Captain Nabi Akramov, was among the Limited Contingent's 21 Heroes of the Soviet Union listed in the Soviet press in early 1985.[103]

While undoubtedly the disproportion of Central Asians evened out in summer 1980, in some instances and some units, the evening out was not felt. A high percentage of Tajiks were sent to Afghanistan in 1981,[104] so they made up a disproportionate number of casualties. The Central Asian population, particularly the Uzbeks, complained that they were bearing too much of the burden of the war and that their boys were the first to die in Afghanistan.[105] An Uzbek soldier said that until 1982, Central Asians were the majority in infantry units, and in the early period, there wasn't a single *mahalla* that did not receive a zinc coffin.[106] According to one source, the cause of discontent was that the Soviet military sought to conduct the funerals without any religious ceremony, which on at least one occasion had caused a riot in Alma-Ata.[107] An intelligence officer said that in Tashkent in summer 1981, the mothers and families of serving or dead soldiers staged a major protest. He claimed this was a key factor in the armed forces' decision to change the composition of the Fortieth Army.[108] Major General Mels Bekboev, deputy commander of the second Muslim Battalion, also attributed the decrease to protests in Central Asia and testified that in spring 1983, an official decree ordered a reduction in the number of Central Asians deployed.[109]

By 1985, however, it seems that objective conditions again compelled the Soviet military authorities to send meaningful numbers of Central Asians to the war. By this time, all mothers were expressing their anxiety at the mounting death toll; as a result of the country's demographic dynamics, Soviet Muslims were 24 percent of the country's potential recruits,[110] almost two-thirds of them Central Asians, causing no little concern in the military.

Throughout the war, there were Central Asians—just as there were citizens of other nationalities, including Slavs—who sought to evade the draft altogether and, in particular, to avoid being sent to Afghanistan (see Chapters 7 and 8). Some claim that the phenomenon was particularly widespread in Central Asia. Although there seem to be no statistics to support this, the MoD daily nevertheless drew attention to "the 'privileged' list" in Uzbekistan's voenkomats; some of those who appeared on it were exempt from military service altogether, while others had the decision to send them to Afghanistan rescinded.[111] Uzbek SSR First Party Secretary Inamjon Usmankhojaev stated in February 1987 that hundreds of Komsomol members in Uzbekistan had been prosecuted for draft dodging.[112]

Many Russian and other Slav officers demeaned the Central Asian soldiers in their units. Unquestionably, the Central Asians who fought in Afghanistan had to endure not only the hardships of service that all soldiers experienced, including the dust and the mines and other "pleasures"—; they also faced humiliation at the hands of officers and fellow soldiers (see Chapter 3). One Uzbek soldier's drunken officer physically injured him for bringing his dinner late. The afganets who remembered this instance said it was one of many.[113] One Uzbek, or Karakalpak, former soldier spoke of the oppressive relations within the Fortieth Army. He was still smarting in 1990 about the offensive way one officer had told a group of Uzbek soldiers that they had bought their driving licenses for a sheep, could not be trusted with technology, and should be consigned to the construction battalion. He was the only member of the group who refused to accept this decision.[114] Central Asian soldiers in Afghanistan were often singled out for hazing. One Tajik interpreter who arrived in Afghanistan in 1985 testified that many Central Asians went over to the mujahidin because they could not take the hazing.[115]

Outside the Muslim Battalion (see below), Central Asian officers in Afghanistan felt discriminated against. One Uzbek deputy battalion chief of staff, who was unable to get promotion throughout his service in Afghanistan, writes that "undeclared restrictions regarding national cadres [i.e., non-Russians] . . . made impossible the advance of national cadres during the course of their service, although they were more talented than some Russian-speaking officers." He felt that promotion was possible only for Russians or for officers with Russian or Tatar wives.[116]

Despite their similar experience at the hands of Slav fellow soldiers or officers, there is no evidence of Central Asian or Muslim solidarity in the ranks of the Fortieth Army. Such cohesion as there was remained within the ethnic group (except perhaps for Kyrgyz and Kazakhs).

One special group of Central Asian soldiers, specifically from the three republics bordering on Afghanistan, merits special attention, as it deployed covertly as spetsnaz (special forces) under the command of the GRU. Central Asian spetsnaz served in two so-called Muslim Battalions, comprising approximately 500 and 750 men, respectively. The first of these played an important role in the Soviet Union's preinvasion operations and in the takeover of Kabul, and both participated in "open battle maneuvers, reconstruction efforts, ambushes, and even 'peacekeeping' missions."[117]

The original Muslim Battalion was formed one month after President Taraki's first appeal for Soviet military involvement (see Chapters 1 and 2). Special Operations Detachment 154 (SpN 00 154), otherwise known as the Muslim Battalion, boasted 520 soldiers, selected from over one thousand applicants who had all served six to twelve months in the Turkestan and Central Asian MDs. It was composed almost entirely of Uzbek, Tajik, and Turkmen (70, 20, and 10 percent, respectively), plus seven Kazakhs and four Tatars, many of them carefully picked specialists, and an antiaircraft platoon manned by Slavs, which trained in Turkmenistan and received instruction in Dari.[118] As Colonel Sharipov, who led the Muslim Battalion's First Company during the December 27 palace assault, put it, "The idea was to put together a unit of Soviet Central Asians who looked like Afghans."[119]

According to Colonel Vasilii Kozlov, the GRU officer who oversaw the unit's creation, "All the Tajiks, approximately half the Uzbeks, and part of the Turkmen knew or could manage Farsi."[120] On December 4, 1979, KGB Chairman Yuri Andropov and CGS Nikolai Ogarkov wrote to the Politburo, "Given the current situation and at the request of Amin consider it appropriate to send to Afghanistan the detachment of the GRU General Staff, the 500 persons prepared for this purpose, in uniform which does not disclose their affiliation to the USSR Armed Forces." SpN 00 154 embarked from Chirchik and Tuzel airfields in Uzbekistan for the Soviet airbase in Bagram, Afghanistan, on December 9 and 10 (two days before the Politburo decided on military intervention). Afghan army uniforms had been sewn for the soldiers in Moscow, and they received forged Afghan identification documents.[121]

The Muslim Battalion played a major role in the assassination of President Amin on December 27, 1979, then left Afghanistan on January 10, 1980. It returned to Chirchik, and from there the soldiers went back to their homes. All of them received state awards. The army did not reveal their roles in the war, and their identity remained secret. Special Operations Detachment 154, the Muslim Battalion, was soon re-formed with new recruits. For the most part it kept its primarily Tajik, Uzbek, and Turkmen ethnic composition and was deployed to Afghanistan in October 1981, along with a second spetsnaz force (177 00 SpN), the second Muslim Battalion.

Special Operations Detachment 177, formed in February 1980 in Kapchagay, Kazakhstan, was also a selective group, comprising soldiers chosen not only for their physical fitness and technical knowledge of how to operate the relevant weaponry and equipment but also by their knowledge of Central Asian languages. In addition to Uzbeks and Tajiks, the force recruited Turkmen, Kazakhs, and Kyrgyz. Its commander was Lieutenant Colonel Boris Kerimbaev (born in Kazakhstan), who wrote a memoir recounting the battalion's activity. The Muslim Battalions were the first two of eight highly trained GRU spetsnaz detachments of the Fifteenth and Twenty-Second spetsnaz brigades involved in the war in Afghanistan. (The other six GRU spetsnaz battalions started entering Afghanistan in early 1984.)[122]

The Muslim Battalions maintained good relations with the local population whose language and customs they knew and shared. These entailed a relatively friendly day-to-day rapport and allowed the enlistment of locals as informers. The relationship notwithstanding, they were, in the words of the deputy commander of one of the battalions, "first of all, Soviet soldiers." Both Muslim battalions took part in fighting, suffering fifty-two and thirty-four losses, respectively.[123]

The establishment of the Muslim Battalions, which were given high-priority assignments and allowed considerable independence of action, seems to indicate once again that the Soviet authorities relied on the fealty of their Central Asian citizens—although it undoubtedly screened each soldier in them carefully. It also served as an antidote to the demeaning attitude of many Russian and Slav officers toward Central Asian soldiers.

Just as they did not regard themselves as Muslims fighting Muslims, so the Central Asian soldiers in Afghanistan did not see themselves as Tajiks, Uzbeks, or Turkmen fighting against co-nationals. Although one scholar, who interviewed ten Central Asian war veterans in the present century, pressed them, none of them indicated that he saw the war in an ethnic light. The deputy commander of the Second Muslim Battalion, Mels Bekboev, said that for his soldiers, it was "an honor to serve" not only because entering the battalion was a selective process, requiring "physical fitness and moral preparation," but also because it led to postwar benefits such as free education. Interviewees insisted that at the time, they believed in their "international duty" and that there was no difference in the way they and soldiers of other nationalities viewed the war.

Many interpreters served in the military, often as part of their regular military service; every unit of the PDPA army that went into an operation had one or two interpreters. The majority of the interpreters were Central Asian soldiers,[124] probably Tajiks, given the closeness of Dari and Tajik. One former student testified that all students of Persian and Pashtu at Tajik State University were supposed to do a year's "internship" abroad as part of the curriculum, which in the 1980s usually meant being dispatched to Afghanistan Often they were sent there a second time after graduation.[125] Most became officers, and not a few of them held responsible positions, serving with Soviet military advisers in the DRA army and in "special psychological operations detachments called *agitotryadi*," which conducted "a vigorous 'hearts and minds' campaign among the Afghan rural population."[126] Some of the interpreters who had not benefited from higher education received professional training in preparation for Afghanistan.[127] The interpreters spoke to Afghans during patrols, interpreted during combat missions, collected intelligence, debriefed informers, and in some cases undertook undercover missions. As one interpreter who served between 1979 and 1981 put it, "Who is the interpreter? A person who knows the situation. A person who knows the history. Literature. Afghan customs. We not only translated, we also explained to these Soviet officers. . . . We told them about the customs, the people, about what you can do and what you must not do. In many cases, the interpreters acted as advisors. Not just as interpreters . . . interpreters played an enormous role during the war."[128]

These men's military careers are further proof that although they, by definition, had frequent contact with the local population, the Soviet high command had no qualms about their loyalty. They too would necessarily have undergone special screening. Some were asked specifically whether they had relatives in Afghanistan.[129]

A number of Central Asian women were part of the Fortieth Army as propagandists among the Afghan population, reaching out especially to women.[130] According to one source, propagandists were "usually though not formally . . . female officers from Central Asia" who served for two years and underwent military training in Tashkent before going to Afghanistan.[131]

Most Central Asian veterans of the Soviet-Afghan War considered the mujahidin enemies. Neither ethnicity nor religious affiliation seems to have influenced their understanding of their role in Afghanistan and they believed that the other side saw the situation similarly. One man from Andijon oblast told a Western scholar, "These people were Uzbeks and Tajiks just like us. And we could speak with them. But we were there as Soviet soldiers. So we had to fight for our country. And they would also see a difference. They told us, 'Yes, you are Tajik but you are Soviet and not real Muslims. If we fight you, we will kill you.'"[132] Two Tajik interpreters remembered Afghans who, finding out they were Tajik, warned them not to participate in combat operations.[133] A Tajik intelligence person said that the Afghans perceived all Soviet soldiers, "Tajiks and Russians, Christians and Muslims" alike, as infidels (kafirs).[134] Other Central Asians sensed that the local population, especially the Afghan Tajiks and Uzbeks, related more positively to them than to other Soviet soldiers "because we were Muslims."[135] A few Central Asian and other "Muslim" soldiers deserted to, or were captured by, the mujahidin; some remained with their captors, and others returned home when the opportunity arose.[136] One Osetian lieutenant, who was captured or deserted, led a group of ten to twelve mostly Tajik, captives/deserters who fought against the DRA and the Fortieth Army.[137]

Soviet Central Asians continued to serve in Afghanistan in various capacities even after February 1989. Shortly after the final troops' withdrawal, 600 Soviet truck drivers, mostly Central Asians, reportedly volunteered, dangers notwithstanding, to drive a large convoy of Soviet aid to the DRA from the Soviet border to Kabul.[138]

One student, many of whose peers went to Afghanistan, testified that Central

Asians did not see the war as "their war," that they were all afraid of being sent there, and that the war had a major influence on her generation. Those who did go returned as different people—more serious, more daring, and in many cases, psychologically affected (*nervoznye*).[139]

The physical and psychological barriers, the mutual fear and hostility, and of course, Soviet military regulations and the realities of war that kept most Soviet Central Asian soldiers apart from the local population held also for those who served as military, though not civilian, interpreters or advisers. Their first encounter with a predominantly Muslim culture evoked little empathy. From their perspective, there was no possibility of their being influenced by their ethnic brethren from over the border, to whom the Soviet Central Asians considered themselves superior. In their view, the Soviet Union had modernized them, given them a good education, and made them technologically far more advanced than the "primitive" Afghans. The Afghans' Islamic practices and traditions were further testimony of their backwardness. Many Central Asians disagreed with the view that they were as good Muslims as the Afghans. As distinct from the Afghans, whose religion was the leitmotif of their insurrection against the Marxist regime in Kabul, "we," they said, "are not real Muslims."[140] In the words of one Soviet correspondent, the border between Soviet Tajikistan and Afghanistan was not "so much a geographic boundary as a border in time, a line between two social and economic systems, between two philosophies. . . . On one side they live in the 1980s, and on the other side, they live in 1366 [by the Muslim calendar] under a feudal system with tribal vestiges."[141] In the words of an Uzbek scholar, for many Central Asians, "Afghanistan served as the possible 'other,' i.e., as an alternative scenario for Central Asian development." Their own progress "is one reason why many feel attached to the Soviet model of development and that model's achievements."[142]

Central Asian Afgantsy

Central Asian soldiers returning from Afghanistan reported that they moved more easily into the normal routines of life than did their European peers. Two vets returning to their native Bukhara in 1981 and 1983, respectively, started working immediately. One of them testified that his parents married him off at once and he "had no time to think about the war and what it did to me."[143]

Not surprisingly, however, the trends prevalent in other parts of the Soviet Union appeared in the Central Asian republics as well. Toward the war's end, for instance, Tajik war veterans were not merely enlisted by the local authorities—the Komsomol, voenkomats, and district soviets—but seem to have felt they had a special responsibility for preparing youngsters for military service. They traveled from school to school, instilling patriotism and encouraging students to improve their physique and their knowledge of Russian.[144]

The veterans demonstrated their pride in having participated in the war both before and after its termination. In 1987, afgantsy took part in the first Day of Remembrance, which the Tajik Supreme Soviet in Dushanbe organized to commemorate Tajikistanis who had perished for Soviet power at home and abroad. This marked the beginning of a process of identifying Afghan War vets with veterans of the Great Patriotic War that strengthened the ties between the former and the party-state.

The veterans also set up their own semiautonomous associations at the local and municipal levels. Some have suggested that in Tajikistan, this development undercut the political clout of the Dushanbe association and foreclosed the establishment of a republic-wide organization, which came into being in independent Tajikistan only in 1992, considerably later than in Uzbekistan or Kyrgyzstan (in 1989 and 1990, respectively). One of the first actions of the Tajik Union of Veterans of the Afghan War (SVAV) was a public denunciation of criticism that the afgantsy were "aggressors and punishers, mercenaries and marauders." The veterans' urge to respond to criticism led them to focus on the postwar years (like their peers elsewhere in the Soviet Union) on their deprivation rather than on their feats and heroism.[145]

The existence of the local associations perpetuated—at least for a while—the veterans' dependence on establishment structures, even after the groups ceased to be the mouthpiece of party-state propaganda. And when these structures disintegrated during the civil war that shook Tajikistan from 1992 to 1997, the associations fell apart as well. The Afghan War vets took sides much the way that the rest of the population did, mostly based on regional and familial ties.[146]

The Uzbek media paid particular attention to the veterans' association in Termez, where not a few afgantsy reportedly sought to remain, as the province of Surkhan-Darya resembled neighboring Afghanistan.[147] It seemed that service in Afghanistan strengthened loyalty to the Soviet Union among the majority of Central Asian soldiers. The Komsomol republican newspapers of the Central Asian republics praised the good deeds of the returning veterans and their contribution to the society around them.[148] They ran recurrent stories about the assistance that the vets rendered their own invalids and the families of the fallen; how they formed clubs, opened museums, and initiated the construction of monuments to comrades killed in the war; and lauded their role in teaching their juniors Soviet values. The chairman of the Afghan veterans' "organizing group" who, perhaps significantly, bore a Slav name (Vasilii Melnichuk), said in Tashkent on May Day 1989 that Uzbekistan's afgantsy had set up "military-patriotic clubs" in all the republic's oblasts, whose members "perform educational work at institutions of higher learning (VUZy), schools and hostels, and at their places of residence. We help the families of those who died and the disabled, and perpetuate the memory of those who did not return from the battlefield."[149] These reports were not sheer propaganda. The Central Asian soldiers returned from the war aware of their better fortune as compared with their neighbors over the border, their relatively advanced education, and their higher standard of living.

The War's Impact—Real and Imagined—on the Soviet "Muslim" Population

Central Asian scholars have stated that the Soviet invasion of Afghanistan shocked the Central Asian republics most acutely since Afghanistan was their immediate neighbor.[150] Yet there is evidence of factors other than proximity. Soviet citizens of traditionally Muslim ethnicities, whose territories were not contiguous to Afghanistan, addressed developments in Afghanistan from the perspective of their Islamic culture and faith. Some hoped that the Afghan civil war would prove to be a starting point for the establishment of an Islamic Afghanistan, in the footsteps of Iran.

Whether as a result of the Islamic revolution in Iran and the Islam-motivated counterinsurgency in Afghanistan or not, samizdat that circulated in Central Asia and the Caucasus contained "calls to avoid military service."[151] With the first reports of open rebellion against the PDPA regime in Kabul in spring 1979, months before the Soviet invasion, an Azeri intellectual reportedly said, "Our hope is in Afghanistan. If the Muslim rebels there succeed in throwing out the Communist government, Moscow must think again. . . . An Islamic Republic of Afghanistan, sandwiched between Iran and Pakistan, would put a community of Islamic nations with 130 million people on the southern border of the Soviet Union. Such a force . . . would . . . strengthen the hand of Soviet Muslims in their dealings with Moscow."[152] The head of Azerbaijan's KGB, Z. M. Yusif-zade, asserted a year after the intervention that "in view of the situation in Iran and Afghanistan, the U.S. special services are trying to exploit the Islamic religion, especially in areas where the Muslim population lives, as one factor influencing the political situation in our country."[153]

A lecturer from Baku informed *Posev* in the mid-1980s that most Azerbaijani Muslims sympathized with the mujahidin. The "rather large" number of funerals, moreover, "aggravated the atmosphere,"[154] for, inevitably, soldiers from Muslim ethnic groups other than Central Asians also fought in Afghanistan. Crimean Tatar leaders too reportedly openly expressed sympathy for the mujahidin.[155]

When, in 1985, the army told Chechen recruits in Astrakhan that they would be trained for Afghanistan, they "categorically refused to go . . . explaining that they did not wish to kill their Muslim coreligionists." The resultant clash with the military led to "wounded and killed on both sides."[156] At the same time, some 2,400 natives of Chechnya fought in Afghanistan; perhaps as a result of this incident, one of them testified that his unit learned of its destination only after it had entered Afghanistan.[157] At the same time, when Major General Johar Dudaev—later the first president of the independent Chechen Republic of Ichkeria—was stationed in Turkmenistan

(1988–1989), the division he commanded conducted massive carpet-bombing sorties against the Afghan opposition.[158]

Muslim religious officials admitted that the war raised difficult questions among Soviet Muslims. An officer back from the war came to the muftiate of European Russia and Siberia in Ufa and asked with bitterness why the Muslim clergy had not intervened to avert bloodshed. The imam responded that although they had appreciated that the war would lead to tragedies, Islam taught the obligation of defending one's country, and also that at the time, everyone was silent. Nonetheless, the imam admitted that it was hard to explain why it was necessary to defend the Soviet Union in Afghanistan.[159] Muslim clergy, moreover, performed the burial services for soldiers killed in Afghanistan. However, unregistered mullahs in Tajikistan's Kulyab oblast reportedly disseminated a fatwa in 1982, prohibiting the burial of "Soviet soldiers killed in Afghanistan according to Muslim rite, as they fought against true Muslims."[160]

The war markedly changed Tashkent itself, the showpiece for Muslim visitors to the Soviet Union. From the war's earliest days, the city was a main transit base. Its streets "became accustomed to the heavy stamp of army boots," its hospitals and clinics "were filled to capacity with 'internationalists,'" and the war "touched the lives of all [the] citizens" of the Soviet Union's fourth largest city."[161] This was all the more true for the towns closer to the border, like Termez, a closed city during the war, from which the army built the Bridge of Friendship in 1982 to carry Soviet tanks and other war materiel and soldiers into Afghanistan, and Tajik border areas that Afghan opposition groups occasionally bombarded (see Chapter 2). Both Termez and Dushanbe also housed hospitals that treated wounded soldiers of the Fortieth Army.[162] One journalist from Tashkent said that students visited the hospitalized soldiers, and the stories the vets told spread through the city.[163] The "incessant sound of cargo planes landing at Dushanbe airport" throughout the war's duration served as "a reminder" to the city's inhabitants of "the proximity and scope of the conflict."[164]

Tashkentis blamed the war for the dearth of merchandise in the shops. They knew that wares from their factories went to Afghanistan, so attributed their increasingly low standard of living to the war.[165] Nonetheless, it seems unquestionable that the Soviet Central Asians' socialization was sufficiently strong that their identification with their education and their modernization withstood the trials.[166]

In fact, immigrants from Tashkent and Samarkand who reached Israel in late 1980 and early 1981 recalled that these cities' inhabitants generally supported Soviet policy regarding Afghanistan and demonstrated no sign of solidarity with the Afghan people.[167] Similarly, a 1980 *New York Times* article reported that "all over the Moslem southern crescent of the Soviet Union, the echoes of the military intervention in Afghanistan still resound but with few audible overtones of discontent or protest. . . . There seems little support here for an idea sometimes advanced in the West that the

Soviet Union may have withdrawn Tadzhik and Uzbek reservists from Afghanistan because of dangers they might be 'infected' by the Moslem fervor of the rebels." The report noted that Central Asians showed a wider acceptance of the Soviet military intervention in Afghanistan than Russians "in Moscow's critical intellectual circles."[168] Soviet Central Asians explained that they had witnessed their conditions improve under Moscow's rule, and generally identified with the Soviet attempt to transform Afghanistan in the same way. An American correspondent writing from Uzbekistan said, "People in this remote region see the Soviet Union as a friend attempting to prevent the re-imposition of a feudal order on a neighboring country that has strong ethnic links . . . and is as economically backward as the Tadzhik and Uzbek republics once were."[169] Even when disapproval of the war increased in the later 1980s (see Chapter 7), there were no indications that reservations emanated from empathy with the mujahidin.[170]

The war in Afghanistan "strengthened the position of Central Asia within the Soviet system—partly as a showcase and partly as a strategic hinterland," bringing Central Asia increased electrification and a good road network—needed to expedite the transfer of troops, war materiel, and supplies to the Afghan border, as well as energy and financial subsidies.[171] This moral and material boost might explain the far broader support for the decision to intervene among Central Asians than among the Soviet population at large. In our survey, almost 60 percent of Central Asians thought in the war's early stages that Moscow needed to intervene, as against 30 percent of Russians; 30 percent still thought so at the war's end, while less than 15 percent of Russians did. Fifty percent of Central Asians thought early on that the method and form of the intervention contributed to the Soviet Union's international prestige, the highest percentage in our sample. Significantly, however, only about 35 percent believed at the war's beginning that the Soviet Union had a moral right to intervene, as against nearly 50 percent of Russians (see Tables 7.5 and 7.9).

Toward the war's end, General Aleksandr Liakhovskii—personal aide to the senior Soviet military representative in Kabul, head of the MoD Operations Group in Afghanistan, Valentin Varennikov—proposed political discussions with one of the most inveterate Afghan leaders, who controlled the northeastern sector of the country. He recommended creating an autonomous Tajik area in northern Afghanistan with direct trade and cultural and economic ties with Soviet Tajikistan. Soviet ambassador Yuli Vorontsov and Varennikov, who were both well acquainted with the situation in the field, endorsed Liakhovskii's ideas,[172] indicating that they had no qualms about encouraging such ties. They did not seem to share the view that Afghan opposition leader Gulbuddin Hekmatyar expressed in May 1987: "If the mujahidin persistently continue to fight, the day will soon come when the occupied lands of Soviet Central Asia will be liberated."[173]

There was no way to prevent media from crossing the border. Several sources testify that early in the war, one could hear Afghan opposition broadcasts throughout Soviet Central Asia, and, at least as of 1982, smugglers brought mujahidin materials—cassettes and brochures in Russian and Uzbek—from Afghanistan.[174] Tajikistan authorities arrested five people that year for circulating antiwar leaflets (presumably the same brochures).[175] In 1983, a Tajik Party CC Secretary claimed that everyone could hear forty hours of broadcasts in Dari and Farsi a week and accused Afghan students studying in Dushanbe of disseminating religious literature and cassettes.[176] A CRA report in March 1984 noted an increase in religious literature entering Tajikistan due to growing ties with Afghanistan, and in summer 1984, with CIA help, "dozens of mujahideen" brought 100,000 copies of the Qur'an in Uzbek to Uzbekistan.[177] In 1983, a Western reporter stated that the Afghan Islamic resistance was broadcasting "on at least one short-wave transmitter that [could] be picked up in Tajikistan,"[178] although there is no evidence of how many Soviet Tajiks listened to these broadcasts. Iranian radio too was providing Central Asians with an alternative view of the war and specifically of the opprobrium it generated among Islamic peoples.[179] By the end of the 1980s, one-third of Turkmenistan's younger generation reportedly listened to Turkmen-language broadcasts from Afghanistan and Iran, while Afghan mujahidin doubled their efforts to smuggle subversive materials and weapons into the Soviet Union following the Soviet troops' withdrawal.[180]

In this context, it behooves us to address one crucial question: Did the Soviet-Afghan War stimulate nationalism and Islamic fundamentalism in Soviet Central Asia? Undoubtedly the Islamic revival, whose inception predated the coup that brought a Marxist-Leninist party to power in Kabul in 1978 and led to the Soviet intervention,[181] gathered momentum during the war, especially in Uzbekistan and Tajikistan. In the view of KGB Major General Viktor Spol'nikov, who had served in Tajikistan from 1980 to 1982, the Islamic revival in Central Asia in the mid- to late 1980s would have occurred without the war, against the backdrop of both the disintegration of the Soviet state and the situation in Central Asia and Tajikistan—a "deformed and weak economy, overpopulation, unemployment, low level of mass culture, religious fanaticism and arrogance of local intellectuals" with "real power and economics in the hands of traditional leaders." But the war accelerated it.[182]

At the same time, *Ogonek* editor Vitalii Korotich testified that assigning Soviet Tajiks to prepare propaganda materials for their co-nationals in Afghanistan renewed the Tajik intelligentsia's acquaintance with Arabic script, which became a central feature of Tajik nationalist activity in the later 1980s.[183] Those who had taken Oriental studies had already learned Arabic/Persian script, but in Afghanistan, they became aware of Persian poetry and other, particularly Afghan and Iranian, prose and poetry that was nowhere to be found in the Soviet Union. It made them realize they were part of a regional Iranian-Persian culture, laying the groundwork for "a rather inclusive idea of Tajik nationalism which had a meaningful impact on the evolution of their national identity."[184] Tajik soldiers reportedly brought back Tajik and Iranian literature of "renowned poets and philosophers" that led Tajiks to revisit their culture and the influence of Soviet rule.[185] In 1989, Tohir Abdujabbor, who had served in Afghanistan as an interpreter, cofounded the Rastokhez (Revival) Popular Movement, supporting Tajik cultural and national rebirth. A mechanic from Bukhara concurred that the events in Afghanistan caused a renaissance of national pride and a return to religion among Uzbeks as well.[186] Jumma Namangoni, the founder of the IMU (Islamic Movement of Uzbekistan), probably the most radical Islamist political movement in Soviet territory at the turn of the decade, had fought in Afghanistan as a paratrooper in the last year of the war; reportedly the experience radicalized him.

Apparently there was disagreement within the ranks of Central Asian Islamists regarding the war's implications for Soviet Central Asia. After tracing the beginnings of re-Islamization since the first half of the 1970s, some scholars contended that the revolution in Iran and the armed resistance of the Afghan mujahidin to the Soviet armed forces took on symbolic meaning for the new generation of Islamic theologians, especially the young Uzbek reformers (*ulama*) who referred to themselves as "Mujaddidiya."[187] The ulama rejected the stance of Muhammadjon Hindustonyi, the doyen of nonestablishment Islam, who approved the intervention on the grounds that its goal was to save Afghanistan from chaos and disorder. Hindustonyi contended that opposing the DRA government was not jihad but merely led to the destruction of mosques, the confiscation of property, and the murder of "those who pray," as well as of women and children. This reflected Soviet propaganda's message comparing the Afghan resistance to the Basmachi, who had fought against the Soviet takeover of Central Asia in the name of Islam (see Chapter 6). Hindustonyi's more radical pupils, who, as of the early 1980s, heard Radio Iran and Radio Liberty or the Voice of America in Uzbek, adopted an opposite position: they charged their former mentor of opting for an apolitical stance and foregoing the mandatory jihad against the Soviet system.[188]

In early 1986, "radical" Islamists, generally people with a modern education, organized a demonstration in Tajikistan in favor of the Afghan mujahidin. They contended that all faithful Muslims should join the war on the side of the mujahidin and should establish an Islamist political framework in Central Asia. (For the arrest of one of its leaders, Said Abdullo Nuri, see above.) In March 1987, another demonstration in favor of the Afghan mujahidin took place, again in Tajikistan, in Qurghonteppa.[189]

Those same Central Asian scholars who noted that the Central Asian republics felt the brunt of the Afghan War most acutely point out that during its course, Islamic networks were reactivated, especially in the Ferghana Valley. They attribute this to the war. Thus, they note, "The Central Committee of the Kyrgyz CP grew seriously concerned over the religious involvements of southerners [the traditionally more religiously inclined inhabitants of southern Kyrgyzstan], that had been gaining momentum since the 1979 invasion of Afghanistan."[190]

This accords with the understanding both of the KGB and in mujahid circles that people in Tajikistan supported the Afghan opposition. A 1980 report from Dushanbe noted sympathy for the "rebels" among the "nationalist intelligentsia." Although they did not "care much about Islam," they criticized the attitude to Islam of Babrak Karmal and the PDPA cadres.[191] This support grew over the decade, whether from Islamic or nationalist motives. One student of the Tajik political scene at the end of the Soviet period contends that "not all" of the "many young Tajik intellectuals" who had served as interpreters in the war "returned with their devotion to the Soviet regime intact. The impact of the war on people's minds was so great and the trauma of it such, even for an intelligentsia "not slow to admit its debt to Russia," that the "hitherto . . . generous benefactor now appeared to young Tajiks as the cause of their country's innumerable problems."[192] One interpreter at the PDPA CC said they all believed at first that the Soviet Union was genuinely helping the Afghans to modernize. During his service (1984–1986), however, he wrote a report focusing on mistakes and failures, both Afghan and Soviet—for which he was penalized and sent to work in the Afghan periphery. Both he and his wife, who spent several months in Kabul and was also an Orientalist, believed that the Afghan experience played a major role in the evolution of nationalism among Soviet Tajiks and of a critical view of Soviet policies.[193] Just before the Soviet Union's demise, Tajik poet and reformer Bozor Sobir stated in the republican parliament that no Tajik should take pride in being a Hero of the Soviet Union for having fought his brother Muslims in the Afghan War. While one Tajik vet endorsed Sobir's position in a letter to the press, stating that Tajiks who fought in Afghanistan were fighting people of the same race, blood, and language,[194] other Afghan War veterans staged a rally in Dushanbe to protest Sobir's critical remarks.

In early 1982, the leader of the Afghan Islamist party, Hezb-e Islami, Gulbuddin Hekmatyar, claimed that volunteers from Soviet Tajikistan had crossed the border to fight with the resistance.[195] In the same year, Jemiat-e Islami, the predominantly Tajik Afghan opposition political organization, claimed to have 2,500 card-carrying members in Tajikistan.[196] Even if the number was exaggerated, the idea of a militant Islamic party having any membership at all within the Soviet Union was clearly dynamite.

According to a report of the Moscow-based Council of Religious Affairs, "extremist mullahs" criticized the war, charging Moscow with having invaded Afghanistan in order to turn the Afghans into infidels. In the context of the war, the report stated, "the most reactionary elements of the unregistered clergy (namely descendants of *ishans* [Sufi teachers and leaders] operating in Central Asia, the leaders of about 400 *murid*

[Sufi novices or adepts] brotherhoods functioning in the North Caucasian republics, and a few more extremist mullahs) are inciting the population to refuse to serve in the Soviet army."[197] Influenced by "provocative rumors regarding events in Afghanistan," there were instances in Dagestan and in Uzbekistan's Surkhan-Darya oblast of refusals to serve.[198] It is not clear whether, as one Western scholar maintains, the war "illustrated to the leaders of Islamic revivalism in Soviet Central Asia" the commitment of the Afghan Islamists and inspired them as responsible Islamic leaders to seek out the sources of the mujahidin's Islamic convictions, which they found in the works of Muslim Brethren, like the brothers Sayyid and Muhammad Qutb and Sayyid Abu `Ala Mawdudi.[199] Another scholar claims that Arab students in Dushanbe brought their works to Tajikistan even before the war, although they became acquainted with Muhammad Iqbal in Afghanistan.[200] Be this as it may, the men influenced by these writings were still a small peripheral group, though they assumed considerable importance, in Tajikistan at least, in the 1990s, after the Soviet-Afghan War was over.

In the "Muslim" republics, Gorbachev's glasnost and democratization did not take root, and the new political structures did not stimulate nationalist and separatist inclinations. However, members of traditionally Muslim ethnicities turned to Islam in the void that the erosion of the Soviet belief system created, just as in other parts of the Soviet Union, people turned to the Orthodox Church and other traditional faiths. Moreover, statements of political protest arose here, as elsewhere throughout the Soviet Union. Candidate People's Deputy Mukhimjon Azizov stated at the May Day parade in Tashkent in 1989 that he had strived in his election platform "to ensure that the possibility of deploying a military contingent outside our country only be decided by a national referendum."[201]

The Soviet-Afghan War continued to affect the areas bordering Afghanistan after its conclusion. Over a year after the final withdrawal, the deputy commander of the Central Asian Border District Troops maintained that as a result of the war and the Soviet withdrawal, the border between Afghanistan and Soviet Central Asia had become porous. In his words, "The border is different now. . . . Thirty mines exploded on the territory of one border troop unit in a single day." Moreover, "drugs and other contraband are smuggled across the border. Emissaries from the Afghan side try to draw citizens of the Central Asian republics into shady enterprises and urge them to wage jihad, holy war against the infidels."[202]

In our survey, almost 80 percent of Afghan War vets thought that the war affected the civil war in Tajikistan that began in 1992, with 34 percent saying that the Afghan War was its primary cause and 43 percent that it was a secondary factor.

While it is generally accepted that interregional conflicts within Tajikistan were the primary cause of its civil war, the close contact between Tajikistan and Afghanistan during the Soviet-Afghan War and the experiences there of many Tajik intellectuals almost certainly influenced, directly and indirectly, political developments in Tajikistan. As Tajik nationalism became a focus of Tajik discourse in the Soviet Union's last years, many secular Tajiks, who had served in Afghanistan as interpreters and advisers, came to appreciate the significance of Dari and Afghan-Persian culture for their own Tajik language and culture, as well as of Islam in Tajik national culture and identity. Similarly, when Tajik opposition figures were exiled to Afghanistan during the civil war, they were able to use their Afghan experiences to find assistance.

The Soviet-Afghan War undoubtedly had a greater effect on the three Central Asian union republics bordering Afghanistan than on the rest of the Soviet Union. And of the three, Tajikistan probably topped the list. It featured the most penetrable frontier, which was apparently why most of the mujahidin incursions into Soviet territory occurred in that republic. A particularly large contingent of Tajiks served in Afghanistan during the war, notably in military intelligence (the GRU) and in the civilian administration, and Tajik afgantsy played a significant role in the nationalist movements of the late 1980s. Tajikistan also had the largest group of co-ethnics over the border (estimated at approximately 3 million) and the Tajik language is very close to Dari, one of Afghanistan's two official languages and the lingua franca in Kabul. Having the war rage so close to their homes must have provoked second thoughts among Central Asians about their earlier belief in the well-being that Soviet rule had brought them.

Chapter 10

The War and the Demise of the Soviet Union

The Soviet-Afghan War was a key episode in the process that led to the Soviet Union's final collapse. It brought about the country's international isolation and, more important, presaged the de facto rejection of the Brezhnev Doctrine that had "legitimized" the introduction of troops to protect "socialist" regimes such as the PDPA's in Kabul. This laid the ground for Gorbachev's New Thinking in foreign policy, which included the recognition of the price of empire.[1]

As for New Thinking—or New Political Thinking—in the domestic arena, as *Pravda* correspondent Yuri Glukhov pointed out on the day of the final withdrawal, it was not the outcome of "hypothetical notions"; the schools in which it was "learned" were Afghanistan and Chernobyl.[2] And the withdrawal, another *Pravda* article noted, was "perhaps the most real victory—one that the people can see and feel—in the revolutionary struggle we call 'restructuring' (perestroika)." The time had come to answer "some agonizingly difficult questions . . . for the sake of those into whose lives Afghanistan infiltrated."[3]

Indeed, the war's true costs for the Soviet system were primarily domestic, especially against the backdrop of perestroika and glasnost. It undermined the previous almost absolute power of the General Secretary and the Politburo and the ability of a small group of men to make major decisions, such as plunging the country into war. It undercut the prestige of the military, one of the main pillars on which the regime rested, and spoiled the army's sacrosanct image.[4] The armed forces' limited effect in Afghanistan underscored the gap between reality and the constantly propagated might of the Soviet Union, while its protracted presence there undercut the system's presentation of the army's role as the defender of the mother country and its population. Moreover, the large contingent of physically and psychologically crippled young men who appeared in Soviet cities and towns throughout the country was a destabilizing factor and belied the myth of the armed forces as a school that prepared young men morally and physically for life.[5]

The war also highlighted the fact that people would no longer countenance censorship that prevented them from knowing what their country was doing and what was happening to their husbands, sons, and brothers. Inevitably, too, the war cost the Soviet Union huge sums while Soviet citizens struggled to make ends meet—nothing new in Soviet history but a situation that people were increasingly unwilling to tolerate. They were no longer prepared to swallow the assurance of their nation's status as a superpower—the carrot that the Soviet Union's leaders offered its citizens in return for their material deprivation. Soviet citizenry was largely in agreement that the costs of the Afghan War contributed to the lowering of their standard of living and so favored withdrawal.

Finally, the war spotlighted a long list of the moral and other ills that plagued late Soviet society: the inequality that enabled the nomenklatura to keep their sons from being sent to Afghanistan and the concomitant bribery, chicanery, and injustice; the drugs and crime; the ethnic tensions, notably between Russians and non-Russians and between Slavs and traditionally Muslim nations; the inadequacies of Soviet medicine and medical technology; the inhumane face of a bureaucracy that could not satisfy even the minimal needs of the returning vets. The war heightened the people's awareness of these ills, paving the way for the development of a civil society under glasnost. Moreover, Gorbachev's simultaneous use of withdrawal to garner popular support, and of glasnost to legitimize withdrawal, exposed the cynicism of the perestroika leadership's political program, thus helping to unleash forces that Gorbachev could not control.

The war and its effects play a part in almost every interpretation of the 1991 collapse of the Soviet Union. Archie Brown analyzes the components of "a communist system," of which the Soviet Union was the archetype, whose raison d'être Gorbachev's reforms had undermined: "the supreme authority and unchallenged hegemony" of the party, which, given the second component, "democratic centralism," allotted all power to the summit of the party hierarchy, the epitome of the dictatorship of the proletariat that enabled a small circle of leaders to launch the war in defiance of the advice of the military leadership. The criticism that this decision evoked in 1989 abetted the undermining of the regime. Media appraisals of both the war and the lot of the returning afgantsy reflected the pluralism and debate that Gorbachev encouraged within the party and throughout the rest of society. Moreover, the failure to give the PDPA the decisive support that it needed highlighted the shallowness of the Soviet claim to stand at the head of an international communist movement.[6]

Some contend that behind Gorbachev's reformism, and ultimately the collapse of the system, was his awareness that the country's economic weakness made it impossible to claim the Soviet Union as a viable superpower. While it was President Ronald Reagan's Star Wars program that underscored the disparity between the two countries, it was the effects and implications of the Soviet-Afghan War that undercut the foundations on which that comparative status was predicated.

Scholars have also attributed the Soviet Union's disintegration to the "national question." The disturbances that shook the national republics in the Soviet Union's last three years demonstrated the establishment's inability to satisfy the growing ethnic awareness of its various national groups. In their samizdats, the Ukrainians and Balts, for example, contended that their soldiers had borne disproportionate losses in the war. Certainly, too, ethnic tensions frequently surfaced among the soldiers in Afghanistan, as elsewhere in the Soviet military. A leading analyst of Russian nationalism insists that the bleeding wound of Afghanistan "served gradually to sap the fading imperial will of the Russian people . . . of a willingness to support the use of Russian lives to preserve the so-called 'outer' Soviet empire."[7]

The new terms of reference enabled a context in which Soviets could voice criticism of the war. At the same time, that vocal criticism strengthened the frameworks and instruments that contributed to the regime's collapse as glasnost got out of hand. Control of all media and art forms was a sine qua non of democratic centralism.

Once the last Soviet soldier had left Afghan territory, protest no longer centered on the need to withdraw the troops. The focus now moved to analyzing the decision-making process and resolving what and who was guilty for the death of thousands of young Soviet citizens and tens of thousands of Afghans, among the war's other negative consequences. Whereas some—notably in the establishment—sought to place all the blame on the four Kremlin leaders now conveniently deceased, others delved deeper, seeking not only to blame but also to understand, in order to prevent the recurrence of similar digressions from normative policymaking. In the words of social psychologist Dmitrii Ol'shanskii, it was not solely the Fortieth Army that was sent to Afghanistan. "We were all sent there," the entire society that asked no questions. "The decision regarding our participation in the Afghan war was approved by society." The public believed that the introduction of troops was necessary. Thousands of young people asked to do their army service in Afghanistan and were disappointed if they could not. Mothers of boys killed there spoke at schools about the feats of their sons and took pride in their medals. "Neither the war's beginning nor its continuation contradicted the will of the majority of society."[8]

Riding the upheaval that accompanied the chaos of the late Gorbachev period, the MoD journal *Voennaia mysl'* admitted that "the use of the army contrary to the interests of the people has grave results. An example is the situation created within society around the use of the limited contingent of Soviet troops in Afghanistan." Placing the onus of its consequences on the military leadership and the army was an oversimplification. "In light of the political outcome of the fighting conducted by Soviet troops in Afghanistan, it is of utmost importance that the procedure for the use of the armed forces beyond the country's borders without appropriate resolutions by the organs of government and in special circumstances by authorization of the President of the USSR has now been guaranteed by law."[9] Another MoD source sought similarly to assess the rights and wrongs of the original intervention and of the Fortieth Army's prolonged stay in Afghanistan. It stated categorically that the DRA army could not have withstood the onslaught of the opposition without outside assistance, and had Moscow refrained from introducing an army, the country would have been lost to the insurgents. Whether the Kremlin should or should not have intervened was therefore a purely political question, not one that the military could resolve. Two things, however, were clear—that a small group of politicians should not have made the decision behind closed doors and that the Fortieth Army's protracted endeavor to solve Afghan domestic issues, while in no way reflecting on the honor of the soldier-internationalists, was historically unjustified and morally inexcusable in light of the great loss of life.[10]

The Soviet journalist perhaps most associated with reporting the war's true face, Artem Borovik, reflecting on the influence of wars in Russian history, said, several months before the war's end, "Interestingly, perestroika . . . began in the very middle of the Afghan War. Perhaps this happened because Afghanistan helped us become powerfully aware of the blatant contradictions in which our ideals find themselves and of what we have brought about in Afghanistan."[11] After the war ended, yet before the Soviet Union's final disintegration, Borovik opined, "We rarely stopped to think how Afghanistan would influence us—despite the hundreds of thousands of Soviet soldiers and officers and the scores of diplomats, journalists, scholars, and military and political advisers who passed through it. . . . It is relatively easy, however, to assess Afghanistan's effects on the people who worked and fought there . . . who were thrown into a country where bribery, corruption, profiteering, and drugs were no less common than the long lines in Soviet stores" and diseases that "can be far more dangerous than hepatitis, particularly when they reach epidemic proportions."[12] Or, in the words of another journalist whose name is linked to reporting on Afghanistan, Aleksandr Prokhanov, "In society, the questions are growing. They cannot be avoided. They are asked in families and in private conversations, they are beginning to be heard in public meetings." He predicted that the issue would remain on the agenda, for "the greater part of our generation tragically passed through Afghanistan, which sowed tragedy and pain in families and a special 'Afghan upsurge' in those who returned from the villages at war."[13]

Riding public opinion and given the ambiguous position of the political elite in the later years of Gorbachev's rule, it was not surprising that the Congress of People's Deputies, elected in the atmosphere of glasnost and democratization, officially condemned the invasion of Afghanistan (on December 25, 1989; see Chapter 4).

A Trigger for Reassessment and Change

In November 1989, the MoD daily admitted that while the war was over, it still troubled Soviet society.[14] A paper on the rehabilitation of the war's veterans recognized that the war and its outcome had highlighted the contradictions between "the conservative forces, the adherents of totalitarianism and militarism, and the democratic forces, the adherents of liberalization of the economy and cutting down the armed forces," with the two sides adopting opposing positions on the war. Indeed, one of the war's consequences—more precisely, of its failures in the eyes of some veterans and society—was "the evolution of a national-patriotic movement oriented toward revenge in the realm of foreign policy and the use of force in the domestic arena for suppressing movements for acquiring national sovereignty."[15]

Senior Soviet analyst Igor' Beliaev said the intervention's consequences were "negative. First of all, for the Soviet Union." The intervention was an error because those who should have done so did not in fact "consider all possible results before dispatching Soviet soldiers south of our frontier." The actions and policies of the Soviet leadership should have been guided by realism. Anatolii Gromyko (son of former Foreign Minister Andrei Gromyko) added that "the Afghan experience" demonstrated that situations must be analyzed by "collective reason, not solely that of politicians and diplomats, but also of parliamentarians, scholars, the Soviet, and the world public." The time had come not just for discussion, but also for nationwide referenda.[16] Answering a correspondent's question on the genesis of Gorbachev's New Political Thinking, Shevarnadze claimed that at the time of the intervention, he and Gorbachev—both then Politburo candidate members—"said to themselves that it was necessary to change everything."[17]

The perceptions that the political, social, and cultural elites in the Gorbachev period created (as shown in Chapter 7) aimed to use the war in Afghanistan "to forward reform in five main areas: 'reclaiming' Russian and Soviet history; redefining relations with Islam; and an interlocked trinity of reassessments of the ends of the USSR's foreign policy, the means by which it should attain them, and the procedures by which that policy should be formulated." In the context "of a decay in the legitimacy of the regime and the cohesion of the elites," the war thus became a "contributory factor for these processes" and "in some small measure, at least" encouraged the downfall of the Soviet Union. The war, "or rather its mythologized doppelganger," became "a powerful idiom in late Soviet politics" as "a textbook example of the habits and failings of the old order, and one framed in a very emotive and dramatic context."[18]

The discussion in the press about the economic cost of the war (see Chapter 6) in the context of *khozraschet*—profit-and-loss accounting, one of the slogans of perestroika—demonstrated a growing sense that the regime should use public expenditure to improve the material condition of the USSR and its people by an accountable and open process. Gorbachev claimed, "We put an end to the foreign policy that served the utopian aim of spreading communist ideas around the world . . . inflicted on the people an intolerable burden of military expenditure, and dragged us into adventures like the one in Afghanistan."[19]

In this way, the Afghan War contributed to both the Soviet retreat from globalism and the move from a closed oligarchy toward democratic accountability. It created a role for those experts whom Brezhnev and his colleagues had failed to consult. They now pointed out that the Soviets had entered Afghanistan without understanding Islamic societies and that the instructions issued political officers, which included guidelines on how to deal with the Afghans, had overlooked Islam entirely. Under glasnost, the experts used Afghanistan to demand their place in domestic and foreign policymaking. Interviewed in May 1989, Iurii Gankovsky of the Institute of Oriental Studies stated explicitly that no one had consulted the experts on Afghanistan before deciding to intervene and that "the quality of the information" on which the decision rested "sometimes did not match the events" and "sometimes" was supplied by "incompetent people." As an infantry officer and war veteran, he felt competent to pass judgment that nobody "could have threatened our power without risk to themselves" and that even though "a hostile government in power in a neighboring country could not have been to our liking," it "does not follow . . . that we had to react to the situation as we reacted in 1979."[20] Not everyone, however, concurred. The MPA journal contended that the Kremlin had behaved responsibly and had considered the negative consequences of intervening militarily in Afghanistan, lamely citing as proof the earlier refusals to comply with Taraki's and Amin's military requests.[21]

Some observers noted that the discussion of accountability for the intervention helped to change the all-powerful status of the Politburo, specifically giving clout to the Congress of People's Deputies and the Supreme Soviet. In the view of one anonymous radio commentator, "With the formation of these new state bodies, and with public opinion now playing a role of no small importance in the nation's life, a leadership that theoretically would attempt something like the Afghan war would be doomed."[22]

On the day that the last Soviet troops left Afghanistan, *Pravda* warned against discarding the Afghan experience "offhand. . . . We have become wiser. We have shattered many stereotypes." The introduction of troops into Afghanistan "was connected with securing our southern border." True, one could question "the Brezhnev leadership's assessment of the extent of the military threat," and one could now say that "henceforth such vitally important questions as the use of troops must not be decided behind closed doors, in secret, without authorization by the country's parliament."[23] The following day, it noted that the Soviet Union had to travel "a long and difficult road in order to appreciate" that the path to peace lay not in interference in Afghanistan's internal affairs but in compromise and national dialogue. "It was even harder to translate our understanding into action. But we did it, and today draws a line, as it were, on the era of stagnation."[24] A year later, *Izvestiia* wrote, "We are seeking a political assessment of the Afghan War, not just of the introduction of troops. . . . We will try to see to it that all those who led us into the war are called to account—not [just] the dead who are long gone."[25]

This was also the main message of Kim Tsagolov's "Open Letter to the Mother of a Soldier Who Died in Afghanistan," which *Pravda* published in fall 1989. It was easy, he maintained, to blame the deceased leaders for introducing Soviet troops into Afghanistan. But they had not made their decision in haste; they had ordered the army to bring troops to the Afghan border months before the intervention (see Chapter 2). The leadership had relied on information that was based not on fact but on disinformation. Those lower down in the hierarchy, who laid the ground for the intervention, were no less to blame than the leaders. The Soviet Union and its population had paid a heavy price for the war's prolongation long after it was clear that it could not be won. It was not the country and the army that were to blame, but individuals. The Soviet troops had fought valiantly; such failures as there were lay at the door of the politicians. The afgantsy and their families suffered insults; there was no personal touch to help families of those who died—no letter from a senior commander, no recognition of individual needs, like erecting suitable tombstones for the fallen or finding housing for the vets. Movies showed the afgantsy as cruel and insensitive, but the reality was different, as manifest in their care for the families of fallen comrades, or the disabled, and other comrades in trouble. At first the media had given half-truths, hiding the fact that Soviet troops were engaged in combat; later they went to the other extreme, which was also a half-truth. The whole truth, however bitter, had to be told.[26]

The war prompted acrimonious exchanges in the Congress of People's Deputies, elected in March 1989 in the Soviet Union's first contested all-union elections (see Chapter 4). At its first convocation—May 25 to June 9—the hard-liners attacked the Congress's leading dissident member, Academician Sakharov, for his charge, in an interview with *Ottawa Citizen*, that Soviet pilots had fired on Soviet soldiers to prevent Afghan rebels from taking them captive. In the words of Hedrick Smith, "The humbling of Sakharov was an emotional but calculated display of the power and passions of the right wing. The Old Guard was intent on humbling the reformers on national television and undercutting their power by casting them in the public's eyes as anti-patriotic." Serhii Chervonopysky, a Komsomol official whom Ukraine's 100,000 afgantsy had elected chairman of the republican council of reservists a year earlier, accused Sakharov of discrediting the Soviet armed forces and "attempting to disrupt the sacred unity of the army, the people, and the Party." Gorbachev and the entire Politburo "joined in a standing ovation for Chervonopysky's censure," giving the hard-liners "free rein, and speaker after speaker heaped opprobrium on Sakharov. 'Who gave him the right to insult our children?' demanded a fifty-year-old farmworker." Former CGS Akhromeev said, "'Not a single order or anything like it was issued at the General Staff and the Ministry of Defense, nor did we receive such savage instructions from the political leadership. . . . All of this is a pure lie, a deliberate untruth, and Academician Sakharov will not find any documents to substantiate it.'" And a "twenty-five-year-old teacher from outside Tashkent told Sakharov, 'You have insulted the entire army, the entire people. . . . I have nothing but contempt.'"

Sakharov did not retreat. "The Afghan war was a criminal adventure . . . a terrible sin," he asserted. "I spoke out against sending troops to Afghanistan [see Chapter 1] and for this I was exiled to Gorky. I am proud of this exile to Gorky, as a decoration that I received. . . . I have not apologized to the Soviet army, for I have not insulted it. I have insulted those who gave criminal orders to send Soviet troops to Afghanistan." He insisted that no one could accuse him of false accusations until there was an objective investigation of his charges.[27] *Moscow News* published an article entitled, "We Should Tell the Whole Truth about This War," in which two Afghan vets reported that they had cabled Sakharov confirming that one of them had been in an incident where a Soviet helicopter fired unguided missiles at Soviet and DRA troops, while the other had been with troops who had been fired on by another Soviet force. There had, then, been mistakes of this nature, and clearly some Western source had interpreted them in the sense Sakharov had reported.[28]

Telling the truth about the war meant disclosing the background of the decision to send Soviet troops to Afghanistan, explaining why the war had been so protracted, and being meticulous about media reporting of unpleasant, thorny issues both in real time and post-factum. Gromov, who had been elected to the Congress of People's Deputies, could not avoid taking part in the discussion. His position was that Moscow could not stand aside in the face of the war that the opposition was conducting against the Afghan people. Yet he did not deny that the intervention had been based on distorted information. Clearly, "in the future, we should ask society and the people whether such campaigns are worth undertaking."[29] This in turn led to the government's publishing the numbers of Soviet casualties. It was not solely the war's veterans who doubted these data. One member of the Congress of People's Deputies extrapolated from partial information that the total figures must have been considerably higher than the official ones.[30]

In December 1989, then, the Congress of People's Deputies adopted the censure of the intervention that the Supreme Soviet Committee on International Affairs recommended and authorized all necessary measures to prevent the recurrence of similar misdoings (see Chapter Four).

The Congress of People's Deputies boasted a disproportionately large presence of Afghan War veterans—120 delegates out of 2,250[31]—indicating that the afgantsy, or many of them, believed that they had a role to play in public affairs and that others shared this belief. Some afganets delegates represented establishment institutions; others won in straight elections, sometimes "on a clear 'afganets ticket,' stressing either military-patriotic education or abhorrence of the war." They were a heterogeneous group, from military candidates like Defense and State Security Committee member Colonel Valerii Ochirov, to "party hack agitators" like Serhii Chervonopysky, to L'viv Deputy Yurii Sorochyk and "veteran turned pacifist Vasilii Katrinich." Deputy Senior Sergeant Yurii Shatrovenko, perhaps the closest to being the "'typical afganets deputy,'" highlighted three areas for concern: the role of the army and its need for public support; youth affairs, "mixing authoritarian views on draft-dodging and military and civil indiscipline with an appreciation of the genuine problems of finding accommodation and meaningful work"; and the need for the afgantsy and the country to "be told, once and for all, whose fault the war was, and see that justice was done." This assortment of afgantsy candidates' platforms in both the USSR and the Russian elections incorporated "general concerns of the time: physical conditions, control of the organs of coercion, moral justice, and the danger of civil anarchy."[32]

Afgantsy were also represented in the Supreme Soviet, which in April 1990 created the Committee for the Affairs of Soldier-Internationalists, headed by decorated afganets Pavel Shet'ko. It had twenty-six members, thirteen of them afgantsy, and its mandate included protecting the interests of internationalists who had been deployed in Vietnam, Egypt, and Ethiopia and helping other "fraternal allies."[33] Within three months of its formation, the committee secured a 50 percent tax discount for afgantsy and a total exemption from taxation for enterprises operating under the aegis of their organizations. It developed links with the Ministry of Health to support war invalids; began negotiations with Mossovet (the Moscow City Council) to set up memorials in the city; and tried to get information on POWs, some of whom had married Afghan women and had families, so as to inform their parents that they were alive. Shet'ko went to Pakistan with a delegation to free two POWs. Over time, he also traveled to the United State to meet Vietnam veterans, politicians, and rehabilitation experts. Eventually the committee initiated a framework for the care and provision of veterans. The committee, moreover, felt that the government's draft program for providing help to the afgantsy "lacked both an appropriate mechanism and an appreciation of the different needs of different veterans, as opposed to some notionally 'average' soldier-internationalist."[34] Its secretary explained that its primary assignment was to give binding statutory authority to the various resolutions designed to assist the veterans.[35]

A year after the elections and the month after becoming head of the Supreme Soviet Committee for the Affairs of Soldier-Internationalist, Shet'ko summed up afganets activity in the Congress's first two sessions. He noted that two veterans were members of the commission to investigate the "tragic events" in Tbilisi (in April 1989) and that they were represented on the commissions looking into the Gdlian and Ivanov "cotton affair" in Uzbekistan and the decision to send troops into Afghanistan. Veteran delegates had held two briefings on the issue of an amnesty for soldiers who had committed crimes in Afghanistan, a prerequisite for liberating Soviet POWs, and they had succeeded in turning the vote in favor of an amnesty.[36] Now the task was to assist veterans in need of help—to promote their "social and psychological adaptation," treat PTSD, set up rehabilitation centers, and collaborate with veteran associations (see Chapter 8).

The afgantsy returned from the war, in the words of one source, "Russian patriots" critical of the Soviet system, to whom Gorbachev's reforms provided "the perfect environment for the blossoming of their influence." As SVA chairman Aleksandr Kotenov wrote, "The overwhelming majority of Afghan veterans returned home with an enhanced sense of justice and a desire to base their lives on the principles of honesty, truth, and genuine rights. . . . They are an emotional, thoughtful, and explosive group who have been cleansed of dogma and cheap catchphrases."[37]

> The heterogeneity of the afgantsy became evident around issues not directly related to them as a group, where they found themselves siding with liberals, conservatives, and radicals. They were torn between endeavors to put an end to the ills of Soviet society with its corruption, nepotism, and endless bureaucracy—like the mayor of the Russian city of Riazan', a former political officer in the Fortieth Army, who waged war against the corruption of the party apparatchiks—and opposition to perestroika and glasnost on the grounds that Gorbachev's reforms were leading to anarchy and Western values and fashions. Afganets sensitivity regarding the honor of the army placed many of them in the Russian neoconservative nationalist camp.[38]

Discussing afgantsy in Soviet society, one source claimed that they had "unquestionably" filled and continued to fulfill an "'emancipatory' role . . . the role of a social eye-opener, of a liberator from the slumber of ignorance." They were a "catalyst of the socio-political process" given expression in "awareness of the genuine national interest that naturally does not tie up with military expansion into a neighboring country; the growth of national-patriotism as a result of military failure, of the hurt to national awareness."[39]

In parallel, nationalists in the various union republics, seeking every possible means to "redefine and relegitimise themselves," used the war for their own ends. The Lithuanian Youth Association's Juventus Academica, for example, compared the Soviet occupation of the Baltic States and Afghanistan, while the Lithuanian samizdat journal *Aušra* maintained that the army had selected nationalist-minded students to serve in the war. Similarly, Ukrainian samizdat made comparisons with the forced collectivization of Ukraine in the early 1930s. Muslim groups portrayed the war as a crime against Islam, even though the official Moscow-appointed Muslim religious functionaries had sanctioned it. Toward the end of the Gorbachev period, even former party leaders and functionaries like Leonid Kravchuk, who had been Ideological Secretary of the Ukrainian CP CC and was to become independent Ukraine's first president, endeavored to enlist the afgantsy by championing their rights and seeking to incorporate them in the Ukrainian armed forces.[40]

Academician Oleg Bogomolov also figured in the debate over the war's morality and the culpability of those responsible for it. In 1990, he wrote an article contending not only that the war had been a mistake but also that responsibility was partly his for not having opposed it more vigorously.[41] Issues of blame and morality were "systematic of the decay underlying the legitimacy of the Soviet state." The war played a part in the decay, "but on the whole . . . reflected the general alienation of both the masses and the rank-and-file Party members who always represented the social basis of the Soviet order. The purchase of exemptions from service in Afghanistan was just part of the wider issue of corruption; the mulish short-sightedness of intervention just part and parcel of the ossification of policy and the 'imperialist internationalism' of the old order; the manifold shortcomings of the war effort just a microcosm of the collapse of the planned economy experiment." And when under glasnost "the masses lost their apathy and the *aktiv* [activists] their cohesion and will, the state's base also crumbled."[42]

Four Soviet commentators participating in a 1990 Western symposium on the war provided additional insights into its after-effects. All four agreed that those who decided on intervention had not understood Afghanistan. One of them, Hero of the Soviet Union and member of the Supreme Soviet Security and Defense Committee Air Force Colonel Valerii Ochirov, asserted that "a purely military intervention cannot be successful" in Afghanistan and that the troops "became both victim and hostage of inept politicians." Another, Artem Borovik, dwelled on the lack of coordination among the three Soviet missions in Kabul: the embassy, the KGB, and the Fortieth Army command. In his view, moreover, "in Afghanistan we bombed" not only rebel detachments and caravans "but our ideals as well." A third, Aleksandr Prokhanov, contended that the war had generated an antiarmy campaign among the Soviet public that weakened the military, and engendered the negative responses when the army tried to restore order first in Georgia (in April 1989) and later in Azerbaijan (in January 1990). Their conclusion was that the Afghan War, like the Crimean and Russo-Japanese wars of 1853–1856 and 1904–1905, respectively, "undermined the rationale and legitimacy of the governing system and led to substantial reform." Afghanistan was not the sole source of perestroika, but the war had an important role in eroding the Soviet leadership's ability to reach major decisions while ignoring the constraints of public opinion.[43]

A former political adviser to the PDPA CC thought similarly: the Afghan War had changed the Soviet Union, just as previous wars had resulted in far-reaching reforms and revolutions. The vets' return constituted a new danger, planting within the populace a large number of people who had their own psychology. Not surprisingly, most of those connected to the August coup (see below) had experienced Afghanistan; their approach to politics was that of people who had been through a war. He dubbed the dissolution of the Soviet Union the country's "rapid Afghanization."[44]

The Social Aspect: Crime, Drugs, and Weapons

Many in the Soviet Union perceived the war as having created a generation of drug and alcohol addicts (see Chapters 7 and 8). The prevalence of alcoholism in the Soviet Union, however, has a long history and needs no corroboration; indeed, alcoholism had reached epidemic levels by the mid-1980s, with 40 million certified alcoholics in 1985, when Gorbachev initiated his anti-alcohol campaign. By the 1970s, the wide use of narcotics—the source of many of which was Afghanistan[45]—was also causing official concern, prompting the regime to pass a series of antidrug laws.[46] Disaffected youth made up the largest group of drug users, and we cannot attribute the increasing addiction rates solely, or even mainly, to the war.[47] The fact that drugs received little media coverage before glasnost does not mean that they were not a major problem, but that the topic, like so many others, was swept under the carpet. Former soldiers who continued to use marijuana or who moved on to heroin and other drugs did so against the backdrop of social factors prevalent in Soviet society, not solely as a reflection of psychological wounds.

There seem to be no statistics or well-founded estimates on the prevalence of drink and drugs among the veterans. In our survey, we found that some afgantsy thought only a small minority resorted to drugs; others didn't "know anyone . . . back from Afghanistan who doesn't smoke and drink. Weak cigarettes don't help either."[48] Many remained drug addicts after returning home. One Soviet general told a Western ambassador that half of the Soviet force in Afghanistan had become drug addicts.[49] An instructor at the Moscow MVD Higher Police School writing on the use of drugs in the Soviet military found Afghan veterans among those who admitted to using drugs and were "knowledgeable about heroin and LSD."[50] Although to some afgantsy it had been clear that on returning home they would have to take to drink in order to forget "all this,"[51] others were driven to drugs, as well as to alcohol and crime, by the obstacles they encountered in adjusting to civilian life.[52] One veteran says that after more than twenty years, he could not get used to civilian life and "drinks a lot."[53]

In Afghanistan, the demand for drugs among the soldiery had been a major—although not the sole—stimulant to crime (see Chapter 3) and to the erosion of blind adherence to regulations. Back in civilian life, the veteran had requirements that were frequently not easily met, whether they were for drugs, alcohol, cigarettes, or spare parts for his car. If he could not satisfy his needs legally, the mentality he had developed in Afghanistan could dispose him to act illegally once again.

In addition to the greater availability of narcotics, it was also easier to obtain weapons during the 1980s, again partly, but not only, as a result of the war. As the security situation throughout the country deteriorated in the last years of the Soviet Union's existence, various media articles contended that private citizens had no problem procuring arms if they so desired. One official estimate spoke of between 15 and 17 million unregistered guns in the Soviet Union, many of them used for hunting.[54] Some of these weapons were "picked up on battlefields and restored in private workshops—or during spells of moonlighting in state factories," or were caches of World War II weapons, some taken from mass graves. Others were modern military equipment "stolen from army and police arsenals or pilfered from trains carrying military goods." Indeed, there was "a lively black market in military hardware."[55] Officers, truck drivers, and others who were successful in smuggling weapons into the Soviet Union found them a ready source of ill-earned wealth.

While there were afgantsy who turned to crime (see Chapter 8), and many were more prone to be trigger-happy than most other Soviet citizens of their age group, the majority of them—notably members of veteran associations—condemned organized crime and even acted, often illegally, against it (see Chapter 8).

The Domestic Implications of the Soviet Withdrawal

Unquestionably, "the inability of the Soviet military to win the war decisively condemned it to suffer a slow bloodletting." This process exposed the weakness not only of the military but of "the Soviet political structure and society itself. The employment of a draft army with full periodic rotation of troops back to the Soviet Union, enabled the travails and frustrations of war and the self-doubts of the common soldier to be shared by the entire population," the caveats on speaking notwithstanding. "The problems so apparent in the wartime army soon became a microcosm for the latent problems afflicting Soviet society. . . . The messages of doubt were military, political, ethnic, and social. In the end they were corrosive and destructive."[56]

This became evident when the MoD announced a call-up of reservists in southern

Russia in January 1990 to restore order in Azerbaijan, a traditionally Muslim Soviet union republic. Citizens filled the streets of Russian cities protesting the mobilization. They called on afgantsy not to take part in the fighting. "Your hands which have already held weapons must not hold them again."[57] A revolt of reservists' mothers bred a new organization, Mothers against Mobilization. The Afghan War had elicited an unwillingness to risk Russian lives to preserve the Soviet empire[58] and "made Russians averse to the use of the military to deal with interethnic conflict within the Soviet Union."[59] At a mothers' picket in the Russian city of Stavropol—shown on TV against a backdrop of Azerbaijan with "a haunting resemblance" to films of the Afghan War—the placards read, "No More Afghanistans." One woman shouted, "We don't want the people of those republics to call us occupiers. We don't need a second Afghanistan," while another cried, "I won't give my son for this!" A Western correspondent reported from Moscow that "the storm of protest" and the MoD's quick cancellation of the call-up "underscored the depth of . . . [the] 'Afghanistan syndrome,' a mood of isolationism driven" largely by the legacy of the Afghan War—"bruised lives, drug abuse and cynicism."[60] (For the origins of mothers' protests and their link to the Afghan War, see Chapter 7.)

It was not solely the performance of the Limited Contingent that upset the balance between the military and society that the regime had nurtured since 1945. The MoD's "military-theoretical journal" devoted an article to this relationship just months before the Soviet Union's breakup. It contended that in a democratic state that operates to the benefit of the predominant majority, deploying the army against the people's interests is fraught with dire consequences. The Afghan intervention made clear that the army's use must be anchored in law.[61]

The constant reassessment of the war led to new insights regarding some of the forces behind its inception and conduct, whether or not these were intentional. One was a resurgence of national, racial, or cultural/"civilizational" identity among the Soviet citizenry. After the war was over, one article quoted an afganets as saying, "We didn't know why we were fighting in the DRA. Only now do we know, and this time we, all of us in the Christian world, must win."[62]

Certainly, too, the presence of a large number of former soldiers, young men with a sense of their strength and growing acrimony and frustration, was more than likely to become a focus for fomentation, especially against the backdrop of high glasnost and the troubled late Gorbachev period.

The Afgantsy as a Social and Political Force

Many of the returning soldiers played an active role in the transformations that shook the Soviet Union under Gorbachev. In the words of a document composed for the Supreme Soviet Committee of Internationalist-Soldiers, "Problems of the Social

Rehabilitation of the Participants of the War in Afghanistan," the afgantsy helped to emancipate society, helped it to see more clearly. They became "a real catalyst of the socio-political process underway in our country." This was reflected in "the recognition of [our] genuine national interests which naturally were not linked to military expansion into a neighboring country; and in the enhancement of national patriotism as a result of the military failure that wounded the national consciousness." They were also an obstacle to the tranquility of some civilians and many officials and became "a target of criticism on the part of those inclined to consider them guilty of our social misfortunes." Nor were they just "the hostages of an unjust war"; they had lived the long list of the unmet needs and difficulties that they faced upon their return. This made their lives a torture and sometimes led to tragedy.[63]

Having, as they did, a number of urgent practical problems (such as the lack of housing), whether particular to veterans or common to all young members of the Soviet working class, the former soldiers cooperated to achieve their goals. Perestroika and glasnost seemed to offer new avenues for lobbying, and the afgantsy could be expected to comprise a significant political force. But the quest for resources in a resource-poor state was a no-win venture. The veterans and their supporters sought to meet their needs by uniting on a local basis and by acting as individuals or within circles of friends (see Chapter 8).

It might have turned out differently had the veterans represented a united force, but as we have seen, they did not. The values with which the afgantsy had been indoctrinated—the beliefs that they had been sent into Afghanistan to promote—had become obsolete by the end of the 1980s, but the afgantsy failed to appreciate why this was so.[64] This was a major factor in their anger at the perception that their war was futile. A conservative assessment of their dilemma in mid-1990 spoke of the state's "repudiation" of these "statists" (*gosudartsvenniki*), although they had proved themselves in battle and shown their willingness to die on behalf of the state and the ideas that it preached. Rather than protecting these men whom it feared, the state left them to "social and national elements" (see below). The afgantsy endeavored to create an afganets movement or brotherhood but instead became a divisive, conflict-ridden group. The eventual failure of their associations, one study suggested, stemmed from their partial symbiosis with the establishment, which kept them from becoming a social and political force as the state and its institutions fell apart.[65]

Admittedly, in real time, the picture looked somewhat different. A study done in 1990 or 1991 (the book appeared in 1993) opined that the afgantsy "now make up quite a large social force. . . . Deceived, seared in the flames of battle, and neglected by the society that had sent them into a war fought on alien soil for alien ideals, these [afgantsy] are now reaching maturity, and the country's destiny will be in the hands of their generation. . . . Both the 'right' and the 'left', the new political parties and social organizations, are trying to use the [afgantsy] for their own ends, to exploit their strength, their status, and their feelings of anger and bitterness in their political games."[66]

Developments, however, supported the view that the afgantsy did not become a meaningful social and political force. Even with the large group of veterans in the Congress of People's Deputies in 1989, the vets failed to win much practical backing. The continued decay of state power and the dwindling of resources further weakened their situation. An indication of the afgantsy's marginalization was the place allotted them in the speech of Tajik Komsomol CC First Secretary A. Yukubov in fall 1989, which was devoted to the problems of young people in the republic. It contained merely a short reference to those of the Afghan war vets, adding that "we should erect a monument to those who died in the land of Afghanistan."[67]

Meanwhile, in March 1989, the veterans established an "all-union" or countrywide association, the Union of Veterans of Afghanistan—the SVA. By 1991, official sources spoke of it as including four hundred Afghan veteran associations.[68] At its 1991 conference in Perm, SVA chair Aleksandr Kotenov claimed that the group had over 300,000 members, with 185 regional sections, nine republican SVAs, organizations in every union republic except Estonia, and an annual budget of 7 million rubles and $960,000.[69] (One knowledgeable scholar contends that SVA membership must have been significantly lower because every large Russian city boasted veterans' associations not associated with it.[70]) In addition to helping the families of those who died and providing medical care and treatment, including wheelchairs and "the best technology in prostheses" for the disabled, the SVA aided veterans economically, socially, and professionally. It ran its own factories, although not only afgantsy worked in them, and maintained contact with veterans' organizations abroad (in the United States, France, and Korea), which sought to help with their experience, especially in social and psychological rehabilitation. Its chair noted that the SVA also boasted its own psychological service.[71]

In parallel, the All-Union Association of Reserve Soldiers' Councils, Soldier-Internationalists, and Military-Patriotic Unions came into being. The association emphasized military-patriotic education and economic activity and had a loose, more confederal structure. Its central body, the coordinating council, was "less intrusive and dirigiste" than the SVA, and so aroused fewer misgivings among the various regional groups. Within a year, it had united 124 regions, 4,000 clubs, and 2,000 soldier-internationalist councils. It too concentrated on "specific practical projects," such as prostheses, rehabilitation centers, and psychotherapy sessions for parents of fallen soldiers.

Neither nationwide organization managed to win political recognition for its claims. Given the "increasingly angry" public mood that resulted from "hunger, shortage, disillusion and an apparent policy impasse in the Kremlin," the afgantsy received "short shrift." The successful afgantsy groups were those able to retain momentum on a local level. The Leningrad Association of Veterans of the War in Afghanistan (LAVVA), formed in winter 1989–1990, was one such body. "Its aims were three—to foster co-operation between local veterans' groups, to co-ordinate common enterprises such as the establishment of a database (on relevant laws, contacts, etc.) and a common programme of self-help, and to provide legal and social protection to afgantsy." LAVVA "continued to expand [its] economic arm and lobbied the local authorities for social provisions." It developed in conjunction with the local military establishment and played a part in the formation of the Union of Afgantsy of veterans serving within the Leningrad MD (see the following section).[72]

At the same time, afgantsy were publishing their own media. Of these, the most important were the Orenburg veterans' *Kontingent*, whose first issue appeared in August 1989; the establishment-backed SVA publication *Pobratim*, the first number of which came out in December 1989; and the Leningrad *K sovesti*. By late 1991, the print runs of these papers had already fallen.[73]

Given the Soviet Union's economic crisis in its last years and the regime's struggle to remold itself in order to retain power and ultimately to survive, it was almost inevitable that the state would abandon the Afghan War vets and their associations. Appreciating that their input was unwelcome and the chances of their receiving their due benefits diminishing—although actual receipt of benefits varied from region to region, those that were more prosperous being visibly more forthcoming[74]—it was hardly surprising that most veterans and their associations lost their interest in politics. They were far more preoccupied with helping one another and raising their families.

Yet sometimes their activity acquired a political hue, perhaps in the context of their general belief that the government, the bureaucracy, and the population at large had let them down. On the one hand, afgantsy involvement in party and state institutions was considerable (especially in the Komsomol), and many served in the militia as druzhinniki. On the other hand, by 1990, afgantsy groups were "campaigning for what they consider[ed] social justice." This came in many stripes, as some maintained "close contacts with Pamyat societies," while at the other end of the spectrum, the Sakharov Union of Democratic Afghan War Veterans defended "democratic activities," including acting as bodyguards for democratic organizations under attack from Pamyat.[75] Some afgantsy became vigilantes by virtue of their employment in security frameworks (see Chapter 8) or of their association with gangs such as the Liubery or Kaskad that sought to mend society through military discipline and martial arts.[76]

Along with this wide gamut of views and positions came a mushrooming of organizations and frameworks for social and political activity, both "all-union" and republican. As the Soviet Union began to disintegrate, central bodies—including those of the afgantsy—had "to compete or co-operate with republican counterparts." One member of the USSR Supreme Soviet Committee for Internationalists' Affairs, Yuri Romanov, also chaired the Russian Conference of Representatives of Participants in the War in Afghanistan and the Parents and Families of Servicemen Killed in Afghanistan, which "ended up playing second fiddle" to the Russian Supreme Soviet Committee for Invalid Affairs, War and Labor Veterans and the Social Protection of Servicemen and their Families, which Aleksandr Rutskoi chaired. In parallel, the USSR Council of Ministers established its own State Commission of Soldier-Internationalists' Affairs, a measure that both the USSR Supreme Soviet Committee and the Union of Veterans of Afghanistan denounced. The mixture of liberalization and decay in late Soviet politics produced a "counter-productive scramble to create newer, different bodies as a surrogate to concerted action" that persisted after the Soviet Union's demise.[77]

A number of political parties in the successor states continued to call for assistance to the Afghan War veterans. In Tajikistan, the draft program of the Socialist Party—as the Communist Party renamed itself in September 1991—committed itself to do "all in its power to create normal living conditions [and] improve pension benefits for war and labor veterans and participants in the Afghan War." In January 1992, the ruling Democratic Party of Turkmenistan undertook to do much the same.[78] A veteran who lived in Minsk and received an apartment noted that Belarus did not abandon its veterans.[79]

Some Afghan War vets departed from the general pattern and focused on issues not even indirectly linked to the war. The top brass who had supported Gorbachev's reforms in the late 1980s (see Chapter 5) opposed both the obdurate conservatism and the extreme liberalism of some of their juniors, but Gorbachev increasingly considered their reformism, which aimed to modernize the existing order, unsatisfying and displaced most of the group's members. Against the backdrop of the general turmoil that characterized the political arena in Gorbachev's last years and of the inefficacy of sectorial, afganets-centered activity, it was inevitable that these higher-placed veterans would seek to participate in both all-union and national, republic-based politics. Several of the Fortieth Army's seven commanders and eleven generals, who had served as chief military adviser to the DRA forces, "appalled by the humiliations inflicted on their army and their country," became involved in the politics surrounding the collapse of the Soviet Union and the emergence of the new Russia.[80]

Even before their involvement, several of them had taken sides in the mounting confrontation between those who sought to preserve the traditional Soviet body politic and the reformists, led by Gorbachev's more radical advisers. These included Volodymyr Ivashko, who had served as a political instructor in Afghanistan in 1980, became the CPU's Ideological Secretary in 1986, and in 1989, succeeded Shcherbytsky as the CPU's First Secretary, as well as Aleksandr Rutskoi.[81]

Gromov, who had delivered a keynote address to the Nineteenth Party Conference in June 1988 and in 1989, had been one of the few senior officers elected, not nominated, to the Congress of People's Deputies. In late 1990, he became First Deputy Minister of the Interior, and in this position, when it became clear that the CPSU was "beyond resurrection," became involved in plans to seize power, cosigning the open letter to *Sovetskaia Rossiia* (July 23, 1991) that was in effect the manifesto for the August Coup (see the next section). He subsequently somehow extricated himself from all blame for the putsch and was appointed deputy commander of the ground forces.[82]

Gromov was one of a number of Soviet military leaders who sought to offset the criticism of the army's role in Afghanistan and consequently of the Soviet armed forces. In March 1989, he warned against the false conclusions about the war that dissident commentators with inadequate credentials were drawing.[83] Others included Deputy CGS General Vladimir Lobov, who in fall 1989 criticized "some mass media" for besmirching the honor of the military and campaigning to demoralize young people in the army; Marshal of the Soviet Union Viktor Kulikov, who accused *Ogonek* journalists for their "sociopolitical activity" in maliciously criticizing the army; and Defense Minister Dmitrii Yazov, who asked military writers to defend the army against attacks by other sectors of society.[84]

Along with political activity, in the Soviet Union's last years, there was military or paramilitary action in a number of union republics in which the afgantsy were visible, often on both sides. As commander of the Trans-Caucasus MD, Igor' Rodionov was charged with quelling the demonstration in Tbilisi in April 1989. Varennikov, the commander of the ground forces, was sent in January 1990 to deal with the anti-Armenian pogroms that swept Baku, and in 1990 and 1991, he coordinated the attempts to subdue the Baltic republics, most notably in Vilnius (January 1991).[85] One afganets "leader" told Gorbachev "that he must use whatever means necessary to impose order and he could then count on the army to support him."[86] This offered a notable contrast to the position of the Russian population at large, which was unwilling to risk Russian lives outside Russia (see above). The paratroop regiment sent from Azerbaijan to deal with the situation in Tbilisi in April 1989 had fought in Afghanistan until the end.[87] Commenting on this, writer Boris Vasil'ev bemoaned the use of Afghan War units at home, for their experience of fighting guerrillas taught them to resort to punitive functions.[88]

Moreover, when in 1990 and 1991 Gorbachev decided to restore order in Vilnius, Riga, and Baku by using forces led by Afghan War generals, OMON, at both the national and the republican level, which had recruited a sizable quota of afgantsy (see Chapter 8), became Moscow's instrument against nationalists in the local militias. The Kyrgyzstan OMON that had afgantsy in its ranks from the start played a major role in quelling the ethnic disturbances between Kyrgyz and Uzbeks in Osh in June

1990. Afgantsy were almost certainly also represented in the MVD special troops that the government had used to quell the ethnic disturbances that troubled Uzbekistan's Ferghana Valley the previous summer.

The predominance of afgantsy generals in the top posts of the military establishment persisted after the breakup of the Soviet Union, when they took key positions in the CIS's main trouble spots. Just over a year after the breakup, Pavel Grachev was minister of defense; Georgii Kondrat'ev, who had been First Deputy Commander of the Fortieth Army (1986–1988), his deputy; Aleksandr Lebed' was commander of the Fourteenth Army in Cisdnistria; Viktor Sorokin was commander of the Operative Group of Russian forces in Abkhazia; Mukhriddin Ashurov, commanded the 201st motor-rifle division, the Russian force in Tajikistan; while Aleksandr Rutskoi, Boris Yeltsin's vice president, oversaw the crises created when Chechnya declared independence, and in South Osetia and Cisdnistria.[89]

Veterans found themselves defending nationalist causes in union republics where local politics deteriorated into clashes with the center, notably in the Trans-Caucasus and the Baltics. Nationalism provided ideals to which they could pledge allegiance and offered employment where their experience was an asset. Some 450 veterans took part in the Tbilisi demonstration in April 1989 and, with the consent of both the population and the military, helped "with night-time patrols" in the tense situation that arose following the military's killing of citizens. In the words of the chairman of the Tbilisi council of internationalist soldiers, "We're taking on the function of intermediaries in resolving possible conflict situations."[90] Boris Vasil'ev praised the Tbilisi afgantsy's mutual help and solidarity under harsh conditions.[91] When rioting broke out in Dushanbe in February 1990, the deputy chairman of the Supreme Soviet Committee for the Affairs of Soldier-Internationalists, Rezo Odzhiev, flew there, quickly "knocked together afgantsy self-defense detachments and the situation 'normalized.'" (This, at least, was the committee secretary's version.)[92] Veterans also joined defenders of the Lithuanian parliament in early 1991 when Soviet troops and OMON riot police stormed key buildings in Vilnius. They trained young volunteers in urban combat skills, and the Lithuanian Union of Veterans of the Afghan War told the USSR Supreme Soviet Committee for Soldier-Internationalists' Affairs that it would organize an "armed rebuff" if Soviet forces tried to occupy the country.[93] Not all afgantsy who joined the militia, however, were eager to use their arms. One Uzbek militia sergeant, who had served two years in Afghanistan, believed that all conflict situations must be solved without resort to arms.[94]

It was not only in Tbilisi that afgantsy faced each other in an armed clash. Afgantsy became heavily involved on both sides in Armenian-Azerbaijani warfare in Nagorno-Karabagh in 1990–1991, and in a Russian force comprising afganets helicopter pilots and tankists that took up positions in between and shot at both. The bullets they had survived in Afghanistan finally overtook them in the Caucasus.[95] According to a psychologist from Dagestan, the situation in the Caucasus resembled Afghanistan, and therefore afgantsy were attracted to conflicts in the region.[96] Those seeking to form a Ukrainian army in early 1991 turned to afgantsy as a vital source of recruits and an active constituency of support. Elsewhere, afgantsy joined the Russian national legion in South Ossetia, Chechen-Ingush insurgents, the Dniester Guard, the so-called new Cossacks, and "any one of a dozen other military or paramilitary nationalist groupings."[97]

In fall 1991, the Adolat (Justice) Party groups that began forming in the Ferghana Valley in Uzbekistan included Afghan War veterans. The local clergy and elders, the *aksakals*, controlled these groups, which were part of an informal Muslim self-government structure that helped to provide material assistance to the community; they introduced *zakat*, the traditional Muslim tax intended to redistribute public wealth in favor of the poor.[98]

Afganets involvement in military strife occurred in the immediate post-Soviet period as well, whether the impetus was personal or identity motivated. One veteran from Belarus, who had been sent to Afghanistan in 1986, opted to go to Transdnistria when war broke out there in the 1990s—he wanted to continue fighting.[99] Afgantsy fought in Georgia's war with Abkhazia in 1993, where they formed a special unit and served as instructors, as the other soldiers "knew nothing about fighting a war."[100]

Indeed, the veterans saw themselves as having played a role in the unfolding interethnic hostilities in the Soviet Union's last years and in the immediate aftermath of its demise.[101] Asked their opinion on this issue in 1992–1993, about 70 percent gave a positive response.

Still in 1992–1993, according to our survey, the afgantsy were relatively sanguine regarding their position in society and potential for creating change (Table 10.1).

By this time, the Committee for Internationalist-Soldiers Attached to the Council of the Heads of Government of the Commonwealth of Independent States (CIS), headed by Ruslan Aushev, had been established (in March 1992), while afgantsy associations at the union republic level continued to exist after the union republics became successor states. Army General Valentin Varennikov, Hero of the Soviet Union Aleksandr Rutskoi, head of the ROC Metropolitan Pitirim, and CGS General Mikhail Moiseev attended the founding conference of the Russian Federation SVA (November 1990).[102] These organizations, however, did not necessarily have a free hand. In 1995, Aleksandr Kotenov resigned as chairman of the SVA in protest against government interference in the organization's affairs.[103] Others attained clout and status. As late as 2000, the antigovernment Afghanistan War Veterans' Party received 8 percent of the vote in the elections to Kyrgyzstan's Legislative Assembly.[104]

However, as a result of ongoing conflicts between the successor states, coordinated

Table 10.1. The afgantsy were the group that united most readily, thanks to their common military past, and so they became an influential social force

Year of service	Average level of agreement
80	4.33
81	4.5
82	5.6
83	4.72
84	5.17
85	4
86	3.26
87	4.75
88	4.3
89	4.55

Note: The level of agreement ranges from 0 to 6.

activity between the afgantsy's respective organizations was difficult. For example, the United Council of the Georgian Federation of Veterans viewed the chairman of the Union of Afgantsy-Internationalists' intention to represent Georgia in the May 2014, parade planned by the Russian Boevoe bratstvo (Fighting Brotherhood) as no less than treason, since Abkhazia and South Osetia (Samachablo), both of which had broken off from Georgia, were to participate as independent states.[105]

There were other reasons as well for clashes between, and within, afganets organizations—notably their financial resources and dealings. Some heads of Afghan veteran organizations became very rich, while only a small part of the money reached the disabled ex-servicemen for whom it was intended.[106] Internal rivalries within the afganets movement—whether based on competition for resources, political differences, or personal animosities—continued to undermine its ability to affect developments. Göransson shows how in Tajikistan, these rivalries continued to trouble the vets' organizations well into the twenty-first century.[107]

Galeotti sums up his study of the veterans' "political activity" (until the early 1990s):

> The afganets movement's dynamic mirrored that of the mothers [see Chapter 7], taking advantage of freedoms offered by glasnost, trying to fight for some share of resources in the period of democratization, then pushed back into the ghetto in the face of hard times and disinterest on the part of society as a whole. In many ways, indeed, it reflected the evolution of Soviet—or at least, Russian—society, with its transition from

informal groups within the existing structures to independent groupings, co-operatives, and unions—a brief explosion of equal parts of idealism and pragmatism and then the slow, sullen retrenchment as times became even harder.[108]

At the same time, the position of afgantsy on the side of democracy, their siding with the people, which arose from rethinking the army's role in Afghanistan, contributed significantly to a reappraisal of the afgantsy in public opinion, promoting their rehabilitation as a group, if not as a social or political force, within Soviet/Russian society.[109]

The August 1991 Coup

The Afghan War created a new military elite that found itself drawn into the political life of the later Gorbachev period, during which the status and role of the military in the Soviet system became a major issue. Although Gromov, as the Limited Contingent's last commander, stole a great deal of the limelight, the most prominent among these military figures was Aleksandr Rutskoi, who had served in Afghanistan in 1985–1986, and again in 1988, as deputy commander of the Fortieth Army's air force. He returned a Hero of the Soviet Union after flying 428 combat missions and being shot down twice and enrolled in the Voroshilov General Staff Academy in Moscow. In 1989, he became deputy chairman of the Russian nationalist Otechestvo Society and in March 1990 was elected to the Russian Republic Supreme Soviet, where he chaired the committee on the rights of invalids and veterans. In April 1991, he announced a new movement, Communists for Democracy, which sought a sovereign Russia and a genuine form of democratic socialism, and he supported Boris Yeltsin, who a month later selected him as his running mate in Russia's first presidential elections. Following Yeltsin's success, Rutskoi established the Democratic Party of Communists of Russia (DPKR). The August Coup elevated Rutskoi and pushed the DPKR formally to renounce communism and move toward constituting itself as the "left-democratic" Party of Free Russia.[110]

Former commanders from Afghanistan, like Rodionov and Varennikov, who were called on to deal with the internal unrest that troubled the Soviet Union in its last years were caught up in events by virtue of their military posts. When in late 1990, Gromov became First Deputy Minister of the Interior, he presided over the militarization of the police forces and the expansion of the MVD interior army—including the OMON special-purpose detachments—commanded by Colonel General Iurii Shatalin, who had been his superior in Afghanistan and brought with him several army units, including a motor-rifle division commanded by fellow afganets major general, Vladimir Neverov.

After their experiences in Afghanistan, some afgantsy officers, perhaps the majority, were both convinced that Russia had the right to protect its interests by every means possible and eager to implement the lessons learned from fighting "local wars." The politicians had only to apply the strength that the army had proved. Officers like Lieutenant General Pavel Grachev, who became commander of the airborne forces (VDV) in late 1990, and his deputy, Major General Aleksandr Lebed', were eager to see their "arms of service given greater prestige and resources and thus for the Soviet army to expand the scope and role of its so-called 'projection' forces, the sort of units which, in one captain's words, 'can go and fight a war on someone else's territory.'"[111]

Given their activity in the last years of the Soviet Union's existence, it is hardly surprising that afgantsy came out onto the streets to resist the putsch in August 1991 and were among its instigators. Indeed, some have contended that key members of the State Committee for the State of Emergency (the putschists), notably Oleg Baklanov, deputy head of the new Security Council, and KGB chief Vladimir Kriuchkov, were themselves "heroes of the Afghan War": although they had not fought there, they had visited frequently as overseers and were deeply involved in its management.[112]

Those who resisted the system's transformation and the loss of power to the republics emphasized the importance of statehood and patriotism. Varennikov, now both C-in-C of the ground forces and deputy defense minister, was among the fifty-three people who, in December 1990, called for a state of emergency and presidential rule in conflict zones if constitutional means proved ineffective. Afgantsy generals were among those military leaders who accused Gorbachev of cowardice, demagogy, treachery, and responsibility for the collapse of Soviet power. This perspective led ultimately to the August 1991 coup, which sought to preserve the status quo without transferring real powers to the union republics.[113] It seems likely that the generals who had fought in Afghanistan and whose advice Gorbachev had thwarted—notably regarding the implementation of withdrawal and Operation Typhoon—lacked confidence in either his order of preferences or his ability to follow through.

The accusations were followed by the letter of July 23, 1991, to the conservative newspaper, *Sovetskaia Rossiia*, "A Word to the People," that was close to being a call to arms. The letter expressed the conviction that the army would not allow the destruction of the mother country and would "act as a reliable guarantor of security and as the mainstay of all the healthy forces of society." Varennikov and Gromov, among others, signed it.

In fact, it was Varennikov who incited Shatalin "to deploy his (disproportionately afganets) MVD troops to seize power." The coup successfully frustrated, CoS Moiseev, Varennikov, Gromov, and Shatalin were removed from their posts. Varennikov was arrested, Moiseev and Shatalin retired, Gromov returned to the MoD, and Akhromeev committed suicide.[114]

Some have attributed the coup's failure to lessons learned from the Afghan War: mistrust of the senior military and political leadership with their incompetence and corruption and "an unspoken but visible collective determination never to let the armed forces be used for misguided political adventures at home or abroad."[115]

The Afghan veterans' prominence was not limited to one side. Among the senior officers, Pavel Grachev began to acquire a political profile when, in January 1991, he publicly opposed the use of paratroopers in ethnic conflicts. Although he and Gromov were at first among the coup's adherents, they reportedly backed down when they realized it would lead to bloodshed; their about-face played a significant role in its failure. Another opponent of the coup was the commander of the Leningrad MD, whose team included a disproportionate share of afgantsy, including First Deputy Commander Lieutenant General Valerii Mironov, who had been Gromov's commander in Afghanistan at one stage.

Afgantsy were also to be found in the streets. Thousands of them gathered to defend Boris Yeltsin and the Russian parliament building. They "quickly organized to prevent provocateurs, just plain drunks, and hotheads from starting trouble with the armoured personnel carriers and tanks that surrounded them; to isolate conflicts and minimize casualties if they did break out; and if a clear-cut attack did happen, to fight to the death."[116] One of the three who died in Moscow defending the parliament was a war veteran. In parallel, the Leningrad afgantsy set up a committee to support Mayor Sobchak's authority and defended it in over 250 manned barricades. The committee's links with the Leningrad MD enabled LAVVA to convince the local military authorities "to defy the putschists' orders to impose martial law in the city during the putsch." Moreover, the regular broadsheets LAVVA produced under the banner of its newspaper, *K sovesti,* became "an information lifeline, a means of promulgating the city government's decrees."

According to Galeotti, the coup failed because of the "informal connections" linking officers on both sides and the collapse of the military and security forces' "functional unity."[117] Almost certainly, the reasons emanate from various other factors that are irrelevant to our discussion. Yet even an assessment stemming from an entirely different angle notes two factors pertinent to the war, one of them tangent to Galeotti's, namely, the lack of cohesion within both the army and the KGB—the two bodies from which the coup's instigators came; the other, a vehement popular consensus that a small group of leaders operating without institutional controls must not again decide the Soviet citizenry's political destinies.[118]

The war itself, as distinct from those who fought it—that is, the introduction of Soviet troops, the conduct of the war, and the protracted delay in withdrawing the Limited Contingent—played its part in sounding the Soviet regime's death knell. The war demonstrated, and made it essential to transform, the arbitrary and authoritarian nature of the decision-making process and to apply direct controls to the actions of the leadership. It also mobilized public opinion against many of the Soviet regime's injustices and inefficiencies, including the misrepresentation of facts in the media. This boosted the atmospherics of glasnost and perestroika that were essential to Gorbachev's perception of the need for far-reaching political—and economic—reform. It led to disenchantment with the military and to the undermining of morale within the Soviet armed forces. And it exacerbated ethnic and social animosities between the center and the periphery. These factors put the Afghan War on the list of Russia's wars that engendered far-reaching domestic transformations.

The anomaly of a controlled economy that bred low productivity and technological backwardness; the hegemony of the party with its rigid hierarchy, corrupt bureaucracy, and defunct ideology that provided its sole legitimization; and the composition of the Soviet empire that could not cater to ethnic diversity and growing demands: these were the factors that led to the Soviet Union's disintegration. The Soviet-Afghan War, in contrast, was not a root or systemic cause, but it played a role in the unraveling. The war almost certainly precipitated the Soviet Union's final collapse. In many ways, it reflected the forces that sealed the fate of the world's second superpower. It served as a catalyst, giving momentum to processes that it had not set in motion.

Certainly, as one student of the topic noted, Afghanistan became associated in the minds of Soviet citizens with the collapse of the Soviet Union, with losing the Cold War, and with "the breakdown of the domestic fabric of Soviet power." It led to a general discrediting on the home front of

> the policies and politics of dealing with the war inside the USSR. . . . Mismanagement of the episode led the citizens to question the foundations on which the CPSU had placed their Motherland. Its authority was undermined in the late 1980s when the extent of its lies and misrepresentation of everything to do with the war . . . became clear. In addition, the inability of the welfare state to provide for those who had been injured or traumatized and the ineffectiveness of the public officials to facilitate the reintegration into society of the men and women who had worked in Afghanistan, revealed the shortcomings—objective and subjective—of a crumbling system.[119]

Writing just a year after the final withdrawal—before almost anyone had foreseen the country's disintegration—a Russian political scientist and social psychologist stated unequivocally, "Our country is not the same after going through this war." He elaborated, "The Afghan fiasco significantly weakened the influence of the ideological-military complex. Any other scenario would have made it difficult to initiate perestroika."[120] And two Russian scholars, analyzing the Soviet soldiers' and officers' violation of their oath by refusing to obey the orders of the top brass and siding with the people and the forces of democracy, attributed their actions in the 1991 August

Coup to a rethinking of the role that the army had filled in Afghanistan—and in Tbilisi, Baku, and Vilnius. In this view, the army had ceased to be a "dutiful tool in the hands of the politicians" and become "the most important democratic institution of the lawful state and civil society."[121]

Writing two decades later, another Russian analyst summed up the consequences of the war. He believed that its financial burden precipitated the Soviet Union's bankruptcy, that it contributed to the erosion of the "entire political system," and that it destroyed "the foundations of interethnic peace" within the country and, ultimately, its "national security and territorial integrity." In his view, the war filled a key role in the breakdown of the country.[122] While these assessments seem exaggerated, the fact that recognized scholars could formulate them in important forums is indicative of trends in the Russian public sphere.

Thus, the Soviet-Afghan War accelerated the Soviet Union's final collapse, for the intervention and the subsequent refusal to withdraw were not only unwise and immoral. They also underscored the arbitrary and authoritarian nature of the decision-making process and the necessity of changing it. They made no less essential the need to apply direct controls to the actions of the leadership. The war mobilized public opinion against many of the regime's inequities and misrepresentations, including the media's falsification of facts. It led to the people's disenchantment with the military and to the undermining of discipline within the Soviet armed forces.

The war affected mechanisms of pristine party control that, at least partly as a result of the war, slipped into the limbo of glasnost. It also influenced various aspects of Soviet political life in the 1980s, specifically the way the regime operated. As a result of the war, glasnost entered an arena that was, in retrospect, preparing for it. Letters from citizens to the central press, the CPSU CC apparatus, and other authorities are one example. In the late 1960s, legislation had created frameworks to give citizens the sense that they could vent criticisms or complaints without fearing retribution, while ensuring that the party authorities regulated the letters' publication, and so possible influence on public opinion and decision making.[123] As early as 1981, the Politburo addressed the issue of letters that the CC received about the way the war's casualties were interred, but it resolved not to heed their content. By 1984, a poignant *Komsomol'skaia pravda* article highlighting the dismal lot of a returning invalid resulted in a flood of letters identifying with the vet and calling for the party-state to rectify the situation in which local authorities could disdain the vets' hardships. The party responded by informing the public that the relevant officials had been punished. (A year earlier, the paper had begun running a daily column on the war in response to readers' letters.) When Gorbachev became General Secretary, the letters from mothers and soldiers drew his attention to the war and, he read to the Politburo some of the (signed) letters that had inundated the CC and newspapers. He ultimately used these letters to push toward withdrawing the Soviet troops from Afghanistan, just as he exploited letters to justify other policies he advocated. (In parallel, once he decided on withdrawal, the papers did not publish the thousands of letters opposing it.)

By studying the ways that the Soviet-Afghan War encompassed various aspects of late Soviet government and society, then, we have touched on a number of topics that were of paramount importance in the 1980s, topics on which the war had no direct bearing but that it affected. One of these was the ethnic unrest that surfaced in the second half of the decade, mainly in Ukraine, the Caucasus, and the Baltics, to the accompaniment of a rampant nationalism in Russia. Both were evident in army life and were heightened by the unnatural conditions of Afghanistan. Another was the enhanced predilection of Soviet youth for Western culture that so enraged the returning afgantsy, who found their peers shaking off the chains of Soviet cultural production and the values that impelled it. A third was the prevailing corruption in both the armed forces and civilian life—as officialdom and citizenry alike sought ways to circumvent the rules that in theory governed their lives and dictated their behavior. All three were omens of a failing system, of a regime that, however much it endeavored to reform in order to get back on its feet, was, in its very fabric, incapable of tolerating meaningful transformation. To use Yakovlev's analysis, they were indications of the "alienation of practices and ideals from people's real interests."[124]

Introducing troops into Afghanistan and leaving them there for nine years were, on the surface, foreign policy decisions, for their perpetrators originally saw them as aspects of Soviet Third World policy and the Soviet Union's jostling with the United States for global status. (Indeed, some have suggested that had the Carter administration mitigated its reaction instead of augmenting military aid to the insurgents, canceling grain exports to the Soviet Union, and banning the Olympic Games, the war might have been averted and the Soviet force withdrawn in February 1980.[125]) Yet like earlier wars on which Imperial Russia had embarked in not dissimilar circumstances—the Crimean War of 1854–1856, the Russo-Japanese War of 1904–1905, and even World War I, which provided the backdrop to the fall of the empire—the long-term domestic impact of the Soviet-Afghan War was infinitely more far-reaching than its international implications, for it provided the mis-en-scène for changing the political system and Russian/Soviet society. The war and the way the Soviet leadership handled it became a focus of confrontation in the Soviet political arena. More, they appear to have been the last straw in the burden that Soviet overextension, overinvolvement in the Third World, and overemphasis on armaments and the military budget inflicted on its citizens while ignoring their welfare. When Gorbachev introduced reforms, the people, finally given the chance, decided that instituting them required abolishing the system.[126]

Less than a year after the final disintegration of the Soviet Union, *Krasnaia zvezda* published an article with extracts from some of the most secret documents connected to the war, noting that it was a tragedy not just for the disabled but "for all of us, for it was in its way the prologue to the times in which we are presently living."[127]

Notes

Introduction

1. Westad, "Concerning the Situation in 'A,'" 131.

2. Borovik, *The Hidden War*, 13–14. I refrain from discussing Borovik's hypothesis regarding the "inherent morality" of the Soviet nation or its system and ideology.

3. Yurchak, *Everything Was Forever, Until It Was No More.*

4. Carrère d'Encausse, *Decline of an Empire,* 265.

5. Suny, *The Revenge of the Past*, 139.

6. The discussion at this three-day symposium appeared in print: "The Intervention in Afghanistan and the Fall of Détente," Nobel Symposium, September 17–20, 1995. See especially 202–227.

7. Galeotti, *Afghanistan: The Soviet Union's Last War*, 2–3, 166.

8. Ol'shanskii, "'Afganskii sindrom'" (The Afghan syndrome), 10.

9. One inside source testified that there is no KGB documentation of the decision to introduce troops and replace DRA president Hazifullah Amin with Babrak Karmal. Andropov ordered his few handwritten notes destroyed—Shebarshin, *Ruka Moskvy: razvedka ot rastsveta do raspada*, 125.

10. "The Intervention in Afghanistan," 203. Shulman was special assistant to the secretary of state, 1977–1981; General William Odom was former director of Soviet affairs at the National Security Council.

Chapter 1

1. By 1979, Brezhnev, "incoherent from arteriosclerosis and tranquillizer overdoses," was working just three hours a day. Kotkin, *Armageddon Averted*, 30. For Brezhnev's declining health throughout the 1970s, see Zubok, *A Failed Empire*, 241–242.

2. Born in 1914, he was the youngest of the three (Ustinov and Gromyko were born 1908 and 1909, respectively).

3. For the presence of Soviet Central Asians in Afghanistan as advisers and experts, before and after April 1978, see Naby, "The Ethnic Factor in Soviet-Afghan Relations," 249–252.

4 For a vivid, detailed account of the Soviet reaction to the "April Revolution" from Day One until the intervention twenty months later, see Snegirev and Simunin, *Virus A*. The authors spell out the story of a Greek tragedy whose finale was written on the wall by the very composition of its actors.

5. Afghanistan Task Force, Foreign Affairs and National Defense Division, *Afghanistan: Soviet Invasion and U.S. Response*, 5.

6. Ivanov, "Ogranichennyi kontingent," *Sovetskii voin*, no. 14 (July 1991), 19. For a detailed list of the eighteen requests, see Liakhovskii, *Tragediia i doblest' afgana*, 87–88.

7. CWIHP, *Bulletin*, issues 8–9 (Winter 1996/97), 136–145.

8. Mendelson, *Changing Course*, 47; Ivanov, "Ogranichennyi kontingent," *Sovetskii voin*, no. 15 (August 1991), 12–19; *CWIHP Toward an International History*, 41–46; Taraki–Kosygin conversation, where Taraki suggested this ruse.

9. It was apparently accepted practice before the outbreak of a war to send KGB sabotage troops trained to operate on enemy territory as advance units. Knight, *The KGB*, 227. And see the book of an interpreter in General Gorelov's team of advisers who arrived in Kabul in July 1979 and was allotted to the DRA army's Fourth Tank Brigade: Greshnov, *Afganistan: zalozhniki vremeni*.

10. *CWIHP Bulletin*, issues 8–9 (Winter 1996/97), 144. The entire territory of the Soviet Union was divided into sixteen MDs.

11. "The Intervention in Afghanistan," 74.

12. Ivanov, "Ogranichennyi kontingent," *Sovetskii voin*, no. 14 (July 1991), 19.

13. *CWIHP Bulletin*, issue 3 (Fall 1993), 67–69. The report was commissioned by the Politburo, March 17, 1979—Documents on the Soviet Invasion of Afghanistan, e-Dossier No.4, CWIHP, November 2001, 140.

14. *International Herald Tribune*, April 14–15, 1979, quoted in Arnold, *The Soviet Invasion in Perspective*, 81.

15. Ustinov report to CPSU CC, November 5, 1979—*CWIHP Bulletin*, issues 8–9, 158. Pavlovskii's sixty-three-man delegation included twelve generals and six colonels. Before leaving for Afghanistan, Pavlovskii called Ustinov and asked whether the Soviet Union was "going into Afghanistan." He was told "not under any circumstances." Mendelson, *Changing Course*, 49.

16. Igor' Beliaev and Anatolii Gromyko, "Tak my voshli v Afganistan" (How we entered Afghanistan), *Literaturnaia gazeta*, September 20, 1989, 14.

17. Brown, *The Gorbachev Factor*, 55.

18. Lyakhovskiy, *Inside the Soviet Invasion*, 17. In connection with the possibility of Islamic extremism reaching Central Asia from Afghanistan, a Soviet colonel was said in early 1980 to have told his counterpart in the DRA Defense Ministry that "we don't want to have to fight this sore on our own territory." *Ha'arets*, May 16, 1980.

19. Vassiliev, *Russian Policy in the Middle East*, 252.

20. The document itself is dated November 29, which is clearly an error, as the Politburo discussed it on October 31, and referred to as having been written on October 29. For further details of the means that the KGB employed beginning October 1979 to discredit Amin with Brezhnev and its preparations for a coup against Amin, see Mitrokhin, *The KGB in Afghanistan*, especially 86–92.

21. *CWIHP Bulletin*, issues 8–9, 159; "The Intervention in Afghanistan," 90–91.

22. Lyakhovskiy, "Inside the Soviet Invasion," 14–15. For the Muslim Battalion, see Chapters 2 and 9.

23. Westad, "*Concerning the Situation in 'A',* 130–131, and Zubok, *A Failed Empire*, 258–264. Georgii Arbatov, head of the Institute of the USA and Canada, said in 1989 that the apparent failure of détente certainly "played a role" in the decision to intervene. Cohen and Heuvel, *Voices of Glasnost*, 319.

24. Quoted in Westad, "*Concerning the Situation in 'A',*" 130.

25. Vasilii Safronchuk, "Afghanistan in the Amin Period," *International Affairs* (Moscow) 2 (1991) 79–96, quoted in Mendelson, *Changing Course*, 51–52.

26. Lyakhovskiy, "Inside the Soviet Invasion," 12, 14, 24. From 1987 to February 1989, Liakhovskii served as chief adviser to General Valentin Varennikov, head of the MoD Operations Group in Afghanistan. Sergei Krakhmalov, military attaché to the Soviet embassy in Kabul from March 1980 to April 1985, similarly attributes the way the decision was made to serious flaws in the decision-making mechanism (see Chapter 4).

27. For example, Krakhmalov, *Zapiski voennogo attashe*, 218. See also the testimony of a known Soviet expert on Afghanistan at the Institute of Oriental Studies: Vladimir Skosyrev, "A Lesson Worth Learning: War in Afghanistan through a Historian's Eyes," *Izvestiia*, May 5, 1989, 5. R. Moscow; FBIS-SOV-89–089, May 10, 1989, 31–34 (see Chapter 10).

28. "The Intervention in Afghanistan," 99–100.

29. Mendelson, *Changing Course*, 51; Nikolai Ivanov, "Ogranichennyi kontingent," *Sovetskii voin*, no. 17 (1991), 13, 16–17, writes that Amin demanded an ambassador who had no connection with any previous Afghan leader or regime or with the KGB or MVD, and that Gromyko chose Tabeev because he wanted "a Muslim [sic!] who knows the traditions, customs and ways of the East." Gai and Snegirev, *Vtorzhenie*, 51, claim that Suslov said the Kremlin wanted an ambassador with a Muslim-sounding name. Ivanov says too that Suslov was involved in the appointment of Magometov.

30. Gorelov was replaced at Brezhnev's behest for not having protected Taraki.

31. According to Mitrokhin, Amin asserted that Puzanov and Gorelov, together with Pavlovskii and head of the KGB group in Afghanistan, Boris Ivanov, were involved in an attempt to lure him into a trap. Mitrokhin, *The KGB in Afghanistan*, 74.

32. Gai and Snegirev, *Vtorzhenie*, 78–79; Beliaev and Gromyko, "Tak my voshli v Afganistan," 14.

33. Interview with Pavlovskii a decade later: "Afganistan ne dolzhen povtorit'sia" (Afghanistan must not be repeated), *Voennyi zhurnal*, no. 1 (1990), 2–3. See also Gai, "Afganistan: kak eto bylo, *Vecherniaia Moskva*, September 12, 1989, 1n 4.

34. Rubtsov, "Sovetskii Soiuz v 'Neob"iavlennoi' voine v Afganistane," 128. For Pavlovskii's report, see Lyakhovskiy, *Inside the Soviet Invasion*, 7–8. Both Pavlovskii and Gorelov later told Gai and Snegirev that they had opposed Soviet military intervention in Afghanistan: Gai and Snegirev, *Vtorzhenie*, 68–72.

35. Vassiliev, *Russian Policy in the Middle East*, 256.

36. Lyakhovskiy, *Inside the Soviet Invasion*, 8, 19–20. Andropov opined that Zaplatin must be recalled from Kabul prior to removing Amin, whom Zaplatin reportedly supported: Ivanov, "Ogranichennyi kontingent," *Sovetskii voin*, no. 17 (September 1991), 21. Apparently Zaplatin was the first individual outside the GS who registered his disapproval of the invasion: Ivanov, "Ogranichennyi kontingent," *Sovetskii voin*, no. 18 (September 1991), 16–17.

37. Safronov, "Kak eto bylo," 67.

38. Braithwaite, *Afgantsy*, 77, 80; Ivanov, "Ogranichennyi kontingent," no. 17 (September 1991), 21, and "M. A. Suslov: 'My tak reshili'" (M. A. Suslov: 'This is how we decided'), *Pobratim*, no. 3 (February 1990), 4–5.

39. Varennikov, "Afganskaia epopeia," 3; Ivanov, "Ogranichennyi kontingent," no. 17 (September 1991), 19–21.

40. "The Intervention in Afghanistan," 177; Westad, "*Concerning the Situation in 'A',*" 130.

41. Lyakhovskiy, "Inside the Soviet Invasion," 17–18, 23; Ivanov, "Ogranichennyi kontingent," no. 18 (September 1991), 13. Ogarkov had previously been at odds with his minister over the budget for the armed forces, which must have diminished any chances of making himself heard on Afghanistan. In an interview with Sarah Mendelson in 1993, Varennikov maintained that the GS had "categorically opposed the intervention" because it ignored important aspects of the Afghan domestic situation, including "the tradition, the ethnic groups, the nationalities, the tribal relations, the Islamic religion." Mendelson, *Changing Course*, 67 n. In 1989, however, Varennikov said that, given the threat to the Soviet Union's southern border, the decision to send in troops was appropriate: quoted by V. Skosyrev, "Urok, kotoryi stoit usvoit'" (A lesson worth internalizing), *Izvestiia*, May 4, 1989, 5.

42. "The Intervention in Afghanistan," 170.

43. Grau, "The Soviet-Afghan War," 134.

44. Vassiliev, *Russian Policy in the Middle East*, 253.

45. "The Intervention in Afghanistan," 87.

46. Shilo, "Posledstviia vvoda sovetskikh voisk v DRA," 2.

47. Miller, *Beyond Afghanistan: Changing Soviet Perspectives on Regional Conflicts*, 3.

48. Westad, "*Concerning the Situation in 'A',*" 130–131.

49. Rubtsov, "Sovetskii Soiuz v 'Neob"iavlennoi' voine v Afganistane," 132. In a speech to the Supreme Soviet on October 23, 1989, Shevarnadze maintained that he and Gorbachev learned about the intervention from the media.

50. Nahaylo, *The Ukrainian Resurgence*, 44–45.

51. Krakhmalov, *Zapiski voennogo attashe*, 219. Kosygin's absence might be explained by ill health: he resigned in October 1980 and died two months later. CC International department official Karen Brutents testified that Kosygin was in hospital on December 12: "The Intervention in Afghanistan," 75.

52. Gromyko, *Memories*, 240.

53. Beliaev and Gromyko, "Tak my voshli v Afganistan," 14.

54. "The Intervention in Afghanistan," 77, 83.

55. Yakovlev, *The Reformation in Russia*, 149.

56. "Kak prinimalos' reshenie," 41; Lyakhovskiy, "Inside the Soviet Invasion,"19. The Fortieth Army's embryo already existed; see Chapter 2. For the law on military service, enacted October 12, 1967, see https://www.lawmix.ru/sssr/4523, accessed October 10, 2017.

57. Lyakhovskiy, "Inside the Soviet Invasion," 18, and "Kak prinimalos' reshenie," 42. This thirteen-page article was published in the official MoD organ by Varennikov's group and can be taken as the MoD position on the actual conduct of the war two years after its completion. In 1993, Varennikov implied that the Kremlin accepted the GS proposal—Varennikov, "Afganskaia epopeia"—but clearly this was not the case.

58. Lyakhovskiy, "Inside the Soviet Invasion," 16–19.

59. Diary of Chernyaev, December 30, 1979, NSArch, quoted in ibid.

60. Rubtsov, "Sovetskii Soiuz v 'neob"iavlennoi' voine v Afganistane," 137. A CPSU CC and Soviet government decree of January 2, 1980, stipulated the size of the force—CWIHP *Toward an International History*, 110–111: "2,000 laborers and office workers, including 1,000 servicemen" would complement it.

61. "Kak prinimalos' resehenie," 43.

62. *CWIHP: Toward an International History*, 2:95–97.

63. Gleason, *The Central Asian States*, 102—103.) Gleason does not give his source.

64. Yuri Andropov, Andrei Gromyko, Dmitrii Ustinov and Boris Ponomarev to the CC CPSU, December 31, 1979. *CWIHP Bulletin*, issues 8–9, 160–161.

65. Safronov, "Kak eto bylo," 67.

66. "The Intervention in Afghanistan," 188.

67. Varennikov at the Lysebu symposium—"The Intervention in Afghanistan," 77; Dobrynin, *In Confidence*, 440.

68. Cherkasov, "'Afgan' nachinalsia tak"; interview with Major-General Ivan Riabchenko, 7.

69. Grau, *The Bear Went Over the Mountain*, xxviii.

70. "Kak prinimalos' reshenie," 42.

71. Lyakhovskiy, *Plamia Afgana*, quoted in *CWIHP Toward an International History*, 120–121; Ivanov, "Ogranichennyi kontingent," *Sovetskii voin*, no. 10 (May 1991), 13–14.

72. O. Bogomolov, "Kto zhe oshibalsia?" (Who was mistaken?), *Literaturnaia gazeta*, March 16, 1988, 10.

73. "The Intervention in Afghanistan," 193.

74. Rubenstein, *Soviet Dissidents*, 272–273. See also *Posev*, no. 6 (1985), 16. Press attacks on Sakharov mentioned that he was not being allowed to reside in Moscow but made no mention of Afghanistan: *Izvestiia*, January 23, 24, 1980, 6; *Pravda*, January 29, 1980, 6; and even a lengthy piece in *Literaturnaia gazeta*, January 30, 1980, 9: A. Borisov, "Klevetnik i farisei" (Slanderer and Pharisee). Sakharov testified in 1989 that he was told specifically that his protest against the introduction of troops into Afghanistan was the reason for his exile; see Chapter 10. For other dissidents who protested the invasion in early 1980, see document 119 of the Moscow Helsinki Watch Group, referred to in Alekseeva, *Istoriia inakomysliia*, 281.

75. Ivanov, "Ogranichennyi kontingent," 14–15, and AFP in English, July 29, 1980. Daily Report, July 30, 1980.

76. Kuzio, "Opposition in the USSR to the Occupation of Afghanistan," 107.

77. "Sitting 'for Afghanistan'," *Posev*, no. 6 (1985), 16, and Alekseeva, *Istoriia inakomysliia v SSSR*, 265, 276. For the opposition of Mazur and Malyshev, see also Andriushchenko, "Chto sovetskie grazhdane dumali o voine v Afganistane i kak KGB borolsia s nedovol'nymi."

78. Julia Wishnevsky, "The Samizdat Almanac of Soviet Feminists," Report on the USSR, RL, April 15, 1980; quoted in Pinnick, "When the Fighting Is Over," 144, and RL Arkhiv Samizdata 5400, quoted in Kuzio, "Opposition in the USSR to the Occupation of Afghanistan," 106.

79. "Afghan Echoes in the Republics," *Soviet Nationality Survey*, vol. 2, no.4, April 1985; *Arkhiv samizdata*, no. 3875, *Vypusk* 6/80, and *Vesti iz SSSR. Prava cheloveka* pod red. Kronida Liubarskogo. Mionkhen, 1982, vol. 10, no. 36, quoted in Alekseeva, Istoriia inakomysliia v SSSR, 67, 68.

80. Mitrokhin, *The KGB in Afghanistan*, 107.

81. Andriushchenko, "Chto sovetskie grazhdane dumali o voine.

82. Gennady Bocharov in an interview with CBS, apparently in 1989 or 1990. Bocharov, *Russian Roulette*, 181.

83. Vassiliev, *Russian Policy in the Middle East*, 257, and Bocharov, *Russian Roulette*, 55–56.

84. "Ob afganskoi voine, sovetskoi presse i rabote NTS" (The Afghan War, the Soviet press and the work of the NTS [the Russian émigré association Narodnyi trudovoi soiuz]), *Posev*, no. 9 (1983), 12; Braithwaite *Afgantsy*, 243.

85. Alekseeva, *Istoriia inakomysliia v SSSR*, 284.

86. Kuzio, "Opposition in the USSR to the Occupation of Afghanistan," 106, 107.

87. "Rasskazyvaiut ob Afganistane," *Posev*, no. 7 (1985), 21.

88. Smith, *The New Russians*, 26–27.

89. Interviews with the author, February 1982.

90. According to General Mahmut Gareev, who played a leading role in the command of the Turkestan MD throughout most of the 1980s and became Afghan President Najibullah's aide when the Fortieth Army withdrew, the Soviets had a moral right to try to save the Afghan people from reactionary Islamist fundamentalism and a strategic necessity to prevent the United States from getting a hold in Afghanistan. Yet Moscow's intervention should have been political and economic, not military. The introduction of Soviet troops caused major damage both to the Soviet Union and to Afghanistan. Gareev, *Moia poslednaia voina*.

91. Lyakhovskiy, "Inside the Soviet Invasion,"23. The quote from Shebarshin, taken from his *Iz zhizni nachal'nika razvedki* (Moscow: Terra, 1994), is brought by Liakhovskii. Ibid.

92. Krakhmalov, *Zapiski voennogo attashe*, 304–305. Mujahidin, literally "those engaged in fighting a jihad," was the most common appellation of the opposition to the Marxist regime in Afghanistan.

93. Ivan Demidov, "Rossiia ne dolzhna podderzhivat' tol'ko odnu iz konfliktuiushchikh storon" (Russia must not support just one of the conflicting parties), *Nezavisimaia gazeta*, September 8, 1992, 1, 4. Both Gorbachev and Shevarnadze were Politburo candidate members in December 1979 and had no vote in that body.

94. Mendelson, *Changing Course*, 39, 41, 62. Mendelson's assessment was not very different from the verdict in the 1990s, after the war was over, of Boris Gromov, the last commander of the Soviet force in Afghanistan, who commented that the Soviet leadership saw the war as yet a further stage in the struggle against the United States, a means of blocking the spread of Islam following the Iranian revolution, and evidence of the superiority of the socialist system. Previous interventions—in Hungary, Czechoslovakia, Cuba, and Vietnam—had gone ahead without serious complications. Boris Gromov, *Ogranichennyi kontingent*, 21.

Chapter 2

1. Grau, *The Bear Went Over the Mountain*, xvi, xxviii–xxix. Grau based his edited volume on a handbook published by Moscow's Frunze Military Academy.

2. Sarin and Dvoretsky, *The Afghan Syndrome*, 87.

3. Kvachkov, *Spetsnaz Rossii*, 95–96.

4. "Kak prinimalos' reshenie" 42–43.

5. Maiorov, *Pravda ob afganskoi voine*, 123.

6. "Kak prinimalos' reshenie," 42 and 44.

7. Blank, "Imagining Afghanistan: Lessons of a 'Small' War," 469.

8. Grau, *The Bear Went Over the Mountain*, xix–xx.

9. David M. Glantz, "Introduction," in Grau, *The Bear Went Over the Mountain*, xii–xiii.

10. The GRU was a department of the General Staff of the Soviet armed forces; the KGB had its own spetsnaz, "Alfa."

11. Alexiev, *Inside the Soviet Army in Afghanistan*, 5–6.

12. Gromov, *Ogranichennyi kontingent*, 115. For preparations beginning April 1979, see Ivanov, "Ogranichennyi kontingent," *Sovetskii voin* nos. 14 and 15 (July and August 1991), 12–21, 12–22 respectively.

13. For the formation of the Muslim Battalion, see Zhou, "The Muslim Battalion," 305–307; and Chapter 9.

14. Cherkasov, "'Afgan' nachinalsia tak, " 6–7.

15. In preparation for a 1983 CPSU CC plenum that devoted considerable attention to the lack of Russian fluency on the Soviet periphery, the Uzbek and Kyrgyz authorities maintained

that more effective Russian-language instruction would improve the performance of Central Asian soldiers in the Soviet armed forces. See, e.g., an article by the Uzbek SSR Minister of Education, "For the Future Fighting Man: The Russian Language and the Military-Patriotic Upbringing of Young People," *Pravda vostoka*, May 15, 1983, 3. Several days later, a Republic Scientific and Practical Conference for the Study of the Russian Language opened in Samarkand to discuss improving Russian-language education, specifically among young men before their induction into the army—"Iazyk nashego edinstva i sotrudnichestva: s respublikanskoi nauchno-prakticheskoi konferentsii po izucheniiu russkogo iazyka" (The language of our unity and cooperation: From the republican practical-scientific conference on study of the Russian language), *Pravda vostoka*, May 21, 1983, 1–2. Three years later, the Soviet government daily noted that "many recruits do not speak Russian well enough to serve anywhere except in manual-labor battalions that dig ditches or pave roads." *Izvestiia*, December 10, 1986.

16. Lyakhovskiy, *Inside the Soviet Invasion*, 35. 39; Gromov, *Ogranichennyi kontingent*, 115–116. Liakhovskii both fought in Afghanistan and, after being wounded, served on the Fortieth Army GS. He was allowed access to classified military, KGB, CPSU CC, and Politburo materials. His two books on the war "reveal the bureaucratic realities" of the CC, the military-industrial commission (VPK), the foreign ministry, and the GS, and emphasize "the misuse of soldiers and officers, rescuing their honor and dignity from the mix of personal and political motives among the party and military elites that perpetrated the disaster." Odom, *The Collapse of the Soviet Military*, 441–442.

17. Mitrokhin, "The KGB in Afghanistan," 112.

18. *Der Spiegel*, June 16, 1980—DR/FBIS III, June 20, 1980, R1–R3.

19. Lyakhovskiy, *Inside the Soviet Invasion*, 39. For the disorder and inadequacies that surrounded preparations in the Turkestan MD, see David Gai, "Afganistan: kak eto bylo" (Afghanistan: how it was), *Vecherniaia Moskva*, September 12, 1989, 4; and Pardaev, *Afganskaia komandirovka*, 55–61.

20. Reich, "Faces of the Lithuanian *Afganai*," 192.

21. Ol'shanskii, "'Afganskii sindrom,'" 11.

22. Lyakhovskiy, *Inside the Soviet Invasion*, 30 and 34.

23. Gai, "Afganistan: kak eto bylo," *Vecherniaia Moskva*, September 12, 1989, 4.

24. Pardaev, *Afganskaia komandirovka*, 97.

25. O. Odnokolenko, "TsK KPSS: 'Sovershenno sekretno,' 'Osobaia papka.' Kto tebia vydumal, 'Afgan'?" *Krasnaia zvezda*, October 7, 1992.

26. Blank, "Imagining Afghanistan: Lessons of a 'Small' War," 469, 471.

27. Maiorov, *Pravda ob afganskoi voine*, 269.

28. Gai, "Afganistan: kak eto bylo," *Vecherniaia Moskva*, September 12, 1989, 4.

29. Interview with David Fierman, August 2, 2016.

30. Cherkasov, "'Afgan' nachinalsia tak . . . ," 8, and Bocharov, *Russian Roulette*, 7–8.

31. Grau, *The Bear Went Over the Mountain*, xviii, xxviii, 200.

32. Krakhmalov, *Zapiski voennogo attashe*, 217.

33. "The Intervention in Afghanistan," 84; Varennikov, "Afganskaia epopeia," 3.

34. Gromov, *Ogranichennyi kontingent*, 118; Gai and Snegirev, *Vtorzhenie*, 116; Liakhovskii, *Tragediia i doblest' afgana*, 123.

35. G. Ustiuzhanin, "'Pokhoronku' ne dognal" (He arrived after the announcement of his death), *Sovetskii voin*, no. 18 (September 1990), 69.

36. Greshnov, *Afganistan: zalozhniki vremeni.*

37. Baumann, *Russian-Soviet Unconventional Wars*, 136–138.

38. Gai and Snegirev, *Vtorzhenie*, 264—265; Gromov, "Zashchishchali, obuchali, stroili," 13.

39. Grau, "The Soviet-Afghan War," 134.

40. McMichael, "Soviet Tactical Performance and Adaptation in Afghanistan," 76.

41. Safronov, "Kak eto bylo," 70.

42. Alexiev and Wimbush, *Ethnic Minorities in the Red Army: Asset or Liability?* 245–246.

43. Gromov, "Zashchishchali, obuchali, stroili," 13.

44. See the testimony of the first VDV division commander to enter Afghanistan in 1979: Cherkasov, "'Afgan,'" 8. The chief military adviser in Afghanistan Maiorov (*Pravda ob afganskoi voine*, 75–76) states this was one of his major objectives. For specific instructions to this effect later on in the war, see below.

45. Bocharov, *Russian Roulette*, 28–29.

46. Pashkevich, *Afganistan: voina glazami kombata*, 49.

47. Alexievich, *Zinky Boys*, 98.

48. McMichael, "Soviet Tactical Performance and Adaptation in Afghanistan," 94.

49. Grau, *The Bear Went Over the Mountain*, 75.

50. Gromov, "Zashchishchali, obuchali, stroili," 15.

51. Safronov, *Kak eto bylo*, 68; see also Allen and Shakel, "Tribal Guerrilla Warfare against a Colonial Power," 590–617.

52. Gai, "Afganistan: kak eto bylo," *Vecherniaia Moskva*, September 16, 1989, 4.

53. Author's interview with Turdibay Shadmonov, Tashkent, May 21–22, 2014.

54. A. Gromyko, I. Andropov, D. Ustinov. and V. Zagliadin to Politburo, April 7, 1980. *CWIHP Bulletin*, 8–9, 170–172.

55. "Informatsiia iz Kabula" (Information from Kabul), *Pravda*, June 22, 1980, 4; "Stavka na napriazhennost" (Counting on tension), *Pravda*, June 25, 5; and "Kliuch k politicheskomy uregulirovaniiu" (Key to a political settlement), *Pravda*, July 2, 1980, 4. For the decision to send some units home, see Chapter 4.

56. Gai and Snegirev, *Vtorzhenie*, 148. Two tactical missile divisions had been withdrawn in February. A. Volkov, "40-ia armiia—Istoriia sozdaniia, sostava, izmeneniia struktury" (The 40th Army—History of its formation, composition and changes of structure), http://old.old.rsva-ural.ru.

57. Rubtsov, "Sovetskii Soiuz v 'Neob"iavlennoi' voine v Afganistane, 139.

58. Krakhmalov, *Zapiski voennogo attashe*, 242.

59. Ivan Radikov of St. Petersburg European University to the author, October 7, 2017.

60. See the description of "this inglorious war" of one colonel who fought in Afghanistan from early 1980 to the end of 1981. Chernyshev, "I raniat nas oskolki toi voiny . . . " 43. Also see Chapter 3.

61. "Afganistan: podvodia itogi" (Afghanistan: Summing up), *Ogonek*, no. 12, March 1989, 7–8.

62. Maiorov, *Pravda ob afganskoi voine*, 9.

63. Mitrokhin, *The KGB in Afghanistan*, 116.

64. Blank, "Imagining Afghanistan: Lessons of a 'Small' War," 469.

65. "Afghanistan under the Soviets: Five Years," *Department of State Bulletin* (*DSB*; January 1985), 43. Rodric Braithwaite, *Afgantsy*, 234, agrees that the Soviets "seem to have used some kind of tear gas . . . but reports of the systematic use of lethal gases were never verified."

66. RFE/RL 12/82.

67. Maiorov, *Pravda ob afganskoi voine*, 219. This was CGS Ogarkov's reply to remonstrations by the chief military adviser in Kabul that the Hague Convention prohibited these bombs.

68. Report of senior officers to Ustinov, the first signature being that of Army General Maiorov. May 10, 1981. *CWIHP Toward an International History*, 232.

69. Ol'shanskii, "'Afganskii sindrom,'" 13. Ol'shanskii served in Kabul from 1985 to 1987 on behalf of the CPSU as head of the PDPA Institute for Social Sciences.

70. Sarin and Dvoretsky, *Afghan Syndrome*, 111. By late 1980, these advisers, according to Braithwaite, *Afgantsy*, 150, numbered 1,600 to 1,800, 60 to 80 of them generals. Advisers served in forty-seven garrisons of the PDPA Army; battalions might have three or four advisers, brigades, five or six, and divisions eleven to fifteen. Oliker, *Building Afghanistan's Security Forces in Wartime: The Soviet Experience*, 43.

71. Krakhmalov, *Zapiski voennogo attashe*, 277.

72. Laruelle and Rakisheva, eds., *Interv'iu s voinami internatsionalistami afganskoi voiny*, 135.

73. Gai, "Afganistan: kak eto bylo," *Vecherniaia Moskva*, October 30, 1989, 4.

74. *CWIHP Toward an International History*, 214–219, quoting from Liakhovskii, *Tragediia i doblest'*. For the plan, see ibid., appendix 3.

75. Grau, *The Bear Went Over the Mountain*, 7–8.

76. Ibid., 101.

77. McMichael, "Soviet Tactical Performance and Adaptation in Afghanistan," 80–82.

78. Maiorov, *Pravda ob afganskoi voine*, 60–65, 266.

79. Kvachkov, *Spetsnaz Rossii*, 96.

80. I have put this in parentheses only because it is extraneous to the topic of the book, not because it was a minor effect of the war.

81. "Moi pobeg—zaplanirovannaia sluchainost,'" *Posev*, no. 12 (1986), 12. For the hostility of the population, see also Chapter 3.

82. Alexievich, *Zinky Boys*, 88, 156.

83. Mitrokhin, *The KGB in Afghanistan*, 118–121.

84. Krakhmalov, *Zapiski voennogo attashe*, 285, 306.

85. Gai, "Afganistan: kak eto bylo," *Vecherniaia Moskva*, October 30, 1989, 4.

86. Leading Afghans told Maiorov that no foreigner could conquer Afghanistan (although it could be bought). He noted that the Muslim committees and the opposition controlled 60% to 65% of the country. Maiorov, *Pravda ob afganskoi voine*, 235, 241.

87. Gai and Snegirev, *Vtorzhenie*, 202–206; Braithwaite, *Afgantsy*, 239–241.

88. I. Shchedrov to the CC CPSU, November 12, 1981, from the Center for Preservation of Contemporary Documentation, Moscow, fond 5, opis 84, delo 855 (translated by Svetlana Savranskaya, National Security Archive).

89. Safronov, "Kak eto bylo," 68.

90. "Kak prinimalos' reshenie," *VIZh*, no. 7 (1991), 45.

91. Galeotti, *Afghanistan*, 199–200. Blank, "Imagining Afghanistan," 474–475, enlarges on what he considers an unprecedented feat: running a war involving the projection and maintenance of a 100,000-man force by satellite communication.

92. A British war photographer saw Soviet companies and platoons signaling each other with flags, "thereby betraying their positions." Lieven, *Chechnya: Tombstone of Russian Power*, 277.

93. Lapshin, *Afganskii dnevnik*, 104.

94. Kline, "The Conceding of Afghanistan," 132.

95. Sarin and Dvoretsky, *The Afghan Syndrome*, 94, 104.

96. Gai and Snegirev, *Vtorzhenie*, 259–260.

97. "Mesto sluzhby: Afganistan" (Duty station: Afghanistan), *Voennye znaniia*, no. 3 (1981), 4–5, quoted in Peter Kruzhin, "*Voennye znaniia*,. reports on the conditions that the Soviet troops experienced in Afghanistan." RL 176/812, April 23, 1981, 2–3.

98. Grau, *The Soviet-Afghan War*, 43.

99. Sarin and Dvoretsky, *The Afghan Syndrome*, 100, 107.

100. Grau, *The Bear Went Over the Mountain*, 52.

101. Blank, "Imagining Afghanistan," 474.

102. Bocharov, *Russian Roulette*, 32.

103. Girardet, "Russia's War in Afghanistan," 85, 92–97. Girardet probably wrote this in 1983 or 1984.

104. Grau, *The Bear Went Over the Mountain*.

105. Grau, "The Soviet-Afghan War," 141.

106. Galeotti, *Afghanistan*, 197–198.

107. Bocharov, *Russian Roulette*, 35–36.

108. Quoted in Göransson, "At the Service of the State," 100.

109. E.g., Gai, "Kak eto bylo," *Vecherniaia Moskva*, September 16, 1989, 4.

110. McMichael, "Soviet Tactical Performance and Adaptation in Afghanistan," 84–91.

111. Gromov, *Ogranichennyi kontingent*, 273.

112. Alexiev and Wimbush, *Ethnic Minorities in the Red Army*, 245–246.

113. Grau, *The Bear Went Over the Mountain*, xix.

114. Galeotti, *Afghanistan*, 17–18. On November 14, 1984, U.S. UN Ambassador Jeanne Kirkpatrick accused the Soviet Union of "using—for the first time since World War II—high-saturation bombing from airplanes based in the Soviet Union." *DSB* (January 1985), 46.

115. *CWIHP Toward an International History*, 266—269, from Liakhovskii, *Tragediia i doblest'*, 242–245.

116. Sokolov report, June 1984. *CWIHP Bulletin*, issue 14–15, 249–250, from Liakhovskii, *Plamia afgana*, 284–285.

117. Report, September 22, 1984. *CWIHP Toward an International History*, 262–264, from Liakhovskii, *Tragediia i doblest'*, 285–288.

118. "Afganistan: podvodia itogi," *Ogonek*, no. 12 (March 1989), 30.

119. Grau, "The Soviet-Afghan War," 135, 139.

120. Allan and Stahel, "Tribal Guerrilla Warfare against a Colonial Power," 603.

121. Drew Middleton, "Russians in Afghanistan: Changes in Tactics," *New York Times*, November 3, 1985, 20–21.

122. Grau, *The Bear Went Over the Mountain*, 122–123.

123. Blank, "Imagining Afghanistan," 379.

124. Kiianenko, "Boevoe primenenie VVS v Respublike Afganistan," 23–28.

125. Gromov, *Ograniochennyi kontingent*, 267.

126. Grau, *The Bear Went Over the Mountain*, passim, especially 100–101, 139, and McMichael, "Soviet Tactical Performance and Adaptation in Afghanistan," 98.

127. Kalinovsky, *A Long Goodbye*, 38–39, especially n. 87.

128. Shebarshin, *Ruka Moskvy*, 111–112.

129. *CWIHP Toward an International History*, 270, from Liakhovskii, *Tragediia i doblest'*, 289.

130. Liakhovskii, *Tragediia i doblest'*, 291, 294.

131. Gromov, *Ogranichennyi kontingent*, 175, 218.

132. Krakhmalov, *Zapiski voennogo attashe*, 299.

133. Varennikov, "Afganskaia epopeia"; see also "Afganistan: podvodia itogi," 7–8. I found no corroboration of a pullout at this time.

134. Gromov, *Ogranichennyi kontingent*, 175. This GS group, comprising five officers, which Gromov headed until April 1986, operated in Afghanistan in addition to the MoD Operations Group. MoD document reproduced in Liakhovskii, *Tragediia i doblest'*, 89.

135. The Russian Wikipedia attributes this testimony to afganets Colonel V. M. Chizhikov, but gives no reference.

136. Zdaniuk, "Ukhodim bez boia, no s poteriami," 3–4. The exchange with Yazov probably occurred when he was deputy DM, for he became minister the same month that Dubynin left Afghanistan.

137. Gromov, *Ogranichennyi kontingent*, 174.

138. USIS Official Text, December 19, 1985. (Actually, Soviet losses were reportedly down from 1984.)

139. Edward Girardet, "Afghanistan: Soviets get tougher," *Christian Science Monitor*, December 27, 1985 (reprinted USIA Addendum, AD857, January 3, 1986).

140. Laruelle and Rakisheva, , eds., *Interv'iu s voinami internatsionalistami afganskoi voiny*, 363.

141. Blank, "Imagining Afghanistan," 478–479.

142. See the CPSU CC greeting to the returning soldiers: "Voinam internatsionalistam vozvrashchiushchikhsia iz Demokraticheskoi Respubliki Afganistana" (To the internationalist fighting men returning from the Democratic Republic of Afghanistan), *Pravda*, October 14, 1986, 1.

143. "V Ministerstve oborony SSSR (In the USSR Ministry of Defense), *Pravda*, November 6, 1986, 2. (Braithwaite, *Afgantsy*, 14, gives the number of troops withdrawn in 1986 as 15,000, but this seems to be erroneous.)

144. "Konstruktivnyi shag," *Pravda*, October 10, 1986, 5.

145. "Kak prinimalos' reshenie," 51.

146. Report, April 20, 1987. *CWIHP Toward an International History*, 308, from Liakhovskii, *Tragediia i doblest'*, 252.

147. Kiianenko, "Boevoe primenenie VVS v Respublike Afganistan," 25.

148. In the first attack, on March 8, the border settlement of Pyanj was shelled, and in the second, on April 8 and 9, Moskovskii (between Pyanj and Kulyab), See Roy, *The New Central Asia*, 154; Borovik, *The Hidden War*, 42–43. TASS acknowledged both attacks. "Zaiavlenie TASS" (TASS statement), *Izvestiia*, April 22, 1987, 4.

149. Kalinovsky, *A Long Goodbye*, 43.

150. Laruelle and Rakisheva, , eds., *Interv'iu s voinami internatsionalistami afganskoi voiny*, 372, and Bill Keller, "Home from Afghanistan; Russia's Divisive War," *New York Times Magazine*, February 14, 1988.

151. "Tiazhelye boi" (Heavy fighting), *Posev*, no. 6 (1983), 16. See also Alexiev and Wimbush, *Ethnic Minorities in the Red Army* 250.

152. Najibullah reckoned that seeking to solve all problems by military means would entail a struggle of twenty to thirty years. Memorandum of KGB Chairman Viktor Chebrikov, Foreign Minister Eduard Shevarnadze, Defense Minister Sergei Sokolov, and CPSU CC Secretary for International Relations Anatoly Dobrynin to Politburo, November 13, 1986; *CWIHP Bulletin*, issue 14–15, 250–252.

153. Gromov, *Ogranichennyi kontingent*, 254, 258.

154. Ivanov, "Generalom stal na voine," 27.

155. Borovik, *The Hidden War*, 245.

156. "Afganistan: podvodia itogi," *Ogonek*, no. 12 (March 1989), 30.

157. Varennikov's proposals for the way the Afghans should use their forces after the Soviet withdrawal—*CWIHP Bulletin*, 14/15, 258–259, from Liakhovskii, *Pliama afgana*, 407–409.

158. "Afganistan: podvodia itogi," *Ogonek*, no. 12 (March 1989), 30.

159. Gromov, *Ogranichennyi kontingent*, 298–305, and "Zashchishchali, obuchali, stroili," 11. See also Sarin and Dvoretsky, *Afghan Syndrome*, 109–110.

160. Gai and Snegirev, *Vtorzhenie*, 268.

161. Grau, *The Bear Went Over the Mountain*, 74–75.

162. The accords comprised bilateral agreements between the governments of Afghanistan and Pakistan and a "Declaration" that the U.S. and the Soviet Union signed as guarantors of the agreements. For the Accords, see Klass, "Afghanistan: The Accords."

163. "Afganistan: podvodia itogi," *Ogonek*, no. 12 (March 1989), 30.

164. A. Gorokhov, B. Kotov, and V. Okulov, "Den' nadezhd i trevog" (Day of hopes and anxieties), *Pravda*, May 15, 1988, 1, 6. The MoD commission that summed up the war spoke of 25 garrisons. "Kak prinimalos' reshenie," *VIZh*, no. 7 (1991), 52.

165. Borovik, *The Hidden War*, 235; see also V. Izgarshev and V. Okulov, "Zastava smeniaet karaul" (The outpost relieves the guard), *Pravda*, January 18, 1989, 6.

166. *CWIHP Toward an International History*, 380—382, from Liakhovskii, *Tragediia i doblest'*, 384–385.

167. *CWIHP Bulletin*, 14/15, 260–264, from Liakhovskii, *Pliama afgana*, 450–452, 485–486.

168. For the operation and its background, see "Shevarnadze: 'Voennye byli pravy' (The military were right), *Sovershenno sekretno*, no. 9 (1992), 2–4; Braithwaite, *Afgantsy*, 284–290, and Kalinovsky, *A Long Goodbye*, 167–169; and Chapter 4.

169. Russian TV, January 28, 1992—FBIS-SOV-92–024, quoted in Mendelson, *Changing Course*, 121.

170. TASS, "From the USSR Ministry of Foreign Affairs Press Center," CDSP XL:35 (1988), 19.

171. Douglas Clarke, "Soviets Reported to Be Using New Type of Bomb," RFE/RAD Background Report/109, June 16, 1988. (The Americans had used FAE5s in Vietnam – ibid.) And Russian TV, January 28, 1992 – FBIS-SOV-92-024, quoted in Mendelson, *Changing Course*, 121.

172. *CWIHP Toward an International History*, 444, from Liakhovskii, *Pliama afgana*, 455–456.

173. Ibid., 482, from Liakhovskii, *Pliama afgana*, 543.

174. See, for example, Okulov and P. Studenikin, "Opalennye Kandagarom" (Singed by Kandahar), *Pravda*, August 10, 1988, 6; and Braithwaite, *Afgantsy*, 290–291.

175. CWIHP Toward an International History, 514–518, from Liakhovskii, *Tragediia i doblest'*, Appendix 11.

176. "Press-Konferentsiia E. A. Shevarnadze" (E. A. Shevarnadze press conference), *Pravda*, April 15, 1988, 6.

177. Gromov, *Ogranichennyi kontingent*, 334, and the film *Poslednyi soldat* (The last soldier; 2004). Gromov had made a similar statement at the Nineteenth CPSU Conference in June 1988. "XIX vsesoiuznaia konferentsiia KPSS" (The Nineteenth All-Union CPSU Conference), *Pravda*, July 2, 1988, 7.

178. Report on interview with Tsagolov, "The Politicians Lost the War," *Argumenty i fakty*, September 30–October 6, 1989, 4–5; FBIS-SOV-89–193, October 6, 1989, 16–18.

179. Rubtsov, "Sovetskii Soiuz v 'neob"iavlennoi' voine v Afganistane, 141.

180. Pardaev, *Afganskaia komandirovka*, 75, 416. *Shuravi* is a literal translation of "Soviets."

181. Krakhmalov, *Zapiski voennogo attashe*, 242, 305.

182. V. Cherkasov, "'Afgan' nachinalsia tak . . . ," 6.

183. "Kak prinimalos' reshenie," *VIZh*, no. 7 (1991), 44.

184. "The Intervention in Afghanistan," 194, 213–214, 232.

185. Lyakhovskiy, *Inside the Soviet Invasion of Afghanistan*, 25, 29.

186. "Kak prinimalos' reshenie," 46, 49.

187. Grau, *The Bear Went Over the Mountain*, 204–205.

188. Galeotti, *Afghanistan*, 193.

189. Altogether, during the course of the war, the Soviets lost 118 planes and 333 helicopters. G. Krivosheev, ed., *Rossiia i SSSR v voinakh XX veka*, 540.

190. Galeotti, *Afghanistan*, 194–197. Both Kalinovsky—*A Long Goodbye*, 43—and Galeotti discredit claims that the Stingers changed the war's course.

191. Liakhovskii and Zabrodin, *Tainy afganskoi voiny*, 214. For the development of carpet bombing toward the war's end, see Chapter 9, n. 158.

192. Krakhmalov, *Zaapiski voennogo attashe*, 302–303.

193. Gromov, "Zashchishchali, obuchali, stroili," 11–15.

194. "Kak prinimalos' reshenie," 52.

195. Borovik, *The Hidden War*, 247–249.

196. Safronov, "Kak eto bylo," 71.

197. This negligence seems to have held for the United States as well, with change occurring only after 9/11 and the 2003 intervention in Iraq. Jones and Smith, "Whose Hearts and Whose Minds? The Curious Case of Global Counter-Insurgency," 84–85.

198. Galula, *Counterinsurgency Warfare: Theory and Practice*.

Chapter 3

1. The term *limited contingent* had also been used for the force that invaded Czechoslovakia in 1968.

2. Krivosheev, ed., *Rossiia i SSSR v voinakh XX veka*, 535. David Glantz in his introduction to Grau, *The Bear Went Over the Mountain*, xiv, basing himself on Liakhovskii, *Tragediia i doblest'*, gives the figure as 642,000.

3. Former political adviser to the PDPA CC Dmitrii Ol'shanskii, "Afganskii sled" (Vestiges of Afghanistan), *Rossiia* no. 8 (67), February 19–25, 1992.

4. Meeting with workers in Irkutsk—Moscow TV, May 14, 1989—FBIS-SOV-89-092, May 15, 1989, 59.

5. For example, Ivanov, "Ogranichennyi kontingent," *Sovetskii voin*, no. 10 (1991), 13; Fane, "After Afghanistan: The Decline of Soviet Military Prestige," 15, n. 1; and afganets member of the Congress of People's Deputies V. V. Yakushin. Third session of the USSR Supreme Soviet, *Izvestiia*, CDSP XLII:7, 6.

6. Kalinovsky, *A Long Goodbye*.

7. Krakhmalov, *Zapiski voennogo attashet*, 242. Gromov, *Ogranichennyi kontingent*, 254, says that the force was at its largest in 1987: 120,000. An Afghan source claims that the Fortieth Army reached a peak of 150,000 in 1985, with another 30,000 situated "along the border," "used for making attacks inside Afghanistan"—Es'haq, "The Present Situation in Afghanistan, 119. (Es'haq was adviser to mujahid commander Ahmed Shah Massoud.) Rofi Pardaev also gives this figure. *Afganskaia komandirovka*, 62. Pardaev claims there were 85,000 Soviet soldiers in Afghanistan as early as February 1980, their number escalating to 135,000 by early 1984 and to 150,000 in 1985. One Western source also speaks of 30,000 to 40,000 troops deployed in bases in Central Asia for special operations in Afghanistan. Girardet, *Afghanistan: The Soviet War*, 33.

8. "Kak prinimalos' reshenie" (How the decision was made), *VIZh*, no. 7 (1991), 43. Krivosheev, *Rossiia i SSSR v voinakh XX veka*, 536, speaks of up to 104,000 plus 5,000 to 7,000 civilians.

9. Excerpt from Politburo meeting, April 1, 1988, https://nsarchive2.gwu.edu/rus/text_files/Afganistan/, accessed January 10, 2017. CGS Akhromeev testified that when the Soviet troop withdrawal began on May 15, 1988, there were 100,300 Soviet soldiers in that country. TASS,

"Vremia konstruktivnykh reshenii" (Time of constructive decisions), *Pravda*, May 27, 1988, 7; another source, "Kak prinimalos' reshenie," 52, says 106,000.

10. Galeotti, *Afghanistan: The Soviet Union's Last War*, 30. For the committee, see Chapters 8 and 10.

11. Gromov, *Ogranichennyi kontingent*, 128.

12. Lyakhovskiy, *Inside the Soviet Invasion*, 39, and *Tragediia i doblest'*, 90.

13. "Kak prinimalos' reshenie," 43. According to Pardaev, *Afganskaia komandirovka*, 62 to 75 percent comprised the fighting force and 25 percent the rear units and military advisers of the DRA army.

14. Pardaev, *Afganskaia komandirovka*, 63. A NATO estimate in 1986 gave a slightly different composition, noting the 103rd Guards Airborne division, the 201st Motor Rifle division, an air assault brigade, two helicopter attack regiments, two helicopter transport regiments, three motorized rifle regiments and a rocket launcher regiment, comprising together 80,000 of the estimated 120,000-strong force. *The Sustainability of the Soviet Army in Battle*, 406.

15. A motor-rifle regiment, for instance, should have 2,315 men; a battalion, 455; a company, 103; and a platoon, 28.

16. Grau, *The Bear Went Over the Mountain*, 76.

17. Gromov, *Ogranichennyi kontingent*, 157.

18. Author's interview with Turdibay Shadmonov, Tashkent, May 21–22, 2014.

19. Krivosheev, ed., *Rossiia i SSSR v voinakh XX veka*, 539. The figure was highest between May 1985 and December 1986, when it reached a 5,743 average.

20. Author's interview with Turdibay Shadmonov.

21. Pardaev, *Afganskaia komandirovka*, 62, says the killed, wounded, and discharged were replenished from the approximately 50,000 troops in reserve in the Turkestan MD.

22. For life in the Soviet armed forces, see Sergei Zamascikov, "Insiders' Views of the Soviet Army," *Problems of Communism* 37 (1988), 110–116, reviewing three books on Soviet army life. Galeotti, *Afghanistan*, 35, writes, "Since 1976 dysentery, hepatitis, and other infectious intestinal disorders had been an increasingly common aspect of [Soviet] conscript life, due to improper refuse disposal, inadequate sewage, sloppy food handling and contaminated water." Hunger was "a feature of army life."

23. The climate undoubtedly took a heavy toll on the health and well-being of the soldiers. Gai and Snegirev, *Vtorzhenie*, 258–259.

24. Pavlov, "Byt soldat afganskoi voiny v 1979–1989 gg., 12.

25. Bocharov, *Russian Roulette*, 9.

26. Pavlov, "Byt soldat," 13.

27. Alexievich, *Zinky Boys*, 20.

28. According to one testimony, the soldiers' uniforms made them easy targets for the opposition. Greshnov, *Afganistan: zalozhniki vremeni*. Greshnov says it was manifest early on that the intervention had not been properly prepared; nobody had considered what the troops were to eat and drink, where they were to sleep, and with what they would fight.

29. Alexievich, *Zinky Boys*, 168.

30. Ibid., 49; Galeotti, *Afghanistan*, 192–193.

31. For example, Borovik, *The Hidden War*, 157–158.

32. Alexievich, *Zinky Boys*, 121, 169.

33. Gai and Snegirev, *Vtorzhenie*, 267–268.

34. Alexievich, *Zinky Boys*, 120–121.

35. M. Bektasov, "Homeland is More Precious than Life," *Turkmenskaia iskra*, February 19, 1989—JPRS-UPA-89-038, 100–102.

36. Alexievich, *Zinky Boys*, 169.

37. This was a fixed question in the questionnaire to the 71 afgantsy interviewed for Laruelle and Rakisheva, (eds.), *Interv'iu s voinami internatsionalistami afganskoi voiny*. Very few respondents gave unequivocally positive replies.

38. See, for example, Bocharov, *Russian Roulette*, 30, 33; Iu. Ivanov, "Kogda prikhodit pochta polevaia" (When the field post arrives), *Komsomolets Uzbekistana*, January 14, 1989.

39. See, for example, Pavlov, "Byt soldat," 18.

40. For the central role of mail and newspapers, and the shooting down of one plane carrying post, see Iu. Ivanov, "Kogda prikhodit pochta polevaia," *Komsomolets Uzbekistana*, January 14, 1989.

41. V. Skrizhalin, "Our Sons Are Serving There," *Krasnaia zvezda*, January 9, 1983, 1, translated in CDSP XXXV:9, 2.

42. Konnov, "Pravda i vymysel ob afganskoi voine," 52.

43. Galeotti, *Afghanistan*, 37–39.

44. Gai and Snegirev, *Vtorzhenie*, 270–271.

45. Braithwaite, *Afgantsy*, 85, and Rubtsov, "Sovetskii Soiuz," 140. Colonel General Sultan Magometov, who filled this post at the time of the invasion (see Chapter 1), was followed in turn by Army Generals A. M. Maiorov, M. I. Sorokin, and G. I. Salimanov, and Colonel Generals V. A. Vostrov and M. M. Sotskov.

46. David Gai, "Afganistan: kak eto bylo" (Afghanistan: How it was), *Vecherniaia Moskva*, October 30, 1989, 4.

47. Lyakhovskiy, *Inside the Soviet Invasion*, 34–35; Vasiliy Mitrokhin, *The KGB in Afghanistan*, 118.

48. Gai and Snegirev, *Vtorzhenie*, 90.

49. "The Sustainability of the Soviet Army in Battle," 407.

50. Grau, *The Bear Went Over the Mountain*, 207.

51. Alexievich, *Zinky Boys*, 44.

52. Galeotti, *Afghanistan*, 171–172.

53. Aleksandr Prokhanov, "Zapiski na brone" (Notes on an armored personnel carrier), *Literaturnaia gazeta*, August 28, 1985, 14.

54. According to some sources, Mikhail Zaitsev was also commander of the Fortieth Army sometime in 1985, but this seems erroneous. He was commander of the Southern Direction of the Soviet Armed Forces as of 1985, so the Fortieth Army fell under his jurisdiction.

55. Verstakov, *Afganskii dnevnik*, 172–174. For earlier campaigns in the Panjshir, see Chapter 2.

56. Braithwaite, *Afgantsy*, 124–125.

57. Author's interview with three afgantsy, Tashkent, June 26, 1991.

58. Bocharov, *Russian Roulette*, 139–147.

59. Iu. Chernyshev, "I raniat nas oskolki toi voiny . . . " (And splinters from that war are wounding us . . .), *Armiia*, no. 21, November 1991, 42.

60. Gromov, *Ogranichennyi kontingent*, 271.

61. Ibid., 266–267. On reporting misinformation, see Chapter 2.

62. See, for example, Protasov, "Po dolgu internatsionalistov."

63. Alexievich, *Zinky Boys*, 49.

64. Odom, *The Collapse of the Soviet Military*, 248.

65. Borovik, *The Hidden War*, 157–160.

66. Report on interview with Kim Tsagolov, "Afganistan, voinu proigrali politiki" (Afghanistan, the politicians lost the war), *Argumenty i fakty*, September 30–October 6, 1989, 4–5.

67. Jones, *Red Army and Society*, 85–88.

68. Galeotti, *Afghanistan*, 187–188.

69. Braithwaite, *Afgantsy*, 126.

70. Liakhovskii, *Tragediia i doblest'*, 291–295 quoted in Odom, *The Collapse of the Soviet Military*, 250, 442 n. 51.

71. Tkachenko, *Afganistan bolit v moei dushe*, 229.

72. Sarin and Dvoretsky, *The Afghan Syndrome*, 104.

73. Pavlov, "Byt soldat," 9.

74. Cherkasov, "'Afgan' nachinalsia tak," 7.

75. Tkachenko, *Afganistan bolit v moei dushe*, 29.

76. Odom, *The Collapse of the Soviet Military*, 248.

77. Alexievich, *Zinky Boys*, 41.

78. "Iz doklada dlia razvedki SShA," *Pobratim*, no. 9 (1990), 4.

79. Laruelle and Rakisheva, , eds., *Interv'iu s voinami internatsionalistami afganskoi voiny*, 170.

80. Verstakov, "Afganskii dnevnik," *Sovetskii voin*, no. 16 (August 1990), 20.

81. Pashkevich, *Afganistan: voina glazama kombata*, 3–4, 27–29.

82. Grau, *The Bear Went Over the Mountain*, 138–139.

83. Jones, *Red Army and Society*, 95–96.

84. Galeotti, *Afghanistan*, 200–202.

85. Alexievich, *Zinky Boys*, 45.

86. Laruelle and Rakisheva, eds., *Interv'iu s voinami internatsionalistami afganskoi voiny*, 280.

87. Braithwaite, *Afgantsy*, 134.

88. Alexievich, *Zinky Boys*, 70.

89. Sarin and Dvoretsky, *The Afghan Syndrome*, 92–93.

90. V. Filatov, "Eto nashi rebiata" (These are our boys), *Krasnaia zvezda*, May 30, 1987 (quoted in Alexiev, *Inside the Soviet Army in Afghanistan*, 10). According to Odom, criminals were recruited to the Fortieth Army "either in lieu of jail terms or after being released from prison." Odom, *The Collapse of the Soviet Military*, 247. For stories of officers and soldiers sent to Afghanistan as a means of punishment or retribution, see "Afganskie zarisovki" (Afghan sketches), *Posev*, no. 3 (1985), 27.

91. See G. Krivosheev, "O vseobshchennosti voinskoi sluzhby" (Universality of military service), *Krasnaia zvezda*, August 31, 1989, 2. According to one such person, the reason was the lack of potential conscripts given the particularly low birth rate in the 1960s—the outcome, in turn, of the birth deficit during the Great Patriotic War. Interview with Vadim Altskan, Jerusalem, June 2014.

92. "XIX konferentsiia KPSS. Vystuplenie tovarishcha Gromova B. V." (19th Party Conference. Speech of B. V. Gromov), *Pravda*, July 2, 1988, 7.

93. For a searing critique of the Soviet health situation, see Feshbach and Friendly, *Ecocide in the USSR.*

94. Exceptions to the rule persisted throughout the war. One soldier went to Afghanistan in 1985 with only six weeks of military training.

95. Sarin and Dvoretsky, *The Afghan Syndrome*, 92–93. For a vivid account of the grueling experiences of the recruits as they were thrown into combat, see Bocharov, *Russian Roulette*, 20–24.

96. Sarin and Dvoretsky, *The Afghan Syndrome*, 88–90.

97. Alexievich, *Zinky Boys*, 22–23.

98. Gai, "Afganistan: kak eto bylo," *Vecherniaia Moskva*, September 12, 13, 1989, 4.

99. Bocharov, *Russian Roulette*, 34.

100. Ibid., 137–138.

101. Gai and Snegirev, *Vtorzhenie*, 288, and below.

102. According to some sources, women accounted for 70 percent of nurses, dentists, and doctors in the medical brigades. Tkachenko, *Afganistan bolit*, 39. For an article devoted to these women medics, see A. Gorokhov and V. Okulov, "Fel'dsher batal'ona" (The battalion paramedic), *Pravda*, October 28, 1988, 8.

103. V. Okulov, "Afganistan zhivet v moei dushe" (Afghanistan lives in my soul), *Pravda*, February 3, 1988, 6, quoted in Swartz, "The Soviet-Afghan War in Russian Literature," 99.

104. Alexievich, *Zinky Boys*, 24, 184–185.

105. Ibid., , 134, 149, 151–155. A Kazakh nurse tells a similar story, Laruelle and Rakisheva, eds., *Interv'iu s voinami internatsionalistami afganskoi voiny*, 118.

106. Alexievich, *Zinky Boys*, 73.

107. Pinnick, "When the Fighting Is Over: The Soldiers' Mothers and the Afghan Madonnas," 150, 152.

108. Alexievich, *Zinky Boys*, 138.

109. Galeotti, *Afghanistan*, 40–41.

110. Gai and Snegirev, *Vtorzhenie*, 279–290.

111. Ibid., 285. One broadcast for soldiers entitled "I serve the Soviet Union" noted that the Fortieth Army suffered more losses from sickness than from military operations. "Iz doklada dlia razvedki SShA" (From a report for U.S. Intelligence), *Pobratim*, no. 9 (1990), 4.

112. Borovik, *The Hidden War*, 136. For a poem about the medics in Afghanistan, see Verstakov, "Afganskii dnevnik," *Sovetskii voin*, no. 16 (August 1990), 18–19.

113. Zubar'ev, "Organizatsiia khirurgicheskoi pomoshchi i reabilitatsiia ranenykh," 18–22.

114. Alexievich, *Zinky Boys*, 21–25.

115. Galeotti, *Afghanistan*, 67.

116. Feshbach and Friendly, *Ecocide in the USSR*, 169.

117. Alexievich, *Zinky Boys*, 48.

118. Borovik, *The Hidden War*, 134–135.

119. Author's interview with Turdibay Shadmonov.

120. Bocharov, *Russian Roulette*, 87–103.

121. Galeotti, *Afghanistan*, 202–203.

122. Grau, *The Bear Went Over the Mountain*, 196.

123. Verstako, "Afganskii dnevnik," *Sovetskii voin*, no. 15 (1990), 17.

124. Gai and Snegirev, *Vtorzhenie*, 271–274.

125. RFE/RL 12/82.

126. E.g., "My vypolnili svoi dolg . . . " (We fulfilled our duty . . .), *Podvig*, Vypusk (Issue) 34, 1989, 13.

127. Mikhail Reshetnikov, rector of the East European Institute for Psychoanalysis in St. Petersburg, interview to the news site Rosblat, http://www.rosbalt.ru/piter/2009/02/14/618431.html, accessed April 12, 2015.

128. *Kniga pamiati*, http://www.rsva-ural.ru/library/mbook.php?id=364, accessed June 3, 2015. Reshetnikov's report to the General Staff said 70 percent were sons of workers and farmers and 20 percent sons of junior white-collar workers. An officer who fought in Afghanistan, apparently in the mid-1980s, testified similarly. "My vypolnili svoi dolg . . . " *Podvig*, issue 34 (1989), 13.

129. Galeotti, *Afghanistan*, 29–30, 228.

130. "My vypolnili svoi dolg . . . ," *Podvig*, issue 34, 1989, 13.

131. Borovik, *The Hidden War*, 84.

132. Alexievich, *Zinky Boys*, 44.

133. Gromov, *Ogranichennyi kontingent*, 286.

134. Daugherty, "Ethnic Minorities in the Soviet Armed Forces," 168.

135. Gromov, *Ogranichennyi kontingent*, 284; Sarin and Dvoretsky, *The Afghan Syndrome*, 88; Rubtsov, "Sovetskii Soiuz," 140.

136. For Mikhail Reshetnikov's report, see above.

137. Jones, *Red Army and Society*, 195, 207 n. 73.

138. Gromov, *Ogranichennyi kontingent*, 284.

139. For the breakdown of casualties according to nationality, see Krivosheev, *Rossiia i SSSR v voinakh XX veka*, 536, 538.

140. Speech by G. A. Borovik at the Nineteenth Party Conference, *Pravda*, July 2, 1988, 3.

141. Author's interview with Turdibay Shadmonov.

142. Artem Borovik, *Afganistan. Eshche raz pro voinu*, 149.

143. Daugherty, "Ethnic Minorities in the Soviet Armed forces," 175.

144. Belarussian afganets Pavel Shet'ko too insisted at the Congress of People's Deputies that there was complete fraternity among the troops, quoted in V. Izgarshev, "Afganskaia bol'" (Afghan pain), *Pravda*, August 27, 1989, 6.

145. "Hazing on trial," *Izvestiia*, August 9, 1990, 6, CDSP XLII:32, 24.

146. Cherniaev Diary, NSA, August 27, 1985, quoted in Kalinovsky, *A Long Goodbye*, 49. Cherniaev read about this in a CPSU CC Secretariat protocol.

147. Tkachenko, *Dorogie moi . . .*:, 195. Almost certainly *Uzbek* here is a generic term for all Central Asians or even Muslims.

148. Quoted in Szayna, *The Ethnic Factor in the Soviet Armed Forces*, 44.

149. Interview with Evgenii Krasnik, Carmiel (Israel), n.d.

150. "Samizdatskoe interv'iu" (Samizdat interview), *Posev*, no. 5 (1985), 11.

151. For example, one infantry soldier. Interview with Oleg Rybak, Carmiel (Israel), n.d.

152. For instance, the speech at the All-Army Conference in the Kremlin of Komsomol secretaries of a Fortieth Army reconnaissance company secretary. "Rodine—nash ratnyi trud" (To the mother country—our martial labor), *Krasnaia zvezda*, May 29, 1984, 4.

153. The low morale in the Fortieth Army contrasted dramatically with the high morale of the Afghan opposition. As one afganets testified, ten mujahidin were equal to fifty Soviet soldiers. Laruelle and Rakisheva, eds., *Interv'iu s voinami internatsionalistami afganskoi voiny*, 325.

154. E.g., in units totally irrelevant to the situation—interview with David Feierman, Kfar Sava, Israel, June 26, 2016. He served from February to September 1980 in an antiaircraft unit whose soldiers had no idea why they were in Afghanistan because the opposition had no aircraft.

155. In the words of one of them, that "tomorrow his bunk might be empty." Laura Tsagolova, "Snova snitsia voina" (Dreaming of the war once again), *Sobesednik*, no. 3 (January 1988), 11.

156. The euphemism was designed to differentiate between the Soviet-German war and World War II and in so doing to obliterate all memory of the Soviet Union's two-year collaboration with Nazi Germany in the wake of the Molotov-Ribbentrop Pact.

157. Alexievich, *Zinky Boys*, 110, 114. For the Black Tulips, see Chapter 7.

158. *Krasnaia zvezda*, December 17, 1983, quoted in "Obostrenie vnutrennykh problem v okkupatsionnoi armii" (Exacerbation of internal problems in the occupation army), *Posev*, no. 4 (1984), 14.

159. Aleksandr Prokhanov, who dubbed the war a "war of the impoverished classes," was one of many who voiced this opinion. Miller, *Afghanistan: Changing Soviet Perspectives on Regional Conflicts*, 7

160. Bocharov, *Russian Roulette*, 110.

161. "'Afgan' nachinalsia tak . . . ," *Sovetskii voin* no. 23 (December 1989), 6–8. Gromov, *Ogranichennyi kontingent*, 115.

162. Author's interview with Turdibay Shadmonov.

163. James P. Sterba, "Russians Said Replacing Ethnic Reservists in Kabul," *International Herald Tribune*, February 4, 1980, 2.

164. Iu. Li, "'Afganskaia aventiura"? ('Afghan adventure'?), *Komsomolets Uzbekistana*, July 14, 1989.

165. Laruelle and Rakisheva, eds., *Interv'iu s voinami internatsionalistami afganskoi voiny*, 127.

166. Ibid., 53, 204.

167. Chernyaev, *My Six Years with Gorbachev*, 25.

168. Borovik, *Afganistan. Eshche raz pro voinu*, 250–251.

169. Tkachenko, *Dorogie moi* . . . , 8—9.

170. Amstutz, *The First Five Years of Soviet Occupation*, 178.

171. Krakhmalov, *Zapiski voennogo attashe*, 244.

172. Quoted Galeotti, *Afghanistan*, 141.

173. Konnov, "Pravda i vymysel ob afganskoi voine," 51.

174. Gromov testified that the command made every effort to keep soldiers from feeling cut off from events at home, providing them with newspapers and exposing them to other media. "XIX vsesoiuznaia konferentsiia KPSS" (The Nineteenth All-Union CPSU Conference), *Pravda*, July 2, 1988, 7.

175. Alexievich, *Zinky Boys*, 89; "My vypolnili svoi dolg . . . " *Podvig*, issue 34, 1989, 11. See also G. Ustiuzhanin, "'Pokhoronku' ne dognal" (He arrived after notification of his death), *Sovetskii voin*, no. 18 (September 1990), 70.

176. Borovik, *The Hidden War*, 92; *Ogonek*, no. 4 (January 1988), 12.

177. Michael Dobbs, "Ex-Soldier Takes on Powerful Foe," *Washington Post*, November 14, 1990, A1.

178. USIA Addendum AD854, January 17, 1986, quoting *Baltimore Sun*, January 10, 1986.

179. Alexievich, *Zinky Boys*, 56, 136. One vet recalled soldiers drinking unclean water in order to get sent home. Author's interview with Turdibay Shadmonov.

180. Borovik, *The Hidden War*, 54–55.

181. Ibid., 91.

182. Ibid., 56.

183. Robert Gillette, "A Brutal War Revealed in Soviet Songs," *Los Angeles Times*, April 17, 1983. The paper brings several particularly poignant samples, some of them quite lengthy.

184. Tarasov, ed., *Moskvichi iz kluba 'Dolg'*, 30–31.

185. Braithwaite, *Afgantsy*, 192.

186. Tkachenko, *Dorogie moi* . . . , 21.

187. Swartz, "The Soviet-Afghan War in Russian Literature," 114. Verstakov, *Afganskii dnevnik*, 241, heard soldiers singing "home-made" compositions already in January 1980.

188. For details of such performances, see Krakhmalov, *Zapiski voennogo attashe*, 291–298.

189. Pavlov, "Byt soldat," 17. Kobzon reportedly flew to Afghanistan at least eight times, giving concerts from morning to evening, each one a "genuine festival." Gennadii Bocharov, "Afgan," *Literaturnaia gazeta*, no. 7, February 15, 1989, 13.

190. "Pod zvezdami afganskimi" (Under Afghan stars), http://afgan.kz/vet/art.htm, accessed February 12, 2018.

191. Swartz, "The Soviet-Afghan War in Russian Literature," 244.

192. Poliakov, *Sto dnei do prikaza* (first published 1987 in *Iunost'*), 89. For hazing in the Soviet armed forces, see also Solnyshkov, "Dedovshchina: tip otnosheniia 'znachimomu drugomu.'"

193. Odom, *The Collapse of the Soviet Military*, 48.

194. Maklak, "*Dedovshchina* on Trial."

195. V. Rybakov interview with a Russian POW, "'Budu zdes' zhit', budet u menia sem' ia . . . '" ('I'll live here, I'll have a family '), *Posev*, no. 2 (1983), 18–21.

196. Odom, *The Collapse of the Soviet Military*, 287–288.

197. Alexievich, *Zinky Boys*, 50–51.

198. Ibid., 58.

199. Ibid., 116–120.

200. Nemirovskii, "Ekho afganskoi voiny," 57.

201. Borovik, *The Hidden War*, 215.

202. Rybakov, "'Budu zdes' zhit', budet u menia sem'ia . . . ,'" *Posev*, no. 2 (1983), 20.

203. Sapper, *Die Auswirkung des Afghanistan-Krieges auf die Sowjetgesellschaft*, 134. Sapper says 60 percent of all POWs, but he clearly means of those who deserted.

204. Laruelle and Rakisheva, , eds., *Interv'iu s voinami internatsionalistami afganskoi voiny*, 135, 325.

205. Nemirovskii, "Ekho afganskoi voiny," 57. One-fifth of the Krasnodar respondents and a number of Maklak's interviewees related positively to hazing as a process of attaining masculinity. Maklak, "*Dedovshchina* on Trial," 697.

206. According to one source, "Most of the troops, both officers and soldiers, sell not just ammunition and articles of MTO, but also their personal weapons. " "Iz doklada dlia razvedki SShA," *Pobratim* no. 9 (1990), 4. One of my interviewees knew NCOs (*praporshchiki*) who "sold vehicles, fuel, even weapons to regular Afghans." Interview with Turdibay Shadmonov, Tashkent.

207. Interview with the head of the Military Tribunal Directorate, *Izvestiia*, May 4, 1989, 3. FBIS-SOV-89–090, 87–90.

208. E.g., *Trud*, May 23, 1984. FBIS III, May 29, 1984, V3; *Argumenty i fakty* no. 8 (1989); "Otkuda prishli narkotiki, kotorye sozhgli pod Kabulom" (Whence came the narcotics burned near Kabul), *Komsomolets Turkmenistana*, December 5, 1989.

209. M. Slutskii, "Ne spit granitsa" (The border knows no sleep), *Komsomolets Turkmenistana*, October 26, 1989.

210. Borovik, *The Hidden War*, 185–186; see also Yuri Teplyakov, "The Other Face of the War," *Moscow News* no. 37, September 17, 1989.

211. Tkachenko, ed., *Dorogie moi* . . . , 54, 58, 62, 88, 175.

212. Alexievich, *Zinky Boys*, 183.

213. RFE/RL Daily Report no. 76, April 19, 1990, quoting *Rabochaia gazeta*, April 8, 1990. Odom, *The Collapse of the Soviet Military*, 290.

214. E.g., one soldier who arrived in 1986. *Interv'iu s voinami internatsionalistami afganskoi voiny*, 324.

215. *Kniga pamiati o sovetskikh voinakh, pogibshikh v Afganistane*, passim.

216. Liakhovskii, *Tragediia i doblest'*, accessed April 18, 2017, 205–206. CGS Ogarkov's military reform divided the Soviet Union's Theaters of Military Operations into four Directions, each covering a number of MDs. The Turkestan MD, to which the Fortieth Army was officially subordinate, was included in the Southern Direction.

217. Quoted in Behrends, "'Some Call Us Heroes," 724.

218. "Na afganskom fronte—bez peremen" (On the Afghan front—without a break), *Posev*, no. 2 (1983), 16.

219. Borovik, *The Hidden War*, 2.

220. Tkachenko, *Dorogie moi* . . . , 12, 74, 96–97, 238.

221. Ibid., 9–10.

222. Naturally, we have to take evidence drawn from deserters or captured soldiers with a grain of salt; I have used such sources only where other sources of information substantiate them.

223. USIA Addendum File no. 23, June 6, 1986, 42–43.

224. Interview with Oleg Rybak, Carmiel (Israel), n.d. Very few soldiers seem to have had such an opportunity.

225. Grau, *The Bear Went Over the Mountain*, 207.

226. Vladimir Shcherban, "Desant na karavannoi trope" (Assault on a caravan trail), *Izvestiia*, September 18, 1987, 6.

227. Borovik, *The Hidden War*, 84–85, 235.

228. Bocharov, *Russian Roulette*, 97.

229. Galeotti, *Afghanistan*, 51.

230. Alexievich, *Zinky Boys*, 171.

231. Gai, "Afganistan: kak eto bylo," *Vecherniaia Moskva*, September 12, 1989, 4.

232. Quoted from N. Traver, *Kife* (1989), 161, in Galeotti, *Afghanistan*, 50–51.

233. Boris Kalachev, "Etomy ne mesto v stroiu" (There's no place for this in the ranks), *Literaturnaia gazeta*, no. 43, October 26, 1988, 12.

234. Alexievich, *Zinky Boys*, 80, 93–94.

235. Borovik, *The Hidden War*, 186.

236. Pardaev, *Afganskaia komandirovka*, 421–422.

237. E.g., the testimony of one soldier who served from 1985 to 1987, Laruelle and Rakisheva, eds., *Interv'iu s voinami internatsionalistami afganskoi voiny*, 232.

238. Aaron Einfrank, "Bitter Racial Violence Rages in Afghan War," *Washington Times*, November 14, 1985, reproduced USIA Addendum no. 47 (AD 858), November 22, 1985.

239. "The other enemy," *Haarets*, November 8, 1985, 14, quoting the *New York Times*.

240. Testimony of an artillery captain—Alexievich, *Zinky Boys*, 80.

241. *Ogonek*, no. 41 (October 1991), 12–13.

242. Gai, "Afganistan: kak eto bylo," *Vecherniaia Moskva*, September 12, 1989, 4.

243. Grau, *The Bear Went Over the Mountain*, 207.

244. Alexievich, *Zinky Boys*, 80.

245. Gennady Zhavoronkov, "We should tell the whole truth about this war," *Moscow News* (*Moskovskie novosti*), July 23, 1989 (no. 30), 9. The Soviet soldiers had grown up on stories of Islamist peasant "Basmachi" fighting the Bolshevik regime in Soviet Central Asia in the 1920s and 1930s.

246. Bocharov, *Russian Roulette*, 26–27.

247. See, for example, Tsagolova, "Snova snitsia voina," *Sobesednik*, no. 3 (January 1988), 11.

248. Gai, "Afganistan: kak eto bylo," *Vecherniaia Moskva*, September 12, 1989, 4.

249. For instance, in the *spetsnaz* toward the war's end—Laruelle and Rakisheva, eds., *Interv'iu s voinami internatsionalistami afganskoi voiny*, 364, 389.

250. Gai, "Afganistan: kak eto bylo," *Vecherniaia Moskva*, September 12, 1989, 4.

251. Laruelle and Rakisheva, eds., *Interv'iu s voinami internatsionalistami afganskoi voiny*, 318.

252. Author's interview with Turdibay Shadmonov.

253. Genrikh Borovik, "Vremia" broadcast, Moscow TV, February 16, 1989. FBIS-SOV-89–032.

254. Ustiuzhanin, "'Pokhoronku' ne dognal," *Sovetskii voin*, no. 18 (September 1990), 69.

255. Gai, "Afganistan: kak eto bylo," *Vecherniaia Moskva*, September 12, 1989, 4.

256. Laruelle and Rakisheva, eds., *Interv'iu s voinami internatsionalistami afganskoi voiny*, 18, 78.

257. Pavlov, "Byt soldat," 8.

258. Laruelle and Rakisheva, eds., *Interv'iu s voinami internatsionalistami afganskoi voiny*, 206.

259. Alexievich, *Zinky Boys*, 118–119.

260. Odom, *The Collapse of the Soviet Military*, 249.

261. Maiorov, *Pravda ob afganskoi voine*, 242–254. Maiorov's insistence that the criminals were Fortieth Army soldiers and call for their arrest cost him his CPSU CC membership.

262. Alexievich, *Zinky Boys*, 6, 18. See also Behrends, "'Some Call Us Heroes,'" 726.

263. Laruelle and Rakisheva, eds., *Interv'iu s voinami internatsionalistami afganskoi voiny*, 19, 109.

264. Interview with Vladimir Gross, n.d.

265. Alexievich, *Zinky Boys*, 117–118.

266. Konnov, "Pravda i vymysel ob afganskoi voine," 51. Konnov spelled out the sums for killing a soldier and an officer or for destroying an APC, a tank, and a helicopter.

267. Alexievich, *Zinky Boys*, 170–172.

268. Philips, "A Soviet Estonian Soldier in Afghanistan," 110–111.

269. Borovik, *The Hidden War*, 186.

270. For one such, see Bocharov, *Russian Roulette*, 67–74.

271. Laruelle and Rakisheva, eds., *Interv'iu s voinami internatsionalistami afganskoi voiny*, 130.

272. Borovik, *The Hidden War*, 255–256, 259.

273. E.g., Laruelle and Rakisheva, eds., *Interv'iu s voinami internatsionalistami afganskoi voiny*, 272.

274. Ibid., 136.

275. V. Verstakov, "Afganskii dnevnik," *Sovetskii voin*, no. 16 (August 1990), 20.

276. TASS, "Strogo sobliudat' obiazatel'stva" (To strictly observe obligations), *Pravda*, May 26, 1988, 5. Lizichev also spoke of 35,478 wounded and 311 missing.

277. The official MoD *Kniga pamiati* (Book of memory), which appeared in 1995, lists over 14,000 who died—in alphabetical order—but contains no figures. But it is not comprehensive; I found names of soldiers KIA who are not included. The Ministry of Defense of the Russian Federation published the volume in the format that the Soviet MoD announced in 1990, "Sozdaetsia kniga Pamiati pavshikh na zemle Afganistana" (Memorial volume of those who fell in Afghanistan), *Pobratim*, no. 6 (1990), 7.

278. Gromov, *Ogranichennyi kontingent*, 336; Liakhovskii and Zabrodin, *Tainy afganskoi voiny*, 213–215. For the breakdown by year, age, and rank, see V. Izgarshev, "Afganskaia bol'" (Afghan pain), *Pravda*, August 17, 1989, 6. (The MoD figures in December 1992: 14,251 dead; 17,980 invalids; 400,000 suffered various illnesses, 280,000 of them infectious diseases).

279. Greshnov, "Afganistan: Zalozhniki vremeni." Greshnov, who served in Afghanistan as an interpreter, endeavored in 1986 to get data about casualties. A sister in the Kabul military hospital told him that in just the surgery department of her hospital, 98 had died in June 1985, 112 in July, and over 120 in August, after which time the numbers diminished.

280. These figures apparently do not include Soviet civilian advisers and specialists killed while carrying out their duties, Krakhmalov, *Zapiski voennogo attashe*, 270–271.

281. Krivosheev, ed., *Rossiia i SSSR v voinakh XX veka: Poteri vooruzhennykh sil*, 537.

282. Liakhovskii and Zabrodin, *Tainy afganskoi voiny*, 74, 80. According to one authoritative Western source, accidental deaths were often written off as battle casualties, for example, thirty soldiers who drowned bathing in the River Kochka in Badakhshan Province. Braithwaite, *Afgantsy*, 177.

283. Fogel', "Osobennosti propagandy SSSR vo vremia voennoi aktsii v Afganistane."

284. Sarin and Dvoretsky, *The Afghan Syndrome*, 93.

285. Cherkasov, "'Afgan' nachinalsia tak . . . ," *Sovetskii voin* no. 23 (December 1989), 8, and Bocharov, *Russian Roulette*, 7–8. Gai gave examples of soldiers killed as a result of carelessness or bravado. "Afganistan: Kak eto bylo," *Vecherniaia Moskva*, December 26, 1989, 4.

286. Pashkevich, *Afganistan: voina glazami kombata*, 4. Pashkevich lost two men who ignored his instructions and left the compound, presumably to get grapes, and stepped on a mine. Ibid., 47.

287. Molly Moore (quoting Hero of the Soviet Union Valerii Ochirov), "A Post-Afghan Syndrome?" *Washington Post*, October 1, 1989, D1.

288. Krivosheev, ed., *Rossiia i SSSR v voinakh XX veka*, 538. The disabled were divided into three categories: first degree, who became totally dependent, 672; second degree, somewhat dependent but able to work under special conditions, 4,216; and third degree, partially handicapped, 5,863. For GS data, 1989. Liakhovskii and Zabrodin, *Tainy afganskoi voiny*, 213. At the war's end, there were said to have been 6,377 invalids. Moscow TV, June 21, 1989, FBIS-SOV-89–122, June 27, 1989, 19.

289. Grau, *The Bear Went Over the Mountain*, xiv.

290. Galeotti, *Afghanistan*, 68.

291. This belief persisted into the twenty-first century, see Laruelle and Rakisheva, eds., *Interv'iu s voinami internatsionalistami afganskoi voiny*, 79.

292. Interview with Oleg Rybak, Carmiel (Israel), n.d. In Rybak's view, 95 percent of the casualties could have been avoided.

293. Interview with Evgenii Krasnik, Carmiel (Israel), n.d.

294. Interview with Lev Shepper, Carmiel (Israel), n.d. For the irritation of officers in the field at these generals, see the description of General Zaitsev's tour of Afghanistan. Liakhovskii, *Tragediia i doblest'*, 205–206.

295. "'First Aid' in Combat," *Agitator armii i flota* no. 10 (May 1989), 15–17. JPRS-UMA-89–017, July 13, 1989, 43.

296. Alexievich, *Zinky Boys*, 59, 60, 101.

297. Ibid., 55–56.

298. *Izvestiia*, February 5, 1989.

299. Alexievich, *Zinky Boys*, 3, 14.

300. Gromov, *Ogranichennyi kontingent*, 269.

301. Elena Tasheva, "Vestochka iz Zhenevy" (News from Geneva), *Komsomolets Uzbekistana*, February 15, 1990.

302. "Tret'ia voennaia vesnia" (The third spring of the war), *Posev* no. 3 (1982), 10, and E. Romanov, "1416 dnei" (1416 days), *Posev* no. 2 (1984), 10, 12. The POWs' tales corroborate this charge (see below).

303. Gromov, *Ogranichennyi kontingent*, 283.

304. Alexievich, *Zinky Boys*, 4, 22.

305. In 1987, over forty years after World War II ended, the Soviet media were still debating whether soldiers who had gone missing or been taken prisoner should be rehabilitated.

306. Sarin and Dvoretsky, *The Afghan Syndrome*, 167–170.

307. Braithwaite, *Afgantsy*, 257–259.

308. TASS, June 13, 16, 1988, and Reuters, June 22, 1988, quoted in Bren West, "Soviet Prisoners of the Afghan Resistance," RL 267/88, June 23, 1988.

309. Quoted in Braithwaite, *Afgantsy*, 257.

310. Laruelle and Rakisheva, eds., *Interv'iu s voinami internatsionalistami afganskoi voiny*, 172.

311. This seems to be the same organization as the Soviet Public Coordinating Committee for the Release of Soviet Servicemen Taken Prisoner in Afghanistan. See Chapter 7.

312. Izgarshev, "Afganskaia bol'," *Pravda*, August 17, 1989, 6. The GS provided this figure. Braithwaite, *Afgantsy*, 333, and Gromov, *Ogranichennyi kontingent*, 323, gave slightly different figures.

313. A. Oliinik, "Nasha gorech' i nasha bol'" (Our rancor and our pain), *Krasnaia zvezda*, February 1, 1992, 1. According to an SVA representative in Afghanistan in 1991, 69 of the 323 missing soldiers had returned to the Soviet Union; of the others, some 40 were known to be alive in Afghanistan (the names of 18 of them were known); just a few were known to be dead. V. Andrianov, "Eshche raz o probleme plennykh" (The problem of prisoners once again), *Pobratim*, no. 11 (1991), 7. The International Committee for the Release of the Soviet Prisoners of War said about 75 remained alive in Afghanistan and Pakistan in 1991. Sarin and Dvoretsky, *The Afghan Syndrome*, 167–170.

314. For example, "Tiazhelye boi" (Heavy fighting), *Posev*, no. 6 (198), 15, 16. There is, however, no concrete evidence that a high proportion of Central Asians deserted apart from deserters' stories, whose veracity is necessarily suspect.

315. A soldier who served from 1984 to 1986 said many Russians who went over to the mujahidin adopted Islam and were reported MIA. Laruelle and Rakisheva, eds., *Interv'iu s voinami internatsionalistami afganskoi voiny*, 171–172.

316. Tasheva, "Vestochka iz Zhenevy," *Komsomolets Uzbekistana*, February 15, 1990.

317. Liakhovskii and Zabrodin, *Tainy afganskoi voiny*, 74.

318. N. Sautin, "Behind the Scenes of Subversion: The Return," *Izvestiia*, December 2, 1984, 6. CDSP XXXVI:48, 7–9.

319. "Gulag v Shveitsarii?" (Gulag in Switzerland?), *Posev*, no. 8 (1982), 2–3; USIS Official Text, U.S. Department of State Special Report December 19, 1985. Altogether, according to MID, eleven POWs passed through this "reception center," which closed in 1986: eight returned home while three went to the West. *Izvestiia*, June 18, 19—FBIS-SOV-89-119. June 22, 1989, 31–32.

320. "Memorandum de Lord Bethell Concernant la Situation des Soldats Soviétiques Prisonniers," 132–137.

321. TASS, "Varvarskoe postuplenie" (Barbaric crime), *Pravda*, May 15, 1985, 5, and Krakhmalov, *Zapiski voennogo attashe*, 274.

322. Krakhmalov, *Zapiski voennogo attashe*, 272–273.

323. Reuters, June 22, 1988, quoted in Bren West, "Soviet Prisoners of the Afghan Resistance," RL 267/88, June 23, 1988.

324. He seems to be the person mentioned in *Moscow News* in the article by Yuri Teplyakov (see note 210).

325. Borovik, *The Hidden War*, 124–132.

326. Ibid., 173–179. This former prisoner and his friend from Kharkov (see following paragraph) were apparently the two whose story was reported in *Pravda*—V. Izgarshev, "Trudnyi put' domoi" (A hard road home), July 21, 1988, 6—who decided to return to the Soviet Union immediately upon hearing of the amnesty.

327. Borovik, *The Hidden War*, 180–190.

328. Ibid., 215–216.

329. Gromov, *Ogranichennyi kontingent*, 344–345.

Chapter 4

1. Fogel', "Osobennosti propagandy SSSR vo vremia voennoi aktsii v Afganistane."

2. "The Second Congress of USSR Peoples' Deputies," *Izvestiia*, December 26, 1989, 3–6. CDSP XLI:10, 15–16. For the Joint Committee report, see below.

3. For example, Brezhnev at the Twenty-Sixth CPSU Congress in February 1981 (see below) and Defense Minister Ustinov on Soviet Army Day in February 1982. For an earlier use of the term in the Soviet press, see Chapter 6, and for a novel by this name, see Chapter 7.

4. Fogel', "Osobennosti propagandy SSSR vo vremia voennoi aktsii v Afganistane."

5. This was the clear impression of General Aleksandr Maiorov, appointed chief military adviser in Kabul in June 1980, Maiorov, *Pravda ob afganskoi voine*, 9.

6. *CWIHP Bulletin*, 8–9, 163—164, and https://nsarchive2.gwu.edu/rus/text_files/Afganistan/, accessed January 10, 2017.

7. "The Intervention in Afghanistan and the Fall of Détente," 143–144.

8. The draft comprised fifteen Articles. https://nsarchive2.gwu.edu/rus/text_files/Afganistan/, accessed January 10, 2017.

9. Archive of the President of the Russian Federation—f.3, op.120, d.44, ll.73 and 77–80; *CWIHP Bulletin*, 8–9, 165–166.

10. Liakhovskii, *Tragediia i doblest'*, 124, accessed online April 18, 2017.

11. "Otvety L. I. Brezhneva na voprosy korrespondenta gazety 'Pravda'" (L. I. Brezhnev's replies to a *Pravda* correspondent), *Pravda*, January 13, 1980, 1.

12. "Rech' L. I. Brezhneva" (L. I. Brezhnev's speech), *Pravda*, February 23, 1980, 1–2.

13. "Edinstvo naroda—velikaia sila" (Unity of the people—a great force), *Pravda*, February 12, 1980, 2.

14. "Nepokolebimym kursom mira. Vstrecha izbiratelei s B. N. Ponomarevym" (On the unshakable road of peace. Voters' meeting with B. N. Ponomarev), *Pravda*, February 5, 1980, 3.

15. "Priem L. I. Brezhnevym P. V. Narasimkha Rao" (Brezhnev receives P. V. Narasimkha Rao), *Pravda*, June 7, 1980, 1.

16. *CWIHP Bulletin*, 8–9, 167–168. Deputies of the four original official members of the commission apparently participated in its functioning. According to Mendelson, *Changing Course*, 48, CGS Nikolai Ogarkov and First Deputy Foreign Minister Georgii Kornienko were actually members of the Afghanistan Commission.

17. *CWIHP Bulletin*, 8–9, 170–172.

18. Gromov, *Ogranichennyi kontingent*, 128.

19. *CWIHP Bulletin*, 8–9, 174.

20. Ibid., 8–9, 175–176. For the withdrawal of these units, see Chapter 2.

21. Ivanov, "Ogranichennyi kontingent," *Sovetskii voin*, no. 10 (May 1991), 15. These were units that were irrelevant to Afghanistan; see Chapter 2. Ivanov speaks of a withdrawal of 5,000 troops in 1981, but I found no corroboration of any such withdrawal and he is probably referring to the units withdrawn in June 1980 (prior to Sakharov's Open Letter).

22. "Zaiavlenie Sovetskogo Soiuza i Demoktraticheskoi Respubliki Afganistana" (Statement of the Soviet Union and the Democratic Republic of Afghanistan), *Pravda*, October 20, 1980, 1–2. There seems to have been some disagreement about the formulation of the statement, for it was published four full days after it had been drawn up.

23. Westad, "*Concerning the Situation in 'A*,'" 131.

24. "Doklad L. I. Brezhneva" (L. I. Brezhnev's report), *Pravda*, February 23, 1981, 3.

25. "Rech' tovarishcha L. I. Bezhneva (Comrade L. I. Brezhnev's speech), *Pravda*, May 23, 1981, 2.

26. Maiorov, *Pravda ob afganskoi voine*, 271–272, 279–281.

27. Vassiliev, *Russian Policy in the Middle East*, 266.

28. *CWIHP Toward an International History*, 212.

29. Ibid., 236—237. The Politburo charged three high-ranking officials to deal with this—Politburo member Mikhail Zimianin, MPA chief Aleksei Epishev, and chief of the CC Administrative Organs Department, Nikolai Savinkin.

30. Shebarshin, *Ruka Moskvy*, 2012, accessed online, February 5, 2017. See also Chapter 2.

31. I. Shchedrov to the CC CPSU, November 12, 1981, from the Center for Preservation of Contemporary Documentation, Moscow, fond 5, opis 84, delo 855. Translated by Svetlana Savranskaya, National Security Archive.

32. For similar instructions issued a year earlier, see Chapter 2.

33. Shebarshin, *Ruka Moskvy*, 151–153.

34. Gai and Snegirev, *Vtorzhenie*, 207–208.

35. Krakhmalov, *Zapiski voennogo attashe*, 306.

36. *Afganistan v nashei sud'be*, 99.

37. Vassiliev, *Russian Policy in the Middle East*, 266.

38. CC Politburo Session, March 10, 1983. *CWIHP Bulletin*, 8–9, 177. Andropov's bottom line contradicts Liakhovskii's contention that Andropov was the first in the Kremlin to realize that it had erred in Afghanistan and sought hard to find a way to leave with dignity. Liakhovskii, *Tragediia i doblest'*, 189.

39. CC CPSU decree of July 8, 1983, quoted in CWIHP, 256—257, from Liakhovskii, *Pliama afgana*, n.p.

40. Krakhmalov, *Zapiski voennogo attashe*, 298.

41. Sarin and Dvoretsky, *The Afghan Syndrome*, 124. A short report of Andropov's meeting with Perez de Cuellar noted that the secretary general told TASS that he "saw support from the Soviet side for my efforts to solve the Afghan problem." TASS, "Vizit sovershen" (Visit concluded), *Pravda*, March 30, 1983, 4.

42. Chernenko's speech, "Aktual'nye voprosy ideologicheskoi, massogo-politicheskoi raboty partii" (Actual questions regarding the Party's ideological and mass-political work), *Pravda*, June 15, 1983, 1–3; Andropov's speech, "Rech' General'nogo sekretar'ia Tsentral'nogo Komiteta KPSS tovarishcha Iu. V. Andropova (Speech of CPSU Central Committee General Secretary Comrade Iu. V. Andropov), *Pravda*, June 16, 1983, 1–2. Chernenko made do with a vague reference to the mother country's demand of its soldiers to fulfill their "international duty" and their consequent performance of "exploits worthy of the military fame of their fathers and grandfathers." Chernenko, "Aktual'nye voprosy ideologicheskoi," 3.

43. "O mezhdunarodnom polozhenii i vneshnei politike" (The international situation and foreign policy), *Pravda*, June 17, 1983, 2–3.

44. Mendelson, *Changing Course*, 73–75; see also n. 38. Major General Kim Tsagolov claimed that Andropov realized that the intervention had been a mistake. Ivan Demidov, "Rossiia ne dolzhna podderzhivat' tol'ko odnu iz konfliktuiushchikh storon" (Russia must not support just one of the conflicting parties), *Nezavisimaia gazeta*, September 8, 1992, 1, 4. One source contends that "several subunits" were withdrawn from Afghanistan under Andropov. Rubtsov, "Sovetskii Soiuz v 'neob"iavlennoi' voine v Afganistane," 141; I found no corroboration of this.

45. N. Egorychev, "Afganistan stoil nam. . . . " (Afghanistan cost us . . .), *Kommersant vlast*, no. 46, November 25, 2002. https://www.kommersant.ru/doc/352676, accessed May 15, 2015.

46. Vasil'ev, *Rossiia na Blizhnem i Srednem Vostoke*, 263.

47. In 2010, Nikita Mendkovich of Moscow's Center for the Study of Contemporary Afghanistan (TsISA) stated that nobody was yet in a position to gauge the Soviet Union's outlay in support of the 1978 Afghan Revolution. "Finansovyi aspekt Afganskoi voiny 1979—1989 gg."

48. White, *Gorbachev and After*, 106.

49. Sarin and Dvoretsky, *The Afghan Syndrome*, 146. Shevarnadze, *The Future Belongs to Freedom*, 58, also gives this figure.

50. Soviet citizens traveling abroad received one dollar for six rubles, which was also considered an underestimate.

51. Mendkovich, "Finansovyi aspekt," 2–3.

52. See note 45.

53. Liakhovskii, *Tragediia i doblest' Afgana*, 611.

54. Chernyaev, *My Six Years with Gorbachev*, 145.

55. Mendelson, *Changing Course*, 94, 114–115.

56. N. Ryzhkov to M. S. Gorbachev, January 8, 1988, https://nsarchive2.gwu.edu/rus/text_files/Afganistan/, accessed January 10, 2017. By 1987, "economic aid and other expenses" were also meaningful: 1,258 million rubles.

57. Gromov, *Ogranichennyi kontingent*, 332–333.

58. The Soviet Union issued no official figures for its defense budget, although in 1989, Gorbachev told the Congress of People's Deputies that military expenditure for that year would be 77.3 billion rubles, 9 percent of the GNP.

59. Author's interview with Turdibay Shadmonov.

60. Yu. Bandura, "When There Aren't Enough *dushmany*," *Izvestiia*, December 1, 1984, 5. CDSP XXXVI:48, 9–10.

61. U.S. Department of State Paper on Afghanistan, *Afghanistan: Two Years of Occupation*, December 23, 1981, 14.

62. Nicholas Daniloff, "Kremlin Stand: No Afghan Pullout without Victory," *U.S. News & World Report*, December 24, 1984, 29–30.

63. "V druzhestvennoi obstanovke" (In a friendly atmosphere), *Pravda*, April 22, 1986, 4.

64. "Sovmestnoe sovetsko-afganskoe kommiunike" (Joint Soviet-Afghan communiqué), *Pravda*, April 25, 1986, 4.

65. Gromov, "Zashchishchali, obuchali, stroili," 11–15. Other officers gave different statistics for the Fortieth Army's construction work—for example, "Zdrastvuete, synov'ia" (Greetings, sons!, *Komsomolets Uzbekistana*, February 8, 1989).

66. Harrison, "A Breakthrough in Afghanistan?" 10.

67. Gennadii Musaelian, "Bessilny dollary i puli" (Dollars and bullets are powerless), *Sovetskaia Rossiia*, March 1, 1985, 3.

68. USIA Addendum File Log no. 9, February 28, 1986, quoting a U.S. Department of State report. See also *Soviet Nationalities Survey* no. 12. U.S. Department of State Bureau of Intelligence and Research.

69. Grau, *The Bear Went Over the Mountain*, 140.

70. See. for example, a CPSU CC document on Afghanistan, dated May 1988 CWIHP, 397–398.

71. Karp, "Afghanistan: Seven Years of Occupation," 16. The DRA government provided the figure for Soviet economic technicians.

72. Galeotti, *Afghanistan*, 161.

73. For example, V. Skosyrev interview with Elena Arefeva of IMEMO, "From Dogmatism to Realism," *Izvestiia*, July 19, 1989, 5. CDSP XLI:28, 10–11.

74. Congress of USSR People's Deputies, Verbatim report, *Izvestiia*, June 11, 1989, 2–8. CDSP XLI:33, 23.

75. Rubtsov, "Sovetskii Soiuz," 119. There is a slight discrepancy between Rubtsov's figure of $8.05 billion and that of Mendkovich, 8.46.

76. Kotkin, *Armageddon Averted*, 61.

77. *Washington Post*, April 17, 1988, quoted in Galster, "Rivalry and Reconciliation in Afghanistan," 1535–1536. Liakhovskii accepted the story—*Tragediia i doblest'*, 204–205—accessed April 18, 2017, and I suspect that Kotkin relied on the same source. Georgii Arbatov, head of the Institute of the United States and Canada, and former CGS Akhromeev denied having any memory of this instruction. Mendelson, *Changing Course*, 102.

78. Chernyaev, *My Six Years with Gorbachev*, 25–26.

79. Vassiliev, *Russian Policy in the Middle East*, 273.

80. Mendelson, *Changing Course*, 94. Ron Suny agrees that with the country "bogged down" in Afghanistan, "economic modernization" was impossible, so Gorbachev decided to withdraw; perestroika dictated concessions abroad. Suny, *The Revenge of the Past*, 127, 139. Certainly, withdrawal benefited Gorbachev's foreign relations, but I reject the implication of Kotkin's assertion that it came about as part of "a strategy to defuse the superpower confrontation," although Kotkin continues "thereby reducing the strain on the Soviet Union and raising his own profile."

81. Mendelson, *Changing Course*, 102–103.

82. Mickiewicz, *Changing Channels*, 57.

83. Rubtsov, "Sovetskii Soiuz," 142; Brown, *The Gorbachev Factor*, 234–235; Kalinovsky, *The Long Goodbye*, 162–165.

84. This position was not universally accepted. Major General Kim Tsagolov blamed Gorbachev for not withdrawing as soon as he came to power for he knew the war was pointless—Demidov, "Rossiia ne dolzhna podderzhivat' tol'ko odnu iz konfliktuiushchikh storon."

85. Chernyaev, *My Six Years with Gorbachev*, 42–43. Without a transcript of the October 1985 meeting or meetings, it is unclear whether they discussed Afghanistan at one meeting or two.

86. See, for example, "Shel parnishke v tu poru devatnadtsatyi god . . . " (Then a nineteen year-old lad went . . .), *Pobratim*, no. 4 (1990), 2.

87. For the party's study of public opinion prior to, and particularly under, Gorbachev, see White, Gill, and Slider, *The Politics of Transition*, 180–182, 199.

88. Shevarnadze, *The Future Belongs to Freedom*, 47.

89. " Doklad tovarishcha Gorbacheva" (Comrade M. S.Gorbachev's report), *Pravda*, February 26, 1986, 8. (The report covered pp. 2–10.) Indeed, the U.S. administration was adamant throughout that there could be no question of halting the flow of military equipment to the mujahidin; for example, see Elie David Krakowski, Special Assistant to the Assistant Secretary of Defense for International Security Policy, in a lecture at the Jaffee Center for Strategic Studies, Tel-Aviv University, December 8, 1986.

90. "Konstruktivnyi shag: Sovetskie voiny-internatsionalisty vozvrashchaiutsia iz Afganistana" (A constructive step: Soviet internationalist-soldiers return from Afghanistan), *Pravda*, October 10, 1986, 5.

91. "Voinam internatsionalistam vozvrashchaiushchimsia iz Demokraticheskoi Respubliki Afganistana" (To the internationalist soldiers returning from the Democratic Republic of Afghanistan), *Pravda*, October 14, 1986, 1.

92. *CWIHP Bulletin*, 8–9, 178–181; Chernyaev, *My Six Years with Gorbachev*, 89–90.

93. B. Piadyshev, "Kak eto bylo . . . Rasskazyvaet prezident Afganistana Najibulla" (The way it was—as told by Afghan President Najibullah), *Pravda*, November 28, 1989, 4.

94. TASS, "V druzhestvennoi obstanovke"(In a friendly atmosphere), *Pravda*, December 13, 1986, 2.

95. CC CPSU Politburo transcript, November 13, 1986, CWIHP Bulletin, issues 8–9, Winter 1996/1997, 178–181. The other commission members were KGB Chairman Viktor

Chebrikov, DM Sergei Sokolov, head of the CC International Department Anatolii Dobrynin, Gosplan Chairman Nikolai Talyzin, and head of Gosagroprom Vsevold Murakhovskii.

96. "Afghanistan: A Voice from Moscow," 18.

97. Mendelson, *Changing Course*, 108, 116.

98. Ol'shanskii, "'Afganskii sindrom'," *Literaturnoe obozrenie* no. 3 (1990), 12.

99. Chernyaev, *My Six Years with Gorbachev*, 106.

100. Brown, *The Gorbachev Factor*, 234.

101. The Soviet central press repeatedly reported such violations—e.g., "Zaiavlenie MID SSSR" (Foreign Ministry statement), *Pravda*, May 29, 1988, 5. Traditionally, such statements provided the backdrop to Soviet reneging on international or bilateral agreements between states.

102. Brown, *The Gorbachev Factor*, 234.

103. See statement by Politburo member and CPSU CC Secretary Lev Zaikov: V. Izgarshev, "Na Sovete Oborony . . . " (At the Defense Council . . .), *Pravda*, November 27, 1989, 2.

104. "Zaiavlenie General'nogo sekretar'ia TsK KPSS M. S. Gorbacheva po Afganistanu" (statement of CPSU CC General Secretary M. S. Gorbachev on Afghanistan), *Pravda*, February 9, 1988, 1.

105. "Interv'iu agentsvu Bakhtar" (interview to the Bakhtar [news] agency), *Pravda*, January 7, 1988, 4.

106. "Zaiavlenie MID SSSR," *Pravda*, May 29, 1988, 5.

107. Chernyaev, *My Six Years with Gorbachev*, 145–146.

108. Kalinovsky, *A Long Goodbye*, 169. And see Chapter 2.

109. USIS Official Text, December 18, 1986, quoting Deputy Assistant Secretary of State Robert Peck at a question-and-answer session at the State Department.

110. "Press-konferentsiia E. A. Shevarnadze" (E. A. Shevarnadze press conference), *Pravda*, April 15, 1988, 6.

111. Fogel', "Osobennosti propagandy SSSR vo vremia voennoi aktsii v Afganistane."

112. CC CPSU Letter on Afghanistan, May 10, 1988, CWIHP, 386–400. Translated from Liakhovskii, *Tragediia i doblest' afgana*.

113. " Doklad M. S. Gorbacheva" (f M. S. Gorbachev's report), *Pravda*, June 29, 1988, 3.

114. "XIX vsesoiuznaia konferentsiia KPSS" (The Nineteenth All-Union Party Conference), *Pravda*, July 2, 1988, 7, 8. Baklanov's criticism of the intervention and war evoked a hostile reaction; rather than the usual applause, his remarks were met with "noise in the hall." See also Tismaneanu, "The Neo-Leninist Temptations," 45.

115. Vera Tolz, "The USSR this Week," RL 213/88, May 20, 1988, 2. Sevruk made the statement to Reuters.

116. See note 45.

117. The 2,250 deputies of the Congress of People's Deputies were elected in the first contested elections in the country since 1918. Its first convocation, which met from May 25 to June 9, 1989, chose from its midst a two-tier Supreme Soviet that would sit for eight months of the year; the old Supreme Soviet had convened for eight days per year and acted as a rubber stamp. Brown, *The Gorbachev Factor*, 178–195 passim.

118. Congress of USSR People's Deputies, Verbatim report, *Izvestiia*, June 3, 1989, 1–7. CDSP XLI:28, 15–16.

119. For instance, Congress of USSR People's Deputies, Verbatim report, *Izvestiia*, June 10, 1989, 3—11, June 11, 1989, 8. CDSP XLI:31, 19 and 33, 27.

120. Excerpt from Politburo meeting, January 24, 1989. https://nsarchive2.gwu.edu/rus/text_files/Afganistan/, accessed January 10, 2017.

121. "Interv'iu E. A. Shevarnadze afganskomy agentstvu Bakhtar" (E.A. Shevarnadze Interview to Afghan Bakhtar Agency), *Pravda*, August 8, 1989, 4.

122. "At the Supreme Soviet," *Izvestiia*, October 24, 1989. CSDP 41:43, 3, and Gai, "Afganistan: kak eto bylo" (Afghanistan: How it was), *Vecherniaia Moskva*, October 30, 1989, 1.

123. Kamrany and Killian, "Effects of Afghanistan War on Soviet Society and Policy," 129.

124. "Soobshchenie Komiteta Verkhovnogo Soveta po mezhdunarodnym delam o politicheskoi otsenke resheniia o vvode sovetskikh voisk v Afganistan" (Report of the Supreme Soviet Committee on International affairs on [its] political assessment of the decision to introduce Soviet troops into Afghanistan), *Pravda*, December 25, 1989, 3; *Izvestiia*, December 26, 1989, 3–6.

125. "The Second Congress of USSR Peoples' Deputies," *Izvestiia*, December 26, 1989, 3–6. CDSP XLII:10, 18; and Shilo, "Afganistan 30 let spustia," 3. The Congress's resolution was entitled "Political Assessment of the Decision to Introduce Troops into Afghanistan in December 1979."

126. Third session of the USSR Supreme Soviet, *Izvestiia*, February 16, 1990. CDSP XLII:7, 6.

127. Mendelson, *Changing Course*, 122–126.

128. Danilova, "Voennosluzhashchie, voiny-internatsionalisty, veterany: dinamika pravovogo statusa," 78. Only the unit number was indicated in demobilization papers, a practice that continued well into the 1980s, viz., the military tickets of veterans in Qurghonteppa ("Qurghonteppa files")—Göransson, "At the Service of the State," 228.

129. Tsentral'nyi Komitet KPSS i Sovet Ministrov SSSR, Postanovlenie ot 17 ianvaria 1983 g. N 59–27 (CC CPSU and the USSR Council of Ministers, resolution of 17 January 1983). http://zakon2.rada.gov.ua/laws/show/v9027400–83. (The women who served in Afghanistan, according to one source, were not included in this decree and were at no stage entitled to privileges. Pinnick, "When the Fighting Is Over," 150.)

130. Postanovlenie ot 26 iiul' 1984 N 812, O merakh po dal'neishemu uluchsheniiu material'no—bytovykh uslovii uchastnikov Velikoi Otechestvennoi voiny i semei pogibshikh voennosluzhashchikh (Measures for further improving the everyday material circumstances of participants in the Great Patriotic War and of the families of those killed on military service [the section concerning veterans of Afghanistan was classified], http://zakon2.rada.gov.ua/laws/show/v0812400–84, which Professor Natalia Danilova of Aberdeen University kindly sent to me. It was only in 1988 that the government finally acknowledged all Soviet personnel who served in Afghanistan between 1979 and 1989 as Afghan War vets entitled to identical privileges. Danilova, "Voennosluzhashchie" 81.

131. "Sevruk: 'Ia ne byl bossom' . . . " (I was not the boss), *Pobratim*, no. 11 (1991), 6; for officialdom's cavalier and callous attitude to returning veterans, see also *Pravda*, April 4 and August 5, 1987, quoted in Chapter 6.

132. A. Titarenko, "'Ia vas v Afganistan ne posylal . . . ' ('I didn't send you to Afghanistan'), *Pravda*, August 20, 1987, 2.

133. *Tajikistan-i Soveti*, August 29, 1987 quoted SWB I, SU/8679 B/6, September 22, 1987.

134. Göransson, "At the Service of the State," 170.

135. "Zaiavlenie General'nogo sekretaria TsK KPSS M. S. Gorbacheva po Afganistanu," *Pravda*, February 9, 1988, 1.

136. Quoted in Gai, "Afganistan: kak eto bylo," *Vecherniaia Moskva*, September 12, 1989, 1.

137. CC CPSU Letter on Afghanistan, May 10, 1988, CWIHP, 386–400. Translated from Liakhovskii, *Tragediia i doblest' afgana*.

138. "Obrashchenie TsK KPSS k sovetskim voinam-internatsionalistam, vozvrashchaiushchiesia iz Respubliki Afganistan" (CC CPSU address to internationalist-soldiers returning from Afghanistan), *Pravda*, May 15, 1988, 1.

139. " Doklad M. S. Gorbacheva" (M. S. Gorbachev's report), *Pravda*, June 29, 1988, 3.

140. O merakh po uluchsheniiu meditsinskogo obespecheniia voinov-internatsionalsitov, August 5, 1988, http://lawrussia.ru/texts/legal_673/doc673a391x924.htm, accessed November 21, 2017.

141. "V Politbiuro TsK KPSS" (In the CPSU CC Politburo), *Pravda*, October 21, 1988, 1.

142. R. Ignat'ev, "Stamped 'secret,'" *Izvestiia*, July 15, 1988, 6, CDSP XL:28, 24–25.

143. "L'goty voinam-afgantsam" (Privileges for afgantsy-soldiers), *Izvestiia*, March 14, 1989.

144. Postanovlenie SM SSSR (USSR government resolution), September 8, 1988, spelled out in *Izvestiia*, September 9, 1988. Radio Moscow announced on September 7, 1988, that the government resolved to give a "personal pension" to war invalids and families of fallen soldiers who were their sole breadwinners.

145. "Dlia voinov-afgantsev" (For afgantsy), interview of T. Khudiakova with V. A. Kaznacheev, *Izvestiia*, September 10, 1988, 1.

146. Tkachenko, ed., *Dorogie moi* . . . , 228.

147. See, for example, V. Izgarshev, The Afghan Pain Is Not Subsiding," *Pravda*, November 15, 1988, 4. CDSP XLI:46, 32.

148. I. Korolkov and R. Lynyov, "Urgent Measures. From What Sources?" *Izvestiia*, August 2, 1989, 1 and 3. CDSP XLI:37, 16. Invalids, however, were acknowledged as owed benefits accorded to GPW invalids. See a/m Ministry of Health decree.

149. "L'goty voinam-afgantsam," *Izvestiia*, March 14, 1989, and V. Izgarshev, "The Afghan Pain Is Not Subsiding," *Pravda*, November 15, 1989, 4. CDSP XLI:46, 32.

150. Tkachenko, ed., *Dorogie moi* . . . , 250.

151. Pavlov, "Byt soldat afganskoi voiny."

152. Alexievich, *Zinky Boys*, 56.

153. Galeotti, *Afghanistan*, 55–56; Sarin and Dvoretsky, *The Afghan Syndrome*, 172.

154. V. Izgarshev, "Afganskaia bol'" (Afghan pain), *Pravda*, August 17, 1989, 6.

155. Izgarshev, "The Afghan Pain Is Not Subsiding."

156. TASS, "Rukovodiastvuias' printsipami gumanizma" (Guided by the principles of humanism) *Pravda*, July 5, 1988, 6.

157. Quoted in Sella, *The Value of Human Life in Soviet Warfare*, 130.

158. "Obrashchenie TsK KPSS, Prezidiuma Verkhovnogo Soveta SSSR, Soveta Ministrov SSSR k sovetskim voinam, vernushimsia iz Afganistana" (Address of the CPSU CC, the USSR Supreme Soviet Presidium and the USSR Council of Ministers to the Soviet soldiers returning from Afghanistan), *Pravda*, February 16, 1989, 1.

159. The draft was submitted for examination at the Supreme Soviet Presidium on August 16. TASS, "Zakon—osnova zhizni pravogo gosudarstva" (The law—the foundation of the life of a law-abiding state), *Pravda*, August 17, 1989, 2–3. See also *Izvestiia*, November 30, 1989, 1, and RFE/RL DR no. 226, November 29, 1989.

160. Paul Goble, "Amnesty Granted for Afghan Crimes," RFE/RL Daily Report no. 226, November 29, 1989.This clause was apparently not always honored; see Chapter 3. According to Procurator-General Aleksandr Sukharev, 4,307 soldiers had been "made criminally responsible over 10 years, mainly for selfish crimes—theft, black marketeering, crimes against persons, and military breaches, including grave ones. . . . In recent years, taking into account the extenuating circumstances, the numerous appeals for these convicts to be pardoned, and the fact that many of them have already served a considerable part of their sentence, the USSR Procurator's Office has reopened the cases of the former Afghanistan troops, and has raised the issue of mitigating, or lifting, the sentences." Consequently, just 420 were still being held "in places of incarceration." Moscow Domestic Service in Russian, October 2, 1989. FBIS-SOV-89–190, 56.

161. *Sovet Turkmenistany*, February 5, 1989. JPRS-UPA-89–044, July 10, 1989.

162. For the Belarussian SSR Supreme Soviet presidium decree on pensions for, and other aid to, the republic's 434 disabled afgantsy, see *Sovetskaia kul'tura*, April 29, 1989, 3.

163. "Problemy sotsial'noi reabilitatsii uchastnikov voiny v Afganistane," 12.

164. Galeotti, *Afghanistan*, 93.

165. Aleksandr Prokhanov, "Kto zashchitit zashchitnikov?" *Sovetskii voin* no. 12 (June 1990), 3.

166. See above and R. Moscow in English, October 5, 1989, FBIS-SOV-89–193, October 6, 1989, 18.

Chapter 5

1. The Soviets had sent relatively small forces to fight in "national-liberation" wars in several Third World countries since 1945, but never an entire army.

2. Jones, *Red Army and Society*, 94.

3. Safronov, "Kak eto bylo," 68.

4. Blank, "Imagining Afghanistan," 472, provides examples that confirm this aspect of Soviet military thought.

5. "It Is Time to Open the Safes," interview with Major-General Iurii Grekov—*Krasnaia zvezda*, May 23, 1989, 2; FBIS-SOV-89–105, June 2, 1989, 74–77.

6. Testimony of former deputy head of the Foreign Ministry Middle East Department, E. D. Pyrlin–Vassiliev, *Russian Policy in the Middle East*, 259.

7. Krakhmalov, *Zapiski voennogo attashe*, 295.

8. Interview with Mikhail Reshetnikov, http://www.rosbalt.ru/piter/2009/02/14/618431.html, accessed April 12, 2015.

9. McMichael, "Soviet Tactical Performance and Adaptation in Afghanistan," 99–100.

10. Foreword to Grau, *The Bear Went Over the Mountain*, n.p.

11. Glants, Introduction, in Grau, *The Bear Went Over the Mountain*, xiv.

12. Blank, "Imagining Afghanistan," 475.

13. Gai, "Afganistan: kak eto bylo" (Afghanistan: How it was), *Vecherniuia Moskva*, September 16, 1989, 4.

14. McMichael, "Soviet Tactical Performance and Adaptation in Afghanistan," 99.

15. "The Sustainability of the Soviet Army in Battle," 404–415.

16. Steve Sego, "US Experts Discuss Soviet Army in Afghanistan," RL 302/87, July 24, 1987, 3.

17. "V interesakh zdorov'ia voinov" (In the interest of soldiers' health), *Krasnaia zvezda*, January 7, 1984.

18. First Deputy Chief of the Central Military Medical Administration Lieutenant General I. Sinopal'nikov drew attention to this during the war in *Agitator armii i flota* no. 23 (1987), quoted "'First Aid' in Combat" (see the following note).

19. "'First Aid' in Combat," *Agitator armii i flota*" no. 10 (May 1989), 15–17. JPRS-UMA-89–017, July 13, 1989, 43.

20. Glants, Introduction, in Grau, *The Bear Went Over the Mountain*, xiv. For the implications of the Soviet withdrawal for Soviet society, see Chapter 10.

21. S. Taransov, "How Officers Live," *Izvestiia*, October 20, 1989, 2. CDSP XLI:42, 30, revealed that an MoD survey conducted among officers disclosed an atmosphere of crisis.

22. V. Sosnitskii, "Prinimaetsia . . . ne edinoglasno," 2.

23. See, for example, N. Malyshev, "Meroi real'nogo boia."

24. Valerii Konovalov, "Afghanistan and Mountain Warfare Training," RL 118/88, March 17, 1988. One Western analyst based his study of the Soviet war effort on sixty articles in Soviet

military journals, mostly apparently as of 1985. McMichael, "Soviet Tactical Performance and Adaptation in Afghanistan," 83.

25. "XIX konferentsiia KPSS. Vystuplenie tovarishcha Gromova B. V." (Nineteenth Party Conference. Speech of B. V. Gromov), *Pravda*, July 2, 1988, 7.

26. Gromov, "Zashchishchali, obuchali, stroili," 11–15.

27. N. Sautin, "Za bar'erom zvuka" (Beyond the sound barrier), *Izvestiia*, August 21, 1988, 3.

28. Blank, "Imagining Afghanistan," 483.

29. Glants, Introduction, in Grau, *The Bear Went Over the Mountain*, xiv.

30. Grau, "The Soviet Combined Arms Battalion—Reorganization for Tactical Flexibility," 2. The quote is from A. Bagaev, "S pozitsii teorii upravleniia" (From the position of control theory); *Voennyi vestnik*, no. 1 (1989), 49–50.

31. Grau, *The Bear Went Over the Mountain*, 206.

32. Drew Middleton, "Afghan War: Soviet Called Bogged Down," *New York Times*, December 8, 1982; McMichael, "Soviet Tactical Performance and Adaptation in Afghanistan," 91, 100–101.

33. Kiianenko, "Boevoe primenenie VVS v Respublike Afganistan," 28.

34. E.g., Shatrov, "Uchit'sia voennomy delu nastoiashchim obrazom," 72.

35. Malyshev, "Meroi real'nogo boia," 34–39.

36. Fortieth Army commanders, for example, balked at what they perceived as the outdated, stereotype suggestions of General Zaitsev, which they believed would cause disproportionate casualties—Liakhovskii, *Tragediia i doblest'*, accessed online April 18, 2017, 205.

37. P. Kruzhin, "'Afgantsy': put' naverkh?" ('Afgantsy': The upward route?), *Posev*, no. 2 (1986) 14–15.

38. *Krasnaia zvezda*, June 11, 21, 1988, quoted in Valerii Konovalov, RL 425/88, September 19, 1988.

39. Galeotti, *Afghanistan*, 194–195.

40. Odom, *The Collapse of the Soviet Military*, 250.

41. Meeting of Politburo, November 13, 1986. CWIHP 8—9, 178.

42. Lapshin, *Afganskii dnevnik*, 104.

43. Vera Tolz, "The USSR This Week: Union of Democratic Afghan Veterans Speaks Out," RL Bulletin 2.15, April 13, 1990, 30.

44. Kiziun, "Vooruzhennye Sily i obshchesto: vzaimosviaz', protivorechiia i puti ikh razresehniia," 2–3.

45. G. Krivosheev, "O vseobshchennosti voinskoi sluzhby" (The universality of military service), *Krasnaia zvezda*, August 31, 1989, 2.

46. In 1971, just 1.1 percent of draftees did not wish to serve; by 1979 their proportion was 7 percent, and by 1989, 18 percent. Murray Feshbach, "The Soviet Military's Recruitment Nightmare," *Washington Post*, August 19, 1990, C4. Iurii Poliakov wrote his novella, "A Hundred Days until the Order," on the subject of "nonregulation relationships," that is, hazing and maltreatment of recruits and clashes in the armed forces between different social and ethnic groups, in the early 1980s. It was published in late 1987 after high-ranking military officials delayed it. Viacheslav Kondrat'ev, A painful subject, *Literaturnaia gazeta*, February 10, 1988, 4.

47. BBC/SWB SU/0785, June 8, 1990, as/3.

48. Krakhmalov, *Zapiski voennogo attashe*, 305.

49. Lieven, *Chechnya: Tombstone of Russian Power*, 205.

50. *Nedelia*, no. 14, May 1–7, 1989. FBIS-SOV-89–091, May 12, 1989, 72.

51. Galeotti, *Afghanistan*, 176–181.

52. Gromov, "Zashchishchali, obuchali, stroili," 11–15

53. "It Is Time to Open the Safes," 2; FBIS-SOV-89–105, June 2, 1989, 74–77.

54. Grau, "The Soviet-Afghan War," 148–149.

55. Kvachkov, *Spetsnaz Rossii*, 105.

56. A. Kovenskii, "Chto eto—otstuplenie?" (What is this—a retreat?), *Posev* no. 2 (1986), 15; and *Krasnaia zvezda*, June 29, 1988.

57. Gromov, *Ogranichennyi kontingent*, 345.

58. Galeotti, *Afghanistan*, 187–189; see also *Sunday Telegraph*, February 19, 1989.

59. P. Studenikin, "Tam, za Gindu-Kushem," *Pravda*, September 11, 1988, 1, 3.

60. Ivan Dynin, "Komandir, prinimai reshenie!" (Commander, take the decision!), *Sobesednik*, no. 10, March 1986, 5.

61. Galeotti, *Afghanistan*, 209–210.

62. Lieven, *Chechnya*, 201–202, 338; and see Chapter 10. "The Soviet Military's Recruitment Nightmare" (see n. 45) confirms the far greater percentage of draft dodgers in Moscow as against rural regions.

63. For the reform of the military and the public debate that preceded and accompanied it, see Odom, *The Collapse of the Soviet Military*, 146–172, 184–200.

64. Blank, "Imagining Afghanistan," 474.

Chapter 6

1. Parta, "The Audience to Western Broadcasts to the USSR during the Cold War," 89. Despite jamming, the "voices" played a major role in information that domestic censorship sought to hide. Jamming ceased only in 1988. Vladimir Ostrogorsky, "No More Jamming," *Moscow News*, no. 51, December 18, 1988, 5; and censorship as of August 1, 1990. "Law of the USSR: On the Press and Other News Media," *Izvestiia*, June 20, 1990, 3; CDSP XLII:25, 16–20.)

2. Downing, "Trouble in the Backyard: Soviet Media Reporting on the Afghan Conflict," 9. For samizdat publications, see below.

3. Mickiewicz, *Changing Channels*, 11.

4. Parta, "The Audience to Western Broadcasts to the USSR during the Cold War," 88–92.

5. Mickiewicz, *Split Signals*, 222.

6. Fogel', "Osobennosti propagandy SSSR vo vremia voennoi aktsii v Afganistane."

7. To quote Kinsburskii and Topalov, "Reabilitatsiia uchastnikov afganskoi voiny v obshchestvennom mnenii," 105. The "experts" gave 1985 as a turning point, but things were changing well before that; see below.

8. A. Maslennikov, "Naprasnye potugi" (Vain attempts), *Pravda*, December 23, 1979, 5.

9. Fogel', "Osobennosti propagandy SSSR vo vremia voennoi aktsii v Afganistane," 69, and "[Vladimir] Sevruk: 'Ya ne byl bossom' . . . " (I wasn't the boss . . .), *Pobratim*, no. 11 (1991), 6.

10. "Obrashchenie pravitel'stva Afganistana" (Address of the government of Afghanistan), *Pravda*, December 29, 1979, 4.

11. Bocharov, *Russian Roulette*, 53–55; Verstakov, *Afganskii dnevnik*, 305. (Verstakov's previous, censored, diary had appeared in 1983.)

12. V. Okulov and P. Studenikin, "Opalennye Kandagarom" (signed by Kandahar), *Pravda*, August 10, 1988, 1, 6.

13. Gai and Snegirev, *Vtorzhenie*, 282–283.

14. Bocharov, *Russian Roulette*, 52–56, 62–63.

15. Verstakov, *Afganskii dnevnik*, 5.

16. P. Studenikin, "'Ia vas v Afganistan ne posylal . . . '" (I didn't send you to Afghanistan), *Pravda*, August 5, 1987, 3.

17. Verstakov, "Afganskii dnevnik," 17.

18. Mikhail Leshchinskii, "Pokaiannaia ne budet . . . " (There will be no confession . . .), *Pobratim*, no. 10 (1991), 8.

19. Brown, *The Gorbachev Factor*, 125–126, 163. For these statements, see the following section.

20. Galeotti, *Afghanistan: The Soviet Union's Last War*, 229.

21. Cohen and Heuvel, *Voices of Glasnost*, 220.

22. Mickiewicz, *Changing Channels*, 57–58.

23. T. Zaslavskaia, "Perestroika i sotsiologiia" (Perestroika and sociology), *Pravda*, February 6, 1987, 2–3.

24. Albert Plutnik, "O pol'ze govorit' pravdu" (The benefit of telling the truth), *Izvestiia*, October 12, 1988, 3.

25. Albert Plutnik, "Lish' by ne bylo voiny . . . " (If only there weren't a war . . .), *Izvestiia*, May 9, 1988, 3.

26. For instance, V. S. Rodin, "Na strazhe sotsialistecheskikh zavoevanii" (Guarding socialist achievements), *Turkmenskaia iskra*, February 23, 1980; Iu. P. Maksimov, "Moguchii strazh sotsialisticheskikh zavoevanii" (Mighty guardian of socialist achievements), *Pravda vostoka*, February 21, 1980, 3.

27. It still appeared in spring 1980: *Literaturnaia gazeta*, March 12, 1980, and *Pravda*, March 20, 1980.

28. P. Studenikin, "In a Country of Mountains and Hopes," *Pravda*, April 14, 1981, 6. CDSP XXXIII:15, 7; B. Tulepbaev, "The collapse of the Basmachi," *Pravda*, January 19, 1982, 3, commenting on I. Mints, ed., *Basmachestvo: Voznikovenie, sushchnost', krakh* (Basmach: origin, essence, collapse; Moscow: Nauka, 1981). For use of "*Basmachi*" among the troops in Afghanistan, see Chapter 3.

29. Interview with Kahramon Radjabov, Institute of History, Tashkent, May 14, 2014.

30. McNair, *Glasnost', Perestroika and the Soviet Media*, accessed online, February 6, 2018.

31. Sapper, *Die Auswirkung des Afghanistan-Krieges*, 201.

32. Galeotti, *Afghanistan*, 89, 142.

33. "'Mesto sluzhby—Afganistan'" (Duty station—Afghanistan), *Posev*, no. 4 (1983), 12.

34. Inna Rudenko, "Dolg," *Komsomol'skaia pravda*, February 26, 1984, 4.

35. "Sevruk: 'Ia ne byl bossom' . . . ".

36. Sapper, *Die Auswirkungen des Afganistan-Krieges*, 207.

37. "Po zakonu dolga" (According to the law of duty), *Komsomol'skaia pravda*, March 13, 1984, 2.

38. Pinnick, "Public Opinion in Russia on the Ex-USSR's Afghanistan War Veterans," n. 10.

39. Fogel', "Osobennosti propagandy SSSR vo vremia voennoi aktsii v Afganistane." According to Bocharov (see above) some of these "concessions" had been implemented before Gorbachev.

40. "Kto tebia vydymal, 'Afgan'?" (Who thought you up, 'Afghan'?), *Krasnaia zvezda*, July 10, 1992.

41. Excerpt from memorandum to Politburo, November 26, 1985. https:/nsarchive2.gwu.edu/rus/text_files/Perestroika/1985.11.26%20Gorbachev's%20Letter%20to%20CC%20CPSU.pdf, accessed December 22, 2019.

42. https:/nsarchive2.gwu.edu/rus/text_files/Yakovlev/1985–12–25-Imperativ-Politicheskogo-Razvitiya%20(Glasnost'Glasnost").pdf, December 25, 1985, accessed December 22, 2019.

43. V. Skosyrev, "Hopes and Doubts: Who Is 'For' and Who Is 'Against' a Political Settlement around Afghanistan," *Izvestiia*, December 26, 1987, 4. FBIS-SOV-87–251, December 31, 1987, 19–20.

44. Tolz, "The Impact of *Glasnost*."

45. Kotkin, *Armageddon Averted*, 68.

46. Stenogramma soveshchaniia provedennogo t. Iakovlevym A. N., February 22, 1988 (Transcript of a meeting chaired by Com. A. N. Yakovlev), https://nsarchive2.gwu.edu/rus/text_files/Afganistan/, accessed January 10, 2017.

47. The first such reference I have found came less than six weeks after the introduction of Soviet troops. V. Sidenko, "Neob"iavlennaia voina protiv Afganistana" (The undeclared war against Afghanistan), *Pravda*, February 5, 1980, 4.

48. Downing, "Trouble in the Backyard," 14. For the Afghan population's "glowing reception" of the Soviet troops, Downing refers to items in *Krasnaia zvezda* and *Literaturnaia gazeta* (March 11 and 19, 1980, respectively). See also Valentin Sharov, "Mezhdunarodnye otnosheniia: . . . Militaristskii udar" (International relations: . . . A militarist blow), *Pravda*, March 9, 1980, 4.

49. "Zaiavlenie pravitel'stva Demokraticheskoi Respubliki Afganistana," *Pravda*, January 2, 1980, 4.

50. "Otpoved' klevetnikam" (Reproof to slanderers), *Pravda*, January 2, 1980, 4.

51. S. Kondrashov, "Chto gotoviat iz odnoi 'utki'" (What is being cooked up from one 'canard'), *Izvestiia*, January 24, 1980, 5.

52. Mark Frankland quoted Bovin, "Explaining Afghanistan," *Jerusalem Post*, August 10, 1980, 6. Bovin reportedly wrote in similar vein in the Italian Communist *l'Unità*, April 25, 1980.

53. "Afghanistan: A Difficult Decade," *Izvestiia*, December 23, 1988, 5, CDSP XL:51, 10.

54. "Mesto sluzhby" Afganistan" (Duty station: Afghanistan), *Voennye znaniia* no. 3 (1981), 4–5, quoted in Peter Kruzhin, "*Voennye znaniia* Reports on Conditions Experienced by Soviet Troops in Afghanistan," RL176/81, April 23, 1981.

55. P. Studenikin, "V strane gor i nadezhd" (In a country of mountains and hopes), *Pravda*, April 14, 1981, 6.

56. V. Skrizhalin, "Let There Be Peace under the Olive Trees," *Krasnaia zvezda*, January 17, 1984, 3. CDSP XXXVI:3, 19.

57. For example, *Krasnaia zvezda* spoke of the mild winter in Afghanistan and the troops' tents being sturdy and comfortable; for another piece containing half-truths, see V. Skrizhalin, "Our Sons Are Serving There: On the Spurs of the Hindu Kush," *Krasnaia zvezda*, January 12, 1983, 1—CDSP XXXV:9, 2.

58. "Mesto sluzhby—Afganistan" (Duty station—Afghanistan), *Komsomol'skaia pravda*, August 7, 1981.

59. *Krasnaia zvezda*, February 24, 1983, quoted in Downing, "Trouble in the Backyard," 18.

60. V. Snegirev, "Net na granitse tishiny" (There is no quiet on the border), *Komsomol'skaia pravda*, September 26, 27, 1981, 3.

61. T. Gaidar, "Iz afganskogo bloknota: V doline piati l'vov" (From an Afghan notebook: In the Valley of the Five Lions), *Pravda*, August 3, 1982, 6. Many Soviet correspondents in Afghanistan entitled their reportage "From an Afghan notebook" or "Afghan diary." I henceforth ignore these designations.

62. Urban, *The War in Afghanistan*, 109, believes that throughout 1982, the Soviets had 600 to 700 fatalities in the Valley.

63. E.g., Moscow TV Service in Russian, September 29, 1984. FBIS III, October 3, 1984, D3. For a 1983 Moscow TV program, see https://www.youtube.com/watch?v=YBf8T-sirdE, accessed November 1, 2017.

64. "Tret'ia voennaia vesnia" (The war's third spring), *Posev*, no. 3 (1982), 11.

65. For the incident, see Gai and Snegirev, *Vtorzhenie*, 162. The Soviet press item "Soobshchenie agentstva Bakhtar" (Report of Bakhtar Agency) appeared almost three weeks after the event. *Pravda*, November 19, 1982, 5.

66. E.g., "The Bandits' Monstrous Activities," *Krasnaia zvezda*, February 6, 1983, 3—CDSP XXXV:9, 4.

67. For example, I. Dynin, "S veroi v budushchee" (With faith in the future), *Krasnaia zvezda*, December 28, 1982, 3.

68. V. Baikov, "Kto vooruzhaet afganskuiu kontrrevoliutsiiu" (Who is arming the Afghan counter-revolution), *Pravda*, May 7, 1983, 4; Oleg Kitsenko, "Otpor vmeshatel'stvu" (Rebuff to intervention), *Pravda*, April 4, 1983, 5, spoke only of imperialist intervention, with no mention of a Soviet presence in Afghanistan.

69. (TASS) "Po puti preobrazovaniia" (On the path of reorganization), *Pravda*, July 7, 1983, 4.

70. For instance, Iu. Teplov and V. Strizhalin, "The Enemy's Attacks Are Doomed to Failure," *Krasnaia zvezda*, February 27, 1983, 3. CDSP XXXV:9, 6.

71. For example, "Goriachee nebo" (Hot skies), *Krasnaia zvezda*, August 3, 1985, 3.

72. Moscow Television, April 27, 1985—FBIS III, April 29, 1985, D2—D7.

73. L. I. Sannikov, ed., *Smoliane—internatsionalisty*, 280.

74. Editorial note, "Zvezdy na kryl'iakh" (Stars on their wings), *Pravda*, August 15, 1982, 2.

75. I. Dynin, "Aist, ptitsa dobraia" (Aist, a friendly bird), *Trud*, February 24, 1983, 4. CDSP XXXV:9, 4–5. (Stovba wrote poetry under the pseudonym Aist, an acronym for Aleksandr Ivanovich Stovba.) *Krasnaia zvezda* reported the death of a Soviet military interpreter serving with the DRA force as early as September 30, 1981.

76. V. Snegirev, "Stationed in Afghanistan: Road to the pass," *Komsomol'skaia pravda*, February 5, 1983, 4.

77. "Helicopter pilots," *Krasnaia zvezda*, December 21, 1983. FBIS III, December 27, 1983, D9–10; V. Skrizhalin, "Mgnoveniia podviga" (Moments of exploit), *Krasnaia zvezda*, January 8, 1984, 2.

78. G. Ustinov, "Golubye kombinezony" (Blue overalls), *Izvestiia*, August 2, 1984, 5.

79. Nicholas Daniloff, "Afghan Conflict: How Kremlin Glorifies It," *U.S. News & World Report*, October 3, 1983.

80. For example, V. Sukhodolsky, "The Third Battalion," *Krasnaia zvezda*, April 21, 1984. 5—FBIS, May 8, 1984, D2—D6.

81. For example, B. Lalaev, "They Helped Their Afghan Friends," *Krasnaia zvezda*, October 16, 1984. FBIS III, October 18, 1984, D4. Dmitriy Pogorzhelskiy, "To Clear the Land of Lurking Death," *New Times*, no. 37, September 1984, 28–30.

82. V. Baikov and V. Okulov, "Sladkaia voda Porandy" (Poranda's sweet water), *Pravda*, July 15, 1984, 4.

83. G. Ustinov, "Afghanistan—Reporting from the Panjshir Valley: In the Lair of the Five Lions," *Izvestiia*, July 31, 1984, 5. CDSP XXXVI:32, 1.

84. E.g., "Vy takzhe nadezhnye" (You are also reliable), *Komsomol'skaia pravda*, July 11, 1984, 2; "Sappery idut vperedi" (Sappers go in front), *Krasnaia zvezda*, July 12, 1984, 2; Editorial note, "Ver' drugu kak sebe" (Trust your friend as yourself), *Komsomol'skaia pravda*, December 27, 1984, 2; P. Studenikin, "Afganskii dnevnik: I snitsia im Salang . . . " (Afghan diary: They dream of Salang), *Pravda*, July 24, 1984, 6; "Award for bravery," *Krasnaia zvezda*, August 16, 1984. FBIS-SOV-84–164, V4, and "Our Correspondent's Report"—Moscow TV, June 6, 1984. FBIS III, June 11, 1984, D2–D3.

85. For example, V. Skrizhalin, "Zdes' sluzhat vashi synov'ei" (Your sons serve here), *Krasnaia zvezda*, November 29, 1984, 2.

86. N. Sautin, "The Return," *Izvestiia*, December 2, 1984, 6; CDSP XXXVI:48, 7–9.

87. For instance, A. Oliinik, "In the Firing Line," *Krasnaia zvezda*, September 25, 1984. FBIS III, October 18, 1984, D3–D4.

88. "Obrecheno na proval. Na chego vedetsia neob"iavlennaia voina protiv Afganistana?" (Doomed to failure: Why an undeclared war is being waged against Afghanistan), *Pravda*, February 14, 1985, 4.

89. Strizhalin, "Let There Be Peace under the Olive Trees.

90. Borovik, *The Hidden War*, 118–120.

91. See, for example, a special page entitled "S chego nachinaetsia dolg" (From what duty begins), *Komsomol'skaia pravda*, December 27, 1984, 2.

92. Murad Nepesov, "Nov' drevnogo Afganistana" (The virgin soil of ancient Afghanistan), *Sotsialisticheskaia industriia*, January 1, 1985.

93. P. Kruzhin, "O geroiakh Sovetskogo Soiuza" (Heroes of the Soviet Union), *Posev*, no. 4 (1985), 31–32.

94. Wise, "The Soviet Domestic Impact of the War in Afghanistan," 12–13, 15–17.

95. Mickiewicz, *Changing Channels*, 57.

96. Rubtsov, "Sovetskii Soiuz v 'Neob"iavlennoi' voine v Afganistane (1979–1989)," 142.

97. TASS, "Varvarskoe prestuplenie" (Barbaric crime), *Pravda*, May 15, 1985, 5. This was shortly after Gorbachev came to power, almost certainly not yet attributable to new influences.

98. P. Studenikin, "Goriachaia zemlia" (Burning ground), *Pravda*, August 22, 1985, 6.

99. P. Studenikin, "Snova snitsia Salang" (Dreaming of Salang again), *Pravda*, September 10, 1985, 6.

100. Iu. Protasov, "Po dolgu internatsionalistov" (In accordance with the duty of internationalists), *KVS*, no. 24 (December 1985), 27–31.

101. P. Studenikin, "Batal'ion idet v gory" (The battalion goes into the mountains), *Pravda*, September 26, 1985, 6; I. Taranenko, "Trudnoe nebo" (Arduous sky), *Pravda*, October 15, 1985, 6; M. Zemskov, "Shagnuli v bessmertie" (They stepped into immortality), *Pravda*, October 19, 1985, 3; "They Served in Afghanistan," R. Moscow and Soviet television, October 18, 1985—SWB, SU/8091/A3/1—3, October 25, 1985.

102. Daniloff, "Afghan War Finally Hits Soviets' Home Front." For the letter of the Armenian mother, whose son had been killed covering a truck carrying civilian cargo, see *Krasnaia zvezda*, September 5, 1985, 2. A U.S. State Department Special Report wrote similarly: USIS Official Text, U.S. Department of State Special Report, December 19, 1985, 12, and see Craig Karp, "Afghanistan: Seven Years of Soviet Occupation," 83.

103. "Esli potrebuetsia, v stroiu ikh zamenish' ty!" (If necessary, you will replace them in the services!), *Sobesednik*, no. 40, September 1986, 8–9.

104. USIA Addendum Press and Publication Service, no. 37, September 13, 1985. See also a *Pravda* editorial, "Dolg kazhdogo grazhdanina" (Every citizen's duty), September 14, 1985, 1, and *Krasnaia zvezda*, December 5, 1985. The latter two articles made no mention whatever of Afghanistan.

105. USIS Official Text, U.S. Department of State Special Report, December 19, 1985, 12.

106. P. Kushnichenko, "Nakazana za vziatku" (Punished for bribe), *Turkmenskaia iskra*, July 8, 1983.

107. *Pravda*, May 19, 1987, quoted in *Haarets*, May 20, 1987 ("'Pravda': Officials help their sons' evasion of military service").

108. A. Simurov and P. Studenikin, "Ne v dushe blagodarnosti . . . " (Not in a spirit of gratitude . . .), *Pravda*, November 25, 1987, 6.

109. Karp, "Afghanistan: Seven Years of Soviet Occupation," 14.

110. Jukes, "The Soviet Armed Forces and the Afghan War," 90.

111. "Zaiavlenie TASS" (TASS statement), *Pravda*, April 19, 1987, 4; and A. Karpov, "On the Border," *Izvestiia*, April 22, 1987, 6. CDSP 39:16, 17–8. For the incursion, see Chapter 2.

112. TASS, "Udary po bandam" (Attacks against the bands), *Pravda*, September 30, 1985, 5, for instance, quoted the Afghan Bakhtar news agency as saying that the DRA army was dealing "a crushing blow" to the counterrevolution.

113. For example, TASS, "Razgrom banditskogo lokova" (Bandit lair wiped out), *Pravda*, May 2, 1986, 5.

114. Chernyaev, *My Six Years with Gorbachev*, 25.

115. Konnov, "Pravda i vymysel ob afganskoi voine," 51.

116. "The Kabul Government Claims It Has Opened the Road to Khost Besieged by Rebels," *Ha'arets*, December 29, 1987.

117. Pashkevich, *Afganistan: voina glazami kombata*, 27, 48.

118. Aleksandr Prokhanov, "Zapiski na brone" (Notes aboard an armored personnel carrier), *Literaturnaia gazeta*, August 28, 1985, 14.

119. E.g., Vladimir Snegirev, "Afganistan, aprel' 1986 goda . . . " (Afghanistan, April 1986 . . .), *Sobesednik*, no. 17 (April 1986), 8–9.

120. V. Andrianov and V. Panov, "Chem bogat Grigorii Kolos?" (What makes Grigory Kolos Rich?), *Komsomol'skaia pravda*, September 4, 1985, 2.

121. Gai and Snegirev, *Vtorzhenie*, 253–254.

122. For example, Ivan Dynin, "Chetvertaia granata" (The fourth grenade), no. 2, January 1986, 5, on an officer killed in battle; Aleksandr Prokhanov "My budem pomnit's etot boi . . ." (We shall remember this battle . . .), no. 4, January 1986, 8–9 (Significantly Prokhanov did not use the word *voina*, war); Novakovskii Boris, "V pis'makh mnogo ne rasskazhesh'" (You don't tell much in letters), no. 27, July 1986; and Liana Minasian, "Nepravda, drug ne umiraet . . . " (It's not true, a friend doesn't die), no. 30, July 1986, 5.

123. Vladimir Misiuchenko, "Gore i dolg" (Sorrow and duty), *Sobesednik* no. 50, December 1986, 8–9; and see Laura Tsagolova, "Snova snitsia voina" (Dreaming of the war once again), *Sobesednik*, no. 3, January 1987, 11.

124. Nahaylo, *The Ukrainian Resurgence*, 73, and "Ukrainian Mother Protests Soviet Media Coverage of the War in Afghanistan," RL 34/87, January 22, 1987.

125. P. Studenikin, "'Ia vas v Afganistan ne posylal . . . '" ('I didn't send you to Afghanistan'), *Pravda*, August 5, 1987, 3. (For Verstakov's specific shameful recollection, see above.)

126. Kotkin, *Armageddon Averted*, 70.

127. Mendelson, *Changing Course*, 108–109; Yurchak, *Everything Was Forever, Until It Was No More*, 2—3.

128. Quoted in Mendelson, *Changing Course*, 113. See Chapter 4.

129. Kim Selikhov, "Trudnym putem" (On a hard path), *Literaturnaia gazeta*, October 14, 1987, 14.

130. Artyom Borovik, "Diary of a Reporter," *Ogonek*, nos. 28, 29, 30 (July 1987), quoted in Smith, *The New Russians*, 103; the full title was "Vstretimsia na trekh zhuravlei: Iz bloknota reportera" (Let us meet at the Three Cranes: From a reporter's diary).

131. Smith, *The New Russians*, 103—104. The quote is from his conversation with Korotich, June 7, 1988.

132. Mendelson, *Changing Course*, 114.

133. Smith, *The New Russians*, 165–169.

134. Bonnell and Freidin, "The Role of Television Coverage in Russia's August 1991 Coup," 812–813.

135. Tsagolova, "Snova snitsia voina," *Sobesednik*, no. 3 (January 1988), 11.

136. E.g., Alexander Usvatov, "They Must Come Home!" *New Times* no. 25 (June 1988), 5–6, on five former POW vets who addressed a press conference at *Literaturnaia gazeta*'s offices.

137. A. Iziumov and A. Kortunov, "Sovetskii Soiuz v meniaiushchemsia mire" (The Soviet Union in a changing world), *Mezhdunarodnaia zhizn'*, no. 7, 1988, 60.

138. R. Vedeniapan, "Zhdut materi synovei" (Mothers await their sons), *Komsomol'skaia pravda*, August 9, 1988.

139. Galeotti, *Afghanistan*, 90–92, 143–144.

140. Artem Borovik, "Chto zhe my navtorili?" (What have we been up to?), *Sobesednik*, no. 38 (1989), 10.

141. Ivan Demidov, interviewing Tsagolov in 1992, said his earlier interview led to a witch hunt by the MPA that ended with him being dismissed from the army. "Rossiia ne dolzhna podderzhivat' tol'ko odnu iz konfliktuiushchikh storon" (Russia must not support just one of the conflicting parties), *Nezavisimaia gazeta*, September 8, 1992, 1, 4.

142. "Afganistan: predvaritel'nye itogi" (Afghanistan: Preliminary results), *Ogonek*, no. 30, 1988, 25–27.

143. Alexander Pumpyansky, "Defeat or Victory? Lessons to be drawn," *New Times*, no. 30 (July 1988), 13–14.

144. See his article "Zapiski na brone," *Literaturnaia gazeta*, August 28, 1985, 14.

145. Aleksandr Prokhanov, "Afganskie voprosy" (Afghan questions), *Literaturnaia gazeta*, February 17, 1988, 1, 9.

146. Vladimir Dashichev, "Vostok—zapad: poisk novye otnoshenii" (East-West: The search for new relations), *Literaturnaia gazeta*, May 18, 1988, 14. Dashichev headed the International Relations Department at the Institute of Economics of the World Socialist System.

147. Demidov, "Rossiia ne dolzhna podderzhivat' tol'ko odny iz konfliktuiushchikh storon."

148. Borovik, "Chto zhe my navtorili?", *Sobesednik*, no. 38 (1989), 2, 10.

149. Bill Keller, "Soviet Secret Party Document Admits Error in Afghanistan," *International Herald Tribune*, June 18–19, 1988, 1–2.

150. Author's interview with Aleksandr Bovin, Tel Aviv, August 1992.

151. Aleksandr Dobrotov, "'Eta vstrecha peretriakhnula vsiu moiu zhizn" (This encounter shook up my entire life), *Komsomol'skaia pravda*, January 8, 1986; quoted in RL 241/86, July 24, 1986, 3–4.

152. E.g., the Tajik SSR government *Tojikistoni soveti*, August 29, 1987. SU/8679/B/6; September 22, 1987.

153. E.g., On April 4, 1987, *Pravda* published an article by P. Studenikin entitled "V chas ispytaniia: proidia dorogami Afganistana, oni vernulis' domoi s obstrennym chuvstvom otvetsvennosti za dela i zaboty Rodiny" (In the hour of trial: Having passed through the roads of Afghanistan, they returned home with a sharpened sense of responsibility for the affairs and concerns of the mother country), relating the story of three afgantsy who had acquitted themselves unfalteringly in battle and whom the local bureaucracy had then maltreated. (This is the article that engendered "I didn't send you to Afghanistan.")

154. P. Studenikin, "'Ia vas v Afganistan ne posylal . . . " (I didn't send you to Afghanistan . . .), *Pravda*, August 5, 1987, 3.

155. A. Simurov and P. Studenikin, "Ne v dushe blagodarnosti . . . " (Not in a spirit of gratitude . . .), *Pravda*, November 25, 1987, 6.

156. G. Apresian, "Afgantsy, "*Literaturnaia gazeta*, August 8, 1988, 11.

157. E.g., *Bakinskii rabochii*, July 8, 1988; *Pravda Ukrainy*, July 10, 1988; *Izvestiia*, July 15, 1988.

158. See note 1.

159. "Spriatannaia voina (The hidden war), *Ogonek*, no. 52 (December 1989), 27, and Borovik, *The Hidden War*, 256.

160. David Gai, "Afganistan: kak eto bylo" (Afghanistan: how it was), *Vecherniaia Moskva*, December 26, 1989, 4.

161. Borovik, *The Hidden War*, 279–280. Indeed, the editor-in-chief of *Nash sovremennik* accused the liberal press—*Iunost'*, *Ogonek*, *Moskovskie Novosti* and *Moskovskii komsomolets*—of driving a wedge between society and the military—"Is Nash Sovremennik Up-to-date?"—*Krasnaia zvezda*, December 20, 1989, 4—CDSP XLII:2, 34–35.

162. Borovik, "Spriatannaia voina," *Ogonek*, Nos. 46 and 49–52 (1989).

163. G. Bocharov, "Afgan," *Literaturnaia gazeta*, February 15, 1989, 13–14.

164. Vladimir Snegirev, "Pro voinu" (About the war), *Komsomol'skaia pravda*, February 9, 1989, 4.

165. Safronov, "Kak eto bylo" (How it was), *Voenno-istoricheskii zhurnal*, no. 5 (1990), 71.

166. For discussion of the evolution of public opinion, see Brown, *The Gorbachev Factor*, 18–19.

Chapter 7

1. How and why the term gained currency is not clear. In the war's early stages, the planes were dubbed "Gruz (Cargo) 200." See N. Ivanov "Tsvety skorbi" (Shades of grief), *Sovetskaia Rossiia*, February 15, 1990, 4.

2. Downing, "Trouble in the Backyard: Soviet Media Reporting on the Afghan Conflict," 7.

3. Kotkin, *Armageddon Averted*, 68.

4. Bill Keller, "Home from Afghanistan; Russia's Divisive War," *New York Times Magazine*, February 14, 1988.

5. Konnov, "Pravda i vymysel ob afganskoi voiny," 52. Konnov was relating his personal experience.

6. Interview with Mikhail Reshetnikov, http://www.rosbalt.ru/piter/2009/02/14/618431.html, accessed April 12, 2015.

7. Braithwaite, *Afgantsy*, 238.

8. Cherniaev, *Sovmestnyi iskhod: dnevnik dvukh epokh*, 391, quoted in Braithwaite, *Afgantsy*, 238.

9. Ol'shanskii, "Afganskii sled."

10. Andriushchenko, "Chto sovetskie grazhdane dumali o voine v Afganistane i kak KGB borolsia s nedovol'nymi."

11. E.g., an All-Union Center for the Study of Public Opinion on Social and Economic Questions came into being in early 1988, headed by Academician Tat'iana Zaslavskaia, and the biweekly *Argumenty i fakty* regularly published opinion polls on a wide range of questions, enabling people to express their views as citizens and consumers.

12. Konnov, "Pravda i vymysel ob afganskoi voiny," 50.

13. For her testimony, see the film *Poslednyi soldat* (The last soldier), directed by Sergei Seregin, script by Aleksandr Liakhovskii and Petr Silantiev, 2004.

14. E.g., in Bukhara, officials interred the 120 casualties in different cemeteries. Interview with Timurid Akebirov, Bukhara, May 11, 2014.

15. Testimony of a physician from Perm—RFE/RL 12/82. See also an item in a prestigious

Moscow paper that wrote about one boy from Kirov oblast' killed in 1980 who had "Perished heroically in Afghanistan," engraved on his tombstone. G. Apresian, "Afgantsy'" (The 'afgantsy'), *Literaturnaia gazeta*, August 8, 1988, 11.

16. Andriushchenko, "Chto sovetskie grazhdane dumali o voine v Afganistane."

17. . Ibid.

18. Gennadii Bocharov, "Afghan," *Literaturnaia gazeta*, no. 7, February 15, 1989, 13.

19. Quoted in Gai and Snegirev, *Vtorzhenie*, 207.

20. *Der Spiegel*, June 16, 1980. DR/FBIS III, June 20, 1980, R1.

21. Girardet (quoting a samizdat report), "Russia's War in Afghanistan," 108.

22. Interviews with the author, February 1982.

23. Braithwaite, *Afgantsy*, 255–256.

24. Borovik, *The Hidden War*, 170.

25. Bocharov, *Russian Roulette*, 30.

26. Alexievich, *Zinky Boys*, 17, 97, 170.

27. Tkachenko, *Afganistan bolit v moei dushe*, 197.

28. See n. 1.

29. Braithwaite, *Afgantsy*, 254–255.

30. Alexievich, *Zinky Boys*, 8. Some families also reported the stench from the coffins, even "little white worms dropping [from them] on to the floor." Ibid., 124.

31. Gai and Snegirev, *Vtorzhenie*, 278–279. The authors bring a document prepared for CGS Ogarkov in 1983 on this sore issue.

32. "Rasskazyvaiut ob Afganistane" (Stories about Afghanistan), *Posev*, no. 7 (1985), 21.

33. Alexievich, *Zinky Boys*, 83, 87. Unfortunately, like many other stories in Alexievich's book, this one is undated.

34. *The Black Tulip* (1987).

35. P. Studenikin, "'Ia Vas v Afganistan ne posylal . . . '" (I didn't send you to Afghanistan), *Pravda*, August 5, 1987, 3.

36. Bohdan Nahaylo, "Radio Kiev Provides Glimpse of Extent of Soviet Casualties in Afghanistan," RL 448/87, October 27, 1987.

37. Galeotti, *Afghanistan*, 30.

38. Testimony of a Leningrad film director who met Soviet soldiers wounded in Afghanistan. RFE/RL 12/82.

39. Amstutz, *Afghanistan: The First Five Years of Soviet Occupation*, 238.

40. Raleigh, *Soviet Baby Boomers*, 263.

41. Alexievich, *Zinky Boys*, 34. For the effect of the public's apathy on the soldiers serving in Afghanistan, see Chapter 3.

42. Michael Binyon, "The Huge Price Russia Is Being Forced to Pay," *Economist*, December 20, 1980.

43. Ibid.

44. "Terroristicheskie nalety i besplodnye razgovory" (Terrorist raids and futile negotiations), *Posev*, no. 5 (1982), 16.

45. Robert Gillette, "Soviet Coffins Bring Afghan War Home," *Los Angeles Times*, March 20, 1983.

46. Raleigh, *Soviet Baby Boomers*, 252–267, 361.

47. Wise, "The Soviet Domestic Impact of the War in Afghanistan," 2.

48. Alexievich, *Zinky Boys*, 108.

49. Sannikov, ed., *Smoliane—internatsionalisty*, 281.

50. "'Mesto sluzhby—Afganistan'" (Duty station—Afghanistan), *Posev*, no. 4 (1983), 12.

51. Gai and Snegirev, *Vtorzhenie*, 206–207.

52. Robert Gillette, "Soviet Veterans Bitter after Afghan War Duty," *Los Angeles Times*, April 4, 1983.

53. Letters to Viktor Yankin, *Komsomol'skaia pravda*, March 22, 1984, 2. FBIS III, March 26, 1984.

54. Ol'shanskii, "Afganskii sled."

55. Odom, *The Collapse of the Soviet Military*, 247–248.

56. Grau, *The Bear Went Over the Mountain*, 207. See also Chapter 6.

57. Alexievich, *Zinky Boys*, 122. For corruption of the voenkomats, see Chapter 3.

58. "Soviet General Took Bribes and Released from Service in Afghanistan," *Ha'arets*, July 7, 1987.

59. Gillette, "Soviet Coffins Bring Afghan War Home."

60. Michael McGuire, "Soviets See No Light in Afghan Tunnel," *Chicago Tribune*, September 2, 1985.

61. SAAOR Research Memorandum RM 6–85, September 1985. There is higher support in the SAAOR poll because Soviet citizens allowed to travel tended to tilt toward approval of regime policy. SAAOR believed that the far higher rate of disapproval in the second poll emanated from different criteria for the in-between categories. Galeotti, *Afghanistan*, 141, notes that the survey results were "processed through a computer simulation designed to correct for such weightings and model the opinions of the broader urban population."

62. Parta, *Discovering the Hidden Listener*, 48.

63. "Opinions on Afghanistan," RFE/RL 7/85, 10. In Russian slang, *chukchi*—the name of a small group of people inhabiting northeast Siberia—is used as a synonym for the "primitive and uncivilized" Soviet Central Asians.

64. Kuzio, "Opposition in the USSR to the Occupation of Afghanistan," 106, 107.

65. Quoted in Bohdan Nahaylo, "Ukrainian Mother Protests Soviet Media Coverage of the War in Afghanistan," RL 34/87, January 22, 1987. For other mentions of Afghanistan in dissident journals, see "References to Afghanistan in Samizdat," RL 143/84, April 6, 1984, and "Ukrainian Samizdat Journal Gives Details of Casualties in Afghanistan," RL 9/85, January 10, 1985.

66. Galeotti, *Afghanistan*, 27.

67. Quoted in Taras Kuzio, "Samizdat against the Afghan War," USIA addendum AD858, February 21, 1986.

68. Nicholas Daniloff, "Afghan War Finally Hits Soviets' Home Front," *U.S. News & World Report*, December 16, 1985, 35.

69. Sallie Wise, "'A War Should Never Have Happened': Soviet Citizens Assess the War in Afghanistan," RL 226/88, June 1, 1988, and "The Soviet Domestic Impact of the War in Afghanistan, 5–12.

70. *Argumenty i fakty*, no. 20, May 20–26, 1989, 4–5. FBIS-SOV-89–099, May 24, 1989, 65.

71. Parta, *Discovering the Hidden Listener*, 49–51, and "The Audience to Western Broadcasts to the USSR during the Cold War," 91.

72. V. Rybakov, "Krovavye sobytiia" (Bloody events), *Posev*, no. 8 (1985), 17.

73. "Afghanistan: A Voice from Moscow," 18.

74. Wise, "A War Should Never Have Happened."

75. "Shel parnishke v tu poru devatnadtsatyi god . . ." (Then a nineteen year-old lad went . . .), *Pobratim*, no. 4 (1990), 2. The man had written a similar letter in June 1985.

76. Chernyaev, *My Six Years with Gorbachev*, 25, 42.

77. *Argumenty i fakty*, no. 20, May 20–26, 1989, 4–5. FBIS-SOV-89–099, May 24, 1989, 65.

78. Keller, "Home from Afghanistan."

79. "Poslednii soldat ogranichennogo kontingenta sovetskikh voisk v Afganistane vernulsia na rodinu" (Last soldier of the Limited Contingent of Soviet troops in Afghanistan returned to the mother country), *Komsomolets Uzbekistana*, February 16, 1989.

80. Keller, "Home from Afghanistan."

81. Galeotti, *Afghanistan*, 31–32.

82. Fane, "After Afghanistan: The Decline of Soviet Military Prestige," 5.

83. For criticism leveled against the military as the 1980s drew to a close—perhaps as a prelude to the cuts in military expenditure enforced in late 1989—see V. Ostalskii, "Is There a Military-Industrial Complex in the USSR?" *Izvestiia*, October 16, 1989, 7, and N. Sautin, AWOL soldier, October 21, 1989, 6. CDSP XLI:42, 21.

84. Parta, *Discovering the Hidden Listener*, 89–90. Two surveys that the Soviet Institute of Sociological Research and Western media organizations conducted jointly found 25 and 27 percent, respectively, holding the former view and 33 and 37 percent the latter.

85. Bernard E. Trainor, "Afghans and the Soviet Psyche: Military Myths Fade as the Troops Pull Out," *New York Times*, February 15, 1989, A12.

86. "Vystuplenie tovarishcha Gromova B. V." (Speech of Comrade B. V. Gromov), *Pravda*, July 2, 1988, 7.

87. E.g., *Pravda*'s military department, "'Chto s nami stalo?'" (What has become of us?), *Pravda*, May 22, 1988, 6.

88. *New York Times*, February 7, 1989, quoted in Rakowska-Harmstone, "The Soviet Armed Forces: The Challenge of Reform and the Ethnic Factor," 33.

89. Bocharov, *Russian Roulette*, 76–83.

90. "Pravda vysshee sensatsii" (The truth is above sensations), *Sovetskaia Rossiia*, November 15, 1989, 4, quoted in FBIS-SOV-89–223, November 21, 1989, 103.

91. Galeotti, *Afghanistan*, 62.

92. Yuli Kosharovsky, "*We Are Jews Again": Jewish Activism in the Soviet Union*, ed. Ann Komaromi (Syracuse, NY: Syracuse University Press, 2017), 154, 233. Several refuseniks expressed this belief explicitly in interviews I conducted with them (*refuseniks* was the term used for Jews refused exit permits from the Soviet Union.)

93. Galeotti, *Afghanistan*, 153–154. A November 1989 survey conducted in Moscow found most respondents likened the Soviet "mission" in Afghanistan to that of the United States in Vietnam. "'Afgantsy' sredi nas" (The 'Afgantsy" amongst us), *Pobratim*, no. 3 (February 1990) 4–5.

94. "Problemy sotsial'noi reabilitatsii uchastnikov voiny v Afganistane," 6–8.

95. Testimony of Dima Adamsky, then a boy in his early teens growing up in Vilnius, February 12, 2013.

96. Galeotti, *Afghanistan*, 58–59, 227–228. For vigilante groups or gangs, see Chapter 8.

97. This was the first conclusion drawn from a survey conducted in Moscow in November 1989 (see n. 93).

98. Interview with Dr. Madridin Magomed-Eminov, Moscow, June 27, 1991.

99. *Afganistan v nashei sud'be*, 164.

100. Znakov, "Psikhologicheskoe issledovanie stereotipov ponimaniia lichnosti uchastnikov voiny v Afganistane."

101. Larisa Vyshinskaia, "Pro ety voinu" (About this war), *Sobesednik*, no. 9, February 1989, 6–7.

102. Quoted Riordan, "Teenage Gangs, 'Afgantsy' and Neofascists," 130.

103. Pikov, ed., *Voina v Afganistane*, 308–309. The sociological service at Gosteleradio conducted this survey.

104. Pinnick, "Public Opinion in Russia on the Ex-USSR's Afghanistan War Veterans since 1991," 1–2.

105. "Problemy sotsial'no reabilitatsii uchastnikov voiny v Afganistane," 11–12.

106. M. Voronin, "Soldiers of the Fatherland," *Sovetskaia Belorussiia*, April 21, 1989, 4. FBIS-SOV-89–108, June 7, 1989, 72–73.

107. *Afganistan v nashei sud'be*, 44.

108. Quoted in Konovalov, "Pesni veteranov Afganistana," 11.

109. Alexievich, *Zinky Boys*, 56–57, 148.

110. V. Dashkevich, "Ostorozhno! Zaplacheno krov'iu . . ." (Careful! Paid for in blood . . .), *Krasnaia zvezda*, October 21, 1988, 2.

111. For instance, a song that Golubye berety performed, which appeared in anthologies (and on CDs) "Ordena ne prodaiutsia" (Awards are not for sale). Oushakine, "'War das etwa alles umsonst?' Russlands Kriege in militärischen Liedern," 194.

112. Galeotti, *Afghanistan*, 152.

113. Kinsburskii and Topalov, "Reabilitatsiia uchastnikov afganskoi voiny v obshchestvennom mnenii," 104–107.

114. Konnov, "Pravda i vymysel ob afganskoi voine," 52.

115. Compare Danilova, "The Development of an Exclusive Veterans' Policy," 903. Few afgantsy complained about the World War II vets' attitude to them. See Figure 8.4.

116. V. Izgarshev, "Afganskaia bol'" (Afghan pain), *Pravda*, August 17, 1989, 6. See also "'Chto s nami stalo?'"

117. M. Kil'kinskii, "Vsegda li prav 'afganets'?" (Is the Afghan vet always right?), *Izvestiia*, September 7, 1988, 6.

118. Alexievich, *Zinky Boys*, 77–78.

119. *Sotsialisticheskaia industriia*, June 26, 1988, quoted in Valerii Konovalov, "Reintegrating Afghan Veterans into Civilian Life," RL 425/88, September 19, 1988.

120. Braithwaite, *Afgantsy*, 319.

121. Yuri Stasiuk in an interview in 2015:file:///D:/Document/Doc/Afghanistan/afgantsy/Yuri%20Stasiuk.htm, accessed November 2, 2015.

122. G. Apresian, "Afgantsy," *Literaturnaia gazeta*, August 8, 1988, 11.

123. Larisa Vyshinskaia, "Pro ety voinu" (About this war), *Sobesednik* no. 9, February 1989, 6–7.

124. Galeotti, *Afghanistan*, 76–77.

125. For example, "Miloserdie—ne meloch'!" (Charity is no small matter!), *Pobratim*, no. 4 (1990), 5.

126. *Afganistan v nashei sud'be*, 146–148.

127. *Krasnaia zvezda*, July 19, 1988, quoted in Galeotti, *Afghanistan*, 83.

128. E.g., "Nesdaiushchiesia" (Those who don't give up), and Dina Rakhimova and Liliana Galleva, " . . . I stol'ko nedostatkov!" (. . . And so many shortcomings!), *Komsomolets Uzbekistana*, July 12, 1989.

129. Pinnick, "Public Opinion in Russia," 4.

130. Congress of USSR People's Deputies, verbatim report, *Izvestiia*, June 10, 1989, 3–11. CDSP XLI:31, 19. Preparations for the MoD Book of Memory were indeed begun in 1989. See Chapter 3.

131. E.g., "Vspomnim vsekh poimenno" (We shall remember them all by name), *Komsomolets Uzbekistana*, June 27, 1989, 1; "Razmyshlenii" (Reflections), *Komsomolets Uzbekistana*, July

12, 1989; Maksim Radov, "Otriad imeni Rasulova" (The Rasulov detachment), *Komsomolets Uzbekistana*, July 21, 1989; Maksud Akramov, "Pamiati internatsionalistov" (In memory of the internationalists), *Komsomolets Uzbekistana*, July 21, 1989; L. Katanova, "My etoi pamiati verny" (We are true to this memory) and M. Slutskii, "Ulitsa mladshego syna" (Street of the younger son), *Komsomolets Turkmenistana*, March 30, June 8, 1989.

132. "V TsK VLKSM" (At the Komsomol CC), *Komsomolets Uzbekistana*, February 18, 1989.

133. This finding contrasted sharply with those of the November 1989 survey, where the majority of respondents opined that society related to the afgantsy "unfairly." "'Afgantsy' sredi nas," *Pobratim*, no. 3 (February 1990) 4–5.

134. Levinson, "Otchet ob issledovanii 'Obshchestvennoe mnenie o problemakh uchastnikov voennykh deistvii v Afganistane.'"

135. Ol'shanskii, "Smyslovye struktury lichnosti uchastnikov afganskoi voiny," 121–129.

136. "Problemy sotsial'noi reabilitatsii uchastnikov voiny v Afganistane," 20.

137. Pavel Felgengauer, "Unfinished War Could Go On Forever," *Current Digest of the Post-Soviet Press* XLVI:7, 31, quoted in Pinnick, "Public Opinion in Russia," 1

138. Andriushchenko, "Chto sovetskie grazhdane dumali o voine v Afganistane."

139. Radio Liberty, SAAOR, SBN 1–86, quoted in Kuzio, "Opposition in the USSR to the Occupation of Afghanistan," 102.

140. Charlotte Astor, "Soviet Anti-Draft Protests Reported," USIA addendum no. 26 PPS, June 28, 1985.

141. Daniloff, "Afghan War Finally Hits Soviets' Home Front."

142. Kuzio, "Opposition in the USSR to the Occupation of Afghanistan," 109.

143. For example, in Estonia in 1987: Kozlov and Mironenko, eds., *Kramola: Inakomyslie v SSSR*, 196.

144. "Demonstration in Moscow against Continued Soviet Presence in Afghanistan Forcibly Dispersed," *Ha'arets*, December 27, 1987. Despite glasnost, sixteen people were arrested in the two demonstrations.

145. Stephen M. Meyer, "From Afghanistan to Azerbaijan, Discord Undermines the Red Army," *New York Times*, January 28, 1990, E3; Rakowska-Harmstone, "The Soviet Armed Forces," 8.

146. Galeotti, *Afghanistan*, 161. The first letter was published in *Sotsialisticheskaia industriia*, May 8, 1988.

147. AS 6299, *Doverie*, no. 7, September 1988, *Materialy samizdata*, Vypusk 47/88. See also "Trudno byt' Bogom. Eshche raz ob Afganistane i ne tol'ko o nem" (It's difficult to be God. Once again about Afghanistan and not only that), [June 1988], AS no. 6291:3.

148. Quoted in Dobbs, "In Service of the Motherland," *Washington Post*, September 7, 1991.

149. AFP in English, April 29, 1989, FBIS-SOV-89–083, May 2, 1989, 48–49.

150. *Literaturnaia gazeta*, April 20, 1988, 14. In June, the same paper published an appeal of afgantsy to do everything possible to liberate the POWs (see Chapter 8) and that same month, *New Times* (no. 26) printed an article entitled "They Must Come Home!"

151. TASS, June 13, 1988, quoted in Bren West, "Soviet Prisoners of the Afghan Resistance," RL 267/88, June 23, 1988.

152. Enver Akhmedzyanov, "The Search for Soviet Captives in Afghanistan Gains Speed," *Moscow News*, no. 47, November 20, 1988, 5. There were also rallies calling for the release of the Soviet POWs outside the U.S. consulate in Leningrad. AFP in English, April 29, 1989. FBIS-SOV-89–083, May 2, 1989.

153. P. Studenikin, "Tam, za Gindu-Kushem" (There, beyond the Hindu-Kush), *Pravda*, September 11, 1988, 1, 3.

154. N. Palkin, "What They Discussed in Islamabad," *Izvestiia*, December 8, 1988, 3. CDSP XL:49, 23. Two POWs had been united with their families days before. TASS, "In the Embrace of Family," *Pravda*, November 29, 1988, 5.

155. R. Moscow, January 9, 1989. FBIS-SOV-89–007, January 11, 1989, 20.

156. "Zalozhniki voiny" (Hostages of war), *Komsomol'skaia pravda*, October 17, 1989, 4. FBIS October 20, 1989. A Hope delegation visited Pakistan in the early summer in order to rescue POWs. M. Kozhukhov, "We Aren't Losing Hope," *Izvestiia*, July 3, 1989, 4.

157. *Izvestiia*, June 18, November 20, 1989, FBIS-SOV-89–119, June 22, 1989, 31–32, and RFE/RL daily report no. 222, November 21, 1989. Initiatives to help liberate the POWs also occurred at the republican level—e.g., *Komsomolets Uzbekistana*, April 11, 1989.

158. M. Bektasov described the tribulations of one such soldier, a Turkmen, taken captive in 1981 who escaped in 1984, in "The Homeland Is More Precious Than Life," *Turkmenskaia iskra*, February 10, 1989, 3. JPRS-UPA-89–038, June 6, 1989, 100–102.

159. For example, "Three Versions of One Homecoming," *New Times*, no. 17, April 24–30, 1990.

160. E. Gams, "Finding Out the Truth," *Argumenty i fakty*, no. 44, November 4–10, 1989, 7. CDSP XLI:50, 17. For doubts about figures for wounded and sick, see Chapter 3.

161. Interview of Iurii Filatov with Irina Dzherelievskaia, *Afganistan v nashei sud'be*, 43, 45.

162. Sh. Zhaksybaeva, "Mat' soldata" (A soldier's mother), *Izvestiia*, August 8, 1990, 6.

163. Analysis of servicemen's deaths in the 1980s showed almost 7,000 per annum (about 50 percent higher than in the U.S. army). While the MoD "alleges that the majority of these men perish through their own fault"—suicide, negligence and accidents—"thousands of parents believe that their sons were killed through some official negligence or murder. . . . A Soviet officer having access to the statistics of the Ministry of Defense has informed us that 'many more soldiers die under mysterious circumstances than the military recognizes even in the reports destined for official use.'" According to "official confidential statistics . . . 18 percent of such deaths are suicides, 5.5 percent are the result of crimes, 13.5 percent . . . a result of accidents, 17 percent from not observing industrial safety, 21 percent from disease, 15 percent from road accidents, and 9.5 percent from careless handling of firearms." Sarin and Dvoretsky, *The Afghan Syndrome*, 175.

164. Peter Gumbel, "Red Army Faces a Formidable Foe: Mothers of Recruits," *Wall Street Journal*, January 30, 1990, A1.

165. "Sovet materei i vdov" (Council of mothers and widows), *Krasnaia zvezda*, October 17, 1989, 1.

166. N. Burbyga, "Gore, kotoroe nel'zia zabyt' (Grief that cannot be forgotten), *Izvestiia*, August 10, 1990, 7.

167. K. Lesoto, "Komandirovka na voinu" (War assignment), *Komsomol'skaia pravda*, February 26, 1988.

168. Editorial, "Dva adresa" (Two addresses), *Komsomol'skaia pravda*, February 22, 1984, 4.

169. In 1990–1991, before the Soviet Union fell apart, republican media deplored the government's failure to support young widows and their small children or to provide health care for soldiers' mothers. See Elena Verina, "Problem trebuiut reshenii" (Problems demand solutions), *Komsomolets Uzbekistana*, February 8, 1990, and E. Karpova, "Kto zhe otvetit?" (Who will provide the answers?), *Komsomolets Kirgizii*, February 13, 1991, 9.

170. A first excerpt appeared in 1981: "Vstrechi na Maivande" (Meeting at Maivand), *Literaturnaia gazeta*, April 21, 1981, 7. The full novel appeared in the conservative journal *Oktiabr'*, no. 1 (1982).

171. Akram Sharipov, "Put' ot Puli-Charkhi" (The road from Puli-Charkhi; the name of

a Kabul prison), *Pravda*, May 4, 1984, 4. The Soviet Writers' Publishing House brought out Kim Selikhov's book, *Neob"iavlennaia voina* (The undeclared war). In 1987, Selikhov visited the Soviet troops in Afghanistan, including one remote outpost that impressed him greatly. Kim Selikhov, "Afganistan: trudnym putem" (Afghanistan: On a difficult path), *Literaturnaia gazeta*, October 14, 1987, 14.

172. Swartz, "The Soviet-Afghan War in Russian Literature," 53.

173. Yurchak, *Everything Was Forever, Until It Was No More*, 215–216. The song "Get Your Filthy Hands off My Desert" compared the Afghan intervention with wars that the Soviets considered "imperialist."

174. "Afganistan v sovetskoi presse" (Afghanistan in the Soviet press), *Posev*, no. 4 (1984), 19.

175. A few, however, were composed earlier; for example, *Krasnaia zvezda* correspondent Viktor Vozovikov's *V gorakh dolgo svetaet* (Light in the mountains lasts long; Moscow: Voenizdat, 1990) was written between 1981 and 1983.

176. Swartz, "The Soviet-Afghan War in Russian Literature," 152–163.

177. They appeared respectively in *Moskva* 9, 10 (1986), 33–155, 11–106; and *Oktiabr'* 9 (1986), 3–55. Prokhanov wrote the novel in 1984 when he was in Herat. *Risunki batalista*, 7. His heroes were soldiers of the Limited Contingent. Aleksandr Prokhanov, "My budem pomnit' etot boi . . ." (We shall remember this battle . . .), *Sobesednik*, January 4, 1986, 8–9.

178. The recordings were entitled *Vremia vybralo nas*. Pesni voinov internatsionalistov" (Time chose us. Songs of internationalist fighters)—V. Verstakov, "Vspomnim, tovarishch . . . " (Let's remember, Comrade . . .), *Pravda*, December 27, 1988, 6.

179. Sapper, *Die Auswirkung des Afghanistan-Krieges auf die Sowjetgesellschaft*, 326–327.

180. Galeotti, *Afghanistan*, 72.

181. Semenov, *Bol'*, 39.

182. http://poetryrain.com/authors/evtushenko-evgeniy/11134, accessed March 16, 2015.

183. Swartz, "The Soviet-Afghan War in Russian Literature," 203–205, 222–223. Swartz devotes an entire chapter of his thesis to Prokhanov's belletristica. For Prokhanov's post–Afghan War writing, see, for example, *Tretii tost* (The third toast; Moscow: Molodaia gvardiia, 2003).

184. *Podvig*, Vypusk (issue) 34 (Moscow: Molodaia gvardiia, 1989).

185. Swartz, "The Soviet-Afghan War in Russian Literature," 164–167, 186–190. The reference is to Ivanov's "Ogranichennyi kontingent," *Sovetskii voin*, nos. 10–19/20 (May–October 1991).

186. Poliakov, *Sto dnei do prikaza*. Poliakov's book contains only two—incidental—mentions of the Afghan War.

187. Swartz, "The Soviet-Afghan War in Russian Literature," 264, 328–329. Swartz has three chapters on Ermakov's work.

188. Swartz, "The Soviet-Afghan War in Russian Literature," 111.

189. Verstakov, *Afganskii dnevnik*, 241, and "Vspomnim, tovarishch . . . ," *Pravda*, December 27, 1988, 6.

190. I. Dynin, "Aist—ptitsa dobraia" (The stork—a friendly bird), *Trud*, February 24, 1983, 4. For reportage surrounding Stovba's death, see Chapter 6.

191. According to Braithwaite, *Afgantsy*, 193, the majority were officers.

192. Verstakov, "Afganskii dnevnik," 20.

193. Swartz, "The Soviet-Afghan War in Russian Literature," 112–114. The quote is taken from I. M. Dynin, *Posle Afganistana* (Moskva: Profizdat, 1990), 51.

194. Verstakov, "Vspomnim, tovarishch . . . ," *Pravda*, December 27, 1988, 6.

195. Ol'shanskii, "'Afganskii sindrom,'" *Literaturnoe obozrenie*, no. 3 (1990), 15.

196. Robert Gillette, "A Brutal War Revealed in Soviet Songs," *Los Angeles Times*, April 17,

1983. Gillette provided the texts of "Gunner's song," "Why We Shed Our Blood," "By Order of the Party," and untitled songs, one of a dying political officer, another of a mountain ambush, and a third of combat on the outskirts of Kabul.

197. Verstakov, *Afganskii dnevnik*, 243.

198. Author's interview with Dima Adamsky, then in his early teens. February 12, 2013.

199. Konovalov, "Pesni veteranov Afganistana," 5.

200. A. Prokhanov, "Zapiski na brone" (Notes aboard an armored personnel carrier), *Literaturnaia gazeta*, August 28, 1985, 14.

201. Verstakov, *Afganskii vestnik*, 244, and Swartz, "The Soviet-Afghan War in Russian Literature," 116–118. Both Tkachenko and Karpenko told Swartz that the government had censored their first books of Afghan songs—*Kogda poiut soldaty* (When soldiers sing) and *Razgovory so smert'iu* respectively. For the Ashkhabad convention, see Chapter 8.

202. https://www.youtube.com/watch?v=YBf8T-sirdE, accessed January 6, 2018. The report is undated.

203. Galeotti, *Afghanistan*, 146–149.

204. Swartz, "The Soviet-Afghan War in Russian Literature," 125, 132.

205. Braithwaite, *Afgantsy*, 193.

206. Swartz, "The Soviet-Afghan War in Russian Literature," 138–140.

207. Karpenko's second volume of poems, *Tret'ia storona medali* (The third side of the medal), appeared in 1991.Vyacheslav Ogryzko, "Neobyknovennaya Sud'ba Poeta Aleksandra Karpenko: Chast' 1, Razgovory so Smertyu" (The unusual fate of the poet Aleksandr Karpenko: Part 1, conversations with death). http://www.proza.ru/2011/03/07/1110, accessed December 15, 2017.

208. Galeotti, *Afghanistan*, 146–149.

209. Oushakine, "'War das etwa alles umsonst?' Russlands Kriege in militärischen Liedern," 194.

210. V. Verstakov, "Vspomnim, tovarishch . . . , " *Pravda*, December 27, 1988, 6. The article was titled after Kirsanov's popular song, "Vspomnim, tovarishch, my Afganistan" (Let's remember, Comrade, we are Afghanistan).

211. Swartz, "The Soviet-Afghan War in Russian Literature," 150–151.

212. Ol'shanskii, "'Afganskii sindrom.'" *Literaturnoe obozrenie* no. 3 (1990), 15.

213. Oushakine, "'War das etwa alles umsonst?' Russlands Kriege in militärischen Liedern," 188–189.

214. "Afghanistan: A Voice from Moscow," 19.

215. Laruelle and Rakisheva, eds., *Interv'iu s voinami internatsionalistami afganskoi voiny*, 84, 324.

216. Vyshinskaia, "Pro ety voinu," *Sobesednik* no. 9 (February 1989), 6–7.

217. "The Pain of a Nonfiction Film," *Nedelia*, October 10–16, 1988, 6. CDSP XL:44, 5.

218. Iu. Antonov, "Shram na pamiati" (A scar on [our] memory), *Sovetskaia kul'tura*, June 24, 1989, 2.

219. Directed by Nikita Tiagunov, "Noga" won numerous awards.

220. P. Tkachenko, "How Are Things Going, My Friend and Brother?—The 'Afghan' Theme in Certain Works of Belles Lettres, Films and Public-Affairs Journalism" *Krasnaia zvezda*, November 5, 1988, 3. CDSP XL:44, 10–11.

221. This was one aspect of what has been described as living *vne* (outside), that is, outside the Soviet system and its all-pervasive discourse—see Yurchak, *Everything Was Forever, Until It Was No More*, 128–133.

Chapter 8

1. I published some of the findings of this chapter in "The Varied Reintegration of Afghan War Veterans in their Home Society," *Journal of Soviet and Post-Soviet Politics and Society* 1, no. 2 (2015):19–56.

2. *Afganistan v nashei sud'be*, 124–125.

3. Petrone, "Coming Home Soviet Style," 351.

4. Alexievich, *Zinky Boys*, 181.

5. Galeotti, *Afghanistan*, 32–34.

6. Yurchak, *Everything Was Forever, Until It Was No More*, 129 and passim.

7. Alexievich, *Zinky Boys*, 19, 36.

8. Stanislav Oleinik, "Afganskii sindrom." http://artofwar.ru/o/olejnik_s_a/afganskij_sindrom.shtml, accessed April 12, 2015.

9. Tishakov, "Voevavashie deti, nevoevavshikh otsov," 27.

10. Galeotti, *Afghanistan*, 45–46.

11. A. Prokhanov, "Zapiski na brone" (Notes aboard an armored personnel carrier), *Literaturnaia gazeta*, August 28, 1985, 14.

12. Semenova, "Travmirovannaia pamiat' kak resurs formirovaniia kollektivnoi identichnosti: sluchai byvshikh afgantsev," 63–87.

13. Sergei Nebrenchin, "Nasha obshchaia tragediia" (Our common tragedy), *Literaturnaia Rossiia*, November 24, 1989, 8, 9, 14.

14. In 1991, the MPA chief, Colonel General Nikolai Shliaga, "Skol'ko nas?" (How many are we?), *Pobratim*, no. 11 (1991), said there were 540,000 afgantsy in the Soviet Union,which would be the official figure. For estimates of the Fortieth Army's size, see Chapter 3. This is a minimum figure. See ibid.

15. Göransson, "At the Service of the State," 226. Elsewhere, Göransson speaks of Tajikistan's afgantsy as a mosaic of different ranks, functions, ethnicities, religions, native languages, regional affiliations, and social backgrounds (111).

16. See, in addition to my own survey, my interview with Dr. Madridin Magomed-Eminov, Moscow, June 27, 1991, whose team conducted a random survey of 15,000 afgantsy in different parts of the country; "Posle Afganistana" (After Afghanistan), *Komsomol'skaia pravda*, December 21, 1989, 2, based on interviews with 15,000 people "almost half of them" afgantsy; and Nemirovskii, "Eko afganskoi voiny," 55–66. The last survey, conducted at Krasnoiarsk State University, interviewed 320 afgantsy.

17. Philips, "A Soviet Estonian Soldier in Afghanistan," 112, 115.

18. Laruelle and Rakisheva, eds., *Interv'iu s voinami internatsionalistami afganskoi voiny*, 115.

19. Questionnaire of Georgian vet Nukri Gordeiani, Tbilisi, 2014.

20. Laruelle and Rakisheva, eds., *Interv'iu s voinami internatsionalistami afganskoi voiny*, 386.

21. "Tiazhelye boi" (Heavy fighting), *Posev*, no. 6 (1983), 15–16.

22. "Moi pobeg—zaplanirovannaia sluchainost'" (My escape—a planned chance), *Posev*, no. 12 (1986), 11.

23. Interview with Mark Brailovskii, Kfar Sava, n.d. The interviews without dates were part of the survey conducted in 1993.

24. Interview with Vladimir Gross, Holon, n.d.

25. Also interviews with two soldiers from *Frunze*, sent to Afghanistan at the beginning of the war, 2015.

26. Interview with Lev Shepper, Carmiel, n.d.

27. Gai, "Afganistan: kak eto bylo," *Vecherniaia Moskva*, September 12, 13, 1989, 4.

28. Alexievich, *Zinky Boys*, 85, 150, 169.

29. E.g., Laruelle and Rakisheva, eds., *Interv'iu s voinami internatsionalistami afganskoi voiny*, 386. This was in 1987.

30. Alexievich, *Zinky Boys*, 28.

31. David Gai, "Afganistan: kak eto bylo" (Afghanistan: How it was), *Vecherniaia Moskva*, September 13, 1989, 4. The vet recalling this was a paratrooper in the original force in December 1979.

32. Strel'tsova, *Vozvrashchenie iz Afganistana*, 110–111, quoted in Swartz, "The Soviet-Afghan War in Russian Literature," 84.

33. Alexievich, *Zinky Boys*, 94.

34. Interview with Valerii Fruktman, Kfar Sava, n.d.

35. "Ver' drugu, kak sebe" (Trust your friend as yourself), *Komsomol'skaia pravda*, December 27, 1984, 2. Also an Uzbek who served there from 1986 to 1988. Laruelle and Rakisheva, eds., *Interv'iu s voinami internatsionalistami afganskoi voiny*, 323. Just two or three out of 400 refused to go.

36. Alexievich, *Zinky Boys*, 54, 57, 70, 93.

37. Bocharov, *Russian Roulette*, 24–26.

38. Alexievich, *Zinky Boys*, 30–31, 43–44.

39. Laruelle and Rakisheva, eds., *Interv'iu s voinami internatsionalistami afganskoi voiny*, 76.

40. Tarasov, ed., *Moskvichi iz kluba "Dolg,"* 5–24.

41. Alexievich, *Zinky Boys*, 118–119.

42. Tkachenko, ed., *Dorogie moi . . . . Pis'ma iz Afganistana*, Introduction, 15.

43. For the censorship of letters home, see Chapter 3.

44. For the frustration of the soldiers who were unable either to identify or locate those who killed their comrades, see, for example, G. Ustiuzhanin, "'Pokhoronku' ne dognal," *Sovetskii voin*, no. 18 (September 1990), 69.

45. Sannikov (ed.), *Smoliane—internatsionalisty*, 194, 284, 288.

46. Alexievich, *Zinky Boys*, 157–160.

47. Behrends, "Some Call Us Heroes, Others Call Us Killers," 719–720, 728.

48. Andriushchenko, "Chto sovetskie grazhdane dumali o voine v Afganistane."

49. This theme is stressed in Danilova, "Die Veteranen des sowjetischen Afghanistankriegs: Gender und Neuerfindung der Identität."

50. Tkachenko, *Dorogie moi . . .* , 194.

51. Aleksandr Prokhanov, "My budem pomnit' etot boi . . . " (We shall remember this battle . . .), *Sobesednik*, January 4, 1986, 9.

52. Interview with a Russian soldier from Kirgiziia who served in 1981–1982 and with Academician Iurii Buriakov, Tashkent, May 13, 2014, whose son who was killed in 1986 had written home that he was in Siberia. Also see Laruelle and Rakisheva, eds., *Interv'iu s voinami internatsionalistami afganskoi voiny*, 97.

53. A soldier in *The Black Tulip* (1987) relates that he had not told his mother that he lost an arm.

54. Not even for the funeral of a parent. Laruelle and RakishevaRakisheva, eds., *Interv'iu s voinami internatsionalistami afganskoi voiny*, 316.

55. Interview with Evgenii Krasnik, Carmiel (Israel), n.d.

56. Alexievich, *Zinky Boys*, 51, 56.

57. Jonathan Steele, "Soviet Hero Declares War on the Party," *Guardian*, November 13, 1990, quoted in Galeotti, *Afghanistan*, 141.

58. Bill Keller, "Home from Afghanistan; Russia's Divisive War," *New York Times Magazine*, February 14, 1988.

59. See, for example, A. Gorokho and V. Okulov, "Im snitsia granitsa . . . " (They dream of the [Soviet] border), *Pravda*, May 27, 1988, 8.

60. Tarasov, ed., *Moskvichi iz kluba "Dolg"*, 40.

61. Much of this section addresses the afgantsy from the Soviet Union's European republics, especially the three Slav republics. Svetlana Alexievich, for instance, from whose book I took a good deal of testimony and who hails from Belarus, seems to have spoken solely with such people. I discuss the Central Asian soldiers specifically in Chapter 9.

62. Alexievich, *Zinky Boys*, 43, 133, 138, 146.

63. Tishakov, "Voevavashie deti, nevoevavshikh otsov," 26.

64. Larry Heinemann, Introduction in Alexievich, *Zinky Boys*, xiii. For one such ceremony, organized by the old school of a wounded veteran and duly reported in the local newspaper, see Bocharov, *Russian Roulette*, 45–46.

65. P. Studenikin, "Tam, za Gindu-Kushem" (There, beyond the Hindu-Kush), *Pravda*, September 11, 1988, 1, 3.

66. V. Matusevich, "Zdrastvui, Rodina!" (Greetings, mother country!), *Pravda vostoka*, January 4, 1989. On the eve of the final withdrawal, those who had come to meet the soldiers found that Termez had insufficient dwellings, food, and transport. A. Kruzhilin, "Domoi, na sever! (Home, to the north!), *Komsomolets Uzbekistana*, February 14, 1989.

67. "K mestu postoiannoi dislokatsii . . ." (To the permanent distribution point . . .), *Komsomolets Uzbekistana*, February 10, 1989.

68. "Obrashchenie TsK KPSS, Prezidiuma Verkhovnogo Soveta SSSR, Soveta Ministrov SSSR k sovetskim voinam, vernushishimsia iz Afganistana" (Address of CPSU CC, USSR Supreme Soviet Presidium and USSR Council of Ministers to Soviet servicemen returning from Afghanistan), *Pravda*, February 16, 1989, 1.

69. The soldiers' ceremonial reception and meeting with relatives in Termez and Kushka were relayed in all the media, including Moscow TV. FBIS-SOV-89–031, February 16, 1989, 23–24. See also "'Shuravi' i drugie" (The "shuravi" and others), *Komsomolets Uzbekistana*, February 18, 1989, and "Vstrechai, Rodina, synovei!" (Mother country, meet your sons!), *Komsomolets Turkmenistana*, February 16, 1989.

70. V. Artemenko and V. Okulov, "S voiny—domoi" (From the war—home!), *Pravda*, February 16, 1989, 4.

71. See, e.g., "Zdravstvuite, synov'ia!" (Greetings, sons!), *Komsomolets Uzbekistana*, February 8, 1989; A. Rybak, "S vozvrashcheniem, rebiata!" (Welcome back, lads!), *Komsomolets Turkmenistana*, February 11, 1989.

72. "Rodnoi bereg" (Home bank), *Komsomolets Uzbekistana*, February 11, 1989.

73. Pikov, ed., *Voina v Afganistane*, 340–341; Strel'tsova, *Vozvrashchenie iz Afganistana*, 12–13, quoted in Swartz, "The Soviet-Afghan War in Russian Literature," 103. See also "Ordena i platskarta" (Medals and train tickets), *Komsomolets Uzbekistana*, February 18, 1989.

74. "Na Salange—geroi! A v Soiuze? . . ." (At Salang—heroes! And in the Soviet Union? . . .), *Pobratim*, no. 3 (February 1989), 2.

75. Konnov, "Pravda i vymysel ob afganskoi voine," 52.

76. Alexievich, *Zinky Boys*, 27–28.

77. Gennady Zhavoronkov, "We Must Tell the Whole Truth about This War," *Moscow News*, no. 30, July 23, 1989, 9.

78. Alexievich, *Zinky Boys*, 21.

79. Laruelle and Rakisheva, eds., *Interv'iu s voinami internatsionalistami afganskoi voiny*, 112.

80. *Komsomolets Uzbekistana*, May 25, 1988, quoted in Valerii Konovalov, "Reintegrating Afghan Veterans into Civilian Life," RL 425/88, September 19, 1988.

81. Alexievich, *Zinky Boys*, 26. For some of the more poignant stories, see ibid., 69, 113, 148–150, 160–161.

82. *Sotsialisticheskaia industriia*, June 26, 1988, quoted in Konovalov, "Reintegrating Afghan Veterans into Civilian Life."

83. "Posle Afganistana" (After Afghanistan), *Komsomol'skaia pravda*, December 21, 1989, 2.

84. Laruelle and Rakisheva, eds., *Interv'iu s voinami internatsionalistami afganskoi voiny*, 14.

85. Alexievich, *Zinky Boys*, 160–161.

86. http://www.gr-oborona.ru/texts/1056965230.html#ixzz3XAFaDllH, accessed April 12, 2015. The song appeared in 1990.

87. P. Tkachenko, "How Are Things Going, My Friend and Brother?" *Krasnaia zvezda*, November 5, 1988. CDSP XL:44, 10; Konnov, "Pravda i vymysel ob afganskoi voine," 52.

88. Laruelle and Rakisheva, eds., *Interv'iu s voinami internatsionalistami afganskoi voiny*, 79. A similar sentiment was expressed by an afganets in the film *Afganskii izlom* (Afghan fracture).

89. *Komsomol'skaia pravda*, August 7, 1988, quoted in *Ha'arets*, August 8, 1988.

90. Göransson, "At the Service of the State," 99. No date is given for this demonstration.

91. *Express Chronicle*, no. 52, December 24, 1989; *Sovset*, December 28, 1989.

92. Alexievich, *Zinky Boys*, 69.

93. For example, one Tajik interpreter admitted that there were occasional instances of smuggling goods and gold into the Soviet Union. Laruelle and Rakisheva, eds., *Interv'iu s voinami internatsionalistami afganskoi voiny*, 128.

94. Reminiscences of Aleksandr Lupoukov in 2014: "Kto my afgantsy?" (Who are we, the Afgantsy?). http://artofwar.ru/l/lupookow_a_n/text_0320.shtml, accessed July 6, 2015. Lupoukov had been in charge of the ward for infectious diseases in a field hospital in Afghanistan.

95. "Posle Afganistana," *Komsomol'skaia pravda*, December 21, 1989, 2.

96. Sarin and Dvoretsky, *The Afghan Syndrome*, 148.

97. "Rasskazyvaiut ob Afganistane" (Stories about Afghanistan), *Posev*, no. 7 (1985), 21.

98. Philips, "A Soviet Estonian Soldier in Afghanistan," 102.

99. Alexievich, *Zinky Boys*, 24, 26, 146. Nor were officers exempt from nightmares. Artem Borovik, *Spriatannaia voina* (Moskva: Sovershenno Sekretno, 2000), 197. The book first appeared in 1989 and differs slightly from the English *The Hidden War*.

100. G. Ustiuzhanin, "'Pokhoronku' ne dognal," *Sovetskii voin*, no. 18 (September 1990), 69.

101. Alexievich, *Zinky Boys*, 26, 149.

102. Borovik, *The Hidden War*, 99–100.

103. "Posle Afganistana," *Komsomol'skaia pravda*, December 21, 1989.

104. Reich, "Faces of the Lithuanian *Afganai*," 192.

105. Nemirovskii, "Ekho afganskoi voiny," 57.

106. Alexievich, *Zinky Boys*, 129.

107. Author's interview with Nugzar Kakhniauri (Tbilisi), September 9, 2014.

108. "My vypolnili svoi dolg . . . ," *Podvig*, issue 34 (1989), 10–11.

109. Aleksandr Drobotov, "'Eta vstrecha peretriakhnula vsiu moiu zhizn'" (This encounter shook up my entire life), *Komsomol'skaia pravda*, January 8, 1986, 4.

110. *Sobesednik*, March 12, 1986, 5.

111. Juris Podniecs, Abram Kletskin, and Evgenii Margolin, "Nashi soavtory," *Avrora* no. 9 (1987), 20, quoted in Riordan, "'Afgantsy'—Return of the Lost Generation," 22–23.

112. Alexievich, *Zinky Boys*, 26.

113. "Posle Afganistana," *Komsomol'skaia pravda*, December 21, 1989.

114. Gai and Snegirev, *Vtorzhenie*, 253. For one who, demobilized in 1982, succeeded in returning in 1984, see *Ogonek*, no. 4 (January 1988), 12; for another, see Borovik, *The Hidden*

War, 94. "I have a lot of friends here. Some serve, some lie at rest. . . . I can't go back to the world. I tried. It doesn't work." Or an ensign on his second tour of duty in Afghanistan, "I'm sick to hell of everything back there." He had returned because he had "a physical, almost love-like craving for this 'godforsaken land,'" Ibid., 113.

115. Grau, *The Bear Went Over the Mountain*, 208.

116. Quoted in Alexiev, *Inside the Soviet Army*, 58.

117. Gai, "Afganistan: kak eto bylo," *Vecherniaia Moskva*, September 16, 1989, 4.

118. Quoted in Svetlana Aleksievich, "Don't Say You Have Not Been in That War," *International Affairs* (Moscow), 36, no. 1 (1990): 135.

119. Sarin and Dvoretsky, *The Afghan Syndrome*, 148.

120. Alexievich, *Zinky Boys*, 148.

121. Konovalov, "Reintegrating Afghan Veterans into Civilian Life," 2.

122. A veteran from Novosibirsk replying to the *Komsomol'skaia pravda* poll: "Posle Afganistana," *Komsomol'skaia Pravda*, December 21, 1989.

123. Nemirovskii, "Eko afganskoi voiny," 63.

124. K. Tsagolov, "Nuzhna polnaia pravda . . . Otkrytoe pis'mo materi pogibshego voiny v Afganistane" (The full truth is needed . . . Open letter to the mother of a soldier who died in Afghanistan), *Pravda*, September 15, 1989, 3.

125. Ol'shanskii, "'Afganskii sindrom,'" 16–17.

126. Petrone, "Coming Home Soviet Style," passim, especially 365.

127. Interview with Magomed-Eminov, June 21, 1991.

128. *Molod' Ukrainy*, June 19, 1986, quoted in RL 241/86, June 24, 1986, 2.

129. Quoted in Behrends, "'Some Call Us Heroes, Others Call Us Killers,'" 724.

130. Sarin and Dvoretsky, *The Afghan Syndrome*, 170.

131. Danilova, "Die Veteranen des sowjetischen Afghanistankriegs," 222.

132. Nemirovskii, "Ekho afganskoi voiny," 57.

133. Alexievich, *Zinky Boys*, 190.

134. Pavlov, "Byt soldat afganskoi voiny v 1979–1989 gg.," 4.

135. V. Artemenko and P. Studenikin, "Odnoi gruppy krovi" (The same blood type), *Pravda*, September 28, 1988, 3.

136. Galeotti, *Afghanistan*, 86–87.

137. Alexievich, *Zinky Boys*, 155–157.

138. *Moskvichi iz Kluba 'Dolg'*, 95–100.

139. Sarin and Dvoretsky, *The Afghan Syndrome*, 173. The newspaper presumably was *Krasnaia zvezda*, of which Sarin was deputy managing editor.

140. A. Pankratov, "Odnazhdy vecherom posle voiny" (One evening after the war), *Komsomol'skaia pravda*, March 17, 1989. The article asserted that in the man's neighborhood (raion) in Kazan, not a single afganets had received an apartment over the previous five years.

141. "Posle Afganistana," *Komsomol'skaia pravda*, December 21, 1989, 2. From time to time, the media published stories of afgantsy who committed or attempted suicide out of despair at not getting housing. One afganets poured gasoline on himself and set himself on fire after being promised an apartment that was eventually given to someone else after he had finished the construction work himself. E. Kessariiskii and E. Z. Vasil'ev, "Chelovek v ogne" (Man on fire), *Pravda*, September 7, 1989, 6.

142. While officially nobody was unemployed, in the late 1980s, there were a large number of "unoccupied" people among the "able-bodied population," especially in the Trans-Caucasus and Central Asia. Viktor Shirokov, "Person without a Job," *Pravda*, October 31, 1989, 2. CDSP XLI:44, 6–7.

143. Galeotti, *Afghanistan*, 57.

144. Liakhovskii and Zabrodin, *Tainy afganskoi voiny*, 214.

145. "Skol'ko nas?" (How many are we?), *Pobratim*, no. 11 (1991), 1.

146. Interview with Major General Iurii Grekov: *Krasnaia zvezda*, May 23, 1989, 2; FBIS-SOV-89–105, June 2, 1989, 74–77.

147. B. Gromov, "'Priznaiu lish' diktaturu zakona,'" (I only recognize the dictatorship of the law), *Pobratim*, no. 11 (1991), 4. For the story of an afganets who made a career in the Georgian MVD, see Nikolai Dolgopolov, "Poedinok" (The duel), *Sobesednik* no. 17, April 1986, 12–13.

148. "The Afghan Fracture: How Ukrainian Soldiers of the Undeclared War Live" (interviews of the Ukrainian site Argumenty i fakty with Afghan veterans). www.aif.ua/society/people/963886, accessed July 6, 2015.

149. Galeotti, *Afghanistan*, 58–61; Konovalov, "Reintegrating Afghan Veterans into Civilian Life"; K. Vladimirov, "Zakalennyi afganom" (Hardened by Afghan), *Na postu* (Tashkent), June 25, 1991, 5; and B. Uraev, "Nashla nagrada voina" (Soldier's reward found), *Komosomolets Turkmenistana*, February 2, 1989. For one of many media articles describing these voluntary vigilante groups and the need to enlist them in the struggle against crime, especially juvenile delinquency, see Aleksandr Radov, "Deti Detochkina" (Detochkin's children), *Komsomol'skaia pravda*, October 17, 1986, 2. Yuri Detochkin, hero of a film from the mid- to late 1960s, stole cars from corrupt officials and anonymously gave the proceeds from selling them to orphanages.

150. Danilova, "Die Veteranen des sowjetischen Afghanistankriegs," 226.

151. Volkov, "The Russian Mafia: Rise and Extinction," 163–164.

152. Interview with Magomed-Eminov, June 27, 1991.

153. Galeotti, *Afghanistan*, 61; Sapper, *Die Auswirkung des Afghanistan-Krieges auf die Sowjetgesellschaft*, 165.

154. Konovalov, "Reintegrating Afghan Veterans into Civilian Life."

155. Mikhail Reshetnikov, rector of the East European Institute of Psychoanalysis, St. Petersburg, in an interview with the RF Rosbalt information and analysis agency. http://www.rosbalt.ru/piter/2009/02/14/618431.htm, accessed April 12, 2015.

156. Alexievich, *Zinky Boys*, 56; Radio Moscow, September 7, 1988.

157. Interview with Pavel Shet'ko, August 25, 1993.

158. Heinemann, Introduction, Alexievich, *Zinky Boys*, xii–xiii.

159. Galeotti, *Afghanistan*, 77.

160. "S"ezd narodnykh deputatov SSSR" (Congress of USSR People's Deputies; verbatim report), *Izvestiia*, June 3, 1989, 5. For the Congress of People's Deputies, see Chapter 4.

161. See, for example, "Tibor pomeshchaet pomoshch'" (Tibor promises help), *Pravda*, September 29, 1989, 5.

162. Alexievich, *Zinky Boys*, 172.

163. Sarin and Dvoretsky, *The Afghan Syndrome*, 170–171.

164. E.g., N. Belan, "Synov'ia, a ne pasynki" (Sons, not stepsons), *Krasnaia zvezda*, May 28, 1988, 4.

165. Sarin and Dvoretsky, *The Afghan Syndrome*, 174.

166. V. Alekseeva, "Nadeemsia na vstrechu" (We hope for a meeting), *Komsomolets Uzbekistana*, February 15, 1990. The story had appeared in the raion newspaper.

167. Reich, "Faces of the Lithuanian *Afganai*," 192.

168. G. Apresian, "Afgantsy," *Literaturnaia gazeta*, August 8, 1988, 11.

169. Alexievich, *Zinky Boys*, 89.

170. One veteran arrived at the hometown of a fallen comrade and sat on a bench for three

hours before being able to enter the home of the boy's parents. Igor' Lavintsov, "Razgovor s drugom" (Conversation with a friend), *Sobesednik*, no. 9 (February 1986), 13.

171. Vladimir Misiuchenko, "Gore i dolg" (Woe and duty), *Sobesednik* no. 50 (December 1986), 8–9.

172. *Komsomolets Turkmenistana*, August 8, 1989.

173. Galeotti, *Afghanistan*, 85.

174. E.g., one father in Karakalpakiia—"Pis'mo otsa" (A father's letter), *Komsomolets Uzbekistana*, July 12, 1989.

175. N. Burov, "Misfortune That Cannot Be Forgotten," *Izvestiia*, August 10, 1990, 7. CDSP XLII:33, 33.

176. Pinnick, "When the Fighting Is Over: The Soldiers' Mothers and the Afghan Madonnas," 147–148.

177. Iurii Lapshin, *Afganskii dnevnik*, 96.

178. A. Goncharov, "Temnye okna" (Dark windows), *Krasnaia zvezda*, December 10, 1987.

179. V. Izgarshev, "Afganskaia bol'" (Afghan pain), *Pravda*, August 17, 1989, 6.

180. Alexievich, *Zinky Boys, 150.*

181. Pinnick, "When the Fighting Is Over," 149.

182. This is a recurrent refrain in the interviews conducted with afgantsy in the 2000s. See, for example, Laruelle and Rakisheva, eds., *Interv'iu s voinami internatsionalistami afganskoi voiny*, passim.

183. Philips, "A Soviet Estonian Soldier in Afghanistan," 105–106, and Laruelle and Rakisheva, eds., *Interv'iu s voinami internatsionalistami afganskoi voiny*, 323.

184. Alexievich, *Zinky Boys*, 136.

185. Liakhovskii and Zabrodin, *Tainy afganskoi voiny*, 74

186. Gai and Snegirev, *Vtorzhenie*, 253–254.

187. "Moi pobeg—zaplanirovannaia sluchainost'," 12.

188. Laruelle and Rakisheva, eds., *Interv'iu s voinami internatsionalistami afganskoi voiny*, 127.

189. Ibid., 363.

190. Cherkasov, "'Afgan' nachinalsia tak . . . ," 8.

191. *Afganistan v nashei sud'be*, 9.

192. E.g., Laruelle and Rakisheva, eds., *Interv'iu s voinami internatsionalistami afganskoi voiny*, 135.

193. *Ha'arets*, March 18, 1988, reproducing an article from the *New York Times.*

194. Pavlov, "Byt soldat," 5, and Laruelle and Rakisheva, eds., *Interv'iu s voinami internatsionalistami afganskoi voiny*, 7, 16. Pavlov does not say how many people he interviewed, but tells us that nearly all of them were rank-and-file soldiers with secondary education.

195. Laruelle and Rakisheva, eds., *Interv'iu s voinami internatsionalistami afganskoi voiny*, 117.

196. Vera Saikina, "Afganskii al'bom generala Kondrat'eva" (The Afghan album of General Kondrat'ev), *Komsomolets Uzbekistana*, February 15, 1990. Lieutenant General Georgii Kondrat'ev was first deputy commander of the Turkestan MD.

197. Alexievich, *Zinky Boys*, 34.

198. For example, one Estonian veteran. "Samizdatskoe interv'iu" (A samizdat interview), *Posev* no. 5 (1985), 11–12.

199. Oushakine, "'War das etwa alles umsonst?' Russlands Kriege in militärischen Liedern," 195.

200. A Kazakh vet interviewed in the 2000s stated this specifically. Laruelle and Rakisheva, eds., *Interv'iu s voinami internatsionalistami afganskoi voiny*, 81, 84.

201. Alexievich, *Zinky Boys*, 160–161.

202. "Posle Afganistana," *Komsomol'skaia pravda*, December 21, 1989, 2.

203. Yurchak, *Everything Was Forever, Until It Was No More*, 4–10.

204. *Afganistan v nashei sud'be*, 8.

205. *Sobesednik*, no.23 (June 1987), 3, quoted in Riordan, "'Afgantsy'—Return of the Lost Generation," 5.

206. Sarin and Dvoretsky, *Afghan Syndrome*, 127–128.

207. Tsagolov, "'Nuzhna polnaia pravda . . . ,'" *Pravda*, September 15, 1989, 3.

208. M. Semenova, "I zhizn', i slezy, i liubov'" (Life, tears and love), *Komsomolets Turkmenistana*, May 9, 1989, 4.

209. Alexievich, *Zinky Boys*, 149–150, 77–78.

210. *Komsomolets Uzbekistana*, July 4, 1989.

211. Nemirovskii, "Ekho afganskoi voiny," 56.

212. RFE-RL SBN, February 1985, 11–12.

213. Izgarshev, "Afganskaia bol'," *Pravda*, August 17, 1989, 6; V. Dolganov, I. Korolkov and R. Lynev, "Urgent Measures. From What Sources?" *Izvestiia*, August 2, 1989, 1. CDSP XLI:37, 16. For the discussion at the Congress of People's Deputies, see Chapter 4.

214. Semenova, "I zhizn', i slezy, i liubov,'" *Komsomolets Turkmenistana*, May 9, 1989.

215. E.g., an interview with two St. Petersburg afgantsy on the twenty-fourth anniversary of the final withdrawal. http://ok-inform.ru/obshchestvo/sobytiya/1090-v-afganistan-prikazom-volya-zavela.html, accessed April 12, 2015. Göransson, "At the Service of the State," 31, tells us that in the second decade of the twenty-first century, Tajik afgantsy were still trying to achieve the same legal status as the Great Patriotic War vets.

216. Alexievich, *Zinky Boys*, 185, 189.

217. Boris Baidachnyi, "Zakon—est' zakon" (Law is law), *Pobratim*, no. 6 (1990), 2.

218. E.g., Drobotov, "Eta vstrecha peretriakhnula vsiu moiu zhizn." See also Chapter 6.

219. Konovalov, "Reintegrating Afghan Veterans into Civilian Life."

220. Alekseevich, *Tsinkovye mal'chiki*, 187–192.

221. P. Studenikin, "V chas ispytaniia" (In the hour of trial), *Pravda*, April 4, 1987, 6.

222. Radov, "Deti Detochkina," *Komsomol'skaia pravda*, October 17, 1986, 2.

223. *Sobesednik*, no. 1 (1987).

224. *Molodaia gvardiia*, no. 8, 1987 (quoted RL n.d.)

225. "XIX konferentsiia KPSS. Vystuplenie tovarishcha Gromova B. V." (Nineteenth Party Conference. Speech of B. V. Gromov), *Pravda*, July 2, 1988, 7.

226. *Komsomolets Turkmenistana*, March 2, 1989.

227. "Posle Afganistana," *Komsomol'skaia pravda*, December 21, 1989.

228. Alexievich, *Zinky Boys*, 129. Until September 1990, the government did not formally acknowledge as war veterans or grant l'goty to the tens of thousands of Soviet soldiers and officers who served in Egypt between 1969 and 1972. See also Chapter 10.

229. Alexievich, *Zinky Boys*, 128, 193.

230. "The Afghan Fracture: How the Ukrainian Soldiers of the Undeclared War Live" (Interviews of the Ukrainian site Argumenty i fakty with Afghan veterans): www.aif.ua/society/people/963886. See also the 1991 film, "Afganskii izlom."

231. "Posle Afganistana," *Komsomol'skaia pravda*, December 21, 1989.

232. Ibid., December 21, 1989, 2. We must remember, however, that those who viewed the veterans positively were precisely the category one would expect to answer the poll.

233. Ibid.

234. Tishakov, "Voevavashie deti, nevoevavshikh otsov," 27.

235. Reich, "Faces of the Lithuanian *Afganai*," 189, and Göransson, "At the Service of the State," 29.

236. Tolz, *The USSR's Emerging Multiparty System*, 26–29. Galeotti attributes their full legalization to 1987, but I have been unable to find a relevant law in that year beyond the draft noted above.

237. Vladimir Iakovlev, "Proshchanie s Bazarovym" (Taking leave from Bazarov), *Ogonek*, no. 36 (September 1987): 4–5, and Butterfield and Sedaitis, "The Emergence of Social Movements in the Soviet Union," 1.

238. Wise, "The Domestic Impact of the War in Afghanistan," 19.

239. L. Galbas, "'Our Pain and Our Glory': Social Strategies of Legitimization and Functionalization," 104, quoting "Perepiska s ministerstvami, vedomstvami, veteranskimi organizatsiami voinov-internatsionalistov, voinami-uchastnikami voiny v Afganistane," 1992, vol. 1, 61.

240. E.g., Göransson, "At the Service of the State," 231ff. One article traces the early stages of afgantsy clubs in Arkhangel'sk prior to the eventual formation of an official association in 1987. Nina Chugunova, "Znaesh', kak tebia zhdali . . ." (Know how they awaited you . . .), *Ogonek*, no. 18 (April 1989), 10–11.

241. Igor' Cherniak, "Ne iskat po zemle zhizni sladkoi" (They are not looking for a sweet life in the country), *Sobesednik*, no. 49 (December 1987), 4, quoted in Riordan, "Teenage Gangs, 'Afgantsy,' and Neofascists," 132.

242. *Molod' Ukrainy*, June 10, 1986, quoted in RL 241/86, June 24, 1986, 1.

243. Göransson, "At the Service of the State," 226.

244. For example, A. Chizhenok, "Nas pomniat, znachit, my nuzhny" (We are remembered, that means we are needed), *Sovetskaia Rossiia*, April 30, 1986, 2, and S. Novoprudskii, "Sila dukha i sila voli" (Strength of the soul and strength of will), *Komsomolets Uzbekistana*, January 18, 1989.

245. Between 1984 and late 1989, it lost 11 million members. Rakowska-Harmstone, "The Soviet Armed Forces: The Challenge of Reform and the Ethnic Factor," 9–10.

246. Riordan, "Teenage Gangs, 'Afgantsy' and Neofascists," 130–131, quoting Igor Korolkov, "Iz boia ne vyshli," *Sobesednik* no. 49 (December 1987), 4.

247. Keller, "Home from Afghanistan"; Laura Tsagolova, Igor' Cherniak, "Muzhskoi razgovor" (Male conversation), *Sobesednik*, no. 47 (November 1987), 2; also see *Komsomolets Uzbekistana*, March 30, 1990.

248. See above and, for example, Moscow Television Service, March 31, 1984: Daily Report, April 19, 1984.

249. Galeotti, *Afghanistan*, 62.

250. *Sunday Times*, November 22, 1987.

251. Sapper, *Die Auswirkung des Afghanistan-Krieges auf die Sowjetgesellschaft*, 173. The last figure, provided by Yazov, covered all internationalist soldiers, including those who fought elsewhere over the years; the non-afgantsy, however, were well under 10 percent of the aggregate number.

252. Galeotti, *Afghanistan*, 104–105, 108–109.

253. Sieca-Kozlowski, "The Post-Soviet Russian State Facing War Veterans' Psychological Suffering," 15.

254. Göransson, "At the Service of the State," 245.

255. M. Chunikhin, "Narodnoe spasibo" (The people's thanks), *Krasnaia zvezda*, May 26, 1987, 1–2.

256. For example, a report from the Baltic MD. A. Khokhlov, "Daite vremia!" (Give time!), *Za rodinu*, January 25, 1990.

257. Galeotti, *Afghanistan*, 104–107, 124–125.

258. *Moskvichi iz Kluba 'Dolg.'*

259. A. Kotenev, "I vot vernulis'" (And now they're back), *Pravda*, March 10, 1989, 2.

260. Z. Yuldashev and N. Kahharov, "Deistvovat'! Ne boiat'sia trudnostei" (To act! Not to fear difficulties), *Komsomolets Uzbekistana*, January 31, 1987.

261. Nina Chugunova, "Znaesh', kak tebia zhdali . . . ," *Ogonek*, no. 18 (April 1989): 10–11. Also *Sobesednik*, no. 47 (November 1987), and *Komsomo'skaia pravda*, January 31, 1988, quoted in Riordan, "'Afgantsy'—Return of the Lost Generation," 26–27.

262. In 1989, in the Turkmen city of Bayram-Aly, for instance, they met weekly in the afganets café to discuss who needed help and what they could do for the families of their fallen comrades. *Komsomolets Turkmenistana*, January 19, 1989. In one Turkmen kolkhoz, ten vets met in April 1989 to discuss their problems and experiences, the first meeting of afgantsy in a raion that had sent 169 boys to the war, N. Kuliev, "Shkola zhizni—Afganistan" (Afghanistan—school of life), *Komsomolets Turkmenistana*, April 25, 1989.

263. "Obrashchenie" (Appeal), *Literaturnaia gazeta*, June 22, 1988, 9.

264. Galeotti, *Afghanistan*, 109–110.

265. Smith, *The New Russians*, 431.

266. Alexievich, *Zinky Boys*, 19.

267. Interview with David Feierman, Kfar Sava, Israel, July 26, 2016. Feierman chaired the association of one of Cheliabinsk's seven raiony, 1991–1994.

268. Elena Verina, "Problemy trebuiut reshenii" (Problems demand solutions), *Komsomolets Uzbekistana*, February 8, 1989.

269. Tkachenko, *Dorogie moi . . .*, 228.

270. *Komsomolets Uzbekistana*, January 18, 1989.

271. Ibid., April 7, 1989.

272. *Pravda*, October 1, 1987, 1–2, spoke of local officials frequently allocating to disabled veterans apartments that were on the outskirts of cities and in areas with few amenities.

273. The founders of *Dolg* dreamed from the start of building an afganets MZhK (young persons' housing complex), *Moskvichi iz Kluba 'Dolg'*, 99.

274. Galeotti, *Afghanistan*, 111–112. The first afganets MZhK was completed in Leningrad with accommodation for 200 veterans, 80 of them invalids and another 80 Great Patriotic War veterans. Ibid. For one afganets initiative to construct their own housing so they could live together (in Kaluga), see Laura Tsagolova, "Snova snitsia voina" (Dreaming of the war once again), *Sobesednik*, no. 3 (January 1988): 11.

275. Swartz, "The Soviet-Afghan War in Russian Literature," 118, and Galeotti, ibid.

276. "Budny polny zabot" (Everyday life full of worries), *Komsomolets Uzbekistana*, May 31, 1990, 2.

277. "Vstrecha detei" (Meeting of children), *Vechernii Donetsk*, December 6, 1990, 1.

278. E.g., A. Ishchenko, "Vspomnit' o voine . . ." (To remember the war . . .), *Komsomolets Kirgizii*, February 27, 1991, 1.

279. Third Session of the USSR Supreme Soviet, *Izvestiia*, February 16, 1990. CDSP XLII:7, 6.

280. Alexievich, *Zinky Boys*, 195.

281. Galeotti, *Afghanistan*, 69.

282. Heinemann, Introduction to Alexievich, *Zinky Boys*, xiii.

283. Znakov, "Psikhologicheskoe issledovanie stereotipov ponimaniia lichnosti uchastnikov voiny v Afganistane."

284. Tkachenko, *Dorogie moi . . .*, 228.

285. The term was coined as an analogy to "Vietnam syndrome," the original meaning of

which, in the United States in the early 1970s, was identical, and which later became synonymous with PTSD (until Henry Kissinger and then President Reagan started to use the term to refer to American society's aversion to fighting foreign wars).

286. Interview with Dr. Magomed-Eminov, June 27, 1991.

287. "Sindrom frontovika," *Pobratim*, nos. 4 and 5 (1990), 5.

288. Ol'shanskii, "'Afganskii sindrom,'" 18.

289. Ol'shanskii, "Smyslovye struktury lichnosti uchastnikov afganskoi voiny," 120–131.

290. Laruelle and Rakisheva, eds., *Interv'iu s voinami internatsionalistami afganskoi voiny*, 79.

291. Sieca-Kozlowski, "The Post-Soviet Russian State Facing War Veterans' Psychological Suffering," 14, 16, 25. The author's quotes are from A. Maklakov, S. Chermianin, and E. Chustov, "Problemy prognozirovaniia psikhologicheskikh posledstvii lokal'nykh voennykh konfliktov," *Psikhologicheskii zhurnal* 19, no. 2 (1998), 15–25.

292. Wise, "The Soviet Domestic Impact of the War in Afghanistan," 18–19.

293. Galeotti, *Afghanistan*, 62–63.

294. See, e.g., "Vspomnim vsekh poimenno . . ." (We shall remember them all by name . . .), *Komsomolets Uzbekistana*, June 27, 1989, 1. The article's motto was a short poem that began, "I know it's not my fault," and ended "All the same, all the same, all the same . . . "

295. "Problemy sotsial'noi reabilitatsii uchastnikov voiny v Afganistane," 14–17.

296. Kinsburskii and Topalev, "Reabilitatsiia uchastnikov afganskoi voiny v obshchestvennom mnenii," 104–107. See also Zakharov, "Struktorno-funktsional'nye osnovy mediko-sotsial'noi reabilitatsii ranenykh i bol'nykh," 7.

297. Alexievich, *Zinky Boys*, 187–188.

298. Alekseevich, *Tsinkovye mal'chiki*, 193–250.

299. R. Moscow in English, October 5, 1989. FBIS-SOV-89–193, October 6, 1989, 19.

300. Rubtsov, "Sovetskii Soiuz v 'Neob"iavlennoi' voine v Afganistane (1979–1989): osmyslenie proshlogo," 117.

301. *Novye aspekty psikhoterapii posttravmaticheskogo stressa: metodicheskie rekomendatsii.*

302. Quoted Galeotti, *Afghanistan*, 68.

303. Report on interview with Tsagolov, "Voinu proigrali politiki" (The politicians lost the war), *Argumenty i fakty*, September 30–October 6, 1989, 4–5. FBIS-SOV-89–193, October 6, 1989, 16–18.

304. Reshetnikov interview with the RF Rosbalt information and analysis agency. http://www.rosbalt.ru/piter/2009/02/14/618431.html, accessed April 12, 2015.

305. Interview with Magomed-Eminov.

306. Ruslan Pavlov, writing in 2015 of the veterans in Cheliabinsk Region. "Byt soldat. . . . ," 3.

307. Two St. Petersburg veterans, interviewed on the twenty-fourth anniversary of the final withdrawal, testified that while they had recovered from these effects (although still suffering from nightmares connected with the war), many others had not and had taken to drink or other wayward distractions, as nobody had helped them adjust to civilian life. http://ok-inform.ru/obshchestvo/sobytiya/1090-v-afganistan-prikazom-volya-zavela.html, accessed April 12, 2015.

308. Braithwaite, *Afgantsy*, 321.

309. "The War Syndrome," published anonymously on the web in 2006—http://www.privatelife.ru/2006/os06/n5/3.html.

310. Laruelle and Rakisheva, eds., *Interv'iu s voinami internatsionalistami afganskoi voiny*, 112.

311. Oleinik, "Afganskii sindrom."

312. An Uzbek afganets whom I interviewed in 2014 said categorically that nobody among the Uzbek veterans ever had psychological problems—nightmares—or treatment. Most Uzbek veterans, he said, just got on with their lives. They weren't afraid of blood; they had all seen sheep

being killed when they were children. Author's interview with Turdibay Shadmanov, May 21, 22, 2014. Other interviews I conducted in Uzbekistan confirm that this was the rule; I heard, however, in casual conversation of Uzbek afgantsy totally unable to take up a permanent job or live a normal life. A Georgian afganets I interviewed in Kutaisi in 2014 told me of a friend who had similar difficulties and eventually committed suicide.

313. Petrone, "Coming Home Soviet Style," 365.

Chapter 9

1. See, for example, Laruelle and Rakisheva, eds., *Interv'iu s voinami internatsionalistami afganskoi voiny*, 79.

2. In 1979, the approximately 15 million strong population of Afghanistan reportedly included 7 million Pashtuns, 3 million Tajiks, 1.5 million Uzbeks, and some 300,000 Turkmen. One Soviet source gave slightly higher figures for each of the last three ethnic groups. Safronov, "Kak eto bylo," 66.

3. Aleksandr Liakhovskii compares the methods that the PDPA used to gain control of Afghanistan with those of the Bolsheviks in the 1920s, whose mistakes and criminal actions in failing to implement economic and social reforms capable of attracting peasants to the side of Soviet power pushed them into joining the Basmachi movement. Lyakhovskiy, *Inside the Soviet Invasion of Afghanistan*, 3.

4. "The Intervention in Afghanistan and the Fall of Détente," 96–97.

5. Opponents of withdrawal in February 1980 suggested too that it might lead to a dramatic growth of Muslim extremism near the Soviet border. See Chapter 4.

6. Altogether, Moscow's approach to Islam was ambiguous and sought to differentiate between domestic and foreign Islam. Islam was both conservative and resisted "new ideas and social progress"—and therefore required repression at home—and represented "a form of expression of the working people's protest against a system that dooms them to poverty and ignorance," a criterion that by definition was not applicable to the Soviet system. Igor' Beliaev, "Islam i politika" (Islam and politics), *Literaturnaia gazeta*, January 14, 1980, 14. The latter standpoint enabled Moscow to support the Iranian revolution of the ayatollahs. Ro'i, "The Impact of the Islamic Fundamentalist Revival of the Late 1970s on the Soviet View of Islam."

7. Gromov, *Ogranichennyi kontingent*, 21.

8. Aleksandr Prokhanov, "Afganskie voprosy" (Afghan questions), *Literaturnaia gazeta*, February 17, 1988, 1, 9.

9. The resolution was based on an identically entitled memo that Andropov, Gromyko, Ponomarev, and CPSU CC Secretary Mikhail Zimianin had presented the CC the day before. CRA memorandum, January 19, 1982. GARF, f.6991, op. 6, d.2761, ll.134—138. See below.

10. E. Ligachev and V. Stukalin to the CPSU Central Committee, November 10, 1983. TsKhSD f.5, o.89, d.82, l.74.

11. Kalinovsky, *A Long Goodbye*, 50.

12. Epkenhans, *The Origins of the Civil War in Tajikistan*, 191.

13. V. Rabiev, "Going Nowhere," *Kommunist Tadzhikistana*, February 12, 1987, 3. CDSP XXXIX:9, 11. Nuri's arrest came in the wake of earlier arrests of 50 harakat sympathizers. Epkenhans, *The Origins of the Civil War in Tajikistan*, 192.

14. Hetmanek, "Islamic Revolution and Jihad Come to the Former Soviet Central Asia," 366. Khujand was an oblast in northern Tajikistan.

15. V. Rabiev, "*V klassu . . . s Koranom*?" (Into the classroom . . . with a Qur'an?), *Kommunist Tadzhikistana*, January 31, 1987, 2. As of the mid-1980s, it became common to use the term '*Wahhabi*' to designate the opposition to establishment Islam.

16. Igor' Beliaev, "*Islam i politika*," *Literaturnaia gazeta*, May 13 and 20, 1987, 13, 12 respectively. To the best of my knowledge, attributing to Muslim elements any contribution whatever to the Alma-Ata demonstrations was a complete canard that reflects the article's source and motivation. *Zheltoqsan* (December) became an important slogan of the Kazakh nationalist revival in Gorbachev's last years.

17. Atkin, "Islamic Assertiveness and the Waning of the Old Soviet Order," 56–57, and "Tajikistan: Reform, Radicalism and Civil War," 620.

18. Interviews with immigrants to Israel, early 1982.

19. Interview with Nariman Abdullaev, Tashkent, May 16, 2014.

20. "Deistvovat' na vsekh napravleniiakh" (To act in all directions), *Kommunist Tadzhikistana*, December 30, 1987, 2.

21. During these two years, the media in Tajikistan devoted considerable attention to illegal Islamic activity.

22. "Deistvovat' na vsekh napravleniiakh," *Kommunist Tadzhikistana*, December 30, 1987, 2.

23. Ebon, *KGB: Death and Rebirth*, 161.

24. Kalinovsky, *A Long Goodbye*, 186.

25. E.g., Yu. Dmitriyev and O. Kyvatkovskiy, "Night Caravan. Armed Groups of Smugglers Neutralized Thanks to Soviet Border Guards' Vigilance," *Trud*, May 23, 1984, 4. FBIS III, May 29, 1984, V3–V6.

26. Urban, *War in Afghanistan*, 130.

27. Mitrokhin, *The KGB in Afghanistan*, 112–116. See also below.

28. Olcott, "Soviet Islam and World Revolution," 488.

29. This held similarly for a host of Third World Muslim countries. See, for example, my article, "The Role of Islam and the Soviet Muslims in Soviet Arab Policy."

30. See, e.g., Tashkent International Service in Uzbek, March 21, 1984. FBIS III, March 26, 1984, D3–D4.

31. See, for example, a Tashkent radio item on DRA awards to Uzbek experts. Tashkent International Service, March 21, 1984. FBIS, March 26, 1984, D3–D4.

32. "Torzhestvo v Kabule" (Festivities in Kabul), *Pravda*, April 27, 1983, 4.

33. A. Rasul Amin, "A General Reflection on the Stealthy Sovietisation of Afghanistan," 54–57. See also note 2.

34. Roy, *The New Central Asia: The Creation of Nations*, 168.

35. A. Rozyev, "Spetsreis agitpoezda" (Special propaganda train) and "Spetsreis" (Special train), *Komsomolets Turkmenistana*, January 28, 1989, February 23, 1989, 6, and *Sovet Turkmenistany*, February 7, 9, 1989, 4. JPRS-UPA-89–044, July 10, 1989.

36. Nissman, "Turkmenistan: Just like Old Times," 646.

37. Atkin, "Religious, National and Other Identities in Central Asia," 58. Hundreds of Afghan students were studying in Dushanbe in 1986. "An der sowjetischen Grenze zu Afghanistan" (On the Soviet border with Afghanistan), *Neue Zürcher Zeitung*, October 11/12, 1987.

38. Fogel', "Osobennosti propagandy SSSR vo vremia voennoi aktsii v Afganistane," 68.

39. "Gorizonty sotrudnichestva" (Horizons of cooperation), *Kommunist Tadzhikistana*, June 21, 1988, 3.

40. R. Moscow, December 30, 1987. FBIS-SOV-87–251, December 31, 1987, 23.

41. Roy, "The Sovietization of Afghanistan," 56. According to Alexandre Bennigsen, over 25,000 Afghans were reportedly studying in the Soviet Union in 1984. "Les rapports entre Russes et musulmans se sont dégradés en Asie centrale soviétique," *Le Monde*, November 15, 1984. Bennigsen gives no source, and the figure might be exaggerated.

42. Bui Fong Din' and Shrikh Mohamad, "Vladi ot voiny" (Far from the war), *Komsomolets Uzbekistana*, January 7, 1989.

43. "Tashkent in Early January," *Komsomol'skaia pravda*, January 5, 1989, 1. CDSP XLI:3, 24–25; "At the Uzbek Ministry of Foreign Affairs," *Pravda vostoka*, January 21, 1989, 1. JPRS-UPA-89–022, April 6, 1989, 93.

44. Tasar, "The Central Asian Muftiate in Occupied Afghanistan, 1979–87," 213.

45. Chronicle of events in Afghanistan, April–June and July–September 1981. https://nsarchive2.gwu.edu/rus/text_files/Afganistan/—accessed January 10, 2017.

46. Tasar, "The Central Asian Muftiate," 217. Tasar's article describes in detail the SADUM effort to propagate in Kabul the Soviet example of church-state relations. Ibid., 213–226.

47. TASS, "Poezdka zavershena" (Trip concluded), *Izvestiia*, September 7, 1980, 5.

48. TASS in English, October 24, 1985. FBIS III, October 28, 1985, D11.

49. *Ogonek*, no. 25, June 1990, quoted in RFE/RL DR, no. 118, June 22, 1990.

50. Tashkent International Service, September 27, 1983. FBIS, October 4, 1983, September 20, 1984. FBIS-SOV-84–187.

51. Moscow TV, September 15, 1984/FBIS-SOV-84–182, September 18, 1984.

52. RFE-RL SBN, February 1985, 11–12.

53. Beginning in 1983, massive arrests swept Uzbekistan.

54. Author's interview with Pavel Palazhchenko, November 17, 1994.

55. CWIHP *Bulletin* 8–9 (Winter 1996/1997): 145–146.

56. Rubtsov, "Sovetskii Soiuz v 'neob"iavlennoi' voine v Afganistane," 139.

57. Most respondents in interviews with afgantsy from Central Asia confirmed that this was the case. Laruelle and Rakisheva, eds., *Interv'iu s voinami internatsionalistami afganskoi voiny*, passim.

58. Liakhovskii and Zabrodin, *Tainy afganskoi voiny*, 57–58.

59. Communication to the author of Rofi Pardaev, Tashkent, May 31, 2014. See also below and *Komsomolets Uzbekistana*, July 4, 1989.

60. "Vstrechi v rodnoi shkole" (Encounters in their home school), *Komsomolets Turkmenistana*, March 2, 1989.

61. James P. Sterba, "Russians Said Replacing Ethnic Reservists in Kabul," *International Herald Tribune*, February 4, 1980, 2.

62. Quoted in Zhou, "The Muslim Battalions: Soviet Central Asians in the Soviet-Afghan War," 322; see also "Obostrenie vnutrennikh problem v okkupatsionnoi armii" (Exacerbation of internal problems in the occupying force), *Posev*, 4 (1984), 15.

63. Laruelle and Rakisheva, eds., *Interv'iu s voinami internatsionalistami afganskoi voiny*, 317.

64. Author's interview with Ibrohim Isrofilod, Dushanbe, January 29, 1992; Laruelle and Rakisheva, eds., *Interv'iu s voinami internatsionalistami afganskoi voiny*, 130.

65. Laruelle and Rakisheva, eds., *Interv'iu s voinami internatsionalistami afganskoi voiny*, 21.

66. Amstutz, *Afghanistan: The First Five Years of Soviet Occupation*, 170.

67. Quoted, *Ha'arets*, May 16, 1980.

68. Marat, *The Military and the State in Central Asia*, 40.

69. Christian Bleuer has eloquently elaborated on this point in his "Muslim Soldiers in Non-Muslim Militaries at War in Muslim Lands," 493–496.

70. Extrapolating from this story, Odom, *The Collapse of the Soviet Military*, 248, speaks of "occasional mutinies," but I am inclined to discard the story altogether. Odom's testimony is based on an account in Alexiev, *Inside the Soviet Army in Afghanistan*, 43, whose sources appear doubtful. Aaron Einfrank, "Bitter Racial Violence Rages in Afghan War," *Washington Times*, November 14, 1985, reprinted in USIA addendum no. 47, AD 890, November 22, 1985, and

Taras Kuzio, "Racism in the Russian Army," AD 853, January 17, 1986 (reprinted from *Soviet Analyst*), tell of fighting that blew up an ammunition depot, leading to at least 450 deaths and the evacuation of the base. A more plausible estimate suggests 80 killed.

71. Smith, *The New Russians*, 305.

72. Interviews with Soviet emigrants to Israel in August 1981 who had visited friends in Tashkent the previous summer.

73. Wimbush and Alexiev, *Soviet Central Asian Soldiers in Afghanistan*.

74. Göransson, "At the Service of the State. Soviet-Afghan War Veterans in Tajikistan, 1979–1992," 200–201; Laruelle and Rakisheva, eds., *Interv'iu s voinami internatsionalistami afganskoi voiny*, 212. This soldier served from 1979 to 1981.

75. Interview with Ikhtyor Tashpulatov, June 12, 2014 (Bukhara). Other Central Asians felt similarly. One Kazakh, for example, said that whereas in the Soviet Union people used machinery for plowing, the Afghans were still using wooden plows. Laruelle and Rakisheva, eds., *Interv'iu s voinami internatsionalistami afganskoi voiny*, 33.

76. Zhou, "The Muslim Battalions," 325.

77. Göransson, "At the Service of the State," 99.

78. Interview with Tuymorod Akebirov, Bukhara, May 11, 2014.

79. Göransson, "At the Service of the State," 199–200

80. Braithwaite, *Afgantsy: The Russians in Afghanistan*, 233.

81. Göransson, "At the Service of the State," 200.

82. Laruelle and Rakisheva, eds., *Interv'iu s voinami internatsionalistami afganskoi voiny*, 325. The source for this was a soldier who served from 1986 to 1988.

83. Compare ibid., 30.

84. Ibid., 214.

85. Ibid., 78.

86. Zhou, "The Muslim Battalions," 322.

87. Interview with Ikhtiyor Tashpulatov, June 12, 2014.

88. Interview with Tuymurod Akebirov, June 11, 2014.

89. Zhou, "The Muslim Battalions," 327.

90. E.g., Laruelle and Rakisheva, eds., *Interv'iu s voinami internatsionalistami afganskoi voiny*, 232. This particular soldier served from 1985 to 1987.

91. Ibid., 389.

92. Sarin and Dvoretsky, *The Afghan Syndrome*, 88.

93. Alexiev and Wimbush, *Ethnic Minorities in the Red Army*, 253.

94. This has been my experience with Uzbek, and that of Markus Göransson with Tajik, afgantsy respondents.

95. Göransson, "At the Service of the State," 146–147.

96. N. Korotkikh, "Da budet Vam mir . . ." (Yes, you'll have peace . . .), *Komsomolets Uzbekistana*, January 19, 1989.

97. For this last point, see Göransson, "At the Service of the State," 197.

98. Alexiev and Wimbush, *Ethnic Minorities in the Red Army*, 251.

99. Ibid., 246.

100. Göransson, "At the Service of the State," 140–144.

101. Laruelle and Rakisheva, eds., *Interv'iu s voinami internatsionalistami afganskoi voiny*, 133–135.

102. "My vypolnili svoi dolg" (We fulfilled our duty), *Podvig*, issue 34, 1989, 13.

103. P. Kruzhin, "O geroiakh Sovetskogo Soiuza" (The Soviet Union's heroes), *Posev*, no. 4 (1985), 31–32.

104. Göransson, "At the Service of the State," 131–132. Göransson claims that 1981 was the year of the largest mobilization of Tajik soldiers for Afghanistan throughout the war. Ibid., 234.

105. Smith, *The New Russians*, 305.

106. Laruelle and Rakisheva, eds., *Interv'iu s voinami internatsionalistami afganskoi voiny*, 317.

107. Hosking, *A History of the Soviet Union*, 447.

108. Zhou, "The Muslim Battalions," 323. I was unable to get corroboration or further information of such protest from Tashkentis whom I interviewed in 2014.

109. Ibid., 324.

110. Jones, *Red Army and Society*, 189.

111. G. Ivanov, "What's behind the Perfunctory Reply?" *Krasnaia zvezda*, July 21, 1986, 2. CDSP XXXVIII:21, 20.

112. Nahaylo, "When Ivan Comes Marching Home: The Domestic Impact of the War in Afghanistan," *American Spectator*, July 1987, 16.

113. Laruelle and Rakisheva, eds., *Interv'iu s voinami internatsionalistami afganskoi voiny*, 271.

114. *Komsomolets Uzbekistana*. April 25, 1990, 1, and Alexiev and Wimbush, *Ethnic Minorities in the Red Army*, 252–253.

115. Interview with Ibrohim Isrofilod, Dushanbe, January 29, 1992.

116. Pardaev, *Afganskaia komandirovka*, 236–237.

117. Zhou, "The Muslim Battalions," 304.

118. Testimony of the political officer of one of the battalion's companies. Laruelle and Rakisheva, eds., *Interv'iu s voinami internatsionalistami afganskoi voiny*, 287–288, and Zhou, "The Muslim Battalions," 305.

119. Zhou, "The Muslim Battalions," 305.

120. Quoted in ibid., 306. Farsi or Persian would include Tajik and Dari.

121. Ibid., 307–308.

122. Ibid., 311.

123. Ibid., 313–314, 321–322.

124. According to one detailed survey, two to three interpreters were also attached to each corps and division. Oliker, *Building Afghanistan's Security Forces in Wartime: The Soviet Experience*, 43–44.

125. Göransson, "At the Service of the State," 125–126.

126. Alexiev and Wimbush, *Ethnic Minorities in the Red Army*, 246.

127. Testimonies of Tajik afgantsy. Laruelle and Rakisheva, eds., *Interv'iu s voinami internatsionalistami afganskoi voiny*, 183.

128. Quoted in Göransson, "At the Service of the State," 199–200.

129. Laruelle and Rakisheva, eds., *Interv'iu s voinami internatsionalistami afganskoi voiny*, 168.

130. For the reminiscences of one of these, see "Ia vospominaiu utrennii Kabul" (I remember Kabul in the morning. http://www.afgan.kz/vet/nailja3.htm, accessed February 12, 2018.

131. Marat, *The Military and the State in Central Asia*, 40–41.

132. Quoted in Finke, "Central Asian Attitudes towards Afghanistan," 64.

133. Laruelle and Rakisheva, eds., *Interv'iu s voinami internatsionalistami afganskoi voiny*, 16. 262.

134. Ibid., 206. Similar testimony was given by another soldier who served as a truck driver. Ibid., 317.

135. E.g., ibid., 170, 246.

136. For one story of a Turkmen soldier who made it back home, see M. Bektasov, "The Homeland Is More Precious Than Life," *Turkmeskaia iskra*, February 19, 1989, 3—JPRS-UPA-89–038, June 8, 1989, 100–103. See also Chapter 3.

137. Borovik, *The Hidden War*, 226.

138. V. Snegirev, "V noch' pod Novyi god" (On the night of the New Year), *Pravda*, March 22, 1989, 5.

139. Interview with Nodira Mustafaeva, Tashkent, May 21, 2014.

140. Interviews with the author.

141. Borovik, *The Hidden War*, 42.

142. Dadabaev, *Identity and Memory in Post-Soviet Central Asia*, 104.

143. Interviews in Bukhara with Tuymurod Akebirov and Ikhtiyor Tashpulatov, June 11, 12, 2014. For other testimonies that Central Asians tended not to be troubled by PTSD, see Chapter 8.

144. RL 260/88, May 24, 1988.

145. Göransson, "At the Service of the State," 47, 246–248.

146. Ibid., 280.

147. "'Shuravi' i drugie" (The "shuravi" and others), *Komsomolets Uzbekistana*, February 18, 1989.

148. I perused both *Komsomolets Uzbekistana* and *Komsomolets Turkmenistana* for the years 1987 to 1991.

149. "Strana, kolonny Pervomaia" (The country: The columns of May 1), *Pravda*, May 2, 1989, 2.

150. Shozimov, Beshimov, and Yunusova, "The Ferghana Valley during Perestroika," 178. The three scholars came from Tajikistan, Kyrgyzstan, and Uzbekistan, respectively.

151. E.g., a report from the Chechen-Ingush ASSR in May 1979, quoted in Kalinovsky, *A Long Goodbye*, 47–49.

152. Fred Coleman, "Moscow Looks South," *Newsweek*, April 2, 1979, 45.

153. *Bakinskii rabochii*, December 19, 1980, quoted in Knight, *The KGB*, 296.

154. "Rasskazyvaiut ob Afganistane" (Stories of Afghanistan), *Posev*, no. 7 (1985), 21.

155. Karp, "Afghanistan: Six Years of Soviet Occupation," 12.

156. Khovanski, "Afghanistan: The Bleeding Wound," 3. Khovanski gives no source for this information.

157. http://chechnyatoday.com/content/view/277498, accessed December 12, 2017.

158. Pavel Grachev testified in an interview in 2001 that Dudaev actually initiated and developed carpet bombing of Afghan targets in 1988 and 1989 and that he and Grachev met several times in Afghanistan to synchronize joint operations of the air force and the paratroop division Grachev commanded. http://www.trud.ru/article/15-03-2001/21092_pavel_grachev_menja_naznachili_otvetstvennym_za_vo.html, accessed December 12, 2017.

159. Aiupov, "Zvezdy pod polumesiatsiem," 66.

160. CRA memo "Situation of Religion in the USSR and Observance of Legislation on Religion in 1982," June 2, 1983. TsKhSD f.5, op. 89, d.82, l.41, and V. A. Kuroedov to the CPSU Central Committee, September 16, 1983; TsKhSD, f.5, op. 89, d.82, l.60.

161. Bocharov, *Russian Roulette*, 75.

162. The Dushanbe hospital dedicated a section for these soldiers as early as 1980. *Der Spiegel*, June 16, 1980. DR/FBIS III, June 20, 1980, R1.

163. Author's interview with Alik Yakubov, June 17, 1991 (Tel Aviv).

164. Dudoignon, "Political Parties and Forces in Tajikistan, 1989–1993," 55.

165. Interview with Nuriman Abdullaev, Tashkent, May 14, 2014.

166. This has been confirmed by the research of Mark B. Göransson, "At the Service of the State," passim.

167. Summary of conversations conducted with these immigrants in August 1981.

168. *New York Times*, April 6, 1980.

169. R. W. Apple Jr., "In Soviet Central Asia, Afghan War Is Always Close," *New York Times*, November 6, 1980.

170. Opposition to the war jumped markedly in Central Asia between 1984 and 1987. See Chapter 7. It will be remembered that in spring 1987, the war spilled over into Tajik territory.

171. Roy, *The New Central Asia*, 126–127.

172. Braithwaite, *Afgantsy*, 287.

173. Quoted in Borovik, *The Hidden War*, 10.

174. *Sovetskaia Kirgiziia*, June 30, 1984, quoted in Alexandre Bennigsen, "Les rapports entre Russes et musulmans se sont dégradés en Asie centrale soviétique," *Le Monde*, November 15, 1984.

175. Bohdan Nahaylo, "When Ivan Comes Marching Home: The Domestic Impact of the War in Afghanistan," *American Spectator* (July 1987): 15.

176. G. Bobosadykova, Information on the implementation of the two abovementioned CPSU CC resolutions, October 11, 1983—TsKhSD f.5, op. 89, d.82, ll.70–71.

177. Kalinovsky, *A Long Goodbye*, 50.

178. Girardet, "Russia's War in Afghanistan," 87.

179. Nahaylo, "When Ivan Comes Marching Home," 15.

180. Annette Bohr, "Turkmenistan under Perestroika: An Overview," Radio Liberty, *Report on the USSR*, March 23, 1990, 19.

181. For the beginnings of this revival, see Khalid, *Islam under Communism*, 144–146; Babadjanov with Malikov and Nazarov, "Islam in the Ferghana Valley between National Identity and Islamic Alternative," 306–310; Ro'i, *Islam in the Soviet Union*, 357–359.

182. Spolnikov, "Impact of Afghanistan's War on the Former Soviet Republics of Central Asia," especially 109–113.

183. Interview with the author, June 19, 1989 (Tel-Aviv).

184. Tim Epkenhans to the author, October 22, 2018.

185. Rustam Shukurov, "Tadzhikistan: muki vospominaniia" (Tajikistan: the pain of recollection), 234, quoted in Marat, *The Military and the State in Central Asia*, 39.

186. RFE-RL SBN 2–85, May 1985, 12.

187. Babadjanov, "Islam in the Ferghana Valley: between National Identity and Islamic Alternative," 308.

188. Bakhtiyar Babajanov to the author, April 2014. See also Bakhtiyar Babajanov and Muzaffar Kamilov, "Muhammadjon Hindustani and the Beginning of the 'Great Schism' among Muslims of Uzbekistan," 202–203.

189. Mullujonov, "The Role of the Islamic Clergy in Tajikistan," 6.

190. Shozimov, Beshimov and Yunusova, "The Ferghana Valley during Perestroika," 178, 196.

191. *Der Spiegel*, June 16, 1980. FBIS III, June 20, 1980, R1.

192. Dudoignon, "Political Parties and Forces in Tajikistan, 1989–1993," 55.

193. Muzaffar and Saodat Olimov to the author, April 24, 2009.

194. Atkin, "Tajikistan: Ancient Heritage, New Politics," 376.

195. Quoted in Naby, "The Uzbeks in Afghanistan," 13.

196. Broxup, "Recent Developments in Soviet Islam," 34.

197. Council of Religious Affairs memo, June 2, 1983; TsKhSD, f.5, op. 89, d.82, l.38.

198. Iu. Andropov, A. Gromyko, B. Ponomarev, and M. Zimianin, "O meropriiatiiakh po protivodeistviiu popytkam protivnika ispol'zovat' 'islamskii faktor' vo vrazhdebnykh Sovetskomy Soiuza tseliakh" (Measures to counteract the adversary's attempts to use the 'Islamic

factor' for ends hostile to the Soviet Union), September 23, 1981. The memorandum was prepared for the CPSU CC apparatus.

199. Olcott, "Islam and Fundamentalism in Central Asia," 34.

200. Tim Epkenhans to the author, October 22, 2018. Also see Ro'i, *Islam in the Soviet Union*, 358.

201. "Strana, kolonny Pervomaia," *Pravda*, May 2, 1989, 2.

202. R. Moscow in English, June 11, 1990. FBIS-SOV-90–113, June 12, 1990, 16–17, and `Grant Apresian, "Voina posle voiny" (The war after the war), *Literaturnaia gazeta*, June 20, 1990, 9.

Chapter 10

1. In the words of John B. Dunlop, the war led to "imperial indigestion." "Russia: In Search of an Identity?" 31.

2. Yu. Glukhov, "Podvodia chertu" (Drawing a line), *Pravda*, February 15, 1989, 1, 4.

3. V. Artemenko and V. Okulov, "S voiny—domoi!" (Home from the war!), *Pravda*, February 16, 1989,

4. An MoD and MPA study of the social structure of officers and their families conducted in the latter half of 1989 found that 36 percent of the officers were concerned about the falling prestige of the armed forces. S. Taranov, "How Officers Live," *Izvestiia*, October 24, 1989, 2. CDSP XLI:42, 30.

5. Sapper, *Die Auswirkung des Afghanistan-Krieges auf die Sowjetgesellschaft*, 363.

6. Brown, *The Gorbachev Factor*, 310–315.

7. Dunlop, "Russia: In Search of an Identity?" 31, 44.

8. Ol'shanskii, "Afganskii sindrom," 11–12.

9. Kiziun, "Vooruzhennye Sily i obshchestvo: vzaimosviaz', protivorechiia i puti ikh razresheniia," 2–3.

10. Safronov, "Kak eto bylo," 71.

11. Evgenii Stepanov interviewed Borovik for *Sobesednik*, no. 38 (1989), 10.

12. Borovik, *The Hidden War*, 13–14. And see the Introduction to this book.

13. Aleksandr Prokhanov, "Afganskie voprosy" (Afghan questions), *Literaturnaia gazeta*, February 17, 1988, 1 and 9.

14. A. Oliinik, "Kak prinimalos' reshenie" (How the decision was taken), *Krasnaia zvezda*, November 18, 1989, 3.

15. "Problemy sotsial'noi reabilitatsii uchastnikov voiny v Afganistane," 20–21. The commission's head, Pavel Shet'ko, gave me this unpublished paper in 1991.

16. Igor' Beliaev and Anatolii Gromyko, "Tak my voshli v Afganistan" (How we entered Afghanistan), *Literaturnaia gazeta*, September 20, 1989, 14.

17. RFE/RL Daily Report, no. 138, July 23 1991, 5–6.

18. Galeotti, *Afghanistan*, 155, 228.

19. Gorbachev, *The August Coup*, 119.

20. V. Skosyrev, "A Lesson Worth Learning: War in Afghanistan through a Historian's Eyes," *Izvestiia*, May 5, 1989, 5. R. Moscow; FBIS-SOV-89–089, May 10, 1989, 31–34.

21. "Kak prinimalos' reshenie," 42.

22. R. Moscow in English, October 5, 1989. FBIS-SOV-89–193, October 6, 1989, 19.

23. Iu. Glukhov, "Podvodia chertu," *Pravda*, February 15, 1989, 1, 4.

24. V. Artemenko and V. Okulov, "S voiny—domoi!" (Home from the war!), *Pravda*, February 16, 1989, 4.

25. N. Burov, "Misfortune That Cannot Be Forgotten," *Izvestiia*, August 10, 1990, 7. CDSP XLII:33, 33.

26. Kim Tsagolov, "'Nuzhna polnaia pravda . . . ' Otkrytoe pis'mo materi pogibshego voiny v Afganistane" ('The full truth is needed . . . .' Open letter to the mother of a soldier who died in Afghanistan), *Pravda*, September 15, 1989, 3.

27. "S"ezd narodnykh deputatov SSSR" (Congress of People's Deputies, Verbatim report), *Izvestiia*, June 3, 1989, 2, 5; Smith, *The New Russians*, 469–470, quoting Congress, June 2, 1989/FBIS, July 26, 1989. *Izvestiia*, March 3, 1989, 3, had already published a MID disclaimer under the caption "Information and Disinformation."

28. Gennady Zhavoronkov, "We Should Tell the Whole Truth about This War," *Moscow News* (*Moskovskie novosti*), no. 30, July 23, 1989, 9. For such incidents, see also Chapter 2.

29. Radio Moscow, May 21, 1989. FBIS-SOV- 89–087, May 22, 1989, 71–72.

30. E. Gams, "Finding Out the Truth," *Argumenty i fakty*, no. 44, November 4–10, 1989, 7. CDSP XLII:50, 17. For the opinion of the afgantsy on this issue, see Table 8.2.

31. Pikov, ed., *Voina v Afganistane*, 308. Galeotti, who gives no source, claims there were fifty-six afgantsy members, but he seems to be mistaken.

32. Galeotti, *Afghanistan*, 125–127; Nahaylo, *The Ukrainian Resurgence*, 195.

33. In 1987, calls began to appear in the media about the need to recognize and recompense veterans (some 50,000 in all) who had been dispatched to countries where Soviet troops had been deployed and involved in hostilities, including Spain, North Korea, Syria, Egypt, Angola, and Vietnam. These deployments had until then been state secrets, so that those involved were not acknowledged as internationalists or war veterans and had not been eligible for l'goty. In November 1989, *Pravda* published the list of these countries. V. Izgarshev, "Afghan Pain Is Not Subsiding," *Pravda*, November 15, 1989, 4; CDSP XLI:46, 32.

34. Boris Baidachnyi, "Zakon—est' zakon" (The law—is law), and Alla Burlakova, "SSSR—SShA: vstrecha veteranov" (The USSR and the U.S.: Mmeeting of veterans), *Pobratim*, no. 6 (1990), 2; Galeotti, *Afghanistan*, 122–124; and interview with Pavel Shet'ko, August 25, 1993. For the committee's members, see "Postanovlenie Verkhovnogo Soveta SSSR ob obrazovanii komiteta Verkhovnogo Soveta SSSR po delam voinov internatsionalistov" (USSR Supreme Soviet decree on forming the USSR Supreme Soviet Committee for the affairs of internationalist-soldiers), *Pobratim*, no. 5 (1990), 1. For the lot of the POWs in both Afghanistan and Pakistan, see "O sud'be nashikh plennykh" (The fate of our prisoners), *Pobratim*, no. 12 (1991), 8.

35. Baidachnyi, "Zakon—est' zakon."

36. The Supreme Soviet passed the amnesty, announced in July 1988, into law on November 28, 1989. See Chapter 4.

37. Melnick, "The Russian 'Afgantsy': Asset to the Russian Armed Forces," 435. Melnick quoted Kotenov's article in *Pravda*, September 29, 1993, 3.

38. Michael Dobbs, "Ex-Soldier Takes on Powerful Foe," *Washington Post*, November 14, 1990.

39. "Problemy sotsial'noi reabilitatsii uchastnikov voiny v Afganistane," 9.

40. Galeotti, *Afghanistan*, 229–230.

41. For his January 1980 criticism, see Chapter 1. *Aktiv* usually refers to party activists, but it is also used in a broader sense for foremost activists—the "vanguard"—in other collectives or "public organizations" such as a kolkhoz or an industrial plant.

42. O. Bogomolov, "Ne mogy sniat' s sebia vinu" (I cannot shake off the guilt), *Ogonek*, no. 35 (1990), 2–3.

43. Miller, *Beyond Afghanistan: Changing Soviet Perspectives on Regional Conflicts*, 5–14.

44. Ol'shanskii, "Afganskii sled."

45. From time to time during the 1980s, the Soviet media raised the issue of drugs smuggled into the country from Afghanistan, not necessarily in connection with the war; for instance "Night Caravan. Armed Group of Smugglers Neutralized Thanks to Vigilance of Soviet Border Guards," *Trud*, May 23, 1984, 4. FBIS III, May 29, 1984, V3–6. Yet the war apparently enhanced the cultivation of hemp and opium poppy, and the drug business, in Afghanistan—e.g., "Otkuda prishli narkotiki, kotorye sozhgli pod Kabulom" (Whence came the drugs burned near Kabul), *Komsomolets Turkmenistana*, May 12, 1989.

46. For a survey of the drug problem in the Soviet Union in the 1970s and 1980s, see Kramer, "Drug Abuse in the Soviet Union," 28–41.

47. Often articles in the Soviet media on the drug problem discussed it as a social ill that stood on its own merit, making no mention whatever of the war, let alone suggesting the war as a major factor in its aggravation—e.g., *Meditsinskaia gazeta*, April 9, 1986, 3, which revealed that the Ministry of Public Health included a permanent committee for the control of narcotics; A. Mostovoi, "When the Poppies Bloom"—*Komsomol'skaia pravda*, June 8, 1986, 2 (CDSP XXXVIII:22); "Dangerous Weakness: Narcotics and Drug Addicts—Three Aspects of the Problem"—*Literaturnaia gazeta*, August 20, 1986, 11

48. Alexievich, *Zinky Boys*, 19.

49. Murray Feshbach to the author, November 18, 2013.

50. Boris Kalachev, "There's No Place for This in the Military," *Literaturnaia gazeta*, October 26, 1988, 12. CDSP XLI:5, 17.

51. The film *The 9th Company*, first shown in 2005.

52. An article published anonymously in 2006 under the title "The War Syndrome." http://www.privatelife.ru/2006/os06/n5/3.html, accessed April 12, 2015.

53. "The Afghan Fracture: How the Ukrainian Soldiers of the Undeclared War Live" (Interviews of the Ukrainian site Argumenty i fakty with Afghan veterans), www.aif.ua/society/people/963886; accessed July 6, 2015.

54. "Vokrug ruzh'ia . . ." (Guns around . . .), *Kazakhstanskaia pravda*, September 18, 1987, quoted in Aaron Trehub, "Privately Owned Weapons in the Soviet Union," RL/536/88, December 5, 1988.

55. Trehub, "Privately Owned Weapons," 3–4.

56. David M. Glantz, Introduction, in Grau, *The Bear Went Over the Mountain*, xiv.

57. *Kontingent* no. 3 (1991), 1, quoted in Pinnick, "When the Fighting Is Over," 149.

58. Dunlop, "Russia: In Search of an Identity?" 44.

59. Ann Sheehy, " A Bankrupt System: Nationalism and Personal Ambitions," in Tolz and Elliot eds., *The Demise of the USSR*, 8.

60. Bill Keller, "Cry of 'Won't Give My Son!' And Soviets End the Call-Up," *New York Times*, January 20, 1990, A6.

61. Kiziun, "Vooruzhennye Sily i obshchestvo: vzaimosviaz', protivorechiia i puti ikh razresehniia," 2–3.

62. Galeotti, *Afghanistan*, 160.

63. "Problemy sotsial'no reabilitatsii uchastnikov voiny v Afganistane," 9–11.

64. Galbas, "Strategies of Legitimization and Functionalization," 103.

65. Göransson, "At the Service of the State," passim.

66. Sarin and Dvoretsky, *The Afghan Syndrome*, 147, 149.

67. *Kommunist Tadzhikistana*, September 28, 1989, 1. JPRS-UPA-89–064, December 6, 1989, 30.

68. "Skol'ko nas" (How many are we?), *Pobratim*, no. 11 (1991), 3. Defense Minister Yazov provided this figure.

69. "Spravka o Soiuze veteranov Afganistana," June 15, 1991; see also *Pobratim*, no. 12 (1991), 1.

70. Sapper, *Die Auswirkung des Afghanistan-Krieges auf die Sowjetgesellschaft*, 188–189.

71. Author's interview with SVA chairman Aleksandr Kotenov, Moscow, June 27, 1991.

72. Galeotti, *Afghanistan*, 113–118.

73. Sapper, *Die Auswirkung des Afghanistan-Krieges auf die Sowjetgesellschaft*, 190. *Pobratim* was down from 125,000 to 100,000 copies.

74. Laruelle and Rakisheva, eds., *Interv'iu s voinami internatsionalistami afganskoi voiny*, 19.

75. Tolz, *The USSR's Emerging Multiparty System*, 99, quoting *Moscow News*, no. 13 (1990).

76. Riordan, "'Afgantsy': Return of the Lost Generation," 24.

77. Galeotti, *Afghanistan*, 124–125.

78. Babak et al., eds., *Political Organization in Central Asia and Azerbaijan*, 275, 346.

79. Interview with Iurii Stasiuk, http://people.onliner.by/2015/02/11/afgan, accessed February 11, 2015.

80. Braithwaite, *Afgantsy: The Russians in Afghanistan*, 124.

81. Nahaylo, *The Ukrainian Resurgence*, 228.

82. According to Archie Brown, *The Gorbachev Factor*, 276, Gromov had "the good sense not to commit himself fully to the *putschists*."

83. Gromov, "Zashchishchali, obuchali, stroili," 5.

84. Swartz, "The Soviet-Afghan War in Russian Literature," 66.

85. Braithwaite, *Afgantsy*, 309–310.

86. Brown, *The Gorbachev Factor*, 280; *Izvestiia*, June 3, 1989, 1–7.

87. Braithwaite, *Afgantsy*, 308. Soldiers killed nineteen civilian demonstrators in Tbilisi and two hundred in Baku.

88. In an interview to *Molodezh' Gruzii*, May 9, 1989. JPRS-UPA-89–046, July 27, 1989, 84–85.

89. Vladimir Gubar'ev et al., "General'skaia repetitsiia" (General rehearsal), *Moskovskie novosti* no. 14, April 4, 1993, 10.

90. "The Situation in Tbilisi," *Izvestiia*, April 14, 1989, 7. CDSP XLI:41:15, 8. See also *Sotsialisticheskaia industriia*, April 15, 1989, and *Sovetskaia Rossiia*, April 19, 1989.

91. Interview to *Molodezh' Gruzii.*

92. "Zakon—est' zakon." A Tajik source confirmed that the "selfless action" of three or four dozen afgantsy led by Odzhiev saved Dushanbe from numerous crimes and clashes. Umed Babakhanov, "Uroki na zavtra" (Lessons for tomorrow), *Komosomolets Tadzhikistana*, April 6, 1990, 2.

93. Galeotti, *Afghanistan*, 54, 136–137.

94. K. Vladimirov, "Zakalennyi afganom" (Hardened by Afghan), *Na postu* (Tashkent), June 25, 1991, 5.

95. Prokhanov, "Kto zashchishchit zashchitnikov?" 3.

96. Interview with Magomed-Eminov, June 27, 1991.

97. Galeotti, *Afghanistan*, 54, 137.

98. See Ro'i, "Islam in the FSU—An Inevitable Impediment to Democracy?" 109.

99. Interview with afganets Iurii Stasiuk: http://people.onliner.by/2015/02/11/afgan, accessed November 2, 2015.

100. Author's interview with Nugzar Kakhniauri (Tbilisi), September 9, 2014, and with a group of four afgantsy in Kutaisi, September 14, 2014. Kakhniauri also told of the veterans' participation in the Tbilisi demonstration.

101. For the vets' opinion regarding the war's impact on the evolution of the civil war in Tajikistan, see Chapter 9.

102. Moiseev had succeeded Akhromeev as CGS in 1988.

103. Braithwaite, *Afgantsy*, 317.

104. Levitin, "Liberalization in Kyrgyzstan: 'An Island of Democracy,'" 207. Although the party received 8 percent of the votes, it was allotted just 2 percent of the seats.

105. C:\Users\user\Documents\Afghanistan\afgantsy\Грузинские ветераны-«афганцы» отмежевались от марша российского «Боевого братства».htm, July 9, 2013, accessed July 15, 2014. Gromov had set up *Boevoe bratstvo* in 1997 and, although a nongovernment organization, it maintained close ties to the powers-that-be in the Russian Federation.

106. Braithwaite, *Afgantsy*, 317–318.

107. Göransson, "At the Service of the State," 62.

108. Galeotti, *Afghanistan*, 118–119.

109. Kinsburskii and Topalev, "Reabilitatsiia uchastnikov afganskoi voiny v obshchestvennom mnenii," 104–107.

110. Galeotti, *Afghanistan*, 127–130.

111. Ibid., 210.

112. Ol'shanskii, "Afganskii sled."

113. Braithwaite, *Afgantsy*, 308–311. Braithwaite quotes, among others, Valentin Varennikov, *Nepovtorimoe*, vol. 5 (Moskva: Sovetskii pisatel', 2002), 192 ff., 230.

114. Galeotti, *Afghanistan*, 178–181; Brown, *The Gorbachev Factor*, 269–271, 291.

115. Blank, *Operational and Strategic Lessons of the War in Afghanistan*, viii. Blank quoted from Victor Yasman, "Mastering an Identity Crisis," RFE/RL *Report on the USSR*, January 4, 1991, 9.

116. Larry Heinemann, Introduction to Alexievich, *Zinky Boys*, xiv; Michael Dobbs, "Coup Lifted War Heroes to Top of Russian Military," *Washington Post*, September 27, 1992.

117. Galeotti, *Afghanistan*, 117–118, 137–138, 182–184.

118. Brown, *The Gorbachev Factor*, 300.

119. Pinnick, "When the Fighting Is Over," 143.

120. Ol'shanskii, "'Afganskii sindrom,'" 9,d 18.

121. Kinsburskii and Topalev, "Reabilitatsiia uchastnikov afganskoi voiny v obshchestvennom mnenii."

122. Shilo, "Posledstviia vvoda sovetskikh voisk v DRA dlia strany i region," 2, 4.

123. For such legislation, see White, Gill, and Slider, *The Politics of Transition*, 194–196.

124. Aleksandr Yakovlev, "Perestroika or the 'Death of Socialism,'" in Cohen and Vanden Heuvel, *Voices of Glasnost*, 62.

125. "The Intervention in Afghanistan and the Fall of Détente," 249–250.

126. Ibid., 251.

127. O. Odnakolenko, "Kto tebia vydumal, 'Afgan'?" (Who thought you up, "Afghan"?), *Krasnaia zvezda*, July 10, 1992.

Bibliography

Primary Sources

Cold War International History Project (CWIHP) Bulletin, no. 3 (Fall 1993), no. 8–9 (Winter 1996/97) and no. 14/15 (Winter 2003–Spring 2004).

CWIHP Toward an International History of the War in Afghanistan, 1979–1989, vol. 2 (2002) e-Dossier No. 4, CWIHP, November 2001.

Kniga pamiati o sovetskikh voinakh, pogibshikh v Afganistane (Moskva: Ministerstvo Oborony, 1995), http://www.rsva-ural.ru/library/mbook.php?id=364.

Laruelle, Marlène, and Botogaz Rakisheva (eds.), *Interv'iu s voinami internatsionalistami afganskoi voiny* (Interviews with internationalist soldiers of the Afghan War; Central Asian Program 2nd Series, George Washington University, 2015). Some of the interviews appear—mostly in part—in Marlène Laruelle, Botagaz Rakisheva, Gulden Ashkenova, and Artemy M. Kalinovsky, "An Oral History of the Soviet—Afghan War: Interviews with Central Asian Afgantsy," in *The Central Asian—Afghan Relationship*, edited by Marlène Laruelle. Lanham, MD: Lexington Books, 2017.

Secondary Sources

"Afghanistan: A Voice from Moscow." *Monthly Review* 39, no. 4 (1987): 15–20.

Afghanistan Task Force. Foreign Affairs and National Defense Division. *Afghanistan: Soviet Invasion and U.S. Response*, issue brief IB80006. January 1980.

Alexiev, Alexander. *Inside the Soviet Army in Afghanistan* (R-3627-A). Santa Monica, CA: Rand, 1988.

Alexiev, Alexander R., and S. Enders Wimbush, eds. *Ethnic Minorities in the Red Army: Asset or Liability?* Boulder, CO: Westview, 1988.

Alexievich, Svetlana. *Zinky Boys: Soviet Voices from the Afghanistan War*. New York: Norton, 1990.

Allan, Pierre, and Albert Stahel. "Tribal Guerrilla Warfare against a Colonial Power." *Journal of Conflict Resolution*, no. 4 (1983): 590–617.

Almqvist, Borje. "The Afghan War in 1983: Strengthened Resistance versus Soviet 'Nazi' Tactics." *Central Asian Survey* 3, no. 1 (1984): 23–46.

Amin, A. Rasul. "A General Reflection on the Stealthy Sovietisation of Afghanistan." *Central Asian Survey* 3, no.1 (1984): 47–61.

Amstutz, J. Bruce. *Afghanistan: The First Five Years of Soviet Occupation*. Washington, DC: National Defense University, 1986.

Arnold, Anthony. *The Soviet Invasion in Perspective*. Stanford, CA: Hoover Institution Press, 1986.

Atkin, Muriel. "Islamic Assertiveness and the Waning of the Old Soviet Order." *Nationalities Papers* 20, no. 1 (1992): 55–74.

———. "Religious, National and Other Identities in Central Asia." In *Muslims in Central Asia: Expressions of Identity and Change*, edited by Jo-Ann Gross. Durham, NC: Duke University Press, 1992.

———. "Tajikistan: Reform, Radicalism and Civil War." In *New States, New Politics: Building the Post-Soviet Nations*, edited by Ian Bremmer and Ray Taras, 602–627. Cambridge: Cambridge University Press, 1997.

Babadjanov, Bakhtiyar, with Kamil Malikov and Aloviddin Nazarov. "Islam in the Ferghana Valley: Between National Identity and Islamic Alternative." In *Ferghana Valley: The Heart of Central Asia*, edited by S. Frederick Starr, 296–372. Armonk, NY: M. E. Sharpe, 2011.

Babajanov, Bakhtiyar, and Muzaffar Kamilov. "Muhammadjon Hindustani and the Beginning of the 'Great Schism' among Muslims of Uzbekistan." In *Islam in Politics in Russia and Central Asia: Early 18th to Late 20th Centuries*, edited by Stephane Dudoignon and Hisar Komatsu. New York: Kegan Paul, 2004.

Babak, Vladimir, Demian Vaisman, and Aryeh Wasserman, eds. *Political Organization in Central Asia and Azerbaijan: Sources and Documents*. London: Frank Cass, 2004.

Baumann, Robert F. "Russian-Soviet Unconventional Wars in the Caucasus, Central Asia, and Afghanistan." *Leavenworth Papers* no. 20, 1993.

Behrends, Jan Claas. "'Some Call Us Heroes, Others Call Us Killers.' Experiencing Violent Spaces: Soviet Soldiers in the Afghan War." *Nationalities Papers* 43, no. 5 (2015): 667–681.

Bennigsen, Alexandre. "Muslims, Mullahs, and Mujahidin," *Problems of Communism* (November–December 1984): 28–44.

Blank, Stephen. "Imagining Afghanistan: Lessons of a 'Small' War." *Journal of Soviet Military Studies* 3, no. 3 (1990).

———. *Operational and Strategic Lessons of the War in Afghanistan 1979–1990*. Newport, RI: U.S. War and Navy College Strategic Studies Institute, September 1991.

Bleuer, Christian, "Muslim Soldiers in Non-Muslim Militaries at War in Muslim Lands: The Soviet, American and Indian Experience." *Journal of Muslim Minority Affairs* 32 (2012): 492–506.

Bocharov, Gennady. *Russian Roulette: Afghanistan through Russian Eyes*. New York: HarperCollins, 1990.

Bonnell, Victoria E. "Voluntary Associations in Gorbachev's Reform Program." In *The Soviet System in Crisis*, edited by Alexander Dallin and Gail W. Lapidus. Boulder, CO: Westview Press, 1991.

Borovik, Artyom. *The Hidden War: A Russian Journalist's Account of the Soviet War in Afghanistan*. New York: Atlantic Monthly, 1990.

Braithwaite, Rodric. *Afgantsy: The Russians in Afghanistan, 1979—1989*. London: Profile Books, 2011.

Bremmer, Ian, and Ray Taras, eds. *New States, New Politics: Building the Post-Soviet Nations.* Cambridge: Cambridge University Press, 1997.

Brown, Archie. *The Gorbachev Factor.* New York: Oxford University Press, 1996.

Broxup, Marie. "Recent Developments in Soviet Islam." *Religion in Communist Land* 11, no. 1 (1983).

Burger, Robert B., and Michael Bathurst. "Controlling the Soviet Soldier: Some Eyewitness Accounts." College Station: Center for Strategic Technology, Texas A&M University, 1983.

Butterfield, Jim, and Judith B. Sedaitis. "The Emergence of Social Movements in the Soviet Union." In *Perestroika from Below: Social Movements in the Soviet Union* , edited by Judith B. Sedaitis and Jim Butterfield. Boulder, CO: Westview Press, 1991.

Carrère d'Encausse, Hélène. *Decline of an Empire.* New York: Harper, 1982.

Cassidy, Robert M. *Russia in Afghanistan and Chechnya: Military Strategic Culture and the Paradoxes of Asymmetric Conflict.* Carlisle Barracks, PA: Strategic Studies Institute, 2003.

Chernyaev, Anatoly S. *My Six Years with Gorbachev.* University Park: Pennsylvania State University Press, 2000.

Chernysh, Mikhail, "Historical Trauma and Memory: The Case of the Afghan War." *Inter* 6 (2011): 77–87.

Cohen, Stephen F., and Katrina Vanden Heuvel. *Voices of Glasnost.* New York: Norton, 1989.

Collins, Joseph J. "Afghanistan: The Empire Strikes Out." *Parameters* 12, no. 1 (1982): 32–41.

———. "The Soviet-Afghan War: the First Four Years." *Parameters* 14, no. 2 (1984): 49–62.

Dadabaev, Timur. *Identity and Memory in Post-Soviet Central Asia: Uzbekistan's Soviet Past.* Abingdon: Routledge, 2016.

Dalziel, Stephen. *Perestroyka, Glasnost' and the Soviet Military.* Sandhurst: Soviet Studies Research Center, RMA, September 1986.

Danilova, Natalia. "The Development of an Exclusive Veterans' Policy: The Case of Russia." *Armed Forces and Society* 36, no. 5 (2010): 890–916.

———. "Die Veteranen des sowjetischen Afghanistankriegs: Gender und Neuerfindung der Identität." In *Sovietnam: Die UdSSR in Afghanistan 1979–1989*, edited by Tanja Penter and Esther Meier, 213–229. Paderborn: Ferdinand Schoningh, 2017. (in German)

Daugherty, Leo J. III. "Ethnic Minorities in the Soviet Armed Forces: The Plight of Central Asians in a Russian-Dominated Military." *Journal of Slavic Military Studies* 7, no. 2 (1994): 155–197.

Davis, Robert B. "Drugs and Alcohol Use in the Former Soviet Union: Selected Factors and Future Considerations." *International Journal of the Addictions* 29, no. 3 (1994): 303–323.

Dobrynin, Anatoly. *In Confidence.* Seattle: University of Washington Press, 1995.

Downing, John H. "Trouble in the Backyard: Soviet Media Reporting on the Afghanistan Conflict." *Journal of Communications* 38, no. 2 (1988): 5–32.

Dudoignon, Stéphane A. "Political Parties and Forces in Tajikistan, 1989–1993." In *Tajikistan: The Trials of Independence*, edited by Mohammad-Reza Djalili, Frédéric Grare, and Shirin Akiner, 52–85. New York: St. Martin's Press, 1997.

Dunlop, John B. "Russia: In Search of an Identity?" In *New States, New Politics: Building the Post-Soviet Nations*, edited by Ian Bremmer and Ray Taras, 29–95. Cambridge: Cambridge University Press, 1997.

Ebon, Martin. *KGB: Death and Rebirth.* New York: Routledge, 1994.

Epkenhans, Tim. *The Origins of the Civil War in Tajikistan.* Lanham, MD: Lexington Books, 2016.

Es'haq, Mohammad. "The Present Situation in Afghanistan (June 1986)." *Central Asian Survey* 6, no. 1 (1987): 119–139.

Fane, Daria. "After Afghanistan: The Decline of Soviet Military Prestige." *Washington Quarterly* (Spring 1990): 5–16.

Feifer, Gregory. *The Great Gamble: The Soviet War in Afghanistan*. New York: HarperCollins, 2009.

Feltham, Ann, and Artk Mairoyan. "Drug Abuse in the Soviet Union." Discussion paper series 11. Colchester: University of Essex, September 1991.

Feshbach, Murray, and Alfred Friendly Jr. *Ecocide in the USSR: Health and Nature under Siege*. New York: Basic Books, 1992.

Finke, Peter. "Central Asian Attitudes towards Afghanistan." In *Ethnicity, Authority and Power in Central Asia: New Games Great and Small*, edited by Robert L. Canfield and Gabriele Rasuly-Paleczek, 61–76. London: Routledge, 2011.

Galbas, Michael. "'Our Pain and Our Glory': Social Strategies of Legitimization and Functionalization." *Journal of Soviet and Post-Soviet Politics and Society* 1, no. 2 (2015): 91–132.

Galeotti, Mark. *Afghanistan: The Soviet Union's Last War*. London: Frank Cass, 1995.

Galula, David. *Counterinsurgency Warfare: Theory and Practice*. 1964. Reprint, Westport, CT: Praeger Security International, 2006.

Galster, Steven. "Rivalry and Reconciliation in Afghanistan: What Prospects for the Accords?" *Third World Quarterly* 10 (1988): 1505–1541.

Gareyev, Mahmut. "The Afghan Problem: Three Years without Soviet Troops." *International Affairs* (Moscow) 38, no. 3 (1992): 15–24.

Girardet, Edward R. *Afghanistan: The Soviet War*. New York: St. Martin's Press, 1985.

———. "Russia's War in Afghanistan." *Central Asian Survey* 2, no. 1 (1983): 83–109.

Gleason, Gregory. *The Central Asian States: Discovering Independence*. Boulder, CO: Westview, 1997.

Göransson, Markus Balasz. "At the Service of the State. Soviet-Afghan War Veterans in Tajikistan, 1979—1992." PhD diss., Aberystwyth University, 2015.

Gorbachev, Mikhail. *The August Coup: The Truth and the Lessons*. New York: HarperCollins, 1991.

Graffy, Julian, and Geoffrey A. Hosking, eds. *Culture and the Media in the USSR Today*. London: Macmillan, 1989.

Grachev, Andrei. *Gorbachev's Gamble*. Cambridge: Polity Press, 2008.

Grau, Lester W. *The Bear Went Over the Mountain: Soviet Combat Tactics in Afghanistan*. London: Frank Cass, 1998.

———. "The Soviet-Afghan War: A Superpower Mired in the Mountains" *Journal of Slavic Military Studies* 17, no. 1 (2004): 129–151.

———. "The Soviet Combined Arms Battalion—Reorganization for Tactical Flexibility." Fort Leavenworth, KS: Soviet Army Studies Program, September 1989.

Gromyko, Andrei. *Memories*. London: Hutchinson, 1989.

Gross, Natalie. "Youth and the Army in the USSR in the 1980s," *Soviet Studies* 42 (1990): 481–498.

Hammond, Thomas R. *Red Flag over Afghanistan* Boulder, CO: Westview Press, 1984.

Harrison, Selig S. "A Breakthrough in Afghanistan." *Foreign Policy* (Spring 1983): 3–26.

Hetmanek, Allen. "Islamic Revolution and Jihad Come to the Former Soviet Central Asia: The Case of Tajikistan." *Central Asian Survey* 12 (1993): 365–378.

Hosking, Geoffrey. *A History of the Soviet Union*. London: Fontana Press and Collins, 1985.

"The Intervention in Afghanistan and the Fall of Détente." Nobel Symposium, Lysebu, September 17–20, 1995. Oslo: Norwegian Nobel Institute, 1996.

Isby, David S. "Afghanistan 1982: The War Continues." *International Defence Review,* no. 11 (November 1982): 1523–1528.

Johnson, A. Ross, and R. Eugene Parta, eds. *Cold War Broadcasting: Impact on the Soviet Union and Eastern Europe.* Budapest/New York: Central University Press, 2010.

Jones, Anthony, Walter Connor, and David Powell. *Soviet Social Problems.* Boulder, CO: Westview Press, 1991.

Jones, David Martin, and M. L. R. Smith. "Whose Hearts and Whose Minds? The Curious Case of Global Counter-Insurgency." *Journal of Strategic Studies* 33, no. 1 (2010): 81–121.

Jones, Ellen. *Red Army and Society. A Sociology of the Soviet Military.* Boston: Allen & Unwin, 1985.

Jukes, Geoffrey. "The Soviet Armed Forces and the Afghan War." In *The Soviet Withdrawal from Afghanistan,* edited by Amin Saikal and William Maley, 82–100. Cambridge: Cambridge University Press, 1989.

Kalinovsky, Artemy. "The Blind Leading the Blind: Soviet Advisors, Counter-Insurgency and Nation-building in Afghanistan." CWIHP working paper 60 (January 2010).

———. "Central Asian Soldiers and the Soviet War in Afghanistan: An Introduction." In *The Central Asian-Afghanistan Relationship: From Soviet Intervention to the Silk Road Initiatives,* edited by Marlène Laruelle, 3–19. Lanham, MD: Lexington Books, 2017.

———. *A Long Goodbye: The Soviet Withdrawal from Afghanistan.* Cambridge, MA: Harvard University Press, 2011.

Kamrany, Nake M., and David T. Killian, "Effects of Afghanistan War on Soviet Society and Policy." *International Journal of Social Economics* 19 (1992): 129–151.

Karp, Craig. "Afghanistan under the Soviets: Five Years." *Department of State Bulletin* (January 1985): 42–45.

———. "Afghanistan: Seven Years of Occupation." *Department of State Bulletin* (February 1987): 1–21.

Khalid, Adeeb. *Islam under Communism.* Berkeley: University of California Press, 2007.

Khovanski, Sergei. "Afghanistan: The Bleeding Wound." *Détente* no. 6 (Spring 1986): 2–4.

Klass, Rosanne. "Afghanistan: The Accords," *Foreign Affairs* 66, no. 5 (1988): 922–945.

Kline, David. "The Conceding of Afghanistan." *Washington Quarterly* (Spring 1983): 130–139.

Knight, Amy W. *The KGB: Police and Politics in the Soviet Union.* Boston: Unwin Hyman, 1988.

Konovalov, Valerii. "Reintegrating Afghan Veterans into Civilian Life." RL 425/88, September 18, 1988.

Kotkin, Steven. *Armageddon Averted: The Soviet Union's Collapse, 1970–2000.* Oxford: Oxford University Press, 2001.

Kramer, John M. "Drug Abuse in the USSR." In *Social Change and Social Issues in the Former USSR,* edited by W. Joyce. London: Palgrave Macmillan, 1992.

Kuzio, Taras. "Opposition in the USSR to the Occupation of Afghanistan." *Central Asian Survey* 6, no. 1 (1987): 99–117.

Laruelle, Marlène, ed. *The Central Asian-Afghanistan Relationship.* Lanham, MD: Lexington Books, 2017.

Levitin, Leonid. "Liberalization in Kyrgyzstan: 'An Island of Democracy." In *Democracy and Pluralism in Muslim Eurasia,* edited by Yaacov Ro'i, 187–213. London: Frank Cass, 2004.

Lieven, Anatol. *Chechnya: Tombstone of Russian Power.* New Haven: Yale University Press, 1998.

Lyakhovskiy, Aleksandr Antonovich. "Inside the Soviet Invasion of Afghanistan and the Seizure of Kabul, December 1979." CWIHP working paper 51. December 2007.

Maklak, Alena. "*Dedovshchina* on Trial. Some Evidence concerning the Last Generation of 'Sons' and 'Grandfathers.'" *Nationalities Papers* 43 (2015): 682–699.

Mathers, Robert S. "Green, Red and White: The Problems of Muslim Soldiers in Today's Russian Army." *Journal of Slavic Military Studies* 16:4 (December 2003): 12–32.

Manaev, O. "A Vicious Circle in Soviet Media Audience Relations." *European Journal of Communication* 4 (1989): 287–305.

Marat, Erica. *The Military and the State in Central Asia: From Red Army to Independence.* London: Routledge, 2010.

McMichael, Scott R. "Soviet Tactical Performance and Adaptation in Afghanistan." *Journal of Soviet Military Affairs* 3, no. 1 (1990): 73–105.

McNair, Brian. *Glasnost, Perestroika and the Soviet Media.* New York: Routledge, 1991.

Melnick, A. James. "The Russian 'Afgantsy': Asset to the Russian Armed Forces." *Journal of Soviet Military Studies* 8:2 (1995): 432–437.

"Memorandum de Lord Bethell Concernant la Situation des Soldats Soviétiques Prisonniers Détenus par la Résistance Afghane." *Central Asian Survey* 3, no. 2 (1984): 132–137.

Mendelson, Sarah E. *Changing Course: Ideas, Politics and the Soviet Withdrawal from Afghanistan.* Princeton: Princeton University Press, 1998.

Mickiewicz, Ellen. *Changing Channels: Television and the Struggle for Power in Russia.* Durham: Duke University Press, 1999.

———. *Split Signals: Television and Politics in the Soviet Union.* New York: Oxford University Press, 1988.

Miller, Eric (Rapporteur). *Beyond Afghanistan: Changing Soviet Perspectives on Regional Conflicts.* Alexandria, VA: Center for Naval Analysis, 1990.

Mitrokhin, Vasiliy. "The KGB in Afghanistan." CWIHP working paper 40 (February 2002).

Mullojonov, Parviz. "The Role of the Islamic Clergy in Tajikistan." Tokyo, 1999.

Naby, Eden. "The Ethnic Factor in Soviet-Afghan Relations." *Asian Survey* 20 (1980): 237–256.

———. "The Uzbeks in Afghanistan." *Central Asian Survey* 3:1 (1984): 1–21.

Nahaylo, Bohdan. *The Ukrainian Resurgence.* London: Hurst, 1999.

Nissman, David. "Turkmenistan: Just Like Old Times." In *New States, New Politics: Building the Post-Soviet Nations*, edited by Ian Bremmer and Ray Taras, 635–653. Cambridge: Cambridge University Press, 1997.

Nobel Symposium 1995. *The Intervention in Afghanistan and the Fall of Détente.* Lysebu September 17–20, 1995. Oslo: Norwegian Nobel Institute, 1996.

Odom, William E. *The Collapse of the Soviet Military.* New Haven: Yale University Press, 1998.

Olcott, Martha Brill. "Islam and Fundamentalism in Central Asia." In *Muslim Eurasia: Conflicting Legacies,* edited by Yaacov Ro'i , 21–39. London: Frank Cass, 1995.

———. "Soviet Islam and World Revolution." *World Politics* 23, no. 2 (1982).

Oliker, Olga. *Building Afghanistan's Security Forces in Wartime: The Soviet Experience.* Santa Monica, CA: RAND, 2011.

Olkhovsky, Paul. *After Afghanistan: Two Opposing Views on the Soviet Military.* Arlington, VA: Center for Naval Analysis, January 1991.

Oushakine, Serguei. "'War das etwa alles umsonst?' Russlands Kriege in militarischen Liedern." In *Sovietnam: Die UdSSR in Afghanistan 1979–1989,* edited by Tanja Penter and Esther Meier, 187–212. Paderborn: Ferdinand Schoningh, 2017.

Parta, R. Eugene. "The Audience to Western Broadcasts to the USSR during the Cold War." In *Cold War Broadcasting: Impact on the Soviet Union and Eastern Europe*, edited by A. Ross Johnson and R. Eugene Parta. Budapest: Central University Press, 2010.

———. *Discovering the Hidden Listener: An Empirical Assessment of Radio Liberty and Western Broadcasting to the USSR during the Cold War.* Stanford, CA: Hoover Institution, 2008.

Petrone, Karen. "Coming Home Soviet Style: The Reintegration of Afghan Vets into Soviet

Everyday Life." In *Everyday Life in Russia Past and Present*, edited by Choi Chitterjee et al., 350–367. Bloomington: Indiana University Press, 2007.

Philips, James."Afghanistan: Islam versus Marxism." *Journal of Social and Political Studies* 4, no. 4 (1979).

Philips, Peter. "A Soviet Estonian Soldier in Afghanistan." *Central Asian Survey* 5, no.1 (1986): 101–115.

Pinnick, Kathryn. "Public Opinion in Russia on the Ex-USSR's Afghanistan War Veterans since 1991." Paper presented at the V World Congress for Central and East European Studies, Warsaw, August 6–11, 1995.

———. "When the Fighting Is Over: Soldiers' Mothers and the Afghan Madonnas." In *Post-Soviet Women: from the Baltic to Central Asia*, edited by Mary Buckley, 143–156. Cambridge: Cambridge University Press, 1997.

Rakowska-Harmstone, Teresa. "The Soviet Armed Forces: The Challenge of Reform and the Ethnic Factor." Unpublished paper, 1990.

Raleigh, Donald J. *Soviet Baby Boomers*. New York: Oxford University Press, 2012.

Reich, Anna, "Faces of the Lithuanian *Afganai*," *Journal of Soviet and Post-Soviet Politics and Society* 1, no. 2 (2015): 187–195

Rigby, T. H., "The Afghan Conflict and Soviet Domestic Politics." In *The Soviet Withdrawal from Afghanistan*, edited by Amin Saikal and William Maley, 67–81. Cambridge: Cambridge University Press, 1990.

Riordan, Jim, "'Afgantsy'—Return of the Lost Generation," unpublished manuscript. N.d.

———. "Teenage Gangs, 'Afgantsy" and Neofascists." In *Soviet Youth Culture*, edited by Jim Riordan, 122–142. London: Macmillan, 1989.

———. "Disabled Afgantsy: Fighters for a Better Deal. In *Social Change and Social Issues in the Former USSR*, edited by Walter Joyce, 136–157. New York: Macmillan, 1992.

———. "Soviet Youth: Pioneers of Change." *Soviet Studies* 40 (1988): 556–572.

Ro'i, Yaacov. "The Impact of the Islamic Fundamentalist Revival of the Late 1970s on the Soviet View of Islam." In *The USSR and the Muslim World*, edited by Yaacov Ro'i, 149–177. London: George Allen & Unwin, 1984.

———. *Islam in the Soviet Union*. London: Christopher Hurst and Columbia University Press, 2000.

———. "Islam in the FSU—An Inevitable Impediment to Democracy?" In *Democracy and Pluralism in Muslim Eurasia*, edited by Yaacov Ro'i, 101–116. London: Frank Cass, 2004.

———. "The Role of Islam and the Soviet Muslims in Soviet Arab Policy." *Asian and African Studies* 10, no. 2 (1974–1975): 157–189, and no. 3 (1975): 259–280.

Roy, Olivier, "The Lessons of the Soviet/Afghan War." *Adelphi Papers*, no. 259, 1991.

———. *The New Central Asia: The Creation of Nations*. New York: New York University Press, 1997.

———. "The Sovietization of Afghanistan" In *Afghanistan and the Soviet Union: Collision and Transformation*, edited by Milan Hauner and Robert L. Canfield, 48–58. Boulder, CO: Westview, 1989),

Rubenstein, Joshua. *Soviet Dissidents: Their Struggle for Human Rights*. Boston: Beacon Press, 1980.

Rubinstein, Alvin Z. "The Soviet Union and Afghanistan." *Current History* (October 1983): 318–321, 337–338.

Sapper, Manfred, *Die Auswirkungen des Afghanistan-Krieges auf die Sowjetgesellschaft*. Hamburg: LIT, 1994.

Sarin, Oleg, and Lev Dvoretsky. *The Afghan Syndrome: The Soviet Union's Vietnam*. Novato, CA; Presidio, 1993.

Sella, Amnon. *The Value of Human Life in Soviet Warfare*. London: Routledge, 1992.

Shevarnadze, Eduard. *The Future Belongs to Freedom*. London: Free Press, 1991.

Shozimov, Pulat, Baktybek Beshimov, and Khurshida Yunusova. "The Ferghana Valley during Perestroika." In *Ferghana Valley: The Heart of Central Asia*, edited by S. Frederick Starr, 178–204. Armonk, NY: M. E. Sharpe, 2011.

Sieca-Kozlowski, Elisabeth. "The Post-Soviet Russian State facing War Veterans' Psychological Suffering." *Journal of Power Institutions in Post-Soviet Societies*, no. 14/15 (2013): 1–18.

Smith, Hedrick. *The New Russians*. New York: Random House, 1990.

Spolnikov, Victor. "Impact of Afghanistan's War on the Former Soviet Republics of Central Asia," In *Central Asia: Its Strategic Importance and Future Prospects*, edited by Malik Hafeez, 95–115. New York: St. Martin's Press, 1994.

Starr, S. Frederick, ed. *Ferghana Valley: The Heart of Central Asia*. Armonk, NY: M. E. Sharpe, 2011.

Suny, Ronald Grigo. *The Revenge of the Past: Nationalism, Revolution and the Collapse of the Soviet Union*. Stanford: Stanford University Press, 1993.

The Sustainability of the Soviet Army in Battle. Soviet Studies Research Centre, RMA, Sandhurst, September 1986.

Swartz, Howard M. "The Soviet-Afghan War in Russian Literature." PhD diss., Oxford University, 1992.

Szayna, Thomas S. *The Ethnic Factor in the Soviet Armed Forces: The Muslim Dimension*. Santa Monica, CA: Rand 1991.

Tasar, Eren. "The Central Asian Muftiate in Occupied Afghanistan, 1979–87." *Central Asian Survey* 30, no. 2 (2011): 213–226.

Tismaneanu, Vladimir. "The Neo-Leninist Temptations: Gorbachevism and the Party Intelligentsia." In *Perestroika at the Crossroads*, edited by Alfred L. Rieber and Alvin Z. Rubinstein, 31–51. Armonk. NY: M. E. Sharpe, 1991.

Tolz, Vera. *The USSR's Emerging Multiparty System*. Westport, CT: Praeger, 1990.

Tolz, Vera, and Iain Elliot, eds. *The Demise of the USSR*. New York: Macmillan, 1995.

Urban, Mark. *War in Afghanistan*. New York: St. Martin's Press, 1990.

U.S. Department of State Paper on Afghanistan. *Afghanistan: Two Years After*. December 23, 1981.

Valenta, Jiri. "Soviet Decision Making on Afghanistan, 1979." In *Decision Making for Soviet Security*, edited by Jiri Valenta and William Potter, 218–236. London: Unwin Hyman, 1984.

Vassiliev, Aleksei. *Russian Policy in the Middle East: From Messianism to Pragmatism*. Reading: Ithaca Press, 1993.

Westad, Odd Arne. "*Concerning the Situation in 'A'*: New Russian Evidence on the Soviet Intervention in Afghanistan," CWIHP Documents on the Soviet Invasion of Afghanistan, e-Dossier no. 4 (November 2001): 128–131.

White, Stephen, Graeme Gill, and Darrell Slider. *The Politics of Transition: Shaping a Post-Soviet Future*. Cambridge: Cambridge University Press, 1993.

Wimbush, S. Enders, and Alex Alexiev. *Soviet Central Asian Soldiers in Afghanistan* . Santa Monica, CA: RAND, January 1981.

Wise, Sally. "The Soviet Domestic Impact of the War in Afghanistan." Paper prepared for Canadian Association of Slavists Annual Conference, 1989.

Yakovlev, Aleksandr. *Hareformatsia berussia: Mibrit hamoatsot lehever ha`amim* (The reformation in Russia: From the Soviet Union to the Commonwealth of States). Tel-Aviv: Ma`ariv, 1996.

Yurchak, Alexei. *Everything Was Forever, Until It Was No More: The Last Soviet Generation.* Princeton: Princeton University Press, 2006.

Zhou, Jiayi. "The Muslim Battalions: Soviet Central Asians in the Soviet-Afghan War." *Journal of Slavic Military Studies* 25 (2012): 302–328.

Zubok, Vladislav M. *A Failed Empire: The Soviet Union in the Cold War from Stalin to Gorbachev.* Chapel Hill: University of North Carolina Press, 2007.

Russian-Language Sources

"Afganistan ne dolzhen povtorit'sia" (Afghanistan must not be repeated), *Voennyi zhurnal*, no. 1 (1990): 2–3.

Afganistan v nashei sud'be. Novosti, 1989.

Aiupov, O. "Zvezdy pod polumesiatsiem" (Stars under the half crescent). *Sovetskii voin*, no. 18 (September 1990): 64–67

Alekseeva, Liudmila. *Istoriia inakomysliia v SSSR.* Vest': Vilnius-Moskva—VIMO, 1992.

Amirov, V. M. "Lokal'naia voina v zerkale rossiiskoi voennoi pressy: kontseptosfera i pragmatika dvukh diskursov," *Izvestiia UrGU*, no. 52 (2007): 87–96.

Andriushchenko, Eduard. "Chto sovetskie grazhdane dumali o voine v Afganistane i kak KGB borolsia s nedovol'nymi" (What Soviet citizens thought of the war in Afghanistan and how the KGB fought against the malcontents). February 13, 2019. https://www.currenttime.tv/a/ussr-kgb-archives-people-about-afghanistan/29766199.html.

Bikbaev Ravil'. *Brigada ukhodit v gory.* EKSMO, 2010.

Borovik, Artem. *Afganistan. Eshche raz pro voinu* (Afghanistan. Once again about the war). Moskva: Mezhdunarodnye Otnoshehiia, 1990.

Cherkasov, V. "'Afgan' nachinalsia tak . . . " (How Afghanistan began). Interview with Ivan Riabchenko, *Sovetskii voin* no. 23 (December 1989): 5–8.

Cherniaev, Anatolii. *Sovmestnyi iskhod: dnevnik dvukh epokh, 1972—1992.* Moskva: ROSSPEN, 2008.

Danilova, Natalia. "Voennosluzhashchie, voiny-internatsionalisty, veterany: dinamika pravovogo statusa" (Servicemen, internationalist-soldiers, veterans: The dynamic of legal status). *Sotsiologicheskie issledovaniia* 10 (2001): 77–85.

Egorychev, N. G. "Napravlen poslom." In *Ot ottepeli po zastoia.* Moskva: Sovetskaia Rossiia, 1990, 153–178

Fogel', S. G. "Osobennosti propagandy SSSR vo vremia voennoi aktsii v Afganistane (1979—1989 gg.)" (The specifics of Soviet propaganda at the time of the military operation in Afghanistan, 1979–1989). *Art of War* 2, no. 13 (2009).

Gai, David, and Vladimir Snegirev. *Vtorzhenie: Neizvestnye stranitsy neob"iavlennoi voiny* Moskva, SP: IKPA, 1991.

Gareev, Mahmut. *Moia poslednaia voina: Afganistan bez sovetskikh voisk.* Moskva: INSAN, 1996.

Greshnov Andrei., *Afganistan: zalozhniki vremeni.*Moskva, 2006. http://www.artofwar.net.ru/profiles/greshnov_andrei_b/view_book/afganistan_zalojniki_vremeneni, accessed January 22, 2017.

Gromov, B. V. *Ogranichennyi kontingent.* Moskva: Progress-Kul'tura, 1994.

———. "Zashchishchali, obuchali, stroili" (We protected, we taught, we built). *Voenno-istoricheskii zhurnal* no. 3 (March 1989): 11–15.

Ivanov, N. "Generalom stal na voine" (He became a general at war). *Sovetskii voin* no. 1 (January 1990): 26–27, 70–71.

———. "Ogranichennyi kontingent" (The Limited Contingent), *Sovetskii voin* nos. 10–19/20 (May–October 1991).

"Kak prinimalos' reshenie" (How the decision was taken). *Voenno-istoricheskii zhurnal*, no. 7 (1991): 41–50.

Kaledin, Sergei. "Stroibat." *Novyi mir* no. 4 (1989): 59–89.

Karpenko, Aleksandr. *Tret'ia storona medali*. Moskva: Profizdat, 1991.

Kiianenko, A. A. "Boevoe primenenie VVS v Respublike Afganistan" (Operational use of the air force in the Republic of Afghanistan). *Voennaia mysl'* no. 8 (1991): 23–28.

Kinsburskii, A. V., and M. N. Topalov. "Reabilitatsiia uchastnikov Afganskoi voiny v obshchestvennom mnenii" (The rehabilitation of the participants of the Afghan War in public opinion). *Sotsiologicheskie issledovaniia* no. 1 (1992).

Kiziun, N. F. "Vooruzhennye Sily i obshchesto: vzaimosviaz', protivorechiia I puti ikh razresehniia" (The armed forces and society: Interrelationship, contradictions and ways of solving them). *Voennaia mysl'* no. 6 (1991): 2–7.

Klimov, V. "Skalpel' i slovo" (Scalpel and words). *Sovetskii voin* no. 14 (July 1991): 58–61

Konnov, Boris. "Pravda i vymysel ob afganskoi voine" (Truth and fabrication about the Afghan War). *Dialog* (Tashkent) no. 11 (1991): 49–52.

Kozlov, Vladimir, and Sergei Mironenko, eds. *Kramola: Inakomyslie v SSSR pri Khrushcheve i Brezhneve, 1953—1982 gg.* Moskva: Materik, 2005.

Kornienko, Georgii. *Kholodnaia voina*. Moskva: Mezhdunarodnye otnosheniia, 1995.

Krakhmalov, Sergei. *Zapiski voennogo attashe*. Moskva: Izd. Dom "Russkaia razvedka," 2000.

Krivosheev, G., ed. *Rossiia i SSSR v voinakh XX veka: Poteri vooruzhennykh sil*. Moskva: Voenizdat, 2001.

Kvachkov, Vladimir. *Spetsnaz Rossii*. Moskva: Russkaia Panorama, 2007.

Lapshin, Iurii. *Afganskii dnevnik*. Moskva, 2004.http://militera.lib.ru/db/lapshin_um/index.html, accessed January 19, 2018.

Levinson, A. G. "Otchet ob issledovanii 'Obshchestvennoe mnenie o problemakh uchastnikov voennykh deistvii v Afganistane'" (Report on investigation of public opinion on the problems of the participants in military activity in Afghanistan). Unpublished. October 26, 1990.

Liakhovskii, Aleksandr. *Plamia afgana* (Afghan flame). Moskva: ISKON, 1999.

———. *Tragediia i doblest afgana*. Moskva: Iskon, 1995 ; 2nd ed. Yaroslavl': NORD, 2004. royallib.ru, accessed April 18, 2017.

Liakhovskii, Aleksandr, and Viacheslav Zabrodin, *Tainy afganskoi voiny*. Moskva: Planeta, 1991.

Maiorov, Aleksandr. *Pravda ob afganskoi voine*. Moskva: Pravo cheloveka, 1996.

Malyshev, N. "Meroi real'nogo boia" (A measure for real warfare). *Kommunist vooruzhennykh sil* no. 8 (1988): 34–39.

Mendkovich, Nikita. "Finansovyi aspekt Afganskoi voiny 1979–1989 gg." (The financial aspect of the Afghan War of 1979–1989). afganistan.ru, accessed May 15, 2015.

Nemirovskii, V. G."Ekho afganskoi voiny" (Echo of the Afghan War). *Sotsiologicheskie issledovaniia* no. 10 (1990): 55–66.

Novye aspekty psikhoterapii posttravmaticheskogo stressa—metodicheskie rekomendatsii. Kharkov, 1990.

Ol'shanskii, D. "Afganskii sindrom." *Literaturnoe obozrenie* no. 3 (1990): 9–18.

———. "Smyslovye struktury lichnosti uchastnikov afganskoi voiny" (Ideational personality structures of participants in the Afghan War). *Psikhologicheskii zhurnal* 12, no. 5 (1991): 120–131.

———. "Psikhologiia sovetskikh soldat v Afganistane i posle vozvrashcheniia na rodinum." *Voprosy. psikhologii.*

Pardaev, Rofi. *Afganskaia komandirovka* (Afghan mission). Tashkent, 2013.

Pashkevich, M. M. *Afganistan: voina glazami kombata.* M.: Voenizdat, 1991.

Pavlov, Ruslan (Cheliabinsk). "Byt soldat afganskoi voiny 1979–1989gg. Po vospominaniem ee uchastnikov" (The everyday life of the soldiers of the Afghan War 1979–1989; reminiscences of its participants). 2015. http://urokiistorii.ru/node/52433, accessed April 12, 2015.

Pikov, N. I., ed. *Voina v Afganistane* (The war in Afghanistan). Moskva: Voenizdat, 1991.

Podvig. Issue 34. Moskva: Molodaia gvardiia, 1989,

Poliakov, Iurii. *Sto dnei do prikaza* (One hundred days until the [discharge] order). Moskva: Astrel', 2009.

"Problemy sotsial'noi reabilitatsii uchastnikov voiny v Afganistane" (Problems of the social rehabilitation of the participants of the war in Afghanistan). Paper prepared for the Supreme Soviet Committee for the Affairs of Soldier-Internationalists, 1991. [The Russian Academy of Sciences Institute of Sociology published a much longer paper by the same title in 1993.]

Prokhanov, Aleksandr. "Kto zashchitit zashchitnikov?" (Who will defend the defenders?). *Sovetskii voin*, no. 12 (June 1990), 1–3.

———. *Risunki batalista.* Moskva: Molodaia gvardiia, 1989.

Protasov, Iu. "Po dolgu internatsionalistov" (In accordance with the duty of internationalists). *KVS*, no. 24 (December 1985): 27–31.

Ptichkin, S. "Na rokovoi poslednem rubezhi" (On the fateful last border). *Sovetskii voin*, no. 17 (September 1990).

Rubtsov, Iurii. "Sovetskii Soiuz v 'neob"iavlennoi' voine v Afganistane (1979–1989): osmyslenie proshlogo." *Novaia i noveishaia istoriia*, no. 1 (2009), 48–70. Reproduced in *Rossiia i musul'manskii mir*, nos 203/204, nos. 5 and 6 (203 and 204; 2009: 121–143, 107–119.

Rybakov, Vladimir. *Afgantsy.* London, 1988.

Safronov, V. G. "Kak eto bylo" (How it was). *Voenno-istoricheskii zhurnal*, no. 5 (1990), 66–71.

Sannikov, L. I., ed. *Smoliane—internatsionalisty.* Smolensk: Smiadyn', 2000.

Semenov, Dmitrii. *Bol'.* Moskva: 1990.

Semenova, Viktoriia. Travmirovannaia pamiat' kak resurs formirovaniia kollektivnoi identichnosti: sluchai byvshikh afgantsev" (Traumatized memory as a resource for shaping collective identity: The case of the former afgantsy). In *Vlast' vremeni: sotsial'nye granitsy pamiati*, edited by V. N. Iarskii and E. R. Iarskii-Smirnovoi, 63–87. Moskva: Variant, TsPGI, 2011.

Shatrov, V. "Uchit'sia voennomy delu nastoiashchim obrazom" (Teaching military art in present-day form). *Kommunist vooruzhennykh sil*, no. 8 (1988).

Shebarshin, Leonid. *Ruka Moskvy: razvedka ot rastsveta do razvala.* Moskva: Algoritm, 2012.

Shilo, N. I. "Afganistan 30 let spustia: Posledstviia vvoda sovetskikh voisk v DRA dlia strany i regiony" (Afghanistan—30 years after: The consequences for the country and the region of introducing Soviet troops into the DRA). *Vestnik MGIMO Universiteta*, no. 2 (2010): 1–9.

Snegirev, Vladimir, and Valerii Semunian. *Virus A: kak my zaboleli vtorzheniem v Afganistan.* Moskva: Rossiiskaia gazeta, 2011.

Solnyshkov, Aleksei. "Dedovshchina: tip otnosheniia 'znachimomu drugomu'" (Dedovshchina: A category of attitude to the 'significant other'). *Sotsiologiia prava: deviantnoe povedenie* (2004): 45–53.

Sosnitskii, V. "Prinimaetsia . . . ne edinoglasno" (Getting down to it . . . not unanimously). *Sovetskii voin*, no. 1 (January 1989).

Stasiuk, Iurii. "Peremolotyi Afganistanom: istoriia minchanina . . . " https://people.onliner.by/2015/2/11.afgan

Strel'tsova, Nina. *Vozvrashchenie iz Afganistana.* Molodaia gvardiia, 1990.

Tarasov, Andrei, ed. *Moskvichi iz kluba "Dolg."* Moskva: Moskovskii rabochii, 1988.

Teplov, Leonid. *Kreshchenie—povestki i rasskazy molodykh pisatelei o sovremennoi armii.* 1990.

Tishakov, Iu. "Voevavashie deti, nevoevavshikh otsov" (Children who fought of fathers who didn't). *Sovetskii voin* 11 (June 1989): 28–29.

Tkachenko, Petr. *Afganistan bolit v moei dushe*. . . Moskva: Molodaia gvardiia, 1990.

———, ed., *Dorogie moi . . . : pis'ma iz Afgana.* Moskva: Profizdat, 1991.

Ustiuzhanin, G. "'Pokhoronku' ne dognal" (He arrived after notification of his death). *Sovetskii voin,* no. 18 (September 1990): 68–70.

Varennikov, Valentin. "Afganskaia epopeia. Analiz i vyvody" (The Afghan epic: Analysis and conclusions). *Patriot,* no. 5–6 (1993).

Vasil'ev, Aleksei. *Rossiia na Blizhnem i Srednem Vostoke: ot messianstva k pragmatizmy.* Moskva: Nauka, 1993.

Verstakov, Viktor. *Afganskii dnevnik.* Moskva: Voenizdat, 1991.

———. "Afganskii dnevnik" (Afghan diary). *Sovetskii voin,* no. 16 (August 1990): 13–23.

———. *Pylaet gorod Kandagar, stikhi i pesni.* Molodaia gvardiia, 1990.

Zakharov, Vasilii. "Struktorno-funktsional'nye osnovy mediko-sotsial'noi reabilitatsii ranenykh i bol'nykh" (Structural and functional basis of the medical and social rehabilitation of the wounded and the sick). *Problemy reabilitatsii,* no. 1 (1999).

Zdaniuk, V. "Ukhodim bez boia, no s poteriami" (We will leave without fighting, but with losses). *Sovetskii voin,* no. 10 (October 1992): 2–5.

Znakov, Vasilii. "Psikhologicheskoe issledovanie stereotipov ponimaniia lichnosti uchastnikov voiny v Afganistane " (Psychological study of stereotypes of understanding the personality of participants of the war in Afghanistan). *Voprosy psikhologii,* no. 4 (1990): 108–116.

Zubar'ev, Petr. "Organizatsiia khirurgicheskoi pomoshchi i reabilitatsii ranenykh v nachal'nom periode boyevykh deistvii v Afganistane" (The organization of surgical aid and the rehabilitation of the wounded at the beginning of the military action in Afghanistan). *Problemy reabilitatsii,* no. 1 (1999): 18–22.

Index

In this index *fig* refers to figures and *t* to tables.

INTERNATIONAL HISTORY
PROJECT SERIES

Edited by James G. Hershberg

Guns, Guerillas, and the Great Leader: North Korea and the Third World
Benjamin R. Young
2021

Between Containment and Rollback: The United States and the Cold War in Germany
Christian F. Ostermann
2021

The Whole World Was Watching: Sport in the Cold War
Edited by Robert Edelman and Christopher Young
2019

Trust, but Verify: The Politics of Uncertainty and the Transformation of the Cold War Order, 1969–1991
Edited by Martin Klimke, Reinhild Kreis, and Christian F. Ostermann
2016

Jimmy Carter in Africa: Race and the Cold War
Nancy Mitchell
2016

The Euromissile Crisis and the End of the Cold War
Edited by Leopoldo Nuti, Frédéric Bozo, Marie-Pierre Rey, and Bernd Rother
2015

The Regional Cold Wars in Europe, East Asia, and the Middle East: Crucial Periods and Turning Points
Edited by Lorenz Lüthi
2015

Poland's War on Radio Free Europe, 1950–1989
Paweł Machcewicz, translated by Maya Latynski
2015

A full list of titles in the Cold War International History Project series is available online at www.sup.org/cwihp.

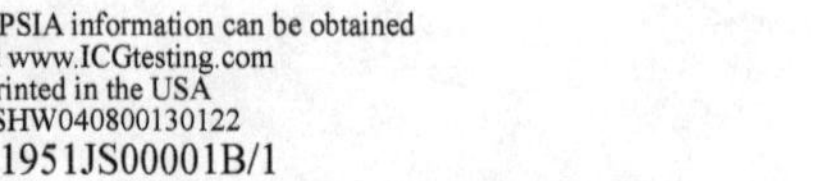
CPSIA information can be obtained
at www.ICGtesting.com
Printed in the USA
JSHW040800130122
21951JS00001B/1

9 781503 628748